THE ANNOTATED LUTHER

Volume 6

The Interpretation of Scripture

Additional Praise for The Annotated Luther Series

"The Annotated Luther series represents a finely crafted synthesis between readable primary texts and some of the best secondary scholarship. A superb editorial team, under the leadership of Hillerbrand, Stjerna, and Wengert, has made seventy-five selections, ranging from major treatises to sermons and letters, and beautifully laid these out in six volumes, together with state-of-the-art analyses and explanatory notes. Luther the theologian, the biblical interpreter, the pastor, the social/political thinker—all are given their due, and the resulting multidimensional portrait combines balance with a newly sharpened focus. In sum, a signal achievement."

—**Denis R. Janz** | Loyola University New Orleans

"The advent of The Annotated Luther series should be cause for celebration among scholars, pastors, students, and others eager to have easy access to so many of Luther's key writings. The appealing layout, rich images, and erudite annotations will make The Annotated Luther the go-to resource for learning about Luther's work and context."

—**Hans Wiersma** | Augsburg College

THE ANNOTATED LUTHER

Volume 6
The Interpretation of Scripture

VOLUME EDITOR
Euan K. Cameron

GENERAL EDITORS
Hans J. Hillerbrand
Kirsi I. Stjerna
Timothy J. Wengert

Fortress Press
Minneapolis

THE ANNOTATED LUTHER, Volume 6
The Interpretation of Scripture

Fortress Press Publication Staff: Scott Tunseth, Project Editor; Alicia Ehlers, Production Manager; Laurie Ingram, Cover Design; Michael Moore, Permissions.

Copyeditor: David Lott
Series Designer and Typesetter: Ann Delgehausen, Trio Bookworks
Proofreader: Paul Kobelski, The HK Scriptorium

Library of Congress Cataloging-in-Publication Data is available.

ISBN: 978-1-4514-6274-6
eISBN: 978-1-4514-6525-9

The paper used in this publication meets the minimum requirements of American National Standard for Information Sciences—Permanence of Paper for Printed Library Materials, ANSI Z329, 48-1984.

Manufactured in the U.S.A.

Contents

Series Introduction

Engaging the Essential Luther

Even after five hundred years Martin Luther continues to engage and challenge each new generation of scholars and believers alike. With 2017 marking the five-hundredth anniversary of Luther's *95 Theses*, Luther's theology and legacy are being explored around the world with new questions and methods and by diverse voices. His thought invites ongoing examination, his writings are a staple in classrooms and pulpits, and he speaks to an expanding assortment of conversation partners who use different languages and hale from different geographical and social contexts.

The six volumes of The Annotated Luther edition offer a flexible tool for the global reader of Luther, making many of his most important writings available in the *lingua franca* of our times as one way of facilitating interest in the Wittenberg reformer. They feature new introductions, annotations, revised translations, and textual notes, as well as visual enhancements (illustrations, art, photos, maps, and timelines). The Annotated Luther edition embodies Luther's own cherished principles of communication. Theological writing, like preaching, needs to reflect human beings' lived experience, benefits from up-to-date scholarship, and should be easily accessible to all. These volumes are designed to help teachers and students, pastors and laypersons, and other professionals in ministry understand the context in which the documents were written, recognize how the documents have shaped Protestant and Lutheran thinking, and interpret the meaning of these documents for faith and life today.

The Rationale for This Edition

For any reader of Luther, the sheer number of his works presents a challenge. Well over one hundred volumes comprise the scholarly edition of Luther's works, the so-called Weimar Ausgabe (WA), a publishing enterprise begun in 1883 and only completed in the twenty-first century. From 1955 to 1986, fifty-five volumes came to make up *Luther's Works* (American Edition) (LW), to which Concordia Publishing House, St. Louis, is adding still more. This English-language contribution to Luther studies, matched by similar translation projects for Erasmus of Rotterdam and John Calvin, provides a theological and historical gold mine for those interested in studying Luther's thought. But even these volumes are not always easy to use and are hardly portable. Electronic forms have increased availability, but preserving Luther in book form and providing readers with manageable selections are also important goals.

Moreover, since the publication of the WA and the first fifty-five volumes of the LW, research on the Reformation in general and on Martin Luther in particular has broken new ground and evolved, as has knowledge regarding the languages in which Luther wrote. Up-to-date information from a variety of sources is brought together in The Annotated Luther, building on the work done by previous generations of scholars. The language and phrasing of the translations have also been updated to reflect modern English usage. While the WA and, in a derivative way, LW remain the central source for Luther scholarship, the present critical and annotated English translation facilitates research internationally and invites a new generation of readers for whom Latin and German might prove an unsurpassable obstacle to accessing Luther. The WA provides the basic Luther texts (with some exceptions); the LW provides the basis for almost all translations.

Defining the "Essential Luther"

Deciding which works to include in this collection was not easy. Criteria included giving attention to Luther's initial key works; considering which publications had the most impact in his day and later; and taking account of Luther's own favorites, texts addressing specific issues of continued importance for today, and Luther's exegetical works. Taken as a whole, these works present the many sides of Luther, as reformer, pastor, biblical interpreter, and theologian. To serve today's readers and by using categories similar to those found in volumes 31–47 of Luther's works (published by Fortress Press), the volumes offer in the main a thematic rather than strictly chronological approach to Luther's writings. The volumes in the series include:

Volume 1: *The Roots of Reform* (Timothy J. Wengert, editor)
Volume 2: *Word and Faith* (Kirsi I. Stjerna, editor)
Volume 3: *Church and Sacraments* (Paul W. Robinson, editor)
Volume 4: *Pastoral Writings* (Mary Jane Haemig, editor)
Volume 5: *Christian Life in the World* (Hans J. Hillerbrand, editor)
Volume 6: *The Interpretation of Scripture* (Euan K. Cameron, editor)

The History of the Project

In 2011 Fortress Press convened an advisory board to explore the promise and parameters of a new English edition of Luther's essential works. Board members Denis Janz, Robert Kolb, Peter Matheson, Christine Helmer, and Kirsi Stjerna deliberated with

Fortress Press publisher Will Bergkamp to develop a concept and identify contributors. After a review with scholars in the field, college and seminary professors, and pastors, it was concluded that a single-language edition was more desirable than dual-language volumes.

In August 2012, Hans Hillerbrand, Kirsi Stjerna, and Timothy Wengert were appointed as general editors of the series with Scott Tunseth from Fortress Press as the project editor. The general editors were tasked with determining the contents of the volumes and developing the working principles of the series. They also helped with the identification and recruitment of additional volume editors, who in turn worked with the general editors to identify volume contributors. Mastery of the languages and unique knowledge of the subject matter were key factors in identifying contributors. Most contributors are North American scholars and native English speakers, but The Annotated Luther includes among its contributors a circle of international scholars. Likewise, the series is offered for a global network of teachers and students in seminary, university, and college classes, as well as pastors, lay teachers, and adult students in congregations seeking background and depth in Lutheran theology, biblical interpretation, and Reformation history.

Editorial Principles

The volume editors and contributors have, with few exceptions, used the translations of LW as the basis of their work, retranslating from the WA for the sake of clarity and contemporary usage. Where the LW translations have been substantively altered, explanatory notes have often been provided. More importantly, contributors have provided marginal notes to help readers understand theological and historical references. Introductions have been expanded and sharpened to reflect the very latest historical and theological research. In citing the Bible, care has been taken to reflect the German and Latin texts commonly used in the sixteenth century rather than modern editions, which often employ textual sources that were unavailable to Luther and his contemporaries.

Finally, all pieces in The Annotated Luther have been revised in the light of modern principles of inclusive language. This is not always an easy task with a historical author, but an intentional effort has been made to revise language throughout, with creativity and editorial liberties, to allow Luther's theology to speak free from unnecessary and unintended gender-exclusive language. This important principle provides an opportunity to translate accurately certain gender-neutral German and Latin expressions that Luther employed—for example, the Latin word *homo* and the German *Mensch* mean "human being," not simply "males." Using the words *man* and *men* to translate such terms would create an ambiguity not present in the original texts. The focus is on linguistic accuracy and Luther's intent. Regarding creedal formulations and trinitarian language, Luther's own expressions have been preserved, without entering the complex and important contemporary debates over language for God and the Trinity.

The 2017 anniversary of the publication of the *95 Theses* is providing an opportunity to assess the substance of Luther's role and influence in the Protestant Reformation. Revisiting Luther's essential writings not only allows reassessment of Luther's rationale and goals but also provides a new look at what Martin Luther was about and why new generations would still wish to engage him. We hope these six volumes offer a compelling invitation.

Hans J. Hillerbrand
Kirsi I. Stjerna
Timothy J. Wengert
General Editors

Abbreviations

ANF	Ante-Nicene Fathers
AWA	Archiv zur die Weimarer Ausgabe
b. Yebam.	Babylonian Talmud, tractate *Yebamot*
BC	*The Book of Concord*, ed. Robert Kolb and Timothy J. Wengert (Minneapolis: Fortress Press, 2000)
Brecht	Martin Brecht, *Martin Luther*, 3 vols., trans. James L. Schaaf (Minneapolis: Fortress Press, 1985, 1990, 1993)
BSLK	*Die Bekenntnischriften der evangelisch-lutherischen Kirche.* 11th ed.
CA	*Augsburg Confession*
CL	*Luther's Werke in Auswahl*, ed. Otto Clemen, et al. (Bonn, 1912–33; Berlin, 1955–56)
CR	*Corpus Reformatorum*
CRR	Classics of the Radical Reformation. 12 vols. Waterloo, ON, and Scottdale, PA: Herald Press, 1973-
EA	[Martin Luther], *Dr. Martin Luther's sämmtliche Werke*, ed. Ernst Ludwig Enders, 2nd ed., 68 vols. (Frankfurt am Main: Heyder & Zimmer, 1862-1885)
FC	*Formula of Concord*
LC	*The Large Catechism*
LW	*Luther's Works* [American edition], ed. Helmut Lehmann and Jaroslav Pelikan, 55 vols. (Philadelphia: Fortress Press, and St. Louis: Concordia, 1955-86)
MA[3]	*Martin Luther.* Ergänzungsbände Werke (Munich, 1954-)
MLBJP	Brooks Schramm and Kirsi Stjerna, *Martin Luther, the Bible, and the Jewish People* (Minneapolis: Fortress Press, 2012)
MLStA	*Martin Luther: Studienausgabe*, ed. Hans-Ulrich Delius, 6 vols. (Berlin & Leipzig: Evangelische Verlagsanstalt, 1979-99)
MPL	*Patrologiae cursus completes, series Latina*, ed. J.-P. Migne, 1st ed., 217 vols. (Paris 1844-55, 1862-65)
MSA	Philipp Melanchthon, *Melanchthons Werke in Auswahl* [*Studienausgabe*], ed. R. Stupperich, 7 vols. (Gütersloh: Mohn, 1951-75)
PE	*Works of Martin Luther* (Philadelphia edition, 1915–43)
Raeder	Siegfried Raeder, "The Exegetical and Hermeneutical Work of Martin Luther," in *Hebrew Bible/Old Testament: The History of Its Interpretation.* Vol. 2, *From the Renaissance to the Enlightenment*, ed. Magne Sæbø (Göttingen: Vandenhoeck & Ruprecht, 2008)
SA	*The Smalcald Articles*

SC	*The Small Catechism*
SD	*Solid Declaration*
S-J	*Luther's Correspondence*, 2 vols., ed. Preserved Smith and Charles M. Jacobs (Philadelphia, 1913–18)
SMRT	Studies in Medieval and Reformation Thought
SRR	*Seminary Ridge Review*
STh	Thomas Aquinas, *Summa Theologica*
TAL	The Annotated Luther, 6 vols. (Minneapolis: Fortress Press, 2015–17)
Thompson	John L. Thompson, ed., *Reformation Commentary on Scripture: Old Testament I: Genesis 1–11* (Downers Grove, IL: IVP Academic, 2012)
WA	*Luthers Werke: Kritische Gesamtausgabe [Schriften]*, 73 vols. (Weimar: H. Böhlau, 1883–2009)
WA 40/1	In epistolam S. Pauli ad Galatas Commentarius ex praelectione D. Martini Lutheri collectus. [1531] 1535: Prefatio D. Martini Lutheri, 1535.
WA 40/1 [Hs]	In epistolam S. Pauli ad Galatas Commentarius ex praelectione D. Martini Lutheri collectus. [1531] 1535: Annotationes Martini Lutheri in epistolam Pauli ad Galatas, 1531.
WA 40/1 [Dr]	In epistolam S. Pauli ad Galatas Commentarius ex praelectione D. Martini Lutheri collectus. [1531] 1535: [Annotationes Martini Lutheri in epistolam Pauli ad Galatas], 1535.
WA 40/2 [Dr]	In epistolam S. Pauli ad Galatas Commentarius 1531 (1535): [Druck].
WA Br	*Luthers Werke: Kritische Gesamtausgabe: Briefwechsel*, 18 vols. (Weimar: H. Böhlau, 1930–85)
WA DB	*Luthers Werke: Kritische Gesamtausgabe: Deutsche Bibel*, 12 vols. (Weimar: H. Böhlau, 1906–61)
WA TR	*Luthers Werke: Kritische Gesamtausgabe: Tischreden*, 6 vols. (Weimar: H. Böhlau, 1912–21)
Wander	*Deutsches Sprichwörter-Lexikon*, ed. K. F. Wander, 5 vols. (Darmstadt: Wissenschaftliche Buchgesellschaft, 1964)
y. Sanh.	Jerusalem Talmud, tractate *Sanhedrin*

REFORMATION EUROPE
in the 16th century
Holy Roman Empire boundary
Provincial boundary
ATLANTIC OCEAN
SCOTLAND
Edinburgh
IRELAND
York
ENGLAND
London
North Sea
NORWAY
SWEDEN
Stockholm
DENMARK
Copenhagen
Baltic Sea
ESTONIA
LIVONIA
KURLAND
Königsberg
PRUSSIA
POMERANIA
Hamburg
BRANDENBURG
POLAND
Ghent
ARTOIS
NETHERLANDS
FLANDERS
HESSE
COLOGNE
SAXONY
SILESIA
LUXEMBOURG
BOHEMIA
Paris
Mainz
UPPER PALITANATE
LOWER PALITANATE
MORAVIA
Nantes
Orleans
BAVARIA
FRANCE
Augsburg
AUSTRIA
Vienna
IMPERIAL HUNGARY
Budapest
FRENCH COMTE
SWISS CONFEDERATION
TYROL
CARINTHIA
BOURBON LANDS
SAVOY
Milan
Trent
CARNIOLA
HUNGARY
Pavia
Venice
Mohacs
Valladolid
Toulouse
Avignon
Genoa
NAVARRE
VENETIAN REPUBLIC
PORTUGAL
SPAIN
Florence
PAPAL STATES
Madrid
Barcelona
Lisbon
CASTILE
Toledo
ARAGON
CORSICA (TO GENOA)
ITALY
OTTOMAN EMPIRE
BALERIC ISLANDS
Rome
Seville
SARDINIA (TO SPAIN)
Naples
NAPLES
Granada
GRANADA
Tangier
Mediterranean Sea
SICILY (TO SPAIN)
Algiers
Bizerte
0
300 Miles
Tunis
Lucidity Information Design, LLC

LUTHER'S GERMANY
Major political subdivisions
N
Baltic Sea
DENMARK
Wolgast
Hamburg
POMERANIA
Stettin
Bremen
Elbe
Amsterdam
NETHERLANDS
Magdeburg
Wittenberg
POLAND
Mansfeld
Eisleben
Torgau
Brussels
Cologne
Eisenach
Leipzig
Marburg
Erfurt
Breslau
Oder
Schmalkalden
LUXEMBOURG
Prague
Worms
Nuremberg
Metz
Regensburg
Rhine
Strassburg
Danube
Augsburg
FRANCE
AUSTRIA
Vienna
Zürich
Salzburg
SWISS
CONFEDERATION
HUNGARY
Milan
Venice
VENETIAN
DOMINION
0
200 Miles
Adriatic Sea
Florence

Introduction to Volume 6

EUAN K. CAMERON

O das gott wollt, meyn und aller lerer ausslegung untergiengen, unnd eyn iglicher Christenn selbs die blosse schrifft und lautter gottis wortt fur sich nehme![a]

Would to God that my exposition and that of all doctors might perish and each Christian for him or herself make the Scriptures and God's pure word his norm.[b]

Martin Luther wrote a vast amount of theology, both pastoral and controversial. He reflected at length, in conversation, in correspondence, and in his other writings, on the extraordinary events of his life and the story of the Reformation. To call him prolific is to understate the case greatly. And yet, for Luther by far the most important text in his life was the text of Scripture itself. He read the Bible often and intensively: he could quote it readily and compare passages fluently. When he took up his professorial position in Wittenberg, Luther chose to lecture continuously on books of the Bible, and only on books of the Bible. He declined to provide running, focused commentary on other theological texts, whether the Scholastics or even the early

a Luther's Christmas Postil as in WA 10/1:728.

b LW 52:286.

fathers, though he knew both genres well, and cited them regularly in his exegetical work. At times, as in the passages quoted above, Luther expressed the wish to see the entire carapace of interpretation inherited from the past, as well as his own commentary and exposition, to be discarded in favor of the reading of Scripture on its own. This desire became all the more realistic when Luther's great translation of the entire Bible into High German, begun with his translation of the New Testament (known as the "September Testament") in 1522, was completed with the publication of the entire Luther Bible in 1534.

As Luther remarked on several occasions, however, both in the preface to the New Testament and in his Christmas Postils, one needed to approach Scripture in the right spirit and with the right orientation. Too many mistaken guides and false signposts were around; no one knew how to read Scripture correctly. Moreover, the right spiritual orientation was needed, the "quiet, contemplative mind" that few could attain to without Luther's interpretative guidance. For those who could, Luther was more than willing, at least in the early days, to allow them to read for themselves: "And so, my dear Christians, get to it, get to it, and let my exposition and that of all the doctors be no more than a scaffold, an aid for the construction of the true building, so that we may ourselves grasp and taste the pure and simple word of God and abide by it; for there alone God dwells in Zion."[c] Nevertheless, Luther devoted an enormous amount of effort to explaining Scripture in the course of his career. He wrote prefaces to his own translations of books of the Bible: some of those prefaces grew into small but significant theological expository treatises of their own, including a miniaturized version of Luther's key message on the justification of sinners (in the preface to Romans), treatises on ethical and moral questions, and even on world history (as in Luther's long introduction to the book of Daniel).[d] He delivered commentaries through his university lectures, many of which were collected and published in his own time. He preached many, many sermons, almost certainly more than are recorded, on passages of Scripture. Numerous other expository and consolatory writings do not fit neatly into the

c LW 52:286.

d See Luther's prefaces to *Daniel* and *Romans*, as edited in this volume by Euan Cameron, pp. 375–412 and 457–80.

Title page woodcut by Lucas Cranach the Younger illustrating Luther's complete German Bible. Printed in Wittenberg in1541 by Hans Lufft.

categories of preface, commentary, and sermon, but incorporate elements from one or the other.

Volume 6 of The Annotated Luther includes selections, which inevitably amount to a tiny percentage of all that Luther wrote, from his various writings about, around, and in dialogue with Scripture. It is astonishing just how comprehensive an image of Luther the expositor, controversialist, and pastor may be formed from the biblical writings alone. Discussion of Luther's short controversial piece, the *Open Letter on Translating*, provides a special insight into Luther's thinking, as his theology informed his reading and translating of Scripture and vice versa.

This introduction must draw attention to a huge gap in the volume. This gap cannot be filled for obvious reasons, but must not under any circumstances go unremarked or unnoticed. One cannot present the Luther Bible itself. Luther's greatest achievement in biblical studies was his translation of the entire Bible into uniquely powerful, dramatic German. Lutheran preachers for centuries afterward would constantly quote from this edition. In the non-Lutheran German reformed world, those whom Luther had habitually denounced as *Schwärmer* and whom his successors would equally crudely denounce as "Calvinists," would depend to an overwhelming degree on the Luther Bible even after other translations became available.[e] The Luther Bible is Luther's most powerful and durable achievement, but by its very essence it cannot be translated. Its character resides in its German language. No English Bible can be the Luther Bible.

This introduction will not endeavor to describe or paraphrase all the expository work carried out by the contributors to the volume for each text individually. Rather, it will draw out certain themes and perspectives on Luther's writings on Scripture, which the selections in this volume help to illuminate. Luther's attitudes to Scripture evolved in the course of his career. When he presented his first lectures on the Psalms, Luther used a particular expository technique that he soon discarded. By the 1530s, when he delivered his commentaries on Galatians and Genesis, his approach to Scripture was quite different. Luther's priorities shifted as the events of the early Reformation forced him to defend his vision against different kinds of adversaries. The balance and the interaction between the motives of pastoral consolation, controversy, and theological instruction, which often combined in the same text, require careful reflection.

One final preliminary observation should be made. Several of the LW volumes most connected with questions of Scripture appeared in print before the corresponding volumes of the Weimar edition *Deutsche Bibel* series. Consequently, the LW editors could not use the remarkably thorough and detailed scholarship applied by the WA DB editors to the material in the origi-

e See Bruce Gordon, "German Bibles outside the Lutheran Movement," in *The New Cambridge History of the Bible: Volume 3, 1450–1750*, ed. Euan Cameron (Cambridge: Cambridge University Press, 2016), 263–84, and esp. 263, 272, 275.

nal Latin and German. In those specific areas, this new edition offers an opportunity to bring the insights of the Weimar editors to the attention of an English-speaking readership.

Luther and the Message of Scripture

Luther's attitude toward Scripture evolved in the course of his career, most noticeably in the 1510s as his style of expository lecture changed with each series that he delivered in the lecture halls in Wittenberg. In the first series of lectures on the Psalms (the *Dictata super psalterium*, 1513–1515), Luther followed medieval expository techniques with the earnest commitment and overpreparation that one recognizes as the work of a newly minted doctor and professor. Diagrams, graphic contrasts between one point and another, and multiple explorations of the same point abound. His exegesis of Psalm 72, edited in this volume by Mickey Mattox, follows a rather cumbersome application of the fourfold exegesis method, or *Quadriga*, which Luther would soon discard.[f] One is reminded of David Curtis Steinmetz's image that a reader of these lectures feels like someone who walks continuously around an apple tree, picking one piece of fruit on each revolution: "At the end of the day his baskets are full but his head is swimming."[g]

By the lectures on Romans delivered from 1515 onward (represented here in Piotr Małysz's edition of Luther's lectures on Romans 3)[h] Luther was already manifesting the preoccupation with a focused explanation of the justification of sinners that would dominate his work thereafter. Nevertheless, one senses in the Romans lectures an expositor who is still monastic, who still envisages his task as the earnest guiding of devout consciences; the urgency and fervor of his later writings is not yet visible, even though many key ideas have already made their appearance. By the time of the lectures on Galatians from 1518 (here

f See Mattox on Psalm 72 in this volume, pp. 229–45.

g David C. Steinmetz, *Luther and Staupitz: An Essay in the Intellectual Origins of the Protestant Reformation* (Durham: Duke University Press, 1980), 92–93.

h See this volume, pp. 481–99.

represented by Simo Peura and Kirsi Stjerna's edition of Gal. 2:15-16),[i] Luther's approach to expounding Scripture acquired its thrust and edge as the primary theological concern became dominant. The reciprocal relationship between the Bible and Luther's theology of justification has been interpreted in different ways by different commentators, including the contributors to this volume. To put it in the most critical way possible: Martin Luther, having—as he himself attested—struggled over a long period to discern the Scripture message of justification, found that message in the radical *theological* disjunction between the freely given forgiveness of God and the actual sinful state of all humanity, including those who had been saved by grace. God's forgiveness saved the sinner from condemnation; the indwelling Spirit gradually healed and repaired fallen human nature, but never completely in this life. Growth in holiness was a consequence of God's favor, not a cause of it. In the technical language of theological historians, the forgiveness is denoted by the term *justification* and the process of healing and renewal by *sanctification*. Luther rarely, if ever, used these terms in that precise sense. When Luther made the distinction, however, for instance in the preface to Romans, between "grace" and "the gifts," he expressed this idea with great lucidity.[j]

Having found this insight and formulated it in what he believed was a watertight fashion, Luther then saw the message of justification in Scripture wherever he looked: in the Psalms, in the Prophets, in the gospels, and above all in Paul's epistles. As Kenneth Appold has recently remarked, on one hand, Luther was bringing his theological concerns and convictions to the reading of Scripture and allowing them to dictate how he read and interpreted the Bible. On the other hand, Luther only attained to this interpretative principle through passionate and serious scriptural study in the first place.[k] A feedback loop was surely operating here, but into this loop Scripture was integrated as both the source and the method of Luther's theology.

i See this volume, pp. 535–55.

j See the *Preface to Romans* in this volume, p. 461.

k See Kenneth G. Appold, "The Importance of the Bible for Early Lutheran Theology," in Cameron, ed., *New Cambridge History of the Bible*, 3:439–61, at 442–45.

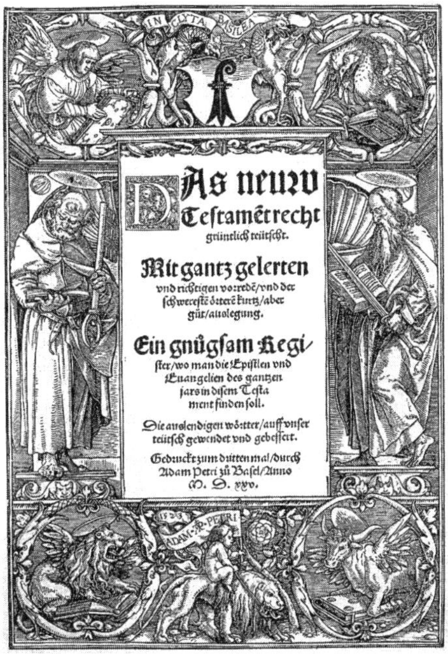

Hans Holbein's ornate woodcut provided the border for Adam Petri's reprint of Martin Luther's translation of the New Testament, published in 1523. The version shown here is from a third printing in 1525.

The Authority of Scripture

> The more it seems to conflict with all experience and reason, the more carefully it must be noted and the more surely believed.[1]

It is important to locate Luther in relation to the authority of Scripture, in an age where the churches seem prone to crude divisions between those who claim to hold to the authoritative text (in practice usually only a few texts, on hot-button issues of cultural ethics) and those who try to read the text in its historical and cultural setting. Martin Luther was quite clear that

1 Exposition of Gen. 2:22, in LW 1, as edited in this volume, p. 119, by Kirsi I. Stjerna and Else Marie Wiberg Pedersen. Parts of Luther's *Lectures on Genesis* from 1535 onward are edited in this volume by Jussi Koivisto, Kirsi I. Stjerna, and Else Marie Wiberg Pedersen.

the Bible from time to time said things that completely baffled human reason. In his exposition of Genesis 2, he displayed little patience with those who tried to explain the creation of Eve from Adam's rib philosophically, by speculating on how many ribs Adam had in his first creation, or wondering whether the male rib cage was asymmetrical. Such attempts were entirely beside the point. God could disrupt and rearrange the created order exactly as God wished to do. Something miraculous must not be "explained away" or spuriously integrated into a system of natural philosophy. We are simply called to accept that God's power transcends all natural laws. With a point that was psychologically valid if not biologically correct, Luther remarked that the ordinary process of human procreation, gestation, and birth were in themselves miraculous and incomprehensible; only their very familiarity prevented us from being amazed by them.[m]

At the same time, while Luther was precritical in his reading of Scripture (as some contributors to the volume have remarked), he was not entirely uncritical. In relation to the process by which the books of the Bible came to be compiled, he was even in some manner protocritical. In his prefaces to the Prophets and in particular to Isaiah, Luther demonstrated both that there were several clear messages in the text, and that these messages were presented in a remarkably disordered fashion. He speculated that the prophets Isaiah and Jeremiah might not have been the last ones to organize the text as we now have it. Although his beliefs about prophetic authorship precluded him from discerning two or three different "Isaiahs," as modern-era scholarship has done, Luther observed a clear disjunction in the voice of Isaiah around chapter 40.[n] At the same time, Luther the translator could not fail to be aware of the different resonances of the Vulgate and the Hebrew texts of the Hebrew Bible. At times he dedicated some effort to reconciling the different readings.[o] No superficial fundamentalist reading of Scripture, as though its meaning were transparent without effort, can take any comfort from the work of Martin Luther. Discerning the text requires real, hard work, and he of all people knew that.

m See the commentary on Genesis in this volume, pp. 119–24.

n See Brooks Schramm's annotations on Isaiah 53, this volume, pp. 349–73.

o See this volume, pp. 347.

Luther's knowledge of the text of Scripture was not perfect. It could hardly have been otherwise, given that he wrote at the very beginnings of modern critical scholarship on the texts, and that his relationship with some of the most advanced Hebrew scholars of his age, such as Sebastian Münster (1488–1552), was often problematical. Anglophone readers who have not been exposed to the Luther Bible from childhood are from time to time surprised by the way that Luther renders some of the more poetic passages of Hebrew Scripture. Subsequent scholarship made important inroads into the medieval understanding of what those texts mean and how they should be read. Even the 1611 King James Bible would in some places mark an advance in terms of Hebrew philology over some of Luther's readings. Some of these critical challenges may be observed in this edition, for instance in the debate over whether to read verse 14 of Psalm 118 as "the Lord is my strength and my might" or, more traditionally, as "the Lord is my strength and my song."[p]

Luther's use of Scripture can still astonish with its lucidity and clarity, for instance in his often profound psychological insights. When he discussed how the prophets denounced the "idolatry" of the Hebrew people of their own age, Luther argued that the "idolaters" who worshiped golden images undoubtedly believed that by so doing they were worshiping the one true God. They did not literally think that the works of their hands were divine. Rather, they worshiped the true God, but with artifices and ceremonies completely different from those that God had commanded them to observe. In the same way, Luther argued, medieval Christians believed that they were worshiping the true God incarnate in Jesus Christ when they conducted a whole range of ceremonies and "works" that God had nowhere required of them.[q]

p See Erik Herrmann on Psalm 118:14 in this volume, pp. 286–88.

q See Schramm on the *Preface to the Prophets* in this volume, pp. 323–30.

The Pastor, the Teacher, and the Conversationalist

There were, in a sense, many Luthers. His ministry seems at times to oscillate erratically across a broad quadrant. At one extreme, Luther writes as a devout pastor seeking to console the afflicted conscience. He makes accessible to every Christian believer the wonderful message of redeeming grace; and that message of consolation never strays far from his work as a constructive biblical theologian. In order to console, he teaches. At the other end of the scale, Luther often manifests himself as the angry, fervent controversialist, frustrated by what he was convinced was the *wrong* teaching about the Christian life that was so prevalent in his day. He denounces the misguided teachings of the church of his time, bewails the corruptions that the devil has introduced into the church, and utters dire warnings against those who do not take the messages of law and gospel with the seriousness that they demand. All three Luthers, the pastor, the teacher, and the polemical controversialist are present to the full in the scriptural writings. Sometimes they even appear in the same sentence, as at the end of his exposition of Isaiah 53: "This figure is a solace to the afflicted, but to snoring readers they are nothing but empty words."[r]

This insight matters, since for Luther the message of comfort, the message of instruction, and the message of warning belonged together. All formed part of the business of the academic theologian and the pastoral writer and preacher. Even in the exposition of Psalm 51, in his first set of academic lectures on the Psalms (usually known as the *Dictata super psalterium*), Luther's writing is suffused with a strong spiritual sense. He expects his hearers and students to embrace the utter humility and disregard of the self that is the beginning of the Christian life.[s] The true point of the Mosaic code, Luther argues, is pastoral. Only by confronting the faithful person with a huge array of laws that cannot possibly be kept in their entirety could God bring a person to that level of affliction and despair which was the necessary prelude to receiving the gospel:

r See this volume, p. 374.

s See this volume, p. 232.

> These many laws of Moses were not only given so that no one might choose their own way of doing good and living well, as was said above, but much more so that sins might simply become numerous and be piled up beyond measure. The purpose was to burden the conscience so that the hardened blindness would have to recognize itself and feel its own inability and nothingness in the achieving of good. Such blindness must be thus compelled and coerced through the law to seek something beyond the law and its own ability, namely, God's grace promised in Christ who was to come.[t]

The consoling voice is present also. In his sermon on the incarnation, based on John 1,[u] Luther takes the physical facts of the incarnation very seriously. He sees it as a blessing beyond measure that human beings can look at their bodily nature, even in all its offensive aspects, and say that God chose to assume that very same nature. It would be a cause of blessing even apart from salvation itself.

Luther's consolatory voice could at times take on a rather rough edge. The Luther who consoled the afflicted—or who directed the afflicted to Scripture for consolation—did not typically promise that all will be well in this life. When expounding Psalm 118, which Luther declared to be one of his favorite psalms, Luther made clear that the righteous, the godly, the believers must expect nothing in this life except tribulation and persecution from the devil and those fighting for him. The godly will suffer and die in the eyes of the world; but in their faith and in their utter dependence on God, they will receive and rejoice in the only thing that ultimately matters.[v] For Luther, the future life offered the supreme, in some senses the only, reward for the true Christian.[w]

t LW 35:244. Compare the point in the *Preface to the Old Testament*, as edited by Schramm in this volume, that some of the Mosaic laws were "foolish and useless" (p. 52).

u As edited by Paul Rorem in this volume, p. 435–55.

v See Erik Herrmann's edition of Luther's exposition of Psalm 118 in this volume, pp. 247–317.

w See Piotr Małysz's edition of Luther on 1 Corinthians 15 in this volume, pp. 500–533.

Moreover, the pastoral message could never be communicated without at least implicit, and usually explicit, criticism and correction of what has been taught before, and especially of what was done in the name of religion in the church of the Middle Ages. False religion was that which encouraged people to become proud of their own spiritual attainments, to suppose that they could earn rewards from God through monastic vows, pilgrimages, or other imagined good works. So, for example, in the commentary on Isaiah, the "papacy" figured as the embodiment of mistaken or false religion. Occasional attacks on the Anabaptists and even the *Schwärmer* punctuated Luther's exegesis. The devil, in Luther's eyes, was the most skilled perverter of Scripture, so the faithful believer must always be on his or her guard against distorted interpretation. The pastor and the controversialist reveal themselves as two sides of the same coin.

An unexpectedly strong aspect to Luther's controversial tone emerges when he writes about rulers and princes in his biblical exegesis. Even in 1530, five years after the Peasants' War in Germany, Luther could write with savage criticism of rulers and princes, especially insofar as they trusted in their own strength, prestige, and honor and forgot their dependence on God. A graphic and characteristically earthy example of Luther's thought in this area appears in his commentary on Psalm 118: "For these very same bigwigs who would rob God of his honor by bragging and boasting of their role in suppressing the insurrection [the 1525 rebellion] were at that time the most fear-stricken wretches I have ever seen. Now they forget the God who rescued them when in sheer fright they shit their pants. We still smell the stench whenever one of these bigwigs is near."[x] Any historians who casually refer to the post-1525 Luther as a "flatterer of princes" may do well to reflect on that and many similar passages. Of course, in criticizing the ruling elites so savagely, Luther in no way intended to bring comfort to those among the lower order who rebelled, let alone those among the clergy who encouraged them to do so.

The ultimate conflict that Luther knew himself to be engaged in was the cosmic one between the forces of God and the power of the devil. Although the victory of God could never be in doubt, Luther envisaged the world as the scene of the last struggle of

x Psalm 118:2, as edited by Erik Herrmann in this volume, p. 260.

the last days. Luther read the Bible in the light of an almost overpowering vision of the final conflict. In his work on Daniel and many other "prophetic" writings, as well as in his chronological speculations, Luther envisaged the end times as fairly near. They would come in God's own time, and the only appropriate preparation was the preaching of the gospel and the proclamation of grace.

Despite these examples of vigorous polemic, in the biblical works the argumentative voice does not always ring through quite as stridently as in the works devoted primarily to controversy. Only by reading the exegetical work, comprising as it does such a vast proportion of Luther's output, can one put the disputatious, controversialist Luther into appropriate proportion. An image of Luther dominated by the 1520 Reformation pamphlets or the tracts against the sacramentarians, even if it reflects Luther's true concerns, will nevertheless be imbalanced.

A depiction of the apocalyptic battle of Armegeddon (Revelation 19) from Luther's German New Testament (1523). The rider on the white horse achieves the final victory as the beast is cast into a lake of fire. Woodcut designed by Lucas Cranach the Elder.

The Significance of Luther's Commentary on Genesis

The American Edition of *Luther's Works* began its survey and selection of Luther's writings with eight volumes devoted solely to Luther's massive exposition of the book of Genesis from his lectures delivered in the 1530s. On the face of it, this might have seemed a strange place to begin. The commentary was delivered within the last fifteen years of Luther's life. It addressed a book of the Bible where the old covenant and the law seemed to predominate. Finally, there was some doubt (now largely allayed) as to whether the theology of the commentary derived from Luther or had been "contaminated" (in the eyes of the orthodox) by Philip Melanchthon (1497–1560) and his followers.

As Jussi Koivisto has pointed out, Luther did not see his Genesis commentary as in any way peripheral to his work; if anything, he saw it as his major theological testament, his last great gift to the world of biblical scholarship and interpretation.[y] Like the commentaries of many other sixteenth-century reformers, however, Luther's Genesis commentary does appear to suffer from a certain lack of focus. In this age, commentaries were typically delivered as more or less extempore lectures, and then written down either by the author or an amanuensis. This process left their authors considerable latitude to explore byways or simply to repeat themselves as a new text authorized the rediscovery of a key insight. Even John Calvin (1509–1564), a thinker who habitually structured his work more rigorously than Luther did, fell into the traps of repetition, verbosity, and excessive length in his commentaries.

And yet the Genesis commentary yields precious insights. By comparing Luther's scriptural reading of gender with that inherited from Greek philosophy, one confronts the possibly surprising message that Luther regarded men and women as fully and completely human in their own respective nature: woman was not (as classical philosophy and some medieval antifeminist literature had claimed) an imperfect or somehow malformed man. It is little enough that Luther was slightly less prejudiced than the worst of his predecessors, one might say. Yet, important consequences follow from the theological read that Luther brought to the question of gender. In their prelapsarian state Adam and Eve enjoyed a more perfect equality; the subordination of women to men only ensued as a consequence of the fall.[z] Therefore (with only a modest extrapolation), one might argue that Luther did not envisage gendered superiority and inferiority in heaven. Gender subordination was a secondary attribute, in the same way that sin was something from which to be redeemed. Luther did not draw these conclusions, but they are implicit in his arguments.

Moreover, while Luther in many respects echoed the negative language of medieval Christianity about human sexuality, once again, any negative sentiments were secondary and consequent to original sin: they were not primordial. Adam and Eve were married in Paradise, and enjoyed their physical natures

y See Jussi Koivisto's introduction to Genesis 3 in this volume, p. 146.

z See Genesis 1 and 2, as edited by Kirsi I. Stjerna and Else Marie Wiberg Pedersen in this volume, pp. 67–144.

and their sexual union with neither shame nor sin. Even more strikingly, Luther argued that human reproduction and childbirth are intrinsically good, blessed things; only original sin, with its concomitants of uncontrolled desire and the resulting shame, prevents us from appreciating these beautiful things as they appear in the eyes of God. Finally, by the mid-1530s, if not long before, Luther was convinced that the majority of human beings were created to live in the conjugal state. Some might be called to another pattern of life, but one could not wish that on oneself, or impose it on oneself by choice. Most people needed a sexual partner and the companionship that such partnership brought. Did Luther envisage sexual relationships in heaven (as C. S. Lewis did not, but John Milton did)? We cannot know. What seems clear, though, is that Luther envisaged the glorified human, restored and redeemed, as a fully embodied human being, not as some incorporeal intelligence.

Detail from Jan Gossaert's painting of Adam and Eve (c. 1520)

Luther's Emphasis on Jesus Christ

When one has been studying Luther and the Bible for some time, relatively few things come as a complete surprise. However, aspects of Luther that one may have been tempted to take for granted, or even to play down, appear in sharper relief when the biblical material is taken into account. Historians of the Reformation sometimes like to point out areas in which Luther was *not* paradigmatic for the entire magisterial Reformation, or even for the Lutheran churches as a whole. His preoccupation with demonology, his bitter antagonism toward adversaries on the sacramental question, even the scale and scope of his hostility to Judaism, all seem to have exceeded the norms for his age. It is striking, however, to see in just how many areas Martin Luther really did frame the question and establish the ground rules for debate, and not just in the most obvious and critical area of justification by free grace. His exposition of the book of Daniel (for one) anticipated to a remarkable degree the claims regarding world history that would be made by other reformers, especially those around Philip Melanchthon.[a]

The lesson from reading Luther on the Bible that can most surprise us is one that, in truth, ought not to be surprising in the least. Quite simply, Luther saw Jesus Christ everywhere that he looked in Scripture, even in those areas where modern exegetes are not accustomed to see him. Only in the light of Christ, he argued, could the law of the Old Testament be understood properly.[b] The prophets, he argued with utter conviction, were looking to Christ even if they could not have foretold every aspect of his ministry. Isaiah, however, foresaw Jesus's ministry to a miraculous degree, above all in the suffering servant passages.[c] Maybe more arresting to the modern reader is Luther's conviction that the Psalms contained, in essence, another form of prophecy; and Jesus was the true focus and theme of the Psalms as well.[d]

Not so long ago Christian interpreters and historians were not only untroubled by this relentless christological emphasis on Luther; many regarded it as a good thing, a symptom of the reorientation of piety back toward Jesus, after what was then viewed as a late Middle Ages unhealthily preoccupied with church traditions, the cult of saints and their relics (for instance). More recently, we have become more anxious, especially as it becomes evident just how much Luther's anti-Jewish rhetoric is tied up with his principles of biblical interpretation. Luther inherited a strong medieval tradition of reading the Bible christologically, to which his emphasis on *sola scriptura* added yet greater force and emphasis. Inseparable from that emphasis, in Luther, was his reaction that anyone who refused to see the

a See the *Preface to Daniel* in this volume, pp. 375–79; also Euan Cameron, "The Bible and the Early Modern Sense of History," in Cameron, ed., *New Cambridge History of the Bible*, 3:657–85, esp. 668–72.

b See Luther's *Preface to the Old Testament*, edited by Schramm in this volume, p. 58.

c See Luther's lectures on Isaiah 53, edited by Schramm, in this volume, esp. pp. 248–50.

d See especially Luther's exposition of Psalm 72, in his lectures on the Psalms from 1513–1515, as edited by Mickey Mattox in this volume, pp. 229–45.

prophecies of Jesus in the Hebrew Bible, once they were so clearly demonstrated, must be perverse or, indeed, possessed. While we are rightly appalled by the prescriptions for public policy at the very end of *The Jews and Their Lies* of 1543, it is important to reflect that the bulk of the book consists of debates over biblical interpretation.[e] Luther and the other reformers showed obsessive interest in the "seventy weeks" prophecy in Daniel 9:24-27, because this cryptic passage in what Christian readers understood as prophetic Scripture appeared not only to foretell the coming of the Messiah but to assign a date that could somehow be made to coincide with the ministry of Jesus Christ.

Luther could not, and never did wish, to allow himself the kind of double truth statement, where one might say, on the one hand, that the historical meaning of a text should be that which it held in the time and place where it was written; and, on the other, that a devotional Christian reading of a Hebrew Bible passage may be entertained as a nonexclusive spiritual or poetic reading, especially if such a reading has authority from the New Testament (as, for instance, in Matthew's Gospel). For Luther there was only one truth, and that truth focused on Jesus Christ. Here, if anywhere, one confronts the historical distance between Martin Luther and ourselves. Our religious cultures have long adjusted to the idea that different peoples perceive the divine differently, and perhaps with equal authority and credibility. Such a response was deeply unacceptable to our theological forebears. When we confront Luther on the Bible, we see so many insights that we can still use with benefit, above all Luther's passionate sense of the love of God. But we also witness the sheer remoteness of an age in which the truth of Scripture, unique, absolute, and infinitely precious, soared far above human ability to critique, modify, or qualify it.

e See TAL 5:441–607.

On Translating: An Open Letter

1530

VOLKER LEPPIN

INTRODUCTION[a]

During the sessions of the imperial diet at Augsburg,[1] Luther was lodged at Coburg castle, nearly seventy miles north of Nuremberg, both for safekeeping and for possible consultation, since Coburg was relatively more accessible to Augsburg than was Wittenberg. Like the Wartburg earlier, the Coburg castle—which Luther called "The Wilderness"—became his temporary home from 23 April to 4 October 1530.

Understandably anxious and apprehensive about the outcome of the Evangelical cause at Augsburg, Luther kept characteristically busy. His correspondence was weighty and voluminous, and his writings included a number of longer works in addition to what he had set as his foremost task while at the Coburg, that of translating. On the day of his arrival he wrote to Philip Melanchthon (1497–1560), "Out of this Sinai we shall make a Zion and build three tabernacles: One to the Psalter, one to the Prophets, and one to Aesop."[b]

1. Holy Roman Emperor Charles V (1500–1558) called this imperial diet but did not actually attend. Two key matters were to be addressed by those who gathered at Augsburg: "A defense had to be organized against the Turks, who had advanced as far as Vienna the preceding year. In addition, the religious dissension in the empire had to be overcome . . . [Charles] was concerned about arriving at a uniform, Christian truth, . . . and restoring the unity of the church" (Brecht 2:369).

a This introduction for *On Translating: An Open Letter* follows closely the introduction in LW 35:177–80 with just a few modifications.

b LW 35:177 n.1: "Margaret A. Currie (trans.), *The Letters of Martin Luther* (London: Macmillan, 1909), 208."

A sixteenth-century depiction of the Diet of Augsburg, 1530

Luther set to work immediately on the Prophets, first of all—in view of the continuing threat of the Turks against the empire—translating and preparing for special publication chapters 39 and 40 of Ezekiel, in which he interpreted Gog and Magog to be the Turks, hoping that all the faithful might thereby draw courage and comfort from this passage.[c] In the same letter of 12 May 1530, in which Luther announced his treatise on Ezekiel 38–39 concerning Gog, he also told of his intention to finish the Prophets by Ascension Day and how such had been thwarted by severe illness.[d] By 10 June he was finished with Jeremiah and working on Ezekiel, which proved—with his recurrent headaches—impossible to complete while at the Coburg. Meanwhile, he had taken up Hosea and completed all the Minor Prophets by early September. His wife, Katy, had heard that he was ill, and his letter of 8 September reassured her that he was well, had finished all the Prophets except one, and was working on Ezekiel again.[e]

Meanwhile, doctrinal issues central to the Reformation kept coming into his thoughts and writing, giving added pertinence to his task of translating. What was on his mind needed telling. Resorting to an open letter, Luther formulated his thoughts on translating and sent them to his friend, Wenceslaus Linck (1483–1547), at Nuremberg on 12 September to have them published. Linck turned the letter over to the Nuremberg printer, Johann Petreius (c. 1497–1550),[f] together with his own brief

c See the text of this brief treatise in WA 30/2:(220) 223–36. See also *On War Against the Turk* (1529), TAL 5:335–89.

d Currie, *Letters of Martin Luther*, 211–12.

e Currie, *Letters of Martin Luther*, 246–47. WA DB 2:xii–xiii.

f MA[3] 6:431. WA 30/2:632 incorrectly names Johann Stüchs as the printer.

introduction,[g] dated 15 September 1530, indicating that this was a letter of Luther which Linck had received "through a good friend."

Luther used this open letter to answer two questions that had apparently been put to him by some other "friend." Who that friend may have been we do not know. Nor does it matter, for the letter itself may well have been merely a literary device[h] for airing two doctrinal issues: the matter of justification by faith alone, and the question of intercessory prayer by the saints. Both issues had again come to the fore during the summer at Augsburg, notably in Melanchthon's encounter with Johann Eck (1486–1543) on the *sola fide*.[2] Luther's treatment of the second question is here so cursory (see page 37 where he announces his intention of treating it more fully elsewhere) that we have omitted mention of it in the title altogether.

2. Melanchthon was the leader of the delegation of Saxon theologians who went to the Diet of Augsburg. In Augsburg he received a new publication edited by Catholic theologian Johann Eck, a staunch opponent of the Wittenberg reformers.

His treatment of the first issue (justification by faith alone) involved him in a direct discussion of a basic principle of translation. Luther readily admits that at times it is necessary for the translator to depart from the literal meaning of the words of the original text in order to clarify in the new language their actual sense, and that a careful translation will sometimes therefore convey a meaning quite different from the one conventionally held.[i] His much-criticized translation of Rom. 3:28 is defended as being both theologically and linguistically just and necessary. By way of illustrating and buttressing this claim, Luther also touches on the problems of relinquishing the letters and rendering the sense of Matt. 12:34; 26:8; and the angelic salutation to Mary in Luke 1:28.

Ever since its first publication in 1522, Luther's translation of the New Testament had been drawing not only wide approval but also certain narrow and often envious criticism. Among his

g The editors of LW 35 included Linck's own introduction (see LW 35:181-82), which was omitted at PE 5:10.

h This interpretation is suggested by the editors in both WA 30/2:627 and CL 4:179.

i Cf. *Defense of the Translation of the Psalms*, LW 35:209, 216, 222, where the principle here enunciated with respect to translation of the New Testament is further illustrated in terms of the Old Testament.

sharpest critics was the notorious Jerome Emser (1478–1527), theologian, lawyer, and, for over twenty years, secretary to Duke George of Saxony (1471–1539). Like certain other rulers in the empire, Duke George had forbidden the circulation of Luther's German New Testament in his territory. In order not to be left without a New Testament in German, however, the Duke had commissioned Emser to provide a reliable Roman Catholic version. Emser obliged and, in the year of his death, lived to see the publication of his traditionalist version of the New Testament in German that followed the Latin Vulgate.

Outwardly, it looked almost identical to the folio edition of Luther's translation, even down to some of the Cranach woodcuts. But its introductions and glosses were all designed to cancel out those that accompanied Luther's version. The text of Emser's New Testament was based not on the original Greek text of Erasmus, which Luther had used, but on the Latin Vulgate and the late-medieval German Bible. With these traditional sources as his base, Emser proceeded to "correct" the errors in Luther's German New Testament; he did not claim to offer wholly a "new" version.

Emser's translation, however, was not as traditional as might be supposed. Actually, he had plagiarized much of Luther's translation and then palmed off the finished product as his own. Hence, the deep scorn and hostility that surges through Luther's open letter, here before us.

ON TRANSLATING: AN OPEN LETTER[j]

Wenceslaus Linck:[3] to all Believers in Christ

GOD'S GRACE AND MERCY. Solomon the Wise says, in Proverbs 11[:26], "The people curse him who holds back grain, but a blessing is on the head of him who sells it." This verse should really be understood to apply to everything that can serve the common good and well-being of Christendom. This is why the master in the gospel scolds the unfaithful servant as a slothful rogue for having buried and

Sketch portrait of Wenceslaus Linck

3. Wenceslaus Linck (1483–1547) was a member of the Augustinian hermits. He studied theology in Wittenberg and participated in the same humanist circles as Martin Luther. He served as a dean of the theological faculty from 1512 to 1514, and later followed the call of Staupitz as a preacher in Nürnberg in 1517–1519. In 1520, he became the successor of Staupitz as general vicar of the Augustinian hermits, but left the order to become a pastor in Altenburg in 1523. From 1525 on, he was a pastor in Nürnberg and one of Luther's closest associates.

j This translation is based on Theodore F. Bachman's revision of the translation of Charles Michael Jacobs in PE 5:10–27, in which he followed CL 4:180–93 (see also LW 35:180). Some updates have been made to the text.

hidden his money in the ground [Matt. 25:25-26]. In order to avoid this curse of the Lord and of the whole church, I just had to publish this letter which came into my hands through a good friend.[4] I could not hold it back. For there has been much talk about the translation of the Old and New Testaments.[5] The enemies of the truth charge that in many places the text had been modified or even falsified, whereby many simple Christians, even among the learned who do not know the Hebrew and Greek languages,[6] have been startled and shocked. With this publication it is devoutly to be hoped that, at least in part, the slander of the godless will be stopped and the scruples of the devout removed. Perhaps it may even give rise to further writing on questions and matters such as these. I therefore ask every lover of the truth to take this work seriously to heart and faithfully to pray God for a right understanding of the divine Scriptures, to the improvement and increase of our common Christendom. Amen.

Nuremberg, 15 September 1530.

To the honorable and worthy N., my esteemed lord and friend.

Grace and peace in Christ, honorable, worthy, and dear lord and friend. I have received your letter with the two questions, or inquiries, to which you ask my reply.[7] First, you ask why in translating the words of Paul in Rom. 3[:28], *Arbitramur hominem justificari ex fide absque operibus*, I rendered them thus: "We hold that a human being is justified without the works of the law, by faith alone."[8] You tell me, besides, that the papists are making a tremendous fuss, because the word *sola* (alone) is not in Paul's text, and this addition of mine to the words of God is not to be tolerated. Second, you ask whether the departed saints, too, intercede for us, since we read that angels indeed do intercede for us?

With reference to the first question, you may give your papists the following answer from me, if you like.

First, if I, Doctor Luther, could have expected that all the papists taken together would be capable enough to translate a single chapter of the Scriptures correctly and well, I should certainly have mustered up enough humility to invite their aid and assistance in putting the New Testament into German.[k] But

k LW 35:182 n.5: "Luther regularly availed himself of the best technical consultants he could assemble for assistance in the work of translating."

4. The good friend is none other than Martin Luther himself, as the subscription of the letter shows.

5. The question of translating the Bible was not new in Reformation times. There existed about fourteen Bibles in High German before 1522, when Luther's September Testament was published. In the prefaces to his *Novum Instrumentum*, Erasmus of Rotterdam (1466–1536) had argued for vernacular translations of the Bible. But when Luther's Testament came out, some scholars on the Roman Catholic side criticized it for appearing to promote Luther's doctrines by means of the choice of words in the translation (see the introduction, pp. 21–22).

6. The knowledge of both classic languages was a sign of humanistic education, as proclaimed by Melanchthon in his Wittenberg inaugural lecture of 1518.

7. Most scholars agree that the letter mentioned here is mere fiction.

8. Strangely enough, in his German text, Luther renders a version we do not find in his Bible translation before 1546.

because I knew—and still see with my own eyes—that none of them knows how to translate or to speak German, I spared them and myself that trouble. It is evident, indeed, that from my German translation they are learning to speak and write German, and so are stealing from me my language, of which they had little knowledge before.[9] They do not thank me for it, however, but prefer to use it against me. However, I readily grant them this, for it tickles me that I have taught my ungrateful pupils, even my enemies, how to speak.

Second, you may say that I translated the New Testament conscientiously and to the best of my ability. I have compelled no one to read it, but have left that open, doing the work only as a service to those who could not do it better. No one is forbidden to do a better piece of work. If anyone does not want to read it, he can let it alone. I neither ask anybody to read it nor praise anyone who does so. It is my Testament and my translation, and it shall continue to be mine. If I have made some mistakes in it—though I am not conscious of any and would certainly be most unwilling to give a single letter a wrong translation intentionally—I will not allow the papists [to act] as judges. For their ears are still too long, and their hee-haws[10] too weak, for them to criticize my translating. I know very well—and they know it even less than the miller's beast[11]—how much skill, energy, sense, and brains are required in a good translator. For they have never tried it.[12]

There is a saying, "He who builds along the road has many masters."[13] That is the way it is with me, too. Those who have never even been able to speak properly, to say nothing of translating, have all at once become my masters and I must be the pupil of them all. If I were to have asked them how to put into German the first two words of Matthew's Gospel, *Liber generationis*,[l] none of them would have been able to say Quack![14] And now they sit in judgment on my whole work! Fine fellows! That is the way it was with St. Jerome, too, when he translated the Bible.[15]

l LW 35:183 n.11 reads: "Matt. 1: 1, 'The book of the genealogy' (RSV), was rendered by Luther both in 1522 and in 1546, 'This is the book of the birth [of Jesus Christ].' WA DB 6:14–15. Emser's itemized critique of Luther's New Testament began with this very verse. His point, however, was that Luther's translation introduced a new idea in making David—rather than Jesus Christ—to be 'the son of Abraham.'" See *Annotationes Hieronimi Emsers vber Luthers Newe Testament* (4th ed.; 1529), p. xviii.

9. Here Luther alludes to Hieronymus Emser's Bible translation, which mainly presented the wording of Luther's Testament. One of the few exceptions was the passage in question, Rom. 3:28, where Emser omitted the word *alone*.

10. The German text here has "ycka ycka," which seems to be an onomatopoeia for the jackass's cry.

11. This makes clear again that the question is about jackasses.

12. Actually, there existed a lot of German Bible translations that Luther might have known, but none of them was based on the Hebrew or Greek original; instead, all were based on the Latin version of the Vulgate.

13. Meaning: Who is active in public gains many critics.

14. The German text has "gack," an onomatopoeia for goose.

15. Saint Jerome (c. 347–420), the translator of the Vulgate, was celebrated in the Renaissance, especially by Erasmus, as an example of humanist training and going *ad fontes* ("back to the sources").

Everybody was his master. He was the only one who was totally incompetent. And people who were not worthy to clean his shoes criticized the good man's work. It takes a great deal of patience to do a good thing publicly, for the world always wants to be Mr. Know-it-all.[m] It must always be putting the bit under the horse's tail, criticizing everything but doing nothing itself. That is its nature; it cannot get away from it.

I should like to see a papist who would come forward and translate even a single epistle of St. Paul or one of the prophets without making use of Luther's German translation. Then we should see a fine, beautiful, praiseworthy German translation! We have seen the Dresden scribbler[n] who played the master to my New Testament. I shall not mention his name again in my books as he has his Judge now,[16] and is already well known anyway. He admits that my German is sweet and good.[o] He saw that he could not improve on it. But eager to discredit it, he went to work and took my New Testament almost word for word as I had written it. He removed my introductions and explanations, inserted his own, and thus sold my New Testament under his name. Oh my, dear children, how it hurt me when his prince,[17] in a nasty preface, condemned Luther's New Testament and forbade the reading of it; yet commanded at the same time that the scribbler's New Testament be read, even though it was the very same one that Luther had produced!

16. Emser had died on 8 November 1527. So, his judge, now, was God.

17. He is referring to Duke George, "The Bearded," of Saxony (1471–1539), whose name is affixed to the 1527 preface to Emser's New Testament. However, Luther suspected that Emser was its real author; cf. his letter to Justus Jonas (1493–1555) of 10 December 1527, in S-J II:426–27.

That no one may think I am lying, just take the two Testaments, Luther's and the scribbler's, and compare them; you will see who is the translator in both of them. He has patched and altered it in a few places. And though not all of it pleases me, still I can let it go; it does me no particular harm, so far as the text is concerned. For this reason I never intended to write against it either. But I did have to laugh at the great wisdom that so terribly slandered, condemned, and forbade my New Testament, when it was published under my name, but made it required reading

m Ger.: *Meister Klüglin*, Luther's favorite expression for one who acts as if he or she knows everything better than anyone else.

n Emser (see the introduction, p. 22 above).

o LW 35:184 n.19: "Emser had admitted that Luther's translation 'was nicer and sounded better' than the old version, but added, 'This is why the common folk prefer to read it, and amid the sweet words they swallow the hook before they know it.'" See Arnold E. Berger, *Luthers Werke* (Leipzig: Bibliographisches Institut [no date]), III, 172, n. 2.

when it was published under the name of another. What kind of virtue that is, to heap slander and shame on somebody else's book, then to steal it and publish it under one's own name—thus, seeking personal praise and reputation through the slandered work of somebody else—I leave that for his Judge to discover. Meanwhile I am satisfied and glad that my work (as St. Paul also boasts [Phil. 1:18]) must be furthered even by enemies; and that Luther's book, without Luther's name but under that of his enemies, must be read. How could I avenge myself better?

But to return to the matter in hand! If your papist wants to make so much fuss about the word *sola* (alone) tell him this, "Dr. Martin Luther will have it so, and says that a papist and a jackass are the same thing." *Sic volo, sic jubeo; sit pro ratione voluntas.*[p] We are not going to be the pupils and disciples of the papists, but their masters and judges. For once, we, too, are going to be proud and brag with these jackass heads; and as St. Paul boasts over against his mad raving saints [2 Cor. 11:21ff.], so I shall boast over against these jackasses of mine. They are doctors? So am I. They are learned? So am I. They are preachers? So am I. They are theologians? So am I. They are debaters? So am I. They are philosophers? So am I. They are dialecticians? So am I. They are lecturers? So am I. They write books? So do I.

I will go further with my boasting. I can expound psalms and prophets; they cannot. I can translate; they cannot. I can read the Holy Scriptures; they cannot. I can pray; they cannot. And, to come down to their level, I can use their own dialectics and philosophy better than all of them put together; and besides I know for sure that none of them understands their Aristotle.[18] If there is a single one among them all who correctly understands one *proemium* [preface] or chapter in Aristotle, I'll let myself be punished. I am not saying too much, for I have been trained and practiced from my youth up in all their science and am well aware how deep and broad it is. They are very well aware, too, that I can do everything they can. Yet these incurable fellows treat me as though I were a stranger to their field, who had just arrived this morning for the first time and had never before either seen or heard what they teach and know. So brilliantly do they parade

18. Actually, as early as in his disputation against the Scholastics in 1517, Luther had attacked the use of Aristotle in theology. Nevertheless, he saw himself as an adequate exegete of the ancient philosopher.

p Juvenal, *Saturae* 6:223. Juvenal's original text begins "*Hoc volo.*" The exact form quoted by Luther is found in the fourteenth-century chronicles of Henry Knighton (d. 1396) and Walter of Guisborough (d. c. 1305) in the context of a critique of papal authoritarianism.

about with their science, teaching me what I outgrew twenty years ago, that to all their blatting and shouting I have to sing, with the girl, "I have known for seven years that horseshoe-nails are iron."[q]

Let this be the answer to your first question. And please give these jackasses no other and no further answer to their useless braying about the word *sola* than simply this, "Luther will have it so, and says that he is a doctor above all the doctors of the whole papacy." It shall stay at that! Henceforth I shall simply hold them in contempt, and have them held in contempt, so long as they are the kind of people—I should say, jackasses—that they are. There are shameless nincompoops among them who have never learned their own art of sophistry[19]—like Dr. Schmidt[20] and Dr. Snotty-brat,[21] and their likes—and who set themselves against me in this matter, which transcends not only sophistry, but (as St. Paul says [1 Cor. 1:19-25]), all the world's wisdom and understanding as well. Truly, a jackass need not sing much; he is already well known anyway by his ears.

19. Luther's polemical word for Scholasticism.

20. Johann Fabri/Faber (1478–1541); in German named Heigerlin. As a son of a smith, he took the Latin word for smith as his name: Faber, which, rendered in German again is Schmied or Schmidt. He served as a general vicar in Constance beginning in 1518, fighting against Ulrich Zwingli's (1484–1531) reform as well as Luther's. In 1530 he became bishop of Vienna.

21. The German word *Rotzloeffel*, used here, literally means "snotty spoon." Luther uses it for Johannes Cochlaeus (1479–1552), thinking of the Latin word *cochlear*, spoon. Cochlaeus, chaplain of Georg of Saxony, was one of the most active enemies of Luther.

Johannes Cochlaeus

q LW 35:186 n.25: "*Mit jhener metzen . . . Ich habs fur siben; jaren gewist, das hilffnegel eysen sind.* This obscure expression may possibly derive from a popular folk song."

To you and to our people, however, I shall show why I chose to use the word *sola*—though in Rom. 3[:28] it was not *sola*, but *solum* or *tantum* that I used,[22] so sharply do the jackasses look at my text! Nevertheless I have used *sola fide* elsewhere,[23] and I want both: *solum* and *sola*. I have constantly tried, in translating, to produce a pure and clear German, and it has often happened that for two or three or four weeks we have searched and inquired for a single word and sometimes not found it even then. In translating Job, Master Philip,[24] Aurogallus,[25] and I labored so, that sometimes we scarcely handled three lines in four days. Now that it is translated and finished, everybody can read and criticize it. One now runs his eyes over three or four pages and does not stumble once—without realizing what boulders and clods had once lain there where he now goes along as over a smoothly planed board. We had to sweat and toil there before we got those boulders and clods out of the way, so that one could go along so nicely. The plowing goes well when the field is cleared. But rooting out the woods and stumps, and getting the field ready—this is a job nobody wants. There is no such thing as earning the world's thanks. Even God himself can earn no thanks, with the sun, indeed with heaven and earth, or with his own Son's death. It simply is and remains world, in the devil's name, because it just will not be anything else.

Here, in Rom. 3[:28], I knew very well that the word *solum* is not in the Greek or Latin text; the papists did not have to teach me that. It is a fact that these four letters *s o l a* are not there. And these stubborn jackass heads stare at them like cows at a new gate. At the same time they do not see that it conveys the sense of the text; it belongs there if the translation is to be clear and vigorous.[26] I wanted to speak German, not Latin or Greek, since it was German I had undertaken to speak in the translation.[27] But it is the nature of our German language that in speaking of two things, one of which is affirmed and the other denied, we use the word *solum* (*allein*)[28] along with the word *nicht* [not] or *kein* [no]. For example, we say, "The farmer brings *allein* grain and *kein* money"; "No, really I have now *nicht* money, but *allein* grain"; "I have *allein* eaten and *nicht* yet drunk"; "Did you *allein* write it, and *nicht* read it over?" There are innumerable cases of this kind in daily use.

In all these phrases, this is the German usage, even though it is not the Latin or Greek usage. It is the nature of the German

22. As Luther stresses here, "alone" in his translation did not function as an adjective, but as an adverb.

23. E.g., in his Latin preface to Romans (WA DB 5:621,28). Actually, the formula "*sola fide*" was not invented by the reformers, but can be found in several medieval texts, as in Peter Lombard's (c. 1096–1160) commentary on Romans.

24. Philip Melanchthon was professor of Greek at the University of Wittenberg beginning in 1518 (see also n. 2, p. 21 above).

25. Matthäus Aurogallus (c. 1490–1543), professor of Hebrew in Wittenberg beginning in 1519. He gave the philological foundation for the translation of the Old Testament. The process of translation, as described here by Luther, is witnessed by the minutes that survived.

26. Luther here shows insights into the theory of language, discerning the literal wording and the thing signified behind it. This might be a fruit of his training in the logic of late medieval *via moderna*.

27. What Luther explains here is what we should now call a "target-language-oriented translation."

28. This adverb would be rendered in idiomatic English by either "alone" or "only."

29. In German this phrase is *auff das maul sehen*, which is a very popular quotation in contemporary Germany.

language to add the word *allein* in order that the word *nicht* or *kein* may be clearer and more complete. To be sure, I can also say, "The farmer brings grain and *kein* money," but the words "*kein* money" do not sound as full and clear as if I were to say, "The farmer brings *allein* grain and *kein* money." Here the word *allein* helps the word *kein* so much that it becomes a complete, clear German expression.

We do not have to inquire of the literal Latin, how we are to speak German, as these jackasses do. Rather, we must inquire about this of the mother in the home, the children on the street, the common man in the marketplace. We must watch their mouth[29] and be guided by their language, the way they speak, and do our translating accordingly. That way they will understand it and recognize that we are speaking German to them.

For example, Christ says: *Ex abundantia cordis os loquitur* [Matt. 12:34; Luke 6:45]. If I am to follow these jackasses, they will lay the original before me literally and translate thus: "Out of the abundance of the heart the mouth speaks." Tell me, is that speaking German? What German could understand something like that? What is "the abundance of the heart"? No German can say that; unless, perhaps, he was trying to say that someone was altogether too magnanimous or too courageous, though even that would not yet be correct. For "abundance of the heart" is not German, any more than "abundance of the house," "abundance of the stove," or "abundance of the bench" is German. But the mother in the home and the common man say this, "What fills the heart overflows the mouth."[r] That is speaking good German, the kind that I have tried for—and, unfortunately, not always reached or hit upon. For the literal Latin is a great hindrance to speaking good German.

So, for example, Judas the traitor says, in Matthew 26[:8], *Ut quid perditio haec?* and in Mark 14[:4], *Ut quid perditio ista unguenti facta est?* If I follow these literalistic jackasses I would have to translate it thus: "Why has this loss of ointment happened?" But what kind of German is that? What German says, "Loss of the ointment has happened"? If he understands that at all, he thinks that the ointment is lost and must be looked for and found again; though even that is still obscure and uncer-

r Luther uses a common proverb here: *Wes das hertz vol ist, des gehet der mund uber.*

tain. Now if that is good German, why do they not come out and make us a fine, pretty, new German Testament like that, and let Luther's Testament lie? I think that would really bring their talents to light! But a German would say *Ut quid*, etc., thus: "Why this waste?" Or, "Why this loss?" Indeed, "It's a shame about the ointment." That is good German, from which it is understood that Magdalene[30] had wasted the ointment that she poured out and been extravagant. That was what Judas meant, for he thought he could have used it to better advantage.

30. Luther here follows the traditional view that the nameless woman giving the ointment to Jesus according to Mark 14:3-9 was Mary Magdalene. In John 11:2; 12:1-3 the anointing is attributed to Mary of Bethany.

Again, when the angel greets Mary, he says, "Hail Mary, full of grace, the Lord is with you!" [Luke 1:28]. Up to now that has simply been translated according to the literal Latin.[s] Tell me whether that is also good German! When does a German speak like that, "You are full of grace"? What German understands what that is, to be "full of grace"? He would have to think of a keg "full of" beer or a purse "full of" money. Therefore I have translated it, "Thou gracious one," so that a German can at least think his way through to what the angel meant by this greeting. Here, however, the papists are going wild about me, because I have corrupted the Angelic Salutation;[31] though I have still not hit upon the best German rendering for it. Suppose I had taken the best German, and translated the salutation thus: "God's greeting to you, dear Mary"—for that is what the angel wanted to say, and what he would have said, if he had wanted to greet her in German. Suppose I had done that! I believe that they would have hanged themselves out of tremendous fanaticism for the Virgin Mary, because I had thus destroyed the salutation.

31. The Angelic Salutation was part of the *Ave Maria*, widely used as a prayer by laypeople.

But what do I care? They might rage or rave, I shall not prevent them from translating as they please. However, I shall translate, too, not as they please but as I please. Whoever does not like it can just leave it alone and keep his criticism to himself, for I shall neither look at nor listen to it. They do not have to answer for my translation, nor bear any responsibility for it. Listen well to this! I shall say "gracious [*holdselige*] Mary," and "dear [*liebe*]

s LW 35:191 n.48: The Latin Vulgate reads: *Ave gratia plena*. A New Testament history Bible of the fifteenth century, for example, written in German, simply retains these three untranslated Latin words for the opening of Gabriel's address to Mary, and follows them with a literal German paraphrase: *Ave gratia plena, Maria, du pist vol aller genaden*.

Mary," and let them say "Mary full of grace [*volgnaden*]." Whoever knows German knows very well what a fine, cordial [*hertzlich*] word that word *liebe* is: the dear Mary, the dear God, the dear emperor, the dear prince, the dear man, the dear child. I do not know whether this word *liebe* can be said in Latin or other languages with such fullness of sentiment, so that it pierces and rings through the heart, through all the senses, as it does in our language.

I believe that with the Greek *kecharitomene* [Luke 1:28] St. Luke, a master of the Hebrew and Greek tongues, wanted to render and clarify the Hebrew word that the angel used. And I think that the angel Gabriel spoke with Mary as he speaks with Daniel, calling him *Chamudoth* and *Ish chamudoth, vir desideriorum*, that is, "You dear Daniel"; for that is Gabriel's way of speaking, as we see in the book of Daniel. Now if I were to translate the angel's words literally, with the skill of these jackasses, I should have to say this, "Daniel, thou man of desires" (Daniel, *du man der begirungen*). Or: "Daniel, thou man of passions" (Daniel, *du man der lueste*). That would be pretty German! A German would hear, of course, that *Man*, *Lueste*, and *begyrunge* are German words—though not altogether pure German words, for *lust* and *begyr* would be better. But when the words are thus put together: "thou man of desires," no German would know what is said. He would think, perhaps, that Daniel is full of evil desires.[32] Well, that would be fine translating! Therefore I must let the literal words go and try to learn how the German says that which the Hebrew expresses with *ish chamudoth*. I find then that the German says this, "You dear Daniel," "You dear Mary," or "You gracious maid," "You lovely maiden," "You gentle girl," and the like. For a translator must have a great store of words, so that he can have them on hand in the event that one word does not fit in every context.

32. Indeed, as Luther implies here, *begirunge* and *lueste* have sexual connotations.

And why should I talk so much about translating? If I were to point out the reasons and considerations back of all my words, I should need a year to write on it. I have learned by experience what an art and what a task translating is. Therefore I will tolerate no papal jackass or mule to be my judge or critic, for they have never tried it. He who desires none of my translating may let it alone. If anyone dislikes it or criticizes it without my knowledge and consent, the devil repay him! If it is to be criticized, I shall do it myself. If I do not do it, then let them leave my translation in peace. Let each of them make for himself one that suits—what do I care?

This I can testify with a good conscience—I gave it my utmost in care and effort, and I never had any ulterior motives. I have neither taken nor sought a single penny for it, nor made one by it. Neither have I sought my own honor by it; God, my Lord, knows this. Rather, I have done it as a service to the dear Christians and to the honor of One who sits above, who blesses me so much every hour of my life that if I had translated a thousand times as much or as diligently, I should not for a single hour have deserved to live or to have a sound eye. All that I am and have is of his grace and mercy, indeed, of his precious blood and bitter sweat.[33] Therefore, God willing, all of it shall also serve to his honor, joyfully and sincerely. Scribblers and papal jackasses may[34] blaspheme me, but real Christians—and Christ, their Lord—bless me! And I am more than plentifully repaid, if even a single Christian acknowledges me as an honest workman. I care nothing for the papal jackasses; they are not worthy of acknowledging my work, and it would grieve me to the bottom of my heart if they blessed me. Their blasphemy is my highest praise and honor. I shall be a doctor anyway, yes, even a distinguished doctor; and that name they shall not take from me till the last day, this I know for certain.

On the other hand, I have not just gone ahead anyway and disregarded altogether the exact wording of the original. Rather, with my helpers[t] I have been very careful to see that where everything turns on a single passage, I have kept to the original quite literally and have not lightly departed from it. For example, in John 6[:27] Christ says, "Him has God the Father sealed [*versiegelt*]." It would have been better German to say, "Him has God the Father signified [*gezeichent*]," or, "He it is whom God the Father means [*meinet*]." But I preferred to do violence to the German language rather than to depart from the word. Ah, translating is not every man's skill as the mad saints imagine. It requires a right, devout, honest, sincere, God-fearing, Christian, trained, informed, and experienced heart. Therefore I hold that no false Christian or factious spirit can be a decent translator.[35] That becomes obvious in the translation of the Prophets made

t See annotations above on Melanchthon (n. 2, p. 21) and Aurogallus (n. 25, p. 29).

33. Luther, here, quite surprisingly, connects the question of his translating work with his doctrine of justification.

34. In 1523, Luther, together with Melanchthon, edited a pamphlet commenting on the drawing of a "*Papstesel*," papal jackass, a monstrous creature, allegedly found in the Tiber and interpreted as a sign for the moral and theological decline of the papacy.

35. This means, for Luther, translation is an act of belief, not only of scholarship.

at Worms.[36] It has been carefully done and approaches my German very closely. But Jews had a hand in it, and they do not show much reverence for Christ.[37] Apart from that there is plenty of skill and craftsmanship there. So much for translating and the nature of the languages!

Now I was not relying on and following the nature of the languages alone, however, when, in Roman 3[:28], I inserted the word *solum* (alone). Actually, the text itself and the meaning of St. Paul urgently require and demand it. For in that very passage he is dealing with the main point of Christian doctrine, namely, that we are justified by faith in Christ without any works of the law. And Paul cuts away all works so completely, as even to say that the works of the law—though it is God's law and word—do not help us for justification [Rom. 3:20]. He cites Abraham as an example and says that he was justified so entirely without works that even the highest work—which, moreover, had been newly commanded by God, over and above all other works and ordinances, namely circumcision—did not help him for justification; rather, he was justified without circumcision and without any works, by faith, as he says in chapter 4[:2], "If Abraham was justified by works, he may boast, but not before God." But when all works are so completely cut away—and that must mean that faith alone justifies—whoever would speak plainly and clearly about this cutting away of works will have to say, "Faith alone justifies us, and not works." The matter itself, as well as the nature of the language, demands it.

"But," they say, "it has an offensive sound, and people infer from it that they need not do any good works." My dear, what are we to say? Is it not much more "offensive" that St. Paul himself does not use the term "faith alone," but spells it out even more bluntly, and puts the finishing touches on it by saying, "Without the works of the law"? And in Galatians 1 [2:16] and many other places he says, "Not by the works of the law," for the expression "faith alone" is

36. Luther refers to the translation of the Old Testament prophets made by the Anabaptists Ludwig Hätzer (d. 1529) and Hans Denck (c. 1495–1527), published in Worms in 1527.

37. Indeed, it seems that Hätzer and Denck referred to Jewish counselors for their translation. Luther himself thought that the right translation of the Old Testament would convince the Jewish people to convert to Christianity.

The title page of *Alle Propheten nach Hebraischer sprach*, a German translation of the Old Testament Prophets by Ludwig Hätzer and Hans Denck (Augsburg edition, 1528)

susceptible of another interpretation,[u] but the phrase "without the works of the law" is so blunt, offensive, and scandalous that no amount of interpreting can help it. How much more might people learn from this "that they need not do any good works," when they hear this preaching about the works themselves put in such plain, strong words, "No works," "without works," "not by works"! If it is not "offensive" to preach "without works," "no works," "not by works," why should it be "offensive" to preach "by faith alone"?

And what is still more "offensive," St. Paul is here rejecting not just ordinary works, but "works of the law." Now someone could easily take offense at that all the more and say that the law is condemned and accursed before God, and we ought to be doing nothing but evil—as they did in Rom. 3[:8], "Why not do evil that good may come?" This is the very thing that one factious spirit began to do in our time.[38] Are we to deny Paul's word on account of such "offense," or stop speaking out freely about faith? My dear, St. Paul and I want to give such offense; we preach so strongly against works and insist on faith alone, for no other reason than that the people may be offended, stumble, and fall, in order that they may learn to know that they are not saved by their good works but only by Christ's death and resurrection. Now if they cannot be saved by the good works of the law, how much less shall they be saved by bad works, and without the law! For this reason it does not follow that because good works do not help, therefore bad works do help, any more than it follows that because the sun cannot help a blind man to see, night and darkness must, therefore, help him to see.

I am amazed that anyone can take exception in a matter as evident as this. Just tell me: Is Christ's death and resurrection our work, that we do, or is it not? Of course it is not our work, nor the work of any law either. Now it is Christ's death and resurrection alone that saves us and makes us free from sin, as Paul says in Rom. 4[:25], "He died for our sins and rose for our justification."

38. Luther here has in mind Thomas Müntzer (c. 1489–1525), one of the leaders in the Peasants' War.

u LW 35:196 n.63: "The inference referred to already in this very paragraph was early drawn by Luther's enemies, though he never intended to say that true faith is, or ever could be—much less should be—without good works. His point was not that faith is ever 'alone,' but that 'only' faith without works—hence, the term 'faith alone'—is necessary for justification before God." Cf. the famous passage in his *Preface to Romans*, in this volume, p. 467.

Tell me, further: What is the work by which we lay hold of Christ's death and resurrection? It cannot be any external work, but only the eternal faith that is in the heart. Faith alone, indeed, all alone, without any works, lays hold of this death and resurrection when it is preached by the gospel. Why then this raging and raving, this making of heretics and burning them at the stake, when the matter itself at its very core is so clear and proves that faith alone lays hold of Christ's death and resurrection, without any works, and that his death and resurrection [alone] are our life and our righteousness? Since, then, the fact itself is so obvious—that faith alone conveys, grasps, and imparts this life and righteousness—why should we not also say so? It is no heresy that faith alone lays hold on Christ, and gives life; and yet it must be heresy, if anyone mentions it. Are they not mad, foolish, and nonsensical? They admit that the thing is right, but brand the saying of it as wrong, though nothing can be both right and wrong at the same time.

Moreover, I am not the only one, or even the first, to say that faith alone justifies. Ambrose said it before me,[39] and Augustine and many others.[40] And if a human being is going to read St. Paul and understand him, he or she will have to say the same thing; she or he can say nothing else. Paul's words are too strong; they admit of no works, none at all. Now if it is not a work, then it must be faith alone. What a fine, constructive, and inoffensive doctrine that would be, if people were taught that they could be saved by works, as well as faith! That would be as much as to say that it is not Christ's death alone that takes away our sins, but that our works, too, have something to do with it. That would be a fine honoring of Christ's death, to say that it is helped by our works, and that whatever it does our works can do, too—so that we are his equal in strength and goodness! This is the very devil; he can never quit abusing the blood of Christ.

The matter itself in its very core, then, demands that we say, "Faith alone justifies." And the nature of our German language also teaches us to express it that way. I have in addition the precedent of the holy fathers. And the danger of the people also compels it, so that they may not continue to hang upon works and wander away from faith and lose Christ, especially in these days, for they have been accustomed to works so long they have to be torn away from them by force. For these reasons it is not only right but also highly necessary to speak it out as plainly and fully

39. Ambrosius (339–397). Actually, when the reformers referred to Ambrose as a witness of the right doctrine of justification they usually had in mind Ambrosiaster, author of pseudo-Ambrosian commentaries on Paul, quoted, for example, in CA 6.

40. Augustine (354–430), the patron of Luther's former monastic order, was cited as a main authority by Luther from his early days.

as possible, "Faith alone saves, without works." I am only sorry that I did not also add the words *alle* and *aller*, and say, "without *any* works of *any* laws," so that it would have been expressed with perfect clarity. Therefore it will stay in my New Testament, and though all the papal asses go stark raving mad they shall not take it from me.

Let this be enough for the present. If God gives me grace, I shall have more to say about it in the tract *On Justification*.[41]

Coming to the second question, whether the departed saints intercede for us, I shall give you only a brief answer now, for I am thinking of publishing a sermon on the angels in which, God willing, I shall treat this point more fully.[42]

In the first place you know that under the papacy it is not only taught that the saints in heaven intercede for us—though we cannot know this, since the Scriptures tell us no such thing—but the saints have also been made gods,[43] so that they have to be our patrons, on whom we are to call—some of whom never even existed.[44] To each of these saints some particular power and might has been ascribed. One has power over fire, another over water, another over pestilence, fever, and all kinds of disease. Indeed, God has had to be altogether idle, and let the saints work and act in his stead. The papists themselves are now aware of this abomination; they are quietly putting up their pipes, and presently preening and primping themselves with this teaching about the intercession of the saints. I shall defer this subject for the present, but you can bet I shall not forget it and allow their preening and primping to go unpaid for.

In the second place you know that there is not a single word of God commanding us to call on either angels or saints to intercede for us, and we have no example of it in the Scriptures. For we find that angels spoke with the fathers and the prophets, but none was ever asked to intercede for them. Even the patriarch Jacob did not ask the angel with whom he wrestled for any intercession, but merely took from him the blessing [Gen. 32:24-29]. Actually, we find in the Apocalypse the very opposite: the angel would not allow himself to be worshiped by John [Rev. 22:9]. Thus, the worship of saints shows itself to be nothing but human twaddle, man's own invention apart from the word of God and the Scriptures.

Since in the matter of divine worship, however, it is not proper for us to undertake anything without God's command—whoever

41. This work was never completed; just a fragment survived (WA 30/2:657–76): "*Rhapsodia seu concepta in Librum de loco iustificationis*."

42. Luther here has in mind his Coburg sermon for Saint Michael's Day (WA 32:111–21,553–55).

43. This obviously is not at all a conviction in the medieval or modern Roman Catholic Church, but Luther here echoes a longstanding complaint about the cult of saints as material helpers, which he expressed as early as his exposition of the Ten Commandments, as in WA 1:411–17.

44. As, for example, St. Christopher. WA 32:500,18–33.

does so is tempting God—it is therefore neither to be advised nor tolerated that we[v] should call upon the departed saints to intercede for us or teach others to call upon them. Rather, this is to be condemned, and we should be taught to avoid it. For this reason I, too, shall not advise it and so burden my conscience with other people's iniquities. It was exceedingly bitter for me to tear myself away from [the worship of] the saints, for I was steeped and fairly drowned in it. But the light of the gospel is now shining so clearly that henceforth no one has any excuse to remain in darkness. We all know very well what we ought to do.

Moreover, this is in itself a dangerous and offensive way of worship, because people are easily accustomed to turning from Christ; they quickly learn to put more confidence in the saints than in Christ himself. Our nature is, in any case, all too prone to flee from God and Christ and to trust in mortals. Indeed, it is exceedingly hard for one to learn to trust in God and Christ, though we have vowed and are in duty bound to do so. Therefore this offense is not to be tolerated, whereby those who are weak and of the flesh engage in idolatry, against the First Commandment and against our baptism. Even if you attempt nothing else but to switch people's confidence and trust from the saints to Christ, by both teaching and practice, that will be difficult enough to accomplish—that humanity should come to him and lay hold on him aright. There is no need to paint the devil on the door; he will be on hand anyway.

Finally, we are certain that God is not angry with us, and that we are quite safe, even if we do not call upon the saints to intercede for us, for he has never commanded it. He says that he is a jealous God, visiting their iniquities on those who do not keep his commandments [Exod. 20:5-6]; but here there is no commandment, and hence no wrath to be feared either. Since, then, there is on this side safety and on that side great danger and offense against God's word, why should we give ourselves over from safety into danger, where we have no word of God to sustain, comfort, and save us in time of need? For it is written, "Whoever loves danger will perish by it" [Ecclus. 3:26], and God's command says, "You shall not tempt the Lord your God" [Matt. 4:7].

v Singular pronouns have been rendered as plural in this sentence and the next.

"But," they say, "that way you condemn the whole of Christendom, which till now has everywhere maintained this." I reply: I know very well that the parsons and monks seek this cloak for their abominations. They want to impute to Christendom the damage wrought by their own negligence. Then when we say, "Christendom does not err," we shall be saying at the same time that they, too, do not err; that way they may not be accused of any falsehood or error, since Christendom holds it to be so. Thus, no pilgrimage can be wrong, however manifestly the devil is a party to it; no indulgence can be wrong, however gross the lies that are involved—in a word, there is nothing there but holiness! Therefore to this you should reply, "It is not a question of who is and who is not condemned." They inject this extraneous subject in order to lead us away from the subject at hand. We are now discussing God's word. What Christendom is or does belongs elsewhere. The question here is: What is or is not God's word? What is not God's word does not make Christendom.

This anti-Catholic woodcut (1546) portrays the pope (note the papal crown) as the Antichrist, half bull and half human, trampling books and wielding a sword. From a volume by Rudolf Gwalther (1519–1586).

We read that in the days of Elijah the Prophet there was apparently no word of God and no worship of God in all Israel. For he says, "Lord, they have slain thy prophets and thrown down thy altars, and I am left completely alone" [1 Kings 19:10, 14]. Here King Ahab and others might have said, "Elijah, with talk like that you condemn the whole people of God." However, God had at the same time kept seven thousand [1 Kings 19:18]. How? Do you not think that God could now also, under the papacy, have preserved his own, even though the parsons and monks within Christendom have been mere teachers of the devil and gone to hell? Many children and young people have died in Christ. For even under Antichrist,[45] Christ has forcibly preserved Baptism, the simple text of the gospel in the pulpit, the Lord's Prayer, and the Creed; whereby he preserved many of his Christians, and hence also his Christendom, and said nothing about it to these devil's teachers.

And even though Christians have done some bits of the papal abomination, the papal jackasses have not yet thereby proved that they did it gladly; still less does it prove that they did the right

45. "Antichrist" is Luther's word for the papacy, which he identified with the Antichrist from 1519.

thing. All Christians can err and sin, but God has taught them all to pray in the Lord's Prayer for forgiveness of sins. And God could very well forgive the sins they had to commit unwillingly, unknowingly, and under the compulsion of Antichrist—without saying anything about it to the parsons and monks! This, however, can easily be proved, that in all the world there has always been a lot of secret murmuring and complaining against the clergy, that they were not treating Christendom properly. And the papal asses have valiantly withstood such murmuring with fire and sword, down to the present day. This murmuring proves how happy Christians have been over these abominations, and how right they have been in doing them!

So come right out with it you papal jackasses and say that this is the teaching of Christendom: these stinking lies which you villains and traitors have imposed by force upon Christendom, and for the sake of which you arch-murderers have slain many Christians. Why, every letter of every papal law bears witness to the fact that nothing has ever been taught by the counsel and consent of Christendom. There is nothing there but *districte precipiendo mandamus.*[46] That has been their Holy Spirit. This tyranny Christendom has had to endure; by it, it has been robbed of the Sacrament, and, through no fault of its own, been held in captivity.[w] And the jackasses would palm off on us this intolerable tyranny of their own wickedness, as a willing act and example of Christendom—and so clear themselves!

46. "We command by strict instruction": a phrase often used in papal and episcopal decrees.

But this is getting too long. Let this be answer enough to your questions this time. More another time. Pardon this long letter. Christ our Lord be with us all. Amen.

Martin Luther,
Your good friend.
The Wasteland,[47] 8 September 1530.

47. Luther's codeword for the Coburg castle.

w An allusion to Luther's tract *On the Babylonian Captivity of the Church*, TAL 3:9–129; LW 36:11–126.

Preface to the Old Testament

1545 (1523)

BROOKS SCHRAMM

INTRODUCTION

Translations of the Bible into German had been in circulation since the fourteenth century, but each of these was based on the Latin Vulgate. The impetus to translate the entire Bible into German from the original Hebrew and Greek languages seems initially to have come from Philip Melanchthon (1497–1560), who suggested this to Luther in December 1521 while Luther was visiting Wittenberg from the Wartburg.[a] The translation project—together with its ongoing process of revision[1]—was a work of immense labor and, once begun, occupied Luther until the end of his life.

1. The most substantial revision took place from 1539 to 1541.

Immediately after his completion of the New Testament translation, which had spanned a mere eleven weeks, Luther set to work early in 1522 on the Pentateuch, the first five books of the Old Testament ("The Five Books of Moses"), and the translation was in print by midsummer 1523 under the title *Das Alte Testament Deutsch*. During this initial translation work on the Old Testament, Luther was in close collaboration with Melanchthon,

a See Luther's 18 December 1521 letter to Johann Lang (c. 1487–1548), LW 48:356–57.

Title page of the first part of Luther's translation of the Old Testament. Woodcut illustrations provided by the workshop of Lucas Cranach the Elder. Published by Melchior Lotter in Wittenberg in 1523.

Matthaeus Aurogallus (1490–1543),[2] and Georg Spalatin (1484–1545).[3] Luther's initial plan was to publish the Old Testament in three installments: (1) Pentateuch; (2) Historical Books; (3) Poetic and Prophetic Books. The second part (Joshua–Esther) was in print by January 1524; the poetic books (Job–Song of Songs) and Psalms were in print by the early fall of 1524, but the remaining books (the Prophets and the Apocrypha) were not fully completed until 1534. The first complete printed Luther Bible was actually in Low German—a collaborative project of Luther and Johannes Bugenhagen (1485–1558)—and published in April 1534 in Lübeck by Ludwig Dietz. "The Complete German Bible" in High German (*Die ganze Heilige Schrift Deutsch*) was finally published in September 1534. As evidence of the ongoing work of revision and correction, a total of eleven editions of the Luther Bible appeared from 1534 to 1545 in Wittenberg.[4] The posthumously published edition of 1546 incorporated a handful of Luther's own New Testament revisions that had not been included in 1545.[b]

2. Matthaeus Aurogallus (Goldhahn) taught Hebrew at the University of Wittenberg from 1521 to 1543.

3. In a 13 January 1522 letter to Nicholas von Amsdorf (1483–1565), Luther acknowledged that translating the Hebrew Old Testament would have to be a team project (LW 48:363). As work on the OT translation progressed, the circle of scholars working with Luther—the *collegium biblicum* or "Wittenberg Sanhedrin"—would become broader. (On Luther's Hebrew expertise, see Stephen G. Burnett, "Luther and Hebrew," in *Hebrew Between Christians and Jews*, ed. Daniel Stein Kokin, Studia Judaica [Berlin: de Gruyter, 2015]).

4. At Luther's death, it is estimated that 500,000 complete or partial copies of his Bible were in print.

The title page of the complete Luther Bible: "The Bible, that is the Entire Holy Scripture [in] German. Mart. Luth. Wittemberg. Favored with Electoral Freedom in Saxony. Printed by Hans Lufft, 1534." On one balcony is seated an old man with a halo writing in a book. In front of him hangs a parchment with the words "The Word of the Lord endures for ever."

As did his great predecessor in Bible translation, Jerome,[5] Luther provided the books of the Bible, or groups of books, with explanatory prefaces (*Vorreden*), the purpose of which was to alert the common reader to the central themes to be encountered in the respective books. Not only are these prefaces invaluable, concise resources for understanding what Luther regarded as fundamental for proper reading of the Bible, but they also contain his candid theological evaluations of the respective biblical books in light of the gospel.[c] In addition to the prefaces, the Luther Bibles also contained copious marginal explanatory notes (glosses or annotations), references to parallel biblical

5. Hieronymus, St. Jerome (347–420), the translator of the Latin Vulgate Bible. Because his Old Testament was translated directly from the Hebrew, it superseded the "Old Latin" version, which had been translated from the Greek.

b For further detail on the Luther Bible, see Brecht 2:46–56; 3:95–113; Raeder 2:363–406 (esp. 395–400); M. Reu, *Luther's German Bible* (Columbus, OH: Lutheran Book Concern, 1934), 146–256. The standard study in German is Hans Volz, *Martin Luthers deutsche Bibel: Entstehung und Geschichte der Lutherbibel* (Hamburg: Wittig, 1978).

c See Theodore Bachmann's "Introduction" to *Prefaces to the Books of the Bible* (LW 35:227–32).

texts, and numerous illustrations (often in color).[6] Though directed to the common reader, when the prefaces and marginal notes are taken together, they function as a concise presentation of Luther's own theological interpretation of the Bible.[7]

6. The 1534 Luther Bible contained 117 woodcuts, most of which came from the workshop of Lucas Cranach (1472–1553). Luther had given specific instructions that the illustrations were not to "deface" the text but, rather, "serve" it (Brecht 3:98).

7. "The Luther Bible, with its prefaces and glosses, is an essential document for determining Luther's theological and historical position. It reflects specific situations, with their options and condemnations, together with the whole range of world, church, politics, and society. To a considerable extent, Luther's own church was molded by it, and thereby the Luther Bible became one of the fundamental pillars of the Lutheran church in Germany" (Brecht 3:100).

Das Erst Buch Mose. I.

I.

AM anfang schuff Gott himel vnd erden/Vnd die erde war wüst vnd leer/vnd es war finster auff der tieffe/vnd der Geist Gottes schwebet auff dem wasser.

Vnd Gott sprach/Es werde liecht/Vnd es ward liecht/vnd Gott sahe das liecht fur gut an/Da scheidet Gott das liecht vom finsternis/ vnd nennet das liecht/Tag/vnd die finsternis/Nacht/Da ward aus abend vnd morgen der erste tag.

Vnd Gott sprach/Es werde eine feste zwisschen den wassern/vnd die sey ein vnterscheid zwisschen den wassern/Da macht Gott die Feste/vnd scheidet das wasser hunden/von dem wasser droben an der Festen/Vnd es geschach also/Vnd Gott nennet die Festen/Himel/Da ward aus abend vnd morgen der ander tag.

Vnd Gott sprach/Es samle sich das wasser vnter dem himel/an sondere örter/das man das trocken sehe/ vnd es geschach also/ Vnd Gott nennet das trocken/Erde/vnd die samlung der wasser nennet er/Meere/Vnd Gott sahe es fur gut an.

Vnd Gott sprach/Es lasse die erde auff gehen gras vnd kraut/das sich besame / vnd fruchtbare beume/ da ein iglicher nach seiner art frucht trage/vnd habe seinen eigen samen bey im selbs/auff erden/Vnd es geschach also/Vnd die erde lies auff gehen/gras vnd kraut/das sich besamet/ein iglichs nach seiner art/vnd beume die da frucht trugen/vnd iren eigen samen bey sich selbs hatten/ein iglicher nach se[i]ner art/Vnd Gott sahe es fur gut an/Da ward aus abend vnd morgen der dritte tag.

Vnd Gott sprach/Es werden Liechter an der Feste des Himels/vnd scheiden tag vnd nacht / vnd geben/zeichen/monden/tage vnd iare/vnd seten liecher an der Festen des himels/das sie scheinen auff erden/Vnd es geschach also/Vnd Gott macht zwey grosse liechter/Ein gros liecht/das den tag regire/vnd ein klein liecht/das die nacht regire/dazu auch sternen/Vnd Gott setzt sie an die Feste des himels / das sie schienen auff die erde/vnd den tag vnd die nacht regirten/vnd scheideten liecht vnd finsternis/Vnd Gott sahe es fur gut an/Da ward aus abend vnd morgen der vierde tag.

Zeichen / als der sonnen/vnd monden finsternis / vnd andere wunder am himel. Monden/ als die Jar feste/als new monden/vol monden etc. Tage / als die Ostern / Pfingsten/ etc. vnd bey vns die Quatember/ vnd andere namhafftige tage im iar.

Vnd Gott sprach/Es errege sich das wasser mit webenden vnd lebendigen thiern/vnd mit geuogel das auff erden vnter der Feste des himels fleuget/Vnd Gott schuff grosse walfische vnd allerley thier/das da lebt vnd webt/vnd vom wasser erregt ward/ein iglichs nach seiner art/vnd allerley gefiderts geuogel/ein iglichs nach seiner art/Vnd Got sahe es fur gut an/vnd segnet sie/vnd sprach/Seid fruchtbar vnd mehret euch/vnd erfüllet das wasser im meer/ vnd das geuogel mehre sich auff erden/Da ward aus abend vnd morgen der funffte tag.

Vnd Gott sprach/ Die erde bringe erfur lebendige thier/ein iglichs nach seiner art/viech/gewürm vnd thier auff erden/ein iglichs

A nach

First page of the book of Genesis in the 1534 Luther Bible, showing marginal annotations

The *Preface to the Old Testament* was originally composed for the publication of the Pentateuch in 1523, and, thus, Luther only makes brief allusions to the contents of the remainder of the Old Testament. The title is, therefore, somewhat of a misnomer.[8] Two issues are of central concern in this particular preface. The first is Christian neglect of the Old Testament. Luther wants his readers to know that the Old and New Testaments are actually inseparable and that the New Testament itself constantly points Christians back to the Old.[d] It is in this context that Luther famously states about the Old Testament: "Here you will find the swaddling cloths and the manger in which Christ lies, and to which the angel points the shepherds. Plain and lowly are

8. Toward the end of his life, Luther planned to write a new preface to the entire Bible in which he would strongly criticize the use of rabbinic sources by Christian translators, but this preface never manifested. (See Table Talk #5324, LW 54:408).

d This point is developed at length in *A Brief Instruction on What to Look For and Expect in the Gospels* (1521), TAL 2:25–37; LW 35:117–24.

these swaddling cloths, but precious is the treasure, Christ, who lies wrapped in them." The second is the role of Moses and the problem of the law for Christians. It is in this context that Luther explicates Moses's proper office in the lives of Christians, namely, the revelation of sin and of human inability, and of death as the punishment for the same. On the one hand, Christians should not confuse Moses with Christ or law with gospel; yet, on the other hand, Christians must recognize the indispensable and ongoing role that Moses and the law play in the service of Christ.[e]

Outline of *Preface to the Old Testament*

- Luther's appeal on behalf of the Old Testament
    - The Old Testament is theologically indispensable
- What to expect in the Old Testament
    - Old Testament as law-book (*Gesetzbuch*)
    - New Testament as grace-book (*Gnadenbuch*)
- Brief descriptions of:
    - Genesis
    - Exodus
    - Leviticus
    - Numbers
    - Deuteronomy
- The nature of Moses's law:
    - God does not allow the people self-chosen works
    - Three kinds of laws:
        - Laws regarding temporal goods
        - Laws regarding external worship
        - Laws regarding faith and love
        - Excursus: Why the laws are arranged in disorderly fashion

e On this second issue, see *How Christians Should Regard Moses* (1526), TAL 2:127–51; LW 35:161–74; Heinrich Bornkamm, *Luther and the Old Testament*, ed. Victor I. Gruhn, trans. Eric W. and Ruth C. Gritsch (Mifflintown, PA: Sigler Press, 1997), 120–79; Bernhard Lohse, *Martin Luther's Theology: Its Historical and Systematic Development*, trans. Roy A. Harrisville (Minneapolis: Fortress Press, 1999), 267–76; Hans-Martin Barth, *The Theology of Martin Luther: A Critical Assessment* (Minneapolis: Fortress Press, 2012), 135–56.

- The true meaning of the law, i.e., Moses's proper office
    - The law reveals sin and human inability, and death as punishment
    - Moses apart from Christ
    - Moses in the light of Christ
- Three kinds of students of the law
- The end of the law
    - Deut. 18:15
- The other books of the Old Testament
    - All of them inculcate the office of Moses
        - They bring everyone to Christ via the law
- The "spiritual interpretation" of the Levitical law
- Conclusion
    - Rendering the *Tetragrammaton*
    - Luther's apology for his Bible translation

The Translation

The translation presented here is a revision of LW 35:235–51 and is based on the preface in the 1545 Luther Bible, WA DB 8:11–31 (odd numbers). The conclusion, which did not appear in the 1545 edition, is based on the original preface of 1523, WA DB 8:30–32 (even numbers). Luther's biblical quotes and allusions have been translated directly.[f] Insofar as possible, Luther's terminology has been rendered consistently throughout the translation.

f Direct translations from the Luther Bible may at times differ from the the biblical versions used in LW or quoted in these TAL volumes.

PREFACE TO THE OLD TESTAMENT

THERE[g] ARE SOME who have a low opinion of the Old Testament; they regard it as a book that was given to the Jewish people alone and is now out of date, containing only stories of past times.[9] They think the New Testament is enough and assert that merely a spiritual sense[h] is to be sought in the Old Testament. Origen,[10] Jerome,[i] and many other distinguished people have held this view.[11] But Christ says in John 5[:39], "Search the Scripture,[12] for it bears witness to me."[13] St. Paul commands Timothy to attend to the reading of Scripture,[j] and in Rom. 1[:2] he declares that the gospel was promised by God in Scripture, while in 1 Cor. 15[:3-4] he says that in accordance with Scripture Christ came from David's blood,[k] died, and was raised from the dead. St. Peter, too, points us back to Scripture more than once.

They do this in order to teach us that Old Testament Scripture[l] is not to be disregarded but rather diligently read. For they themselves so strongly base the New Testament upon it, proving the New through the Old, and appealing to it, as St. Luke also writes in Acts 17[:11], saying that those at Thessalonica searched Scripture daily to see whether these things were so that Paul was teaching. Just as the basis and proof of the New Testament are surely not to be disregarded, so the Old Testament is to be highly regarded. And what else is the New Testament but public

g WA DB 8:11; LW 35:235.

h *Geistliche sinn*, i.e., the allegorical sense.

i See n. 5, p. 43 above.

j 1 Tim. 4:13.

k There is no actual reference to Christ's Davidic descent in 1 Corinthians 15. Luther is likely thinking here of Rom. 1:3.

l LW 35:236.

9. See *Brief Instruction* (1521), TAL 2:36; LW 35:123: "But what a fine lot of tender and pious children we are! In order that we might not have to study in the Scriptures and learn Christ there, we simply regard the entire Old Testament as of no account, as done for and no longer valid. Yet it alone bears the name of Holy Scripture."

10. Origen of Alexandria (c. 185–c. 254). Though clearly one of the greatest minds in Christian history, Luther rarely, if ever, has anything good to say about him due to his allegorical method of exegesis.

11. Though not explicitly mentioned, Luther may well have Erasmus (1466–1536) in mind here, for he was the one who regarded the Old Testament as essentially obsolete for Christians and who also viewed Origen as the greatest of all Christian interpreters. In a 1518 letter to the Christian Hebraist, Wolfgang Capito (c. 1478–1541), Erasmus wrote: "Oh, [I wish] that the Church of the Christians would not value the Old Testament so highly. It is almost preferred to the Christian scriptures, although it has been given only for a limited time and consists of nothing but darkness." Quoted in Raeder 2:370.

12. As always in the New Testament, "Scripture" here refers to the Old Testament. Luther actually preferred this New Testament usage, arguing that the Old Testament alone rightly bears the title of "Sacred Scripture," with the gospel being best regarded as an oral or spoken word. See *Brief Instruction*, TAL 2:36; LW 35:123.

13. It is hard to overestimate the significance of this biblical text for preaching and proclamation about Christ, set forth through the sayings in the Old Testament and fulfilled through Christ?[14]

In order that those who are not more familiar with it may have an introduction and instruction for reading the Old Testament with profit, I have prepared this preface to the best of the ability God has given me. I request and faithfully admonish every pious Christian not to be offended by the simplicity of the language and stories frequently encountered there, and not to doubt that, however plain they may seem, these are the very words, works, judgments, and stories of the high divine majesty, might, and wisdom. For this is the Scripture that makes fools of all the wise and prudent and that is open only to the small and simple,[m] as Christ says in Matt. 11[:25]. Therefore let go of your own thoughts and feelings, and regard this Scripture as the highest and noblest sanctuary, as the richest of mines which can never be sufficiently explored, so that you may find that divine wisdom that God lays before you here so simply and plainly, in order to quench all pride. Here you will find the swaddling cloths and the manger in which Christ lies, and to which the angel points the shepherds.[n] Plain and lowly are these swaddling cloths, but precious is the treasure, Christ, who lies wrapped in them.[15]

Know, then, that this book is a book of law,[o] which teaches what one ought and ought not to do.[16] In addition, it provides examples and stories of how these laws are kept or transgressed. Similarly, the New Testament is a gospel or a book of grace,[p] and it teaches how the law is fulfilled. But just as in the New Testament there are also given, beside the teaching about grace, many other teachings which are laws and commandments for governing the flesh, since in this life the Spirit is not perfected and pure grace cannot[q] govern, so also in the Old Testament there are, beside the laws, certain promises and sayings about grace, through which the holy ancestors and prophets who lived under the law were

m WA DB 8:13.

n Luke 2:12.

o *Gesetzbuch.*

p *Gnadenbuch.*

q LW 35:237.

Luther. It functions as the linchpin in any of his arguments for the indispensability of the Old Testament for Christian theology. Closely related in significance is John 4:22: "Salvation comes from the Jews."

14. A programmatic claim by Luther, deeply informed by his reading of Romans: "it appears that Paul wanted in this one epistle to sum up briefly the whole Christian and evangelical doctrine, and to prepare an introduction to the entire Old Testament" (*Preface to Romans*, this volume, p. 479; LW 35:380).

15. This is one of Luther's most beloved statements about the Bible, but it is a double-edged sword. Such a description of the Old Testament makes clear that Luther is as far removed from Marcionism as it is possible to be. Luther elevated the significance of the Old Testament for Christian theology to a degree rarely seen before him, and yet it is this very move that placed him on an unavoidable collision course with Jewish biblical interpretation. (See the similar formulation in *Brief Instruction*, TAL 2:33–34; LW 35:122.)

16. Luther's statement applies to the Old Testament in general, but most specifically to the Pentateuch or the "Five Books of Moses." As will be seen below, Luther regards the remainder of the Old Testament as essentially an explication of the Pentateuch.

preserved, like us, by faith in Christ.[17] Nevertheless, just as the real main teaching of the New Testament is the proclamation of grace and peace through the forgiveness of sins in Christ, so the real main teaching of the Old Testament is the teaching of laws, the disclosing of sin, and the demanding of good. This is what to expect in the Old Testament.

Genesis. Frontispiece depicting the Creation, from the 1534 Luther Bible. Colored woodcut.

17. For Luther, the Old Testament—properly understood—is a Christian book, and the two volumes of the Christian Bible, therefore, constitute a theological unity. This is what enables him to speak of the church as being present already in the Old Testament and to speak of certain Old Testament characters (even Moses!) as Christians. What binds the two volumes of the Christian Bible together is the promise of the coming of the Messiah and faith in that promise. His key claim is that the faith of the Old Testament and the faith of the New Testament are the same. (See Brooks Schramm and Kirsi I. Stjerna, eds., *Martin Luther, the Bible, and the Jewish People: A Reader* [Minneapolis: Fortress Press, 2012], 13).

We come first to the books of Moses.[18] In his first book,[19] Moses teaches how all creatures were created, and—as the primary reason for his writing—where sin and death came from, namely, through Adam's fall, from the devil's malice. But immediately thereafter, before Moses's law comes, he teaches where the help comes from for driving out sin and death, namely, not through the law or one's own works (because there was no law as yet), but rather through the woman's seed—Christ—promised to Adam and Abraham.[20] This was so that faith might be thoroughly praised from the beginning of Scripture above all works, laws, and merits. The first book of Moses, therefore, is made up almost entirely of examples of faith and unbelief, and of the fruits that faith and unbelief produce. It is a very evangelical book.[21]

Thereafter, in the second book,[22] when the world was now full and sunk in blindness so that it was scarcely known any longer what sin was or where death came from, God brings Moses forward with the law and takes a particular people, in order to enlighten the world again through them, and through the law to reveal sin anew.[23] He therefore encompasses this people with all kinds of laws and[r] separates them from all other peoples. He has them build a tent and establishes divine worship. He appoints princes and officials, and provides his people with both laws and persons of the finest sort to govern them both bodily before the world and spiritually before God.[24]

In the third book,[25] the particular issue is the appointment of the priesthood, with its laws and statutes according to which the priests are to act and to teach the people. There we see that the priestly office[26] is instituted only because of sin, to make the same known to the people, and to make atonement before God. Thus, its entire task[s] concerns sins and sinners. For this reason, too, no temporal holding is given to the priests; neither are they ordered or permitted to govern bodily. Rather, they are to care for the people assigned to them who are in their sins.

In the fourth book,[27] after the laws have been given, the priests and princes instituted, the tent and divine worship established, and everything that pertains to the people of God made ready, then the whole thing commences and a test is made as to how well the arrangement operates and how suitable it is. That is why

r WA DB 8:15.

s LW 35:238.

18. In the Luther Bible, the first five books of the OT are called "The First, Second, Third, Fourth, and Fifth Books of Moses."

19. Genesis.

20. A persuasive case can be made that Gen. 3:15, the so-called *Protoevangelium* ("I will put enmity between you and the woman, and between your seed and her seed; he will tread on your head, and you will sting his heel"), was regarded by Luther as the single most important text in the interpretation of the Old Testament. In all editions of the Luther Bible, he included this marginal note for the reader of Gen 3:15: "This is the first gospel and promise of Christ on earth, to the effect that he will overcome sin, death, and hell and save us from the power of the Serpent. In this, Adam believed together with all of his descendants, (and) by which he became a Christian and was saved from his fall" (WA DB 8:45).

21. From 1535 to 1545 Luther would lecture through the entire book of Genesis (*Lectures on Genesis*, LW vols. 1-8), a work that can be regarded as his magnum opus. For a fine study of the Genesis lectures, see John A. Maxfield, *Luther's Lectures on Genesis and the Formation of Evangelical Identity* (Kirksville, MO: Truman State University Press, 2008). See also lectures on Genesis 1:26—2:3; 2:21-25; and 3:1-15 in this volume, pp. 67-201.

22. Exodus.

23. A concise statement describing the divine purpose in the election of the people, Israel.

24. The terms "before the world" (*vor der Welt*; *coram mundo*) and "before God" (*vor Gott*; *coram Deo*) correspond to Luther's distinction between the

this book says so much about the disobedience and the plagues of the people, and why some laws are explained and enhanced. Indeed, this is the way it always goes; laws are quickly given, but when they are to go into effect and become operative, they meet with nothing but pure obstruction, and nothing goes as the law demands. This book is a distinct example of how vacuous it is to try to make people pious with laws; rather, as St. Paul says, the law only brings about sin and wrath.[t]

In the fifth book,[28] after the people have been punished for their disobedience, and God has enticed them a little with grace, in order that by the benevolence of giving them the two kingdoms[u] they might be moved to keep God's law with delight and love, Moses then repeats the entire law. He repeats the stories of what had happened to them (except for that which concerns the priesthood) and explains anew everything that belongs either to the bodily or to the spiritual government of a people. Thus, Moses, as a consummate lawgiver, fulfilled all the duties of his office. He not only gave the law but was also there when it was supposed to be practiced. When things went wrong, he explained and re-established it. But this explanation in the fifth book really contains nothing else than faith toward God and love toward one's neighbor, for all of the laws of God come to[v] that. Therefore, down to the twentieth chapter, Moses, with his explanation, opposes everything that might destroy faith in God; and from there to the end of the book he opposes everything that hinders love.

It[w] is to be noted in the first place that Moses encompasses the people so precisely with laws such that he leaves reason no room to choose any work or to invent its own divine worship. For he not only teaches fear, love, and trust toward God, but he also provides so many ways of outward divine worship—sacrifices, thanksgivings, fasts, mortifications,[x] etc.—that no one needs to choose anything else. Also, he teaches about planting and

two kingdoms or realms, both sets of which describe the tensive nature of human existence. See Bernhard Lohse, *Martin Luther's Theology: Its Historical and Systematic Development*, trans. Roy A. Harrisville (Minneapolis: Fortress Press, 1999), 314–24; Robert Kolb, "Luther's Hermeneutics of Distinctions: Law and Gospel, Two Kinds of Righteousness, Two Realms, Freedom and Bondage," in *The Oxford Handbook of Martin Luther's Theology*, ed. Robert Kolb, Irene Dingel, and L'ubomír Batka (Oxford: University Press, 2014), 168–84.

25. Leviticus.

26. German *Amt* and Latin *officium* are technical terms in Luther and are widespread in the corpus. The terms have their origin in the secular sphere, and Luther uses them to identify a person's particular responsibilities in his or her God-given vocation.

27. Numbers.

28. Deuteronomy.

t Cf. Rom. 4:15.

u On the two kingdoms and two governments in Luther, see *How Christians Should Regard Moses*, in TAL 2:127–51; Lohse, *Martin Luther's Theology*, 151–59; 314–24; Barth, *Theology of Martin Luther*, 313–75.

v LW 35:239.

w WA DB 8:17.

x *Casteien* (*Kasteien*), from Latin *castigare*. The 1523 preface had used *zuchtigen* (*züchtigen*).

tilling, marrying and fighting, governing children, servants, and households, buying and selling, borrowing and repaying, and about everything that is to be done both outwardly and inwardly. He goes so far that some of the statutes can be regarded as foolish and useless.

Dear friend, why does God do that? In the end, because God took the people to be God's very own and wanted to be their God. For this reason God wanted to govern them in such a way that all of their actions before God would surely be right. For if anyone does anything which God's word has not previously specified, it counts for nothing before God and is lost.[29] For in chap. 4[:2] and 12[:32] of the fifth book, God forbids any addition to God's laws; and in chap. 12[:8] God says that they shall not do merely whatever is right in their own eyes. The Psalter and all the prophets also complain that the people are doing good works that they themselves have chosen and that were not commanded by God. For God will not and cannot permit God's own to undertake anything that God has not ordered, no matter how good it may be. For obedience which clings to God's words is the noblest and best of all works.

29. The key to this argument is the phrase "counts for nothing before God"; it is part of a widespread polemic in Luther against human-made (i.e., self-chosen) laws, the following of which is nothing more than self-justification. On the other hand, with regard to human life in general, Luther would never be one to claim that only that is permitted which is expressly commanded in the Bible.

But because this life cannot be without external forms of divine worship, God put these various forms before them and encompassed them with the divine commandment, in order that if they must or would do God any outward service, they might take one of these and not one they themselves had devised. They could then be doubly sure that their work was being done in obedience to God and God's word. In this manner, they are prevented on every hand from following their own reason and free will[y] in doing good and living well. Space, place, time, person, work, and form are all more than adequately determined and prescribed, so that they cannot complain, nor need they follow the example of foreign divine worship.

In the second place, it should be noted that the laws are of three kinds. Some speak only of temporal goods, as in the case of our imperial laws. These are established by God chiefly on account of the evil ones, so that they may not do even worse things. Such laws are more for prevention than for instruction, as when Moses commands that a wife be dismissed with a bill

y LW 35:240.

of divorce.[z] Also, that a husband can get rid of his wife with a "cereal offering of jealousy"[a] and is then permitted to take other wives. All of these are secular[b] laws.

There[c] are some, however, that teach about external divine worship, as has already been mentioned.

Over and above these two are the laws about faith and about love. All other laws must and ought to be measured by faith and by love. That is to say, the other laws are to be kept where their observance does not conflict with faith and love; but where they do conflict with faith and love, they should simply be abrogated.

For this reason we read that David did not kill the murderer Joab,[d] even though he had twice deserved death.[e] And in 2 Sam. 14[:11] David promises the woman of Tekoa that her son shall not die for having slain his brother. Nor did David kill Absalom either.[f] Also, in 1 Sam. 21[:6] David himself ate of the holy bread of the priests. Also, Tamar thought that the king might give her in marriage to her stepbrother, Amnon.[g] From these and similar stories one sees plainly that the kings, priests, and heads of the people often boldly[h] tinkered with the laws, when faith and love required it. Therefore faith and love should be the mistress of all laws and have all of them in her power. For since all laws drive toward faith and love, none of them can be valid or be regarded as law, if they conflict with faith or love.

Thus, even to the present day, the Jews are greatly in error when they hold so strictly and harshly to certain laws of Moses. They would[i] rather let love and peace be destroyed than eat and

z See Deut. 24:1.

a See Num. 5:11-31.

b English translations often render Luther's term *weltlich* as "worldly" or as "temporal." But the latter has its own German equivalent, *zeitlich*, and the former, though accurate, does not quite capture the specific valence of *weltlich*, which for Luther is the counterpart to *geistlich* ("spiritual"). Luther uses *weltlich* for both the Latin *saecularis* and *mundanus*.

c WA DB 8:19.

d See 1 Kgs. 2:5-6.

e See 2 Sam. 3:27; 20:10.

f See 2 Sam. 14:21-24.

g See 2 Sam. 13:13.

h Luther's term *frisch* (lively, brisk) is used here with the sense of *frech* (bold, brash, daring).

i LW 35:241.

drink with us, or do things of that kind, because they do not view the meaning of the law properly. But this understanding is essential for all who live under laws, and not only for the Jews. For Christ also says in Matt. 12[:11-12][j] that one might break the sabbath if an ox had fallen into a pit, and might rescue it. Now that was only a temporal necessity and injury. How much the more should one boldly break all kinds of laws when bodily necessity requires it, provided that nothing is done against faith and love. It is just as Christ says in Mark 2[:25-26], that David did this very thing when he ate the holy bread.

But why does Moses arrange the laws in such a disorderly manner? Why does he not put the secular ones together in one group, the spiritual ones in another, and the ones concerning faith and love in still another? In addition, he sometimes repeats a law so often and inculcates the same kind of thing so many times that it becomes tedious to read it or listen to it. The answer is that Moses writes as the situation demands,[k] such that his book is an image and example of governing and living. For this is the way it happens in real life: sometimes this work has to be done and sometimes another. Insofar as life is to be lived in a godly[l] manner, no one can so arrange their life that they practice purely spiritual laws on one day and purely secular laws on another. Rather, God governs with all the laws mixed together—like the stars in the heavens and the flowers in the fields—such that a person must be ready for anything at any time and do whatever the situation requires.[m] Thus, the book of Moses is a mixture of different kinds of laws.

That he is so insistent and often repeats the same thing is also an indication of his particular type of office. For whoever would govern a people whose lives are to be based on law[n] must constantly persevere, constantly urge, and slave away[o] with the people as with donkeys. For no work of law is ever done out of

j The passage in question speaks of a sheep rather than an ox. Cf. Luke 14:5.

k *Wie sichs treibt.*

l WA DB 8:21.

m *Vnd thun welchs jm am ersten fur die hand kompt.*

n *Ein Gesetzuolck* (*Gesetzvolk*), literally "a law-people."

o Reading with Heinrich Bornkamm, ed., *Luthers Vorreden zur Bibel* (Göttingen: Vandenhoeck & Ruprecht, 1989), 48, taking Luther's *sich bleuen* as *sich plagen*.

delight and love; it is all forced and compelled. Because Moses is a teacher of law, he has to indicate by his insistence that works of law are forced works. He wears the people down through this insistence, until they recognize their illness and their aversion to God's law, and begin to strive for grace, as we shall show.

In[p] the third place, the true meaning of Moses is that through the law he reveals sin and puts to shame all presumption as to human ability. For this reason St. Paul, in Gal. 2[:17], calls him "an officer of sin," and in 2 Cor. 3[:7] he calls his office "an office of death." In Rom. 3[:20] and 7[:7] he says, "Through the law comes nothing but the knowledge of sin"; and again in Rom. 3[:20], "Through works of the law no one becomes pious before God." For through the law Moses can do no more than indicate what one ought and ought not to do. However, he does not provide the strength and ability for such doing and not doing, and thus leaves us stuck in sin.

When we are stuck in sin, death quickly presses in upon us as vengeance and punishment for sin. That is why St. Paul calls sin "death's sting,"[q] because it is through sin that death has all of its rights and power over us. But if there were no law, there would be no sin.[r]

Therefore it is all the fault of Moses's office, who stirs up and rouses sin through the law; and then death follows violently upon sin. It is just and right that St. Paul calls Moses's office an office of sin and death,[s] for through his lawgiving he brings us nothing but sin and death.

And yet this office of sin and of death is good and most essential. For where there is no law of God, there all human reason is so blind that it cannot recognize sin. For human reason does not know that unbelief and despairing of God is sin. Indeed, it knows nothing about the duty to believe and trust in God. Hardened in its blindness, it goes its way and never feels this sin at all. Meanwhile, it does what are otherwise good works and leads an outwardly respectable life. Then it thinks that all is well and that things have been handled satisfactorily. We see

p LW 35:242.

q 1 Cor. 15:56.

r See Rom. 4:15.

s 2 Cor. 3:7.

this in the heathen[t] and the hypocrites, when[u] they live at their best. Also, it does not know either that the evil inclination of the flesh and hatred of enemies are sin. Because it sees and feels that all people are so inclined, it regards these things as natural and right, and thinks it is enough merely to guard against the outward works. So it goes its way, regarding its illness as strength, its sin as right, its evil as good, and never getting anywhere.

See, then, Moses's office is necessary for driving away this blindness and hardened presumption. Now, he cannot drive them away unless[v] he reveals them and makes them known. He does this through the law, when he teaches that one ought to fear, trust, believe, and love God; and, in addition, one ought to have or bear no evil desire or hatred for anyone. But when nature hears this correctly, it must be frightened, for it surely perceives neither trust nor faith, neither fear nor love toward God, and neither love nor purity toward the neighbor. Rather, it perceives pure unbelief, doubt, contempt, and hatred toward God, and pure evil will and desire toward the neighbor. But when it finds these things, then death is quickly before its eyes, wanting to gorge[w] on such a sinner and to gobble them up in hell.

See, then, this is what it means to bring death upon us through sin, and through sin to kill us. This is what it means to stir up sin through the law and set it before our eyes, driving all our presumption into despondency and trembling and despair, so that one can do no more than cry out with the prophets, "I am rejected by God." Or, as it is said in German, "The devil has me; I can never be saved."[x] That is what being cast into hell really means. And that is also what St. Paul means by those short words in 1 Cor. 15[:56], "The sting of death is sin, but the law is sin's power." It is as if he were saying that, being guilty of death, death stings and slays us by the power of sin that is found in us; sin, however, is found in us and gives us so mightily to death by the power of the law which reveals sin to us and teaches us

t Luther often uses the term *Heiden* (heathen) for Gentiles (i.e., non-Jews), but here it clearly refers to non-Christians.

u WA DB 8:23.

v LW 35:243.

w The verb *fressen* (to eat) is properly used only for animals. When used for people it is highly pejorative. English "gorge" is an approximation.

x *Jch bin des Teufels, Jch kan nimer mehr selig werden.*

to recognize it, which before we did not know and therefore felt secure.

Now, see with what force Moses conducts and performs this office of his. For in order to put nature to the utmost shame, he not only gives laws like the Ten Commandments that speak of natural and true sins, but he also makes sins of things that are by nature not sins. Moses, thus, pushes and presses sins upon them in piles. For unbelief and evil desire are by nature sins and worthy of death. But that one is not to eat leavened bread at Passover,[y, z] or not to eat an unclean animal,[a] or that one is not to make a mark on one's body,[b] and everything else that the Levitical priesthood deals with as sin—these[c] are not by nature sin and evil. They become sins only because they are forbidden through the law, a law that can now be abrogated. The Ten Commandments, however, cannot be abrogated, for there is sin here, even if there were no commandments, or even if they[d] were not[e] recognized—just as the heathen's unbelief is sin, even though they do not know or regard it as sin.

Thus, we see that these many laws of Moses were not only given so that no one might choose their own way of doing good and living well, as was said above, but much more so that sins might simply become numerous and be piled up beyond measure. The purpose was to burden the conscience so that the hardened blindness would have to recognize itself and feel its own inability and nothingness in the achieving of good. Such blindness must be thus compelled and coerced through the law to seek

God on Mount Sinai giving Moses the Ten Commandments on stone tablets and the Israelites worshiping the golden calf and reveling at the foot of the mountain. From a 1530 printing of Luther's *Large Catechism*.

y *Auff Ostern.*

z See Exodus 12–13.

a See Leviticus 11; Deuteronomy 14.

b See Lev. 19:28; Deut. 14:1.

c WA DB 8:25.

d I.e., sins.

e LW 35:244.

something beyond the law and its own ability, namely, God's grace promised in Christ who was to come. For every law of God is good and right,[f] even if it only refers to carrying manure or gathering straw. Accordingly, whoever does not keep this good law—or keeps it reluctantly—can neither be pious nor of a good heart. Thus, nature itself can do nothing other than keep it reluctantly. By this good law of God, it must, therefore, recognize and feel its malevolence, and sigh and strive for the aid of divine grace in Christ.

For this reason, then, when Christ comes the law ceases,[30] especially the Levitical law which, as has been said, makes sins of things that by nature are not otherwise sins. The Ten Commandments also cease, not in the sense that they are no longer to be kept or fulfilled, but in the sense that Moses's office in them ceases.[31] It no longer strengthens sin through the Ten Commandments,[g] and sin is no longer death's sting. For through Christ sin is forgiven, God is reconciled, and the heart has begun to be friendly toward the law. Moses's office can no longer chastise the heart for the sin of not having kept the commandments and, thus, for being guilty of death, as it did prior to grace and before Christ came.

St. Paul teaches this in 2 Cor. 3[:7-14], where he says that the brightness in the face of Moses ceases, because of the brightness in the face of Jesus Christ. That is, the office of Moses, which makes us to be sin and shame with the radiance of the knowledge of our[h] malevolence and nothingness, no longer causes us pain and no longer terrifies us with death. For we now have the brightness in the face of Christ.[i] This is the office of grace through which we recognize Christ, with whose righteousness, life, and strength we fulfill the law and overcome death and hell. Thus, the three apostles who saw Moses and Elijah on Mount Tabor were not afraid of them, because of the lovely brightness in the face of Christ.[j] But in Exod. 34[:29-35], where Christ[k]

f See Rom. 7:7-16.

g See Rom. 5:20.

h LW 35:245.

i See 2 Cor. 4:6.

j See Luke 9:32.

k WA DB 8:27.

30. A direct allusion to Rom. 10:4. Luther's translation of the passage in his German New Testament is: "For Christ is the end of the law; whoever believes in him is righteous." By this he understands that the law of Moses terminated at a specific time in history, the time of the coming of Jesus the Messiah. Of equal importance is Gal. 3:24, which Luther interprets as follows: "For the law had its limits until Christ, as Paul says below (Gal 3:24): 'The law, until Christ.'" When he came, Moses and the law ceased. So did circumcision, sacrifices, and the Sabbath. So did all the prophets" (*Lectures on Galatians* [1535], LW 26:7). On the one hand, for Luther, the coming of Christ and the ending of the law is a once-and-for-all-time historical event. On the other hand, it is an ongoing existential event in the daily dying and rising of the individual Christian. See immediately below.

31. This is Luther's distinction between Moses (or the law) apart from Christ and Moses (or the law) in the light of Christ (or in dialectical relation to Christ). In the former, Moses is pure death. In the latter, Moses is the servant of the gospel.

was not present, the children of Israel could not endure the brightness and radiance in Moses's face, so that he had to put a cover over it.

For there are three kinds of students of the law. The first are those who hear the law and despise it, who lead an indifferent life without fear. To these the law does not come. They are signified through the calf-worshipers in the wilderness, on whose account Moses broke the tablets in two.[l] To them he did not bring the law.

The second kind are those who seize it and attempt to fulfill it by their own power, without grace. They are signified through those who could not look at Moses's countenance when he brought the tablets the second time.[m] The law comes to them, but they cannot endure it. Therefore, they put a cover over it[32] and lead a hypocritical life of external works of the law. Yet when the cover is removed, the law makes it all to be sin. For the law indicates that, apart from Christ's grace, our ability is nothing.

The Transfiguration of Christ, **part of an iconostasis in Constantinople style from the mid-twelfth century. Located at St. Catherine's Monastery (Sinai, Egypt). Moses and Elijah flank Jesus at the top with the three apostles below.**

The third kind are those who see Moses clearly, without a cover. These are they who understand the meaning of the law and how it demands impossible things. Here sin comes to power, here death is mighty, here Goliath's spear is like a weaver's beam and its point weighs six hundred shekels of bronze, so that all the children of Israel flee before him unless the one and only David—Christ our Lord—saves us from all of this.[n] For if Christ's brightness did not come alongside this brightness of Moses, no one could bear the radiance of the law, that is, sin and death's terror. These flee away from all works and presumption and learn from the law nothing else except to recognize sin and to sigh for Christ.[o] This is the proper office of Moses and the very nature of the law.[33]

So Moses himself has also indicated that his office and teaching should last until Christ, and then cease, when he says

32. Luther implies that the people put a cover over the law, but see the passage in context (Exod. 34:33-35), where Moses puts a cover or veil over his own face. Luther's reading is influenced by 2 Cor. 3:14.

33. For Luther, both Christ and Moses have a "proper" and an "alien" work, but they are inversely related. See Heinrich Bornkamm, *Luther and the Old Testament*, ed. Victor I. Gruhn, trans. Eric W. and Ruth C. Gritsch (Mifflintown, PA: Sigler Press, 1997), 145–49; Lohse, *Martin Luther's Theology*, 267–76.

l Exod. 32:19.

m Exod. 34:34-35.

n See 1 Sam. 17:7, 24, 32.

o LW 35:246.

in Deut. 18[:15-19], "The LORD your God will raise up for you a prophet like me from among your brothers—him shall you heed," etc.[34] This is the noblest saying and certainly the kernel in the entire Moses, which the apostles also elevated and made much use of, in order to strengthen the gospel and abolish the law.[p] All the prophets, as well, drew heavily upon it. For since God here promises another Moses whom they are to heed, it necessarily follows that he would teach something different than Moses did; and Moses gives up his power and yields to him, so that people will heed him. The same prophet cannot, then, teach law, for Moses has already done that in superior fashion. There would be no need to raise up another prophet on account of the law. Therefore, this was surely said about the teaching of grace and about Christ.

Therefore,[q] St. Paul also calls Moses's law the Old Testament,[r] and Christ does the same when he institutes the New Testament.[35] It is a testament because God promised and alloted to the people of Israel the land of Canaan, if they would keep it. God gave it to them, too, and it was confirmed through the death and blood of sheep and goats. But because this testament was not based on God's grace but rather on human works, it had to become obsolete and cease, and the Promised Land had to be lost again—because the law cannot be fulfilled through works. And another testament had to come which would not become obsolete, which would not be based on our deeds either, but rather on God's words and works, so that it might last forever. Therefore it is confirmed through the death and blood of an eternal person, and an eternal land is promised and given. Let this be enough about Moses's books and office.

What, then, are the other books of the prophets and the histories?[36] Answer: They are nothing else than what Moses is. For all of them inculcate Moses's office; they guard against the false prophets, that they may[s] not lead the people to works, but allow them to remain in the true office of Moses and knowledge of the law. They hold fast to this purpose of keeping the people conscious of their own inability through a right understanding of

34. An absolutely essential prooftext for Luther, which occurs manifold times in the corpus. In his reading, Deut. 18:15 announces the Messiah's displacement of Moses.

35. 1 Cor. 11:25. As a rule, Luther does not equate the Old Testament (the book) with law and the New Testament (the book) with gospel. The law/gospel distinction, rather, applies to the entire Bible, because the Old Testament is saturated with gospel. He does, however, equate the old covenant (Moses/Sinai) with law and the new covenant (Christ/Pentecost) with gospel.

36. Luther now turns to summarize the remaining books of the Old Testament.

p See Acts 3:22; 7:37.

q WA DB 8:29.

r 2 Cor. 3:14.

s LW 35:247.

the law, and thus driving them to Christ, as Moses does. For this reason they also further explicate what Moses said about Christ, and furnish two kinds of examples: of those who have Moses rightly and of those who do not, and also of the punishments and rewards that come to both. Thus, the prophets are nothing else than administrators and witnesses of Moses and his office, bringing everyone to Christ through the law.

Finally, I ought also to indicate the spiritual interpretation[t] set before us by the Levitical law and priesthood of Moses. But there is too much of this to write. It requires space and time and should be expounded with a living voice. For Moses is, indeed, a well of all wisdom and understanding, out of which has sprung all that the prophets knew and said.[37] Furthermore, the New Testament also flows out of it and is grounded upon it, as we have heard. It is my task, however, to give at least some little hint to those who have the grace and understanding to pursue the matter further.

If you would interpret well and confidently, set Christ before you, for he is the one to whom absolutely everything applies.[38] Make the high priest Aaron, then, to be nobody but Christ alone, as does the epistle to the Hebrews,[u] which is by itself virtually sufficient for interpreting all of Moses's figures.[39] Thus, it is also certain that Christ himself is the sacrifice—indeed even the altar[v]—who sacrificed himself with his own blood, as the same epistle announces.[w,x] Now, whereas the Levitical high priest only took away artificial sins through this sacrifice, sins which by nature were not sins, our high priest, Christ, through his own sacrifice and blood, has taken away real sins, sins which by nature are actually sins. He has gone in once for all through the curtain to God to make atonement for us.[y] Thus, you should interpret[z] all that is written about the high priest as referring to Christ personally, and to no one else.

t *Die geistliche Deutung.*

u See Heb. 5:4-5.

v See Heb. 13:10.

w WA DB 8:31.

x See Hebrews 9–10.

y See Heb. 9:12.

z LW 35:248.

37. That the Prophets were expositors and explicators of Moses, i.e., the Pentateuch, rather than bearers of new revelation is something that Luther, whether he realized it or not, had in common with the entirety of rabbinic tradition.

38. In other words, all of the priestly legislation in the Pentateuch applies to Christ.

39. In his appeal to Hebrews, Luther is engaging here in straightforward allegorical interpretation. Luther continued to utilize allegorical interpretation throughout his career, but his tendency was to constrain its use to the making of christological claims. (See Raeder 2:370–78.)

The high priest's sons, however, who are engaged in the daily sacrifice, you should interpret as referring to us Christians, who live here on earth bodily before our father Christ,[a] who is seated in heaven. We are not there with him yet[b] except spiritually by faith. Their office of slaughter and sacrifice signifies nothing else than the preaching of the gospel, through which the old human is slain and offered to God, burned and consumed through the fire of love, in the Holy Spirit. This sacrifice smells very good before God; that is, it produces a conscience that is good, pure, and secure before God. St. Paul applies this interpretation in Rom. 12[:1] when he teaches that we are to offer our bodies to God as a living, holy, and acceptable sacrifice. This is what we do (as has been said) by the constant exercise of the gospel both in preaching and believing. Let this suffice for the present as a brief introduction for seeking Christ and the gospel in the Old Testament.[40]

Whoever[c] reads this Bible should also know that I have been careful to write the name of God, which the Jews call the *Tetragrammaton*,[41] in capital letters; thus, LORD [*HERR*], and

a The title "father Christ" is an extremely rare formulation in Luther. (*Auslegung und Deutung des heiligen Vaterunsers* [1518], WA 9:129,34; *Vorrede über den Propheten Daniel* [1541, 1545], WA DB 11/2:94,8; 11/2:95,8; see also the *Preface to Daniel* in this volume, pp. 375–411).

b Luther's phrase, *vnd nicht hin durch sind bey jm*, is difficult to render.

c WA DB 8:30.

40. In editions of the complete Luther Bible from 1534 on, the Preface ended at this point. The paragraphs that follow were printed only in the earlier editions.

41. The four-letter name of God in the Hebrew Bible, יהוה, Y-H-W-H.

42. The generic Hebrew word (אדני) for "lord, master, mister," or *Herr* in German.

43. In terms of its visual presentation, the Luther Bible thus contained three different forms of the word *Herr*: *HErr* = rendering the *Tetragrammaton*; *HERR* = rendering *Adonai* when referring to God; *Herr* = rendering *Adonai* when referring to human beings, although the different printings are not consistent. Occasionally, the Hebrew Bible uses the compound title for God, אדני יהוה, literally *Adonai (Lord) Yhwh*. In these cases, the Luther Bible renders with *HErr HERR*. As a rule, English translations have followed Luther's practice for rendering the *Tetragrammaton*: LORD, or LORD. (On Luther's attitude toward the *Tetragrammaton*, see "Excursus on the Tetragrammaton," *Operationes in Psalmos*, AWA 2:331–39 and his bitter 1543 anti-Jewish treatise, *On the* Schem Hamphoras *and On the Lineage of Christ*, TAL 5:653–55.)

44. Jeremiah 23:6 was a central Old Testament proof-text for Luther. In his understanding of the text, the *Tetragrammaton* was specifically applied to the Messiah, thus indicating the Messiah's divinity. (See Schramm and Stjerna, *Martin Luther, the Bible, and the Jewish People*, 104–6.)

the second name which they call *Adonai*[42] only half in capital letters; thus, LOrd [*HErr*].[43] For among all the names of God in Scripture, these two alone are assigned[d] to the real, true God; while the others are often ascribed to angels and saints. I have done this so that one can thereby draw the strong conclusion that Christ is true God. For Jer. 23[:6] calls him LORD when he says, "They will call him: 'The LORD, our righteous one'."[44] More of the same can be found in other passages.[45]

Herewith I commend all my readers to Christ and request that they help me obtain from God the ability to carry this work through to a useful end. For I freely admit that I have undertaken too much, especially in trying to translate the Old Testament into German.[46] The Hebrew language, unfortunately, is in such a state of stagnation that even the Jews themselves know little enough about it, and their glosses and interpretations (which I have tested) are not to be trusted.[47] It is my view that if the Bible is to re-emerge, we Christians are the ones who will have to do it, because we have the understanding of Christ,[48] apart from which even the knowledge of the language amounts to

d LW 35:249.

45. During the Bible revision of 1539–1541, Luther introduced the practice of signaling the *Tetragrammaton* in certain New Testament texts as well. E.g., "angel of the LORD" (Matt. 1:20; 2:13; Luke 1:11; 2:9; Acts 8:26); "the temple of the LORD" (Luke 1:9); "the glory of the LORD" (Luke 2:9); and, most provocatively, "I praise you Father, LORD of heaven and earth . . ." (Matt. 11:25 // Luke 10:21). This printing practice ceased soon after Luther's death. (See R. Kendall Soulen, *The Divine Name(s) and the Holy Trinity*, vol. 1: *Distinguishing the Voices* [Louisville: Westminster John Knox, 2011], 92–93.)

46. Luther had no illusions about the demands of the translational enterprise he had undertaken. In a 1522 letter to Hartmut von Cronburg (1488–1549), he stated: "It was necessary for me to take up the task of translating the Bible into German, because otherwise I would have died in the delusion that I was a learned person" (WA 10/2:60,13–15).

47. Luther had already arrived at this conviction in 1523, but it would only grow ever stronger over the coming years. See esp. *On the Last Words of David* (1543), LW 15:267–352.

48. A direct allusion to 1 Cor. 2:16. The Greek text is translated as "Now we have the mind [νοῦς] of Christ." The Vulgate, however, had rendered "mind" with *sensus*: "Now we have the sense of Christ," which came to be interpreted as "Now we [Christians] have the christological sense [of the Old Testament]." This interpretation was fully shared by Luther, and thus, for him, only Christians can understand and interpret the Old Testament properly.

nothing.[49] Because of this lack,[50] many of the old translators and even Jerome made mistakes in many passages. Though[e] I cannot boast of having captured it all, nevertheless, I dare to say that this German Bible is clearer and more accurate at many places than the Latin. So it is true that—if the printers do not (as they tend to do) spoil it with their carelessness[51]—the German language certainly has here a better Bible than the Latin language—and the readers will bear me out in this.[52]

And now, of course, the crap will stick to the wheel,[f] and there will be those rude enough to want to be my master in this work and who will criticize me here and there. They can have at it. I had anticipated from the beginning that I would find ten thousand to criticize my work before I would find even one who could accomplish one-twentieth of[g] what I have.[53] I, too, would like to be very learned and give brilliant proof of my skill by criticizing St. Jerome's Latin Bible,[h] but he in turn could also defy me to accomplish what he has. Now if anyone is so much more learned than I, let them undertake to translate the whole Bible into German, and then let me know what they can do.[i] If they do it better, why should they not be preferred to me?

I thought I was learned—and I know that by God's grace I am more learned than all the sophists in the universities—but now I see that I cannot even handle my own native German language. Nor have I read up to this time a book or letter that contains the proper kind of German.[54] Besides, no one pays any attention to speaking proper German, especially those in the chancelleries and the patchwork preachers and pretentious writers.[j] They think they have the right to change the German language and

e WA DB 8:32.

f A colorful idiom: *Nu wirt sich auch der kot an das rad hengen.*

g LW 35:250.

h See n. 5, p. 43.

i See *On Translating: An Open Letter* (this volume, pp. 19–40; LW 35:183–84; and *Defense of Translation of Psalms*, LW 35:221–23).

j *Die lumpen prediger, vnd puppen schreyber.* The latter phrase occurs only here.

49. Luther's consistently applied translational philosophy was that "the meaning of the whole" constrains "the meaning of the parts." That "whole" was the two-volume Christian Bible and its "meaning" was the saving work of God in Jesus Christ on behalf of sinful humanity. From Luther's perspective, therefore, Jewish interpreters, because they do not read the "whole" (i.e., OT + NT), are always guilty of reading the Bible (i.e., the Old Testament) out of context.

50. I.e., of the messianic understanding.

51. Beginning in 1541, the Luther Bible contained a "Warning to the Printers" in which Luther complained bitterly about the role of greed in the printing of the Bible and about the numerous errors introduced into the text by unauthorized reprints. (See WA DB 8:6–9 and the discussion in Brecht 3:101.) Luther never asked for, or received, any remuneration for his translation of the Bible.

52. Having the Bible in a reliable vernacular translation was a central component in the Reformation's revolution within the Western church. The Council of Trent (1545–1563) would state unequivocally that the Latin Vulgate Bible is and remains the official Bible of the Roman Catholic Church (see "Trent, Council of," in F. L. Cross, ed., *The Oxford Dictionary of the Christian Church* [New York: Oxford University Press, 2005]). For Luther (as opposed to Origen, Augustine, and Jerome) the Hebrew language as such was not holy but became so by virtue of its role as vessel or bearer of the word of God. Thus, "Luther under[stood] his translation of the Bible as a sanctification of the German language by the word of God." Raeder 2:404–5.

coin new words for us every day, such as *behertzigen*,[k] *behendigen*,[l] *erspriеslich*,[m] *erschieslich*,[n] and the like. Yes, dear fellow, there are even *bethoret* and *ernarret*.[o]

In summation, if we would all just work together, we would have enough to do in bringing the Bible to light, one working with the sense,[55] another with the language. For I have not worked on this alone either but have used the services of anyone I could.[56,p] Therefore, I request everyone to cease with their disparagement so as not to confuse the poor people, and help me if they can. If they do not want to do that, then let them take up the Bible themselves and make their own translation. Those who do nothing but disparage and carp are actually not pious and

k *Behertzigen* (*beherzigen*) = to heed or take to heart. Deriving largely from Swabian origin, the term had been used frequently by Jerome (Hieronymus) Emser (1477–1527), German theologian and antagonist of Luther.

l *Behendigen* (*behändigen*) = to place in the hand, or hand in. In a letter from Luther and Andreas Karlstadt (1486–1541) to Duke Frederick of Saxony (1463–1525) dated 18 August 1519, Luther—or perhaps his co-author—had himself used the term *Behendigkeit* (WA Br 1:477,1.410). The use of *behendigen* is documented as early as 1484 in Wetterau (Moritz Heyne, *Deutsches Wörterbuch*, 3 vols. [Leipzig: Hirzel, 1890–1895], 1:324). This and the previous term do not occur in Luther's Bible.

m *Ersprieslich* (*erpriesslich*). Meaning originally to spring forth or sprout, *erspriessen* early came to be used in New High German in the sense of "be useful, profitable, advantageous." The adjective, too, was given this derived meaning from about the beginning of the sixteenth century.

n *Erschieslich* (*erschiesslich*). Luther apparently was unaware that the intransitive verb *erschiessen* was used rather extensively in a sense synonymous with that of *erspriessen*.

o *Bethoret* (*betöret*). *Betören* means to make a fool of, in the sense of infatuate, seduce, or deceive. *Ernarren* means to play the fool, in the sense of be silly, astonish, or amaze. The construction of Luther's sentence conveys a double meaning: not only that these words, too, are recent innovations, but also that all such innovating is sheer folly.

p LW 35:251.

53. On the critics of Luther's Bible translation, see Brecht 3:107–10.

54. On the evolution of the writing of the German language in the various editions of the Luther Bible, see Brecht 2:48–49.

55. Luther is speaking here about the ongoing dialectical relationship between grammar (or philology) and meaning (or the subject matter) in the translational task. While meaning should not contradict grammar, neither should grammar be used to obfuscate the meaning of a passage. The latter was the primary source of Luther's bitter arguments against Jewish interpreters and their Christian Hebraist followers. See Burnett, "Luther and Hebrew"; Raeder 2:403–4.

56. Johannes Mathesius (1504–1565), Luther's first biographer, lived in Luther's house in the summer of 1540 and witnessed the translation team at work on the Bible revision of 1539–1541: "Luther appointed the best people available. They came together weekly for several hours before supper in the Doctor's cloister: Dr. Johann Bugenhagen, Dr. Justus Jonas (1493–1555), Dr. [Caspar] Cruciger (1504–1548), Master Philip [Melanchthon], Matthaeus Aurogallus; Master Georg Rörer (1492–1557), the proofreader, was also there. Many times other doctors and scholars also participated in this lofty work. . . . After Doctor [Luther] had consulted the already published [German] Bible . . . , he came into the consistory with his old Latin and new German Bibles, and he always had the Hebrew text with him as well. Master Philip brought the Greek text with him. In addition to the Hebrew, Dr. Cruciger brought the Chaldean Bible [i.e., the Aramaic paraphrases—

or Targum—in the Rabbinic Bible, published by Jacob ben Chayyim in Venice in 1524–1525]. The professors had their rabbis with them [i.e., the interpretations of Jewish scholars], Dr. Pommer [i.e., Bugenhagen] had a Latin text before him, with which he was quite familiar. Each participant had prepared beforehand for the text to be discussed, by consulting the Greek and Latin texts along with the Jewish interpreters. Thereupon the chairperson [i.e., Luther] proposed a text and asked each one of them what they had to say based on the characteristics of the language or according to the interpretations of the old doctors. Very beautiful and informative speeches were given about this work, some of which have been recorded by Master Georg [Rörer]" (Hans Volz, ed., *D. Martin Luther: Die gantze Heilige Schrifft Deudsch, Wittenberg 1545* [Munich: Rogner & Bernhard, 1972], 105*).

honest enough to really want a pure Bible, since they know that they cannot produce it. Rather, they prefer being know-it-alls[q] in a field not their own, even though they have never even been students in their own field. May the work that God has begun be brought to completion.[r] Amen.

q *Meyster klugling*, a favorite term of Luther's, meaning something like "Mr. Smart Guy."

r See Phil. 1:6.

Lectures on Genesis 1:26—2:3 and Genesis 2:21-25

1535

KIRSI I. STJERNA AND
ELSE MARIE WIBERG PEDERSEN

INTRODUCTION

Solu sexu differet

Luther surmised that men and women differ "only in sex."[a] Even with this understatement, Luther had an instinctive appreciation of the manifold reality of sex/gender differences.[1] This was an area of life that he first observed from his family of origin or friends' lives and when ministering to men and women in Wittenberg, until he finally learned from his own personal life through his marriage to Katharina von Bora.[2] His personal marital relationship and family life became an invaluable source for him on gender relations even though his marriage shocked some of his colleagues and made him the object of spiteful scorn from his Catholic opponents.[3] The bottom line "truth" of the matter for him, however, was to be found in the Bible.[b] In this respect,

a See pp. 73–75 below.

b See Susan C. Karant-Nunn and Merry E. Wiesner-Hanks, *Luther on Women* (Cambridge: Cambridge University Press, 2003). Also, Kirsi Stjerna, "Grief, Glory and Grace: Insights on Eve and Tamar in Luther's Genesis Commentary," SRR 6, no. 2 (Spring 2004): 19–35, for Luther's treatment of a biblical text and issues pertaining to womanhood and gender.

1. Luther goes against the standard view on women's biology held since Aelius Galenus (c. 129–c. 200). According to this view, men and women were biologically identical, although women with their internalized sexual organs were considered a less perfect and deficient version of men, whose externalized organs made them better and stronger. The female ovum was not detected until late in the sixteenth century; and not until the eighteenth and nineteenth centuries did scientists categorize women and men differently according to sex. See Thomas Laqueur, *Making Sex: Body and Gender from the Greeks to Freud* (Cambridge: Harvard University Press, 1990).

2. Katharina von Bora (1499–1552), daughter of an impoverished noble family, spent much of her early life in a convent but left her Cistercian Order with eleven other nuns after her exposure to the writings of Martin Luther, whom she married on 13 June 1525. She became the manager of their large household at the old Black Cloister. She was the mother of their six children (with two miscarriages).

3. Some of Luther's supporters feared that his marriage would jeopardize the cause of the Reformation, and they were right in the sense that Luther was accused of being a pervert by one of his worst critics, Johannes Cochlaeus (1479–1552), and his marriage to a nun was seen as nothing less than harlotry. See Carter Lindberg's article, "Martin Luther on Marriage and Family," *Perichoresis* 2, no. 1 (2004): 27–46.

Adam and Eve in Paradise **(1533)**
by Lucas Cranach the Elder (1472–1553)

Luther's *sola scriptura* principle is reflected in his lectures on Genesis, which are clearly interpreted from a profound christological and soteriological perspective.

A biblical scholar by trade,[c] Luther returned to the complex Genesis chapters 1–3 and joined the long line of interpreters whose impact in the West for understanding sex/gender has been

c On Luther's general exegetical operatives, particularly vis-à-vis the Old Testament and Hebrew interpretations, see Heinrich Bornkamm, *Luther and the Old Testament*, ed. Victor I. Gruhn, trans. Eric W. and Ruth C. Gritsch (Philadelphia: Fortress Press, 1969). Also, Brooks Schramm, "Introduction: Martin Luther, the Bible and the Jewish People," in MLBJP, 10–14.

palpable.[d] His conclusions on gendered human life culminated in his last lectures on the book of Genesis, spanning nearly ten years (1535-1545). Luther intended to replace the traditional picture of humanity, which he found too much derived from Greek philosophy—reflected in his repeated critique of Aristotle—with a biblically derived picture. This comes to the fore when Luther takes it for granted that "male and female" in Genesis 1:27 connects to the image of God, something that was far from always the case in the tradition before him.[e] Standing between two worlds and unable to leave behind the tradition he has inherited, he finds Augustine of Hippo (354-430) helpful[4] as he sets out to wrestle with this stressful material. Yet, Luther abandons allegorical interpretation of Augustine as a proper way to deal with the image of God in woman, as also the double-creation schemes of several of the church fathers.[f]

Diptych with the portraits of Martin Luther and his wife, Katharina von Bora (c. 1529), by artist Lucas Cranach the Elder

4. "It is apparent that the interpretation of the first three chapters was difficult for Luther and he breathed a sigh of relief when he had crossed this 'sea.' He had had an easier time than his predecessors, however, because he had stuck to the literal text and avoided allegories" (Brecht 3:137).

d See Helen Kraus, *Gender Issues in Ancient and Reformation Translations of Genesis 1–4* (Oxford: Oxford University Press, 2011). Also, Mickey L. Mattox, *Defender of the Most Holy Matriarchs: Martin Luther's Interpretation of the Women of Genesis in the Enarrationes in Genesin, 1535–1545* (Leiden: Brill, 2003).

e See Jane Dempsey Douglass, "The Image of God in Women as Seen by Luther and Calvin," in Kari E. Børresen, ed., *Image of God and Gender Models in Judaeo-Christian Tradition* (Oslo: Solum, 1991), 242. Cf. Phyllis A. Bird, "Sexual Differentiation and Divine Image in the Genesis Creation Texts," in Børresen, ed., *Image of God*, 11-31.

f For the traditional rendition of the image of God and woman, see Bird, "Sexual Differentiation"; Anders Hultgaard, "God and Image of Woman in Early Jewish Religion"; and Giulia S. Gasparro, "Image of God and Sexual Differentiation in the Tradition of *Enkrateia*," all in Børresen, ed., *Image of God*, 16-21; 26-30; and 153-63, respectively.

In the few verses, Gen. 1:26—2:3 and Gen. 2:21-25, Luther covers a significant space of theological anthropological territory. He ruminates on the origins and original nature of human beings as men and women. The framework for Luther's deliberation on gender and sex is in his fascination with—and gratitude for—the mystery of creation. Of all the miracles of life, the bringing forth of new human life is in a category of its own. Procreation and the natural conditions for each human birth speak to Luther of the grandness and genius of God's creation. Elsewhere, Luther praises the common life with children and wife, where even the washing of smelly diapers is as an expression of God's creation.[5]

Luther maintains the Augustinian understanding of human beings' inability to know themselves or God in creation as an inherited condition. Human lives are complicated with the so-called original sin, which Luther, however, considers as a relational rather than an ontological burden. In light of how life was in Paradise, Luther deems that human beings' passions and love for one another have become compromised, while still bearing the original design for human happiness that God intended in our relationships with God and one another. Due to sin, sexual desire and even nudity have become tainted with unnecessary shame. In a benign debate on the reading of Genesis 2 with the ancient and medieval teachers of nature, Luther explains the building of a woman from Adam's rib as an equal while being a notably different creature who as God's image has a special vocation to rule the household and to be the nest for her husband.[6]

Luther's depiction includes his marriage charter (that is, his rationale for marriage), his tentative deliberation on the issue of divorce, and his thoughts on celibacy, his old battle call.[7] As with his own writings dealing with the interpretation of the Old Testament, these lectures mirror the ongoing discussions with Jewish theology and ideology. Thus, commenting on Gen. 1:26, Luther discusses the God concept, arguing for the Trinitarian God from his knowledge of the Hebrew *Elohim* and the phrase "Let Us make" in the plural against the fundamental monotheism of Judaism and Islam.[8] Likewise, commenting on Genesis 1:27, he argues for the equal and independent status of the female sex as *imago Dei* from the textual basis, while he distances himself from what he labels Talmudic ideas and also from Aristotle's and other "Gentile" pejorative perceptions of the female

5. Luther in several places accentuates the less glorious or scatological parts of life as integral to the living out of faith, such as a father washing diapers: "God with all the angels and creatures is smiling—not because the father is washing diapers, but because he is doing so in Christian faith" (LW 45:40).

6. The correlation between Luther's interpretation of the equality of the two genders per the Genesis texts and the actual changes—or lack of them—in women's status in sixteenth-century society is ambiguous. Thus, "[P]erhaps Luther's work should be seen as 'change-in-progress,' with some ideas beginning to grow but not yet mature. The ground is fertile but not yet sufficiently prepared" (Helen Kraus, *Gender Issues in Ancient and Reformation Translations of Genesis 1–4* [Oxford: Oxford University Press, 2011], 131, 128-31). The question is complex. We know, e.g., from Luther's will that he wanted Katharina to inherit their property and become guardian of their children (WA Br 9:574-76), even if this was against the Saxon laws at the time, and modifications had to be made to Luther's will. Luther's theological arguments on the equality of women and his personal aspirations to that direction fundamentally clashed with the basic gender norms and ideologies of his time.

7. Luther wrote his most famous text against monastic celibacy four years before he was married: *De votis monasticis iudicium* (*The Judgment of Martin Luther on Monastic Vows* [1521]), LW 44:251-400. Here Luther denounces monastic life as a *status perfectionis*: as a form of contempt for life and the created world it is contrary to the common life of ordinary people who live in real obedience to God's commandments.

sex as not divinely created. Amidst these larger themes, Luther offers reflection on ever-important theological-anthropological topics, such as the balance between human life and nature's products, and the character of sleep, death, and resurrection.

A goldmine for Luther's theology from multiple angles, these lectures and how they were recorded come with peculiar challenges for the reader.

The Fragmented Texts

The first set of Genesis lectures[g] occurred between 1 and 18 June 1535, during which Luther covered Gen. 1:1–3:14. The lectures were soon interrupted due to a sudden onset of plague in July, as recorded by Luther's Wittenberg associate, Veit Dietrich.[9]

The lectures, held in Latin for an academic (and male) audience and not in the vernacular for the open public, commenced again on 25 January 1536, starting with Gen. 3:15, and by the

Etching of Veit Dietrich

g See Jaroslav Pelikan's introduction to LW 1:ix-xii; Brecht 3.

Only as institutions that educate children of both sexes is the monastic life a realization of Evangelical freedom. Cf. Else Marie Wiberg Pedersen, "'Ein fürtrefflicher Munch': Luther and the Living Out of Faith," in Christoph Bultmann, Volker Leppin, and Andreas Lindner, eds., *Luther und das monastische Erbe* (Heidelberg: Mohr Siebeck, 2007), 221-42.

8. Luther's attitude toward Judaism changed over the years from a positive to a mostly negative position. At the same time, Luther without hesitation utilized the insights into the Hebrew language and grammar gained through the Christian Hebraists (among them converts from Judaism) and their engagement with Jewish scholars. See Gregory Miller, "Luther's Views of the Jews and Turks," in Robert Kolb, Irene Dingel, and L'ubomír Batka, eds., *The Oxford Handbook of Martin Luther's Theology* (Oxford: Oxford University Press, 2014), 427-34. In this context, Luther—based on his knowledge of Hebrew—is arguing strictly from his Trinitarian theology.

9. Veit Dietrich (1506-1549), from Nurnberg, served as Luther's secretary and "scriba" at Coburg (1531) and as the dean of the art faculty (1533). He edited Luther's works and sought to interpret both Luther's and Philip Melanchthon's theology. He is one of the sources for the Table Talks from 1531 to 1533.

fall of 1536 he had reached Genesis, chapter 9.[h] Lecturing continued,[10] with interruptions, until 1545.[i]

The published copies of lectures come to us with text-historical problems: with no certainty of the chronology or progress, the authenticity of Luther's voice as the author has been debated, and even contested. From these precious lectures not even raw scribbles from Luther himself survive; the printed lectures rely on an amalgamation of edited listeners' notes.[11]

The reader can, as has been noted, detect editors' additions in the form of admonitions to the "reader,"[12] anachronistic contextual notes from multiple editors' pens, and suspiciously detailed citations from classical authors.[j] Luther at first refused to have his lectures published, as he found them "tumultuous and imperfect." Only after numerous queries did he finally accept, and then without ever going through the material, even though he wrote the foreword to the publication of the first eleven chapters in January 1544.[k] Therefore, whether any of Luther's theological positions became altered in the process of recording and transmitting the lectures remains uncertain.

Considering that Luther's theology matured over the years, straightforward comparisons with the "young" Luther would hardly provide scientific evidence regarding the authorship.

10. Luther typically lectured on Mondays and Tuesdays. After completing his lectures on Psalm 90 on Monday, 31 May 1535, he announced his plans to focus on the books of Moses. He dedicated his last years of working energies for interpreting these books, with a pecial attention to Genesis.

11. The lecture notes from George Rörer (1492–1557) and Caspar Cruciger (1504–1548), unfortunately, did not survive; only those (incomplete) from Veit Dietrich, who published them in a four-volume commentary in 1544–1554, a work completed by Jerome Besold (1522–1562) and Michael Roting (dates unclear) after Dietrich's death (1549).

12. Before Luther died, there was a struggle about the real Luther, but after his death in 1546, a fierce struggle between those who saw themselves as the real Lutherans, the so-called Gnesio-Lutherans, and those who had an affinity for Philip Melanchthon's approach, the so-called Phillipists, arose. The former criticized the latter for abandoning Luther's original theology and bending it in a wrong direction, especially for adding a forensic meaning that Luther never intended. In the twentieth century, Peter Meinhold has been particularly suspicious of the alterations of themes that became disputes in the Lutheran community and what he deems as the footprints of Philip Melanchthon's forensic approach to the doctrine of justification. In this vein, he delivered a detailed interpretation of the authorship of Luther's lectures on Genesis and their printed form. See Peter Meinhold, *Die Genesisvorlesung Luthers und ihre Herausgeber* (Stuttgart: Kohlhammer, 1936), 53-117. The matter is much disputed, and, e.g., Jaroslav

h See LW 1:ix: "From a statement at table, dated 27 October–4 December, 1536."

i The result is collected in WA 42–44; also LW 1–2.

j See LW 1:x. Editors completed many of Luther's citations; e.g., from Augustine, Nicholas of Lyra (1270–1349), and Peter Lombard (1100–1160).

k According to the introduction to WA 42, Luther rejected the first request in 1538 with the words: "*est tumultuaria et imperfecta lectio, qua aliis do ansam cogitandi*" (WA 42:x), which means, "It is a tumultuous and imperfect reading, but I'll give it to others to do what they think."

All things considered, a reader seeking to understand Luther's fundamental theological convictions and conclusive exegetical analysis with the Genesis chapters can rest assured:[13] "The hands are sometimes the hands of the editors, but the voice is nevertheless the voice of Luther."[l]

Pelikan questioned Meinhold's critique of "philippist" changes of Luther's text vis-à-vis Luther's own treatment of Genesis. See James A. Nestingen, "Luther in Front of the Text: The Genesis commentary," *Word & World* 14, no. 2 (1994): 186-94.

13. According to Martin Brecht, assuming that the editors "likely added some things" and "their own theology crept into the work," "we must be very cautious in making use of the lectures on Genesis. Nevertheless, the bulk of this commentary, with its amazing richness of features and allusions, undoubtedly does come from Luther, and his spirit is evident in it. Despite the subsequent alterations, this monumental work may still be regarded as primarily his work" (Brecht 3:136).

The Marvelous Content

Recognizing that the biblical creation story itself stretches the limited human imagination, Luther begins his lectures with arguments on the importance of literal reading of the Scriptures' creation stories. Noting more than once that the creation of Eve, in particular, sounds like a fairy tale, nature alone provides Luther with proofs about both God's existence and the divine design for the reality of all that exists. Adam being created out of a clod or Eve being formed from Adam's rib are no less impossible than the conception of any human baby ever since.

The miracle of semen and human reproduction in general catches Luther's attention, as he seeks biblical answers for the mystery of human existence. In his reasoning, human conception—just like music and stars—is one of those daily miracles to which human beings have become numb. This blindness is due to sin. But the fact that human beings fail to recognize God's work and give thanks for it does not negate the truth of God's wondrous actions for the benefit of the human being, starting from the creation of a man and a woman. The agent behind all that exists is God, and God's Word in particular. In this light, the human-constructed "proofs" or lack of them do not matter. God does what God does, and God did indeed create Eve, the mother of all living.

Like his contemporaries, and theologians before, Luther seeks to articulate a rationale for the existence of a woman, first, and for her calling and relation to the man, second.[14] In his treatment, Eve's creation is presented as equal to that of Adam's, yet different. Luther labors with the biblical evidence of Eve's creation being equally noble as Adam's, the creation order having no impact on the worth of either. Commenting on Genesis 1, Luther consistently spells out that Adam and Eve are equal in

14. Based on sermons, theological treatises, visual arts, and scientific sources, Eve was particularly important for Lutheran theologians seeking to understand the human condition post-fall. Their fascination ranged from female physique, particularly the uterus, to women's "place" in family and society at large. Thus, participating in the medieval debate on women (*querelle des femmes*), Lutherans heavily promoted marriage and related gender roles for women who, in their female bodies, provided a special space for God's work. See Kathleen M. Crowther, *Adam and Eve in the Protestant Reformation* (Cambridge: Cambridge University Press, 2010), esp. 104–6, 110–11, 137–38.

l Pelikan, in LW 1:xii.

creation by further emphasizing that they are equally the image and similitude of God, equal recipients of God's word (as of the commandment), and that they are equally given dominion over the rest of creation, and have equal future glory. There is no hierarchy in God's creation of men and women, but there is a difference in the method used. Commenting on Genesis 2, Luther makes significant conclusions from God's choice of using Adam's rib for Eve and from Adam's immediate reaction to his newly created partner. Luther deems the physical "shared" rib and the

The Creation of Eve (c. 1510)
by Michelangelo (1475–1564)

immediate recognition of the beloved's words of intimacy and love to be God's intention for men and women. With tenderness, he characterizes Eve as the nest and dwelling place for Adam. Although Luther perceives this as compromised because of sin that brought along false awareness of self and the other, and an ongoing power struggle—starting from home and basic gendered relations—he is adamant regarding the great promise of spousal love and domestic harmony.

That Eve "is given to" Adam means that "even today" they are partners both in managing the house with a common interest in their children and property. That God created them male and female in God's image and similitude also means that the female sex may not be excluded from any glory of the human creature, although this sex due to the fall and God's punishment is inferior to the male sex. God created two equal beings with different sexes, Luther asserts, while rejecting both a Jewish notion that the female should be cut from a bi-gendered man and Aristotle's view of woman as an imperfect man. He also firmly rejects those who "maliciously" consider women monsters. Such pejorative ideas about God's "most excellent work" are unreasonable.

Luther grieves for the lack of innocence in the Garden of Eden, a sign of which was shameless nudity and sacred sex. Elsewhere he returns to the effects of sin to all aspects of human life, including sexuality, actually without an alternate view to that of Augustine's (though outside of the lecture hall Luther expresses a most positive view of sexuality as both a practice of Christian love and a creational command, as evidenced in his letters). Hence, Luther's instincts draw him to recognize the goodness of the creator's design in all of human existence. It is remarkable how he writes about the female body, conception, pregnancy, and childbirth with a positive and affectionate curiosity.

Viewing women through the lenses of his medieval notions, Luther considers women's bodies already as a proof for what their calling in life is, so indicated by the word *build* in the biblical narrative: God built a woman to be "the" building for her spouse and family, the foundation and a "safe place," to use modern terms. Even more so, God created a woman with her body to serve as the host for the revelation of the gospel. Without Luther making too many explicit comments in this particular text, and considering Luther's explication (elsewhere) of the role of Mary in the delivery of the gospel promise and the incarnation of the Word, it is clear that he reads women and their bodily existence organically into the salvation message of Christian faith.[15] It was important, thus, to get the details right about the creation of the first woman and of her equality in creation, as it was important for Luther, commenting on the significance of the seventh day, to accentuate the virgin's birth of the Son as *the* proof of God's continuous creation. God did not stop creating on the seventh day, the sabbath, but continued to change and renew creation. Even Luther's own life is a proof of this.

Among other things that Luther touches upon in his explanation of the few verses in Genesis 1 and 2, he reminds the reader

15. In his exposition of Luke 1 in *Magnificat* (1521), Luther emphasizes Mary as the epitome of humanity. He uses Mary as a *Fürstenspiegel*, demonstrating how imperial powers and the demonic are unmasked, while the human is humanized in the lowly maiden. See Luther's *Magnificat* (1521), TAL 4:307–84; LW 21:295–35. See also Else Marie Wiberg Pedersen, "A Man Caught Between Bad Anthropology and Good Theology? Martin Luther's View of Women Generally and of Mary Specifically," in *Dialog: A Journal of Theology* 49, no. 3 (2010): 190–99, esp. 195–98.

Martin Luther (center) with his family and Philip Melanchthon. By L. Schultz after a painting by Gustav Adolph Spangenberg (ca. 1866–75).

of the divine qualities of nature, surmising how the earth is a house and a gift of production and procreation that before sin produced better fruits so that humans would not have overeaten (for example, they would not have eaten meat), but would have led a much more healthy life. Concurrently, he deliberates on sleep, with poignant, related comments on how sweet death would have been without sin, and how the resurrection would have ensued as a painless transfer to another reality. He speaks with the experience of a father of the natural process of children leaving the nest and making their own home, while caring for their aging parents. Quite humorous are Luther's fantasies of the ideal scenario for women's reproduction: without original sin, women would have produced babies without pain and litters at a time. That Luther loved children is evident.[16]

16. Luther's children brought him tremendous joy, just as his loss of two young daughters was the most devastating experience in his life, and the gravest test of his theology. It is evident that his personal experiences as a father illuminated his vision of Paradise and Heaven: in the existence free of sin, children do not suffer.

The reader is left with many authentic, meaningful insights from Luther: human beings have been blessed with the divine gifts of sleep and sex, and human existence is filled with mysteries of God that are, indeed, the very reason behind gender and gendered existence and human love. The reader also discovers charming and entertaining observations, such as that the cursed earth does not produce the quality of fruits as it did before the fall; rather, it produces insects, with the effect that human life is more troublesome. Just imagine a life without flies or mosquitoes as Luther did!

The Annotations

The following annotations are new, with few exceptions. They are written as a teaching or learning companion. Instead of cross-referencing Luther's own words on the matters at stake or engaging contemporary hermeneutics on either Luther or the Bible, the annotations are designed with two interests in mind: first, Luther's interpretation of the central text for Christian anthropology in light of information from gender studies; and second, the framework of the Reformation-era theologians pondering the mysteries of humanness and sex/gender. Comparisons with his contemporaries demonstrate how Luther's evolving views on gender for the most part resonate with those of his peers, and yet reflect peculiarly forward-looking ideas toward a quite radical theological anthropology.

The focus here is to render as inclusive as possible a translation of Luther's words, while also keeping the tensions in the Latin text, to both honor the conventions of modern English and to carve space for and tease out Luther's original instincts in the matters of gender and Christian freedom. Observations and information are included to facilitate renewed engagement with Luther toward modern anthropology that embraces the cherished Genesis texts as sources for promoting equality and integrity of all human beings.[m]

m For a contemporary biblical interpretation, see, e.g., Claus Westermann, *Genesis 1–11*, A Continental Commentary (Minneapolis: Fortress Press, 1994); Phyllis Trible, *God and the Rhetoric of Sexuality*, Overtures to Biblical Theology (Philadelphia: Fortress Press, 1978); and Phyllis A. Bird, *Faith, Feminism, and the Forum of Scripture: Essays on Biblical Theology and Hermeneutics* (Portland, OR: Cascade, 2015).

LECTURES ON GENESIS 1:26–2:3[a]

ELSE MARIE WIBERG PEDERSEN

26. Let Us make a human being
according to our image and likeness.[b]

HERE AGAIN Moses employs a new expression. God does not say: "Let the sea be set in motion," "Let the earth bring forth herbs," or "Let it bring forth." God says: "Let Us make." Therefore he[1] includes an obvious deliberation and plan; he did nothing similar in the case of the earlier creatures. There, without any deliberation and counsel, God said: "Let the sea be put in motion," "Let the earth produce," etc. But here, when God wants to create a human being, God summons divinity to a council and announces some sort of deliberation.

Therefore, in the first place, there is indicated here an outstanding difference between a human being and all the other creatures. The beasts greatly resemble human beings.[c] They dwell together; they are fed together; they eat together; they receive their nourishment from the same materials; they sleep and rest among us. Therefore, if you take into account their way of life, their food, and their support, there is a great similarity.

1. With "he" Luther refers to Moses, whose "new expression" about the creation of the human being, different from the creation of the other creatures, Luther is explaining.

a The text for Luther's treatment of Gen. 1:26–2:3 is drawn from *Luther's Works*, vol. 1: *Lectures on Genesis: Chapters 1–5*, ed. Jaroslav Pelikan, H. C. Oswald, and H. T. Lehmann (St. Louis: Concordia, 1958), 55–82. The translation is revised, with basis in the Latin version of WA 42:41–62, and with regard for inclusive language. The footnotes and annotations are, with few exceptions, chiefly new.

b The Bible verse follows the Latin of the Vulgate: "*Faciamus hominem ad imaginem et similitudinem nostram.*"

c Grammatically, the text has *homo*, human being, in the singular. However, Luther does speak of the human being in the generic, which substantially gives more sense to rendering here in the plural as human beings.

But here Moses points out an outstanding difference between these animals and humankind when he says that human beings were created by the special plan and providence of God. This means that between human beings and the other animals that live a corporeal life, human beings are creatures far superior, especially since their nature had not become depraved yet. Epicurus holds the opinion that humans were created solely to eat and drink.[2] But this is equivalent to making no difference between humans and the rest of the beasts, which also have their desires and follow them. Here the text definitely sets humans apart when it says that in a special deliberation God gave consideration to the creation of humans; and not only that but also to making them in the image of God. This image is something far

Woodcut of Adam and Eve in Paradise
(1509) by Lucas Cranach the Elder

2. Epicurus (341–270 BCE) was a Greek philosopher and citizen of Athens. He perceived the world to consist of an empty space and innumerable atoms in a limited number of forms. The human soul was simply a set of atoms and thus a thing among all others. Since cognitively, the senses were objective and infallible, humans could not ethically fail if only they focused on being in a stable state of pleasure, the highest good, meaning freedom from pain and emotional upheaval. To Epicurus this pleasure was obtained through the practice of virtue. In the Middle Ages, his philosophy was often viewed as hedonistic and opposed to the moral Christian life, though this does not take into account the ethics of moderation in his thought.

different from the concern of the belly, that is, food and drink, for which the beasts also have understanding and appreciation.

Thus, Moses indicates to those who are spiritually minded that we were created for a better life in the future than this corporeal life would have been, even if our nature had remained unimpaired. Therefore, the doctors put it well: "Even if Adam[3] had not fallen through sin, still, after the appointed number of saints had been attained, God would have transferred them from this animal life to the spiritual life."[d] Adam was not to live without food, drink, and procreation. However, these corporeal activities would have come to an end at a predetermined time, after the number of saints had become full; and Adam, with descendants, would have been translated to an eternal and spiritual life. Nevertheless, these activities of corporeal life—like eating, drinking, procreating, etc.—would have been a service pleasing to God; we could also have rendered this service to God without the vice of desire that is there now after sin, without any sin, and without the fear of death. This would surely have been a pleasant and delightful life, a life about which we may indeed think but which we may not attain in this life. Yet, this we have, that we believe in a spiritual life after this life and the end of life in Paradise, which was devised and destined by God, and that we confidently look for it through the merit of Christ.

Thus, attention should be given to the text before us, in which the Holy Spirit dignifies human nature greatly and distinguishes it from all other creatures. Corporeal or animal life was, indeed, to be similar to that of the beasts. Just as the beasts have need of food, drink, and rest to refresh their bodies, so Adam, even in innocence, would make use of them. But what is added—that humanity was created for the animal life, but in such a way that humanity was also made according to the image and likeness of God—this is an indication of another and better life than that of the animals.

Thus, Adam had a twofold life: an animal one and an immortal one, though this was not yet clearly revealed but in hope. Meanwhile Adam would have eaten, drunk, labored, procreated, etc. In brief, I want to call attention to the difference that God makes through divine counsel, by which God discerns between

3. Luther enters into the traditional vocabulary of the "doctors" and replaces "*homo*" with "Adam." However, he mostly uses the noun in the generic sense of Adam as the earth creature (*adam* in Hebrew), being created from the earth (*adamah* in Hebrew). It should be noted that in the Hebrew there is a grammatical distinction between Gen. 1:1–2:3, designated the Priestly account, and Gen. 2:4ff., designated the Yahwistic account: Genesis 1 has the noun without the article (*adam*: humankind), whereas Genesis 2 exclusively has the noun with the article (*ha adam*: the human). See further Phyllis A. Bird, "Sexual Differentiation and Divine Image in the Genesis Creation Texts," in Kari E. Børresen, ed., *Image of God and Gender Models* (Oslo: Solum, 1991), 22.

d Cf. Peter Lombard, *Sententiarum libri quatuor*, II, Dist. XX, *Patrologia, Series Latina*, CXCII, 692–94.

us and the other animals that God lets us live with. Below we shall deal again with these matters at greater length.

Secondly, the word "Let Us make" is aimed at confirming the mystery of our faith, by which we believe that from eternity there is one God and that there are three separate Persons in one divinity: the Father, the Son, and the Holy Spirit.[4] The Jews indeed try to get around this passage in various ways, but they advance nothing solid against it. This passage bothers them to death, to use an expression of Occam, who applies it to irksome and difficult problems which he cannot solve.[5]

The Jews, then, say that God is speaking thus with the angels, likewise with the earth and with other creatures.[6] But I ask: Why did God not do this previously? Second:[7] What concern is the creation of humans to the angels? Third: God does not mention the angels but simply says: "We." Hence, God is speaking of makers and creators. This certainly cannot be said of the angels.

Fourthly, this is also certain: it can in no way be said that we were created according to the image of the angels. Fifthly, here both "Let Us make," in the plural, and "God made," in the singular, appear, whereby Moses clearly and forcibly shows us that

A page of *Genesis* from Lyra's *Postillae perpetuae* (Basel, 1498)

4. Luther utilizes the plural form "let Us make" as the very evidence that God is triune as "one substance in three persons, *una substantia in tres personae*," as already Tertullian (c. 160–220) explained that God is not only creator but also savior and life-giver, and which was the formula given in the credos of the old church: the Nicene-Constantinopolitan Creed (381), the Athanasian Creed (c. 400?), and the Apostolic Creed (c. 600?). Luther's exegesis of the verb is fundamental to his whole exegesis of Genesis 1–3, which is totally trinitarian.

5. William of Occam (c. 1300–c. 1349), who influenced Luther's thought, criticized Thomistic Scholasticism.

6. As Jaroslav Pelikan notes in the introduction to LW 1, Luther's lectures on Genesis were dependent on the Franciscan Bible scholar Nicholas of Lyra (1270–1349) "for the rabbinical learning they display and for at least some of the patristic exegesis they consider" (xi). Luther, who below is referring directly to Lyra, here seems to indirectly refer to him for quoting this exegesis of Gen. 1:26 from a "Rabbi Eben Ezra" found in an incunabulum of 1492: *Postilla fratris Nicolai de lyra de ordine niorum super Genesim Exodum Leuiticum Numeri Deutronomium [sic] Josue Judici Regum & Paralypomenon. Cum additionibus pauli episcopi Burgensis*. See below, n. *b*, p. 98.

7. Luther lists three questions he wants to ask the Jews, while arguing against their rejection of a trinitarian understanding of the one God. Here is the second of the three questions.

within and in the very Godhead and the Creating Essence[e] there is one inseparable and eternal plurality. This not even the gates of hell (Matt. 16:18) can take from us.

Next, when the Jews say that God is speaking with the earth concerning the earth, this is also frivolous. For the earth is not our maker.[f] Moreover, why didn't God rather speak to the sun, since Aristotle says: "The human being and the sun bring humans into existence."[g] However, this does not fit either, as we were not made according to the image of the earth; but we were made according to the image of those Makers who say "Let Us make." These Makers are three distinct Persons in one divine essence. Of these three Persons we are the image, as we shall hear later.

It is utterly ridiculous when the Jews say that God is following the custom of princes, who speak of themselves in the plural number due to reverence. The Holy Spirit is not imitating this court mannerism (to give it this name); nor does Holy Scripture acknowledge this manner of speaking. Consequently, this is a sure indication of the Trinity, that in one divine essence there are three Persons: the Father, the Son, and the Holy Spirit. Thus, not even so far as their activity is concerned, is God separated, because here all three Persons cooperate and say: "Let Us make." The Father does not make one human being and the Son another, nor does the Son make one human being and the Holy Spirit another; but Father, Son, and Holy Spirit are one and the same God, author and creator of the same work.

Nor is it possible to divide God objectively[8] in this manner, since the Father is not known except in the Son and through the Holy Spirit. Therefore, such as there is one God actively, so also objectively. Yet, so far as God's substance or essence is concerned from within, God is Father, Son, and Holy Spirit, three distinct Persons in one divinity.

e Note that the text uses the feminine form of creator (*creatrix*), to match the feminine noun *essentia*, thus not confining God's creative essence to that of the male sex.

f Again the text speaks about the maker in the feminine (*factrix*), again probably to match the feminine noun *terra*, which shows us that in several places the grammar dictates the vocabulary more than does the ideology when it comes to matters of gender and sex.

g Apparently a reference to Aristotle's *De generatione et corruptione*, II, ch. 10.

8. Luther may be referring to the Scholastic concept of objective being, *esse obiective*, according to which what is present to pure thought is not imprinted there as a perception passively received through the senses, but as the terminus of an act of seeing. It is present as the object of our representation, both as immanent (what is represented) and as transcendent (what it is representing). Duns Scotus (c. 1266–1308) determined the objective being as universal, abstract, and immanent to the spirit, as the being of the thing remains the same whether its object exists or not. See further, Barbara Cassin, ed., *The Dictionary of Untranslatables: A Philosophical Lexicon* (Princeton: Princeton University Press, 2014), 725. Luther seems to emphasize that God does not simply exist in this "objective" manner but also in an active manner as the truly existing one and triune God who acts and creates.

These evidences should be precious and welcome to us. Even though both Jews and Turks[9] laugh at us because we are convinced that there is one God and three Persons, nevertheless, unless they are shameless enough to deny the authority of Scripture, they are compelled by this passage as well as by those quoted above to adopt our conviction. They may scoff at these ideas, as the Jews zealously do; but meanwhile there remains in their hearts that little sting: "Why should God say 'Let Us make'?" Likewise: "Why should Moses employ the plural noun *elohim*?"[h] These thoughts they cannot shut out from their minds, even though they can make the attempt and raise questions of various kinds. If it were a matter of wisdom[i] to scoff at such evidences, do you think that we lack the ability to do the same? But among us the authority of Scripture is too great, especially since the New Testament points this out even more clearly. The Son, who is in the bosom of the Father (John 1:18), teaches us the same fact much more clearly and not to believe him is the utmost blasphemy and eternal death. Hence, away with those utterly blinded corrupters of the divine doctrines until the time of their judgment!

But, you say, these evidences are too obscure to prove so important an article of faith. I answer: At that time these statements had to be made so obscurely by divine counsel, or at least because all things were reserved for that future Lord for whose arrival the restitution of all things (Acts 3:21), of all knowledge, and of all revelations was reserved. Thus, what had previously been told through enigmas, as it were, Christ evolved and commanded to be preached in clear language. And yet the holy patriarchs had this knowledge through the Holy Spirit, although not as clear as it is now, when we in the New Testament hear mentioned the Father, the Son, and the Holy Spirit. When Christ came, those seals had to be broken and to be preached with clarity what previously had been communicated in obscure words, solely out of respect for the future Teacher. If the Holy Spirit

h All the places where Luther is commenting on specific Hebrew terminology from the Genesis text as here on the Hebrew word for God (*El*) and in the plural (*Elohim*) the LW has added the Hebrew. However, as the Latin text considered the most correct source does not have the Hebrew, it is left out in this version.

i In keeping with tradition, Luther distinguishes between wisdom (*sapientia*) and acquired knowledge (*scientia*).

9. Cf. n. 7 above. Luther is concerned about one of the most important theological differences between the three monotheist religions: Judaism, Islam, and Christianity, namely, the doctrine of God. Whereas mainstream Christian doctrine teaches the one God as one substance in three persons, Jews and Muslims (here named Turks as was the custom in Luther's time) are fundamentally opposed to the doctrine on the Trinity, criticizing it for jeopardizing the one God and, thus, for being rather polytheist. Luther seems to have experienced the argumentation not only as an objection but even as a ridicule of the Christian message, which increasingly provoked him during his lifetime. While the young Luther had an eye for not least the rationality of the Jews, the old Luther sharpened his rhetoric against the Jews as they did not convert to Christianity. For Luther, the conflict was foremost theological. But it is also important to note that in Luther's context, Christians were not supposed to be "Jew friends." Both imperial law and ecclesial regulations since the late Middle Ages were forbidding Christians and Jews to mingle. "Even willingness to learn Hebrew and Jewish sources was problematic" due to the regulations, as Christian Hebraists experienced. Thus, when Luther and other reformers employed Hebrew and Jewish sources, following the Bible humanist ideal to go *ad fontes*, they were censored and might risk jeopardizing their reform cause. In 1541, for example, one of Luther's most vehement opponents, Johann Eck (1486–1543), wrote a strongly anti-Jewish attack on Luther's collaborator, Andreas Osiander (1498–1552), after he defended the Jews. See MLBJP, 21–33.

had not postponed this clear knowledge to the time of the New Testament, the Arians would have existed long before the birth of Christ.[10] And so in the last days the Holy Spirit wanted to confront the devil with this sun of knowledge, to put a bandage over his eyes, to make him envy humans even more for this clear knowledge, and so to torture him still more.

Saint Augustine Meditates on the Trinity When the Child Jesus Appears Before Him (c. 1475) by Vergós Group

In the third place, it is as if there is stirred up here a sea of questions: What is that image of God according to which Moses says that humans were made? Augustine has much to say in his explanation of this passage, particularly in his book *On the Trinity*.[j] Moreover, the remaining doctors in general follow Augustine, who keeps Aristotle's classification: that the image of God is the powers of the soul—memory, the mind or intellect, and will.[11] These three, they say, comprise the image of God which is in all humans. Just as in the divine relationships,

j Luther is referring to one of Augustine's seminal works, *On the Trinity*, IX–XI.

10. The Arians, named after the Alexandrian presbyter Arius (c. 256–336), was a Christian movement that denied the co-eternal divinity of Christ and the Holy Spirit. According to Arius, the Son was created like all other human beings, not born or generated by the Father. Arius believed that Christ, the Son, became divine only by the will of the Father. According to Arius, only the Father is unbegotten. The Arian controversy was settled at a council in Nicea 325, called by Emperor Constantine the Great (272–337). The Nicene Creed went against Arius, stating that the Son was "of the same substance" (*homoousios*) as the Father. As the Arian movement was strong, the statements of Nicea (325) were restated at the Council at Constantinople (381) and at the Council of Chalcedon (451), both with an enhanced third article on the Holy Spirit. Luther and the Lutheran reformation recognized the trinitarian dogma and included the three ecumenical creeds: the Nicene Creed, the Athanasian Creed, and the Apostolic Creed in the Augsburg Confession. See further, e.g., Günther Gassmann and Scott Hendrix, *The Lutheran Confessions* (Minneapolis: Fortress Press, 1999), 38, 66. Luther here seems to claim that the Arians' history goes way back before the incarnation.

11. Augustine, *On the Trinity*, X, 11–12. The North African bishop Aurelius Augustine of Hippo (354–430) and his doctrine on the triune God, as well as on sin and grace, impregnated the theology of the Western church. During the Middle Ages a diversity of Augustinian trajectories developed,

they say, the Word is begotten from the substance of the Father and the Holy Spirit is the delight of the Father, so, in the case of humans, from the memory comes forth the word of the heart, which is the mind. When this has been brought forth, the will brings out that which it sees as mind and is delighted by it.

Moreover, they say that the similitude lies in the gifts of grace.[k] Just as a similitude is a certain perfection of an image, so, they say, our nature is perfected through grace. And so the similitude of God consists in this, that the memory is adorned with hope, the intellect with faith, and the will with love. In this way, they say, humans are created according to the image of God; that is, humans have a mind, a memory, and a will. Thus, humanity is created according to the similitude of God; that is, the intellect is enlightened by faith, the memory is made confident through hope and steadfastness, and the will is adorned with love.

In the third place,[12] they also make other divisions, such as the memory being the image of the power of God, the mind of God's wisdom, and the will of God's justice, etc. In this manner Augustine chiefly, and others after him, have exerted themselves to think out different kinds of trinities in the human being; for they believed that in this way the image of God could more easily be beheld. However, although these not unpleasing speculations are proposed by keen and leisurely geniuses, they do very little to correctly explain the image of God.[13]

Hence, although I do not condemn or find fault with that effort and those thoughts by which everything is brought into relationship with the Trinity, I am not at all sure that they are very useful, especially when they are subsequently spun out further. For there is also added a discussion concerning free will, which has its origin in that image. This is what they maintain: God is free; therefore, since humans are created according to the image of God, they, too, have a free memory, mind, and will. In this way many statements are carelessly made, statements that are either not properly expressed or later on are understood in a wicked way. Thus, this was the origin of the dangerous opinion that in governing humans God permits them to act under their own impulse. From this assertion came many inconvenient

k This distinction between "image" and "similitude," parallel terms in the Hebrew text, goes back at least to Irenaeus (c. 130–c. 202), *Against Heresies*, V, ch. 6, par. 1.

not all reconcilable with Augustine's own thoughts. When Luther joined the Friary of Augustinian Hermits at Erfurt in 1505, this gave him the choice of following the new humanist tendencies that from the beginning of the sixteenth century called for a revival of classical Latin and the reading of church fathers, such as Augustine, and the Bible rather than Scholastic textbooks. See Bernhard Lohse, *Luthers Theologie in ihrer historischen Entwicklung und in ihrem systematischen Zusammenhang* (Göttingen: Vandenhoeck & Ruprecht, 1995), 24–25.

12. The *tertio* here, "in the third place," seems to be a pedagogical device—either by Luther in his oral presentation or by one of the scribes—to inform the reader that Luther is still treating the "sea of questions" related to the *imago Dei*. Luther has thus reached the third point, after the question of difference between humans/animals and the question of God's Trinity, namely, the question of the trinitarian structure of human capacities, a question on which Luther is not quite in agreement with Augustine. Cf. above, n. 11.

13. Luther is using his famous sarcasm as a rhetorical tool in order to unmask the absurdities of the opponents.

ideas. It is similar to the quotation: "God, who created you without you, will not save you without you."[l] From here the conclusion was drawn that free will cooperated as the preceding and efficient cause of salvation.[m] No different is the assertion of Dionysius, though more dangerous than the former, when he says that although the demons and the human beings fell, nevertheless their natural endowments, such as the mind, memory, will, etc., remained unimpaired.[n] But if this is true, it follows that by the powers of their nature humans can bring about their own salvation.

These very dangerous opinions of the fathers were discussed in all the churches and schools, but I really do not see what the fathers intended to achieve by them. Therefore, my advice is to read them with discretion. They often speak as the result of an emotion and of a particular mood that we do not have nor can have, since we do not have similar situations. And so the inexperienced appropriate everything without discretion, in the sense they give to it and not in the one the fathers had. But I pass over these things and return to the subject.

I am afraid that after this image was lost through sin we cannot understand it to any extent. Memory, will, and mind we have indeed; but they are most corrupted and most gravely weakened, yes, to put it more clearly, they are utterly leprous and unclean. For if these powers are the image of God, it will also follow that Satan was created according to the image of God, since he surely has these natural endowments, such as memory, an intellect higher, and a will more obstinate than we have.[14]

14. This is Luther's most famous formulation and argument against the traditional threefold Augustinian understanding of the human *imago Dei*: memory, intellect/rationality, and will. Luther argues that if the human *imago Dei* is simply expressed in the three abilities of remembering, understanding, and willing, then Satan, who possesses as much memory and even greater intellect and will than humans, is so much more created in the image of God.

Thus, the image of God is something far different, namely, a unique work of God. If some nonetheless assert that these powers are that image, let them admit that they are, as it were, leprous and unclean. Similarly, we still call leprous human beings even though in their leprous flesh everything is almost dead and without sensation, except that they are rather vehemently excited to lust.

l This is an Augustinian aphorism, which can be found in his sermon 169, 13. See William A. Jurgens, *The Faith of the Early Fathers*, vol. 3 (Collegeville, MN: Liturgical Press, 1979), 29.

m According to Aristotle, *Metaphysics*, V, ch. 2, the efficient cause is "that from which the change or the resting from change first begins."

n Luther is referring to Pseudo-Dionysius the Areopagite (c. 650–c. 725). See LW 13:110 n.55.

Therefore, the image of God, according to which Adam was created,[o] was something far more distinguished and excellent, since obviously no disease of sin adhered to his reason or to will. Both the inner and the outer sensations were all of the purest kind. The intellect was most pure, the memory the best, and the will the most sincere—all in the most beautiful tranquility of mind, without any fear of death and without any anxiety. To these inner qualities came further those most beautiful and superb qualities of body and of all the limbs, qualities in which he surpassed all the remaining living creatures. I am fully convinced that before Adam's sin his eyes were so sharp and clear that they surpassed those of the lynx and eagle.[p] Adam was stronger than the lions and the bears, whose strength is very great; and handling them the way we handle puppies. Furthermore, the fruits used as food then were far superior in sweetness and quality, compared to what they are now.

But after the fall death crept like disease into all our senses, so that we cannot understand that image even with our intellect. Adam would not have known his Eve except in the most unembarrassed attitude toward God, with a will obedient to God, and without any evil thought. Now, after sin, we all know how great passion is in the flesh, which is not only passionate in its desire but also in its disgust after it has acquired what it wants. Thus, in both instances we see neither reason nor will unimpaired, but passion greater than that of cattle. Is this not a serious and pernicious disease, of which Adam was free before sin? Moreover, he had greater strength and keener senses than the rest of the living beings. To what extent are humans today surpassed by the boars in their sense of hearing, by the eagles in their sense of sight,

o The text shifts terminology from *homo* (Genesis 1), the human being in the generic, to the male named Adam (Genesis 3), the Hebrew term (*adam*) otherwise used for the earth creature. In the Hebrew text, *Adam* is used without the article for the earth creature (Genesis 1) or with the article for the human (Genesis 2–3). Whether God names the man, *ish*, Adam, when he tells him—after having cursed the serpent and told the woman, *ishah*, that her pain in childbearing will be multiplied—that the earth, *adamah*, is cursed due to him (Gen. 3:17) is not clear. Claus Westermann almost consequently translates *Adam* of Genesis 2–3 into "the man." See Westermann, *Genesis* (London: T&T Clark, 2004), 15, 24.

p Cf. LW 12:19 n.8.

and by the lion in his strength? Therefore no one can grasp how much better nature was then than it is now.

Hence, my understanding of the image of God is this: that Adam had it in his being and that he not only knew God and believed that God was good, but that he also lived a life that was fully divine; that is, he was without the fear of death or of any other danger, and was content with God's grace. Likewise, it appeared in Eve,[15] who speaks with the serpent without any fear, as we do with a lamb or a dog. For this reason, too, God announces the punishment if they should transgress the command: "On whatever day you eat from this tree, you will die by death," as though God said: "Adam and Eve, now you are living without fear; death you have not experienced nor seen. This is my image, by which you are living, just as God lives. But if you sin, you will lose this image, and you will die."

So we see now what great dangers and how many varieties of death and chances of death this wretched nature is compelled to meet with and to endure in addition to the execrable lust and other sinful passions and inordinate emotions that arise in the hearts of all. We are never secure in God; terror and apprehension cause us concern even in sleep. These and similar evils are the image of the devil, who stamped them on us. But Adam lived in supreme bliss and security; not afraid of fire, of water, or of the other discomforts with which this life is beset and of which we are inordinately afraid.

And so let those who wish to do so minimize original sin;[16] it surely appears both from the sins it produces and from the punishments it incurs that it is by far the greatest sin. Consider lust alone. Is it not most monstrous both in its desire and in its disgust? Moreover, what shall we say about hatred against God and about blasphemy? These are the very signs of failures that truly demonstrate that the image of God was lost.

Therefore, when we speak about that image, we are speaking about something unknown. Not only are we not experts, but we perpetually experience the opposite; and so we hear nothing except bare words. In Adam there was an enlightened reason, a true knowledge of God, and a most upright will to love God and the neighbor, so that Adam embraced Eve and at once acknowledged her to be his own flesh. Added to these were other lesser but exceedingly important gifts—if you draw a comparison with our infirmity—namely, a perfect knowledge of the nature of the ani-

15. Luther stresses that Eve has the same substance from God as Adam has.

16. The idea of sin as an original sin committed by Adam and Eve and henceforth transferred to every generation through desire was fully developed by Augustine, though already taught by his teacher Ambrose of Milan (c. 340–397). See, e.g., Augustine's *Enchiridion de Fide, Spe et Caritate*, ch. 8, 25–27. Whereas the Eastern church never adopted Augustine's idea of sin as a hereditary sin transferred through human, sexual lust (Lat.: *libido*) and desire (Lat.: *concupiscentia*), the Western church adhered to it in different forms. For the great significance to the Lutheran reformation of original sin as hereditary sin, see CA 2.

The Fall of Man (Gen. 3:4) by Peter Paul Rubens (1577–1640) and Jan Breughel the Elder (1568–1625)

mals, the herbs, the fruits, the trees, and the other creatures.

If all these qualities are combined, do they not make up and produce the sort of man[q] in whom you would think that the image of God is reflected, especially when you add the rule over the creatures? Just as Adam and Eve acknowledged God as their Lord, so later on they ruled over the other creatures in the air, in the water, and on the earth. Who could adequately describe this glory in words? I believe that Adam could command a lion with a single word, just as we give a command to a trained dog. And he was free to cultivate the soil to produce what he wished. Our later discussions will show that thorns and thistles were not in existence at that time.[17] Similarly, I believe that in those days the beasts were not as fierce as they are now.

But this condition is the fault of original sin, and from it all the remaining creatures derive their vices. I hold that before sin the sun was brighter, the water purer, the trees more fruitful, and the fields more fertile. However, through sin and that awful fall not only our flesh is disfigured by the disease of sin, but everything we use in this life has become corrupt, as we shall point out more clearly below.

But now the gospel has brought about the restoration of that image. Intellect and will indeed have remained, but both very much impaired. And so the gospel brings it about that we are formed once more according to that familiar and indeed better image, because we are born again into eternal life or rather into the hope of eternal life by faith, that we may live in God and with God and be one with God, as Christ says (John 17:21).

And indeed, we are reborn not only for life but also for righteousness, because faith acquires Christ's merit and knows that

17. Luther is referring to his subsequent comments to Gen. 3:17-19 and how the earth is cursed due to Adam.

q The text uses the term *vir*, a male.

through Christ's death we have been set free. From this source our other righteousness has its origin, namely, that newness of life through which we are zealous to obey God as we are taught by the word and aided by the Holy Spirit. But this righteousness has merely its beginning in this life, and it cannot attain perfection in this flesh. Nevertheless, it pleases God, not as though it were a perfect righteousness or a payment for sin but because it comes from the heart and depends on its trust in the mercy of God through Christ. Moreover, this is brought about by the gospel, that the Holy Spirit is given to us, who offers resistance in us to unbelief, envy, and other vices that we may earnestly strive to glorify the name of the Lord and his word, etc.[18]

In this manner this image of the new creature begins to be restored by the gospel in this life, but it will not be finished in this life. But when it is finished in the kingdom of the Father, then the will truly will be free and good, the mind truly enlightened, and the memory persistent. Then it will also happen that all the other creatures will be under our rule to a greater degree than they were in Adam's [and Eve's] Paradise.[19]

Until this is accomplished in us, we cannot have an adequate knowledge of what that image of God was which was lost through sin in Paradise. What we are stating, however, is that faith and the word, as though they point it out from a distance, teach us that glory of the divine image.[20] Just as in the beginning heaven and earth were unfinished bodies, so to speak, before the light had been added, so the godly have within themselves that unfinished image which God on the last day[21] will bring to perfection in those who have believed the word.

Therefore, that image of God was something most excellent, in which were included eternal life, everlasting security, and all good. However, through sin this image was so obscured and corrupted that we cannot grasp it even with our intellect. Although we utter the words, who is there who could understand what it means to be in a safe life, without terrors and dangers, and to be wise, upright, good, and free from all calamities, spiritual as well as corporeal? However, greater than these was the fact that they were empowered for eternal life. They were so created that as long as they lived in this physical life, they would till the ground, not as if they were doing an irksome task and exhausting the body by toil but with supreme pleasure, not as a pastime but in obedience to God and submission to the will of God.

18. Luther is clearly interpreting the creation and the fall in a trinitarian perspective (see pp. 82–83 above). Hence, the christological, soteriological, and pneumatological aspects play a major part in his interpretation of Genesis 1.

19. The text only mentions Adam, but from the context Eve must be understood as part of the pre-fall human being in its bi-gendered state in this formulation. Cf. Luther's comments below on Adam's and Eve's equal dominion in Paradise. *Luther's Lectures on Genesis*, deemed too unsystematic and imperfect to publish at first, probably still has the notion of being an exegesis offered orally. This at least explains the constant and unsystematic shift between mentioning only Adam as the Paradise creature and mentioning both Adam and Eve as equal creatures of God in Paradise.

20. After having stated that one can know nothing about the image of God, Luther gives his notion of how life before the fall would probably have been.

21. The text uses the term *novissimo die* (Lat.), "the newest day," thus pointing to the new life following this life, a spiritual and angelic life as Luther explains in the subsequent passages.

After this corporeal life a spiritual life was expected, in which they would neither make use of physical food nor do the other things which are customary in this life, but would live an angelic and spiritual life. As the future life is pictured to us in Holy Scripture, we shall not drink, eat, or carry on any other physical functions. Hence, Paul says (1 Cor. 15:45): "the first human being was made a living soul"; that is, it lived an animal life, which needs food, drink, sleep, etc. But "the second human being shall be renewed into the life-giving spirit"; that is, a spiritual human being when it reverts to the image of God. It will be similar to God in life, righteousness, holiness, wisdom, etc. Now follows:

Let them have dominion over the fish of the sea, etc.[r]

Here the rule is assigned to the most beautiful creatures that know God and are the image of God, in whom the similitude of the divine nature shines forth through their enlightened reason, through justice and wisdom.[22] Adam and Eve become the rulers of earth, sea, and air. But this dominion is commissioned to them not only by way of advice but also by express command.[23] Here we should first carefully ponder the exclusiveness in this: no beast is told to exercise dominion; but quite simply all the animals and even the earth, with everything brought forth by the earth, are subjected to Adam, whom God by an express verbal command constituted ruler of the entire living creature.[24] Adam and Eve heard the words with their ears when God said: "Have dominion." Thus, the naked human being—without weapons and walls, even without any clothing, solely in their bare flesh[25]—was given the rule over all birds, wild beasts, and fish.

Even this small part of the divine image we have lost, so much so that we do not even understand that fullness of joy and bliss which Adam had by contemplating all the living creatures. Today all our faculties are leprous, indeed dull and utterly dead. Who can conceive of that part, as it were, of the divine nature, that Adam and Eve understood all the dispositions of all animals, their characters and all their powers? What kind of a reign would it have been if they had not had this knowledge? Among the saints there is some knowledge of God in this life, recognized from the word and the Holy Spirit. However, the knowledge of

r The Latin text reads: "*Dominetur piscibus maris*, etc.," thus not following the Vulgate, which does not refer to Adam's and Eve's dominion until later.

22. Again, Luther speaks about both the image and the similitude of God in the tradition of the Old Testament and Augustine. Luther here asserts that the first humans were created in the image of God, while the similitude of divine nature was expressed in their reason, justice, and wisdom. In his treatise *The Freedom of a Christian* (see TAL 1:467–538), Luther determines Christ to have become *similitudo hominis*, the similitude of the human being, while the human being had lost its *imago Dei* to which it was created.

23. Luther stresses that Eve and Adam are equally given dominion over the rest of creation, thereby underlining their creational equality. Luther seems to refute the tradition, seen in most patristic writers, that identifies dominion with the male sex. Likewise, he seems to play with the Scholastic distinctions between *consilia*, e.g., a temporal promise like the monastic vow of poverty, and *praecepta divina* or as here *mandata Dei*, God's eternal command. See, e.g., Thomas Aquinas, STh II.II.q.189.a.1–5. By thus stressing that dominion is commissioned to both Eve and Adam by God's council and express command, Luther is making his own very strong statement.

24. Luther is clearly referring to Adam as the earth creature in this passage, whereas he in the next sentence focuses on how both Adam and Eve heard the words of God: that they should rule in the capacity of *homo nudus*, the in-flesh naked human being without weapons or walls, *sine armis et muris*. In other words, Luther is imagining a very peaceful dominion by the *homo nudus*.

25. By defining the godlike human being as *homo nudus*, bare flesh, Luther is likely making a playful contrast to Adam's and Eve's discovery that they were naked after having eaten the forbidden fruit (Gen. 3:7), when they became shameful about their nudity and covered it.

26. Luther this time points out that the human likeness to God, the *similitudo Dei* (leaving out here the *imago Dei*), such as in wisdom, relates to Adam and Eve as they were before the fall.

nature—that we should know all the qualities of trees and herbs, and the dispositions of all the beasts—is utterly beyond repair in this life.

If, then, we should praise an outstanding philosopher, let us not overlook our first parents as long as they were still pure from sin. They had a most perfect knowledge of God, for how would they not know God whose similitude they had and felt within themselves?[26, s] Furthermore, they had the most dependable knowledge of the stars and of the whole of astronomy.

Eve had these mental gifts in the same degree as Adam, as Eve's utterance shows when she answered the serpent concerning the tree in the middle of Paradise. There it becomes clear enough that she knew to what end she had been created and pointed to the source from which she had this knowledge; for she said (Gen. 3:3): "The LORD said." Thus, she not only heard this from Adam, but her very nature was pure and full of the knowledge of God to such a degree that by herself she knew the word of God and understood it.

Woodcut illustration of Adam and Eve in the Garden of Eden by Erhard Altdorfer (d. 1561) in a 1533/34 printing of the Luther Bible

Of this knowledge we have feeble and almost completely obliterated remnants. The other animals, however, completely lack this knowledge. They do not know their Creator, their origin, and their end; or out of what and why they were created. Therefore, they certainly lack that similitude of God. For this reason the psalm also urges (Ps. 32:9): "Do not become like the horse and the mule."

Thus, even if this image has been almost completely lost, there is still a great difference between the human being and the rest of the animals. Before sin the difference was far greater and more evident, when Adam and Eve knew God and all the creatures and, as it were, were completely engulfed by the goodness and justice

s *Praedicemus primos nostros parentes, cum adhuc essent a peccator puri. Hi enim congnitionem Dei perfectissimam habuerut, quomodo enium nescirent eum, cuius similitudinem in se habebant et sentiebant?* The Latin text confirms that Luther, contrary to modern claims, did engage in the idea of the human being as not only created as the likeness of God (*similitudo dei*) but also as possessing the quality attached to it: the human being by creation had the ability of knowing God due to its likeness to God.

Adam and Eve at the Fall, part of the fresco covering the ceiling of the Sistine Chapel painted by Michelangelo in the years 1508–1512. Michelangelo has the serpent turn into a woman that seems to exchange power with Eve as their left hands, the hand of the devil, touch. By contrast, Luther emphasizes that evil comes from Satan, not from Eve. Hence, in Luther's interpretation we would never find the snake (symbol of evil and Satan) identified with a woman as Michelangelo has done.

of God. As a result, there was between them a singular union of soul and will. No other sight in the whole world appeared lovelier and more attractive to Adam than his own Eve. But now, as the Gentiles say, a wife is a necessary evil.[t] Why they call her an evil can be perceived readily enough; but they do not know the cause of evil, namely, Satan, who has so vitiated and corrupted this nature.[27]

What we achieve in life, however, is brought about, not by the dominion which Adam had but through industry and skill. Thus, we see the birds and the fish caught by cunning and deceit; and by skill the beasts are tamed. Those animals that are most domesticated, such as geese and hens, nevertheless are wild so far as they themselves and their nature are concerned. Hence, even now this sick body has some appearance of the dominion

27. When here referring to the "Gentiles" or "people" (Luther uses the Latin term *gentes*), Luther may be referring to a popular adage. The notion that "a wife is a necessary evil" is not expressing his own view and he finds it far from a Christian notion. Quite to the contrary, Luther stresses that the source of evil is Satan, not a woman/wife as part of tradition since Tertullian maintained. Note also that the text does not say that woman as a creature has been corrupted (as the LW version colors Luther). The Latin text reads that human nature as such has been corrupted: *"Ac cur malum vocent, satis manifeste cernitur, sed causam mali nesciunt, Satanam scilicet, qui hanc naturam sic depravavit et corrupit."*

t This seems to be a reference to Aristotle, *De generatione animalium*, I, ch. 20.

over the other creatures by the favor of God. But it is extremely small and far inferior to that first dominion, when there was no need of skill or cunning, when the creature simply obeyed the divine voice because Adam and Eve were commanded to have dominion over them.

We thus retain the name and word "dominion" as a bare title, but the substance itself has been almost entirely lost.[28] Yet it is a good thing to know and ponder these facts, so that we may have a longing for that coming day when that which we lost in Paradise through sin will be restored to us. We are waiting for that life for which Adam also should have waited. And we duly marvel at this and thank God for it, that although we are so deformed by sin,[29] so dull, ignorant, and dead, as it were, nevertheless, through the favor of Christ, we wait for the same glory of the spiritual life for which Adam would have waited if having remained in the physical life that was endowed with the image of God.

27. And God created humans according to his image, according to the image of God he created them.[u]

Here Moses does not employ the word "similitude," but only "image." Perhaps he wanted to avoid an ambiguity of speech and for this reason repeated the noun "image." I see no other reason for the repetition unless we should understand it for the sake of emphasis as an indication of the Creator's rejoicing and exulting over this most beautiful work made, so that Moses intends to indicate that God was not so delighted at the other creatures as at humans, whom God had created according to the similitude of divinity. The rest of the animals are designated as footprints of God; while humans alone are God's image, as appears in the *Sentences.*[v] In the remaining creatures God is recognized as by God's footprints; but in the human being, especially in Adam,[w] God is truly recognized, because in it there is such wisdom, justice, and knowledge of all things that it may rightly be called a

u The Latin text, following the Vulgate, reads: "*Et creavit Deus hominem ad imaginem suam, ad imaginem Dei creavit illum.*"

v In Peter Lombard, *Sententiae*, II, Dist. XVI, 683–85, is a discussion of the image of God in man.

w The text is again speaking in the generic of Adam, the earth creature, in this passage.

28. Luther continues the tradition that the human being's likeness to God, *similitudo Dei* (Lat.), was almost lost through sin. In tradition it varies if the *imago Dei* or the *similitudo Dei* is totally lost or remains in a weakened form. Bernard of Clairvaux (1090–1153), who was of great inspiration for Luther, has both variations in his theological anthropology. In his treatise *Grace and Free Choice*, Bernard holds that the *similitudo Dei* (identified as the three goods of the soul: dignity, knowledge, and virtue) is lost, while the *imago Dei* (identified as the will to God) is damaged. But in his sermons 80–82 of the *Sermons on the Song of Songs*, Bernard deliberately reverts the order. The image of God (greatness and uprightness) is lost, while the likeness of God (simplicity, immortality, and free choice) is permanent, albeit damaged. For Bernard the variations, of which he adduces several over the years, are "*diversa sed non adversa*," different but not opposite (*Sermones in Cantica Canticorum* [SCC] 81:11; *Sancti Bernardi Opera* [SBO] 2:291). Particularly important in relation to Luther is that Bernard, in his latter variation of image and likeness, asserts that the soul is made "in the image" of the true Image who is the Word (SCC 80:2; SBO 2:277–78).

29. Luther employs the Latin term *deformati* for fallen humanity in continuation of the vocabulary known from the Augustinian tradition, which plays on the root word "form," *forma* (Lat.). The idea is that the human being was originally created in the "form" of God, was "de-formed" by sin, and shall again be "re-formed" through Christ in order to "con-form" with the will of God.

micro-cosmos.[30] It has an understanding of heaven, earth, and the entire creation. And so it pleases God to have made so beautiful a creature.

But without a doubt, just as at that time God rejoiced in the counsel and work by which humans were created, so today, too, God takes pleasure in restoring this divine work through the Son and our liberator, Christ. It is useful to ponder these facts, namely, that God is most kindly inclined toward us and takes delight in this thought and plan of restoring all who have believed in Christ to spiritual life through the resurrection of the dead.

Male and female he created them.[x]

In order not to give the impression that God was excluding the woman from all the glory of the future life, Moses includes both sexes; for the woman appears to be a somewhat different being from the man, having different members and a much weaker nature.[31] Although Eve was a most extraordinary creature—similar to Adam so far as the image of God is concerned,

In this 1534 woodcut, God creates Eve out of Adam's rib while he sleeps (Genesis 2).

x The Latin text follows the Vulgate and reads: "*Masculum et foeminam creavit eos.*"

30. Apart from being a familiar idea in the Renaissance, the idea of man as a μικρόκοσμος was central to Maximus the Confessor (c. 580-662). See Lars Thunberg, *Man and the Cosmos: The Vision of St Maximus the Confessor* (Yonkers, NY: St. Vladimir's Seminary Press, 1985).

31. Luther is following the Hebrew and Latin text when he now translates the human into the bi-gendered male (*masculum*) and female (*foeminam*). However, when he immediately after translates male and female as two sexes with a hierarchical distinction between them as the woman (Lat. *mulier*) having a weaker nature than the man (Lat. *vir*), Luther is following a long tradition rooted in early Judaism, which reads Gen. 1:26-27 with Gen. 2:7, 15-24 as its hermeneutical lens. According to this tradition, woman is inferior to man qua woman, but it is important that one notices that there are actually very different ways of understanding this inferiority both within Judaism and, no less, within Christianity. Kari Børresen has shown how traditional Christian anthropology holds two contrasting tenets: (1) androcentric gender hierarchy or female subordination is established by God's creative order; (2) human equivalence in the sense of women's parity with men is realized through Christ in redemption. This asymmetry between women's creational inferiority and soteriological equality is affronted by what Børresen calls "patristic 'feminists'" such as Clement of Alexandria (d. before 215) and Augustine of Hippo. They define *imago Dei* as an incorporeal and sexless quality, a gender-free quality that enables them to backdate women's Christ-likeness to the creational level, while still seeing women as God-givenly

that is, in justice, wisdom, and happiness—she was nevertheless a woman. For as the sun is more excellent than the moon (although the moon, too, is a very excellent body), so the woman, although she was a most beautiful work of God, nevertheless was not the equal of the male in glory and prestige.[32]

However, here Moses puts the two sexes together and says that God created male and female to indicate that Eve, too, was made by God as a partaker of the divine image and of the divine similitude, likewise of the rule over everything. Thus, even today the woman is the partaker of the future life, just as Peter says

subservient qua female. This split has existed until the twentieth century. See Børresen, "God's Image, Man's Image? Patristic Interpretation of Gen. 1,27 and I Cor. 11,7," Børresen, ed., *Image of God*, 188–207. Cf. Phyllis A. Bird, "Sexual Differentiation and Divine Image in the Genesis Creation Texts," and Anders Hultgaard, "God and Image of Woman in Early Jewish Religion," Børresen, ed., *Image of God*, 11–34 and 35–55.

32. Again, Luther draws on a long tradition when using the sun as metaphor for Adam's higher excellence, while Eve is a very excellent body like the moon. The imagery of the sun and moon was particularly used to designate Christ's (the second Adam) excellence over the also very excellent Virgin Mary (the second Eve) in the ancient and medieval church. See, e.g., Kerstin Bjerre-Aspegren, *Bräutigam, Sonne und Mutter: Studien zu einigen Gottesmetaphern bei Gregor von Nyssa* (Malmö: Gotab, 1977). Luther does not use the imagery in this manner, but here translates it to the relation between man and woman in general. It is important that we remember that Luther is not formulating a politics. He is simply expressing what has been the standard view of the sexes until far into the twentieth century when equality between the sexes became politically correct foremost in the Western world. Yet, one should also notice that Luther, distinct from the standard view of male excellence, emphasizes the excellence of the female sex.

33. In this passage, Luther sums up what he already stated above: The female and male are equal concerning the image and similitude of God and thus equal in ruling, the two factors so that they are joint heirs of the same grace (1 Pet. 3:7). In the household the wife is a partner in the management and has a common interest in the children and the property, and yet there is a great difference between the sexes. The male is like the sun in heaven, the female like the moon, the animals like the stars, over which sun and moon have dominion. In the first place, therefore, let us note from this passage that it was written that this sex may not be excluded from any glory of the human creature, although it is inferior to the male sex.[33] About marriage we shall have something to say below.[34]

closely linked in Luther's phraseology. Luther understands the male and female equality to encompass both their creational state, their actual life in the household (*oeconomia*) with a common ownership, and their eschatological state. They are partners that equally partake in all these aspects. It cannot be overstated that Luther's thoughts in this regard of equaling the female and male are innovative and go against the traditional interpretation through the perspective of Gen. 2:18. Hence, he further in this text rejects Talmudic tales of a bi-gendered creature split apart into male and female, and no less those who, like Aristotle, pejoratively term women "damaged males" or others who term them "monster." Yet, the text presents Luther as ambivalent in his view of women, as when it is again asserted that the female is different from the male, like the moon from the sun. However, one should note that female inferiority is not explicated beyond the metaphor of the sun versus the moon, while Luther is adamant in asserting the co-dominion of male and female. Hence, the emphasis is not on the inferiority of the female but on the equal glory, Luther's point being that the female in all respects equally partakes in the glory of the human creature.

34. Luther is referring to his later comments on Gen. 2:18 according to which post-fall women, unlike Eve, are subject to their husbands as they are also the necessary antidote against sin.

In the second place, there is here an argument against Hilary and others, who maintained that God created everything at the same time.[y] Here our opinion is supported: that the six days were truly six natural days, because here Moses says that Adam and Eve were created on the sixth day. One may not use sophistries with reference to this text. But concerning the order of creation of the human being he will state in the following chapter that Eve was made sometime after Adam, not like Adam, from a clod of earth, but from his rib, which God took out of the side of Adam as he slept. These are all works of time, that is, works that require time. They were not performed in one moment; neither were these acts: that God brings to Adam every animal and that there was not found one like him, etc. These are acts requiring time, and they were performed on the sixth day. Here Moses touches on them briefly by anticipation. Later on he will explain them at more length.

Many scholars also believe that Adam sinned on the sixth day, and they celebrate the sixth day for its twofold fame, namely, that just as Adam sinned on the sixth day, so Christ also suffered on the sixth day.[z] Let them see themselves whether this is true. What Moses clearly states is that the man[a] was created on the sixth day and that a wife was given to him.[35] But to me, as I shall point out below,[36] it seems more likely that Adam sinned on the seventh day, that is, on the sabbath, just as even now Satan disturbs the sabbath of the church when the word is being taught; but not even this can be clearly proved from Moses. Thus, on each side there are reasons against reasons, as Emperor Maximilian used to say.[37] Therefore I leave these matters undecided and within anyone's discretion.[38]

Lyra also relates a Jewish tale, of which Plato, too, makes mention somewhere, that in the beginning man was created bi-gendered and later on, by divine power, was, as it were, split or cut apart, as the form of the back and of the spine seems to prove.[b]

35. The Latin text here peculiarly reads *homo* in distinction from *uxor* (wife), not *Adam* or man (*vir*) distinct from *Eve* or woman (*mulier*). Where the text has not, so far, read Gen. 1:26-27 from the perspective of Gen. 2:18, the Bible verses in question are here co-read with Gen. 2:22-24. It is noteworthy, though, that Luther both here and in his direct comments to Gen. 2:22-24 below avoids the traditional emphasis on the wife having an inferior status as helpmate.

36. Luther is referring to his later comments on Gen. 3:1.

37. Maximilian I (1459–1519) was the Holy Roman Emperor in rule when Luther's case started. Had Maximilian I not died on 12 January, shortly after the Diet of Augsburg, championing his grandson Charles as Roman/German king, Luther's case might have looked very different, according to Heiko Oberman, *Luther: Man between God and the Devil*, trans. Eileen Walliser-Schwarzbart (New Haven: Yale University Press, 1982), 24. See also Luther's comments, LW 13:214–15.

38. Luther asserts that the question whether Adam was created on the sixth or the seventh day is an indifferent matter, an *adiaphoron*, while indicating that the real problem lies elsewhere: the preaching of the word on the sabbath is threatened by Satan.

y Luther seems to be referring to bishop Hilary of Poitiers (c. 315–c. 367), *On the Trinity* XII, ch. 40, *Series Latina* X, 458–59. Cf. Augustine, *De Genesi ad litteram libri* XII, IV,13, in Corpus Scriptorum Ecclesiasticorum Latinorum 28, Sec. 3, I, 133.

z Cf. below, Luther's comments on Gen. 2:3, p. 102.

a It makes more sense to translate the *homo* of the text into "the man."

b Nicholas of Lyra on Gen. 1:27, sec. "e." Cf. above, n. 6, p. 81.

Others have expanded these ideas with more obscene details. But the second chapter refutes these babblers.[39] For if this is true, how can it be sure that God took one of the ribs of Adam and out of it built the woman? These are Talmudic tales, and yet they had to be mentioned so that we might see the malice of the devil, who suggests such absurd ideas to human beings.

This tale fits Aristotle's designation of woman as a "maimed man"; others declare that she is a monster.[40] But let them themselves be monsters and sons of monsters—these men who make malicious statements and ridicule a creature of God in which God took delight as in a most excellent work, moreover, one which we see created by a special counsel of God. These Gentile [pagan] ideas show that reason cannot establish anything sure about God and the works of God but only thinks up reasons against reasons and teaches nothing in a perfect and solid manner.

28. And God blessed[c]

This God did not say about the animals; therefore God includes them here.

Be fruitful[d]

This is a command of God added for the creature. But, good God, what has been lost for us here through sin![41] How blessed was that state of humans in which the begetting of offspring was linked with the highest respect and wisdom, indeed with the knowledge of God! Now the flesh is so overwhelmed by the disease of lust that in the act of procreation the body becomes downright brutish and cannot beget in the knowledge of God.

Thus, the power of procreation remained in human nature, but very much debased and even completely overwhelmed by the disease of lust, so that procreation is only slightly more moderate than that of the brutes. To this we add the perils of pregnancy and of birth, the difficulty of feeding the offspring, and other endless evils, which all teach us the magnitude of original sin. Therefore, the blessing, which remains till now in nature,

c The Latin text understands the Vulgate's *Deus*, God, without mention.

d The Latin heading only uses *fructificate*, "be fruitful," different from the Vulgate's *multiplicamini*, "multiply."

Portrait of Maximilian I, Holy Roman Emperor (1519) by Albrecht Dürer (1471–1528)

39. Both here and in the immediate context Luther's principle of the *sola scriptura* is immanent as an argument for his exegesis, a clear example of an intertextual reading as Genesis 1 is read through the lens of Genesis 2, albeit only as an indication.

40. "*Cum hac fabula convenit, quod Aristoteles appellat mulierem virum occasionatum, et alii monster dicunt.*" Presumably with reference to Aristotle's *De generatione animalium*, I, ch. 20, Luther firmly rejects the pejorative designation of woman as an imperfect male, *mulierem virum*, as a *fabula*, something made up.

41. Again, it is evident that Luther, like the tradition in which he was taught, reads Genesis 1–3 as an entity, not as three separate chapters or narratives. But he does it in his own novel way, as is revealed through the subsequent deliberations: sex and procreation were as integral a part of pre-fall human life as of post-fall life. The difference is that pre-fall human procreation took place with respect and wisdom in a state of blessedness, not in a state of lust as post-fall procreation.

is, as it were, a cursed and debased blessing if you compare it with that first one; and yet, God established it and preserves it. So let us gratefully acknowledge this "marred blessing"; and let us keep in mind that the unavoidable disease of the flesh, which is nothing but disobedience and loathsomeness attached to bodies and minds, is the punishment of sin. Moreover, let us wait in hope for the death of this flesh that we may be set free from these loathsome conditions and may be restored even beyond the point of that first creation of Adam.[42]

42. As can be seen, Luther operates with a first and a second creation of Adam.

And have dominion over the fish of the sea.[e]

We are so overcome by our ignorance of God and the creatures that we cannot establish with certainty what use would have been made of the cattle, the fish, and the other animals in the first creation and state of perfection. We see now that we eat flesh, vegetables, etc. If they were not used in this manner, we would not know why they were created; for we neither see nor have any other use for these creatures. But Adam[43] would not have used the creatures as we do today, except for food, which it would have derived from other, far more excellent fruits. For they[f] under whose power everything had been placed did not lack clothing or money. Nor would there have been any greed among their descendants; but, apart from food, they would have made use of the creatures only for the admiration of God and for a holy joy which is unknown to us in this corrupt state of nature. By contrast, today and always the whole creation is hardly sufficient to feed and support the human being. Therefore, what this dominion consisted of we cannot even imagine.[44]

43. Again, Luther is referring to Adam as the earth creature, the prototype of the first human being that somehow includes the female, in keeping with his firm statement that the male and the female have common dominion over the rest of creation.

44. Luther contrasts the state of innocence in Paradise (where humans would not have eaten animals) with the present state of sin (where the rest of creation does not even make up food enough for humans due to their sinful greed). Luther thus holds a view of creation that goes against a traditional view according to which the divinely ordered human dominion of creation is without limits.

e This time the Latin text follows the Vulgate verbatim.

f The Latin verb is in the singular, but for coherence of the text it is here translated into the plural "they."

29. And God said: Behold, I have given you every herb bearing seed etc.[g]

Here you see how solicitous God is for the human being that was created. First God created the earth like a house in which they should live.[45] Then God arranged the other things divinely regarded as necessary for life. Finally, God gave the gift of procreation to the humans. Now God also provides food that nothing may be lacking for leading a life in the easiest possible manner. Moreover, I believe that if Adam[46] had remained in the state of innocence, their children would have run immediately after birth to the enjoyment of those delights which the initial creation afforded. But it is vain to mention these things; they cannot be acquired by thought, and they are irrecoverable in this life.

And all the trees[47]

Moses seems to be making a difference between the seeds and the green herbage, perhaps because the latter were to serve for the use of the beasts, the former for that of humans. I have no doubt that the seeds we use for food today were far more excellent then than they are now. Moreover, Adam would not have eaten the various kinds of meat, as the less delightful food, in preference to the delightful fruits of the earth, whereas for us nothing is more delicious than meat. From the use of these fruits there would not have resulted that leprous obesity, but physical beauty and health and a sound state of the humors.[48]

But now people do not content themselves with meats, with vegetables, or with grain; and rather often, because of unsuitable food, we face dangers of health. I am saying nothing about those increasingly widespread sins of overindulgence in food and drink which are worse than brutish. The curse which followed because of sin is apparent. It is also likely that only then were the accursed and pernicious insects produced out of the earth, which was cursed because of humanity's sin.[49]

45. The text, shifting between *homo* in the singular, *homini* in the plural, and *Adam*, must be referring to the creation of humankind, and as the following sentence is about their procreation, the subject is here rendered in the plural as "they."

46. Once again Luther must mean Adam the earth creature or humankind, encompassing both the male and the female, matching the *homini*, humans, of the former sentence. As below, Luther is deliberating on what he understands as the initial creation.

47. Interestingly, the Latin heading leaves out the whole wording from the Bible verse, especially the words on animals, because Luther concentrates on the gifts of food to humans.

48. The medieval medical term used here is *sana humanorum temperatura*, which in Luther's rendition, interestingly, mirrors the view on health and a healthy humanity of the early twenty-first century.

49. Luther is referring to Genesis 3 while emphasizing that the earth is cursed due to humanity's sin, whereas humans were not cursed. According to Luther, however, humanity is now having the effects of the curse, such as overindulgence in the products of the earth or irritating insects that in his view are coming from the earth.

g The Latin text follows the Vulgate without rendering the whole wording: "*dixitque Deus: Ecce dedi vobis omnem heram afferentem semen* etc."

But here comes the question of how the granting to Adam of the enjoyment of all the trees of the field harmonizes with the later assignment to it of a single portion of the earth for tilling, the portion called Paradise. It is also asked whether the whole earth is called Paradise, etc. But we shall put off these matters to the second chapter.[50]

50. Luther is referring to his subsequent comments on Gen. 2:17.

31. And God saw all things that he had made,
and they were very good.
And evening and morning became the sixth day.[h]

After God has finished the works, God speaks after the custom of one who has become tired, as if God were to say: "Behold, I have prepared all things in the best way. The heaven I have prepared as a roof; the earth is the flooring; the animals—with all the appointments of the earth, the sea, and the air—are the possession and wealth; seeds, roots, and herbs are the food. Moreover, the human self, the ruler of these, has been created in order to have knowledge of God to make use of the creatures as it wishes, according to its free choice with the utmost certainty, justice, and wisdom.[i] Nothing is lacking. All things have been created in greatest abundance for physical life. Therefore I shall keep a sabbath."

All these good things have, for the most part, been lost through sin; and we, who have kept hardly a shadow of that realm, are today like a corpse of that first human being. Or shall we not say that it has lost everything, becoming mortal after being immortal, a sinner after being righteous, a condemned human after being welcome and well-pleasing? For now the human being is mortal and a sinner. But if these thoughts do not move us to hope and longing for the coming day and the future life, nothing could move us. Let this suffice as an exposition of the first chapter. In the next, Moses will give information about the work of the sixth day, how the human being was created.[51]

51. This formulation confirms that Luther's lectures were given based on the Vulgate, while he was referring to the Hebrew foundation alongside. Again, we see how the text in unison with tradition reads the two different creation narratives of Genesis 1–2 *en bloc*, viewing Genesis 2 as an exposition of Gen. 1:26-27, quite contrary to modern exegesis which, on the other hand, understands the first creation narrative to encompass Gen. 2:4a. See, e.g., Claus Westermann, *Genesis 1–11*, A Continental Commentary (Minneapolis: Fortress Press, 1994), 6–13.

h The Latin text reads the Vulgate almost verbatim: "*Viditque Deus cuncta, quae fecerat, et erant valde bona. Factumque est vespere et mane dies sextus.*"

i *Cum summa securitate, iustitia, sapientia* (Lat.).

CHAPTER TWO

1. And the heavens and the earth were finished, and all the host of them.[j]

Our text has "and all their adornment," but in the Hebrew it is "their army" or "their host," *Zebaam*.[k] The prophets have retained this manner of speech. Therefore they call the stars and the planets the host of the heavens. Thus, it is stated in Jer. 19:13 that the Jews worshiped "the entire heavenly host," that is, the sun, the moon, and the other stars; and in Zeph. 1:5: "I shall destroy those who worship on the roofs the host of the heaven." And Stephen, in Acts 7:42, said: "They served the host of the heaven."

Expressions of this kind the prophets borrowed from Moses, who uses military terminology in this passage and calls the stars and the luminaries of heaven the army or host of heaven; but humans, beasts, and trees he calls the host of the earth. Perhaps he does this in view of future events, because later on God is named the God of the armies or of the hosts, that is, not only of the angels or of the spirits but of the entire creation, which carries on warfare for and serves God. After Satan had been cast away by God on account of his sin, he was filled with such hatred of God and of humans that, if he were able, he would in one moment rob the sea of its fish, the air of its birds, the earth of its fruits of every kind, and would destroy everything. But God created all these creatures to be in active military service, to fight for us without end against the devil, and against humans, as well as serving us and being of use to us.

2. And on the seventh day God completed his work which he had made, and he rested on the seventh day from all his work that he had made.[l]

Here a question arises. Moses says that the Lord rested on the seventh day from the work which he had done, that is, that he

j The Latin text follows the Vulgate almost verbatim: "*Et perfecti sunt coeli et terra et omnis exercitus eorum.*"

k Again, the Hebrew added in the LW version is left out.

l The Latin text here reads different from the Vulgate: "*Consummavitque*

This engraving, by Julius Schnorr von Carolsfeld (1794–1872), depicts God resting with the earth as footstool, following the seven days of creation.

ceased to work on the seventh day. On the other hand, Christ says in John 5:17: "My Father works until now, and I work." Moreover, what Heb. 3:18 and 4:3 state concerning the rest pertains to this passage: "If they shall enter," not indeed into the Land of Promise but "into my rest."

We simply answer in this way: The solution is given by the text itself when it says: "The heaven and the earth were finished." The sabbath, or the sabbath rest, denotes that God ceased in such a way that he did not create another heaven and another earth. It does not denote that God gave up preserving and governing the heaven and the earth which had already been created. For in the preceding chapter Moses very plainly informs us about the manner of the creation when he says that God had created all things through the word: "Let the sea bring forth fish; the earth, herbs, beasts," etc.; likewise: "Grow, fill the earth and the sea." These words are in force until today, and for this reason we see increase[m] without end. Therefore, if the world were in existence for an infinite number of years, the effectiveness of these words would not pass away; but there would be continuous increase through the power of that word or, to express myself so, of the original endowment.[n]

Thus, the solution is easy. God rested from work, that is, God was satisfied with the heaven and earth which had then been created by the word; God did not create a new heaven, not a new earth, new stars, or new trees. And yet God works till now, if indeed the divine has not abandoned the world which was once

Deus in die septimo opus suum, quod fecerat, et quievit in die septimo ab omni opere suo, quod fecerat."

m The Latin term used is *multiplicatio*, the idea of creatures multiplying and filling up the created world.

n The Latin term is *fundatio*, an allusion to the medieval practice of establishing a prebend from which a canon or other ecclesiastical statement was supported. Cf. LW 21:182 n.28.

established, but governs and preserves it through the effectiveness of God's word. God has, therefore, ceased to establish; but not ceased to govern. In Adam humankind[o] had its beginning; in the earth the animal race, to use this expression, had its beginning through the word; and in the sea that of the fish and of the birds had its beginning. But in Adam and in the first little beasts[p] or animals they did not reach their end. Until today there abides the word which was pronounced over humankind: "Grow and multiply"; there abides the word: "Let the sea bring forth fish and birds of the heaven." Almighty, therefore, is the power and effectiveness of the word which thus preserves and governs the entire creation.

Thus, Moses has clearly established that the word was in the beginning. But because all things grow, multiply, and are preserved and governed until now in the same manner as from the beginning of the world, it obviously follows that the word still continues in force and is not dead. Therefore, when he says, "God rested from his work," it is not to be understood of that course of events which involves their preservation and government but simply of the beginning, namely, that God had ceased constructing classes,[52] as they say in common speech, and new species or new creatures.

If you look at my person, I am something new, because sixty years ago I was nothing. Such is the judgment of the world. But God's judgment is different; for in God's sight[q] I was begotten and multiplied immediately when the world began, because this word, "and God said: Let Us make the human being," created me, too.[r] Whatever God wanted to create, God created when speaking. Not everything has come into view at once. Similarly, an arrow or a ball which is shot from a cannon (for it has greater speed) is sent to its target in a single moment, as it were, and nevertheless it is shot through a definite space; so God, through the word, extends divine activity from the beginning of the world to its end. For with God there is nothing that is earlier or later, swifter or slower; but in God's eyes all things are present things. For God is simply outside the scope of time.

o *Genus humanum* (Lat.) here and below.

p The original Latin is *bestiolis seu animalibus.*

q Luther employs his famous Latin terminology *coram Deo.*

r *"Et dixit Deus: Faciamus hominem me quoque creavit"* (Lat.).

52. The Latin verb used is *condere*, "to build, establish, or construct," which gives the notion of God as the constructor. In the following, the text uses *condere*, "to build," *creere*, "to create," and *facere*, "to make," interchangeably. However, the verb *build* plays a particularly significant role when Luther later is explaining the construction of Eve as the archetypal spouse who constitutes the building or house where the spouses together rule and procreate. See Luther's exposition on Gen. 2:22. The Latin noun used for classes is *ordines*, often translated as "orders."

Therefore these words, "God said: 'Let there be, grow, multiply,'" established the creatures as they are now and as they will be to the end of the world. But God ceased creating new ones. God did not create a new earth or a new heaven; but as God wanted the sun and the moon to course, so they still course. Just as at that time God filled the sea with fish, the heaven with flying things, and the earth with cattle, so these are complete, remain up to the present time, and are preserved. It is as Christ says (John 5:17): "My Father is working still, and I work." The word which God spoke in the beginning is still in existence, as Ps. 33:9 says: "He spoke, and it came into being."[s]

But here another objection is voiced, namely: "How can it be true that God has constructed nothing new, when it is certain that the rainbow, or iris, was established at the time of Noah?[t] Likewise, after Adam's fall the Lord threatens that the earth will produce thorns and thistles,[53] which it would not have produced if Adam had not sinned. Likewise, it is stated about the serpent that it would have to creep face down on the ground, although without a doubt, in the state in which it was originally constructed, it walked upright, just as deer and peacocks do today. This is surely a new state of affairs made by a new word. Moreover, if Adam had not fallen into sin, wolves, lions, and bears would not have become ferocious. Absolutely nothing in the entire creation would have been either troublesome or harmful for the human being. For the text plainly states: 'Everything that was created by God was good.' And I ask you how troublesome they are? How many great afflictions of disease affect our body? I am passing over the fleas, the flies, and the spiders, and how great the dangers are from the other fierce and poisonous animals! But even if not one of these things is pertinent, surely this is something supremely new, that a virgin gives birth to the Son of God.[u] Therefore God did not stop on the seventh day. God works not only by preserving creation but also by changing and renewing this creation. Nor is it true, as was stated above, that God has refrained from establishing new classes."[54]

53. Here and below Luther is referring to the curses given to the earth (Gen. 3:18) and to the serpent (Gen. 3:14).

54. Luther combines creation and redemption as a continuous creation. Because God's creation is a *creatio continua*, God does not stop creating on the seventh day, of which Christ's incarnation through the virgin birth is the best evidence.

s The Latin text is referring to Psalm 32, following the Vulgate's numbering.

t Luther is referring to Gen. 9:13.

u *Virgo parit filium Dei* (Lat.).

My answer is: Here Moses is speaking about the uncorrupted nature; if, therefore, the human being had maintained itself in the state of innocence in which it was created, no thorns or thistles or diseases would have come into existence, and beasts would not have become ferocious. This appears clearly enough from the fact that Eve speaks to a serpent with as little fear as we have when we speak to a charming little bird or a fawning puppy. Nor do I have any doubt that the serpent was a most beautiful creature singularly endowed with a reputation for greater cleverness than the remaining beasts, just as little foxes, weasels, etc., have a reputation for cleverness.

Since Adam was still holy and innocent, all the living beings dwelt with him with the greatest delight, ready for every kind of service. If he had remained so, there would have been no fear of the flood; and, in consequence, iris, or the rainbow, would not have come into existence. But because of sin God changed many things. And on the last day there will be a far greater change and a renewal of the entire creature, which, as Paul says (Rom. 8:20), is now subjected to futility because of sin.

Hence, when Moses states that the Lord rested, he is speaking about the original state of the world. Because there was no sin, nothing new was created in it. There were neither thorns nor thistles, neither serpents nor toads; and if there were any, they were neither venomous nor vicious. Thus, he is speaking about the creation of the world in its perfection. At that time the world was pure and innocent because the human being was pure and innocent. Now, when the human being is different on account of sin, the world, too, has begun to be different; that is, the fall of humankind was followed by the depravation and the curse of the creation. "Cursed is the earth," said God to Adam (Gen. 3:17-18), "on your account; thorns and thistles it will bring forth for you." On account of the sin of one single cursed Cain the earth is cursed so that even if it is tilled, it will not yield its best products. Later on there comes the flood because of the sin of the whole world, and the universal humankind is destroyed.[55] A few righteous people were preserved, however, lest the promise concerning Christ should not be fulfilled. But inasmuch as it appears that the earth was disfigured by sin, therefore I for one believe that the light of the sun also was more brilliant and beautiful when it was created, before humans' sin.

In the theological schools the saying is current: "Distinguish

55. Luther here discerns between the first human being, *homo*, who sinned, and the universal humankind, *universus genus humanus*, who is affected by this sin.

the times, and you will bring the Scriptures into harmony."[56] Therefore what we say about the world after that wretched depravity which came in through sin must be far different from what we say about the original pure and unimpaired world. Let us consider an example that is before our eyes. Those who have seen the Promised Land in our time declare that it in no way resembles the favorable description which appears in Holy Scripture. Therefore when Count Stolberg had explored it with special care, he stated that he preferred his own lands in Germany.[57] On account of sin, on account of the wickedness and vileness of humans, the land was made unfruitful, as Psalm 107:34 says. So Sodom, too, was a sort of Paradise before it was destroyed by fire from heaven (Gen. 13:20).

Thus, a curse generally follows sin, but the curse changes things so that the best becomes the worst. Therefore Moses is speaking about the perfection of the creatures as it was before sin. If the human being had not sinned, all the beasts would have remained obedient until finally God would have transferred the human being from Paradise, or from the earth; but after sin all things underwent a change for the worse.

In this way the solution proposed above stands: that in six days God finished divinity's work, that is, that God ceased establishing classes; and whatever God wanted to make was made then. God did not say again: "Let there be a new earth, a new sea," etc. As to the fact that the Virgin Mary gave birth to the Son of God, it is clear that the reason also for this charitable act was the misfortune into which we fell through sin. God performed this marvelous and extraordinary work in such a way that God first revealed through the divine word that God would do it in the future. Similarly, God indicated through the word that other miracles would also take place in the future.[58]

This, then, is the first disquisition concerning the statement that God finished the heaven and the earth and that God made nothing new. Now, that we may learn, this, too, should be explained: What is the sabbath or the rest of God? Likewise, in what manner did God sanctify the sabbath, as the text says?

56. Luther discusses the necessity of this exegetical skill at greater length in his comments on Gen. 33:17 (WA 44:133). For Luther, the distinction between pre- and post-fall had implications for the theological anthropology, as it came to the fore in his controversy with Erasmus of Rotterdam (1466–1536) on the human will in 1525. In his *De servo arbitrio*, as elsewhere, Luther views the God-human relation "from behind," from a post-fall perspective, according to which humankind no longer has its original pure *imago Dei* but is bound to the consequences of sin. At the same time, Luther is adamant that "Christ is the Lord of the Scriptures," as he wrote Erasmus. "Take Christ out of the Scriptures, and what will you find left in them?" See TAL 2:165.

57. Count Henry the Elder of Stolberg had been in the Holy Land in 1461; Count Henry the Younger (1467–1508) in 1493, on a pilgrimage with Frederick the Wise. In his *Table Talk* Luther quotes the elder count as saying: "Is this the Promised Land? I would rather have the Golden Meadow!"—a section of Thuringia (WA TR 1:1223).

58. Luther clearly understands the virgin birth of the Son of God as a miracle in the sense that God continues to create and change. When Mary is mentioned here it is not as part of the Eve-Mary typology, introduced by Tertullian, according to which Mary as the second Eve reverses the evil and death caused by the first Eve. To Luther, the miracle is the continuous creation by God of which the act of salvation of the sinful creature is part.

3. And God blessed the seventh day and sanctified it,
because on it he had rested from all his work
which God created, so that he made it.[v]

In Matthew 12 Christ says that the sabbath was made for humans, not humans for the sabbath.[w] But Moses says nothing here about humans; he does not say in so many words that the sabbath was commanded to the human being; he says that God blessed the sabbath and sanctified it to God's own being. Moreover, God did not do this to any other creature, did not sanctify heaven, earth, or any other creature for God's own being; but the seventh day God did sanctify for God's own being. This has the special purpose of making us understand that the seventh day in particular should be devoted to divine worship. For "holy" is that which has been set aside for God and has been removed from all profane[59] uses. Hence, to sanctify means to set aside for sacred purposes, or for the worship of God. In this manner Moses rather frequently employs the expression, also of sacred vessels.[x]

Madonna under the Fir Tree (1510)
by Lucas Cranach the Elder

It follows, therefore, from this passage that if Adam had remained in the state of innocence, he nevertheless would have held the seventh day sacred.[60] That is, on this day he would have given his descendants instructions about the will and worship of God; he would have praised God; he would have given thanks; he would have sacrificed, etc. On the other days he would have tilled his fields and tended his cattle. Indeed, even after the fall he kept this seventh day sacred; that is, on this day he instructed his family, of which the sacrifices of his sons Cain and Abel give the proof. Therefore, from the beginning of the world the sabbath was intended for the worship of God.

v The Latin text reads: "*Et benedixit Deus diei septimo, et sanctificabit eum, eo quod in eo quievisset ab omni opere suo, quod creavit Deus, ut faceret.*"

w This passage is not from Matthew 12, as the text has it, but from Mark 2:27.

x Apparently, a reference to the usage in passages like Exod. 40:9.

59. Luther uses the term *profane* (Latin: *pro + fanum*) in its original sense, as that which is not consecrated and, therefore, a worldly opposite to the sacred.

60. In this passage the text is speaking of Adam the male solely, as can be seen from the reference to tilling the fields and tending the cattle. The text in this passage matches the agricultural context in which Luther lived. However, in the next passage the subject is again the human being in the generic.

Innocent human nature would have proclaimed the glory and the kindnesses of God in this way: on the sabbath day humans would have conversed about the immeasurable goodness of the Creator; they would have sacrificed; they would have prayed, etc.[y] For this is the meaning of the verb "to sanctify."

Moreover, this also implies the immortality of humankind, as the letter to the Hebrews (8:11) with erudition discusses about God's rest on the basis of Psalm 95:11: "They shall not enter into my rest." For God's rest is eternal. For Adam would have lived for a definite time in Paradise, according to God's pleasure; then he[61] would have been carried off to that rest of God which God, through the sanctifying of the sabbath, wished not only to symbolize for human beings but also to grant to them. Thus the physical life would have been blissful and holy, spiritual and eternal. Now we wretched human beings have lost that bliss of our physical life through sin, and while we live we are in the midst of death.[z] And yet, because the sabbath command remains for the church, it denotes that spiritual life is to be restored to us through Christ. And so the prophets have carefully searched those passages in which Moses intimates the resurrection of the flesh and life immortal.[62]

61. Again, Adam is understood as the earth creature in the generic. The pronoun here is rendered traditionally as "he," but could as well be rendered "it" or even "they," congruent with the subsequent comments referring to human beings as they are now.

62. In this passage Luther interprets the seventh day ecclesiologically, while in the next he interprets it eschatologically.

Then it is also shown here that the human being was foremost created for the knowledge and worship of God. For the sabbath was not ordained for sheep and cows but for human beings, that in them the knowledge of God might be developed and might increase. Hence, although humans lost their knowledge of God, nevertheless God wanted this command about sanctifying the sabbath to remain in force. On the seventh day God wanted humans to be busy both with the word and with the other forms of worship God established, so that we might give first thought to the fact that this nature was created chiefly for acknowledging and glorifying God.

Moreover, this is also written that we might preserve in our minds a sure hope of the future and eternal life. All the things God wants done on the sabbath are clear signs of another life after this life. Why is it necessary for God to speak with us through the word if we are not to live in a future and eternal

y The verbs are in the plural, thus denoting that Luther is talking about human nature and humans in the plural, not solely Adam.

z Cf. LW 13:83 n.16.

life? If we are not to hope for a future life, why do we not live like people with whom God does not speak and who do not know God? But because the Divine Majesty speaks to the human being alone and the human being alone knows and apprehends God, it necessarily follows that there is another life after this life. To attain it we need the word and the knowledge of God. For this temporal and present life is a physical life, such as all the beasts live that do not know God and the word.

This is what the sabbath, or the rest of God, means, on which God speaks with us through the word and we, in turn, speak with God through prayer and faith. The beasts, such as dogs, horses, sheep, and cows, indeed also learn to hear and understand the voice of humans; they are also kept by humans and fed. But our state is better. We hear God, know divine will, and are called into a sure hope of immortality. This is the testimony of the clear promises concerning eternal life that God has revealed to us through the word after giving those obscure indications, like this one concerning the rest of God and the sanctifying of the sabbath. And yet, this one dealing with the sabbath is rather clear. Suppose that there is no life after this life; does it not follow that we have no need of God or of the word? What we need or do in this life we can have even without the Word. The beasts graze, live, and grow fat, although they do not have the word of God or hear it. What need is there of the word to get food and drink that has already been created?

In this etching (1520), Christians gather to hear the preaching of their faith, thus illustrating their obedience to the third commandment to sanctify the sabbath.

Therefore, that God gives the word, that God commands us to occupy ourselves with the word, that God issues orders for sanctifying the sabbath and for the worship—all this clearly proves that there remains a life after this life and that the human being was created not for this physical life only, like the other animals, but for eternal life, just as God, who has ordered and ordained these practices, is eternal.

But here another question arises, on which we touched above, namely, about the time of Adam's fall. When did he fall, on the seventh day or on another? Although nothing certain can be proposed, still I can readily imagine that he fell on the seventh day. On the sixth day he was created; Eve likewise was created toward evening or near the end of the sixth day, while Adam was sleeping. Early in the morning of the seventh day, which had been sanctified by the Lord, God speaks with Adam, gives him directions concerning his worship, and forbids him to eat the fruit of the tree of the knowledge of good and evil. This is the real purpose of the seventh day: that the word of God be preached and heard.[63] Henceforth, both in the Scripture and in common usage the practice remained that the morning time was set aside for prayer and preaching, as Psalm 5:3 says: "In the morning I shall stand before you, and I shall see."

63. Cf. above (pp. 104–5) where Luther discusses whether God rested on the seventh day and not the sixth, emphasizing that the preaching of the word on the sabbath is the most important question.

Thus, early on the seventh day Adam appears to have heard the Lord charge him with the management of household and world affairs, and at the same time forbid him to eat the fruit. Satan was intolerant of this most magnificent creation and arrangement. He also envied humans such great bliss, that an overflowing supply of everything was at hand for them on the earth and that after so blissful a physical life they had the sure hope of eternal life, which Satan himself had lost. And so, perhaps about noon, after God's conversation, he converses with Eve.[64] So it is wont to be to this day. Where the word of God is, there Satan also makes it his business to spread falsehood and false teaching; for it grieves him that through the word we, like Adam in Paradise, become citizens of heaven. And so he successfully incites Eve to sin. Moreover, the text states plainly that when the heat of the day had ended, the Lord came and condemned Adam, together with all his descendants, to death. I am easily convinced that all these events took place on the very sabbath—and that one not complete!—on which Adam lived in Paradise and enjoyed its fruits.

64. The meaning is that Satan converses with Eve about noon after God has been conversing with both Adam and Eve in the morning.

And so through sin humankind lost this bliss.[a] But Adam would not have spent his life in Paradise in idleness if he had remained in the state of innocence. On the sabbath day he would have taught his children; through public preaching he would have bestowed honor on God with the praises which God deserved; and through reflection on the works of God he would have incited himself and others to expressions of thanks. On the other days he would have worked, either tilling the field or hunting. But this would have been far different from the way it is done now. For to us work is something burdensome; but for Adam it would have been a supreme joy, more welcome than any leisure. Therefore, just as the other misfortunes of this life remind us of sin and of the wrath of God, so work, too, and the well-known

a Though the text reads *homo* in the singular, it is here rendered humankind.

hardship of providing sustenance should remind us of sin and rouse us to repentance.

Now Moses proceeds with a clearer description of the human being, after first repeating what he had said in the first chapter.[65] Although these statements appear to be unnecessary, nevertheless the repetition is not altogether unnecessary, because he wishes to continue his account in a connected manner.

65. Until modern biblical scholarship exposed the larger literary complexes of two different creation accounts with each their own style, language, and theological accent, it was the tradition to see Gen. 2:4b-25 as Moses's enhancing repetition of Gen. 1:1–2:4a.

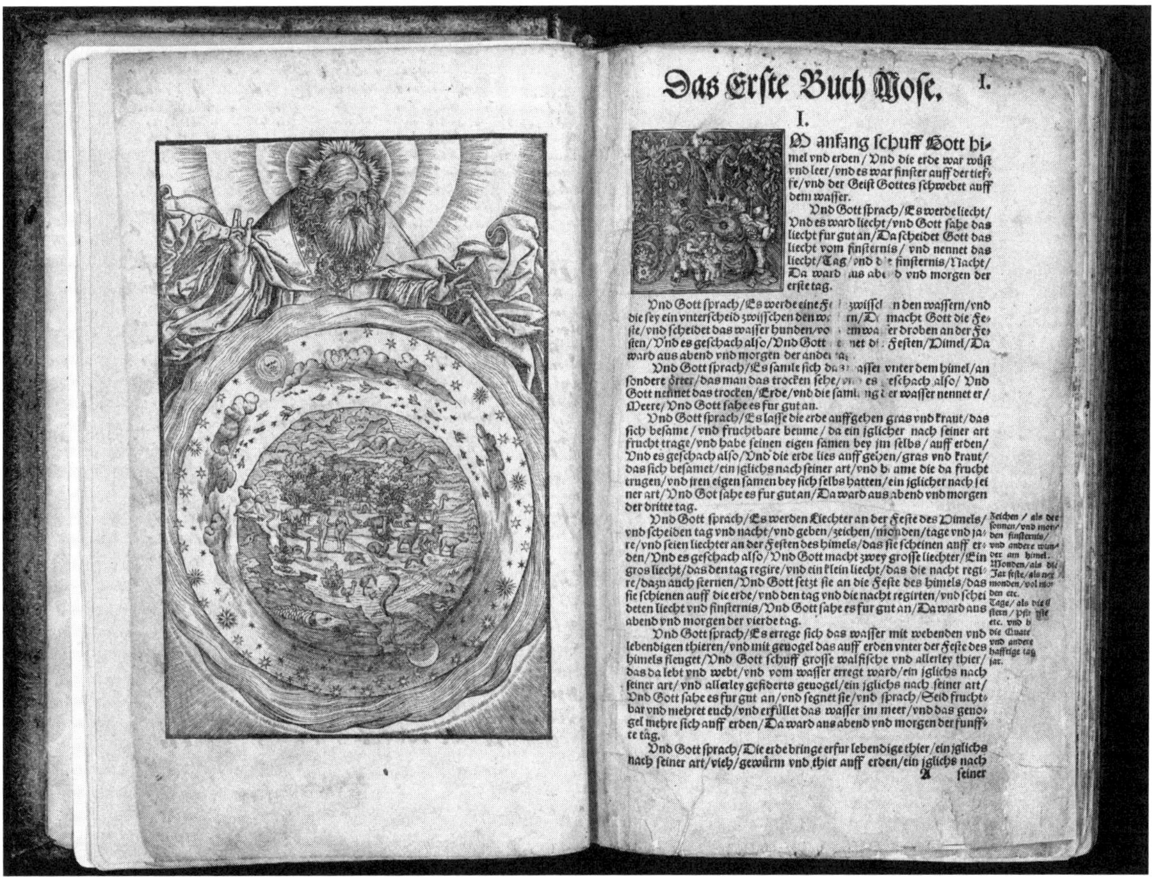

The opening page of Genesis in the Luther Bible. This second edition, printed in 1535 in Wittenberg, featured some hand-colored woodcuts by Lucas Cranach the Younger.

LECTURES ON GENESIS 2:21-25[a]

KIRSI I. STJERNA

21. Then the Lord *God*[b] *sent a deep sleep upon Adam, and when he had fallen asleep, God took one of his ribs and closed the place with flesh.*[c]

HERE, TOO, not only faith but also reason and the situation demand that the time of waking be taken as one time and the time of sleeping as another. Both of these activities have their own intervals. That Adam was created on the sixth day, that the animals were brought to him, that he heard the Lord giving him a command regarding the tree of the knowledge of good and evil, that the Lord sent a sleep upon him—all these facts clearly refer to time and physical life. Therefore it is necessary to understand these days as actual days contrary to the opinion of the doctors of the church.[1] Whenever we see that the opinions of the ancestors are not in agreement with Scripture, we tolerate them with respect and acknowledge them as our ancestors; but we do not because of them disregard the authority of Scripture.[2] Aristotle's statement in the first book of his *Ethics*[d] is elegantly put and true:

1. Luther's word is "fathers" and refers to the teaching fathers of the church.

2. This is Luther's persistent Reformation principle, *sola scriptura*, and his authorization to promote changes that on many occasions signaled a discontinuity with the (at least the immediate medieval) tradition.

a The text for Luther's treatment of Gen. 2:21-25 is drawn from *Luther's Works*, vol. 1: *Lectures on Genesis 1–5*, ed. Jaroslav Pelikan (St. Louis: Concordia, 1958), 122–40. George V. Schick's translation is revised particularly for inclusive language, on the basis of WA 40/2:92–105. The footnotes and annotations are mostly new, with a few exceptions. Beyond the text selection, LW volumes 1–8 are devoted to what is extant from Luther's *Enarrationes in Genesin* (*Lectures on Genesis*), included in WA 42–44, and also in LW 1-2.

b Lat.: *Dominus Deus.*

c Lat.: *carne.*

d Luther refers to the Greek philosopher-scientist Aristotle's (Aristotle of Stagira, 384–322 BCE) landmark opus, *Nichomachean Ethics.*

The Garden of Eden by Lucas Cranach the Elder (1530)

"It is better to defend the truth than to be devoted[e] to those who are our friends and relatives."[3] And this is, above all, the proper attitude for a philosopher. For although both, truth and friends, are dear to us, preference must be given to truth.[4] If a non-Christian[5] maintains that this must be the attitude in secular discourses, how much more must it be our attitude in those which involve the clear witness of Scripture that we dare not give preference to the authority of people over that of Scripture! Human beings can err, but the word of God is the very wisdom of God and the most certain truth.

But so far as this account is concerned, what, I ask you, could sound more like a fairy tale[f] if you were to follow your reason? Would anyone believe this account about the creation of Eve[g] if it were not so clearly[h] told? This is a reversal of the pattern of the entire creation. Whatever is born alive, is born of the male and the female in such a manner that it is brought into the light by

e Lat.: *addictus.*

f Lat.: *fabulosius.* The word *fabula* means a story or a tale.

g Lat.: *de conditione Heuae.* Luther spells Eve's name as *Heuae*, following the Hebrew.

h Lat.: *aperte.* Luther considers the details in the Genesis account convincing and an argument in themselves.

3. *Nicomachean Ethics*, I, ch. 6: "While both are dear, piety requires us to honor truth above our friends." The above-cited statement has been attributed to Aristotle's saying, "Plato is dear to me, but dearer still is truth," but the closest wording is actually found from a much later period; Roger Bacon, *Opus Majus*, pars I, cap. v.

4. In the Greek world, both seeking for the truth and male friendships were highly revered. Luther exhibits his psychological instincts, acknowledging human tendencies toward "people pleasing" and reminds of what is of most importance.

5. With *homo ethnicus* (Lat.), translated as "pagan" in LW 1, Luther means a nonreligious or, rather, a non-Christian person.

the female.[i] Here the woman herself is created from the man[j] by a creation no less wonderful[6] than that of Adam,[k] who was made out of a clod of earth into a living soul.[l] This is extravagant fiction and the silliest kind of nonsense if you set aside the authority of Scripture and follow the judgment of reason.[7] Accordingly, Aristotle declares that no first human being can be inferred to have existed.[m] Reason would compel us, too, to make the same statement if it did not have this text. If you should reach the conclusion that what the uniform experience of all creation proves is true, namely, that nothing comes into existence alive except from a male and a female, then no first human being can be conceded.

The same thing would also have to be stated about the world, which the philosophers have therefore asserted is eternal.[8] But reason with all its force inclines to this conviction even though proofs founded on reason are thought out by which it is demonstrated that the world is not eternal. How can it take its beginning from nothing? Moreover, if you should say that the world had a beginning and there is a time when the world was not in existence, it immediately follows that there was nothing prior to the world.[n] An endless series of other absurdities follows, and these induce philosophers to conclude that the world is eternal. But if you should say that the world is infinite, then immediately another new infinite will also appear, namely, the succession of human beings. But philosophy does not grant the existence of several infinites, and yet it is compelled to grant them because it knows of no beginning of the world and of humans.[o] These

i Lat.: *ut per foeminam edatur in lucem.*

j Lat.: *Hic ipsa foemina ex viro conditur.*

k Lat.: *non minus conditione quam Adam fuit.*

l Lat.: *qui ex gleba terrae factus est in animam viventem.* Luther uses the word *anima* for "soul," in distinction to *corpus*, "body," or *carnis*, "the flesh."

m Lat.: *neque primum neque ultimum hominem dicit posse dari.* LW 1 translates *hominem* as "man." In the following, in similar instances, the word *human* is used. For the quotations from Aristotle, see Thomas Aquinas, STh, part I, q. 46, art. 1 (cf. LW 1:3 n.2).

n On Luther's theology of creation, see Johannes Schwanke, *Creatio ex nihilo: Luthers Lehre von der Schöpfung des Nichts in der grossen Genesisvorlesung (1535–45)* (Berlin: de Gruyter, 2004).

o LW 1 translates *hominem* as "men."

6. Luther's reading parallels that of the twenty-first-century feminist interpreters who note the equality in the creation of the two sexes. E.g., Phyllis Trible: "The parallelism between *ha-adam* [= 'humankind'] and 'male and female' shows further that sexual differentiation does not mean hierarchy but rather equality. Created simultaneously, male and female are not superior and subordinate. Neither has power over the other; in fact, both are given equal power. . . . God proposes, by using a plural verb form, that Adam be given dominion over all the earth: 'let them have dominion' (1:26). Moreover, in the verses that follow our poem God blesses male and female, using the plural 'them,' and the deity consistently speaks 'to them' with plural verb forms (1:28-29) . . . neither is given dominion over the other" (*God and the Rhetoric of Sexuality*, Overtures to Biblical Theology [Philadelphia: Fortress Press, 1978], 18–19).

7. Luther educates the reader, recurrently, about God's creating work including acts and dynamics beyond human comprehension, most specifically the conception of human beings. He draws attention to the many mysteries of divine acts that human beings have grown accustomed to and ignore in their daily comings and goings (such as music or the sound of the River Nile, or the beauty of stars in the night sky). Luther, like Thomas Aquinas (1225–1275)—"Doctor Angelicus," a Dominican friar, the most influential Scholastic theologian, and a legal scholar of the Middle Ages—draws evidence for God's divine work from the reality known by senses.

8. Aristotle speaks of questions "in regard to which we have no argument because they are so vast,

contradictions and the lack of clarity gave the Epicureans[9] the opportunity to say that the world and humanity[p] came into existence without any reason and will also perish without any reason, just as cattle perish, which die as though they had never existed. This leads to another conclusion, namely, that God either plainly does not exist[10] or does not personally care for human affairs. The reason is led into these perplexing mazes of reason when it is without the word and follows its own judgment.[11]

However, it is useful to realize why our reason or wisdom is unable to improve in understanding the creation. For what, I ask, does a philosopher know about heaven and the world if one does not even know from where it came and where it is going?

This large floor mosaic from a Roman villa in Sentinum (now known as Sassoferrato, in Marche, Italy), c. 200–250 CE depicts Aion, the god of eternity, standing inside a celestial sphere decorated with zodiac signs, in between a green tree and a bare tree (summer and winter, respectively). Sitting in front of him is the mother-earth goddess, Tellus (the Roman counterpart of Gaia), with her four children, who possibly represent the four seasons.

p LW 1 translates *hominem* (Lat.) as "man."

and we find it difficult to give our reasons, e.g., the question whether the universe is eternal or no." *Topics*, I, ch. 11 (see LW 1:3 n.3).

9. With "Epicureans" Luther refers to a Greek school of philosophy, founded c. 307 BCE by Epicurus (341–270 BCE) as a reaction against Platonism and with a rejection of superstition and divine intervention. Aiming for pleasure and absence of pain as the highest goal, the state of *ataraxia* was deemed the worthy state of being, achieved by modest living and elimination of pain. Luther is using the word in a sense of "hedonism," a pleasure-seeking attitude and lifestyle, which is actually not what Epicureanism is at its core.

10. Luther is naturally familiar with Thomas Aquinas's "Five Proofs of God's Existence," even if he does not explicitly name that source: God's existence is proven from rational logical conclusions with the observable data from creation, with arguments on (1) Motion, (2) Efficient Causes, (3) Possibility and Necessity, (4) Gradation, and (5) Design.

11. Luther's conclusions echo with twenty-first-century scientists' and philosophers' debates about reality: in the "reductionist" model everything is a sum of its parts, matter, organized by the laws of physics; the "emergence" perspectives assume a higher plan and a "downward causation" of being/s.

Indeed, what do we know about ourselves? We see that we are human beings. But that we have this man for a father and this woman for a mother—this must be believed; it cannot be known in any way. Thus, our entire knowledge or wisdom is based solely on the knowledge of the material and formal cause, although in these instances, too, we sometimes talk disgraceful nonsense.[12] And this is the misery: we obviously cannot point out the efficient and final cause for the world we exist and live in, the object of our cogitation and disputation. Such miserable and inadequate wisdom!

Aristotle declares: "Human being and the sun bring humankind[q] into existence."[r] Beautifully said. But follow this wisdom, and you will arrive at the point where you maintain that human and the sun are eternal and infinite. For you will never find a human being who is either the beginning or the end, just as I cannot find the beginning and the end of my person if I want to gain certain knowledge about this and am not willing to rely on belief. But what sort of wisdom and knowledge is it that knows nothing about the final cause and the efficient cause? So far as our knowledge of the form is concerned, a cow likewise knows her habitat and (as the German proverb has it) looks at and recognizes her door. This also makes clear how awful the fall into original sin[s] was, through which we have lost this knowledge and have become incapable of seeing either the beginning or the end of ourselves.[13]

Plato, Cicero, and other philosophers who belong to the better sort state in their discussions that humans walk with their head erect[14] while the rest of the beings look at the earth with their heads bent down. To human they attribute reason or the ability to understand; and later they reach the conclusion that human is an extraordinary animal created for immortality. But how tenuous and almost useless this is! All this is based on a knowledge of human's form. But if you go on to give consideration to the human's substance, does not reason compel you to

12. See LW 1.124 n.59: Aristotle writes about the material cause as "that from which, as immanent material, a thing comes into being," while the formal cause is "the form or pattern, i.e., the definition of the essence, and the classes which include this . . . and the parts included in the definition" (Aristotle, *Metaphysics*, V, 2).

13. Luther's point echoes that of Calvin about the root cause of human calamity: the original sin's burden comes from not knowing oneself and thus not knowing one's God, and vice versa. (See, e.g., Calvin, *Institutes of the Christian Religion*, ch. 1, section 1.)

14. Luther would have no idea that the words *homo erectus* would be applied in scientific naming of human fossils and evolution.

q Luther uses the words *homo* and *hominem*, which in LW 1 is translated with the word "man."

r A reference to Aristotle, *De generatione et corruptione*, II, ch. 10.

s Lat.: *peccati originalis*. On Luther's treatment of the original sin in light of Genesis 3, see this volume, pp. 152–82.

declare that this being must again be disintegrated and cannot be immortal?

Therefore let us learn that true wisdom is in Holy Scripture and in the word of God. This gives information not only about the matter of the entire creation, not only about its form, but also about the efficient and final cause,[t] about the beginning and about the end of all things: about who did the creating and for what purpose God created. Without the knowledge of these two causes our wisdom does not differ much from that of the beasts, which also make use of their eyes and ears but are utterly ignorant about their beginning and their end.

Therefore this is an outstanding text.[15] The more it seems to conflict with all experience and reason, the more carefully it must be noted and the more surely believed. Here we are taught about the beginning of the human being that the first human did not come into existence by a process of generation, as reason has deceived Aristotle and the rest of the philosophers into imagining.[u] The reproduction of the first humans' descendants takes place through procreation; but the first male was formed and created from a clod of the field, and the first female from the rib of the sleeping man. Here, therefore, we find the beginning; this would be impossible to find through Aristotle's philosophy.

After this beginning was made, there then follows the propagation—which is no less wonderful—through the union of a male and female, whereby the entire human origins[v] is brought into being from a droplet of the human body. In a similar vein Paul, on the basis of this passage, has a clever discourse among the philosophers in Athens (Acts 17:25): "God gives to all ζωὴν καὶ πνοὴν, spirit and life everywhere, and from the blood of one human being God makes the whole humankind[w] that it may dwell on the entire earth, that they may seek God, if perhaps they may feel God or find God, although God is not far from each one of us." Here Paul is speaking of the propagation brought about by the first human when he says "from the blood of one person."

15. The text is "outstanding" because it deals with the ultimate reality questions: the origins and design of the creation of human beings, and the mystery of being human.

t A clear reference to Thomas Aquinas's Five Proofs; see n. 00 above.

u Lat.: Luther uses the word *hominem*, translated in LW 1 as "man."

v Lat.: *genus hominum*, could be translated as "human race."

w Lat.: *genus hominum*, see n. *v* above.

If, therefore, a human being is brought into existence from a droplet of blood, as the experience of all humans on the entire earth bears witness, surely this is not any less miraculous[16] than the first human being's creation from a clod, and the female from a rib of the man.[17]

But why does the creation of Adam and Eve seem so unbelievable and miraculous, while the propagation of a human being, known and seen by all, does not seem so miraculous? Undoubtedly, because, as Augustine says, miracles become commonplace through their continuous recurrence. Thus, we do not marvel at the wonderful light of the sun, because it is a daily phenomenon. We do not marvel at the countless other gifts of creation, for we have become deaf toward what Pythagoras[18] aptly terms this wonderful and most lovely music coming from the harmony of the motions that are in the celestial spheres. But because human beings continually hear this music, they become deaf to it, just as the people who live at the cataracts of the Nile are not affected by the noise and roar of the water which they hear continually, although it is unbearable to others who are not accustomed to it. Without a doubt he took over this very statement from the teaching of the church fathers; however, they had not meant that sound was given off by the motion of the celestial bodies. Rather, they wanted to say that their nature was most lovely and altogether miraculous, but that we ungrateful and insensible people did not notice it or give due thanks to God for the marvelous condition and preservation of God's creation.

Thus, it is a great miracle that a small seed is planted and that out of it grows a very tall oak. But because these are daily occurrences, they have become of little importance, like the very process of our procreation. Surely it is a cause of utmost awe worthy of wonder that a woman accepts[19] semen, that this semen becomes thick and, as Job elegantly said (Job 10:10), it coagulates, and then it receives its form and is nourished until the fetus is ready for breathing air. When the *fetus edito foetu per partem* has been brought into the world by birth, no new nourishment appears, but a new way and method: milk by which the baby is nourished flows now from

A sixteenth-century engraving depicting God as master of creation

16. An example of Luther using human reproduction as a significant proof for God's possibilities in the act of original creation. Luther's fascination with gynecology and pregnancy has theological reasons, supported by personal observations from his marriage.

17. In this sentence, Luther uses the following words for human: *homo, foemella, viri* (Lat.), making a distinction between genders when describing specifically the creation of female from the rib of the male. When speaking of the first human being created, however, Luther consistently chooses the word *homo* ("human") not *vir* ("man"); the LW 1 translation thus unnecessarily translates homo as "man."

18. Pythagoras was a Greek philosopher and a mathematician (c. 570–c. 495 BCE).

19. Lat.: *accipit*, meaning both "receive" and "accept." In Luther's time, "science" was not yet clear about the dynamics

the two breasts, as from a fountain.[20] All these are causes of supreme awe and are wholly beyond our understanding. Because this all happens frequently, however, as if commonplace, we have become deaf to this loveliest music[21] of nature.[x]

This engraving, which appears in a book published 1516, depicts the Madonna nursing her child with three angels surrounding her.

But if we regarded these wonders in true faith and appraised them for what they actually are, they surely would not be inferior to what Moses says here: that a rib was taken from the side of the sleeping Adam and thus Eve was created. If it had pleased God to create us by the same method by which Adam was created from the clay, by now we would not consider this either a miracle; we would marvel more at the method of procreation through the semen of a man.[y] This vulgar gibberish is right, and there was certainly good reason for composing it: "Everything that is rare, we appreciate; what happens every day, we consider ordinary." If the stars did not rise every single night or in all places, what a great gathering of people there would be for this spectacle! Now no one finds it a reason to open a window even.

Therefore our lack of gratitude[22] deserves to be damned. If we believe that God is the efficient and the final cause, should

x See, e.g., Carl F. Schalk, *Luther on Music: Paradigms of Praise* (St. Louis: Concordia, 1988); and also Luther himself, *Preface to the Symphoniae Iucundae* (1538), WA 50:364–74.

y Lat.: *semen viri.*

of the female seed and male seed in the conception of a child. The fact that Luther considers the essential role of the female seed is noteworthy.

20. Luther gleaned important evidence from his own household: his wife, Katharina, breastfed their children and delighted the ex-monk with this miraculous experience, possible only for women; these experiences shaped his view of God's maternal love. Curiously, Luther received advice from a Bavarian lay author, Lady Argula von Grumbach (c. 1492–1554/1568), to pass along to Katharina, on the secrets of breastfeeding and weaning.

21. Luther, a known lover of music, considers music right next to the word of God, a divine gift without comparison. Luther's adoration of the mysteries of creation and the universal metalanguage of music, on the one hand, illuminates his experience of the omnipresence of the divine, and, on the other hand, speaks of his expansive theological core that orients beyond space and time.

22. Luther addresses this fundamental sin particularly in his *Large Catechism*, when explaining the first three commandments, which require proper love and respect of God the creator, and human beings' chronic failure on both accounts since birth.

we not admire God's works, delight in them, and proclaim them always and everywhere? But how many are there who really do this and from their soul?[z] We hear that God took a clod and made a human being; we marvel at this, and because of our amazement we regard it as a fairy tale. But that God now takes a drop from the blood of the father[23] and creates a human being, this we do not marvel at, because it happens daily, while the other creation took place only once—both, however, by the skill and power of the same Author. For God who once formed a human being from a clod now creates human beings[a] from the blood[24] of their parents.

23. Luther repeats Aristotelian misconceptions about the fetus drawing its life mostly from the semen of the father.

24. Since Aristotle, in antiquity and the Middle Ages, human conception was explained from an androcentric view. Male *sperma*, semen, was considered as the hard, form-giving source, and female *membra,* blood, as the soft matter for the new embryo. The male sperm was more decisive in Aristotelian thinking that was adopted by, e.g., Scholastics such as Thomas Aquinas. A competing view came from the Greek philosopher, physician, and writer Galen of Pergamum (129–200/216), who identified ovaries as female testicles also producing seeds for the embryo. In both views, the embryo was understood to feed on the blood of the *membra*. See Manfred Horstmanshoff, Helen King, and Claus Zittel, eds., *Sweat, Blood and Tears: The Changing Concepts of Physiology from Antiquity into Early Modern Era* (Leiden: Brill, 2012).

Woodcut by Jakob Ruf (1505–1558) depicting a fetus in the womb

Aristotle, therefore, babbles in vain that the human and the sun bring human beings into existence. Although the heat of the sun warms our bodies, nevertheless the cause of their coming into existence is something entirely different, namely, the word of God, who gives the command to the husband: "Now your

z Lat.: *vere et ex animo*. LW 1 translates *ex animo* as "from the heart."

a Lat.: *hominem, homines*.

blood shall become a male; now it shall become a female." Reason knows nothing about this word. Therefore it cannot get away from its childish babble about the causes of such important matters. Thus, the physicians, who have followed the philosophers, ascribe procreation to a matching mixture of qualities that act in the predisposed matter.[25] Although reason cannot disprove

Portrait of Hildegard of Bingen (1098–1179). The name of the engraver, William Marshall (d. 1649), appears at the bottom right.

this (for it sees that dry and cold natures are unsuited for generating, while moist and fairly warm ones are better suited), still they have not arrived at the first cause.[26] The Holy Spirit leads us to something higher than nature, higher than qualities and their proper mixture, when she puts before us the word in[b] which everything is created and preserved.

Therefore that a human is developed from a drop of blood, and not an ox or a donkey, happens by virtue of the word uttered by God. And so, as Christ also teaches in the Lord's Prayer (Matt. 6:9),[27] we call God our Father[c] and our Creator, in the words of the Creed. When we look at this Cause, then we can speak chastely, purely and with joy of those things, which, if this Cause

b Lat.: *in quo*.

c A contemporary reader may add here "Mother."

25. Luther builds on existing theories with long roots: see, for example, the German visionary-theologian-scientist-philosopher Hildegard of Bingen (1098–1178), who applies her own branch of the Galenian theory of four humors to explain illnesses and suffering from a loss of equilibrium with the basic elements and substances in nature. She names the basic elements in nature as hot/fire, dry/air, moist/water, cold/earth, and considers each one to correspond with a substance and personality shaped by the dominating liquid: yellow bile/choleric, blood/sanguine, phlegm/phlegmatic, and black bile/melancholic.

26. The theory of humors in its different renditions has inspired caricaturist characterizations from the sparky sanguinic and the driven choleric to the dark melancholic and the tarry phlegmatic personalities. Hildegard's and the medieval thinkers' concern, however, was not a personality type but the order and equilibrium of the cosmos, macro- and micro-.

27. Luther explains the meaning, and proper use, of the Lord's Prayer in his *Large Catechism*; see TAL 2:366–87; BC, 440–56.

is disregarded, we could not mention without filthiness and obscenity.

This discussion also shows how awful the fall into original sin was; without this, the entire human race knows nothing of its origin.[28] Indeed, we see a man and a woman engage in sexual intercourse; we see the woman made pregnant by a droplet of blood; and later, at a definite time, a baby is brought into the world. These are the well-known facts clear before everyone's eyes; and yet without the word reminding and instructing, you would lack actual knowledge of the very activity you are consciously carrying on and with eyes wide[d] open. The philosophers' disputations, which we have already discussed, sufficiently show this. Such horrible blindness and such a pitiful ignorance!

Accordingly, had Adam persevered in innocence, it would have been unnecessary to instruct his descendants about their origin, just as it was unnecessary to instruct Adam about the creation[e] of his Eve: because the moment he looked at her, he understood that she was bone from his bones and flesh from his flesh.[29] That kind of knowledge of themselves and of the remaining creatures would have remained also among their descendants. All would have become aware at once of the final and efficient cause about which we do not know any more than the cattle does.

28. Obliviousness to the realities of life is an expression of the original sin's devastating effects: not knowing one's God as the Creator and thus failure to know oneself. Luther builds on a strong post-Augustine tradition with this fundamental conviction about the existential state of human life, named so theologically with the concept of sin.

29. In an effort to interpret the biblical material on gender relations and the status of women, the question of Adam's reaction has been analyzed from different angles, before and post-Luther. E.g., Dutch-born German poet, painter, and scholar Anna Maria Van Schurman (1607–1678) (*Paraphrase of Genesis* 1–3, *Uitbreiding*, 6.9–22, in John L. Thompson, ed., *Reformation Commentary on Scripture: Old Testament I: Genesis 1–11* [Downers Grove, IL: IVP Academic, 2012], 98), who notes Adam's recognizing in Eve their physical oneness (in flesh) and thereby a rationale for their marital relation and mutual affection: "God willed a fitting wife to make him, to adorn her with His [God's] image so that in marriage she could take him. From one, God makes two, and from those two he [God] again makes one; when man sees her, he knows as well his very flesh and bone. God therefore wills that every man should call his own wife a wo-man and love her more than father and mother as his true companion." This resonates with Luther's reading of Genesis.

d The adjective *wide* is added to the translation.

e Lat.: *de conditione*, literally "of the condition."

f See Acts 7:22. On this well-known patristic theory, see, e.g., Clement of Alexandria, *Exhortation to the Heathen*, ch. 6.

g Lat.: *Faciamus hominem*. Using the plural, Luther names the Holy Trinity in the acts of creation, including the creation of a woman, foreshadowing modern feminist biblical interpretation.

Thus, in the ears of reason, this is a most beautiful and pleasing fairy tale, which the philosophers enjoyed ridiculing when hearing; this is the case with some of them, especially those acquainted with the science and wisdom of the Egyptians.[f] But it is inestimable wisdom for us to know what is taught by this (as the world calls it) foolish fairy tale: namely, that the beginning of the human beings' coming into existence was through the word: namely, God takes a clod and says: "Let Us[g] make a human being."[30] And later God takes a rib of Adam and says: "Let Us[31] make a helper[h] for the man."[i] Now, after the necessary discussion on the content, let us now consider their meaning.[32]

The Lord God, says Moses, caused a תַּרְדֵּמָה [*tardemah*], a "deep sleep," to fall upon Adam. The verb רָדַם [*radam*] means to be overwhelmed by sleep, like when one falls in such a deep sleep that one hears and sees nothing and one's head is nodding.[j] There are different kinds of sleep.[k] Some are deep or heavy and not disturbed by dreams. These are health-giving for they moisten the body well; they are also useful for digestion; they do not fatigue the head either. Others are lighter and, as it were, mixed with

h The word *helper* in English translations of the text has generated important discussion on the original, Hebrew meaning of the word and its sometimes inaccurate translations in English. E.g., on how the word pertains to the female sex, Phyllis Trible writes: "The Hebrew word *ezer* has been traditionally translated 'helper'—a translation that is totally misleading because the English word helper suggests an assistant, a subordinate, an inferior, while the Hebrew word *ezer* carries no such connotation. To the contrary, in the Hebrew Scriptures this word often describes God as the superior who creates and saves Israel. In our story the accompanying phrase, 'corresponding to it' (*kenegdo*), tempers this connotation of superiority to specify identity, mutuality, and equality" (Trible, *God and the Rhetoric*, 90).

i Lat.: *Faciamus homini adiutorium*.

j The plural nouns and verbs are translated here in the singular third person.

k See the *Table Talks*, WA TR 1, no. 508.

30. The wording in Genesis has been scrutinized for a possible rationale for a hierarchy between Adam and Eve, based on the order or the manner of their distinct creation. E.g., according to Brevard Childs: "The threefold repetition of the verb *create* ties closely together the special act of creation with its form of human sexual duality: God created [hu]man in his [God's] own image, in the image of God he [God] created them, male and female he [God] created them. No differentiation is made between male and female in terms of temporal priority or function. Their creation occurs simultaneously and only together is their creative role described. Surely this is a witness of absolute equality" (*Old Testament Theology in a Canonical Context* [Philadelphia: Fortress Press, 1985], 189).

31. In comparison, the German humanist theologian Konrad Pellikan (1478–1556): "Now in fact he [God] did not say 'let us make' as in the case of Adam, but the singular 'I will make.' From this more majestic way of speaking it further appears that the creation of the man was more noble than that of the woman. 'Before him' or 'belonging to him,' he [God] said, so that the woman would defer to man and stand by to assist him, not one who debates or heaps cares upon her husband" (*Commentary on Genesis* 2:18, *Commentaria Bibliorum* (1532) 1:5r, in Thompson, 101). This is clearly not Luther's take on the matter.

32. The interpretation of these words to imply a woman's servitude in partnership to a man has deep roots before and also in the Reformation tradition. John Calvin explains the rationale for woman as the man's companion: "the order of nature implies

periods of waking. In this kind of sleep, dreams are more frequent, but they also hurt the head and are a manifestation of a weaker body.[33]

Moses says that Adam was overcome by the deepest kind of deep sleep,[l] so that, as he lay stretched out on the green earth, he drew long breaths, as people do when they are enjoying a good, sweet sleep. God made this sleep to fall over Adam, says Moses. Sleep is truly a divine and the most beautiful gift which streams down from above like dew and moistens the entire body. While Adam was sleeping this way, God took one of his ribs. The Hebrew word צֵלָע [*tsela*] denotes a rib and a side. Therefore I deem that God did not take a bare rib, but one covered with flesh, since Adam says below: "This is bone from my bones and flesh from my flesh." Moreover, God does this also through the word. We should not suppose that God, like a surgeon, did any cutting. God said: "Let there be a woman made from this bone thus covered with flesh," and it was done. Later God closed this gap in the side with flesh.

Here the nitpickers invoke some debating with their prodigious babble. They claim that the male has more ribs on one side than on the other.[34] But in this matter the physicians are better informed, because they know. Lyra[35] has a discussion on whether that rib was superfluous in the body of Adam.[m] If this was the case, he says, it would be something monstrous; if it was not the case, then Adam would later miss a rib. But Lyra says that this also would be monstrous. Lyra's response follows: Because the rib was extra[n] only for the individual concerned, even after its removal, Adam's body was complete. At the same time, Adam's body needed this extra rib because a woman was to be formed from it.[36]

l Lat.: *Profundo somno opressum*, "a profound sleep oppressed," or "took over."

m LW 1:129 n.67: "This seems inappropriate, for either that rib belonged to the completeness of [Adam's] nature, or it was superfluous. If the first, then his body became imperfect and diminished, which would not be proper for the condition of the first [hu]man, who was simply perfect in both soul and body. If the second, then that rib was a freak in Adam, as a sixth finger would be on a hand, which would be inappropriate in a perfect [hu]man, as was said before." Lyra on Gen. 2:21, sec. "h."

n Lat.: *superfluous*, "extra," "unnecessary."

that the woman should be a helper to the man. Truly, it is a vulgar proverb that 'woman is a necessary evil,' but far better that we should listen to the voice of God, which declares that she was added as the man's companion and partner, to assist him live well" (*Commentary on Genesis* 2:18 in Calvin's Commentaries, 46 vols. [Edinburgh: Calvin Translation Society], 1:129–30 as cited in Thompson, 107–8).

33. The word *ekstasis* in Gen. 2:21, for deep sleep may actually "indicate something other than sleep: a trance-like state, rather than deep unconsciousness"; see Helen Kraus, *Gender Issues in Ancient and Reformation Translations of Genesis 1–4* (New York: Oxford University Press, 2011), 57–59, 65, at 57.

34. In comparison, the French reformer in Geneva, John Calvin (1509–1564), wrote about Adam trading a rib for a companion who would "complete" him: it would be absurd to think that Eve was created from a superfluous rib of Adam, or "that his body would have been mutilated by losing that rib." Instead, "If, however, we should say that the rib from which he [God] would form a second body had been already prepared by the world's creator, I find nothing in this answer that disagrees with divine providence. Yet I am more in favor of a different conjecture, namely, that something was removed from Adam in order that he might embrace with greater kindness a part of himself. Thus, he did lose a rib. But he was repaid for it with a far richer reward, since he obtained a faithful and lifelong companion. Even more, he now saw himself made whole in his wife, where previously he had been but half a self. And in this we see a true likeness of our union with the Son of God, for he

God creates Eve from Adam's rib while he sleeps. Woodcut from a book by Johann Dietenberger (1534).

Our reply to all this is the word: "God said." This statement puts an end to all such debates. Why is it necessary to discuss where the remaining material was found by God who can do anything and creates all things by a single word?[37] These questions have their origin in philosophy and in the science of medicine, where the works of God are disputed without the word. Moreover, the result of this way of proceeding is that the glory of Holy Scripture and the majesty of the Creator are lost. Therefore, passing over these discussions, we shall simply adhere to the account as it is presented by Moses: Eve was created from a rib of Adam, and part of his body was again closed with flesh. Just as Adam was made from a clod, so I was made from a droplet of my father's blood. How my mother conceived me, how I was formed in the womb, and how I grew in increments—all this I leave to the glory of the Creator. For it is truly unbelievable that a human being comes into existence from a drop of blood; and yet it is true. Therefore if there is that power of bringing a human being into existence from a drop of blood, why not also from a clod? Likewise, why not from a rib?

But this sleep of Adam—so sound that he was not aware of what was being done to him—is as if a picture of the transformation which would have taken place in the state of innocence.[38] The righteous nature would have experienced no death but would have lived in the utmost joy, in obedience to God, and in

became weak that the embers of his body might be endowed with strength" (Calvin, *Commentary on Genesis* 2:21, in Thompson, 101).

35. Nicholas of Lyra (1270–1349), a Franciscan scholar from University of Paris, whose groundbreaking biblical exegesis was fundamentally important for Luther.

36. In comparison, Cardinal Cajetan (1469–1534), an Italian Catholic philosopher and a theologian, refutes a literal reading of the words; the woman was not literally from Adam's rib, as that would be absurd and would mean that Adam was a monster (*Commentary on Genesis* 2:21, *Commentarii illustres* [1539], 14–15, in Thompson, 99–100).

37. One of the consistent statements in Luther's theological writing is a reminder of the workings of God's word, from creation to redemption to resurrection.

38. Lat.: *statu innocentiae*. The words about the "innocent status" have in Christian theology referred to the original state of creation without sin. In many ways, Christian theology in the Middle Ages formulated ways to return to, or to restore, the fallen nature to the closest approximate of the state of grace.

admiration of the works of God until the time of the change had arrived. Then Adam would have experienced something similar to this sleep that happened to him as something most delightful while he lay among roses and under the loveliest trees. During that sleep he would have been changed and translated into the spiritual life without experiencing any pain, just as he did not realize that his body was being opened and that a rib, with flesh, was being taken out. Now this corrupt nature suffers death. In the case of godly,[39] a sweet sleep follows this disintegration of the body until we awake in a new and eternal life. Moreover, here Adam, impelled by admiration, says: "This is bone from my bones," and yet he had been so overcome by sweet sleep that he did not realize that it had been taken out of him. So on that day we shall say: "Behold, into what great glory this body, consumed by worms, has suddenly risen!"

We have talked copiously about the creation of Eve, which sounds like a fairy tale to reason, but is the most certain truth. It is revealed in the word of God, which alone, as I said, imparts true information about the two main causes, the effective and the final; knowledge of these, if available, is considered to be of the greatest importance also in matters pertaining to nature. What advantage is there in knowing what a beautiful creature a human being is, if not knowing, namely, that the human being was created to worship God and to live eternally with God? Aristotle says something worthwhile when declaring that the goal of human beings is happiness, which consists in a virtuous life. But in view of the feebleness of our nature, who can reach this goal?[o] Even those who are the most fortunate encounter discomforts of various kinds, which both misfortune and the ill will and meanness of human beings bring on. Peace of mind is necessary for such happiness. But who can always preserve this amid the great changes of fortune? It is vain, therefore, to point out this goal which no one reaches.

The main goal, then, to which Scripture points is that the human being is created in the similitude of God;[p] the human being is therefore created to live with God in eternity. While here on earth, the human being is to preach God, thank God, and

39. Lat.: *piis* can be translated as "pious" or "godly." Here the latter is used in light of Luther's teaching of justification bringing one into union with God in Christ, and thus godliness in *coram Deo*. The word *pious* has been associated more with "piety" and holiness in *coram hominibus* (sanctification).

40. Before and after Luther, biblical interpreters of the two creation stories in the book of Genesis have deliberated on the different emphases regarding the meaning for gendered existence and relations: The first, Gen. 1:1–2:4a (from what is known as the "Priestly" account), depicts a simultaneous creation of male and female: "So God created humankind in God's image . . . in male and female." The second account, Gen. 2:4b–3:24 (the so-called Yahwist account), names woman as the "helper" who was created after the male. The latter source implies an "order of creation" not found in the first.

41. Rabbi Solomon, son of Isaac, acronym "Rashi" (1040-1105).

42. Luther's description of the presumed physical characteristics and differences of men and women rests on his own observations but also on depictions from male theologians over the centuries. The late medieval stereotypes about the (ideal) female body are hardly helpful for contemporary readers who may find them ridiculous if not offensive.

o Aristotle, *Nicomachean Ethics*, I, ch. 4.

p Lat.: *conditus ad similitudinem Dei*.

patiently obey God's word. In this life we hold on to this goal in ever so weak a manner; but in the future life we shall attain it fully. This the philosophers do not know. Therefore the world with its greatest wisdom is most ignorant when it does not take advantage of Holy Scripture or of theology. Human beings know neither their beginning nor their end when they are without the word. I say nothing about the other[q] creatures.

22. And the Lord God built the rib that God had taken from Adam into a woman, and God brought her to Adam.[40]

Here Moses uses a new and unheard-of expression, not the verb "form" and "create," as above, but "build." This induced all the interpreters to suspect that there is some underlying mystery here. Lyra, in common with his Rabbi Solomon,[41] believes that the reference is to the novel form of the woman's body.[r] As the shape of buildings is wider in the lower part but narrower in the upper, so, he says, the bodies of women are thicker[s] in their lower part but more contracted in the upper,[t] while men have broader shoulders and larger chests.[42] But these are nonessential features of the body. Moreover, Scripture says of the entire body that it is a building,[u] just as Christ (Matt. 12:44) calls the body a person's house.[43]

Others look for an allegory and say that the woman is called a building because of an analogy to the church. For as there are various parts in a house—walls, joists or beams, a roof, etc.—so in the church, which is analogous to the body because of the diversity of members, there are different kinds of services and offices. I for my part am not annoyed by what is appropriately applied to Christ and the church. But because these explanations are altogether allegorical, the historical and strict meaning of this passage must be sought and adhered to.[44] A woman, especially a married one, is called a building, not for the sake of allegory but historically. Scripture employs this method of speech everywhere. Thus, Rachel said to Jacob (Gen. 30:3): "Take the maid

q Lat.: *reliquis*, "remaining."

r Lyra on Gen. 2:21, sec. "I."

s Lat.: *craassiora*, literally "fatter."

t Lat.: *contractiora*, translated in LW as "drawn together."

u See, e.g., 1 Cor. 3:16-17.

43. In comparison, Konrad Pellikan writes (*Commentary on Genesis* 2:21, *In Primum Librum Mosis* [1569], 12r, in Thompson, 100): "He [God] cast him into a deep sleep lest he be terrified that he would feel pain from the opening of his side, the removal of a rib or putting his flesh back into place. And so, from the union of the woman with the man, it is as if the man lost no small measure of his solidity, constancy and manly fortitude when his rib bone was removed, in the place of which he acquired a certain softness of the flesh and became smaller and more fragile, accustomed to feminine charm and affection—however reluctantly husbands may have the heart to admit it. Even Christ, the new Adam, endured the ultimate in suffering; and through his death, as a sacred promise, the church of Christ was made his beloved bride."

44. Luther articulates a literal/historical reading as his fundamental approach to biblical exegesis. He criticizes allegorical interpretation, yet allows it when it supports the "plain" reading of the text that, to him, always should point to Christ. Allegory should not be used, however, for doctrinal argumentation.

that I may be built by her." Scripture states the same thing of Sara (Gen. 16:2). And in Exodus it is said of the midwives (Exod. 1:21): "The LORD built them houses"; that is, through the blessing of a family God repaid the kindnesses which they showed to Israel contrary to the king's command. Likewise, in the account about David, when he wanted to build a house for God, he receives the answer (2 Sam. 7:11): "You shall know that the LORD will build you a house."[45]

Abraham sends Hagar and Ishmael away as Sarah and Isaac watch in the background. Woodcut from *The Bible in Pictures* (c. 1860) by Julius Schnoor von Carlosfeld.

Thus, this expression is common in Scripture, that the wife is called a household building because she bears and brings up the offspring. Through sin, we have lost completely the form this building would have had in Paradise; we cannot even fathom it in our thinking. But, as I said above, this present life of ours possesses some small and pitiable remnants of its culture and safeguards as well as of its dominion over the beasts. Sheep, oxen, geese, and hens we govern, although boars, bears, and lions pay no attention to our rule. Similarly, some faint image of this building remains; for he who marries a wife has her as a nest and

45. Luther points to the allegorical interpretation of the words "building" or a "house" for how the "church" is understood. He, however, aims to interpret the words "historically," with a significant theological point about women's role in God's design for creation and redemption: women since Eve and the matriarchs serve in a central role as a home and locus for the historical embodied revelations of God's word; women do that as they give birth to new generations.

46. On many occasions, Luther argues for the beauty and godly design of marriage, from which those forced to live in celibacy were unfairly deprived. This was one of Luther's early Reformation calls: to hinder people from something this normal and God-ordered would be demonic and leads to sin: "It is more than a command, namely, a divine ordinance [*werck*] which it is not our prerogative to hinder or ignore. Rather it is just as necessary as the fact that I am a man, and more necessary than sleeping and waking, eating and drinking, and emptying the bowels and bladder. It is a nature and disposition just as innate as the organs involved in it. Therefore, just as God does not command anyone to be a man or a woman but creates them the way they have to be, so God does not command them to multiply but creates them so that they have to multiply. And whenever people try to resist this, it remains irresistible nonetheless and goes its way through fornication, adultery, and secret sins, for this is a matter of nature and not of choice" (see *On the Estate of Marriage* [1522], TAL 5:42; LW 45:18; WA 10/2:276,21–31).

home where he stays at a certain place, just as birds do with their young in their little nest. Those who, like the impure papists, live as celibates do not have such a home.[46]

This living-together[v] of husband and wife—that they occupy the same home, that they take care of the household, that together they give birth to and bring up children[47]—is a kind of faint image and a relic, as it were, of that blessed[48] living-together because of which Moses calls the woman a building. If Adam had continued in his innocence, his descendants would have married and wandered away from their father Adam to some little garden of their own. There they would have lived with their wives, and together they would have filled the soil and brought up their children. There would have been no need for imposing buildings of hewn stone or for kitchens or for cellars, as we have now. Just as birds live in their little nests, so the first humans would have dwelt here and there in God's work and calling. And the wife would have been the main reason for the husbands' dwelling in fixed habitations. Now in this disaster of sin, when we must have houses because of the severity of the climate, we cannot even imagine the happiness; and yet these pitiable remains are excellent gifts of God, and it is truly wicked to use them ungratefully.

We all realize how much of the dominion, which human beings received in Paradise, was lost after our defilement by sin. And yet what a great blessing it still is that this dominion was turned over to human beings and not to the devil! For how could we withstand our invisible enemy if it had not only the determination to inflict harm but also the power to do so? In one hour, in one moment, we would all be annihilated if Satan stirred up merely the wild beasts against us. Thus, even if the dominion has been almost entirely lost, it is still a very great blessing that some remnants of it are in existence to this day.

Similarly, there are also some remnants in the instance of procreation, although in the state of innocence[w] women would not only have given birth without pain,[x] but their future fertility[y] would also have been far greater. Procreation[49] is now hindered by a thousand diseases, and it happens either that unborn chil-

v Lat.: *cohabitatio.*

w Lat.: *statu innocentuae.*

x Lat.: *sine dolore.*

y Lat.: *futura foecunditas.*

47. Luther writes about the parents' holy duties that continue after the fall in a radically affirming way for a medieval male theologian: "A wife too should regard her duties in the same light, as she suckles the child, rocks and bathes it, and cares for it in other ways; and as she busies herself with other duties and renders help and obedience to her husband. These are truly golden and noble works" (*On the Estate of Marriage* [1522], TAL 5:68; LW 45:40; WA 10/2:296,12–15). Influenced by his experiences with his own children (still a new perspective for a late medieval male theologian), Luther affirmed a fathers' vocation: "Likewise, when a father washes diapers, he may be ridiculed by some as an effeminate fool, but God, with all God's angels and creatures, is smiling—not because that father is washing diapers, but because he is doing so in Christian faith" (ibid.; see also LW 44:12–14; WA 2:169,38–170,7). Luther's personal experience enhances his fundamental appreciation of the biblical narrative of God's creation of men and women.

48. "This is your comfort, that you know and believe how your estate [of marriage] is pleasing and blessed in God's eyes" ("A Marriage Booklet," in the *Small Catechism*, TAL 4:246; BC, 371).

49. Luther is building his arguments on the consequences of the fall on the basis of long tradition that, since Augustine, located the "beginning" of an individual's sin in the birth and the act of procreation, which since the Garden of Eden had become tainted.

dren do not survive the period of gestation or that at times marriages are altogether sterile. These deficiencies and punishments result from Adam's [and Eve's] awful fall and the original sin.[50] In the same way the wife is still the house of the husband, to which he goes, with whom he dwells, and with whom he joins in the effort and work of supporting the family. In this sense it will be stated below (Gen. 2:24): "One[z] will cling to one's wife and will forsake one's father and mother."[51]

But in addition to the countless other troubles caused by sin, this living-together is deformed to an astonishing degree by pervert individuals. There are not only those[a] who think it is clever to find fault with the opposite sex[52] and to have nothing to do with marriage but also those who, after they have married, desert their spouses[b] and refuse to support their children. Through their baseness and wickedness these people lay waste God's building, and they are really abominable monsters of nature. Let us, therefore, obey the word of God and recognize our wives as a building of God. Not only is the house built through them by procreation and other services that are necessary in a household; but the husbands themselves are built through them, because wives are, as it were, a nest and a dwelling place where husbands can go to spend their time and dwell with pleasure.

What Moses adds, "And God brought her to Adam," is a sort of description of engagement,[c] which is worthy of special notice.

z For this familiar statement, Luther uses *homo* for human being as he describes what the "man" does in respect to his wife. While the medieval man Luther could not have foreseen marriage between men or between women, in light of contemporary understanding of marital relations and human nature, the new translation aims beyond heteronormativity.

a LW translates "men."

b LW uses the word "wives" for *coniuges* (Lat.).

c Lat.: *quaedam sponsalium*. The word *sponsalium* can mean "betrothal," "wedding," or "wedding feast," and Luther's word choice here points to the special relationship of Adam and Eve from the first encounter onward."

50. Nakedness had been "most honorable and the unique adornment" of human beings; after the fall, human beings made girdles "for the purpose of covering, as though it were something most shameful, that part of the body which by its nature was most honorable and noble." It was a sin that human beings covered their most honorable parts meant for the most precious act of procreation (LW 1:167–68; WA 42:126). The consequence of sin, thus, is felt in shame and pain in human beings' gendered state and relations. As they transgressed God's will, their mutual relationship became tainted with shame, and an ongoing struggle for power ensued (LW 1:165–66; WA 42:124).

51. In comparison, Wolfgang Musculus, a Reformation theologian (1478–1556), wrote: "This word *kenegdo* signifies that a woman is prepared for the man and placed alongside him so that the companionship and intimacy that they share living together may be undivided, not like that of animals who come together but once a year for procreation and afterwards wander off separately and unrestrained. A wife ought to be so yoked to her husband that she is inseparable from him" (*Commentary on Genesis* 2:18, *In Mosis Genesim* [1554], 74, in Thompson, 104).

52. It is to be noted that Luther on several occasions makes an explicit, theological counterargument against attempts to see women as inferior human beings. He draws from creation the dignity and equality of both sexes, which, in his time, was a progressive position to hold. E.g., "And God saw all that God had made, and look, it was all very good." . . . "So God created human . . . male and female . . . divided humankind into two classes, namely,

Two women working in a kitchen. From *Tacuina Sanitatis*, a late fourteenth-century handbook mainly about health.

Adam does not arbitrarily on his own snatch Eve after she has been created, but he waits for God to bring her to him. As also Christ says (Matt. 19:6): "What God has joined let no human separate."[53] For the lawful joining of a man and a woman is a divine ordinance and institution.

Here, therefore, Moses keeps his own particular expression. "He brought," he says. Who? No doubt, יְהוָה אֱלֹהִים,[d] that is, the entire divinity—Father, Son, and Holy Spirit. These say to Adam: "Behold, this is your bride, with whom you shall inhabit, with whom you shall create children." And without a doubt Adam received her with great pleasure, just as even now in this corrupt nature the mutual love of bridegroom and bride is extraordinary.[54] But then it was without the epileptic and apoplectic

d Lat.: *Iehova Elohim*.

male and female, or a he and a she. This was so pleasing to God who called it a good creation [Gen 1:31]" (LW 45:17; WA 10/2:275,18).

53. Luther, like any medieval Christian teacher, is cautious about the grounds for divorce, but recognizes also valid reasons for it: e.g., sexual unhappiness or incompatibility, "wrong faith," and irreconcilable differences would count. For Luther on reasonable grounds for divorce, see *On the Estate of Marriage* (1522), TAL 5:57-63; LW 45:30-35; WA 10/2:287,13—292,6. See also *On the Babylonian Captivity of the Church* (1520), TAL 3:107-9; LW 36:103-6; WA 6:558,8—560,18.

54. With the Latin words *amore mutuus* and *sponsi et sponsae*, Luther underscores the intimacy and affection between the two partners from the very beginning. It is noteworthy how Luther, since his own marriage in 1525, expresses his delighted appreciation of the expressions of marital love.

desire of marriages today; it was a chaste and delightful love, and the actual intercourse would also have been most honorable and most sacred. But now sin forces and presents itself everywhere, involving the eyes and ears and also all the other senses.[55]

The Infatuated Old Woman
by Lucas Cranach the Elder (c. 1522)

Therefore it should be particularly noted that this passage is not only directed against all the awful abuses of lust; it also gives a [positive] confirmation for marriage in contrast to the wicked ranting with which the papacy has brought it shame. For is it not a great thing that already in the state of innocence God ordained and instituted marriage?[e,f] But now this institution and com-

55. Luther, in Augustinian tradition, sees the impact of original sin tainting all of human existence, including the most beautiful dimension of it, sexuality and love (*On the Estate of Marriage* (1522), TAL 5:77; LW 45:49; WA 10/2:304,9-12. The false awareness caused by disobedience is at the root of sin: not knowing God as God intended, and seeing good as evil and vice versa. The consequences are tragic.

56. This text is a "marriage charter text," also according to David Chytraeus (1530-1600), a Reformation theologian and a historian (*Commentary on Genesis* 2:18-25, *In Genesin* (1576), in Thompson, 99): "The doctrine of marriage is necessary for the whole church. The original establishment of marriage, as well as its true, complete and learned definition, is handed down in this text, which. . . . Marriage is the indissoluble joining of one man and woman who are lawfully able to be joined, it is divinely instituted so that we might come to know that God is a pure and spotless mind. . . . In this way, through the propagation of the human race, God's eternal church is gathered."

57. With the Latin words *coniugium est vitae genus divinum*, Luther underscores the underscores the divine nature of human experiences in marriage in marriage.

e For Luther on marriage, see *On the Babylonian Captivity of the Church* (1520), TAL 3:96-110; LW 36:92-106; WA 6:550,2–553,21; "A Marriage Booklet for Simple Pastors" (1529) in the *Small Catechism*, TAL 4:242-46; BC 367-71; LW 53:110-15; WA 30/3:74-80; *On Marriage Matters* (1530), LW 46:(261) 265-320; WA 30/3:205-48; *Judgment on Monastic Vows* (1521), LW 44:(243) 251-400; WA 8:(564) 573-669.

f On studies on this central Reformation topic, see John Witte Jr., *From Sacrament to Contract: Marriage, Religion, and Law in the Western*

mand are all the more necessary, since sin has greatly weakened and corrupted the flesh. Therefore this comfort stands invincible against all the doctrines of demons (1 Tim. 4:1), namely, that marriage[56] is a divine kind of life[57] because it was ordained by God.[58, g]

Now what has gone into the heads of the tools of Satan and the enemies of Christ who deny that there is any chastity in marriage and declare[h] that the most suited for the ministry of the church are those who live as celibates, because Scripture says (Lev. 11:44): "You shall be pure." Are those who are married then impure? Is God the author and institutor of impurity when bringing Eve to Adam? Is Adam then doing wrong when he allows himself to be persuaded into impurity while in his innocent state he could have avoided marriage? The papacy has truly paid the deserved penalties for such blasphemies, having polluted themselves with a multitude of whores and indulged also in other such loathsome crimes that they are ripe now for the punishment of Sodom and Gomorrah.[59]

When I was a boy, the wicked and impure practice of celibacy[60] had made marriage so notorious that I believed I could not even think about marital life without sinning. Everybody was fully persuaded to think that in order to lead a holy life acceptable to God, one should not marry but live as celibate and take the vow of celibacy. Thus, many who had been married became either monks or priests after their spouses had died. Therefore it was necessary and useful for the church that marriage through the word of God became respected again and received the praises it deserved. As a result, by the grace of God now everyone declares

Tradition (Louisville: Westminster John Knox, 1997); Scott Hendrix, "Luther on Marriage," in Timothy Wengert, ed., *Harvesting Martin Luther's Reflections on Theology, Ethics, and the Church* (Grand Rapids: Eerdmans, 2003), 169–89; John Witte Jr., "The Mother of All Earthly Laws: The Lutheran Reformation of Marriage," in Kirsi I. Stjerna and Brooks Schramm, eds., *Encounters with Luther: New Directions for Critical Studies* (Louisville: Westminster John Knox, 2016), 111–25; and Kirsi I. Stjerna, "Luther on Marriage, for Straight and Gay," in ibid., 126–43.

g See Christopher Brooke, *The Medieval Idea of Marriage* (Oxford: Clarendon Press, 1994); and Merrie E. Wiesner, "Marriage," in Wiesner, *Women and Gender in Early Modern Europe*, 2d ed. (Cambridge, UK: Cambridge University Press, 2000), 71–101.

h The words *negarunt* and *dixerunt* are translated in the present tense.

58. Lat.: *ab ipso Deo ordinatum.* Luther is convinced of this while also arguing that marriage is a human contract. See John Witte Jr., *From Sacrament to Contract: Marriage, Religion, and Law in the Western Tradition* (Louisville: Westminster John Knox, 1997).

59. When naming sins that incur God's punishment, particularly with the corrupt supposedly celibate clergy (all the way to the pope), Luther turns to the example of Sodom and Gomorrah and uses the word *sodomy* as a sign of the end of times. See Christopher Elwood, "A Singular Example of the Wrath of God: The Use of Sodom in Sixteenth-Century Exegesis," *Harvard Theological Review* 98, no. 1 (2005): 67–93; Helmut Puff, *Sodomy in Reformation Germany and Switzerland, 1400–1600* (Chicago: University of Chicago Press, 2003).

60. Luther's criticism of celibacy, one of his first battle calls early in the Reformation turmoil, led him to criticize his church's teaching and practice on multiple levels. It also made Luther an unexpected teacher of marriage, a topic that required his attention on an ongoing basis, not to his delight, if we can believe his own words: "How I dread preaching on the estate of marriage!" "I am reluctant to do it because I am afraid if I once get really involved in the subject it will make a lot of work for me and for others." "But timidity is of no help in an emergency, I must proceed. I must try to instruct poor bewildered consciences, and take up the matter boldly" (*On the Estate of Marriage* [1522], TAL 5:40; LW 45:17; WA 10/2:275,2–4, 8–9).

that it is good and holy to live with one's spouse in harmony and peace even when the spouse is infertile or troubled by other ills.

I do not deny, of course, that there are some who can live chastely without marrying. Because they have a greater gift than ordinary folk, such people can sail by their own wind.[61] But the chastity which the pope recommends to his monks, nuns, and priests is contaminated and polluted with horrible sins. In addition, celibacy has been instituted without the word of God, or, actually, against the word of God, as the present history testifies. How they would triumph, if they could substantiate celibacy from the word of God the same way we can prove that marriage is divinely instituted! How much more vigorously they would then force everyone into their celibacy![62] As it is, they have only this single true commendation for celibacy, namely, that it is a human tradition[63] or, to speak with Paul, a doctrine of demons (1 Tim. 4:1).

23. And Adam said: This, then, is bone from my bones and flesh from my flesh. She will be called Woman[i] *because she has been taken from man.*[j]

The statement which will follow a little later, "Therefore one[k] will forsake one's father and mother," is quoted by Christ as if it had been said by God and not by Adam (Matt. 19:5). But there is no difficulty here; for, because Adam was pure and holy, his utterance is rightly declared to be a divine voice. God spoke through him, and in that state of innocence the words and works of Adam are all truly the words and works of God. Eve is offered to him by God. Therefore just as God's will is ready to establish marriage, so Adam is ready to receive Eve with the greatest pleasure

i Lat.: *Virago*.

j Lat.: *vir*.

k See earlier, n. 45, p. 101, on translating *homo* as "one."

61. Luther considers it a special, unusual gift and calling from God to live an asexual, sexually inactive life. Among men he names "eunuchs" in different categories as those disposed to celibate life. He distinguishes between those who have been eunuchs from their birth and those who have been made eunuchs. See *On the Estate of Marriage* (1522), TAL 5:42; LW 45:18; WA 10/2:277,5).

62. Luther argues against the practice of celibacy in several of his writings, including the *Babylonian Captivity of the Church* (TAL 3), and, e.g., his "Preface to Stephan Klingebeil," in *On Clerical Marriage* (1528), WA 26; LW 59/1, ed. Christopher Boyd Brown (St. Louis: Concordia, 2012), 220–30. See Helen Parish, *Clerical Celibacy in the West, c. 1100–1700* (Farnham, UK: Ashgate, 2010).

63. Luther makes a distinction between human traditions and divine institutions: the former are not binding. That Luther considers marriage a matter of divine institution is worth noticing in light of his context where marital and sexual relations and human love were not considered holy per se. By naming marriage as divinely instituted he immediately elevated its role. At the same time, Luther deems human rules about marriage changeable.

64. Luther's Latin words, *cum summa voluptate et sanctimonia*, point to the coexisting dimensions of desire and sanctity in marriage, one of the expressions of Luther's Reformation anthropology that considers also body, bodily, and sexual desire as holy.

65. Similarly, commending intimacy, friendship, and love, Johannes Oecolampadius (1482–1531),

and sanctity.[64, 65] Thus, even now the bridegroom has a manifest affection for the bride, yet it is contaminated by that leprous lust of the flesh[66] which was not present in blameless[l] Adam.

But it is most worthy of wonder that when Adam looks at Eve as a building made from himself, he immediately recognizes her and says: "This now is bone from my bones and flesh from my flesh."[67] These are not words of a stupid or a sinful human being who has no insight into the works and creatures of God, but rather of a righteous and wise human being filled with the Holy Spirit. He reveals to the world a wisdom so-far unknown: that the effecting cause of the wife and of marriage is God, but that the final cause is for the wife to be the home in the world[m] to her husband. This knowledge is not simply the product of intelligence and reason; it is a revelation of the Holy Spirit.

The word הַפַּעַם, *hapaam*, which means "now" or "this time" or "at last," is not as excessive as it appears to be; it expresses most beautifully the affection of a husband who feels his need for a delightful and full relationship or cohabitation not only in love but also in holiness.[68] It is as if he were saying: "I have seen all the animals. I have carefully considered the females which were provided for the increase and the preservation of their kind, but they mean nothing to me. But this at last is flesh of my flesh and bones of my bones. I desire to live with her and to comply with God's will by procreating descendants." This little word

l *Adam iusto*, "the righteous Adam" is translated as "blameless Adam."

m The word *world* fails to fully convey what all is meant with the Latin *politicum habitaculum*.

a reformer from Palatinate, writes: "God wished to form the woman, Eve, to be the man's companion, so that there should be the most intimate closeness and friendship between the man and the woman. So he took her out of Adam's side, sending sleep on Adam beforehand. . . . By that miracle God wanted to commend to us the highest love and friendship, which the married ought to preserve between them, and finally to teach each one to acknowledge one's spouse as one's own flesh" (*Commentary on Genesis* 2:21–22, *In Genesim* [1536], 39r–v., in Thompson, *Reformation Commentary on Scripture*, 101).

66. The Latin words *leprosa libidine carnis* in Luther's use do not necessarily imply the wickedness of "flesh" in the sense of the body but, rather, point to the misoriented desire inherited in the original sin, concupiscence.

67. With Gen. 2:23, in a similar tone Wolfgang Musculus wrote about God acting as a matchmaker. "This may be considered the betrothal of Eve, who was so recently born. He [God] who had just created her, now betroths her and at the same time acts as her matchmaker. . . . she had already been announced by God's words. . . . So this presentation was nothing other than an act of true matchmaking. And Adam rightly understood this, and when she had been presented to him, he recognized the woman and took her for his partner, saying, 'This is . . .'" (*Commentary on Genesis* 2:18, *In Mosis Genesim* [1554], 70, in Thompson, 102–3).

68. Luther consistently affirms the holiness of spousal love and, in his opinion, as far more valuable than an ascetic or monastic lifestyle. It is safe

indicates an overwhelmingly passionate love.[69] Today that purity and innocence is lost; there still remain the bridegroom's delight and his love for the bride, but because of sin it is impure and imperfect. Adam's love was most pure and most holy and also pleasing to God. Inspired by this love, he says: "This now is bone from my bones, not from wood, not from stone, not from a clod of the earth; I care for it more for it is made from my bones and my flesh."[70] And so he says: *This one will be called Woman, because she has been taken from the man.*

The Cook and His Wife
(c. 1497) by Albrecht Dürer

to conclude that Luther's marriage to Katharina von Bora, along with parenthood, opened to him a holistic perspective on the holiness of daily life and natural human relations. This orientation and conviction of Luther cannot be overemphasized for its novelty in his time and for its lasting promise to new generations of men and women seeking their self-worth and ground of being in their sex and in their gender relations and the many dimensions of human love.

69. Lat.: *Hunc exundantem amoris affectum particula haec ostendit*. Luther uses the word *amor* to stress what kind of love Adam and Eve experienced—sensual, affectionate, and desiring love.

70. According to Wolfgang Musculus (*Commentary on Genesis* 2:18–25, *In Mosis Genesim* [1554], 74, referencing Eph. 5:28-29, in Thompson, 107), God used the rib on purpose: A woman was created "not from Adam's head, lest the woman grow haughty on account of her origin," and not from his feet so that she is not "demoted to . . . the insignificance of a slave." Instead, she is created "rather from Adam's side, so that he would know she was made to be her partner and the inseparable companion of his life, and so that she might legitimately cleave to his side, whence she was taken."

71. According to also John Calvin, Adam recognized Eve as "another self" (*Commentary on Genesis* 2:23, in Thompson, 103): The words "This at last" implied that Adam had been missing something. "And he gives to his wife a name taken from that of man, that by this testimony and this mark he might attest God's wisdom with an everlasting remembrance."

And now, just as Adam through the Holy Spirit understood past events he had not seen and glorified, he praised God for the creation of his mate: so now he prophesies the future when saying that she must be called "Woman."[71] We are not able to imitate the elegance of the Hebrew language. אִישׁ, *ish*, signifies a man. But he says that Eve must be called אִשָּׁה (*ishah*), as if you would call "wife" a "she-man,"[n] a heroic woman who performs virile[72] acts.[73]

Moreover, this designation carries with it a wonderful and pleasing description of marriage, in which, as the jurist also says, the wife shines through her husband's rays. Whatever the husband has, this also the wife has and possesses completely. They share[74] not only their means but also children, food, bed, and home; their will is also the same. Therefore, the husband differs from the wife in no other respect than in sex; otherwise the woman is completely[o] a man. Whatever the man is and has in the home, this also the woman is and has; she differs only in sex.[75] And this is actually something Paul mentions in 1 Tim. 2:13: that she is a "virago" [wo-man/she-man/heroic woman] by origin, because the woman came[76] from the man and not the man from the woman.[77]

n Lat.: *Vir Vira.*

o Lat.: *plane*, "completely" or "clearly."

72. The word used derives from *vir*, meaning "manly" acts. In medieval anthropology, a desirable spiritual goal for women was to rise above their female sex to identify with maleness and virtuosity was considered more possible for men than women (a remnant of logic from the Greek Aristotle).

73. In comparison, Wolfgang Musculus speaks of Eve's four names, two imposed by God, and two by Adam. First, Eve is called *Adam*, as earth is called *adamah*. Second, Eve's feminine sex is designated with the word *neqebah* (derived from perforation, distinct from *zakar* for masculinity). Third, Adam as the husband calls Eve *ishah*, the feminine form of *man*, as in *me-ish*, "taken out of man"—and thus belonging to him. Last but not least Eve is *Havah*, "the mother of all the living." In other words, women created from earth (Adam) are female by sex, and counterparts (*ishoth*) in marriage in which they become mothers of all (Eve). The latter "office" is both an honor and a burden (see *Commentary on Genesis* 2:18–25, *In Mosis Genesim* [1554], 78, in Thompson, 108–9).

74. Lat.: *Sunt communes* indicates the equality in sharing what belongs into marital life.

75. Lat.: *solo sexu differt.* The wording "only" is ironic in light of post-Luther gender studies' revelation of the complexity of sex/gender in human experience and relations.

76. Lat.: *descendit.* Notice the choice of "descend," implying a hierarchical order between the first man and woman.

77. The word *virago* is used instead of (what would appear a more logical choice) *virgo* because of the nuanced difference in meaning. E.g., in Jerome's

Also today we can observe some remnants of this sharing,[p] although wretched ones, if looking back to the first beginning. For if the wife is honest, modest, and devout,[78] she shares in all the cares, endeavors, duties, and functions of her husband.[79] Towards this end she was created in the beginning and is called woman,[q] or, if we were able to say so in Latin, a "she-man."[r] Thus, she differs only in sex from the head[80] of the household, inasmuch as she was taken from the flesh of the man. Although this can be said only of Eve, who was created in this manner, nevertheless in Matt. 19:5 Christ applies it to all wives[81] when saying that husband and wife are one flesh.[82] In this way, although your wife has not been made from your bones, nevertheless, because she is your wife, she is the ruler of the house just as you,[s] with the exception that the wife was made subject to the man[83] by the law given after sin. This punishment is similar to the others that have diminished the glorious conditions of Paradise, of which this text informs us. Moses is namely not speaking of the wretched life of those married now but of the innocence in Paradise. There the governing would have been equally shared, just as Adam prophesies here that Eve must be called "she-man," or "virago"[t] because she performs similar activities in the home. Now the sweat of the face is imposed upon man, and woman ordered to be under her husband's rule.[84,u] Yet there remain remnants, like dregs, of the dominion, so that even now the wife can be called "virago"[v] because of the shared possessions.[85, 86]

p Lat.: *communionis*, "sharing," "partnership," "fellowship."

q Lat.: *virago*, a "heroic woman."

r Lat.: *vira*, a feminine form of the word for "man," *vir*.

s Lat.: *quia uxor est, est domina domus sicut tu*. The translation in LW 1 suggests that the husband is the ruler in relation to wife as the mistress.

t See 77, pp. 139–40.

u Lat.: *uxori mandatur, ut sit sub viro* refers to "mandates" in the law to which wives are subjected.

v See n. 77, pp. 139–40.

Vulgate, "Virgo signifies a girl of marriageable age . . . as well as a woman who is sexually intact. . . ." The words *virgo* and *virago* do not share a root etymologically. *Virgo* would imply a professional virgin, pagan or Christian. See Kraus, *Gender Issues*, 59.

78. Lat.: *Ibi enim, uxor, si modo honesta, pudica et pia sit*. The word *pudica* means also "chaste," and *pia* can mean "religious," "godly," "holy."

79. Lat.: *participat curis, studiis, officiis, actionibus omnibus mariti*. Luther's point emphasizes the equality between men and women in the marital relationship.

80. The term *paterfamilias* means literally the "father of the family" and thus the "head of the family" or "household," in line with patrilinear and patriarchal structuring of medieval life in families and in society.

81. Lat.: *ad omnes uxores hoc accommodat*. Luther uses the word *wife*.

82. Lat.: *Maritum et uxorem esse unam carnem*. Here the word *flesh* is used positively to explain the depth of the union.

83. With the Latin words *viro mulier subiecta est*, Luther makes it explicit: wives are subjected to their husbands.

84. Similarly, Konrad Pellikan concludes that, as created from Adam's rib, a wife should allow herself to be ruled by her source of existence and instructed by her husband; "she should guard loyalty to him as to her very self, and work with him for the household needs without anger or argument. In turn, she should be loved by her husband as another self to him and, like a noble member of his own body, she should be constantly cherished as his heart's most loyal

Portrait of an unknown woman (1525) by an anonymous painter of the Cranach school

24. Therefore a man[w] *will leave father and mother and will cling to his wife.*

Christ (Matt. 19:5) and Paul (Eph. 5:31) apply this statement as a general rule also to our marriages, [lived] after lost innocence. Accordingly, if Adam had prevailed in his innocence, the children that were born would have married, and after leaving their parents' table and home, they would have had their own trees under which they would have lived separately from their parents. At times they would have come to their father, Adam, to sing a hymn and praise God, and then they would have returned to their own homes. Although these remnants have become mutated, there still remains this close bond between spouses, so that a man leaves father and mother rather than his wife. But where something different happens, as when married people

w Lat.: *homo* means "human being," but in this particular case it makes the best sense to translate it as "man."

guardian" (*Commentary on Genesis* 2:23, *Commentaria Bibliorum* [1532] 1:5v, cited in Thompson, 103).

85. Luther's colleague Andreas von Karlstadt (1486–1541) also argued that God had created Adam and Eve as equals but different. Unlike Luther, he stressed the importance of not perverting the created order: "Spouses retain their equality if they remain in the instituted unity, with the woman [helpmate] being obedient and submissive to her husband, holding him in honor and treating him well, always mindful that she has been taken from the man and is called she-man." Similarly, a husband must treat with love his spouse as one from his flesh. By divine order, the husband is the head and the wife should not aspire to become a she-man; that would be a perversion and lead to conflicts (*Regarding Vows*, CRR 8:97–98, in Thompson, 106–7).

86. Luther is distinctive in his esteem of Eve's equality and women's partnership in marriage. He seeks to understand women as women in the big picture of God's plans primarily, and not exclusively in relation to a man, even if his thoughts echo the basic imaginations of his contemporaries about women's realm limited to marriage and household. In comparison, e.g., Wolfgang Musculus argues that wives are specifically *formed* to be helpers of their husbands: for procreating offspring, to offer remedy for husband's temptations with lust, and to manage the household affairs. "Many things have to be managed by her in the absence of her husband, and a worthy matron illumines her home with the splendor of her diligence—just as the moon shines in the absence of the sun" (*Commentary on Genesis* 2:18-25, *In Mosis Genesim* [1554], 74, in Thompson, 105). The latter comment reflects Luther's oft-stated opinions of his wife's leadership abilities.

87. This kind of negative statement about Jewish faith or people is, unfortunately, frequent in Luther's writings. Most commonly he uses the image of a Jew to describe law-abiding faith and works righteousness.

mutually forsake each other, it is not only against this command; it is also an indication of the horrible corruption that has entered human beings through sin and that is supported by Satan, the father of all discord.

Moreover, also the Gentiles [pagans] realized that there was nothing more proper and more advantageous than this intimate marital relationship. Hence, they declare that according to natural law, it is necessary to have a wife and maintain with her an inseparable intimacy until death. Christ, too, states that divorce[x] was granted by Moses because of the hardness of the hearts of the Jews,[87] but that it had not been so from the beginning (Matt. 19:8). These troubles arose later on through sin, just as the instances of adultery, poisoning, and the like, which sometimes occur among married people. Thus, scarcely a thousandth part of that first institution remains; and yet, because of their offspring, husband and wife have their own little nest even now, in accordance with the statement by which this kind of life receives glorious and magnificent support from our first parent, yes, from God, as Christ declares.

The Holy Family by Lucas Cranach the Elder (1509)

This forsaking is not to be understood as though the married children would not have visited their parents at all. The reference is only to living together, namely, that the married children would dwell in their own little nest. Among all the troubles caused by sin is also this, that children are compelled to support their feeble parents in need. While in Paradise our condition would have been different and better, still, this practice would have still been kept: that because of his love for his spouse[y] the husband would choose his own little nest and give up living with his parents, just as the little birds are accustomed to do.

x See n. 53, p. 133.

y Lat.: *propter amorem coniugis.*

This statement is also in the nature of a prophecy. There was no father or mother yet, and no children; nevertheless, through the Holy Spirit, Adam prophesies this way about the married life, about their own home, about the distinctions in the dominion over the entire world, so that individual families might live in their own little nest.

25. But both were naked, the man and his wife, and they were not ashamed.

It seems that this little statement could have been omitted, as it tells of something that is not altogether necessary. For of what importance is it whether they walked around in Paradise naked or clothed? Yet it is an important and necessary little statement; it uses a rather insignificant fact, as appears to us, to show how much evil has come to this nature through original sin. All people, particularly those who live farther toward the north,[88] abhor nudity. Therefore the shyer and more serious people not only criticize the short outfits and [revealing] military garments worn by young people, but also avoid the public baths, even when the private parts are carefully covered both by women and by men. This is now a matter of wisdom and a praiseworthy practice, for what father without committing a crime could uncover himself before his son? But Adam and Eve, says Moses, walked about naked and were not ashamed. Therefore it was not only not shameful to walk about naked; it was even praiseworthy, glorious, and delightful.[89]

We have now lost this through sin. We are indeed born naked into this world and with a hairless skin, although the rest of the animals all bring with them their fur, hair, feathers, and scales. Therefore we must have the shade of houses against the heat of the sun, and a variety of garments against rain, hail, and snow. Adam would have experienced none of these things; but just as the human eyes still have this characteristic that they are affected neither by cold nor by heat, so at that time the entire body would have been protected against cold. And, even better in many ways, Eve, our mother, would have sat among us naked. None of us would have been offended by the nakedness of her breasts and the other parts of the body, which now cause us shame and, because of sin, kindle lust.[90]

Therefore this passage points out beautifully how much

88. Luther apparently refers to people in northern Europe. It is ambiguous on what he bases his assumption.

89. The fall caused fundamental confusion about sex and gender and ignited a false feeling of shame: "Therefore this is an excellent description of the corruption which has taken the place of original righteousness and glory. It was glory for human beings not to realize that they were naked. Moreover, what can be a greater depravity than that the nakedness which formerly was a glory is now turned into the greatest is grace? No one blushes because of healthy and sound eyes. Distorted or weak eyes are regarded as less becoming and bring on shame. So in the state of innocence it was most honorable to go about naked. Now, after sin, when Adam and Eve see that they are naked, they are made ashamed, and they look for girdles with which to cover their disgrace" (LW 1:165–66; WA 42:124).

90. With Genesis 3, Luther describes how, after the fall, Adam and Eve became ashamed of their created state of nudity and their most glorious sexual organs; they sinned further by making themselves girdles to hide their sex, and, eventually, trying to hide from God. "Out of this corruption which followed because of sin there followed another evil. Adam and Eve not only were ashamed because of their nakedness, which previously was most honorable and the unique adornment of human beings, but they also made girdles for themselves for the purpose of covering, as though it were something most shameful, that part of the body which by its nature was most honorable and noble. What in all nature is nobler than the work of procreation? This work was assigned by God neither to the eyes nor to the mouth, which we regard as the more honorable parts of the body, but to that part which sin has taught us to call the pudendum and to cover, lest it be seen" (LW 1:167–68; WA 42:126).

91. Lat.: *summa nostra gloria . . . extrema turpitude.* Luther grieves over the development that the glorious bodiliness and sexuality, expressed in nudity, suffer from depravity since the fall.

evil followed from Adam's sin. For now it would be regarded as extreme insanity if anyone walked about in the nude. Therefore what would have then been our greatest glory is now our extreme shame.[91] It would have been something amazing for the human beings that, while all the animals needed hair, feathers, and scales to cover up their ugliness, the humans alone were created with such prestige and beauty of body that they could walk about with a hairless and naked skin.[z] This glory has perished. For we must cover our bodies with greater effort and care than the rest of the animals—not only because of necessity but rather to avoid shame.[a] The rest of the animals have been covered naturally.[b]

Thus, this chapter presents the work of the sixth day a little more clearly: how by a special counsel the human being was created; how the Garden of Eden was made, in which the human being would be able to live with pleasure; how finally, while the tree of the knowledge of good and evil is forbidden, the outward worship of the future church is established by divine authority—the worship in which they would have testified of their obedience to God, had they avoided the devil's traps. And so during that night, according to the opinion of some, Adam was in Paradise with his Eve until the following sabbath. But the following chapter will tell what happened on the sabbath.

z Translation uses plural third person rather than the pronoun "he."

a See n. 25, p. 91 and n. 50, p. 132 above on post-fall shame.

b Lat.: *a natura.* LW 1 translates this as "by nature."

Lectures on Genesis 3:1-15

1535

JUSSI KOIVISTO

INTRODUCTION

What we call Luther's Genesis commentary (1535–1545) is actually a series of Luther's lectures on Genesis that was later reworked and edited by Luther's colleagues.[a] It is not, therefore, surprising that scholars have long debated the authenticity of Luther's lectures on Genesis. In the twentieth century, Erich Seeberg and Peter Meinhold, in particular, questioned the authenticity of these lectures and aimed to find traces of editorial "improvement" that, as Mickey Leland Mattox suggested, would "conform to the concerns and commitments of the Philippist party in the second generation of Lutheranism, falsely attributing to Luther proofs for the existence of God, arguments for the immortality of the soul, and the justification of astrology." Mattox and Jaroslav Pelikan, however, consider the lectures authentic in spite of the editorial work done by others.[b] I have reached

a For more details, see LW 1:ix–x.

b Mickey Leland Mattox, *"Defender of the Most Holy Matriarchs": Martin Luther's Interpretation of the Women of Genesis in the Enarrationes in Genesin, 1535–1545* (Leiden: Brill, 2003), 263–73; LW 1:x–xii.

The Fall (c. 1550) by Titian (1490–1576)

a similar conclusion based on my studies regarding Luther's understanding of the serpent.[c]

It is also important to notice that this commentary was considered as Luther's theological testament in the decades following the Reformation.[d] It is a successful description of these lectures. This commentary, namely, is not only the best-known late work of Luther regarding the Bible (in addition to *De servo*

c Jussi Koivisto, "Martin Luther's Conception of the Serpent Possessed by the Devil (Gen 3) and the Antecedent Tradition," in *"Wading Lambs and Swimming Elephants": The Bible for the Laity and Theologians in the Late Medieval and Early Modern Era*, ed. Wim François and August den Hollander (Leuven: Peeters, 2012), 137–38. Luther also commented on Genesis in the beginning of the 1520s—probably in his sermons (see also ibid., 132–37).

d Eero Huovinen, *Kuolemattomuudesta osallinen. Martti Lutherin kuoleman teologian ekumeeninen perusongelma* (Helsinki: Suomalaisen teologisen

arbitrio [1525] and *Lectures on Galatians* [1531/1535]), but also the most extensive of his works, with two thousand pages of edited Latin text. Only Luther's first Psalms commentary compares with this work in length.[e] These lectures also were meaningful to later Lutheran generations. In the *Formula of Concord*, for example, his *Lectures on Genesis* (and also *Lectures on Galatians*) were noted as "brilliant" (*praeclarus*).[f]

Luther's Premodern Exegesis

Luther's Genesis commentary was titled in Latin *Enarrationes* (Lat.: *enarratio*, meaning to speak, tell, set forth in detail, to speak in public in detail, an explanation, oral lecturing, or an interpretation).[g] The *enarratio*-exegesis was a usual way to explain the Bible in the Middle Ages and early modern era. This method differs significally from modern exegesis (especially the historical-critical method). Unlike the historical-critical method, it was not strictly about grammatical issues, historical background, and the like. For Luther, *enarratio* meant a host of things, including doctrinal issues such as soteriology, doctrine, and dealing with topical issues (e.g., antinomianism in the Wittenberg community). Another prominent feature of *enarratio*-exegesis was its great length compared to many modern exegetical studies.[h]

In addition to *enarratio*-tradition, Luther's exegesis was influenced by the medieval tradition of sacred texts known as *lectio divina*. For Luther, this meant that engaging the Bible is itself

kirjallisuusseuran julkaisuja 130, 1989) (English: "Participating Immortality. The Ecumenical Elementary Problem of Martin Luther's Theology of Death").

e WA 3-4; WA 42-44; WA 55/1-2.

f *Bekenntnisschriften der evangelisch-lutherischen Kirche herausgegeben im Gedenkjahr der Augsburgischen Konfession 1930* (Göttingen: Vandenhoeck & Ruprecht, 1998), 889 n.44; see also 865-66 nn.61-62.

g Karl Ernst Georges, *Ausführliches lateinisch-deutsches Handwörterbuch aus den Quellen zusammengetragen und mit besonderer Bezugnahme auf Synonymik und Antiquitäten unter Berücksichtigung der besten Hilfsmittel* 1 (Hannover: Hahnsche Buchhandlung, 1998), 2:416.

h John A. Maxfield, *Luther's Lectures on Genesis and the Formation of Evangelical Identity* (Kirksville, MO: Truman State University Press, 2008), 15-16, 18, 23-24. See also Mattox, *"Defender of the Most Holy Matriarchs,"* 2.

a spiritual exercise in which both speaker and hearer are confronted by the word of God.[i] In short, Luther's exegesis and medieval and early modern exegesis did not attempt to separate the spiritual from the academic enterprise. This made exegesis perhaps more scattered than modern exegesis, but, on the other hand, reading medieval and early modern commentaries is very interesting, because they also reveal, for example, what sorts of doctrinal issues were topical at that time.

Readers of Luther's commentaries (especially the opening chapters of Genesis) should also take into consideration that Luther represents the early modern perspective of the world. This perspective did not know anything about evolution, about the true age of the earth and universe, nor even about the exact geometry of the earth. Although Luther's ideas seem outdated in the light of current science, this does not necessarily mean that his ideas regarding Christian faith are outdated. Even modern readers can find Luther's ideas on Christian dogma still relevant or even inspiring. It is also important to remember when reading Luther's commentary on Genesis or the opening chapters of Genesis that they still offer an interesting conversation partner with current science (e.g., regarding human nature)—in spite of scientific progress.[j]

i Maxfield, *Luther's Lectures on Genesis*, 74; see also 66, 80–81; Kenneth Hagen, *Luther's Approach to Scripture as Seen in His "Commentaries" on Galatians 1519–1538* (Tübingen: Mohr, 1993), 49–66, 128, esp. 49–51.

j See more about this dialogue between Genesis 3 and current science: *Four Views on the Historical Adam*, ed. Matthew Barrett, Ardel B. Caneday, and Stanley N. Gundry (Grand Rapids: Zondervan, 2013); *Reading Genesis after Darwin*, ed. Stephen C. Barton and David Wilkinson (Oxford: Oxford University Press, 2009). See also about the origin of Genesis 3 in Bill T. Arnold, *Genesis* (Cambridge: Cambridge University Press, 2009), 63, where he presents an interesting scenario: "the Garden of Eden reflects an old Canaanite myth of a sacred grove, with a tree of life, living waters, guardians at the entrance, and especially a serpent." Arnold considers it possible that this story has been demythologized in order to expose the real nature of Canaanite Baalism, "and not only to expose it, but to universalize the experience for all Israel so that obedience to Yahweh's voice and repudiation of Baalism becomes paramount for all." See also John W. Rogerson, *Genesis 1–11* (Sheffield: JSOT Press, 1991), 194–96, where he represents that the similarities between Gen. 3:1-24 and Ezek. 28:11-19 suggest that a similar story was used in their formation.

About the Story of the Fall

The story of the fall has intrigued artists, writers, and Christian scholars throughout the centuries. Even today exegetes turn to Genesis 2 and 3 and propose fresh interpretations.[k] One reason for the vast interest in the third chapter of Genesis in Christianity is probably the fact that, according to early Christians, Christ was considered as the second Adam who saves and delivers humans from the transgression of the first Adam (cf. Rom. 5:12-21).

Genesis, chapter three, had a special relevance for Luther. For him it was a description of the beginning of the age-old battle between God and the devil for the church. In fact, for Luther, human history itself is defined by this battle.[l] Although many modern exegetes are reluctant to identify the serpent in the story as synonymous with the devil or give any role to the devil in the story,[m] they also usually see it as a story about corruption and fall. And they focus on the etiological nature of the story in order to explain the origin of suffering in the world.[n]

In spite of these differences between Luther and modern exegesis, Genesis 3 can be said to be a tragic story about the fall of humanity from their blissful life with God. Also, the serpent has a special role in the story. Just as God created the world through words (cf. Genesis 1), so the serpent uses the power of words to persuade the woman to see the tree in a new light, a light that will lead her and Adam to death. The words of the serpent, however, are not as effective as God's words, which create reality immediately. In other words, the serpent has to persuade and it cannot simply command something to exist just like God. In this sense I think that Luther is on the right track with his emphasis that the "serpent" poisons the first humans through words.[1]

Luther interprets this story of evil and sin to include a major positive aspect. Already, in the midst of the beginning of the battle, the true winner is announced in the so-called proto-gospel

k Claus Westermann, *Genesis 1–11*, A Continental Commentary, trans. J. J. Scullion, S.J. (Minneapolis: Fortress Press, 1994), 186.

l Maxfield, *Luther's Lectures on Genesis*, 147–57.

m See, e.g., Westermann, *Genesis 1–11*, 238–39.

n See, e.g., Umberto Cassuto, *A Commentary on the Book of Genesis, Part One: From Adam to Noah*, trans. Israel Abrahams (Jerusalem: Magnes Press, 1961), 138–40.

1. Another interesting connection between Luther and some modern exegetes is the way they describe the spiritual life of the first humans and consider them as religious leaders. See, e.g., John H. Walton, "A Historical Adam: Archetypal Creation View," in *Four Views on the Historical Adam*, ed. Matthew Barrett, Ardel B. Caneday, and Stanley N. Gundry (Grand Rapids: Zondervan, 2013), 109, 114–15.

(Gen. 3:15). This short gospel proved, according to Luther, that the seed of the woman (i.e., the Christ) will be born and crush the powers of evil. For this reason, Luther's comments on the fall also include hopeful and consoling aspects.

About the Translation and Annotations

I have omitted from the text especially those parts that are not directly related to the exegetical or theological meaning of Gen. 3:1-15. My aim has been to depict a narrative that leads from the fall to a hope for redemption. The reader will notice that Luther focuses much on the progress of sin that occurs in humans through the fall and the deceptive words of the serpent possessed by the devil.

In the footnotes and annotations I have focused attention primarily on: (1) the influence of church fathers and medieval theologians on Luther and how he evaluated their ideas; (2) Luther's own theological notions; and (3) Luther's exegetical and grammatical remarks on the Genesis text itself and how Luther's ideas may be evaluated in the light of modern commentaries on Genesis.

LECTURES ON GENESIS 3:1-15[o]

[Introduction to the Fall][p]

1[a]. But the serpent was more clever than all the animals of the earth which God had made.

IN THE PRECEDING CHAPTER we heard how man and woman were created on the sixth day according to the image and likeness of God, so that humanity's will[2] was good and sound; moreover, reason or intellect[3] of human beings was sound, so that whatever God wanted or said, they[q] also wanted, believed, and understood the same thing. The knowledge of all the other creatures necessarily followed this knowledge; for where the knowledge of God is perfect, there also the knowledge of the other things that are under God is necessarily perfect.

But these words show how horrible the fall of Adam and Eve was; for through it we have lost a most beautifully enlightened reason and a will in agreement with the word and will of God. We have also lost the glory of our bodies, so that now it is a matter of the utmost disgrace to be seen naked, whereas at that time it was something most beautiful and the unique prerogative of the human race over all the other animals. The most serious loss consists in this, that not only were those benefits lost, but humanity's will turned away from God. As a result, we want and do none of the things God wants and commands. Likewise, we have no knowledge about what God is, what grace is, what righteousness is, and finally what sin itself is. [. . .][r]

o This translation is based on LW 1:141–98, edited by Jaroslav Pelikan. The text has been updated, especially with regard to greater inclusivity.

p Headings in brackets have been added to guide the reader. They do not appear in the original text.

q This singular male pronoun has been translated as a plural pronoun.

r The figure [. . .] indicates commentary text is cut. Here, portions of LW 1:141, para. 2 through 142, para. 2 have been removed.

2. For Luther, the will (Lat. *voluntas*) meant a human ability that was situated both in the highest part of a human being, that is, in his or her spirit and also in the soul. In other words, there is a spiritual will and a more mundane and psychological will. The former wants either divine things (e.g., the will and power to fight against various spiritual anxieties) and the latter more ordinary things (e.g., whether or not to build a house or have a candy). See, e.g., WA 40/1 [Dr]:292,19—295,34. Luther also argued that Christian hope is the subject of the (spiritual) will. See WA 40/1:21,15-18; WA 40/2 [Dr]:26,11-13,28,22-24. Luther thought that an individual does not have true freedom of choice especially in spiritual matters (see *On the Bondage of the Will* [1525], TAL 2:153-257).

3. For Luther, the intellect meant either mundane intellect (e.g., the ability to evaluate various scenarios in everyday life) or spiritual intellect (e.g., the correct understanding of Christ and other spiritual things). WA 40/1:21,15-18; WA 40/2 [Dr]:26,11-13,28,22-24.

From the image of God, from the knowledge of God, from the knowledge of all the other creatures, and from a very honorable nakedness humanity has fallen into blasphemies, into hatred, into contempt of God, yes, what is even more, into enmity against God. I am now saying nothing about the tyranny of Satan,[s] to whom this wretched nature has been subjected because of sin. This should be emphasized, I say, for the reason that unless the severity of the disease is correctly recognized, the cure is also not known or desired. The more you minimize sin, the more will grace decline in value. [. . .]

Therefore[t] in theology let us maintain that reason in human beings is most hostile to God, and that the respectable will is most opposed to the will of God.[4] From this source arise the hatred of the word and the persecution of godly ministers. For this reason, as I said, let us not minimize this evil which human nature has contracted as a result of the sin of our first parents; rather let us emphasize it. Then we shall both regret deeply this state of ours and have a profound longing for Christ, our Physician, who was sent by the Father to heal those evils which Satan brought upon us through sin, and to restore us to the eternal glory which we had lost.

4. Elsewhere, Luther argues that our spiritual abilities are corrupted because of sin, but our natural abilities are (at least to some measure) untouched, because we have the ability to build a house, to hold an office and other such things based on Gen. 1:28. (Cf. WA 40/1 [Dr]:293,19f.)

[Historical Interpretation]

As for the historical event of which Moses gives us an account in this present chapter, I stated my opinion before, that this temptation appears to me to have taken place on the sabbath; thus, Adam and Eve[5] were created on the sixth day, Adam earlier and Eve toward evening. Early on the following sabbath Adam preached to Eve concerning God's will: that the most gracious Lord had created the entire Paradise for the use and enjoyment of people; that, also as a result of God's extraordinary goodness, he

5. Luther identifies Adam and Eve as those humans who were created on the sixth day. He therefore does not differentiate between the first and second creation story nor (naturally) ponder, whether they originate from different sources (cf. modern exegesis). Luther, in addition, speaks here about Eve, although the original text speaks only about a woman; the name Eve is given to her later (Gen. 3:20).

s A good and comprehensive study about Luther's understanding of the devil (or Satan) is Hans-Martin Barth, *Der Teufel und Jesus Christus in der Theologie Martin Luthers* (Göttingen: Vandenhoeck & Ruprecht, 1967); see esp. 190–96 about the fall, where Barth, e.g., says that Luther argued in his *Commentary on Romans* that the original sin came from the external cause (= the devil) to human beings, but sinful deeds can be traced to humans.

t See LW 1:143, para. 3.

had created[6] the tree of life,[u] through the use of which the powers of the body would be refreshed and perpetual youth would be maintained. But one other tree—the tree of the knowledge of good and evil—was forbidden and from it was not permitted to eat. This kind of obedience they showed to their friendly Lord. When Adam said this to Eve, perhaps he led Eve about in Paradise and showed her the forbidden tree.

In this way Adam and Eve, resplendent with innocence and original righteousness, and abounding in peace of mind because of their trust in God, who was so kind, walked about naked while they discoursed on the word and command of God and praised God, just as should be done on the sabbath. But then, alas, Satan interfered and within a few hours ruined all this, as we shall hear.

[Why the Fall Occurred]

Now here, too, a sea of questions arises. Inquisitive people ask why God permitted Satan to tempt Eve. Furthermore, why Satan ambushed Eve through the serpent rather than through a different animal. But who can supply the reason for the things that he sees the Divine Majesty has permitted to happen? Why do we not rather learn with Job that God cannot be called to account and cannot be compelled to give us the reason for everything he does or permits to happen? Why do we not likewise register a complaint with God because the earth does not produce plants and because the trees are not green throughout the year? I am fully convinced that in Paradise there would have been perpetual spring without any winter, without snow and frosts, such as we have today after sin. But these are all things under the divine power and will. To know this is enough. Besides, it is wicked curiosity to investigate these problems in greater detail. Therefore let us, who are clay in God's hands, cease to discuss such questions. Let us not sit in judgment on our God; let us rather be judged by him.[7]

Hence, the answer to all such inquiries must be only this: It pleased the Lord that Adam should be tempted and should test

u "Trees were a nearly universal symbol of life in the ancient Near East, and 'trees-of-life' particularly represented the divine power responsible for fertility in plant life"; see Bill T. Arnold, *Genesis* (Cambridge: Cambridge University Press, 2009), 58.

6. Luther emphasized in his *Lectures on Genesis* that God created the whole world through creative words. See WA 42:13,11–17,23.

7. For Luther, God's goodness is a self-evident fact, in spite of the evilness of the world. The goodness of God is also beyond human comprehension. Although God's goodness is beyond human comprehension, "faith and spirit" believe that God is good even if all humans would be damned. In fact, God's goodness was, for Luther, a matter of faith. Human reason without faith would consider God good only if he would save all people. See WA 18:685,25–686,13; 702,9-20; 707,32–708,23; 784,1-20; 785,31-38.

This picture appears in an edition of the Luther Bible published in 1550. It was quite usual in the beginning of the sixteenth century to make a biblical picture multidimensional. This painting depicts events from Genesis 2–3, including the creation of a woman from Adam's rib, the fall, expulsion from Eden.

his powers. [. . .] Here[v] there is another question. Perhaps it can be discussed with less danger but with greater profit. It is: "Why does Scripture make this account so obscure? Why does it not rather state directly that the angel who had fallen entered the serpent, was speaking through the serpent, and deceived Eve?"[w] But I answer: "This account is so obscure in order that all things might be held over for Christ and for his Spirit, who was to shed light throughout the entire world like the midday sun and to

v See LW 1:145, para. 2.

w There is a long Judeo-Christian history regarding the idea that the serpent was influenced or possessed by the devil. See a thorough explanation of this history in Jussi Koivisto, "Martin Luther's Conception of the Serpent Possessed by the Devil (Gen 3) and the Antecedent Tradition," in *Wading Lambs and Swimming Elephants: The Bible for the Laity and Theologians in the Late Medieval and Early Modern Era*, ed. Wim François and August den Hollander (Leuven: Peeters, 2012), 111–52. This article shows that Luther was influenced by John Chrysostom, Augustine's *De Genesi ad litteram*, and shared many similar ideas regarding the serpent as the Eastern and Western fathers. In addition, he knew such medieval works as *Glossa ordinaria*, Nicholas of Lyra's *Postilla literalis super totam Bibliam*, as well as the complete Bible commentary published under the name of Hugh of St. Cher. Luther, however, was more in accordance with the fathers than medieval tradition regarding the serpent. Luther, e.g., emphasized the cunning of the serpent as a suitable tool for the devil—just as the fathers had done.

open all the mysteries of Scripture." Because this Spirit of Christ was in the prophets (1 Pet. 1:11), the holy prophets understood such mysteries of Scripture.

[Why Temptation Came through the Serpent]

But we said above that as animals have their different endowments, the serpent excelled in the gift of cleverness.[8] For this reason it was more suited for this game of Satan.[x] A sufficiently clear proof of this is this text of Moses, which declares that there was extraordinary cleverness in the serpent, more than in the other animals. We marvel today at the cleverness which foxes display in lying in wait, then also at their wonderful skill in escaping from danger. Sometimes, after it is worn out by running, it throws its tail before the pursuing dogs. When the dogs fall upon it with great vehemence and stop their running, it gains some distance by its wonderful speed and so escapes. There are

x Cf. Westermann, *Genesis 1–11*, 237–39, where he denies, e.g., the possibility that the serpent is a demon or divine being opposed to God, because "the text says nothing about such enmity toward God." Westermann's explanation is that there is no explanation of evil about its origin: "The origin of evil remains a complete mystery." Cf. James McKeown, *Genesis* (Grand Rapids: Eerdmans, 2008), 34: "Throughout the ancient world, the serpent was considered as a divine or semi-divine symbol. In Gilgamesh Epic the hero finds a plant that could give immortality, but while he is swimming in a pond a snake swallows the plant." According to McKeown, snake symbolizes evil in Genesis (35). See also Hermann Gunkel, *Genesis übersetzt und erklärt* (Göttingen: Vandenhoeck & Ruprecht, 1977), 15; Gerhard von Rad, *Genesis: A Commentary* (London: SCM Press, 1985), 87–88: "In the history of religions the snake indeed is the sinister, strange animal par excellence (v. d. Leeuw), and one can also assume that long before, a myth was once at the basis of our narrative"; Arnold, *Genesis*, 62–63: "One possibility is that the mythological figure behind the serpent is Canaanite Baal, appearing in the form most tempting to ancient Israel, that of a serpent." In any case, according to my opinion the serpent is depicted in Genesis hostile toward God and it is, therefore, correct to presume that the serpent represents in the story some kind of God's antagonist—although he is created by God. It is interesting that in the book of Job Satan (= antagonist) has a similar role to the serpent. He is among the sons of God (Job 1:6) and still its name means "antagonist" and it is given the power to harass Job in a grave way.

8. The serpent is called "more crafty" (Lat. *callidior*). The Hebrew equivalent, עָרוּם, is ambiguous: it carries both negative and positive connotations. See *Theological Dictionary of the Old Testament*, ed. G. J. Botterwerck, H. Ringgren, and H.-J. Fabry (Grand Rapids: Eerdmans , 2001), 11:362–63. See also Claus Westermann, *Genesis 1–11*, A Continental Commentary, trans. J. J. Scullion, S.J. (Minneapolis: Fortress Press, 1994), 239: "The cunning of the serpent is proverbial (Mt 10:16); it is associated with its ability to produce poison or to change its skin." See also Gordon J. Wenham, *Genesis* (Waco: Word, 1987), 72, about עָרוּם: "On the one hand it is a virtue the wise should cultivate (Prov. 12:16; 13:16), but misused it becomes wiliness and guile (Job 5:12; 15:5; cf. Exod. 21:14; Josh. 9:4)." See also ibid., 73: "Within the world of Old Testament animal symbolism a snake is an obvious candidate for an anti-God symbol, notwithstanding its creation by God." Cf. Arnold, *Genesis*, 62–63, to Wenham, *Genesis*, 72. Luther does not ponder the negativity or positivity of this notion.

also some other animals whose extraordinary skill and industry we admire. But this quality in the serpent was extraordinary. Therefore it appeared to Satan to be a convenient tool through which to ambush Eve.

[Fall from True Worship]

[1b.] Who said to the woman:
Did God really command you not to eat from every tree of Paradise?

[. . .] [T]he serpent directs its attack at God's good will and makes it its business to prove from the prohibition of the tree that God's will toward humanity is not good. Therefore it launches its attack against the very image of God and the most excellent powers in the uncorrupted nature. The highest form of worship itself, which God had ordained, it tries to destroy. It is, therefore, vain for us to discuss this or that sin. Eve is simply urged on to all sins, since she is being urged on against the word and the good will of God.[9]

Accordingly, Moses expresses himself very carefully and says: "The serpent said," that is, with a word it attacks the word. The word which the Lord had spoken to Adam was: "Do not eat from the tree of the knowledge of good and evil" [Gen. 2:17]. For Adam this word was gospel and law;[10] it was his worship; it was his service and the obedience he could offer God in this state of innocence. These Satan attacks and tries to destroy. [. . .]

For[y] when the gospel is preached in its purity, people have a sure guide for their faith and are able to avoid idolatry. But then Satan makes various efforts and trials in an effort either to draw people away from the word or to corrupt it. [. . .] Therefore[z] Satan here attacks Adam and Eve in this way to deprive them of the word and to make them believe his lie after they have lost the word and their trust in God. Is it a wonder that when this happens, a person later on becomes proud, that he is a scorner of God and of human beings, that he becomes an adulterer or a murderer? Truly, therefore, this temptation is the sum of all temptations; it brings with it the overthrow or the violation of the entire Decalogue.[11] Unbelief is the source of all sins; when

y LW 1:146, para. 3.

z LW 1:147, para 2.

9. For Luther the most severe sin was idolatry and the most important commandment was the first one. Other sins are more or less a consequence of an idolatry. See LC in BSLK (12th ed., 1998), 572:48. Many modern commentators consider—just like Luther—the opening words of the serpent as a distortion of God's word. Modern commentators also emphazise the psychological skilfullness of these words. See, e.g., Von Rad, *Genesis*, 88.

10. Cf. WA 40/1 [Dr]:517,31–527,27; esp. 526,21-22: *Sic ergo Christianus divisus est in duo tempora. Quatenus est caro sub lege est, quatenus Spiritus, sub Evangelio est.* In this long passage from his *Lectures on Galatians* (1531/1535), Luther carefully discusses the relationship between the law and the gospel. According to Luther, God's law hinders evil humans to do more evil deeds and betokens that all humans are (born) sinful and need the gospel (i.e., God's mercy). It is obvious that before the fall the law and gospel had a different role, according to Luther: the prohibition to eat from the tree of knowledge of good and evil was both law and gospel at the same time. In other words, Adam lived in a stage of innocence and therefore obediently and gladly obeyed the only command: it did not cause, e.g., anxiety or hatred like in the fallen world.

11. The Ten Commandments (Exod. 20:1-17; Deut. 5:6-21).

Satan brought about this unbelief by driving out or corrupting the word, the rest was easy for him.

Thus, when Eve had permitted herself to be driven away from the word by a lie, it was very easy to approach the tree and pick fruit[a] from it. [. . .] For the chief temptation was to listen to another word and to depart from the one which God had previously spoken: that they would die if they ate from it. But let us consider Moses's words in their order.

In the first place, Satan imitates God.[12] Just as God had preached to Adam, so he himself also preaches to Eve. What the proverb says is true: "Every evil begins in the name of the Lord." Therefore just as from the true word of God salvation results, so also from the corrupt word of God damnation results. By "corrupt word," however, I do not mean only the ministry of the spoken word but also the inner conviction or opinions that are in disagreement with the word.

Moreover, Moses indicates this by the word: "It said" [Gen. 3:1]. Satan spoke in order to lead them away from what God had said; and after he had taken away the word, he made corrupt the perfect will which humans had previously had, so that he became a rebel. He corrupted the intellect also, so that it doubted the will of God. The eventual result is a rebellious hand, extended against the will of God, to pick the fruit. Next the mouth and the teeth become rebellious. In short, all evils result from unbelief or doubt of the word and of God. For what can be worse than to disobey God and to obey Satan?[13] [. . .]

Thus,[b] a new god is invented by Satan for humans without their even being aware of it. For he also sets a word before them, but not the kind which has been put before us by God, namely, that repentance and remission of sin should be preached in the name of Christ (Luke 24:47). When the word of God is changed or perverted in this way, then, as Moses says in his song (Deut. 32:17), "come new and recent gods, whom our fathers did not worship."[14]

a Luther often uses the Latin word *pomum* (fruit). Cf. Von Rad, *Genesis*, 90: "The tradition about the apple tree derives from Latin Christianity and may be occasioned by the association *malus* ('bad'), *malum* ('apple')."

b LW 1:148, para. 3.

12. Luther discusses many times in his works how the devil imitates either God or Christ (e.g., in his *Lectures on Galatians*). For Luther, the devil imitates God, either leading humans astray or accusing them too severely in the conscience. See WA 40/1 [Dr]:96,10–11; 130,36–131,20; 298,19–299,28; 315,21–322,21.

13. Notice that, for Luther, the original and the first sin is not the actual transgression of God's commandment, but the unbelief preceding it. In fact, in the light of the inner structure of Genesis 3 this is possible and I would say the best interpretation. Before the woman takes the fruit from the forbidden tree, she sees this tree in a new light after she has discussed with the serpent: "So when the woman saw that the tree was good for food, and that it was a delight to the eyes, and that the tree was to be desired to make one wise, she took of its fruit and ate; and she also gave some to her husband, who was with her, and he ate" (Gen. 3:6; NRSV). In other words, the perspective of the woman changes after the discussion: the tree is no longer forbidden, but an instrument to become godlike (including knowledge of both good and evil). This is one of the most central ideas both in Luther's interpretation and also in the text of Genesis 3.

14. For Luther, the struggle of true faith was first and foremost a struggle about the correct biblical interpretation.

It is useful to know these snares. If Satan were to teach that people ought to kill, commit fornication, and disobey their parents, who would not realize that he is suggesting something that is forbidden by the Lord? Therefore it would be easy to be on one's guard against him. But here, when he propounds another word, when he discourses about the will of God, when he uses the names "God," "the church," and "the people of God" as a pretext, then people cannot so readily be on guard against him. But we need the keenest judgment of the spirit to distinguish between the true God and the new god, as Christ distinguished when Satan tried to persuade him to demand that the stones become bread and to hurl himself from the pinnacle of the temple (Matt. 4:3-7). Satan wanted to persuade Christ to attempt something without the word. But he could not deceive Christ as he deceived Eve, for he held to the word and did not allow himself to be led away from the true God to the false, new god.

The source of all sin truly is unbelief and doubt and abandonment of the word. Because the world is full of these, it remains in idolatry, denies the truth of God, and invents a new god. [. . .]

[The Devil's Temptation as Original Sin]

And[c] so this passage helps us to learn that this temptation of the devil was the beginning of original sin, when he led Eve away from the word of God to idolatry, contrary to the First, the Second, and the Third Commandments.[15]

15. As this passage shows, Luther thought that the true cause and beginning to original sin was in the devil. See also WA 18:675,34-37.

Here properly belong these words: "Did God actually command you?" [Gen. 3:1]. This is an instance of the awful boldness of the devil, as he invents a new god and denies the former true and eternal God with such unconcern and assurance. It is as if he were to say: "Surely you are silly if you believe that God has given such a command, for it is not God's nature to be so deeply concerned whether you eat or not. Inasmuch as it is the tree of the knowledge of good and evil, how can such ill will come upon him that he does not want you to be wise?"[d]

c LW 1:149, para. 3.

d Cf. E. A. Speiser, *Genesis: Introduction, Translations and Notes* (Garden City: Doubleday, 1964), 26: "The Heb. stem *yd'* signifies not only 'to know,' but more especially 'to experience, to come to know' . . . in other words, the verb describes both the process and the result." and Von Rad, *Genesis*, 89: "For the ancients, the good was not just an idea: the

Furthermore, this unspeakable villainy is sufficient proof that Satan was the architect of this affair, although Moses makes mention of the serpent only and not also of Satan. Although these statements are ever so veiled, nevertheless, through the enlightenment of the Holy Spirit, the holy fathers and prophets readily saw that this was not an affair of the serpent, but that in the serpent there was that spirit, the enemy of innocent nature, of whom Christ declares clearly in the gospel that he did not stand in the truth and that he is a murderer and liar (John 8:44).[16] It remained for the gospel to present all this with greater clarity and to point out this enemy of God and humanity.

Moreover, the fathers realized this very thing on the basis of the following reasoning: It is certain that at that time all creatures were in perfect obedience, according to the statement (Gen. 1:31): "And God saw all that he made, and it was very good." But here, in the case of the serpent, a spirit betrays itself who is the enemy of God and who corrupts the word of God in order by this means to lead the innocent human being into sin and death.

[The Serpent Possessed by the Devil]

It is clear, therefore, that in the serpent there was something worse, something that could properly be called the adversary of God, a lying and murderous spirit, in whom there is the utmost and most awful smugness. He is not afraid to distort the command of God and to urge man on to idolatry, which he knew would result in the destruction of the entire human race. [. . .]

At[e] first Eve resists the tempter admirably. For she is still being led by that Spirit who was lighting her path, just as we showed above that man was created perfect and according to the likeness of God. But in the end she allows herself to be persuaded.

It is uncertain on what day the fall of the angels occurred, whether on the second or on the third.[17] Only this much can be shown from the gospel, that Satan fell from heaven, inasmuch as Christ declares that he saw him fall from heaven (Luke 10:18).

good was what had a good effect; as a result, in this context 'good and evil' should be understood more as what is 'beneficial' and 'salutary' on the one hand and 'detrimental,' 'damaging' on the other." See also Wenham, *Genesis*, 73.

e LW 1:150, para. 3.

16. Many church fathers, e.g., Chrysostom (c. 347–407), Ambrose (339–397), Tatian (c. 120–c. 180), Irenaeus (c. 125–c. 202), Procopius of Gaza (c. 465–c. 527), and Theophilus of Antioch (d. 183), and Christian scholars used passages such as John 8:44; Rev. 12:9; and Wisd. 2:24 to argue that the devil was involved in the fall or influenced and spoke through the serpent. The connection between the serpent and the devil was also present in Second Temple Judaism, and in the Apocrypha and Pseudepigrapha of the New Testament (e.g., *Arabic Gospel of the Infancy of the Savior* 16; *First Gospel of the Infancy of Jesus Christ* 23). Luther focuses mainly on John 8:44 in proving that the devil influenced through the serpent. In addition, he argues that Genesis 3 itself proves this. How else could it have been possible that the serpent can dispute about the commandment of God unless it was influenced by a higher being? See Koivisto, "Martin Luther's Conception of the Serpent," 118–20, 146–49.

17. The fall of angels is an old Christian idea that is based on some biblical texts (e.g., John 8:44 and Jude 6) and further developed by, e.g., church fathers and medieval scholars. Some church fathers (Tatian, Irenaeus, et al.), for example, tried to respond to the criticism of Celsus, a Greek opponent of Christianity in the second century, by developing (based on the biblical material; e.g., Rev. 12:9) the idea that Eve's assailant was in fact a fallen angel. Celsus criticized Genesis 3 by arguing that the speaking serpent resembles more an old wives' tale than divinely inspired history. Also Augustine (354–430) argued that "collusive prosecuting angels" were deservingly thrown down

We do not know whether the heavens at that time were finished or still crude and unfinished.[18]

But this discussion is not pertinent to this passage. What is pertinent is that we perceive the utmost villainy, combined with an awful smugness, which makes this spirit unafraid to cast doubt on the command of the Divine Majesty, especially when he knows what great misfortune will follow for the whole human race.

Secondly, consideration must be given also to his extraordinary cleverness, which becomes evident immediately, when Satan assails the greatest strength of men and women and battles against the very likeness of God, namely, the will that was properly disposed toward God. The serpent's cleverness, says the text, was greater than that of all the animals on earth.

But this cleverness is superior to the natural cleverness of the serpent because it discusses with man the word and the will of God. This the serpent could not do in its natural state, since it had been placed under the rule of man.[f] However, the spirit who is speaking in the serpent is so cunning that he outwits the man and persuades him to eat the fruit of the forbidden tree. Therefore the one who speaks here is not a creature of God which is good; he is the bitterest enemy of God and of humans. He, too, is a creature of God, but he was not created evil by God. "For he did not stand in the truth," as Christ says in John 8:44. These clear conclusions follow from the gospel and from this text.

Satan's cleverness is perceived also in this, that he attacks the weak part of the human nature, Eve the female, not Adam the male. Although both were created equally righteous, nevertheless Adam had some advantage over Eve. Just as in all the rest of nature the strength of the male surpasses that of the other sex, so also in the perfect nature the male somewhat excelled the female. Because Satan sees that Adam is the more excellent, he does not dare assail him; for he fears that his attempt may turn out to be useless. And I, too, believe that if he had tempted Adam first, the victory would have been Adam's. He would have crushed the serpent with his foot and would have said: "Shut up! The Lord's command was different." Satan, therefore, directs his attack on Eve as the weaker part and puts her valor to the

f Cf. Gen. 1:28; WA 40/1 [Dr]:293,29–32.

from celestial seats in their perversity and pride. See Augustine, MPL 34, *De Genesi contra Manichaeos in libri duo*, cols. 430–31; also Koivisto, "Martin Luther's Conception of the Serpent," 118–20, 125–27, 144–49, esp. 146: ". . . just like the first humans, angels were also originally in a sort of middle stage where they were created in a stage of innocence with a chance to fall from it. If all the angels and humans had remained in this stage of innocence, they would later have been confirmed ('*confirmare*') so as not to fall, as (the Church) fathers suggest according to Luther. Actually, good angels did not fall earlier and they cannot fall from their current being: their good status is confirmed. Still, the first humans and a large number of the angels fell."

18. In *De servo arbitrio* about ten years earlier (1525), Luther also discusses the fall of the devil. However, he uses quite enigmatic expressions about the fall of the devil. According to Luther, God "discovers" the will of the devil to be evil. The will of Satan became evil when it deserted God and sinned. However, why and how this exactly occurred, Luther does not answer. One reason for this is the fact that the Bible does not give a clear answer to this question. See WA 18:711,7–19; 712,26–31.

test, for he sees that she is so dependent on her husband that she thinks she cannot sin.[g]

Here, too, we are reminded of the divine permission, namely, that the devil was permitted to enter beasts, as he here entered the serpent. For there is no doubt that it was a real serpent in which Satan was and in which he conversed with Eve.

The Fall and Banishment of Adam and Eve from Paradise by Michelangelo (sixteenth century). Note that the serpent is depicted as having a woman's face, a feature common in the thought of medieval and early modern theologians.

Some carry on laughable discussions about whether the serpent had a human face.[19] It was a most beautiful little animal; otherwise Eve would not have conversed with it so calmly. However, after sin it was not only the beauty of the serpent that was changed—for God threatens that it will creep on the earth, while previously it walked erect, like a rooster,[20] and that it will eat earth, while previously it lived on the better fruits (Gen. 3:14)—but also that freedom from fear has been lost, for we flee from

g See also Mickey Leland Mattox, *"Defender of the Most Holy Matriarchs": Martin Luther's Interpretation of the Women of Genesis in the Enarrationes in Genesin, 1535–1545* (Leiden: Brill, 2003), 54–57, 63–65, 92, 99, where he, e.g., argues that although Luther, who was experienced in family life, cannot be said to have taken "a position that could be regarded from the standpoint of contemporary sensitivities as proto-feminist," still his ideas on women changed to a more positive direction in regard to Eve's positional relationship to her husband before the fall. In his Genesis lectures, Luther does not typify Eve as the heretic; now the heretic is Satan instead.

19. In some medieval and early modern paintings (e.g., Michelangelo) the serpent was depicted with a human face. Already before Luther this matter was discussed among scholars. However, this is not such a ridiculous question as Luther suggests. The serpent in the story can speak. Because humans are the only creatures on Earth with the ability to speak (at least a language that humans can understand), it is conceivable that the mouth and face of a speaking serpent might differ from that of an ordinary snake and instead resemble human faces. On the other hand, the story does not evidently fit everyday categories, so Luther is therefore correct in that it is impossible to provide an exact description of the serpent's face.

20. The idea of a serpent walking like a rooster may first sound far-fetched, but is actually a plausible interpretation. Namely, later in the story (Gen. 3:14), God metes out a punishment to the serpent to crawl on its belly. Therefore, according to Genesis 3, it is probable that the serpent walked on its feet or moved in some other notional manner. On the other hand, there are also other plausible explanations. See, e.g., Arnold, *Genesis*, 68: "This curse does not mean the serpent once walked upright with legs anymore than it wants the reader to assume the serpent will now literally eat dust as opposed to its previous fare. Rather these are idioms for humiliation. The serpent, who had been characterized as the shrewdest of all the animals, will now become the most humble."

serpents just as the serpents, in turn, flee from us. These wounds of nature were inflicted on account of sin, just as we have lost our nakedness, our upright will, and our sound intellect. And I believe, too, that the serpent has also lost most of its cleverness, which Moses mentions here as an extraordinary gift of the Creator. Just as today the serpent is the evil one among the animals, so I hold that it was then a beautiful, good, blessed, and lovely creature, with which not only man but also the rest of the animals enjoyed living. Therefore it was also best suited for Satan's plan to speak through it and to incite Eve to sin.[21]

This is my idea about the natural serpent, which Satan wanted to misuse and which at that time was a most beautiful little beast, without the poisonous tail and without those ugly scales; for these were added after sin. Similarly, we find in Moses a command that animals which have caused a death should be killed (Exod. 21:28), for no other reason than that Satan sinned through them by bringing death to a human being. Thus, the serpent has been punished, in proof of this fall and devilish villainy.

[Temptation: Is God Inconsistent?]

But so far as grammar is concerned, the Latin translation renders the little expression אַף כִּי with "why."[h] Although this may not be quite right, it does not clash too much with the sense; for the first and foremost temptation occurs when God's counsel is discussed: "Why did God do this or that?" According to my opinion, however, the emphasis is not placed on that little word "why" or on the question but rather on the name אֱלֹהִים ("God"). For this lends greater force to the temptation.[22]

It is as if Satan were saying: "Surely you are very silly if you think that God did not want you to eat from this tree, you whom

h This Hebrew expression can also be translated "Is it really so?" See Matti Liljeqvist, *Heprea-suomi, aramea-suomi: Vanhan testamentin sanakirja* (Saarijärvi: Aikamedia Oy, 2004), 214.

21. The positive characteristics of the serpent, such as beauty, goodness, blessedness, and loveliness, are plausible interpretations, although Genesis 3 describes the serpent only as cunning. The woman, namely, talks with the serpent quite confidentially and seems to speak with it willingly. Therefore, it is probable that the serpent was not intimidating before the fall.

22. Luther is careful to answer questions like why God allowed evil to slither into the world, but he also presented views on how one can find some sense in evil: (a) evil can test the church and its members; (b) we can find some answers to the meaning of the fall through the (enigmatic or mystical) illumination of Christ's Spirit; (c) in the future fulfillment we can comprehend through the light of glory that God, whose judgment in this life is one of incomprehensible justice, proves to be the most righteous in eschatological fulfillment; (d) the omnipotent God uses evil beings "in accordance with his wisdom for his own glory and our salvation." See Jussi Koivisto, *Is Evil Inevitable for Creation and Human Life? Studies on Martin Luther's Biblical Interpretation* (Helsinki, diss., 2012), esp. 164–65. However, one of the most interesting explanation to why-questions regarding evil is from Luther's *Table Talk*, year 1540 (see LW 54:385–86): "If God should be asked at the last judgment, 'Why did you permit Adam to fall?' and he answered, 'In order that my goodness toward the human race might be understood when I gave my Son for the salvation of humanity,' we would say, 'Let the whole human race fall again in order that thy glory may become known! Because thou hast accomplished so much through Adam's fall we do not understand thy ways.'"

he appointed lords over all the trees of Paradise. In fact, he created the trees on your account. How can he, who favored you with all these things, be so envious as to withhold from you the fruits of this one single tree, which are so delightful and lovely?" Satan is seeking to deprive them of the word and knowledge of God that they may reach the conclusion: "This is not the will of God; God does not command this." The words which follow also support this opinion when he says: "You will not die." Satan has staked everything on this one effort to draw them away from the word and faith, that is, from the true God to a false god. [. . .]

Therefore[i] since the main point of the temptation is to bring about doubt whether God said this, the emphasis is more properly placed on the noun "God." The little word "why" makes for a rather weak meaning. Hence, I rather favor the translation: "Did God say: 'You will not eat from every tree of the garden'?" Satan is not really concerned with inquiring about the reason why God said this. He is rather concerned with this: in order for him to deprive Eve of the word, she should reach the conclusion that God simply did not say this. He sees that reason can easily be deceived in this way, when, under the pretense of God's name and word, God and word are lost.[23]

Again he shows his cunning by speaking in general and including all the trees together. It is as if he were saying: "You have the universal rule over all the beasts. Should not God, who gave you this universal rule over all the beasts, also give you all the trees? What you ought to think is: 'Just as God has put the whole earth and all the animals under us, so he has also permitted the use of all the things that spring from the earth.'"

This is surely a great temptation. With it Satan tries to induce Eve's mind[24,j] to reach the conclusion that God is inconsistent.

i LW 1:153, para. 1.

j See also Wilfried Joest, *Ontologie der Person bei Luther* (Göttingen: Vandenhoeck & Ruprecht, 1967), 193, according to which the soul is "the middle between the body and the spirit" (*anima medium inter corpus et spiritum*). Thus, the spirit signifies the relationship with God and the body signifies the presence in the world that is constrained by death. Luther's anthropology is influenced by Origen's (c. 185–c. 254) distinction between spiritual and bodily senses that had a considerable influence on medieval mysticism. See, e.g., Simo Knuuttila, *Emotions in Ancient and Medieval Philosophy* (Oxford: Clarendon, 2004), 126, 133, 144–45, 198, 284; WA 18:774,17f.;

23. For Luther these types of spiritual doubts caused by the devil were the most severe form of anxiety. In his *Lectures on Galatians* (1531/1535), for example, he argues that spiritual tribulations, where an individual suspects God's mercy toward him, may even lead to suicide. Luther, e.g., describes how the devil can transform as "the angel of light" and imitate Christ. A depressed person may think that Christ is haunting and persecuting her. However, this is not the case. Christ is, according to Luther's biblical interpretation, intercessor, comforter, savior, throne of grace, etc. See WA 40/1 [Dr]:96,10f.; 130,36f.; 298,19f.; 315,21f. See esp. 299,14–17.

24. Here the original Latin word for mind is *animus* (also meaning, e.g., soul or spirit or the rational soul); see WA 42:115,30–31. Luther thought that a human being consists of spirit, soul, and body (cf. 1 Thess. 5:23). The spirit is the highest part of human being, because it can understand, e.g., invisible and eternal things. In addition, it is just like a house, where God's word and faith live. He also thought that the wisdom belonged to the spirit. Instead, the soul analyzes more mundane things. It makes rational, everyday decisions and also controls the body. In this mundane or psychical level, human abilities were not corrupted by sin like in the spirit. Luther, on the other hand, thought that when Christian faith enlightens the spirit and gives true wisdom to it, this faith also influences soul and bodily functions. For example, when faith enlightens the spirit, e.g., the mouth works in different way: it does not speak blasphemous things about God, but praises God's mercy instead. See WA 7:550,19f.; WA 40/1 [Dr]:293,19f.; WA 40/2 [Dr]:178,16f.

Accordingly, if he turned over all the other creatures, he also turned over all the trees. Therefore it follows that the command about not eating of the tree is not God's command, or at least is not to be understood as though he did not want anyone to eat from this tree.[25]

Thus, a twofold temptation is put before Eve, by which, however, Satan has the same end in view. The first is: "God did not say this; therefore you may eat from this tree." The second is: "God has given you everything; therefore you have everything in your possession; therefore this one single tree is not forbidden you." However, each aims at the same end: that Eve be drawn away from the word and from faith. This command about not eating from the tree, which was given them by God, is a convincing proof that even if his nature had remained perfect, Adam, together with his descendants, would have lived in faith until he would have been translated from this physical life to the spiritual life.[k] Where the word is, there necessarily faith also is. Here is the word that he should not eat of this tree; otherwise he would die. Therefore Adam and Eve ought to have believed that this tree was detrimental to their welfare. Thus, faith is included in this very commandment.

We who are being brought out of sin into righteousness and from our mortal body to the immortal body also live in faith. But we have a different word, which Adam did not have when his nature was perfect, since he would have been directly translated from the physical life to the spiritual. For this reason I said above that this tree in the middle of the garden would have been like a temple in which this word would be preached: that all the other trees were wholesome, but that this one was destructive. Therefore they should have learned to obey God and to render him the service of refraining from eating of it, since God had forbidden it.

WA 40/1 [Dr]:291,29f.; WA 40/2 [Dr]:111,32f.; 116,20f. See, about Luther's anthropology, Eero Huovinen, *Kuolemattomuudesta osallinen. Martti Lutherin kuoleman teologian elumeeninen perusongelma* (Helsinki: Suomalaisen teologisen kirjallisuusseuran julkaisuja 130, 1989), 43.

k Cf. WA 42:84,15f. See also WA 42:66,7–27, where Luther argues that humans and animals differ from each other: the former have a hope of immortality and they are created as an image and similitude of God.

This proves that Luther sometimes spoke about soul (Lat.: *animus* or *anima*; Ger.: *die Seele*) when he meant spirit or about spirit (Lat.: *spiritus*; Ger.: *der Geist*) when he meant soul. In addition, Luther differentiated between two parts of the soul: (1) the temporal and mortal; (2) the immortal. The former dies in this life, while the latter lives immortally the future life. See WA 5:385,17f.

25. Compare Wenham, *Genesis*, 74–75: "But commentators have often pointed out, the snake was uttering half-truths . . . ," with Von Rad, *Genesis*, 90: "The serpent neither lied nor told the truth. . . . One should also observe that it speaks no summons; it simply gives men the great stimulus from which decision can be made quite freely." Luther therefore transfers the guilt more on the serpent (or more precisely the serpent possessed by the devil) than some modern commentators.

In this way uncorrupted nature, which had the true knowledge of God, nevertheless had a word or command which was beyond Adam's understanding and had to be believed. Moreover, this command was given to Adam's innocent nature that he might have a directive or form for worshiping God, for giving thanks to God, and for instructing his children. Since the devil sees this and knows that this command is beyond the understanding of the human being, he tempts Eve so that she herself may proceed to ponder whether this is God's command and will or not. This is the beginning and the main part of every temptation, when reason tries to reach a decision about the word and God on its own without the word.

It was God's intention that this command should provide humanity with an opportunity for obedience and outward worship, and that this tree should be a sort of sign by which people would give evidence that they[l] were obeying God. But by getting a discussion under way as to whether God had commanded this, Satan is trying to lead man away from this obedience to sin. In this situation the only salvation would have been if Eve had laid emphasis on God's command and had not allowed herself to be drawn away to other discussions about whether God had commanded this, or whether, since God had created everything for the sake of humans, this one tree had been created for their ruin. It seems a matter of wisdom to investigate these questions rather carefully; but the moment the mind engages in discussions of this kind, it is done for. Now let us hear what Eve's reply was.

[Doubt—Beginning of the Fall]

2. To this the woman answered:
Of the fruit of the trees which are in Paradise we eat;
3. but of the fruit of the tree which is in the midst of Paradise
God commanded us not to eat or to touch it, lest perchance we die.

The beginning is rather favorable: she makes a distinction between the remaining trees and this one, and she quotes God's command. But she begins to waver when she comes to the mention of the punishment. She does not mention the punishment

l The masculine singular is here rendered as plural.

as God had stated it. He had simply stated (Gen. 2:17): "On whatever day you will eat from it, you will surely die." Out of this absolute statement she herself makes one that is not absolute when she adds: "Lest perchance[26] we shall die."

This is a striking flaw, and one that must not be overlooked; for it shows that she has turned from faith to unbelief.[27] For just as a promise demands faith, so a threat also demands faith. Eve should have maintained: "If I eat, I shall surely die." On this faith Satan makes such inroads with his crafty speech that Eve adds the little word "perchance." She had been persuaded by the devil that God was not so cruel as to kill them for eating the fruit. To this extent Eve's heart was now poisoned with Satan's venom.[28, m]

For this reason our text here, too, has been poorly translated. It reads as though Eve were quoting her own words; actually, she is quoting God's words, and on her own she is adding to God's

Eve and the serpent, from *Speculum humane salvationis* (Augsburg, 1470)

26. The word "perchance" (Lat.: *forte*) is based on the Latin version of the Bible (= Vulgate) that was widely used in the Middle Ages. However, this word is omitted from the Masoretic and Septuagint texts. Although Luther's translation of the Old Testament is based on the Masoretic text, he still uses the Latin version of the Bible in his *Lectures on Genesis* (1535–1545). The reason for this is probably the fact that Latin was the official language (and lingua franca) in universities and among scholars at that time. In addition, the Latin version of Genesis also fits better with Luther's interpretation than the Masoretic or Septuagint text, because the word *perchance* or *perhaps* (Lat.: *forte*) reflects doubts that Eve (or more precisely the woman) was having. Therefore, it is an indication of sinful transformation before the sinful deed itself. Also modern commentators acknowledge doubts or alterations in her words. See, e.g., Von Rad, *Genesis*, 88.

27. Cf. Genesis 3, where the woman sees (as a result of the persuasion of the serpent) the tree of knowledge of good and evil from a different perspective: it does not represent God's command anymore, but offers knowledge without God instead.

28. Luther's ideas regarding (original) sin as a venom which corrupts Eve's heart resembles a "Manichaean" heresy that is condemned and described in the *Formula of Concord* (FC) in the following manner: "even after the fall human nature is originally created pure and good but that Satan infuses and mixes original sin (as something essential) into this nature from the outside, as poison is mixed with wine." On the other

m See more about Manicheanism and about its influence on Augustine, who had some influence on Luther's theology and is probably the most famous ex-Manichean: e.g., Jason David BeDuhn, *The Manichaean Body: In Discipline and Ritual* (Baltimore: Johns Hopkins University Press, 2000); Jacob Albert Van Den Berg, *Biblical Argument in Manichaean Missionary Practice: The Case of Adimantus and Augustine,* Nag Hammadi and Manichaean Studies 70 (Leiden: Brill, 2010); Johannes van Oort, Otto Wermelinger, and Gregor Wurst, eds., *Augustine and Manichaeism in the Latin West: Proceedings of the Fribourg-Utrecht International Symposium of the International Association of Manichaean Studies (IAMS),* Nag Hammadi and Manichaean Studies 49 (Leiden: Brill, 2001).

word the little word "perchance." And so the deceit of the lying spirit met with success. What he sought to achieve above all—to lead Eve away from the word and faith—this he has now achieved to the extent that Eve distorts the word of God; that is, to use Paul's language, he has turned her away from the divine will, so that she goes after Satan (1 Tim. 5:15). But it is the beginning of one's ruin to turn away from God and to turn to Satan, that is, not to remain constant in the word and in faith. When Satan sees these beginnings, he now exerts himself with his utmost power, as though against a leaning wall, in order to overwhelm her altogether.

hand, FC refers many times to Luther's conception of original sin as poison and leprosy. The part that analyzes original sin even ends at a quotation taken from Luther's lectures on Genesis: "We are poisoned by the venom of original sin from the soles of our feet to the hairs on our head because it befell us in this perfect nature." This may seem contradictory. Luther, however, does not represent the Manichaean heresy. He explicitly condemns Manichaean heresies in his Genesis lectures. See BSLK (12th ed., 1998), 770f., 843f.; Koivisto, *Is Evil Inevitable?*, 117f.; WA 42:159,7f.

[Satanic Oratory]

4. And the serpent said to the woman: You will in no wise die;
5. but God knows that on that day on which you will eat from the tree your eyes will be opened, and you will be like God, knowing good and evil.

This is Satanic oratory, with which he completely overpowers the pitiable woman when he sees that she has turned away from God and is ready to listen to another teacher. When he said above: "God did not give you this command, did he?" he did not openly deny the word; but through the nature of his question he tried to raise a doubt in Eve. Now, after he sees that he has achieved this, he begins with utmost boldness to deny the word of God directly and to charge God with lying and with cruelty. It is not enough for him that Eve added the little word "perhaps"; but out of the little word "perchance" he now makes a negative and says: "You will not die."[29]

Therefore we see here what an awful thing it is when the devil begins to tempt a person. One lapse involves another lapse, and an apparently slight wrong brings about a prodigious lapse. It was something serious to turn away from God and from God's word and to lend her ears to Satan. But what is something far more serious now happens: that Eve agrees with Satan when he charges God with lying, and, as it were, strikes God in the face with his fists. Therefore Eve no longer shows any aversion as in the first temptation; but she joins with Satan in despising God and denying the word of God, and she believes the father of lies rather than the word of God.

29. Luther could have developed his idea of the corruptive words of the serpent further. There is an interesting difference in effective power between the words of God and the words of the serpent: God's words take effect immediately, but the words of the serpent take effect with a time lag (see Genesis 1–3).

Let these events be a warning for us that we may learn what human beings are. For if this happened when nature was still perfect, what do we think will happen to us now? And we have examples before our eyes. For many of those who originally thanked God with us for his revealed word have not only fallen away but have become our adversaries. [. . .]

Thus,[n] so far as the passage before us in Moses is concerned, the words were most simple: "From the tree in the midst of Paradise you shall not eat." But reason did not understand the purpose of these words, why God wanted it to be so. Therefore Eve perishes while she investigates too inquisitively and refuses to be satisfied with what she had heard the Lord command. Thus, this temptation is a true pattern of all temptations with which Satan assails the word and faith. Before the desire to eat of the fruit arose in Eve, she lost the word which God spoke to Adam. If she had adhered to this word, she would have continued in the fear and faith of God. Where the opposite happens and the word is lost, there is contempt of God and obedience to the devil.

All this is useful, that we may learn, as Peter says (1 Pet. 5:9), to stand undaunted in temptation and to resist the tempter while holding on to the word with a firm faith and closing our ears so as not to grant admittance to what is foreign to the word. For truly, these afflictions of Eve and Adam are lessons for us, in order that we may not have the same experiences by being drawn away from the word and from faith.

What follows in the text: "God knows that your eyes will be opened" has a double meaning. On the one hand, it can be understood to mean that Satan said this to stir up resentment against God for not wanting humans to eat so useful a fruit, that in this way Eve might begin to hate God as though he bore them too little good will. Or, on the other hand—and this is how I understand it—he praises God that he might the more easily involve Eve in his treachery. It is as if he said: "Surely God is not such a one that he wants you to live in darkness, as it were, without any knowledge of good and evil. He is good. He does not begrudge you anything that is useful and helpful to you in any way. He will take it calmly that you are like him."

When Satan praises God in this way, then, in truth, he has a razor in his hand to cut man's throat. The fall becomes very easy

n LW 1:157, para. 5.

when the pretense of the word and the will of God are added to what desire suggests. This is the reason why I incline to the understanding that this was said by Satan in order to persuade Eve rather than to stir up resentment against God. Yet I leave it to you to adopt what you please. The gist certainly is that he is trying to lead Eve away from the word and to persuade her to do what had been forbidden by the word. He is a very bitter enemy of the word of God because he knows that our salvation rests on obedience to the word.

[Death Awaits]

Here a question which is not at all senseless is raised: how it happens that Eve is not yet aware of her sin. Although she has not yet eaten the fruit, she has already sinned against the word and faith; for she has turned away from the word to a lie, from faith to unbelief, from God to Satan, and from the worship of God to idolatry. Since this was the main feature of her sin (for picking the fruit was not the main feature), how does it happen that death does not follow immediately? How does it happen that she does not realize her sin? What's more, how does it come that after she herself has eaten the fruit, she does not experience death before she has also persuaded Adam to eat?[30] [. . .]

In[o] the first place, God is long-suffering; therefore God does not punish sin immediately. Otherwise it would happen that we would immediately perish in our sins. This long-suffering of God Satan abuses, since it is advantageous for his purpose that people should not immediately become aware of his sin. And so it happens that because the punishment is delayed, Satan fills the heart with smugness, and humans not only do not become aware that they have committed sin, but are even glad over it and rejoice in their sins.

The very same thing happens to Eve here. Through her unbelief she had fallen from the word into a lie. Therefore before God's eyes she was already dead. Because Satan restrains her mind and eyes, however, she not only does not see death or become aware of it, but gradually she is also more inflamed by her desire for the fruit and delights in this idolatry and sin. If, then, she had not drawn away from the word, looking at the fruit and desiring

30. Luther suggests here evidently that the true fall was to look at the tree in a new light, because of Satanic oratory. This is an excellent and nonstereotypical interpretation of Genesis 3, where the vision of the woman changes twice: (1) when she looks at the tree in a new light; and (2) when her eyes are opened to see the sin she has done. Cf. Wenham, *Genesis*, 75: "Actions hitherto characteristic of creator are now ascribed to the woman. She 'saw . . . that the tree was good,' clearly echoing the refrain of Gen 1, God saw . . . that it was good.'"

o LW 1:159, para. 3

to eat of it would have been something horrible for her. Now she turns this sin over in her mind with pleasure. Where formerly she would have fled if she had seen someone else stretching out his hand toward that tree, she is now impatient of delay, since sin has taken over her lower limbs and has burst forth from her heart. Thus, this delight and desire to eat the fruit are like a disease born of sin, upon which death later follows. Meantime, while Eve is sinning, she does not feel it, as the sequel shows.[31]

31. Just like the sinful transformation corrupts an individual from head to toe, the transformation and renewal of the Holy Spirit liberates from this corruption from head to toe (although imperfectly during this lifetime), according to Luther. Cf. WA 40/2 [Dr]:178,16f.

[Sin: Poison Corrupting All the Senses]

6. And so the woman saw that the tree was good for eating
and beautiful for the eyes and delightful, because it made wise.
She took of its fruit and ate, and she gave to her husband, and he ate.

See how sin is gradually spread to all the senses.[p] After Eve has believed Satan, contrary to God's word, that she will not die, but rather that her eyes will be opened, and she will know evil and good, what does she neglect to do that is needed to make her sin greater? Her eyes cannot be satisfied by the appearance. It is not enough for her that she has the knowledge of God and a sound reason; she wants the knowledge of evil to be added. But this is Satan's very own poison, that she wants to have insight beyond what was commanded. This wisdom is death, and it is hostile to the wisdom of God which was given her in the command; it has the effect that she regards as righteousness what is sin; and what is the utmost folly she imagines to be the highest wisdom.[q]

The emphasis, therefore, lies on what the Latin text nevertheless has omitted, namely, that the tree appeared delightful because it would make people wise.[32] This is what the devil is wont to bring about in all his temptations, that the farther man

32. Luther is correct in saying that the Vulgate does not include (unlike the Hebrew Masoretic text) the reason for the delightment of the tree: "because it made wise." Cf. *Biblia Hebraica Stuttgartensia*, ed. K. Ellinger and W. Rudolph (Stuttgart: Deutsche Bibelgesellschaft), 4.

p The Latin word *sensus* means also understanding, perceiving, observation, thought, instinct, feeling, etc. Luther uses it here probably to refer to five human senses. Cf. WA 40/1 [Hs]:316,2–3 : "Diabolus est, potest sic ludifacere omnes 5 sensus, ut iures veram rem, et tamen merum ludibrium."

q The idea of spiritual vision (whether corrupted or not), which means wisdom, comprehension, or lack of them, is also an old Christian idea. See Augustine and the case of Holy Macarius in *Vitae patrum*, MPL 21, c. 451.; cf. WA 40/1 [Dr]:319,18f.

draws away from the word, the more learned and the wiser he appears to himself. [...] But[r] the temptation involving wisdom is far more effective than those cruder ones involving lust, greed, pride, etc.

The verb הִשְׂכִּיל denotes "to be prudent," from which is derived מַשְׂכִּיל, "wise," "prudent," as in Ps. 14:2: "God looked down from the heaven upon the children of men, whether anyone was understanding and sought God." Also Isa. 52:13: "My servant יַשְׂכִּיל, will deal prudently." In the strict sense it denotes that wisdom by which God is known. But Eve had that light, or sun, in her heart[s] before, because she had the word; then also she had the knowledge of all the creatures. But when that wisdom is not satisfied, it wants to rise higher and know God in a way different from his revelation of himself in his word. Here is the fall, that, after losing the true wisdom, she plunges into utter blindness. [...]

These[t] actions dare not be regarded lightly; for they are, as the saying is, pregnant with the punishments which we endure, such an awful condition of sin and such an awful antipathy to God. We ought to look at and think about these, instead of confining ourselves to the fruit that was plucked and swallowed. Those who look only at the action and not at the sin from which this action followed cannot do otherwise than charge God with cruelty, that because of so small a sin he has inflicted such great punishment on the entire human race. [...]

[Sin against the Word of God]

Thus,[u] we must pay attention to the word. Moreover, this is God's word. And so, just as important as the word is, so important also is the sin which is committed against the word. To this sin our entire nature has succumbed. How could it overcome this sin, since its magnitude is inexhaustible? To overcome this

r LW 1:161, para. 1.

s Luther spoke of the anthropological center of spirituality, e.g., with the following biblical terms: the mind (*mens*), the heart (*cor*), the conscience (*conscientia*), and the spirit (*spiritus*). See Koivisto, *Is Evil Inevitable?*, 49. Cf., e.g., Ps. 34:19; Gal. 3:1; and 1 Tim. 1:19.

t LW 1:162, para. 2.

u LW 1:162, para. 3.

sin, we need God who brings with him inexhaustible righteousness, that is, the Son of God.

And this also reveals Satan's cunning. He does not immediately try to allure Eve by means of the loveliness of the fruit. He first attacks humanity's greatest strength, faith in the word. Therefore the root and source of sin are unbelief and turning away from God, just as, on the other hand, the source and root of righteousness are faith.[v] Satan first draws away from faith to unbelief. When he achieved this—that Eve did not believe the command which God had given—it was easy to bring this about also, that she rushed to the tree, plucked the fruit, and ate it. The outward act of disobedience follows sin, which through unbelief has fully developed in the heart. Thus, the nature of sin must be considered in accordance with its true immensity, in which we have all perished. Now follows the disclosure of the sin together with its punishments.

[Temptation and Sin]

7. Then the eyes of both were opened;
and when they realized that they were naked,
they sewed together leaves of the fig tree and made themselves girdles.

I said above that the pattern of all the temptations of Satan is the same, namely, that he first puts faith to trial and draws away from the word. Then follow the sins against the Second Table.[33] From our own experience we perceive that this is his procedure. The events which now follow deal with the description of sin: what its nature is when it is active, and what it is later on when it lies in the past. For while it is active, it is not felt; otherwise we would be warned by the ill effects which sin brings on, and we would draw back. But because these lie hidden, we proceed

33. Regarding the sins against the Second Table, Luther means sins against neighbor (i.e., sins against commandments 4–10 in the Ten Commandments). The sins against the First Table mean sins against God (i.e., sins against commandments 1–3 in the Ten Commandments). Cf. Deut. 10:1-5; 2 Chron. 5:10.

v Cf. WA 40/1 [Dr]:427,11–24, where Luther compares the incarnation of Christ to the manner in which faith incarnates to action and love. See esp. 11–12, *Quare fides perpetuo iustificat et vivificat, et tamen non manet sola, id est, otiose.* See also Peter Manns, "*Fides absoluta—Fides incarnata.* Zur Rechtfertigungslehre Luthers im Großen Galater-Kommentar," in *Vater im Glauben: Studien zur Theologie Martin Luthers*, Veröffentlichungen des Instituts für europäische Geschichte 131 (Stuttgart: Steiner-Verlag-Wiesbaden, 1988), 8–9.

smugly to the deed itself after we have forsaken our uprightness and faith. Eve trespassed similarly in the instance of the fruit after she had been persuaded, contrary to the word of God, that she would not die, but that her eyes would be opened and she would become wiser. This poison of Satan she drank with her ears; she stretched out her hand to the forbidden fruit; and she ate it with her mouth. And so she sins through all her senses of soul and body, and yet she is not aware of her sin. She eats the fruit with pleasure, and she urges her husband also to do the same.

Eve Tempts Adam (1504),
engraving by Albrecht Dürer

These experiences are alike in all temptations and sins, whether of lust or of anger or of greed. While sin is active, it is not felt. It does not frighten, and it does not bite; but it flatters and delights. And inasmuch as these things happened when nature was still perfect, it is not surprising that they happen likewise to us, who are infected with the poison of original sin from the soles of our feet to the crowns of our heads. [. . .] But when later on sin is revealed through the law, then it weighs too heavily on man.[34]

But before this revelation, while sin is being committed, Eve's eyes are not open; otherwise she would have died rather than touch the fruit. But because her eyes are not yet open and unbelief remains, there remain both the delight in the forbidden fruit and the eagerness and the desire to acquire a wisdom which was also forbidden. Poor Eve is so engrossed in unbelief both in spirit and in body that she does not realize that she is doing evil.[35] [. . .]

As[w] soon as the eyes of Eve are opened, she remembers the law which she had previously forgotten and which commanded them not to eat from the forbidden tree. Before the knowledge of this law she was without sin, just as Paul says in Rom. 7:9: "I was living some time without the law," not because the law was not in existence but because he did not feel the threats and punishments of the law. To himself, therefore, he seemed to be without sin. "For through the law comes the knowledge of sin" [NRSV; Rom. 3:20]. Therefore when the law becomes alive again, sin also becomes alive at the same time.[x]

This Moses points out in the account about our first parents when he says: "Their eyes were opened." It is as if he were saying: "Satan had closed not only the eyes but also the heart of Eve through the unbelief and disobedience of all her members within and without. But after sin was allowed to enter and was committed, he blithely allows their eyes to be opened that they may see what they had done." Here Satan seeks to make another gain, namely, that those who have sinned should perish in despair.[36] [. . .] But[y] what Moses adds—that after eating the fruit they saw that they were naked—is not without a purpose. If it is carefully considered, it contains a beautiful description of original righteousness. [. . .]

[Original Righteousness]

[R]ighteousness[z] was not a gift which came from without, separate from human nature, but it was truly part of that nature,

w LW 1:164, para. 1.

x Cf. Wenham, *Genesis*, 76.

y LW 1:164, para. 4.

z LW 1:165, para. 2.

34. Luther sees an analogy between the fall (to original sin) mentioned in Genesis 3 and how original sin manifests in a fallen world: at first, sin seems harmless (e.g., eating from the forbidden tree or transgressing of the Ten Commandments), but afterwards, when God or God's law reveals it, it terrifies.

35. Although Luther speaks about a new vision regarding the tree, this vision is blindness to the fact that she is committing a sin.

36. Luther distinguishes in his *Lectures on Galatians* (1531/1535) two types of despair: harmful and useful. The former occurs when an individual does not trust in God in various anxieties but also loses, e.g., the passion for life. The latter, holy despair, occurs when an individual understands that they cannot save themselves and are sinful, but still trust in Christ and pray for mercy. This is useful and realistic desperation, because it makes God's mercy necessary. On the other hand, this proper desperation goes hand in hand with the will to overcome sin with the power of God. Luther also accuses, in his *Lectures on Galatians*, Satan as the cause of harmful despair. See WA 40/1 [Dr]:50,12f.; 131,15f.; 320,25f.; 517,31f.; WA 40/2 [Dr]:26,18f.; 92,17f.

so that it was Adam's nature to love God, to believe God, to know God, etc. These things were just as natural for Adam as it is natural for the eyes to receive light. But because you may correctly say that nature has been damaged if you render an eye defective by inflicting a wound, so, after humanity has fallen from righteousness into sin, it is correct and truthful to say that our natural endowments are not perfect but are corrupted by sin. For just as it is the nature of the eye to see, so it was the nature of reason and will in Adam to know God, to trust God, and to fear God. Since it is a fact that this has now been lost, who is so foolish as to say that our natural endowments are still perfect? And yet nothing was more common and received more general acceptance in the schools than this thesis. But how much more foolish it is to make this assertion about the demons, about whom Christ says that they did not stand in the truth (John 8:44) and whom we know to be the bitterest enemies of Christ and of the church![37]

Therefore the perfect natural endowments in humanity were the knowledge of God, faith, fear, etc. These Satan has corrupted through sin; just as leprosy poisons the flesh, so the will and reason have become depraved through sin, and man not only does not love God any longer but flees from God, hates him, and desires to be and live without him.

Therefore this is an excellent description of the corruption which has taken the place of original righteousness and glory. It was glory for Adam not to realize that he was naked.[a] Moreover, what can be a greater depravity than that the nakedness which formerly was a glory is now turned into the greatest disgrace? No one blushes because of healthy and sound eyes. Distorted or weak eyes are regarded as less becoming and bring on shame. So in the state of innocence it was most honorable to go about naked. Now, after sin, when Adam and Eve see that they are naked, they are made ashamed, and they look for girdles with which to cover their disgrace. Yet how much greater disgrace is there in this, that the will is impaired, the intellect depraved, and the reason entirely corrupt and altogether changed! Is this what they mean when they say that our natural endowments are perfect?

a Cf. Von Rad, *Genesis*, 91: "To appear naked before God was an abomination for ancient Israel. In the cult every form of bodily exposure was carefully guarded against (Ex. 20.26)."

37. Compare this to Luther's lectures on Galatians a few years earlier, where he speaks about the natural abilities of a human being in positive tones (WA 40/1 [Dr]:293,19–33). On the other hand, Luther differentiates between mundane and spiritual abilities: the former can be called (at least to some measure) intact, but the latter abilities are corrupted because of the fall (WA 40/1 [Dr]:292,19–295,34). However, this does not mean that Christian faith would not have an influence on mundane things. It even affects positively politics and economics (WA 40/1 [Dr]:106,15f.). A ruler, for example, without the guidance of the (Holy) Spirit may neglect his duties (e.g., he does not punish guilty and protect innocents) and start unjust wars based on his sinful desires. One important and challenging theme is also the question how much Luther thought that an individual has true freedom of choice in mundane things. I think that the best answer to this is given in Marjorie O'Rourke Boyle, "Stoic Luther: Paradoxical Sin and Necessity," in *Archive for Reformation History* 73 (Gütersloh: Gütersloher Verlagshaus Gerd Mohn, 1982), 86–88: "It is the same binary perspectival system that operates in Luther's argument. In the initial occurrence of his necessitarian dogma in the Assertio, he explains that 'from a human perspective [*nobis ad inferna spectantibus*] things appear arbitrary and fortuitous, but from the divine viewpoint [*sed ad superna spectantibus*] all things occur necessarily.'"

But see what follows if you maintain that original righteousness was not a part of nature but a sort of superfluous or superadded gift. When you declare that righteousness was not a part of the essence of a human being, does it not also follow that sin, which took its place, is not part of the essence of a human being either? Then there was no purpose in sending Christ, the Redeemer, if the original righteousness, like something foreign to our nature, has been taken away and the natural endowments remain perfect. What can be said that is more unworthy of a theologian?

Therefore let us shun those ravings like real pests and a perversion of the Holy Scriptures, and let us rather follow experience, which shows that we are born from unclean seed and that from the very nature of the seed we acquire ignorance of God, smugness, unbelief, hatred against God, disobedience, impatience, and similar grave faults.[b] These are so deeply implanted in our flesh, and this poison has been so widely spread through flesh, body, mind, muscles, and blood, through the bones and the very marrow, in the will, in the intellect, and in reason, that they not only cannot be fully removed but are not even recognized as sin. [. . .]

The[c] fact that Adam and Eve walked about naked was their greatest adornment before God and all the creatures. Now, after sin, we not only shun the glance of others when we are naked; but we are also bashful in our own presence, just as Moses states here about Adam and Eve. This shame is a witness that our heart has lost the trust in God which they who were naked had before sin. Therefore even if Adam had been blind, he still would have been afraid to show himself naked to the eyes of God and of others, because through his disobedience his confidence in God was lost.

[. . .] Just as it was part of human nature to walk about naked, full of trust and assurance toward God, and to be pleasing to God and others this way, so now, after sin, mortals are convinced that this nakedness of the innocent nature is offensive to God,

b Cf. this to BC (SD), 532–33, 538, which argues that when God creates human beings, "original sin is transmitted through carnal conception and birth from father and mother through the sinful seed."

c LW 1:167, para. 1.

Luther's Understanding of Stages in Humanity*

Human being in the state of innocence

spirit trust God; spiritual life without corruption of sin
soul very powerful in all measures
body very powerful in all measures

Description of a fallen human nature

spirit superstitious, heretical or/and its object of trust is in something other than true God (e.g., money)
soul works quite well in mundane things (e.g., building a house, working), but cannot be compared to natural abilities before the fall
body works together with soul (e.g., senses like vision, etc.), but has lost glory and power because of the fall

Description of a Christian who fights against sin under guidance of the Holy Spirit

SINFUL "FLESH"	VS.	HOLY SPIRIT
spirit superstitious, etc. (cf. the fallen human being)		**spirit** trusting, believing, and hoping in true God
soul works well in mundane life, but sins		**soul** works well in mundane life, but does not sin
body works well in mundane things but sins		**body** works well in mundane things but does not sin

Human being in future fulfillment

Abilities in every measure surpass previous stages; an individual loving perfectly both God and other humans

* This chart, made by the author, illustrates how Luther understood various stages in humanity and human anthropology in the 1520s and 1530s (for example, see Luther's *Lectures on Galatians* and *Lectures on Genesis*).

to themselves, and to all the creatures; and they provide clothing to cover his body. Is this not a change of nature? The nature indeed remains; but it is corrupted in many respects, inasmuch as confidence toward God has been lost and the heart is full of distrust, fear, and shame.[d] Thus, the parts of our body remain the same. But those which, when they were naked, were looked upon with glory are now covered up as shameful and dishonorable, as a result of the inner revolt; for through sin nature has lost its confidence in God. If we believed, we would not be ashamed.

[Sexual Lust]

Out of this corruption which followed because of sin there followed another evil. Adam and Eve not only were ashamed because of their nakedness, which previously was most honorable and the unique adornment, but they also made girdles for themselves for the purpose of covering, as though it were something most shameful, that part of the body which by its nature was most honorable and noble. What in all nature is nobler than the work of procreation? This work was assigned by God neither to the eyes nor to the mouth, which we regard as the more honorable parts of the body, but to that part which sin has taught us to call the pudendum and to cover, lest it be seen. Moreover, although in the innocent nature the entire work of procreation would have been most holy and most pure, after sin the leprosy of lust has made its way into this part of the body. Hence, those who live outside the married state burn most shamefully. And unless those who live in the married state restrain their passions and carefully guard their relations with each other, they encounter all sorts of temptations.

Are we not, then, going to realize at last what a hideous and awful thing sin is, inasmuch as lust alone can be cured by no remedy, not even by marriage, which was ordained by God as a

d Cf. Von Rad, *Genesis*, 91: "If shame was the sign more of a disturbance in man's relation to other men, then fear before God was the sign of a disorder in his relation to his Creator. Fear and shame are henceforth the incurable stigmata of the Fall in man."

remedy for our weak nature? Most of those who are married live in adultery and sing the familiar little verse about their wives: "I can live neither with you nor without you." This awful disgrace has its source in the most honorable and most excellent part of our body. Most excellent I call it because of the work of procreation, which is a most excellent one inasmuch as it preserves the species. And so through sin the most useful members have become the most shameful.

Assuredly, this would not have been the case in the instances of Adam and Eve. They were full of faith toward God. And so, as often as they would have wanted to beget children, they would have come together, not urged on by that passion which is now in our leprous flesh but admiring God's dispensation and obeying him with the utmost restraint, just as we now come together to hear the word of God and to worship him. All these things we have lost through sin to such an extent that we can conceive of them only in a negative and not in a positive way. From the evil which we have with us we are forced to infer how great the good is that we have lost. However, we owe thanks to God that we still have remnants of the work of procreation, be they ever so corrupted, which the church and state both need. [. . .]

The[e] word תֲּגוֹרָה, which occurs here in the plural, strictly denotes a girdle. From this you will understand that the fig leaves covered every part of the thigh, so that the part which was most honorable before sin was covered as though most disgraceful and unworthy of the eyes of all others. Oh, what an awful fall into sin! The eyes of a human being are opened in such a way that what was most honorable he now looks upon as most disgraceful.

And so it still is. [. . .] Such[f] is simply the habit of people. Even when they have been caught and are being held, they nevertheless try to get off, so that they may not be dismayed but may appear good and righteous. This poison, too, has been infused into our nature through sin, as the passage before us proves.

e LW 1:169, para. 1.

f LW 1:169, para. 3.

[Sin, Cause of Fear]

8. And when they had heard the voice of the Lord *God,*
who was walking in Paradise at the breeze of the day,
Adam and his wife hid among the trees of Paradise
from the face of the Lord.

[. . .] Therefore[g] after their conscience has been convicted by the law and they feel their disgrace before God and themselves, Adam and Eve lose their confidence in God and are so filled with fear and terror that when they hear a breath or a wind, they immediately think God is approaching to punish them; and they hide.[h] I, too, think that by the voice of the Lord, who was walking about, Moses means the wind or the sound of the wind, which preceded the appearance of the Lord. Similarly, in the gospel Christ says of the wind (John 3:8): "You hear its sound." When they heard the leaves rustling as if they were being moved by the wind, they thought: "Behold, now the Lord is coming to demand punishment from us."

Therefore when Moses later adds: "Toward, the wind of the day," it seems to me that he is explaining himself, as if he were saying: "There was a sound like that of the wind of the day," so that emphasis lies on the word "day." He does not refer to the wind in the night, because he wants to lay greater emphasis on the prodigious fear which followed sin, as if he were saying: "They were so fearful that even in the bright light of day they were afraid of the rustling of a leaf." What would have happened if God had come in the dark and during the night? For then the terror is far greater. Just as light makes people courageous, so darkness increases their fear. This fear, which overtook Adam and Eve in the very light of day after their sin, is a clear indication that they had fallen completely from the faith. [. . .]

Here[i] again you see the immensity of original sin, with which we are born and which has been planted in us through the sin of our first parents. Moreover, this detriment also helps us to gain an insight into original righteousness on the basis of what we have lost, or by way of contrast. For in human beings there

g LW 1:170, para. 2.

h Cf. Wenham, *Genesis*, 76: "A more complete transformation could not be imagined. The trust of innocence is replaced by fear of guilt."

i LW 1:171, para. 2.

was the most admirable confidence in God, and they could not have been afraid even if they had seen the heavens collapse. [. . .] Oh,[j] what a grievous downfall, to plunge from the utmost sense of security, from confidence and delight in God into such awful terror that humans shrink from the sight of God more than from the sight and presence of the devil! Adam and Eve were not avoiding the devil; it was God, their Creator, whom they were avoiding! Him they judged to be more troublesome and more dreadful than Satan. But Satan they consider better than God, for they do not avoid Satan. And so this fear is really an avoidance and hatred of God.

[Gradual Growth of Sin]

Moreover, it is worthwhile to note how sin gradually grows until it becomes exceedingly sinful sin, as Paul is wont to call it (Rom. 7:13). First humanity falls from faith into unbelief and disobedience. Then fear, hatred, and avoidance of God follow unbelief, and these bring with them despair and impenitence. For where should the heart in its fright flee from the presence of God? To the devil? This is neither an advantageous nor an advisable thing to do, and yet it turns out this way. And so this account shows that God created human beings[k] and made them lord of all, and yet they avoid God and consider nothing either more hateful or more unbearable than God. Otherwise they would not have turned away from God; they would not have avoided him; and he would not have trembled at the voice of God when he was coming, not at night, not with lightning and thunder, as at Sinai, but in the clear light of day, while a light and delightful breeze was blowing and the leaves of the trees were gently stirring. Thus, there is nothing more grievous, nothing more wretched, than a conscience frightened by the law of God and by the sight of its sins.

This brings about what is worst: that Adam and Eve avoid their Creator and God and take refuge under the protection of the fig trees, both to cover themselves and to hide in the midst

j LW 1:171, para. 3.

k In this paragraph, single male pronouns have been rendered as plural for the sake of inclusivity.

of the trees. What can be termed more horrible than to flee from God and to desire to be hidden from him?

Here again it becomes evident how righteous our will and intellect is after sin! Their very action shows that their will has become depraved, because they have a desire for what was forbidden by God; they aspire to become disobedient to God but obedient to the devil. Nor can we have any doubt that their intellect was depraved when we look at the stratagem by which Adam and Eve think they are safe. Or is it not the height of stupidity, in the first place, to attempt the impossible, to try to avoid God, whom they cannot avoid? In the second place, to attempt to avoid him in so stupid a way, that they believe themselves safe among the trees, when iron walls and huge masses of mountains could not save them? When confidence in God has been lost in this way, there follows an awful fright in the will; and when the superb gifts of wisdom and understanding have been lost, there follows the utmost stupidity, so that they attempt the impossible by the most stupid means. To such an extent original sin is an inexhaustible evil. And yet these instances are, as it were, preludes. For the verdict, which is ghastly and terrible, had not yet been reached.

[Trial Begins]

9. And the LORD God called Adam
and said to him: Where are you?

This is the description of the trial.[38] After Adam has become terrified through the awareness of his sin, he avoids the sight of God and realizes that not only Paradise but the entire world is too narrow to be a safe hiding place. And now, in that mental agony, he reveals his stupidity by seeking relief from sin through flight from God. But he had already fled too far from God. Sin itself is the real withdrawal from God, and it would not have been necessary to add any further flight. Thus, it happens—and this is the nature of sin—that the farther one withdraws from God, the farther that person still desires to withdraw; and having once fled and apostatized keeps on fleeing forever. [. . .]

Accordingly,[l] when Moses says: "He called him," this must be understood to mean that he called Adam to judgment. [. . .]

38. Cf. Arnold, *Genesis*, 66: "So the chapter moves summarily from crime (vv. 1–7) to punishment (vv. 8-24). This is the first time we encounter this theme that extends into the rest of the Primeval History (Gen. 1–11), and indeed throughout the Pentateuch as a whole: 'Creation–Uncreation–Re-creation.'"

l LW 1:173, para. 2.

But[m] it should be noted particularly that Moses specifically says that Adam was called, namely, that he was the only person to whom on the sixth day the word of the Lord regarding the fruit of the forbidden tree was addressed. Therefore just as he alone heard the commandment, so he alone is first called to trial. But because Eve also sinned and fell away from God, she hears the verdict at the same time and shares in the punishment.

The words "Where are you?" are words of the law. God directs them to the conscience. [. . .] He is speaking according to our way of thinking; for he sees us considering how we may withdraw from his sight. Therefore when God says: "Where are you?" it is the same as if he were saying: "Do you think I do not see you?" He wants to show Adam that though he had hidden, he was not hidden from God, and that when he avoided God, he did not escape God. [. . .] He[n] had stupidly hoped to be able to hide; and, behold, he stands before God's judgment seat and is now called in for his punishment.

God calling to Adam (Genesis 3:9) from *Figures de la Bible*, illustrated by Gerard Hoet (1648–1733) and others. Published by P. de Hondt in The Hague (1728).

[Evidence of Sinful Transformation: Adam's Absurd Response]

10. And he said: I heard your voice in Paradise, and I was afraid because I was naked; and I concealed myself.

Just as Adam stupidly began to flee, so he answers most stupidly; so thoroughly had sin deprived him of all discernment and good sense. He wants to inform God that he is naked—God, who created him naked. By this action he confuses himself, betrays and condemns himself with his own mouth. He says that he heard God's voice and was afraid. But had he not heard the voice of the Lord before, when He forbade him to eat of the forbidden tree? Why was he not afraid then? Why did he not hide then? Why did he stand glad and upright when he saw and heard God before him? But now he is terrified by the rustling of a leaf (Lev. 26:36). It follows, therefore, that Adam is no longer the same that he was, but that he has undergone a change and has become a different person, one who is looking for a fictitious reason as

m LW 1:173, para. 3.
n LW 1:174, para. 1.

his excuse. How can it be true that the reason for his fear is the voice, when previously he did not fear the voice but heard God with delight?

[...] He[o] says that the reason for his flight was not that he had sinned, but that he had heard the voice of the Lord and was frightened by it and became ashamed because he was naked. The poor fellow does not reflect that he did not have this fear previously and that he had not been ashamed because of his nakedness. Since it was something that God had created, why is he afraid on account of that which God made? Naked he had previously walked about in the sight of God and of all the creatures in Paradise, assured of God's goodwill and delighting in God. Now he is ashamed because he is naked; he flees from God and conceals himself. All these facts are sure proofs by which Adam condemns himself and betrays his sin.

In the same way the ungodly will condemn themselves at the last judgment, when the dark recesses of human hearts will be revealed and, as though in open books, the evil deeds of every single being will be read. God indeed knows that Adam sinned and that he is guilty of death. However, God questions him so that by his own witness Adam himself may prove himself guilty of having committed sin; for he is fleeing from God, something which in itself is a sin, just as it is a virtue[p] to take one's refuge in God. Although Adam hopes to be able to cover his sin with a lie, he brings this witness against himself when he says that the reason for his flight was the voice of the Lord and his own nakedness.

Let us learn, therefore, that this is the nature of sin: unless God immediately provides a cure and calls the sinners back, they[q] flee endlessly from God and, by excusing their sin with lies, heap sin upon sin until they arrive at blasphemy and despair. Thus, sin by its own gravitation always draws with it another

o LW 1:174, para. 2.

p Lat.: *virtus*, which means also, e.g., strength. Luther thought that various virtues are a gift from God and fruits of the Holy Spirit (cf. Gal. 5:22-23), which are engendered and strengthened, e.g., through a sermon. See, e.g., WA 40/1 [Dr]:351,36f.

q Singular male pronouns in the original text are rendered as plural in this paragraph.

sin and brings on eternal destruction, till finally the sinful persons would rather accuse God than acknowledge their own sin. Adam should have said: "Lord, I have sinned." But he does not do this. He accuses God of sin and says in reality: "You, Lord, have sinned. For I would have remained holy in Paradise after eating of the fruit if you had kept quiet." This is in reality the meaning of his words when he says: "I would not have fled if your voice had not frightened me."

Thus, when one has been accused of sin by God, he does not acknowledge his sin but rather accuses God and transfers his guilt from himself to the Creator. The outcome is that in this way sin grows endlessly unless God through his mercy grants his help.[39] This wickedness and utmost stupidity Adam regards as supreme wisdom. He has become so confused by his fright that he does not realize what he is saying or what he is doing, and by excusing himself he brings the most serious charges against himself and increases his sin to huge proportions.

39. Cf. Koivisto, *Is Evil Inevitable?*, 162: "Luther also deemed that liberation from various forms of evil, including sin, possession, and bewitchment, was only possible through pastoral care or spiritual healing orchestrated by the Holy Spirit."

However, we must not think that this happened to Adam alone. We, each one of us, do the same thing; our nature does not permit us to act otherwise after we have become guilty of sin. We all prefer to accuse God rather than to acknowledge it before God. [. . .]

[Adam in the Midst of Death and Hell]

11.[r] The LORD said to him: But who told you that you were naked? Have you not eaten from the tree about which I had commanded you that you should not eat?

Here Adam's conscience is roused by the real sting of the law. It is as if God said: "You know that you are naked, and for this reason you hid. But your nakedness is my creation. You are not condemning it as something shameful, are you? Therefore it was not the nakedness that perplexed you, it was not my voice that frightened you; but your conscience convicted you of sin because you ate the fruit from the forbidden tree." Here Adam, hard pressed in this manner, was in the midst of death and in the midst of hell. He was compelled to confess that nakedness was

r LW 1:176.

not evil, for it had been created by God. On the other hand, he realized that the evil was this: that now he had a bad conscience because of the nakedness in which he had previously gloried as in a unique adornment, and that he was now terrified by God's voice, which previously he had heard with the utmost pleasure.

To this thought, which the Lord observes in Adam, his words refer. It is as if he were saying: "Since you are aware of your guilt and are terrified, you surely have eaten from the forbidden tree. You did not receive a command about not killing, about not committing adultery, but about not eating the fruit of this tree. Therefore because you are terrified, you prove that you have sinned against this command." Thus, Adam hears from the Lord his very thoughts. He was thinking: "I have eaten the fruit, but I shall not say that I am fleeing for this reason; I shall keep still about the sin and say that I am afraid because I am naked and that I am frightened by God's voice." But while Adam is reflecting on these thoughts, he is forced to accuse himself, and within him he hears his conscience convicting him of a lie and charging him with sin. In addition, the Lord himself now charges him with sin directly and in plain words. But not even in this way is he able to bring the naïve Adam to an acknowledgment of his sin.[40] For he says:

[Don't Blame Me! It Was Her! And It Was You, My Lord!]

12. The woman whom Thou gavest me as a companion gave me from the tree, and I ate.

See how superbly the malice and nature of sin is pictured here. Adam can in no wise be forced into a confession of his sin, but he denies his sin or excuses it as long as he sees that he has any kind of excuse, hope, or pretext left. It is not amazing that in the beginning he hoped to be able to cover his sin and that he accuses God rather than acknowledge that he has sinned. But this is amazing, that he still persists in his excuse after his conscience has convicted him and he himself has also heard his sin from God. He does not say: "Lord, I have sinned; forgive me my debt; be merciful"; but he passes on the guilt to the woman. (It is the nature of sin not to permit the soul to flee back to God but rather to force it into a flight away from God.)[41] [. . .]

40. Cf. Wenham, *Genesis*, 77: "Who told you . . . ? Have you eaten . . . ? These further questions are not those of an ignorant inquirer. Their very formulation suggests the all-knowing detective who by his questioning prods the culprit into confessing his guilt."

41. Cf. Wenham, *Genesis*, 77: "As people are wont in such situations, the man tries to excuse himself by blaming the woman and implying that it was really God's fault for giving him this woman"; and Von Rad, *Genesis*, 92: "The man betrays the woman. The sin they committed in common did not unite men before God but isolated them."

There[s] just is no end to sinning once one has turned away from the word. He had sinned through disobedience and unbelief; now he doubles his great disgrace and blasphemy when he says: "I did not listen to the serpent; I felt no pleasure in looking at that tree; I did not stretch out my hand to pluck the forbidden fruit. All this the woman did whom you did give to me." In short, Adam does not want to acknowledge his sin; he wants to be regarded as pure and innocent.

And so this little section, too, deals with the description or the nature of sin. When there is no promise of forgiveness of sins and no faith, the sinner cannot act otherwise. If God had said: "Adam, you have sinned; but I shall forgive you your sin," then with the utmost loathing Adam would have humbly and frankly acknowledged his sin. But because the hope for the forgiveness of his sins is not yet available, he feels and sees nothing except death itself because of his transgression of the command.[42] [. . .]

Therefore[t] the statement "The woman whom you did give to me" is full of resentment and anger against God, as if Adam were saying: "You have burdened me with this trouble. If you had given the woman some garden of her own and had not burdened me by making me live with her, I would have remained without sin. Therefore the guilt for my having sinned is yours, since you gave me a wife." [. . .]

[Don't Blame Me! It Was the Serpent! And It Was You, My Lord!]

13. And the LORD God said to the woman: Why did you do this? And she answered: The serpent deceived me, and I ate.

Now Eve, too, is put before us as an example; and when she is corrupted by sin, she is not one whit better than Adam. Adam wanted to appear innocent; he passed on his guilt from himself to God, who had given him his wife. Eve also tries to excuse herself and accuses the serpent, which was also a creature of God. Indeed, she confesses that she ate the fruit. "But the serpent," says she, "which you have created and which you have permitted to move about in Paradise, deceived me." Is not this accusing the

s LW 1:177, para. 2.

t LW 1:178, para. 2.

42. Modern exegetes like John H. Walton have focused on the archetypal meaning of Adam as representative of humanity. Walton reminds us that Hebrew as a language developed only sometime after the Israelites came to the land of Canaan after the exodus. Therefore *Adam*, the Hebrew word for humankind, is a literary designation given relatively late. Walton also points out based on Richard S. Hess's study that the Hebrew word *'adam* has several meanings in the opening chapters of Genesis: (1) it does not refer to a personal name (cf. the archetypal individual) when it includes an article; (2) in five occurences without an article it is a clearly a personal name (4:25; 5:1a, 3, 4, and 5); (3) it refers to generic humanity, corporate, and en masse (i.e., including both female and male). See John H. Walton, "A Historical Adam: Archetypal Creation View," in *Four Views on the Historical Adam*, ed. Matthew Barrett, Ardel B. Caneday, and Stanley N. Gundry (Grand Rapids: Zondervan, 2013), 91. Luther considers Adam to be a historical person (naturally, because Luther lived centuries before the idea of evolution and new research regarding the age of humanity and earth), he also considers Adam as some sort of archetype. According to him, Adam's fall is our fall. We as sinful beings fear God's punishment—just like Adam feared—and act just like Adam acted after his fall, trying to minimize the severity of our sins, etc.

Creator and pushing off one's guilt from oneself? So we see that sin is and acts the same everywhere. It does not want to be sin; it does not want to be punished because of sin. It wants to be righteousness. When it cannot achieve this, it puts the guilt on God, so that it accuses God of a lie when he accuses sin.[43]

In this engraving, the monogrammist HA depicts God confronting Adam and Eve after they have eaten from the tree of the knowledge of good and evil. From a 1545 printing of Luther's *Small Catechism for the Priest and Preacher.*

[Demonic Sin]

Thus, out of a human sin comes a sin that is clearly demonic; unbelief turns into blasphemy, disobedience into contempt of the Creator. But I call this a demonic sin and not a human one, because the devil everlastingly hates, accuses, and damns God but exonerates himself; and it is not possible for him to say from his heart: "Lord, I have sinned, forgive me." [. . .]

43. In his *Lectures on Genesis*, Luther clearly avoids giving the impression that, according to him, God could be considered as the origin of sin. Instead, he lays the blame mostly on Satan as the origin of sin (and naturally both Adam and the woman). The reason for this may be that Erasmus of Rotterdam accused him in 1523 of making God the origin of sin in private correspondence between Erasmus and Cuthbert Tunstall (see WA 18:579). Although this accusation was probably an overstatement, these types of accusations did not come out of the blue. Luther emphasized at that time (and especially in *De servo arbitrio* [1525]) that all things occur inevitably or necessarily. By emphasizing the necessity or inevitability of all things, Luther wanted to prove that God is the author and origin of all good and especially salvation in the world. However, when he applied this idea to evil, he really had to work to avoid such conclusions that he thought that God is the origin of evil. Luther managed to avoid this conclusion by emphasizing that human beings cannot judge God's work or God's goodness nor evaluate God, because humans have such a poor capacity compared to God. It was the devil who should be blamed instead. However, the fall of the devil itself remained a mystery for Luther (probably because of the lack of biblical evidence) and he used only enigmatic expressions (e.g., God "discovers" the devil as evil). See, e.g., WA 18:615,31f.; 616,13f.; 636,23f.; 670,25f.; 685,25f.; 692,1f.; 693,28f.; 699,15f.; 702,9f.; 707,32f.; 711,7f.; 712,26f.; 736,27f.; 772,36f.; 771,27f.; 784,23f. See also Koivisto, *Is Evil Inevitable?*, 134f., esp. 156: "Rather than God, it was Satan

Thus,[u] we see Adam and Eve so fallen and sunk in sin that they cannot sink deeper. After unbelief follows the disobedience of all of humanity's powers and parts. After this disobedience follows later on the excuse and defense of sin; and after the defense, the accusation and condemnation of God. This is the last step of sin, to insult God and to charge God with being the originator of sin. Unless hearts are given courage through trust in mercy, this nature cannot be urged on beyond this point if there are successive steps of sin. [. . .]

[God's Fatherly Concern]

But[v] God comes in a very soft breeze to indicate that the reprimand will be fatherly. He does not drive Adam away from himself because of his sin, but he calls him and calls him back from his sin. Yet Adam does not understand or see this fatherly concern, since he is overwhelmed by his sin and terror. He does not notice that God deals far differently with the serpent. He does not call the serpent. Nor—in order in this way to call it to repentance—does he ask the serpent about the sin that has been committed. But he condemns it immediately.

This shows that even then Christ, our Deliverer, had placed himself between God and humanity as a Mediator.[w] It is a very great measure of grace that after Adam's sin God does not remain silent but speaks, and in many words indeed, in order to show signs of his fatherly disposition. With the serpent everything is done differently. And so, although the promise concerning Christ is not yet there, it is already noticeable in the thought and counsel of God.

[. . .]

whom Luther considered actively causing both: his own Fall and the Fall of the first humans. God only permitted these falls, but did not actively cause or was not ontologically involved in them."

u LW 1:179, para. 3.

v LW 1:180, para. 3.

w Cf. Barth, *Der Teufel und Jesus Christus*, 208–10, where he argues, e.g., that for Luther the devil is situated between God and human beings. From this position the Christ, the Mediator, has plunged the devil into peril.

[Execution of Sentence]

[x]14. And the Lord God said to the serpent:
Because you did this, you are cursed among all the living things
and beasts of the earth: on your belly you will walk,
and dust you will eat all the days of your life.

After the trial and the inquiry into the case has been carefully carried out, there now follows the execution of the sentence, as they say, by which there is rendered to each according to his deed, and yet not exactly alike, as we shall hear.[y] Moreover, careful consideration should be given to this passage for two reasons. In the first place, nowhere else in Moses does God, in person, speak as extensively as he does here; in the second place, it does not contain any law about what either the serpent or a human being should do but is devoted entirely to promising and threatening what good and what evil will happen to both.[z]

This, too, should be carefully noted: that after sin no law was put upon Adam, although the perfect nature had its law. But this happened because God sees that nature, which is now corrupt, not only can receive no support from a law but has gone through such a complete convulsion and disturbance that it cannot bear even a syllable of the law. Therefore God does not further burden sin-burdened nature with the law. But he heals sin, like a wound, with a health-giving plaster, that is, with the promise concerning Christ, while he also applies the harsh cautery which the devil had brought on. Just as health-giving plasters also damage the flesh while they effect their cure, so the curative promise is put to Adam in such a way that at the same time it includes a threat, to serve as a cure for the lust of the flesh. But by "lust" I mean not only the hideous prurience of the flesh[44] but also that filthiness of the spirit, as Paul calls it (2 Cor. 7:1), that by nature we

x LW 1:182.

y Cf. Von Rad, *Genesis*, 92: "The penalties are all to be understood aetiologically; in them the narrator gives a reason for disturbing enigmas and necessities, he answers elementary questions about life."

z Cf. Arnold, *Genesis*, 67–68: "The punishments are announced in poetry, which may reflect the cultural expectations for legal verdicts. . . . Indeed, in the Hebrew Scriptures, divine punishment mirrors precisely the sin being punished. Judgment and punishment follow a sort of 'poetic justice,' meaning the penalty inflicted on the sinner matches repayment in kind for the harm done in the offence."

44. Luther usually referred to the notion of the flesh (Lat.: *caro*) as the corrupted human nature (including spirit, soul, and body) or that part of human nature which is corrupted by sin (usually including some parts of spirit, soul, and body) and was not yet purified by the Holy Spirit. See, e.g., Tuomo Mannermaa, *Christ Present in Faith: Luther's View of Justification*, ed. and introduced by Kirsi Stjerna (Minneapolis: Fortress Press, 2005), 58–59: "When talking about the partial aspect of justification, Luther's attention is focused on believers themselves and on the battle between the new and the old in them. Luther states explicitly that Christians live 'partly in the flesh and partly in the Spirit' (*partim carnem, partim Spiritum habent*), which means that they are partly sinners and partly righteous. . . . The flesh is opposed to the Spirit, and the Spirit is opposed to the flesh"; WA 7:550; WA 40/2 [Dr]:178,16f.

are inclined to idolatry, unbelief, smugness, and other horrible sins against the First and the Second Table. There was need of this harsh cautery to keep this depravity of our nature in check.

[God's Figurative Language]

It would be my wish, moreover, that I could treat this text in accordance with its importance; for it contains whatever is excellent in all Scripture. And the first part of the text is entirely in figurative language; God is speaking with the serpent, and yet it is certain that the serpent does not understand these words. These are not words of creation, as were those words above when He said to the animals: "Increase and multiply," and when God said to the earth: "Let the earth bring forth herbs and trees of every kind"; but they are words that threaten and promise. God is not speaking to an irrational nature but to an intelligent nature.

And so God mentions the serpent by name, but he is dealing primarily with Satan, who is in control of the serpent and through it is deceiving the human beings. But on account of the sin of man, who is the lord of the creatures, the animals and trees also perished in the flood, just as subjects often suffer punishment because of the errors of their rulers.[45] Thus, it also happened to the serpent that it was punished because of the sin of the devil, who had misused the serpent for such a great evil; and yet, in a figurative sense, Satan's punishment is meant by the punishment of the serpent. [. . .]

[Satan in Serpent]

For[a] we have the Holy Spirit as our Guide. Through Moses the Spirit does not give us foolish allegories;[46,b] but teaches us about most important events, which involve God, sinful humanity, and Satan, the originator of sin. Let us, therefore, establish in the first place that the serpent is a real serpent, but one that has been entered and taken over by Satan, who is speaking through the serpent.[47] In the second place, let us also establish this: that what God is saying to the serpent, the serpent, being an irratio-

a LW 1:185, para. 3

b For more on allegorical interpretation and exegesis in the Middle Ages, see Henri de Lubac, *Medieval Exegesis*, vol. 1: *The Four Senses of Scripture*, trans. M. Sebanc, Retrieval & Renewal Resourcement in Catholic

45. Luther's commentary on Genesis has surprising similarities with first-century Jewish theologian Philo of Alexandria's *Questions and Answers on Genesis*. See David Clough, "All God's Creatures: Reading Genesis on Human and Nonhuman Animals," in *Reading Genesis after Darwin*, ed. Stephen C. Barton and David Wilkinson (Oxford: Oxford University Press, 2009), 146–47: "Luther's commentary on Genesis agrees strikingly with Philo that we can discern God's provident care for humanity in his making every part of creation with a view to its contribution to a splendid home for human beings." Both Philo and Luther also thought that because animals are subject to humans, they also suffer with humans—just like nations suffer with their rulers (cf. Clough, "All God's Creatures," 147). Cf. Wenham, *Genesis*, 81: "It should be noted that neither the man nor the woman are cursed: only the snake (v 14) and the soil (v 17) are cursed because of man."

46. Luther criticizes in his Genesis lectures, e.g., Origen (c. 185–c. 254), Jerome (c. 347–420), Augustine, and Nicholas of Lyra for those allegories that are not based on the historical meaning of the texts. Luther, however, does not abandon allegorical method as such, but accepts the use of them, if allegories follow the historical meaning of the text. Allegories can even serve as "an ornament or flowers of a kind" for illustrating "the history" (see WA 42:173,4f.).

47. In his *Scholia in librum Genesios*, which were collected by Johannes Poliander [Gramann] (1487–1541) and probably from the year 1523 or 1524, Luther emphasizes that the serpent in Genesis 3 was a real serpent and supports his view with John Chrysostom's *Homilies on Genesis*; WA 9:332,15f.; 335,38f.; WA 63:284. Cf. Chrysostom in MPL 53 *Homiliæ in Genesin*, cols. 125–134; also Von Rad, *Genesis*, 92–93: "So too the serpent; a real serpent is meant; but at the same time, in it and its enigmatic relation to man, man's relation to the evil with which he has become involved becomes vivid." See more about Luther's *Scholia* in Mattox, *"Defender of the Most Holy Matriarchs,"* 261–62.

nal animal, did not understand; but Satan did, and he was the one whom God had especially in mind. Thus, I adhere simply to the historical and literal meaning, which is in harmony with the text. In accordance with this meaning, the serpent remains a serpent, but one dominated by Satan; the woman remains a woman; Adam remains Adam, just as the following events prove. [. . .]

Now[c] what God says to the serpent: "You are cursed among all the animals and beasts of the earth, upon your breast you shall go" does not have the meaning which Augustine and others after him adopt, namely, that by "breast" is meant pride. But because Satan misused the serpent for sin, the serpent is compelled to bear a part of the punishment and is cursed by becoming the most hated among all the beasts. It was not so originally; but now, through the curse, something is added to the nature of the serpent. Although before the curse it was a very pretty little beast, it is now more frightful and more hated than all the other animals. We know from experience that by nature we have a fear of serpents and that by their nature serpents also flee from us. Thus, the serpent is compelled to bear a part of the curse and of the punishment. But these words are not addressed to the serpent alone. God is dealing with Satan, who is hidden within the serpent; the verdict of the last judgment is here announced to him, and he is actually made to stand before the judgment seat of God.

His way of speaking with the serpent is far different from his way of speaking with Adam and Eve, whom he affectionately calls back. "Where are you? Who told you that you are naked?" These words reveal God's love toward the whole human race; even after sin the human being is sought and called, and God converses with him and hears him. This is a sure indication of his mercy. Although these are words which deal with law and

Thought (Grand Rapids: Eerdmans/London: T&T Clark, 1998); Henri de Lubac, *Medieval Exegesis*, vol. 2: *The Four Senses of Scripture*, trans. E. M. Macierowski, Retrieval & Renewal Resourcement in Catholic Thought (Grand Rapids: Eerdmans/London: T&T Clark, 2000); Henri de Lubac, *Medieval Exegesis*, vol. 3: *The Four Senses of Scripture*, trans. E. M. Macierowski, Retrieval & Renewal Resourcement in Catholic Thought (Grand Rapids: Eerdmans, 2009).

c LW 1:185, para. 5.

judgment, they nevertheless indicate a clear hope that Adam and Eve were not to be condemned eternally.

With the serpent and Satan God deals more harshly. God does not call him, and he does not say: "Why did you do this?" But he simply announces the verdict of the court in very harsh words: "Because," says God, "you did this." It is as if he were saying: "You, Satan, have already committed sin previously, and you were condemned when you fell from heaven. To this sin you have now added another, in order to bring humanity into sin through your misuse of the serpent. For this reason the serpent will bear this punishment, that now it alone will lie under the curse, when previously it shared in the blessing which all the other beasts had."

[Serpent before and after Sin]

From this some obvious conclusions follow: that before sin the serpent was a most beautiful little animal and most pleasing to human beings, as little mules, sheep, and puppies are today; moreover, that it walked upright.[d] And so it is due to the curse and not to its nature that it now creeps on the ground, just as it is due to the curse that a woman conceives with shame, gives birth with pain, and brings up her offspring with toil. But if the work of procreation were without the curse, it would be something most honorable; birth would be very easy, and bringing up the offspring would be the greatest joy. Therefore sin has not merely deformed nature most shamefully, but has perverted it in the worst possible manner.[48, e] [. . .] The serpent, which Satan misused for sin, bears this burden because of sin: although it had

48. Many modern exegetes emphasize the etiological nature of Genesis 3. According to them this chapter attempted to explain the following: "Why there was no shame about nakedness at the beginning" (2:25; 3:7, 10); "Why the serpent seems isolated and is often a loner" (3:14); "Why women have such pain in giving birth" (3:16); "Why the serpent must crawl on its belly" (3:24); "Why there is enmity among serpents and humans" (3:24); and so on. It is obvious that one aspect of the story is this kind of etiological nature. This story is intended to describe, e.g., why there are everyday difficulties in human life. It is evident that Luther does not deny this kind of aspect of the story. However, the difference between Luther's lectures and modern commentators is Luther's strong metaphysical emphasis: the devil and sinful human nature are to be blamed for such difficulties because of their transgressions.

d Cf. Arnold, *Genesis*, 68.

e Many modern commentators are more careful to take such strong aspects to the (metaphysical) etiology of the story. See more, e.g., Robert Alter, *Genesis: Translation and Commentary* (New York: Norton, 1997), 13; John Barton and John Muddiman, eds., *The Oxford Bible Commentary* (Oxford: Oxford University Press, 2001), 44; Jacob Benno, *Das Buch Genesis* (Stuttgart: Calwer Verlag, 2000), 101–2; James H. Charlesworth, *The Good and Evil Serpent: How a Universal Symbol Became Christianized* (New Haven: Yale University Press, 2010), 276–79, 294, 310, 315, 322; Westermann, *Genesis 1–11*, 238–39. However, some scholars see a connection between the serpent and some evil force (e.g., the devil or mythological demon): see, e.g., Hermann Gunkel, *Genesis übersetzt und erklärt* (Göttingen: Vandenhoeck & Ruprecht, 1977), 15;

previously been most beautiful, now suddenly, before Adam's eyes, it takes on a snakelike tail, creeps on the ground, and becomes an object of fear for him. If this is so, why shall we have any doubt about man, who himself sinned and drank the poison of sin which was poured into him by Satan? [. . .]

To[f] this curse also belongs the statement: "And the dust of the earth you will eat." [. . .] There are other beasts which also eat earth, but the serpent eats earth in this way; although previously it was superior as regards its cleverness, its beauty, and also its diet, which it shared with the humans, it now bears the punishment that the nature of its diet is changed. [. . .] It[g] dares not eat apples, pears, and nuts, on which even the mice feed; but it consumes the raw earth. These are not my words but those of Moses; they teach that the nature of the serpent was entirely changed and made different.

But although I said—and it is also true—that God is speaking with the serpent in a way that is especially aimed at Satan, as the following events show more clearly, yet I do not agree that, like Augustine, whom Lyra follows, we should allegorically apply to Satan those statements which fit well with the nature of the serpent. For the serpent and Satan are linked together in their sinning; although Satan is the one who does the acting, the serpent is, as it were, his instrument. For the same reason they are also linked together in their punishment. But the serpent bears only its bodily punishment, while for Satan, as the originator and perpetrator, another judgment has been prepared, of which Christ says in John (16:11): "The prince of this world has already been judged." This judgment will follow later.

Some maintain that, like the serpent, the devil no longer walks upright and has lost his earlier form and stature. Although this is correct, it is out of place here and has no bearing on the explanation of the text before us. Moreover, when I say that before the curse the serpent walked upright, this is not to be understood as though it walked about upright as human beings

John Skinner, *Critical and Exegetical Commentary on Genesis* (Edinburgh: T&T Clark, 1951), 71–82: "It is more probable that behind the sober description of the serpent as a mere creature of Yahwe, there was an earlier form of the legend in which he figured as a god or a demon. . . ."

f LW 1:187, para. 2.

g LW 1:187, para. 3.

do, but as a deer or a peacock does. So much for the judgment of the serpent.

What follows pertains properly to the devil. It depicts his judgment far better than those foolish and unsuited allegories. It also gives this sound comfort, that now the devil is no longer in a position to rage and do harm as freely as he would like and as he would do if there were no woman's Seed.

[Judgment of Satan]

15[a]. I shall put enmity between you and the woman and your seed and her seed.

These words deal specifically with the judgment of Satan, and in them sound comfort is given to the godly.[h] [. . .] [W]hen[i] we must make statements about Satan, let us fall back on other Scripture proofs that are pertinent, sure, and strong. Of this sort are John 8:44: "The devil is a murderer and the father of lies," and "He did not abide in the truth"; 1 Pet. 5:8: "He goes about like a roaring lion, seeking whom he may devour"; and John 16:11: "The prince of the world is judged."[49]

h Genesis 3:15 is sometimes referred as the proto-gospel, because it is considered to be the first promise of Christ. See Mattox, *"Defender of the Most Holy Matriarchs,"* 60f., about young Luther's understanding of proto-gospel. Cf. Arnold, *Genesis*, 69: "Although it must be cautioned that messianic prophesy is not intended in 3:15, it remains an attractive appropriation of these words to find their fullest meaning (*sensus plenior*) in a future member of the human race destroying the serpent as part of God's redemptive plan, especially as it might relate to ancient Israel's royal ideology." See also Wenham, *Genesis*, 81–82: "Certainly the oldest Jewish interpretation found in the third century B.C. Septuagint, the Palestinian targums (Ps.-J., Neof., Frg.), and possibly the Onqelos targum take the serpent as symbolic of Satan and look for a victory over him in the days of King Messiah. The NT also alludes to this passage, understanding it broadly in a messianic sense. . . . Certainly, later Christian commentators, beginning with Justin (ca. A.D. 160) and Irenaeus (ca. 180), have often regarded 3:15 as the Protoevangelium, the first messianic prophesy in the OT." Cf. Von Rad, *Genesis*, 93, where he argues that Gen. 3:15 is more like a doom than reason for messianic hope (of the early church): it means a struggle between species "and as such there is no foreseeable hope that a victory can be won by any kind of heroism." According to Von Rad, the "seed" may not be construed personally, but it just means "posterity."

i LW 1:189, para. 2.

49. This is a good example of how Luther uses the passages from the New Testament to interpret Genesis 3 and of how he applies to his allegorical interpretation his so-called *analogia fidei* principle ("analogy of faith"). What exactly Luther meant by this principle, however, is difficult to define, but it is possible to make some conclusions. It could be described as follows: interpretation must follow the promises, the basic teaching, or the consensus of the Bible (e.g., only faith provides salvation, or the serpent was moved by the devil). In addition, the allegorically orientated *analogia fidei* had a pastoral task. According to Luther, following it in interpretation and in teaching not only embellishes the literal teachings of the Bible, but also consoles the distressed conscience. See Koivisto, "Martin Luther's Conception of the Serpent," 130.

Finally, who does not realize that the statement before us deals specifically with Satan, whom the Son of God resists in such a way that he cannot undertake anything with open force as though he had no antagonist? Under this protection the church is safe; Satan not only cannot attack the church with open force, but also in other respects his tyranny and his malevolence have been broken. Otherwise he would not permit a single tree to reach maturity. He would hinder, nay, even choke everything that is brought forth by the earth. In one single moment he would put an end not only to the birth of human beings but also to the preservation of the rest of the animals. Such great eagerness to do harm proves adequately that he is unable to rage with open force, but that whatever he does, he does with trickery and deceit.[50]

50. This passage proves how important Luther considers Genesis 3: it is essentially linked with the cosmological struggle between Satan and Christ.

[Consolation and Hope]

Moreover, this, too, ought to be noted here: that these words are not spoken by God for the devil's sake. God does not regard him worthy of his condemnation, but it is enough that his own conscience condemns Satan. These words are spoken for the sake of Adam and Eve that they may hear this judgment and be comforted by the realization that God is the enemy of that being which inflicted so severe a wound on human beings. Here grace and mercy begin to shine forth from the midst of the wrath which sin and disobedience aroused. Here in the midst of most serious threats the Father reveals his heart; this is not a father who is so angry that he would turn out his son because of his sin, but one who points to a deliverance, indeed one who promises victory against the enemy that deceived and conquered human nature. [. . .]

Thus, the sun of comfort, previously enveloped by black clouds, rises above the clouds and with its most delightful light shines on their frightened hearts. For Adam and Eve not only do not hear themselves cursed like the serpent; but they even hear themselves drawn up, as it were, in battle line against their condemned enemy, and this with the hope of help from the Son of God, the Seed of the woman. Forgiveness of sins and full reception into grace are here pointed out to Adam and Eve. Their guilt has been forgiven; they have been won back from death and have already been set free from hell and from those fears by which they were all but slain when God appeared.

This comfort springs from the fact that God does not curse Adam and Eve as he curses the serpent. Only this happens: that Adam and Eve are set into conflict with this enemy to keep them busy. Therefore even this situation turns out for humanity's good. Moreover, the main point of the comfort is this: Although this enemy fights with cunning and treacheries, the Seed will be born who will crush the head of the serpent. These words point to the ultimate destruction of Satan's tyranny, although it will not pass away without a most bitter conflict being fought for humanity.

This ninth-century ivory plaque from Genoels-Elderen (present-day Belgium) depicts Jesus (the Seed) standing on the heads of two creatures, including a serpent.

But see how uneven the outcome of the battle is. The human being's heel is in danger, but his head is uninjured and undefeated. On the other hand, it is not the tail and not the belly of the serpent but the head itself that is to be crushed and trodden underfoot by the Seed of the woman. But this victory will also be given to us as a gift, as Christ clearly states (Luke 11:22): "The spoils are divided after the defeat of the mighty one." By faith the Christian is made the victor over sin, over the law, and over death, so that not even the gates of hell can prevail against him (Matt. 16:18).

This first comfort, this source of all mercy and fountainhead of all promises, our first parents and their descendants learned with the utmost care. They saw that without this promise procreation would indeed continue to go on among people as well as among the other living beings, but that it would be nothing else than a procreation to death. And so that gift which was given by God to our nature is here made greater, nay, even made sacred; for there is hope of a procreation through which the head of Satan would be crushed, not only to break his tyranny but also to gain eternal life for our nature, which was surrendered to death because of sin. For here Moses is no longer dealing with a natural serpent; he is speaking of the devil, whose head is death and sin. And so Christ says in John 8:44 that the devil is a murderer and the father of lies. Therefore when his power has been crushed, that is, when sin and death have been destroyed by Christ, what is there to prevent us children of God from being saved?

In this manner Adam and Eve understood this text. Their consolation against sin and despair was their hope for this crushing, which was to be brought about in the future through Christ. And through the hope based on this promise they will also rise up to eternal life on the last day.

[Hope of Restoration]

[15b.] And It will crush your head, and you will crush Its heel.[j]

[. . .] This,[k] therefore, is the text that made Adam and Eve alive and brought them back from death into the life which they had lost through sin. Nevertheless, the life is one hoped for rather than one already possessed.[51] Similarly, Paul also often says (1 Cor. 15:31): "Daily we die." Although we do not wish to call the life we live here a death, nevertheless it surely is nothing else than a continuous journey toward death. Just as a person infected with a plague has already started to die when the infection has begun, so—because of sin, and death, the punishment for sin—this life after it has been infected by sin can no longer properly be called life, but death. Right from our mother's womb we begin to die.

51. In addition to his lectures on Genesis, Luther addresses hope extensively in two of his significant works: *Operationes in Psalmos* (1519–1521) and *Lectures on Galatians* (1531/1535). E.g., in his *Lectures on Galatians*, Luther focuses on the relationship between faith and hope. Luther finds five differences between faith and hope: (1) faith guides the intellect and hope guides the will; (2) faith "dictates, directs, teaches and is knowledge"; hope "encourages, summons forth, dares, awaits, and bears"; (3) faith grasps in truth or to the word that promises (good things); hope instead grasps to the content of those promises (e.g., to perfect righteousness in the future); (4) faith is the beginning of (holy) life and exists before various tribulations; hope activates later in tribulations and gives strength to stand various tribulations; (5) faith struggles against (spiritual) errors and heresies; hope struggles against evil emotions and tribulations like anxiety, despair, fear, etc., and expects good things in evil situations. In short, faith is "the brains" and hope is the strength for Luther, although he thought that they naturally include many other aspects as well. See AWA 2:280f.; WA 40/1:21,15f.; WA 40/2 [Dr]:23,12f.

j Cf. Arnold, *Genesis*, 68: "The original sense was something like, 'he will crush (*yĕšûpek*) your head, and you will snap at (*tĕšûpennû*) his heel.'" Cf. Arnold, *Genesis*, 69: "In addition to the complexities of the poetry, 3:15b has a long and complicated interpretation history. Judaism found in these words a messianic hope for victory over Satan, as evidenced by the translations. . . . Although it must be cautioned that messianic prophecy is not intended in 3:15, it remains an attractive appropriation of these words to find their fullest meaning (*sensus plenior*) in a future member of the human race destroying the serpent as part of God's redemptive plan, especially as it might relate to ancient Israel's royal ideology."

k LW 1:196, para. 2.

Through baptism,[l] [however], we are restored to a life of hope, or rather to a hope of life. This is the true life, which is lived before God. Before we come to it, we are in the midst of death. We die and decay in the earth, just as other dead bodies do, as though there were no other life anywhere. Yet we who believe in Christ have the hope that on the last day we shall be revived for eternal life. Thus, Adam was also revived by this address of the Lord—not perfectly indeed, for the life which he lost he did not yet recover; but he got the hope of that life when he heard that Satan's tyranny was to be crushed.

Therefore this statement includes the redemption from the law, from sin, and from death; and it points out the clear hope of a certain resurrection and of renewal in the other life after this life. If the serpent's head is to be crushed, death certainly must be done away with. If death is done away with, that, too, which deserved death is done away with, that is, sin. If sin is abolished, then also the law. And not only this, but at the same time the obedience which was lost is renewed. Because all these benefits are promised through this Seed, it is very clear that after the fall our human nature could not, by its own strength, remove sin, escape the punishments of sin and death, or recover the lost obedience. These actions call for greater power and greater strength than human beings possess.

And so the Son of God had to become a sacrifice to achieve these things for us, to take away sin, to swallow up death, and to restore the lost obedience. These treasures we possess in Christ, but in hope. In this way Adam, Eve, and all who believe until the last day live and conquer by that hope. Death is indeed an awful and undefeated tyrant; but God's power makes nothing out of that which is everything, just as it makes all things out of that

l For more on Luther's understanding of Baptism, see Eero Huovinen, *Fides infantium: Martin Luther's Lehre vom Kinderglauben* (Mainz: Verlag Philipp von Zabern, 1997).

which is nothing.[m] Look at Adam and Eve. They are full of sin and death. And yet, because they hear the promise concerning the Seed who will crush the serpent's head, they have the same hope we have, namely, that death will be taken away, that sin will be abolished, and that righteousness, life, peace, etc., will be restored. In this hope our first parents live and die, and because of this hope they are truly holy and righteous.

Thus, we also live in the same hope. And, because of Christ, when we die, we keep this hope, which the word sets before us by directing us to put our trust in the merits of Christ. It is vain to long for such perfection in this life that we become wholly righteous, that we love God perfectly, and that we love our neighbor as we love ourselves. We make some progress;[52] but sin, which wars in our members (Rom. 7:23) and is present everywhere, either corrupts or altogether obstructs this obedience.

52. According to Luther, it was possible to proceed in righteousness and holiness with the power of the Holy Spirit already during this lifetime—although imperfectly. See, e.g., WA 40/2 [Dr]:178,16f.

Therefore just as our very life can be called a death because of the death which lies ahead of us, so also our righteousness is completely buried by sins. By hope we hold fast to both life and righteousness, things which are hidden from our eyes and our understanding, but will be made manifest in due time. Meanwhile our life is a life in the midst of death. And yet, even in the midst of death, the hope of life is kept, since the word so teaches, directs, and promises. Thus, Ps. 68:20 offers the exceedingly beautiful comfort: "Our God is the God of salvation, the Lord of the issue of death." Let us give this title to God, not only because he grants aid in this temporal life—the devil also does this for those who worship him, as the examples of the heathen show—but because he is the Lord of the issue of death; that is, he frees those who are overwhelmed by death, and transports them into eternal life. This he does, as Moses teaches here, by crushing the head of the serpent.

m See more about Luther's understanding of nothing (Lat. *nihil*), in Sammeli Juntunen, *Der Begriff des Nichts bei Luther in den Jahren von 1510 bis 1523* (Helsinki: Luther-Agricola-Gesellschaft, 1996). Juntunen concludes, e.g., that the notion of nothing is for Luther an expression of the absolute ontological dependence of human beings and even the entire world on God. This means, e.g., that whatever an individual is or does is absolutely dependent on God and God's creative actions (cf. *creatio continua*); see 405.

Accordingly, we now find Adam and Eve restored, not indeed to the life which they had lost but to the hope of that life. Through this hope they escaped, not the first fruits of death, but its tithes; that is, although their flesh must die for the time being, nevertheless, because of the promised Son of God, who would crush the head of the devil, they hope for the resurrection of the flesh and eternal life after the temporal death of the flesh, just as we do. [. . .]

This image of David singing to God
is from a 1519 printing of Luther's *Seven Penitential Psalms*, his first independently published book.

Preface to the Psalter

1528 (1545)[a]

KRISTEN E. KVAM

INTRODUCTION

Luther's 1528 *Preface*[b] *to the Psalter*[1] is an exceptional text within Luther's corpus. It is noteworthy in part because of its deep resonance with the reformer's biography and vocation. As a monk, Luther had been immersed in praying the Psalms, a practice he continued daily even after he left the Augustinian Order.[2] The Psalms also had an important standing in Luther's work as a biblical theologian. Early in his teaching career at the University of Wittenberg, he gave two lecture courses on the Psalms, each lasting for well over a year.[3] Further, the first book he published

a Placing 1528 ahead of 1545 emphasizes the preface's first publication date. The changes made for the preface's second publication in 1545 concerned spelling, paragraphing, capitalization, and punctuation. Since these are not substantial revisions, it seems best to situate the text's date closest to its original historical context.

b A preface (or *Vorrede* in German) offered an author, commentator, or endorser an opportunity to provide guidance for reading the text that followed the prologue. The provision of a preface was a traditional—and ancient—literary practice. For scholarship on this genre, see Kevin Dunn's *Pretexts of Authority: The Rhetoric of Authorship in the Renaissance Preface* (Stanford: Stanford University Press, 1994); Gérard Genette, *Paratexts: Thresholds of Interpretation* (Cambridge: Cambridge University Press, 1997); Tore Janson, *Latin Prose Prefaces: Studies in Literary Conventions* (Stockholm: Almqvist and Wiksell, 1964).

1. The term *Psalter* refers to the book of Psalms as a whole, rather than to particular psalms.

2. Carter Lindberg notes that Luther's monastic experience of the Psalms was formative to his "life long enthusiasm for the psalms as model prayers." See Lindberg's essay "Piety, Prayer, and Worship in Luther's View of Daily Life," in *The Oxford Handbook of Martin Luther's Theology*, ed. Robert Kolb, Irene Dingel, and L'ubomír Batka (Oxford: Oxford University Press, 2014), 417.

3. In August 1513, Luther started his teaching career by lecturing on the Psalms, covering most of the Psalter by the time these lectures ended in late 1515. These lectures, known as *Dictata super Psalterium* (see image on p. 214 in this volume), are published in English translation in LW 10 and 11, where it is noted (10:ix) that they also are referred to as *Initium theologiae Lutheri*

("The Beginning of Luther's Theology"). Luther lectured on the Psalms a second time starting in 1518 or 1519; his summons to the Diet of Worms interrupted these lectures (and Luther's plans to publish them).

4. Luther's *The Seven Penitential Psalms* grew out of his earliest psalm lectures. This was the first book he prepared for publication, which occurred in 1517. LW 14:137–205 offers an English translation of the revised version that Luther published in 1525.

was a German translation and commentary on *The Seven Penitential Psalms*,[4] and he continued to translate and publish groupings of psalms as well as individual ones. In 1524, he published his first translation of the entire Psalter. Finally, while many persons know that Psalm 46 forms the basis for Luther's famous hymn "A Mighty Fortress Is Our God," it is less well known that the first hymnal Luther published in 1524 included six metrical paraphrases of psalms for congregations to sing.

Luther's *Preface to the Psalter* also is remarkable because of its pithy and robust witness to important features of Luther's theology. Students of this text will see a fine example of the dialogue between Luther's reading of Scripture and his theological teachings, including his stress that Scripture ought to be the primary source for shaping practice and understanding.

Luther actually wrote two different prefaces to the Book of Psalms. His first preface to the Psalter was published in 1524.[c] Four years later—in 1528—he wrote a new preface. Adding to the complexity of the history of Luther's prefatory work, the second preface was reissued in 1545 but without substantial changes to the 1528 text.

Although the 1528 preface incorporates some themes Luther had presented in his first *Preface to the Psalter* in 1524, the rhetoric and structure are strikingly different in the 1528 preface. In the 1524 preface, Luther primarily wrote about the richness of the Hebrew language (which he said "may indeed be called a holy tongue") and then explored the meanings of particular Hebrew words and how they would be best rendered into German.[d] In the 1528 preface, however, Luther devoted his attention to the important ways that the Psalter provides examples of how saints have

See also Christopher Boyd Brown's "Introduction to Volumes 59 and 60 [Prefaces I and II]," in LW 59:xvii–xl. For other prefaces by Luther in The Annotated Luther series, see *Preface to the Wittenberg Edition of Luther's German Writings* (1539), TAL 4:475–88; and *Preface to Luther's Latin Works* (1545), TAL 4:489–503; as well as Luther's preface to the *Handbook: The Small Catechism for Ordinary Pastors and Preacher* (1529), TAL 4:212–17.

c Luther's 1524 *Preface to the Psalter* is in English translation in John Walther Reu's *Luther's German Bible: An Historical Presentation Together with a Collection of Sources* (Columbus, OH: The Lutheran Book Concern, 1934; reprint, St. Louis: Concordia, 1984), 202–3.

d Ibid., 202.

spoken to God, with joy and praise as well as sorrow and fear.[e] Comparing the Psalter, which he described as "a little Bible," to legends of the saints and other hagiographical literature, he praised the Psalter for how it offered access to "real, living, active saints," in contrast to what he termed the "speechless" and "half-dead" saints of the legends. Moreover, Luther contended that the Psalter teaches and comforts Christians by showing that they, too, are included in God's communion of saints, whether they are "struck by fear" or "floating on joy."

The Translation

WA DB 10/1 places the 1528 *Preface to the Psalter* side by side with the 1545 preface on pages 98–104. After a careful comparison of the 1528 preface and the 1545 preface confirmed that the revisions in the latter were minimal, the 1545 preface was used as the basis for the following translation. Earlier translations into English were consulted, including one by Charles M. Jacobs with revisions by E. Theodore Bachmann in the section on "Prefaces to the Old Testament" in *Word and Sacrament I* (LW 35:253–57), and another by Charles M. Jacobs, "Preface to the Psalter of 1531," in Johann Michael Reu, *Luther's German Bible: An Historical Presentation Together with a Collection of Sources* (Columbus, OH: The Lutheran Book Concern, 1934; reprint: St. Louis: Concordia, 1984), 202–5.

e For a helpful discussion of the significance of language for Luther, see Johannes von Lüpke's "Luther's Use of Language," in *The Oxford Handbook of Martin Luther's Theology*, ed. Robert Kolb, Irene Dingel, and L'ubmorir Batka (Oxford: Oxford University Press, 2014), 143–55.

Decorative border framing the first word in the book of Psalms. From a book published by Daniel Bomberg in 1524.

PREFACE TO THE PSALTER

MANY HOLY FATHERS[f] praised and loved the Psalter above all other books of Scripture. To be sure, the work itself gives enough praise to its author.[g] We, however, must give evidence of our own praise and thanks.

In years past, so many legends of the saints,[5] and passionals,[6] books of examples,[7] and histories have been circulated that the world has been so filled with them. Hence, the Psalter has lain under the bench[h] and in such obscurity that no one has under-

f Even though many holy mothers also would have loved and praised the Psalter, this translation retains Luther's use of "father."

g The German term translated here as "author" is *Meister* (master). For this translation, Charles Jacobs, in LW 35:253 n.49, cites Wander, 579, "*Meister*," no. 17.

h Luther's phrase *unter der banck lag* could be translated as "neglected" or even "despised" but the metaphor's vivid image is worth retaining.

5. In this list of various genres of hagiography, Luther fittingly refers first to the legends of the saints. During Luther's time, *The Golden Legend* or *Legenda aurea* may have been the most widely read book in Europe (next to the Bible). Compiled by Jacobus de Voragine (c. 1229–1298), this collection of stories about the saints was one of the most translated texts in fifteenth-century Europe, with editions in at least nine vernacular languages. See the 1941 English translation by William Granger Ryan in *The Golden Legend: Readings on the Saints*, 2 vols. (Princeton: Princeton University Press, 1993). For a critical discussion of Renaissance perceptions of this collection, see Sherry L. Reames's *The "Legenda aurea": A Reexamination of Its Paradoxical History* (Madison: University of Wisconsin Press, 1985).

6. *Passionals* were picture books with text that described the lives and sufferings of the saints as well as of Christ Jesus.

7. *Exempel Bücher* were books that portrayed the lives of the saints as examples for Christians to follow.

stood even one psalm correctly. Still the Psalter gave off such an exquisitely excellent scent that all pious hearts felt the devotion and power in the unknown words, and for this reason loved the book.

I hold, however, that no finer book of examples or of legends of the saints[8] has ever come—or can come—to earth than the Psalter. If one should wish that from all the examples, legends, and histories, the best should be selected and brought together and put in the best form, the result would have to be the present Psalter. For here we find not only what one or two saints have done, but what has been done by the one who is the very head of all saints. We also find what all the saints still do—such as the attitude they take toward God, toward friends and enemies, and the way they conduct themselves in all dangers and sufferings. Beyond that there are contained here all sorts of godly and healing teachings and commandments.

8. What is translated as "saints" here and throughout the preface is the German plural *heiliger.* It is interesting to note that, according to Heinrich Bornkamm, Luther translated the plural of Hebrew terms for "the holy" (*qedoshim* and *ḥasidhim*) "from the beginning and without wavering" as "the saints." See his discussion in *Luther and the Old Testament*, trans. Eric W. and Ruth C. Gritsch (Philadelphia: Fortress Press, 1969), 243–44.

In this depiction of Christ's crucifixion, Archbishop Jacobus da Voragine is pictured at left holding his book, *The Golden Legend.* Fresco by Ottaviano Nelli, Chapel of the Trinci Palace, Foligno, Italy.

Luther did so in his 1539 *Preface to the Wittenberg Edition of Luther's German Writings* (TAL 4:479; LW 3:283). See also LW 35:166 n.7, a reference to Wander I, 229.

9. As Luther notes here, the term *Enchiridion* literally means a text that could be held in one's hand. These compact manuals included summaries of law as well as of instruction and advice.

The Psalter ought to be a dear and beloved book, if only because it promises Christ's death and resurrection so clearly—and pictures Christ's kingdom and the condition and nature of all Christendom[i]—that it might well be called a little Bible. The Psalter puts everything that is in the entire Bible most beautifully and briefly; it is truly a fine enchiridion or handbook.[9] It seems to me that the Holy Spirit wanted to take the trouble to compile a short Bible and example book of all Christendom or of all saints, so that whoever could not read the whole Bible would have here almost an entire summary of it, comprised in one little booklet.

But above all this, the Psalter has this excellent virtue and manner: other books make much ado about the works of the saints, but say very little about their words. The Psalter is a gem[j] in this respect: it gives forth so sweet a scent when one reads it because it relates not only the works of the saints, but also their words—how they spoke with God and prayed, and still speak and pray. Compared to the Psalter, the other legends and examples present to us nothing but merely speechless[k] saints; the Psalter, however, pictures for us real, thoroughly living saints.

Compared to a speaking person, a speechless one is to be regarded simply as a half-dead person; and there is no mightier or nobler work of humanity than speech.[l] A human person is most differentiated from other animals by speech, much more than by a human person's shape[m] or any other work. By the woodcarver's art even a block of wood can be given the shape of a human person; and an animal can see, hear, smell, sing, walk, stand, eat, drink, fast, thirst, hunger, and even suffer from frost and a hard bed—as much as a human person.

i This translation retains rendering *Reich* as "kingdom" rather than "reign," and *Christenheit* as "Christendom" rather than "Christianity."

j The term *Ausbund* also means "quintessence" or "paragon."

k Luther's term here is *Stumm;* it can be translated as "silent," but "speechless" better captures the passage's sense of negation.

l To highlight Luther's contrast between *Wort* (word) and *Werk* (work), these terms and their derivatives have been translated primarily in terms related to speech and work, rather than drawing on such wider connotations as "language," on the one hand, and "activity" or "deed," on the other hand.

m The term translated here and in the next sentence as "shape" is *gestalt.*

Moreover, the Psalter does still more than this. It presents to us not the simple, ordinary speech of the saints, but the best of their speech, that which they used when they spoke with God in great earnestness and on the most important matters. Thus, the Psalter lays before us not only their words instead of their works, but their very hearts and the inmost treasure of their souls, so we can look down to the foundation and source of their words and works. We can look into their hearts and see what kind of thoughts they had, how their hearts were disposed, and how they acted in all kinds of situations, in danger and in need. The legends and examples, which boast only of the works and miracles of the saints, do not and cannot do this, for I cannot know how a person's heart is, even though I see or hear of many important works this person does. And just as I would rather hear what a saint says than see the works the saint does, so I would much rather see the saint's heart and the treasure in the saint's soul than hear the saint's words. And this the Psalter gives us most abundantly concerning the saints, so that we can be certain of how their hearts and of the words they sounded to God and to everyone.

A human heart is like a ship on a wild sea, driven by storm winds from the four corners of the world. Here it is struck with fear and worry about coming disaster; there comes grief and sorrow because of present evil. Here it floats on hope and anticipated good fortune; there blows confidence and joy in present blessings.[10] These storm winds teach us to speak earnestly, to open the heart and pour out what lies at the bottom[n] of it. The person who is stuck in fear and need speaks of misfortune very differently than the one who floats on joy; and he who floats on joy speaks and sings of joy quite differently from him who is stuck in fear. It is not from the heart, they say, when a sad person laughs or a glad person weeps. That is, the bottom of the heart is not open, and what is in it does not come out.

What is the greatest thing in the Psalter but this earnest speaking amid such storm winds of every kind? Where does one find finer words of joy than in the praise psalms and thanksgiving psalms? There you look into the hearts of all the saints, as into beautiful and pleasant gardens—yes, as into heaven itself.

10. In relation to the term translated as "blessings," see Luther's discussion of his decisions on translating *Güte* as "favor," "love," and even "showing friendship" in the preface to his first Psalter of 1524, which is rendered in English in Reu, *Luther's German Bible*, 202.

n "Bottom," here and in the paragraph's final sentence, translates Luther's *Grund*.

There you see what fine and pleasant flowers of the heart spring up from all sorts of beautiful and happy thoughts toward God, because of God's blessings.

On the other hand, where do you find deeper, more sorrowful, more pitiful words of sorrow than in the lamentation psalms? There you look into the hearts of all the saints, as into death—yes, as into hell. How gloomy and dark it is there, with all kinds of distressed forebodings about the wrath of God! So, too, when they speak of fear and hope, they use such words that no painter could so depict for you fear or hope, and no Cicero[11] or other orator so portray them.

11. Marcus Tullius Cicero (106–43 BCE) was renowned as an orator and author, philosopher, and politician. Known as "the master of Latin prose," he had a great influence on the Latin language. Luther referred to Cicero frequently; see Robert Rosin's discussion of Luther's relation to Cicero in "Humanism, Luther, and the Wittenberg Reformation," in Kolb, Dingel, and Batka, eds., *Oxford Handbook of Martin Luther's Theology*, 96–98.

And that they speak these words to God and with God, this, I repeat, is the best thing of all. This gives the words double earnestness and life. For when one speaks with human persons about these matters, what he or she says does not come so powerfully from the heart; it does not burn and live, is not so urgent. Hence, it is that the Psalter is the book of all saints; and everyone, in whatever situation that person may be, finds in the psalms words that fit his or her case or situation—that suit him or her as if they were put there just for his or her sake, so that he could not put it better himself, or find better words or wish for better.

And this, too, is good that when these words please a person and suit her or his case, this person becomes sure that they are in the communion of saints,[o] and that it has gone with all the saints as it goes with him or her self, since they all sing with this person one little song. It is especially so if this person can speak these words to God as they have done. This must happen in faith since these words have no flavor to a godless human being.

Finally, there is in the Psalter security and a well-tried guide, so that one can follow in it all the saints without peril. The other examples and legends of the speechless saints present works that one cannot imitate; they present even more works that are dangerous to imitate—works that usually start sects and divisions,[p] and lead away from the communion of saints and rip it apart. But the Psalter holds you away from the divisions and to the communion of saints. For it teaches you—in joy, fear, hope, and

o *Gemeinshaft der heligen*, Luther's phrase here and in the next paragraph, could be translated as "community of saints."

p *Rotten* here could be translated as "disturbances" or even "mobs."

sorrow—to contemplate and speak as all the saints have contemplated and spoken.

In summary, if you would see the holy Christian church painted with living color and shape and put into one little picture, then take up the Psalter. There you have a fine, bright, pure mirror[12] that will show you what Christendom is. Indeed you also will find yourself in it and the true *gnothiseauton*,[13] as well as find God in God's self and all creatures.

12. The image of the Psalter as a mirror has been a beloved metaphor. Athanasius, bishop of Alexandria (c. 296–373), used this image in the fourth century; John Calvin (1509–1564) used it in the sixteenth century.

13. Luther's term reiterates the maxim from ancient Greek philosophy and religion: "Know Thy Self." This important aphorism was inscribed on the Temple of Apollo at Delphi.

Luther at his desk with the portraits of others on the wall, including Katharina von Bora. This seventeenth-century illustration offers an image of "the communion of saints."

Let us see to it then also that we thank God for all these unspeakable blessings. Let us receive them and use them diligently and earnestly, exercising ourselves in them to God's praise and honor, lest we earn something worse with our ingratitude. Heretofore, in the time of darkness, what a treasure it would have been thought if one were able to understand a psalm correctly, and to read or hear it in understandable German, but we did not have that treasure. Yet now, blessed are the eyes that see what we see and the ears that hear what we hear [Luke 10:23].[14] And yet I fear—no, sad to say, we see—that things happen with us as with the Jews in the wilderness, when they spoke about the bread from heaven [Num. 21:5]: "We detest this miserable food."[15] We should remember, however, that alongside this story there also stands the story of how they were plagued and died,[16] lest the same thing happens to us.

To this may the Author[q] of all grace and mercy help us, through Jesus Christ our Lord, to whom be praise and thanks, honor and glory, for this German Psalter and for all God's innumerable and unspeakable blessings into eternity. Amen, Amen.[17]

14. The first part of this sentence quotes Jesus's blessing upon the disciples; the second part develops the blessing in relation to hearing, reversing the criticism of those who do not hear in Luke 10:24. See also Matt. 13:13-17 with its inclusion of a prophecy about not hearing or seeing from the book of Isa. 6:9-10.

15. According to Num. 21:5, the Israelites in the wilderness became impatient and spoke out against God and Moses, including complaining about the manna God sent from heaven. For a discussion of the complexity of Luther's views concerning Jewish people, see MLBJP; and TAL 5.

16. See Num. 21:6.

17. *Amen* comes from a Hebrew word. Signifying an affirmation of trustworthiness and expectation, it often is translated into English as "let it be so" or "truly."

q Luther here has *Vater*, "father."

Lectures on Psalm 51

1513–1515

MICKEY L. MATTOX

INTRODUCTION

The earliest of Martin Luther's academic lectures for which we have a reliable record are those given on the Psalms between 1513 and 1515. The *Dictata super psalterium* were read out to the students and presumably taken down by them verbatim, as was the practice at that time. Indeed, there is much in these lectures to mark them as typically medieval. Most importantly, they were offered for students in a monastic community where the Psalms were prayed corporately several times each day.

Each of the Psalms was deeply familiar to Luther and his students, and their meaning was a matter of constant reflection. Luther's exposition of the Psalms was also offered in a traditional form: he first provided brief notes on the text itself, the so-called glosses; then, in order to bring out the Bible's deeper meanings, he offered "scholia," extended comments that probed the text spiritually and addressed important theological questions. This traditional form of biblical commentary was reflected in the outward appearance of medieval Bibles, where one would see at the center of the page a few lines of Scripture, with generous space between each line and large margins at the sides. The interlinear spaces were filled with glosses that helped clarify meaning, while the generous side margins provided com-

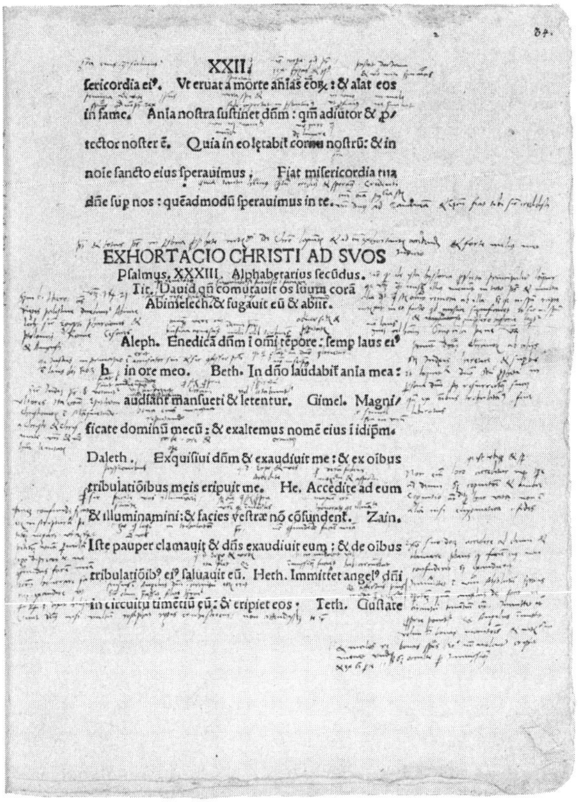
XXII

EXHORTACIO CHRISTI AD SVOS

Psalmus. XXXIII. Alphabetarius secudus.

A page from Luther's copy of *Dictata super psalterium* showing glosses and notes

ments on the text drawn from respected Christian biblical expositors.

Luther's lectures on the Psalms followed the tradition of the "glossed Bible," but just here he also took an innovative step forward. Utilizing the latest technology, he had a Wittenberg printer prepare pages of the biblical text that left the spaces between the lines and at the margins blank, so his students could take down his comments and use them to surround and thus illuminate the biblical text at hand. This new procedure reflected what would become an abiding principle in Luther's theology: that those who would know God should probe and taste the Holy Scripture for themselves.

During his long career as Doctor of Bible in Wittenberg, Luther probed and tasted the Psalms many times. These first lectures, however, have been the object of special interest to scholars because they come from the period several years before before his *95 Theses*[a] thrust him onto the center stage of European history. Here we meet Martin Luther as the pious monk and newly minted Doctor of Theology, lecturing to his monastic brothers in service to their shared pursuit of wisdom and holiness. A central marker of this context is Luther's profound emphasis on humility, which was considered a crucial virtue in all the Western monastic orders. Luther's own group, moreover, the Hermit Order of St. Augustine, had developed a piety that was deeply shaped by their namesake, whose theology emphasized that salvation is a gift of God's grace and therefore not, or at least not in the first place, a divine response to human efforts.[b] Luther's early Psalms lectures reflect just this conviction, especially in his insistence that for every Christian at every stage of the Christian journey the first word of praise to God must be a humbling word

a See TAL 1:13–46.

b See Eric L. Saak, *High Way to Heaven: The Augustinian Platform Between Reform and Reformation, 1292–1524* (Leiden: Brill, 2002), esp. 671.

of confession, a recognition that one is a sinner before God who can only receive God's favor and salvation as a gift.

Psalm 51, on which Luther is commenting below, was an ideal workshop, so to speak, for bringing this distinctive later medieval Augustinian faith and piety to expression. Included among the traditional seven penitential psalms, this psalm of lament takes as its point of departure King David's adultery with Bathsheba (see 2 Samuel 11), and the death and destruction that followed. While Luther surely knew that the psalm is about David and his life, like Christians of all times he also read it as the story of his own life, indeed, of every life. Lecturing his way through this psalm in the open space of the classroom and filling in the open page of his biblical text, Luther was developing his own powerfully distinctive take on such traditional themes as sin and grace, confession and forgiveness, faith and humility. The Christian as she appears here is one who is starkly aware that she stands, as Luther puts it, "before God" (*coram Deo*). In the bright light of God's majesty and holiness, and viewed through the lens of God's own words about human beings, she knows and confesses herself a sinner, and in just this way she "justifies God" in his judgment over her. The sinner in effect echoes God's word of judgment, and as she surrenders to it she finds herself justified before God—set right, that is—and on the path toward salvation.

David looks down from his palace as Bathsheba bathes in a pool. From a 1525 edition of Luther's commentary on the seven penitential psalms, *Die Siben Buosz Psalmen*.

LECTURES ON PSALM 51[c]

THIS PSALM is very widely known; even so, it is certainly very difficult, especially in verse five, on which almost as many interpretations have been offered as there were interpreters.[1] For that reason we wish for now to follow the apostle,[2] who in Rom. 3[:4] uses this passage to prove that every human being is a liar and a sinner, while God alone is true and righteous. This must be understood as referring to those people who have not yet been justified by God and joined to God, since such persons are righteous and true. Therefore he says [Rom. 3:4]: "But God is true, and every human being is a liar,[3] as it is written, 'That you may be justified in your words, and that you may overcome when you are judged.'" And according to some, in what follows he introduces a corollary [Rom. 3:5]: "But if our iniquity serves to commend the righteousness of God, etc." This seems to follow from the words, *Against you I have sinned, that you may be justified* (v. 4), as if he could not be justified unless we sin. But this should be understood in another way by setting forth some theses:

First. All human beings are in sins before God and commit sin; that is, they truly are sinners.

Second. To this God himself bore witness through the prophets and in the end he established the same by the suffering of Christ, for it is on account of the sins of humankind that he made him suffer and die.

Third. God is not made just in himself, but in his words and in us.[4]

c This translation is an updated version of the text in LW 10:235–43.

1. The Psalms, in Luther's day, had been long and rightly recognized as the prayer book of the church, appearing ubiquitously throughout Christian liturgy and worship. They were especially prominent in the daily religious life of monastic communities such as Luther's order, the Hermits of St. Augustine.

Perhaps the best introduction to the Christian use of the Psalms for the life of prayer and devotion is to be found in a letter of St. Athanasius (c. 296–373). See his *On the Incarnation*, rev. ed., trans. by a Religious of C.S.M.V. (Crestwood, NY: St. Vladimir's Orthodox Theological Seminary, 1953), Appendix: "Letter to Marcellinus," 97–119.

2. Luther's interpretation of the Psalms leans heavily on the Greek writings of the apostle Paul, especially the Epistle to the Romans. In his later lectures on Romans (1515–1516) a similar pattern emerges, this time with the Psalms being brought to the aid of understanding Paul. The back and forth between the psalmist and the apostle seen here is a compelling instance of the principle that Holy Scripture is its own interpreter.

3. In Rom. 3:4, Paul first quotes Ps. 116:11, which says that "every human being is a liar," and follows that with a quote from Ps. 51:4.

4. The passive voice Latin verb *iustificatur* here could be rendered either "justified" or "made just." The latter translation makes clear Luther's intent: God is not somehow being "made just" within God's own being; rather, God is being made just in those who are, as mentioned above, being justified by God and joined to God. The words of God are the means by which this justification is accomplished.

In this 1522 printing of Luther's German New Testament, an initial letter D features the apostle Paul holding a book and a sword. Woodcut designed by Lucas Cranach the Elder (1472–1553).

Fourth. We become sinners then when we admit that we are such, for such we are before God.[5]

Thus, it follows: One who is not sinner (that is, one who does not admit herself a sinner) openly attempts to condemn God in his own words, by which he bears witness that we are in sins. And such persons insist that Christ did not die for sins.[6] And so they pass judgment on God and try to make him a liar. But they will neither win nor gain the upper hand; God, however, has prevailed. Of such kind were and are the Jews, down to the present day.[7]

Whence there are many fine statements in the gospel and the apostle's writings which appear to lead us to sin, although they seek nothing else but that we should confess and acknowledge that we are sinners.[8] The psalmist says *Against you alone have I sinned* (v. 4), and so God is made righteous and truthful in his words, by which he declares us to be sinners. And he emerges

5. As justification does not make God in God's self just, so here one is not made a sinner by the confession of sin. Instead, one who confesses sin thereby becomes to herself what in reality she already was, as mentioned in the first thesis.

6. Luther's assertion here that the Christian is one who confesses himself a sinner anticipates the advice he offered in a letter to George Spenlein in 1516: "Beware of aspiring to such purity that you will not wish to be looked upon as a sinner, or to be one. For Christ dwells only in sinners." See *Luther: Letters of Spiritual Counsel*, trans. and ed. Theodore G. Tappert (Philadelphia: Westminster, 1960), 109–11.

7. Scholars have struggled, particularly since the Shoah, to make sense of Luther's harsh criticisms of Jews and Judaism. Some see the Jews as a constitutive element in Luther's theology because they epitomize for him the reverse side of faith and acceptance by God, that is, unbelief and rejection by God. See Thomas Kaufmann, *Luthers Juden* (Stuttgart: Reclam, 2014). For a concise introduction to the problem, see Kaufmann's "Luther and the Jews," in *Jews, Judaism, and the Reformation in Sixteenth-Century Germany*, ed. Dean Philip Bell and Stephen G. Burnett (Leiden: Brill, 2006), 69–104.

8. Luther seems to mean that the Scripture's frequent exhortations to good deeds could lead to sin if they are understood as the means by which we make ourselves just before God.

victorious because he has been falsely judged. And the one who says, "Against you alone have I sinned," excludes the justifications of the law, as if to say: "I am not talking about sins against the ceremonies of the law, for such sins are figurative and removable by the law. Rather, I am talking about those sins which the law can in no way remove, by no sacrifices, no washings or ceremonies. Therefore against you alone have I sinned, because I am making confession about real sins, not shadowy ones."

For *behold, you have loved the truth* (v. 6).[9] And thus the preceding verse expresses what kind of sin it is he is acknowledging, for it is not a figurative one nor one that can be removed by the blood of goats. And to confess sins in such a way means to justify God and make him the victor.[10] The Jews, who want their sins removed by the blood of goats and who think that their sins are merely figurative, reject this even up till now. Wherefore these things conflict with one another:

Denying that one has sin, or not confessing it—and justifying God.

Justifying oneself before God—and glorifying God.[11]

This is why God is not justified by anyone except the one who accuses and condemns and judges herself. For the righteous person is, first of all, one who accuses and condemns and judges herself. Therefore she justifies God and causes him to win out and to prevail. On the contrary, the ungodly and proud person is, first of all, the excuser and defender, the justifier and savior, of himself. For that very reason he automatically says that he does not need God as his Savior, and he judges God in his words and robs him of his justice and accuses him of being a liar and false. But he will not prevail, for God will win out.

But in case someone does not yet understand that no one is righteous before God, who alone is justified, an even clearer expression follows: *Behold, I was conceived in iniquity* (v. 6). "Therefore it is true that before you I am a sinner and have sinned, so that you alone may be glorious in righteousness and you alone may be justified, when all of us are sinners."[12] It is true, for indeed we are unrighteous and unworthy before God, so that whatever we can do is nothing before him. Yes, even faith and grace, through which we are today justified, would not of themselves justify us if God's covenant had not been established. It is precisely for this reason that we are saved: he made a testament and covenant with us that "whoever believes and is baptized shall be saved." But in

9. Here, the truth that God loves is the penitent's confession of sin.

10. The recognition that the Christian's relationship with God begins with a daily surrender, and that in this sense God must always have the victory over us, suggests here both Luther's deep monastic piety and his indebtedness to mystical theology.

11. Not confessing sin means saying that God's judgment of the sinner is unjust; self-justification, in turn, means self-glorification.

12. In the two sentences placed within quotation marks here, Luther briefly glosses the meaning of Ps. 51:6 before commenting further. All human beings are sinners, and all have sinned.

this covenant God is truthful and faithful and keeps what he promised.[13]

Therefore it is true that before him we are always in sins, so that in his covenant and testament which he has established with us he himself might be the one who justifies. Hence, the Hebrew literally says: "Against you alone have I sinned, so that you shall be justified in your word,"[d] that is, in thy covenant. Consequently, God in his covenant does not justify whoever does not sin or does not confess sin, for [as Scripture says] "whoever does not believe, etc. [will be condemned]," in view of which God cannot do it.[14]

However, he says *against you alone* because of legal sins which could also be cleansed by the law, such as touching a dead body, bodily uncleanness, etc. For such sins are sins before the law, and in them it is a matter of sin against Moses rather than against God. He says *I have sinned* (v. 4), namely, in a true and spiritual sin,[15] about which Ps. 19[:12] says: "Cleanse me from my secret sins." And this is the judgment which is the "choice of the king's honor and which the Lord loves,"[e] namely, to accuse and judge oneself. And then the Lord is justified in his words, as Ps. 145[:13] says below: "The Lord is righteous in his words," namely, those in which he shows that all are in sins.

Then follows *that you may be justified* (v. 6). This takes place in those who do not justify themselves but judge that God is righteous and that they, too, are justified by him. Note, however, that he says *that you may be justified*, and not, "that you may be made true," for he is speaking especially against the Jews, as is clear from Rom. 3[:1ff.], who are not ignorant, or at least should not be ignorant, of the fact that all are in sins. But because they believe that they are justified by their own righteousnesses,[16] they make God unrighteous, as though he were doing them an injustice by denying that they can be justified in themselves. Among the Gentiles, however, he is truthful and righteous.[17]

That you may overcome (v. 6). This happens among the wicked and unbelieving by whom God is judged, although they ought

d See LW 10:237 n.1: "Luther cites the Latin translation of J. Reuchlin's *Septem Psalmi poenitentiales Hebraici*. The source usually quoted by Luther under the designation 'Hebr.,' Jerome's *Psalterium iuxta Hebraeos*, here agrees with the Vulgate."

e See Ps. 99:4.

13. Here again Luther draws on the New Testament to shed light on the psalm, in this case appealing to the Gospel of Mark (16:16). But he does so in a way that reflects his training in a later medieval form of theology that emphasized God's covenant as defining the terms of the divine-human relationship. According to this way of thinking, God is eternally free and is under no obligation to save fallen humankind. God has freely chosen, however, to establish a covenant or agreement with fallen humankind, and according to this covenant all people who have faith (believe) and receive grace (baptism) will be saved.

14. The Scripture text Luther alludes to here completes the quotation from Mark 16:16 begun above. God here cannot save the person who will not acknowledge and confess sin because God must remain faithful to the terms of the divine covenant of salvation, announced in God's own words.

15. Luther is distinguishing between "legal sins" that violate only the ritual laws of the Old Testament and "true" or "spiritual" sins against God, such as pride or self-righteousness.

16. The Latin plural here, "their own righteousnesses," suggests that in Luther's understanding the Jews think they are justified by keeping the particular commandments of the Old Testament and in this sense make God unrighteous, a liar.

17. By "Gentiles" here Luther means Christians, who confess themselves sinners before God and so justify God in his judgment over them.

rather to be judging themselves, as do those who say: "Against you have I sinned." But instead they say, "I have not sinned." And so one necessarily condemns God as long as one justifies oneself. Concerning such people Prov. 30[:20] says: "This is the kind that wiping her mouth says, 'I have done no wrong.'"[f] For these two things are in a reciprocal relationship:

Whoever {
- justifies herself condemns God, who throughout Scripture states that she is a sinner, especially Ps. 14[:3], as the apostle cites it in Rom. 3[:10].
- judges herself and confesses her sin justifies God and affirms his truthfulness, because she is saying about herself what God is saying about her.

And so she is now in agreement with God and truthful and righteous, like God, with whom she agrees. For they are saying the same thing. But God says what is true and righteous, and she says the same. Therefore she, too, is righteous and truthful together with God. The others, however, fight with God about the truth, for God asserts that they are ungodly, but they deny it. Thus, either God or they are necessarily lying, for they mutually condemn and judge each other. But God cannot possibly lie. Therefore *that you may overcome when you are judged*, namely, *in your words* (v. 6), for he is not justified or judged in himself. And on the basis of this word the difference between judgment and justification becomes abundantly clear.

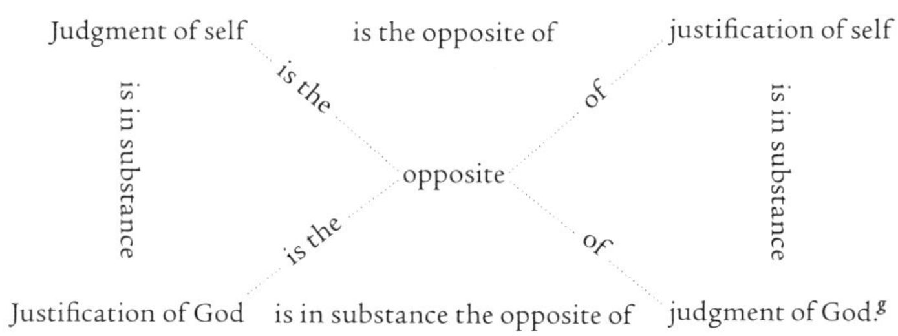

f Luther seems to have quoted this text from memory because the Vulgate has not "the kind that" (*generatio que*) but "the way of an adulterous woman" (*via mulieris adulteriae*).

g This chart appears in Latin in WA 55:272.

Now apply the rules of logic concerning the natures of opposite propositions to these.

1. Every self-accuser justifies God: but, on the contrary, not every justifier of God judges herself, because an ungodly person can glorify God, as demons do.[18]

2. Every self-justifier condemns God: but, on the contrary, not every condemner justifies himself, because the damned judge God and yet do not justify themselves.

3. No self-justifier justifies God: but, on the contrary, whoever is a justifier of God rightly justifies himself.

All of this is what was said in the preceding psalm [50:23], "The sacrifice of praise will glorify Me, and that is the path."[19] Thus, Job [15:15] says: "The heavens are unclean in his sight" and [Job 25:5] "the stars are unclean before him, and the moon does not shine," that is, the saints are not saints before him. So Isa. 40[:17] says: "All the nations are as nothing and are regarded as emptiness by him." For the saints confess above all that they are unclean, always saying: "Against you only have I sinned, that you may be justified." Hence, one bright star among them said [1 Tim. 1:15]: "Jesus Christ came to save sinners, of whom I am the foremost." Behold, how that star is not clean before God, though it shines with such brilliance before men.[20]

And thence arises the fact that [Ps. 68:35] "God is wonderful in his saints." For it is true: Whoever is most beautiful in the sight of God is the most ugly [in her own sight], and, vice versa, whoever is the ugliest is the most beautiful. In this sense: Whoever is most beautiful in his own eyes is the most shameful before God. How so? Because [Ps. 50:23] "the sacrifice of confession will honor Me."[21] Nor is there any adornment or garment of the church that is more excellent than the clothing of confession, for this suits her above all. Thus, the psalm says [Ps. 96:6], "Praise [*confessio*] and beauty are before him"; and again [Ps. 104:1]: "You have put on praise [*confessio*] and beauty"; and [Ps. 111:3] "His work is praise and magnificence." For that reason Ps. 45[:10-11] says, "Hear, O daughter, and see and incline your ear. Be humble, and so the king will desire your beauty."

Therefore, the one who is most attractive in the sight of God is not the one who seems most humble to herself, but the one who sees herself as most filthy and depraved. The reason is that she would never see her own filthiness, unless she had been enlightened in her inmost being with a holy light. But when she

18. Perhaps Luther has in mind here the demons' spontaneous recognition of Jesus as the Messiah, as found at times in the gospels (see, e.g., Luke 4:41). This would correlate with his mention of Philippians 2, below, where it would seem the demons bow the knee and confess that Jesus Christ is Lord.

19. One is on the right path who offers up the sacrifice of praise indicated by the psalmist, and this praise necessarily includes, as Luther explains below, one's confession of sin. In Luther's understanding, the Christian who prays the Psalms in this way follows the authentic path shown by the Hebrew prophets.

20. Luther here takes the "heavens" and the "stars" as allegorical references to the saints, who are always unworthy before God. The words of "that star," St. Paul, quoted here were often cited to show that increasing holiness brings with it an increasing awareness of one's own unworthiness before God. Hence, the greatest saints always see themselves as the greatest sinners. Luther's comments here and in the next paragraph reprise this traditional theme.

21. The psalm has here "sacrifice of praise" (*sacrificium laudis*), which Luther interprets as a "sacrifice of confession" (*sacrificium confessionis*). To praise God, therefore, is to offer God the sacrifice of one's recognition of sin.

has such a light, she is attractive, and the brighter the light, the more attractive she is. And the more brightly she has the light, the more she sees herself as ugly and unworthy.[22]

Therefore it is true: The one who is most depraved in his own eyes is the most handsome before God and, on the contrary, the one who sees himself as handsome is thoroughly ugly before God, because he lacks the light with which to see himself. Thus, the blessed Virgin says [Luke 1:48]: "For he has regarded the lowliness of his handmaid." These things are the marrow of Scripture and the meat of the heavenly grain, more desirable than all the glory of riches [Ps. 119:72]: "The law of thy mouth is better to me than thousands of gold and silver." If given the option, I would not substitute the riches of the whole world for such knowledge [Ps. 19:10]: "These words of God are sweeter than honey and the honeycomb."

Consequently, even the saints do not boast about their own strengths, although they might delight and rejoice in them by referring them to him who gave them. Either one is extremely absurd: both to be proud in poverty and to be proud in someone else's clothes. Those who justify themselves, since they are ungodly, do the first. Those who are righteous, but are proud of their own strengths and want to be seen in them, do the second. Although, as I have said, it is well to rejoice. Hence, we must always fear sin, and we must always accuse and judge ourselves in the sight of God.[23]

For if we judge ourselves, we shall certainly not be judged by the Lord.[h] For we shall not be judged twice for the same thing. God cannot condemn him who has already been judged by himself and, in consequence, by the words of God. For God cannot deny himself [2 Tim. 2:13], but he has judged this sinner, and the sinner has done the same thing.

Therefore God cannot be against one who is thus judging himself. Otherwise he who agreed with him in judgment would be against himself. For that reason it is necessary that God acknowledge and approve his own judgment in that man.[24]

Thus, it is clear that this psalm was composed, strictly speaking, not about David but prophetically in the person of the church.[25] It was written by David as being part of the church, the

h See 1 Cor. 11:31.

22. The illumination to which Luther refers here is divine, that is, it is God's work. The light that illumines the saints internally is the Holy Spirit, and this light reveals one's sin.

23. The Christian here is one who finds herself clothed with spiritual goods as gifts received from God. She may rejoice in these gifts, but the sin of pride always threatens to well up within her. To guard against this temptation she adopts a posture of holy fear, ever confessing her sin and unworthiness before God even as she cautiously rejoices at God's work in her.

24. Here again God is bound in Luther's understanding by what God has announced in his dealings with fallen humankind. What God can or cannot do is not therefore a matter of divine power or freedom, but of God's faithfulness to the terms of his own covenant of salvation. In the language of later medieval theology, the "ordered power of God" (*potentia dei ordinata*), expressed definitively in the divine words of the covenant, restrains the "absolute power of God" (*potentia dei absoluta*), according to which God can, of course, do whatever God wishes. God is bound, then, only by God's own words.

25. Christian approaches to interpreting the Psalms in the Middle Ages sometimes included an effort to identify the true speaker of the Psalms. In this case, one would ask who speaks the words, "Have mercy on me, O God. . . . Against you, you alone, have I sinned." Luther universalizes the psalm here, rendering David's words of repentance the very words that can, indeed must, be spoken by every Christian. All sinners, therefore, are

occasion having been taken from the story which is mentioned in the title, especially from the fact that David, reprimanded by Nathan, immediately acknowledged and confessed his sin, saying [2 Sam. 12:13]: "I have sinned." Hence, it is this very thing which he here adduces. *For I acknowledge my iniquity* (v. 5). There he has come to understand that to accuse himself means to justify God and, consequently, himself as well. Not so Saul. When he was rebuked by Samuel he said [1 Sam. 15:20]: "To the contrary, I have obeyed the voice of the LORD."[26] He was a symbol of the synagogue. Like him it was thrust from the face to the rear,[27] from the life-giving spirit to the dead letter.[28]

In this woodcut illustrating sermons by Johann Eck (1527), Jesus is crucified between two thieves.

called to make these words their very own.

26. To be sure, Saul does actually confess to the prophet Samuel in 1 Samuel 15, but only after initially denying his sin and hearing the prophet's condemnation. However, Samuel does not accept Saul's reluctant confession as sincere, and this seems at least in part to provide the point of departure for Luther's negative use of his example here.

27. That is, from the "face" of God to the "backside," or from God's grace and favor to God's wrath and judgment.

28. Luther is concerned here with fundamental types of the human being's stance before God. In immediately confessing to God and crying out for forgiveness, King David symbolizes faithful Israel and, just so, the Christian church. King Saul, on the other hand, in his self-assertive pride, symbolizes the faithless synagogue, by which Luther seems to mean the Jews after their rejection of Jesus as the Christ. One Jew, then, symbolizes repentance and faith, while the other represents prideful self-assertion and unbelief. One should prefer, therefore, to be a David rather than a Saul.

Luther extends this symbolic reading of biblical figures in the interpretation that follows, where the two thieves crucified with Jesus represent these two types as well: the first is a "Saul" who dies judging and blaspheming against God, but the other is a "David" who submits to God's judgment, condemns himself, and so finds God's forgiveness and dies in the hope of Paradise.

Observe a figure of this matter in Christ hanging on the cross. One robber judges, condemns, and blasphemes him; the other judges himself and justifies Christ, saying [Luke 23:41]: "We indeed justly," that is, *against you alone have I sinned*, "but this man has done no evil," behold, *that you may be justified* (v. 6).[29] Even if he is not justified, but judged, he overcomes nevertheless, and he will be justified, even if by the unwilling. Those who now do not want to accuse themselves and justify God, when they are chosen in gentleness and goodness, will finally do this when they are overcome by power and severity, namely, after death and in the last judgment.[30]

However, this insight is useful not only for this verse or this psalm but for all, wherever there is recollection of the praise and righteousness and glory of God. For God cannot be praised, justified, glorified, magnified, admired, etc., unless we ourselves are at the same time, and even beforehand, disparaged, accused, and put to shame, and vice versa. Where our shame and accusation are in evidence, there the praise of God and the remembrance of his righteousness become a reality.

29. The second of the two thieves here acknowledges that they have been properly condemned for wrongdoing, while Jesus has been wrongly condemned and suffers unjustly.

30. Luther alludes powerfully here to apocalyptic expectations after death or at the end of history, when Christ is met as fearsome judge, and when "every eye will see him, even those who pierced him; and on his account all the tribes of the earth will wail" (Rev. 1:7). In the final consummation, moreover, Christ will be universally acknowledged, even by those who rejected him, for "at the name of Jesus every knee should bend, in heaven and on earth and under the earth . . ." (Phil. 2:10).

A sample of the first kind	"Thy praise reaches to the ends of the earth" etc., Ps. 48[:10] and from the following psalm [Ps. 50:23], "The sacrifice of praise" and "Praise, ye children" [Ps. 113:1] Also, wherever there is Hallelujah
A sample of the second kind	"Let them be confounded and ashamed" [Ps. 35:4; 40:14; 70:2] "When they shall be confounded and put to shame" [Ps. 71:24] "His work is praise and magnificence" [Ps. 111:3]

Create in me a clean heart, O God (v. 12). A wonderful and notable word! I mean, many do not commit sins, but only good deeds, and nevertheless the most subtle kind of pride alone, born of their own virtues, has soiled them.[31] Therefore he does not say, cleanse the hand, eyes, feet, tongue, ears, flesh, because with regard to these someone is perhaps not yet sinning, but only his heart is puffed up and soiled. So also the *right spirit* (that is, I am now speaking tropologically,[32] beyond what was said literally in

31. Persistence in the prayer that God will create within one a clean heart is here placed at the very center of life for all those who, like the young Luther and his brother Augustinians, had devoted themselves to the pursuit of holiness through the disciplines of the monastic life. Why? Because as he notes here, wickedness can subtly posit itself precisely through the pride that grows almost unobserved just below the surface of the good works of such morally serious persons, in their very hearts. Crying out to God, "create in me a clean heart," therefore, brings with it a perpetual return to the wellsprings of the Christian life in the form of the confession of sin, even—no, especially!—for those who are most practiced in the virtues. The most holy persons thus continually confess themselves sinners, in part because they know how dangerous it is not to do so.

32. The tropological sense of Scripture is the meaning that applies to the reader morally, edifying her in the strengths of character that make for a faithful Christian life.

the gloss), for some indeed live in the spirit and mortify the flesh, but their spirit is bent and curved in on themselves[i] for empty glory and pride.[33]

In this engraving from a 1680 publication, St. Augustine holds a flaming heart in his right hand. This great theologian of the heart famously wrote: "You have made us for yourself, O God, and our hearts are restless till they find their rest in you."

Without doubt such were some heretics who led a very chaste life, and today our neighbors, the Bohemians,[34] who outdo us in almost every kind of purity, except for the heart, which spiritual pride has soiled. And this is the devil's choice food. For though he is himself completely unclean, he chooses to dwell in a clean

33. The notion that the beginning of sin is to be found in pride is prominent in the writings of St. Augustine of Hippo (354–430; see the image on this page), the great late ancient patron of Luther's monastic order. Luther reprises it inventively here, noting that pride means making one's self one's first concern. In this way pride corrupts monastic mortifications, making of them not humble self-sacrifices offered out of love for God, but, to the contrary, the ironic means of self-assertion and, therefore, self-justification. In his heart, the prideful monk remains curved in upon himself, focused, that is, on his own achievements and rewards.

34. Luther refers here to heretics in the region known as Bohemia (part of the Czech Republic today). These were followers of Jan Hus (1369–1415), a church reformer who was put to death at the Council of Constance in 1415. After 1520, Luther recognized that his own reforms had much in common with those recommended by Hus. See the image on p. 227.

i The phrase "curved in on oneself" is found both in Augustine and in St. Bernard's mystical theology, and either may be Luther's source. See Étienne Gilson, *The Mystical Theology of Saint Bernard*, trans. A. H. C. Downes (New York: Sheed & Ward, 1940), 54. For the frequent use of the phrase *in se curvatos*, see LW 25:291, 313, 345, 351, 513.

place. He says: "I will ascend the mountain of the north."[35] Thus, it is a horror to consider this bottomless and terrifying judgment of God that many heretics were so learned, outwardly so holy and most skilled in the Scriptures, and on account of this inmost filthiness of the heart alone every such synagogue was rejected and defiled.[36]

But note: If God is to be justified in his words, by which he declares that we are sinners, He must also be justified in his deeds, by which he asserts the same thing. But these works are scourges and crosses. When they come upon us, they are like the word of God accusing and opposing our sin. Therefore they must be received with all fear and humility, and we must confess to him, for he is righteous in his works. For thus he says through the prophets Isaiah and Jeremiah: "I will correct thee in judgment; lest thou seem innocent to thyself" (Jer. 46:28; cf. Isa. 38:16). Always there are left in us also some remnants of

This engraving (c. 1464) depicts the burning of Jan Hus at the Council of Constance in 1415. Hus had received a pass guaranteeing him safe conduct to and from the council, but was nevertheless burned at the stake after his conviction in a heresy trial.

35. Bringing the devil into his discussion of heresy, Luther alludes here to Isa. 14:13. He may have gotten this reference from a sermon of St. Bernard of Clairvaux (1090–1153) (Sermons on the Song of Songs, #17), in which Bernard discusses the ins and outs of life in the spirit and the devil's envy of the human race, citing for support Isa. 14:13. For more on the influence of Bernard of Clairvaux on Luther, see Theo M. M. A. C. Bell, *Divus Bernhardus: Bernhard von Clairvaux in Martin Luther's Schriften* (Mainz: Philipp von Zabern, 1993); Franz Posset, *Pater Bernhardus: Martin Luther and Bernard of Clairvaux* (Kalamazoo, MI: Cistercian Publications, 1999.

St. Bernard of Clairvaux (1090–1153) adores the Man of Sorrows. Woodcut by Lucas Cranach the Elder. Bernard was a lifelong favorite of Luther. Some have attributed key elements in Luther's "evangelical breakthrough" to what he learned reading Bernard.

36. Luther's use here of "every such synagogue" as a symbol for heretics suggests that the Jews function for him archetypally, as those who are guilty of sins, namely, of an evil drive and impulse toward wrath, pride, gluttony, and sloth, which are sins in the sight of God, evil and worthy of condemnation, and therefore they must always be punished. So it was with the Jebusites of old on the borders of the children of Israel. Because of them, since they were unable to drive them out, the Israelites were often punished with wars, famine, etc., yes, and enticed to sins.[37]

O Lord, open my lips (v. 17). This properly belongs to the church, because the mouth of the whole Scripture has now been opened and the praise of Christ is publicly proclaimed. But it is opened by faith, without which it is closed, and silent, as it is written: "I have believed, therefore have I spoken" (Ps. 116:10). For faith opens the mouth especially toward God (thus we are now speaking) and concerning God speaking in truth.

Against you I have sinned (v. 6). Why not "against me"? Does not sin harm me and lead to my wretchedness? But it is "against you," that is, "before you," as if to say [Ps. 143:2]: "Even if I should be innocent and holy before men, still I have sinned before you; I am both a sinner and I have done evil, 'for no man living shall be justified in your sight.'"[j]

<table>
<tr>
<td>Thus to you</td>
<td>I am a liar
I am evil
I am stupid
I am blind
I have fallen
I am wretched
I am nothing</td>
<td>so that you may be</td>
<td>truthful, Rom. 3[:4]: "God is truthful, but every human being is a liar."
good, Luke 11[:13]: "You are evil, only God is good."
wise, 1 Cor. 3[:18]: "Whoever wishes to be wise, let him become a fool."
seeing, John 9[:41]: "If you were blind, you would not have sin."</td>
</tr>
</table>

spiritual pride. Thus, he classes prideful Christians and prideful Jews together as one type. Luther also uses the phrase to shame Christian heretics for, in effect, making the same error as the Jews.

37. Luther here makes the Old Testament story of the attacks of the Jebusites against the people of Israel an allegory for the external afflictions—"scourges and crosses"—God visits upon the faithful in order to purge them of their remaining sin.

j A quote from another of the penitential psalms. See Ps. 143:2.

Lectures on Psalm 72

1513–1515

MICKEY L. MATTOX

INTRODUCTION

Scholars today classify Psalm 72 as a "royal psalm," a prayer that God will bless the kings of Israel (beginning with King David's immediate heir, Solomon) and enable them to rule with justice and to judge the people's affairs with righteousness. According to this psalm of prayer, the kings who do so will bless not only the peoples of Israel, but also, eventually, all the nations of the earth. Thus, the psalm finds its place within the religious national life of God's chosen people, the descendants of Abraham, Isaac, and Jacob (Israel).

In Christian understanding this Old Testament prayer for divine blessings on the kingly rule of David's heirs points prophetically ahead toward David's greater descendant, the Messiah of Israel, who will reign as David's final heir, institute a universal kingdom of justice and righteousness, and in this way truly fill the earth with the glory of God. Thus, the "sweet psalmist of Israel," King David, prophetically prays for God's blessings not only upon his earthly descendants, but also upon that greater heir and the kingdom of God he will one day usher in. The deepest meaning of the psalm becomes clear, then, only in the inauguration of the kingly reign of Jesus Christ.

In his remarks on this psalm, Martin Luther was clearly

This woodcut from a 1544 printing of a German Bible shows King David playing the harp while a dove, an image of the Holy Spirit, hovers nearby. The dove suggests that David prays by the inspiration of the Spirit, which enables him to see—and so to prophesy about—the future reign of Christ.

focused not on the kings of ancient Israel or their enthronement ceremonies, but on its prophetic christological meaning. For Luther Psalm 72 is about the justice and the judgment of God, as well as the kingly rule of the Messiah, Jesus Christ. His initial remarks move directly to verse 2, where the psalmist prays that the king may "judge your people with righteousness, and your poor with justice." He employs a number of standard later medieval exegetical tools in an effort to bring out the text's deeper meanings. First, we see him in good Scholastic fashion making careful conceptual distinctions: between human judgment and God's judgment, for example, or between the final judgment when God will sentence some to eternal damnation and the sort of temporal judgment God makes in separating the wicked and the good within the church, and so on. These distinctions themselves, however, reflect and are embedded within a traditional approach to figuring out the meanings of the biblical text.

Working through the ins and outs of justice and righteousness in this psalm, Luther employs the Quadriga,[a] or fourfold method of interpretation, which was developed in the early church and codified in the Middle Ages. This method recognized in Scripture four possible levels or types of meaning. The first is the literal or historical meaning, according to which, for example, the word "Jerusalem" in the Old Testament refers simply to a city in the Middle East. Following this literal meaning there are three different kinds of figurative meaning: allegorical, tropological, and anagogical.[1] The allegorical meaning builds up the Christian in the virtue of *faith*, teaching her what to believe; that is, it teaches her to believe Christian doctrine as it is taught in the allegorical "Jerusalem," the Christian church. The tropological meaning, on the other hand, speaks to the "Jerusalem" that is the human soul. It edifies believers morally, teaches them what is to be done, and so builds them up in the virtue of *love*. Finally, the anagogical meaning edifies believers in the virtue of *hope*. Naturally, then, it pertains to that hoped-for last day, when Christ returns as fearsome judge and brings all things to their appointed end. This final end is understood to include the establishment of Christ's kingdom, which is itself the eschatological Jerusalem. Thus, the application of the Quadriga encourages the biblical interpreter to learn from Scripture not only stories

a A Latin word that means "four-horse chariot."

1. A common Latin verse helped students memorize the fourfold method of interpretation:

Littera gesta docet
quid credas allegoria
moralis quid agas
quo tendas anagogogia

"The letter, teaches deeds
allegory, what you should believe
tropology, what you must do
anagogy, what you should press on for."

This image of the Last Judgment shows Christ appearing in glory to separate the sheep from the goats (Matthew 25). From a 1540 printing of a volume by Andreas Osiander.

about the past, but, through them, a range of meanings that build the Christian up in the three traditional theological virtues: faith, hope, and love.[b]

As Luther's exegesis here suggests, the Quadriga was not typically applied woodenly, as if each word of Scripture had four possible meanings. Instead, the method at its best led readers like Luther to search out the full range of the Bible's significance for Christian faith. The method was restrained, moreover, by the church's own faith and teaching. The so-called rule of faith (*regula fidei*) as given in the classical ecumenical creeds (the Apostolic or Old Roman Creed, and the Nicene Creed) provided broad guidelines to what the expositor should search for in the text, with the understanding that Scripture as a whole is given in order to build up, to edify, that is, all believers in the "faith which was once delivered unto the saints" (Jude 1:3, KJV). Biblical interpretation was thus an ecclesial enterprise, done within and on behalf of the community of faith. At its best, then, the fourfold method encouraged the wide application of the church's faith to the task of biblical interpretation, as we see here powerfully displayed in the Psalms exegesis of the young Augustinian friar, Martin Luther.

This edition translates the text as revised in WA 55, which differs in several respects, chiefly the ordering of paragraphs in the *scholion*, from the earlier edition of the same lecture in WA 3. As a consequence, the material is differently organized from that found in LW 10:403–14 and may better reflect Luther's intentions.

b The *locus classicus* for this triad is 1 Corinthians 13.

LECTURES ON PSALM 72

The judgment of *men*	in public is	just unjust	in	the heart word deed
	in private is	rash unfair true		

According to Scripture, however, that which is called human judgment is contrary to God's judgment. For they consider only earthly goods, calling evil good, and good evil, according to Isa. 5[:20].[2] In a similar manner this is also the case with *righteousness*.

The judgment of God is anagogical,[3] which some call the "judgment of damnation." In the Scriptures [of the old law, but indeed also in the new] this is rarely called judgment. More often it is called "the revelation of judgment," Rom. 2[:5], and "day of retribution," Isa. 61[:2].

The judgment of God is allegorical, which nevertheless is literal according to prophecy. Some call this the "judgment of distinction," since in every judgment there is distinction and condemnation, a sorting out of the good and a damnation of the wicked. This is what Christ as God is doing secretly in the church, and it is inscrutable. Scripture does not often speak of this either. But what he does openly is something else.

The judgment of God is tropological. This is its most frequent use in Scripture. This is the judgment by which God condemns and causes to condemn whatever we have of ourselves, the whole old man with his deeds [even our righteousnesses, Isa. 64:6]. This is properly humility, yes, humiliation. For it is not the one who regards himself as humble that is righteous, but the one who considers himself detestable and damnable in his own eyes [and condemns and compensates for his own sins], he is righteous. [And he justifies God even where God seems unjust. For

2. In Isaiah 5 the Lord through the prophet Isaiah denounces the wickedness of the people of Israel, including their inability rightly to discern the difference between darkness and light, good and evil. Their wickedness extends so far as to even define wickedness as the good, and vice versa. Thus, human judgment fails in moral matters precisely insofar as people are sinful and inclined to wickedness rather than the good.

3. Anagogical here refers to divine judgment in terms of what it will be in the last judgment at the end of history. Luther labels this anagogical judgment a "judgment of damnation," because some will be damned to eternal punishment.

"the foolishness of God is wiser than men" (1 Cor. 1:25). "Better is the iniquity of a man than a woman doing a good turn" (Ecclus. 42:14).[c] And the injustice of God is better than the justice of men.] "He who is dead is justified," Rom. 6[:7].[4] And it is for this distinctive feature that Scripture uses the word *judgment*, to express the true nature of humility, which is the downgrading and contempt and the complete condemnation of oneself.[5] This is the case especially where the word is coupled with righteousness, as, for example, in Isa. 9[:7]: "To strengthen it with judgment and righteousness," and Isa. 11[:4]: "He shall judge the poor with judgment, and reprove with righteousness for the meek of the land." Ps. 89[:14]: "Righteousness and judgment are the preparation of thy throne." Ps. 97[:2]: "Righteousness and judgment are the establishment of his throne." Ps. 99[:4]: "Thou hast done judgment and righteousness in Jacob." Ps. 33[:5]: "He loves mercy and judgment." Ps. 37:28: "The Lord loves judgment." Ps. 99:4: "The king's honor loves judgment." This is the judgment about which all the prophets cry that the Jews have detested it in ancient times, as they still do today. For "Moab is exceedingly proud" [Isa. 16:6], and they are caught in their pride, for "the ungodly shall not rise in the judgment" [Ps. 1:5]. So also Ps. 96[:13] and 98[:9], "He will judge the world with equity. He will judge the people with righteousness. He comes to judge the earth." Thus, the apostle says, "If we would judge ourselves, we would not be judged by the Lord" [1 Cor. 11:31]. This is called the judgment of God, like the righteousness or strength or wisdom of God. It is that by which we are wise, strong, and humble, or by which we are judged.[6]

But since this judgment comes about in heart, word, and deed, like any virtue, neither one suffices without the other. Again, since faith is sometimes taken for the internal act, sometimes for the gospel itself which teaches faith, or for the objects of faith, so it happens that also judgment may sometimes denote

c A modern translation renders this peculiar text: "Better a man's harshness than a woman's indulgence." It has to do with a father's duty to impose loving discipline on a daughter, where a mother might presumably be inclined to indulge her.

4. This peculiar-sounding reference, that those who are dead are justified, comes from Paul's discussion of baptism in the letter to the Romans, where he identifies the Christian's descent into the waters of baptism with Christ's descent into death. When one's "old self" has in this way been put to death, then forgiveness of sin is effected such that one is justified. The other side of this baptismal logic is the rising up out of the water in imitation of and identification with Christ's rising from the dead, which means rising as a new person ready to "walk in newness of life."

5. Scholars often note that Luther's earliest lectures feature prominently the virtue of humility. Sometimes the argument has been made that this early focus on humility later gave way to a newfound joy in the good news of the saving Christ, a rejoicing, that is, and radical confidence in God's word understood as an unbreakable promise to save. In the monastic context reflected in the Psalms lectures translated here, however, Luther focuses on humility at least in part because the monastic life itself requires humility, both as the sinner's proper posture before a holy God and as a virtue crucial to the success of the monastery as a human community.

6. The language here is quite similar to that found many years later in a famous autobiographical reminiscence in which the elder Luther recalled the process whereby he came to understand the gospel of Christ as good news for sinners. The crucial problem was Paul's insistence in Rom. 1:17 that in the gospel the "righteousness of God" is revealed. How, Luther wondered, can the news that God is righteous be "good news" for men and women

the gospel and the word of God, for it teaches us to exercise and perform such judgment.[7] Ps. 19[:9]: "The judgments of the LORD are true, etc." Ps. 10[:5]: "Thy judgments are removed from his sight." Indeed, the word *judgment* can in every place be taken in the sense of word of God [especially when it is used in the plural (as in Ps. 119:102): "I have not turned aside from thy judgments"], for through the word all judgments of God become whatever they become, since also the Son is the judgment and Word of the Father. Therefore these three are one [1 John 5:8]:

Judgment	Word of God		water	
Judgment	self-condemnation	thus	Spirit	These three are one.
Judgment	fulfillment in deed		blood	

Water	the fleeting word in the mouth
Spirit	in the heart
Blood	punishment in the body.

Whoever condemns and downgrades himself in his heart must also demonstrate and suffer the like in the body.

Thus, we interpret tropologically that passage in Ps. 149:6-9: "Two-edged swords in their hands, to execute vengeance upon the nations"—namely, of the senses—"and chastisements among the peoples"—namely, of the impulses of the flesh—"to bind their kings with chains"—namely, the members of sin reigning in the human being—"and their nobles with fetters of iron. That they should execute upon them the judgment that is written"—namely, tropologically.[8] "This glory is in all his saints," that is, no one is holy who is not glorified by that glory [i.e., God's glory], although only their confusion and shame may appear to worldly people, because they are not wise to the things of the Spirit.[9]

But in its own way it can also be understood allegorically. In that very way the righteousness of God is also threefold: tropologically, it is faith in Christ. Rom. 1:17: "For the righteousness of God is revealed in the gospel from faith to faith." And so it is used most often in the Scriptures. Allegorically, it is the church itself as a whole, as the apostle says, "that we might be made the righteousness of God in Christ" (2 Cor. 5:21). Anagogically, it is

who are unrighteous, i.e., sinners? He writes, "There I began to understand that the righteousness of God is that by which the righteous person lives by a gift of God, namely by faith. . . . Here I felt that I was altogether born again and had entered paradise itself through open gates" (LW 34:337). The righteousness of God, as Luther had come to understand it, is not just what God is but also—and even more importantly for fallen humankind—what God gives to the sinner when through faith she is joined to Christ the Savior and so receives God's own "alien righteousness" as a gift that becomes her own possession.

7. Here Luther notes the semantic range of the word *faith* as Christians commonly use it. It may refer either to one's own subjective belief in Christian truth, or, in a nutshell, to the good news about Jesus the Christ, or, more broadly, to all the truths of faith in which the Christian believes.

8. The words of Psalm 149 are taken here as figurative tropes for the personal moral reform to which the Scripture calls every Christian. The "senses" of the Christian are understood figuratively as the "nations" upon which one must take vengeance; similarly, the "impulses of the flesh" are the "peoples" the Christian must chastise; the "members of sin," likewise, are the "nobles" and "kings" that must be bound with chains. Tropologically, then, the psalm is understood as an exhortation to the individual Christian to persist in the personal quest for holiness through renunciation and asceticism.

9. Note that the glory of the saints is hidden from the world's view. Those who judge matters apart from the

God himself in the church triumphant.[10] Just as righteousness properly has to do mainly with good persons and is in them, so also judgment has to do mainly with wicked persons and is in them. For judgment is spoken with regard to damnation, just as righteousness is spoken with regard to salvation.

A corollary: These prayers in the psalms are most pleasant, even if they are spoken out of a prayerful attitude and not brought forward in the course of prophecy. "Judge me, O LORD" [Ps. 43:1]. "Judge the earth" [Ps. 82:8]. "He will judge the world" [Ps. 98:9]. For in that case these expressions must always be understood as referring to a tropological judgment, so that the meaning is: "Judge me, O LORD," that is, "Give me true humility and mortification of my flesh and self-condemnation, that thus I may be saved by thee in spirit." So also: "O LORD, judge the earth," that is, "Teach people to think meanly of themselves and to condemn and crucify their sins." But if they are brought forward prophetically, the words are terrible and full of horror, so that the meaning would be, "Thou wilt judge and condemn them, etc.," and the words are understood as referring to the anagogical judgment.[11]

The law of Christ, the law of peace, the law of grace, the gospel—this is known by many other names, such as "the way of the LORD" in Ps. 25[:10]: "All the ways of the LORD are mercy and truth" (that is, "grace and truth through Jesus Christ," John 1[:17]). So also we read in Isa. 55[:9]: "As the heavens are higher than the earth, so are my ways higher than your ways." And Ps. 71[:19] says: "Thy righteousness [reaches] even to the highest heavens." Ps. 103[:11-12]: "As far as the east is from the west, so far has he removed our iniquities from us. According to the height of the heaven above the earth, he has strengthened his mercy toward those who fear him," that is, he has lifted up grace above the letter, which has been put down, for it is the law of sin and death. Now, then, it is remarkable how grace, or the law of grace (which is the same thing), is both judgment and righteousness. This must be recognized: It is without doubt so, for he both judges and justifies the one who believes in him. Therefore, any word of God whatever is judgment. But God judges in a threefold way:

Spirit's guidance are unable to see the glory concealed under the saints' outward appearance of shame and disorder. Luther magnifies the grace of God at work in the saints here by stressing that they have been made glorious by God's own glory.

10. Here Luther fleshes out all three of the figurative levels of meaning found in the Quadriga: tropologically, "righteousness of God" refers to the faith that justifies the believer; allegorically, "righteousness of God" refers to the entire company of believers gathered into the church; anagogically, "righteousness of God" refers to God as he is with the saints in heavenly glory.

11. Note how Luther's pastoral reading of these psalms depends on taking them not anagogically, with regard to God's coming judgment, but tropologically, with regard to the Christian's standing before God in the here and now. The anagogical as the future prophetic meaning anticipates the "dread judgment seat of Christ," and can therefore only terrify. The tropological meaning, however, is about the prayerful present, the time during which the saving words of God's judgment and righteousness may still be found.

First, tropologically, for he condemns the works of the flesh and of the world. He shows that all that is in us and in the world is abominable and damnable before God.[12] Thus, whoever clings to him by faith necessarily becomes vile and nothing, abominable and damnable, to himself. And that is true humility. Therefore, that word most fittingly expresses the nature and character of humility. It is not he who makes or calls or considers himself humble, but the one who shows himself to be vile and damnable, and this not only in the heart and in word, but also in deed. [And this is the judgment which he mentions here.][13] Consequently, the scourging and crucifixion of the flesh and the condemnation of all that is in the world are the judgments of God which he carries out with his own through judgment, that is, through the gospel and his grace. And thus, righteousness comes about. For to him who is unrighteous to himself and thus humble before God, God gives his grace. In this manner it is most often taken in the Scriptures. Thus, righteousness in a tropological sense is faith in Christ. Rom. 1:17: "The righteousness of God is revealed therein, etc."[14]

Second, allegorically. For as he discerns between the flesh and the spirit and separates their works, approving the latter for justification and disapproving the former—nay more, even all that we have, especially our own righteousnesses—for condemnation, so he also discerns between believers and nonbelievers. For the grace or rule of Christ is not given indiscriminately to all, as was the case formerly in the law and is even now in earthly things, which God seems to give to all without judgment, and sometimes more to the wicked than to the good. Whence the Jews complained in Ezek. 18[:25]: "The way of the Lord is not just." And in the resultant proverb [Ezek. 18:2]: "The fathers have eaten sour grapes." [And in Jer. 23(:33ff.) they said: "The word of the Lord is a burden," and in the same place he said: "Every man's word shall be his burden."] For God also allowed evils to fall indiscriminately on the good and the wicked. And thus God seemed to make no distinction.

But now the gospel consists of spiritual goods. Therefore, by a most rigid distinction these goods are given only to the good, while spiritual evils fall only on the wicked, just as in the same place he foretold. Thence it is called the judgment of God, because it is contrary to the judgment of men. It condemns what men choose and chooses what men condemn. And this judgment

12. The sense of the phrase "before God" here is "in the presence of God." Behind this stands first a profound recognition of God's holiness and incomprehensible self-sufficiency. "Before God" no creature, and still less a fallen and sinful human being, can claim to be owed anything at all. No one can make God a debtor.

13. Luther sets a high standard here, insisting that self-interested admission of one's sin, either out of fear of punishment or in hope of reward, must in the Christian give way to true contrition, based solely on the recognition of the depth of one's unworthiness. The bracketed words remind us that Luther is still working out the meaning of the words justice and judgment, as found in Psalm 71:2.

14. Faith here is the result of the scourging and crucifixion effected within the Christian herself as she experiences God's just judgment of her sin and unworthiness. The humility that results teaches her to cling by faith to the word of God, which brings her the righteousness of God. The gospel message of the judgment of God is thus the means by which God effects faith in the Christian and so grants to her the gift of justification.

has been manifested to us in the cross of Christ, for as he died and became "the one rejected by the people," so we must bear a similar judgment with him, be crucified and die spiritually, as the apostle explains in Rom. 6[:4-11] and 8[:10-11].[15]

It is to be noted, however, that when I say the gospel is judgment and righteousness, this must be understood as referring to the satisfied or fulfilled gospel. For the gospel fulfilled and perfected in deed is the very judgment and righteousness by which Christ rules the church. Otherwise, if it is taken for just the word of the gospel, then it is only judgment and righteousness in that it shows what is to be condemned and what is to be chosen. That is, to express it in our customary way, the gospel is judgment and righteousness really and formally when it is lived in deed, as the gospel itself teaches us. But it is judgment and righteousness in an exhibiting and teaching function when it teaches us that we must live in that way. They who fulfill the gospel are not under the law, for it is no longer over them, since they have fulfilled it and are now even adequate to it. The law does not rule and is not over those who fulfill it. Rather, they rise up to it and reach it.

[The fulfillment of the law is the death of the law. Rom. 7:1: "Only as long as a man lives."]

[For when the gospel is fulfilled in deed, then the word of God is always incarnated spiritually. The work is the flesh, as it were, and the Word is the Son of God, as it were. Therefore the gospel fulfilled is judgment and righteousness, as well as the work of God, the way of God, etc., just as Christ is all this literally in his person.]

Whence whoever wants to understand the apostle and the other Scriptures prudently ought to understand all that tropologically: truth, wisdom, strength, health, righteousness, by which of course it makes us strong, healthy, righteous, wise, and so on. So also the works of God, the way of God, everything literally is Christ, while morally these things are his faith.

Judgment and *righteousness* in the Scriptures of the old law are very rarely taken literally as referring to the future, but most often, indeed always, as referring to the tropological, the moral, and the allegorical. The reason for this is that the old law prophesied strictly only the first advent of Christ, in which Christ rules with kind and salutary judgment, because it is an advent of grace and kindness.[16] Hence, the apostle, in Rom. 3:21-22, says: "The righteousness of God has been manifested apart from the law

15. The imitation of Christ Luther promotes here is one of identification with Jesus in his cross, suffering, and spiritual death.

16. Here Luther draws attention to the grace and kindness of Christ's first advent, when God came to us "meek and mild," in the form of the child born to Mary. This first advent contrasts sharply with the longed for second advent, when Christ returns and every person must stand before the dread judgment seat of Christ.

and the prophets, . . . even the righteousness of God through faith in Jesus Christ." The new law, however, prophesies particularly concerning future judgment and righteousness, since it prophesies the second advent of Christ, which will be in severe judgment and eternal punishment, as is clear from many passages. John 5:27: "He has given him power to execute judgment." 2 Tim. 4:1: "Who is to judge the living and the dead." Rom. 2:5: "The revelation of God's righteous judgment."

It is clear that he is here speaking about the kindly judgment, because he says: *He will judge the poor of the people* (v. 4). For he condemns them in order that he might save them. Again, to *judge thy people in righteousness* (v. 2). But he judges the ungodly in their unrighteousness. And he aptly says "judge," because Christ did not receive judgment from the Father to no purpose, nor only for himself, but on the contrary for us. For he says "judge thy people."

According to Cassiodorus, an *oppressor* (v. 4) is one who attempts by premeditated scheming to bring another's innocence to guilt.[17] This is the devil's own occupation. In Rev. 12:10 it is written: "The accuser of our brethren, who accused them day and night, has been cast forth to the ground." But as the devil inflicts this evil on the whole human race, just so the Jewish people did with Christ, the tyrants with the martyrs, the heretics with the Catholics, and just so do the slanderers and the proud with the good and the simple to the end of this age. But every oppressor has been and will be humbled by Christ.

As is clear in many downfalls of the saints, even now the devil works to display goods, which they may lack, so that he might manage to insert something of himself into them.

5. *And he shall continue with the sun and before the moon.* Though these words may simply depict Christ's eternity, nevertheless they are also pregnant with other mysteries. The Hebrew reads: "And they will fear thee with the sun and beyond the moon." Hence, also the sun and the moon must here be seen tropologically, allegorically, and anagogically.[18]

Anagogically, the sun is the divinity of Christ, the moon his humanity. Thus, the meaning is that Christ consists of sun and the moon, or, as it says most specifically, "with the sun and before the moon." For Christ is with his divinity and before his humanity.[19] For according to his being man, he is before himself in eternity; but according to his being God, he is only with him-

17. In the Psalms lectures, Luther relied extensively on the commentaries of St. Augustine (354–430) and of the less well known ancient Christian writer Flavius Magnus Aurelius Cassiodorus Senator (c. 490–585). Lecturers in premodern Christianity routinely turned to the writings of esteemed Christians when developing their own interpretations of the Bible. Luther is not working in these lectures, then, equipped solely with the Bible and his own keen insight. To the contrary, he is drawing on the ancient traditions of scriptural interpretation to offer his own distinctive reading of the Psalms. For the remarks of Cassiodorus that Luther references here, see *Cassiodorus—Explanation of the Psalms*, vol. 2, trans. P. G. Walsh (Mahwah, NJ: Paulist, 1991), 186.

18. Luther here takes the differences between the Hebrew and the Latin text as suggestive of different levels of allegorical meaning. From 1506, Luther had been studying Hebrew, using a Hebrew lexicon in these early lectures to explore the insights that could be gained through the study of the Hebrew words and grammar. For Luther's use of Hebrew in the Psalms lectures, see Siegfried Raeder, *Grammatica Theologica: Studien zu Luthers Operationes in Psalmos* (Tübingen: J. C. B. Mohr, 1977).

19. In the classical Christian teaching about Christ (Christology), the Son is eternally begotten of the Father in the unity of the Holy Spirit. Eternally, therefore, the one God is these three persons: Father, Son, Holy Spirit. Of these three, only the Son became incarnate in the womb of the Virgin Mary. And this becoming incarnate did not cause the Son to come into existence. To the contrary, he existed eternally prior to and apart from his

self. Yet now he remains in both eternally, namely, continuing both as God and as man in himself, and as such in his believers through faith. But the Hebrew is like this: "They will fear thee (namely, with filial fear[20]) with the sun (that is, the Son) with the same reverential worship; and beyond the moon, that is, worshiping him more in his divinity than as man in himself.

[The Hebrew easily agrees with this, for Christ (is said to remain) with the sun and before the moon. He is to be believed in as God and man, and to be worshiped and feared in this way. But as far as he is man, he is beyond the moon before himself, because he is God. For it is believed that he is something beyond the moon before the humanity, namely, God. And this is said in opposition to the heretics. But if it is simply understood in the literal sense, the question arises whether it can also be said like this: "He will remain with the sun," that is, like the sun? As Ps. 9(:6) says: "Their memory has perished with the sound," that is, like the sound, or in the manner of a sound. So here "with the sun" means in the manner of the sun, or like the sun, for the sun does not pass through changes in its light as the moon does. Thus, Christ remains the same through all the times of the church, while some flourish and others decline. Therefore he says "beyond," or "before," the moon, that is, more than the moon and above the moon, that is, the church, which experiences various changes in growth and decrease. Yet Christ is the same; he is always the sun.]

Allegorically, the sun is Christ, while the moon is his church.[21]

Tropologically, the sun is the believer's soul, while the moon is his flesh. For as the moon, according to the astronomers, is always bright in one half of its sphere, namely, in that part which is turned toward the sun, from which it gets all its light, so the church is always half-lighted, that is, according to the soul, while according to the flesh it is dark before the world. Many other mysteries in the movement of the moon can be gathered from the Scriptures at random. In Prov. 7[:20] we read: "In the day of the full moon."

Therefore Christ remains in this way with his humanity and before the moon, that is, in the presence of the church, which always has him before herself, because she receives her light from him. Or because he is before and prior to the church and is her head. For the sun does not have its light from the moon, but the moon from the sun. Therefore the moon is not before the sun,

appearance in the flesh. Luther's words here reflect this ancient Christian teaching. The psalmist's phrase "with the sun" anagogically denotes that the Son is co-eternal with the Father, while "before the moon" means that he became human in time. As God he is eternal, but as man temporal. Thus, as Luther continues here, as God he is "before himself," that is, prior to his own humanity.

20. St. Augustine made a famous distinction between two different kinds of fear. "Servile fear" is the kind of dread the slave experiences when confronted by the master. "Filial fear," on the other hand, refers to the dread and reverence a son or daughter has in relation to father or mother. Luther is speaking of the latter here, interpreting the psalm as a prophecy that Christ's people will offer him "reverential worship" as God.

21. The analogy Luther presents here, between the sun and the moon, on the one hand, and Christ and the church, on the other hand, presents itself as plausible at least in part because in Latin the words "sun" and "Christ" are both masculine gender nouns, while "moon" and "church" are feminine gender nouns. The masculine sun is its own light and glory just as Christ, as God, is also his own light and glory. The feminine moon, on the other hand, reflects the sun's light and glory even as the church reflects the light and glory of her Lord, Jesus Christ.

but the sun before the moon.[22] Tropologically, he remains with the sun, that is, the faithful soul, before its flesh, that is to say, in spirit.

6. *He will come down like rain upon the fleece, etc.* First, he will become incarnate without a human work.[23] Therefore Mic. 5[:7] said of the apostles: "The remnant of Jacob will be in the midst of many peoples like dew from the Lord and like drops on the grass, which do not wait for man nor tarry for the children of men." As Christ was conceived by the Holy Spirit, so every believer is justified and reborn by no human work but entirely by the grace of God and the activity of the Holy Spirit. Second, Lyra and Cassiodorus[d] suggest that just as the fleece receives the rain and gives it back while remaining unharmed, so the Virgin conceived and gave birth without loss of virginity. For both we sing in the sequence: "With the Holy Spirit bringing down the dewfall, Gabriel singled out the almond tree that was to produce the divine blossom."[24] But the fact that first the fleece and then the earth was sprinkled with the dew signifies, according to Augustine, first the synagogue and then the Gentile world.

7. *Until the moon be taken away*, both the literal and the mystical one. But the moon is literally taken away when it becomes full, as the sun presently is. For now it is always half-shining, and by a foreign light, but then it will shine with its own light.[25] The alternating of light in it will come to an end, as Isa. 30[:26] says: "The light of the moon will be like the light of the sun, and the light of the sun will be sevenfold, as the light of seven days." I do not understand this, as many do, as referring to the first days, when they say that the sun was seven times brighter than it is now but was darkened because of Adam's sin, so that now it hardly shines with one-seventh part. Nor does the Isaiah passage say this, nor does it demand this understanding, but it says that the light of the sun will be seven times the light of the sun, as the

22. Here the sun is "before" the moon as a source of light to its reflection. Analogously, Christ is "before" the church both as the source of her reflected light and in priority over the church, as her "head."

23. Luther's language here suggests that he is speaking of the initial act of conception whereby the Virgin Mary became pregnant. If that is correct, then he means by "without human work" simply that Jesus was conceived without an act of sexual intercourse, that is, without a human father, but instead by the Holy Spirit.

24. Luther quotes here a well-known sequence hymn, which was chanted during the celebration of the Mass. This particular one was sung during the Christmas season (Epiphany). It praised the Virgin Mary as a new "tree of life," like the one that stood in the Garden of Eden before the exile of Adam and Eve. Mary was thus the tree, as we have it here, that produced the "divine blossom," that is, her son Jesus, who would bring redemption and new life to fallen humankind.

25. Luther and his contemporaries were well aware that only one side of the moon was visible. One side was illuminated, the other dark. Here again, then, he takes these facts regarding nature as figures of spiritual realities.

d Nicholas of Lyra (c. 1270–1349). For Cassiodorus, see n. 17, p. 238 above.

light of seven days, that is, as if seven days were one day and out of this sevenfold light of days one light were to come into being. However, it can easily be granted that the light of the sun is seven times brighter than the light of the moon. Therefore as much as the moon will increase, so much also the sun in brightness.[26]

Thus, the church, as the spiritual moon, will be "taken away," when it will shine like the sun according to the body and when it will shine in the bright vision of God according to the soul, in which it already shines by faith. This vision will surpass the brightness of faith seven times and more. In the meantime, however, while it is bright in its middle part (that is, according to the spirit through faith), which is the ray coming down on it from Christ, the Sun, and is dark in its other part (that is, according to the body), righteousness and an abundance of peace will always arise. So 1 Cor. 13:10 says: "When that which is perfect has come, that which is in part will be done away."

Behold a miracle. In all the prophets, when the peoples which are converted to Christ are specifically enumerated, only southern ones are mentioned, like Ethiopians, Arabians, and Egyptians.[27] On the contrary, when evils are prophesied, almost always northern peoples are mentioned, such as Gog, Magog, Tubal, Meshech, and Dedan. This demonstrates the difference between both groups of peoples. The southerners are the ones to whom the sun draws near through faith, while the northerners are the ones from whom the sun withdraws because of unbelief. And as the sun performs this judgment in the whole world, so Christ does the same with the whole human race. Thus, the reason is given why the Ethiopians are brought in before others, namely, because of the mystery. For the Ethiopians denote those who have the most ardent faith. As the sun is nearest to the Ethiopians and they have been stained blackest of all by it, so those who are most fervent in their faith in Christ are nearest

26. Light or illumination in Christian theology often symbolizes the divine or the experience of God's self-revelation. In St. Paul's first letter to Timothy, for example, Jesus Christ is said to dwell "in unapproachable light," and Paul himself was blinded by "a light from heaven" when he met the risen Christ on the road to Damascus (Acts 9:3-9). In the traditional Christian imagination, the heavens above are illumined by the sun, moon, and stars, and these in turn point beyond themselves toward the "unapproachable" light in which their Creator dwells. Luther clearly thinks of the sun and moon in just this way. In this case he rejects a venerable interpretation of Isaiah 20 (which he is using to try to understand Ps. 72:7), according to which the sevenfold increase of light mentioned in Isaiah 30 refers back to the original, pristine world of the first creation, before the darkening brought about by the sin of Adam and Eve. The "seven days" Isaiah mentions, then, do not refer back to the days of the creation and divine rest, but forward to a future increase in the brightness of the sun, an increase that both reflects and is the reality of the world divinized, a bright realm of participation in the light of God that exceeds even the great light of its first creation. At the same time, however, Luther also thinks that this text refers allegorically to the church, which will "shine like the sun," and tropologically to the faithful soul, which in the eschatological fulfillment will be illumined by the brightness of vision rather than only by faith.

27. Here the difference between north and south is taken as symbolic of the difference between faith and unbelief. Thus, the southern peoples, nearer as they are to the sun and so more

to him, and he to them. Therefore they are especially stained by him when they acknowledge themselves to be black and humble themselves before him, as in Song of Sol. 1[:4]: "I am black but beautiful."

10. *Of Tarshish.* It was said above, in connection with Psalm 48, that this is sometimes used for the sea. So it appears to be taken here, because he adds, *and of the islands*, as if to say, the kings of the sea and the islands which are in the sea. Hence, the Mediterranean Sea is meant, on whose southern shore are the kingdoms of Egypt, Africa, Numidia, Mauretania, Libya, and Cyrene. On the other side and on the northern shore are the realms of Spain, France, Italy, Greece, Asia, Ionia, Pamphylia, Lycia, Cilicia, Antioch, Syria, etc. All these are situated on the shore of our sea, that is, the Mediterranean. And all of them will serve gloriously under the faith in Christ.

illumined by it, symbolize those peoples who receive the good news of Christ in faith. Conversely, the northern nations with their distance and annual withdrawal from the sun each winter symbolize unbelief. Similarly, dark-skinned peoples symbolize those nearest to God because the darkness of their skin results from their constant nearness to the sun and so is analogous to the spiritual darkness the faithful come to acknowledge within themselves as they draw near to Christ in faith. In this case, then, southern and dark are superior to northern and light. It is important to note that in Luther's thought neither one's geographical location nor one's skin color determines one's relation to God. All peoples everywhere and of every color are invited to let the bright glad tidings of Christ shine in them through faith.

A leaf from the *Gunda Gunde Gospels* (Ethiopia, c. 1540)

Where we have "kings of the Arabians," the Hebrew has "kings of Sheba (expressed by a thick and foaming Swabian S) and Seba (expressed by a thin and slender S)."[28] The difference between them is that the first "Sheba" denotes Fertile Arabia and gets its name from Sheba, the son of a son, that is, a grandson, of Cush, who was the son of Ham, per Gen. 10[:7]. In Latin it is called Sabea, where incense and myrrh are native. [It extends to the shore of the Red Sea on the east side.] Vergil said, "The frankincense-shrub belongs only to the Sabeans."[29] This is what Scripture calls Fertile Arabia. So below, "He shall be given some of the gold of Arabia" [Ps. 72:15]. The Hebrew has "Sheba," which is Fertile Arabia. From there came the queen of Sheba who visited Solomon in 1 Kings 10[:7ff.]. But the second "Seba" is a royal city of Ethiopia, and gets its name from Seba, a son of Cush himself. Hence, in Hebrew Cush is called an Ethiopian because he is the ancestor of the Ethiopians.

It is thought that the wise men who came to the newborn Christ came from these two places. The same thing can be the meaning of the first part of the verse, namely, "the kings of Tarshish," that is, of the Red Sea, which only the Arabians of Fertile Arabia, or the Sabeans, possess on both shores, and consequently also the islands in between. And so the second part would be a repetition of the same thought for greater clarity. But the first is better, since it agrees with Isa. 60[:5-7], which says: "When the multitude of the sea [as if to say, "the kings of Tarshish"] shall be converted to thee, the strength of the Gentiles shall come to thee [as if to say, "and the islands"]. The dromedaries of Midian and Epha. All they from Sheba shall come, bringing gold and frankincense." Again, "all the flocks of Kedar shall be gathered together unto thee; the rams of Nebaioth shall minister to thee." These words in some manner express what and of what kind these gifts are, for he wants us to think of men who are to be converted, namely, to the service of Christ. Hence, threefold Arabia, which the Latins call stony, desert, and fertile, is in Scripture labeled in this way, that Fertile Arabia is always called Sheba, and Desert Arabia keeps its own name because Arab means desert, while Stony Arabia has not just one name, but is sometimes called Midian, Epha, Nebaioth, and Kedar, but more often Kedar. And the Ishmaelites, Ammonites, Moabites, Midianites, and Edomites are all in Arabia.

28. Luther notes here that the Vulgate text reads "kings of the Arabians," and he then compares that to what is found in the original Hebrew, which he either knew from St. Jerome's *Quaestiones Hebraicae* or from his own study of the Hebrew text.

29. The mention of the ancient Roman poet Vergil (70–19 BCE) here reminds us that Luther was intimately familiar with a wide range of non-Christian authors from Greek and Roman antiquity and sometimes used their works to shed light on the Bible.

Engraving of the *Adoration of the Magi* (1501) by Albrecht Dürer

16. *There will be* {
a strong support (Septuagint)
memorial wheat (Jerome)
an abundance of wheat (Lyra)
a cake of wheat (Paul of Burgs)
a little bit of grain (Kimchi)[30]
} *on the*

earth on the tops of the mountains, in Chaldean,[e] "on the heads of the priests." All of these come out the same way. For "above the mountains" he called the apostles and their successors. But the top, or the pinnacle, of the mountains is their head. On this pinnacle Christ in the sacrifice of the Mass is the grain and the heavenly bread in the sacramental form.

30. Luther lists here the various possible translations of the Hebrew of verse 16, beginning with the Greek translation in the Septuagint version of the Old Testament, followed by three well-known Christian biblical scholars, and, lastly, by the reading of David Kimchi (1160–1235), a Jewish scholar whose works on the Old Testament were often consulted by Christians.

e Luther's mention of Chaldean here refers to the Targum, paraphrases of the Old Testament in the Aramaic language.

First, "a strong support," because "bread strengthens a man's heart," Ps. 104[:15]. And Christ in this sacrament is the unique and singular strong support of the whole Christian faith and religion. Remove this sacrament, says Bonaventure,[31] and there will be a confused paganism and idolatry throughout the church.

Second, it is "a wheat to be remembered," for it was instituted in memory of the Lord's suffering. Therefore it is called a memorial of the Lord.

Third, "an abundance," because such a sacrament is abundantly provided throughout the world.

Fourth, "a cake." This rather gives expression to the form and shape (the rite and ceremonies) of the sacrament.

Fifth, "a little bit." This indicates the amount of bread. However, the fact that the Septuagint preferred to write "strong support" was done because they clearly did not want to surrender so holy a sacrament to the pagans.

They of the city shall flourish like the grass of the earth. Because of its fleeting existence, grass has a bad meaning.[32] Isaiah 40[:6-7]: "All flesh is as grass, and all its glory as the flower of grass. The grass withers and the flower of the grass fades. Indeed, the people is grass," namely, because of mortality and transitory existence. But with respect to its origin it has a good meaning. In the first place, as grass comes up without human endeavor, so also the children of the church. Second, as the grass comes up suddenly all over the earth, so the faithful spring up throughout the world, for "his word runs swiftly" [Ps. 147:15]. As the grass in spring is a most delightful sight in the meadows, so it was with the early church in the martyrs. That was the most delightful time of the church, when there were so many flowers and fragrant grass everywhere. Thus, "the vines in flower yield their sweet smell" [Song of Sol. 2:13].

31. Luther thought highly of St. Bonaventure (1221-1274), a Franciscan who had been canonized a saint only one year before Luther's birth.

32. Here again Luther points out how something good in itself—in this case, grass—can be used symbolically in Scripture to illustrate something bad—in this case human, mortality. Per Isaiah 49, our lives are fleeting, just as the bright green grass of spring withers and dies in the late summer heat. Fascinatingly, however, Luther immediately turns the symbol around and notes how new grass can also represent such good spiritual realities as the "springing up" of those who respond to the word in faith, their universality across the earth, and even the "fragrant grass" of the holy martyrs. In mentioning the martyrs here Luther seems to allude vaguely to the well-known saying of Tertullian (c. 150–c. 220), the first Latin-writing Christian theologian, in his *Apologeticum*, that "the blood of the martyrs is the seed of the church."

Commentary on Psalm 118

1530

ERIK H. HERRMANN

INTRODUCTION

Luther's interpretation of the Psalms stretches back to his time as a monk, when the daily prayers in the canonical hours were shaped by the Psalter. Regarded as the entry point into the Bible,[1] the Psalms were approached not only as a devotional prayer book but as a prophetic text through which Christ was promised and presaged. It is not surprising, then, that his inaugural lectures as a university professor were based on the Psalms.[a] For two years, 1513–1515, Luther navigated this "dark and holy labyrinth," interpreting what were admittedly difficult poetic texts in order to better understand the message of the Scriptures. At that time, Luther frequently appealed to the traditional medieval hermeneutical method, namely, that the Scriptures could be interpreted by a fourfold sense: literal, allegorical, tropological, and anagogical. Luther viewed the Psalms as a "hard nut," their meaning inaccessible unless split open against the "Rock" which is Christ. For this reason, Luther interpreted the Psalms in these lectures as prophecies about the time of Christ or the very words of Christ himself. To read them merely as examples of faith and

1. Cassiodorus (c. 485–c. 585): "It is proper that one enters into the divine law through the Psalter," cited by Gerhard Ebeling, "Luthers Psalterdruck vom Jahre 1513," in *Lutherstudien* 1 (Tübingen: Mohr/Siebeck, 1971), 69. Cf. Jerome, *Ep.* 107, 12.

a Cf. LW 10 and 11.

piety within the Old Testament was to prefer the "letter" to the "spirit."[2]

Luther would eventually move away from these traditional approaches to the Psalter. Lecturing on Paul, and with the help of Augustine's writings, the distinction of "letter" and "spirit" would become the dialectic of law and gospel. As such, the Psalter not only contained prophecies of Christ but also the prayers of God's ancient people, which were models of faith in midst of both joy and suffering. When he lectured again on the Psalms in 1519, his interpretation reflected this new hermeneutic.[b]

When it came to Luther's reform of *Geistlichkeiten*, that is, the various devotional practices common in late medieval piety,[c] his translation of the Psalter into German was his answer to the popular *Legenda aurea*—the "Lives of the Saints" literature.[3] Rather than the *works* of the saints, the Psalms offered their *words*, "how they spoke with God and prayed, and still speak and pray. Compared to the Psalter, the other legends and examples present to us nothing but mere silent saints; the Psalter, however, pictures for us real, living, active saints."[d] Following his program of reform which sought to return the reading of the Bible as the central Christian practice for faith and piety, Luther argued that the Psalms were to be the constant companion of the Christian, for they drew one into the communion of saints and into Christ, the head of all the saints. They might as well be called "a little Bible."

These assumptions continued to stand behind his ongoing interpretation of the Psalms throughout his career. Of particular value to Luther was Psalm 118. In 1529, he gratefully received from the poet Eoban Hess (1488–1540) a Latin versification of the psalm. "I read it and reread it daily," Luther effused. At the end of 1529, he published a brief commentary on the same poetic version. Shortly afterwards, he announced his intention to work

2. 2 Cor. 3:6, "For the letter kills, but the Spirit gives life." Two contrasting but helpful analyses of Luther's hermeneutical approach in his first Psalms lectures are the following: Gerhard Ebeling, "The Beginnings of Luther's Hermeneutics," *Lutheran Quarterly* 7 (1993): 129–58, 315–38, 451–68; and James Samuel Preus, *From Shadow to Promise: Old Testament Interpretation from Augustine to the Young Luther* (Cambridge: Harvard University Press, 1969).

3. Cf. LW 35:253: "Over the years a great many legends of the saints, and passionals, books of examples, and histories have been circulated; indeed the world has been so filled with them that the Psalter has been neglected. . . . I hold, however, that no finer book of examples or of the legends of the saints has ever come, or can come, to earth than the Psalter. If one were to wish that from all the examples, legends, and histories, the best should be collected and brought together and put in the best form, the result would have to be the present Psalter."

Woodcut (1526) portrait of Eoban Hess attributed to Albrecht Dürer

b WA 5:19–673.

c See Scott Hendrix, "Martin Luther's Reformation of Spirituality," in *Harvesting Martin Luther's Reflections on Theology, Ethics, and the Church* (Grand Rapids: Eerdmans, 2004), 240–60.

d LW 35:254f.

up a larger commentary on the *Confitemini*.[4] But this work was complicated by the imperial summons to Augsburg for which a statement on the controverted doctrines and practices were to be presented. At the elector's request, Luther, Johannes Bugenhagen (1485-1558), Justus Jonas (1493-1555), and Philip Melanchthon (1497-1560) all set to work. The result would be the *Confessio Augustana* (the *Augsburg Confession*).

4. A common liturgical title for Psalm 118, from the first verse in the Vulgate: *"alleluia confitemini Domino quoniam bonus quoniam in saeculum misericordia eius."*

So that Luther could be near the diet, the elector sent him to the Coburg castle. Although visitors would come, Luther often felt the loneliness of the place, isolated from his colleagues. It is in this context that he would turn again to the Psalms for solace, especially Psalm 118. Shortly after arriving at the Coburg, he had verse 17 written on the wall of his chamber: "I shall not die, but I shall live, and recount the deeds of the LORD." During the following months, Luther resumed his commentary on Psalm 118. The context of the diet was particularly fitting for this text, which trumpets confidence in God's provisions and goodness in the face of the powers of princes: "It is better to take refuge in the LORD than to put confidence in mortals. It is better to take refuge in the LORD than to put confidence in princes" (Ps. 118:8-9). Luther would cite passages from the psalm in his letters to Melanchthon, who continued to be anxious about the course of the diet. As such, the commentary on Psalm 118 had the character of a parallel confession to that which was presented at Augsburg. Although every effort and measure was taken to clearly confess the Evangelical faith before the emperor, the preservation of the church belongs to Christ alone: "Christ himself brought us the word; we did not invent it. He must preserve it, for we cannot do so with our

The twenty-one articles of the Augsburg Confession illustrated by Wenceslas Hollar (1607-1677)

might and skill. Christ instituted, founded, and built Christendom. He must also protect and promote it."[e]

Psalm 118

1 O give thanks to the LORD, for he is good;
his steadfast love endures forever!
2 Let Israel say,
"His steadfast love endures forever."
3 Let the house of Aaron say,
"His steadfast love endures forever."
4 Let those who fear the LORD say,
"His steadfast love endures forever."
5 Out of my distress I called on the LORD;
the LORD answered me and set me in a broad place.
6 With the LORD on my side I do not fear.
What can mortals do to me?
7 The LORD is on my side to help me;
I shall look in triumph on those who hate me.
8 It is better to take refuge in the LORD
than to put confidence in mortals.
9 It is better to take refuge in the LORD
than to put confidence in princes.
10 All nations surrounded me;
in the name of the LORD I cut them off!
11 They surrounded me, surrounded me on every side;
in the name of the LORD I cut them off!
12 They surrounded me like bees;
they blazed like a fire of thorns;
in the name of the LORD I cut them off!
13 I was pushed hard, so that I was falling,
but the LORD helped me.
14 The LORD is my strength and my might;
he has become my salvation.
15 There are glad songs of victory in the tents of the righteous:
"The right hand of the LORD does valiantly;

e See page 263 below.

[16] the right hand of the LORD is exalted;
the right hand of the LORD does valiantly."
[17] I shall not die, but I shall live,
and recount the deeds of the LORD.
[18] The LORD has punished me severely,
but he did not give me over to death.
[19] Open to me the gates of righteousness,
that I may enter through them
and give thanks to the LORD.
[20] This is the gate of the LORD;
the righteous shall enter through it.
[21] I thank you that you have answered me
and have become my salvation.
[22] The stone that the builders rejected
has become the chief cornerstone.
[23] This is the LORD's doing;
it is marvelous in our eyes.
[24] This is the day that the LORD has made;
let us rejoice and be glad in it.
[25] Save us, we beseech you, O LORD!
O LORD, we beseech you, give us success!
[26] Blessed is the one who comes in the name of the LORD.
We bless you from the house of the LORD.
[27] The LORD is God,
and he has given us light.
Bind the festal procession with branches,
up to the horns of the altar.
[28] You are my God, and I will give thanks to you;
you are my God, I will extol you.
[29] O give thanks to the LORD, for he is good,
for his steadfast love endures forever.

COMMENTARY ON PSALM 118

Preface[5]

TO THE VENERABLE LORD, Fredrick, Abbot of Saint Giles of Nuremberg, my gracious lord and patron.[6] Grace and peace in Christ, our Lord and Savior!

My venerable and dear lord and patron:

While I should like to show my gratitude to you for your love and favor to me, I am, by earthly standards, a beggar. Besides, even if I had much, there is nothing special I could do for you in your position. And so I turned to my wealth, which I treasure so much, and took up my beloved psalm, the beautiful *Confitemini*, putting down on paper the thoughts which came to me. I am quite idle here in the wilderness;[7] and yet, in order to spare my head, I need to pause and rest occasionally in the hard work that I hope to complete soon, the translation of the Prophets into German.[8]

These thoughts of mine I decided to send you as a gift. I have nothing better. Though some may consider this a lot of useless drivel, I know it contains nothing evil or un-Christian. This is my own beloved psalm. Although the entire Psalter and all of Holy Scripture are dear to me as my only comfort and source of life, I fell in love with this psalm especially. Therefore I call it my own.[9] When emperors and kings, the wise and the learned, and even saints could not aid me, this psalm proved a friend and helped me out of many great troubles. As a result, it is dearer to me than all the wealth, honor, and power of the pope, the Turk, and the emperor. I would be most unwilling to trade this psalm for all of it.

But lest anyone, knowing that this psalm belongs to the whole world, raise his eyebrow at my claim that this psalm is mine, may he be assured that no one is being robbed. After all, Christ is mine, and yet he belongs to all believers. I will not be jealous but will gladly share what is mine. Would to God all the world would claim this psalm for its own, as I do! Peace and love could not compare with such a friendly quarrel. Sad to say, there are few,

5. The English translation for this edition is a revision of that which is found in LW 14:43–106. The revisions are based on WA 31/1:65–182. Annotations and footnotes are the work of the editors but are also informed by notes included in previous critical editions.

6. Fredrick Pistorius (d. 1553), the last abbot of St. Aegidius (in English, St. Giles) Benedictine monastery in Nuremberg, was supportive of Luther already in the early 1520s. The city council allowed him to retain his title and accommodations even after he married and turned to the Evangelical cause. In 1527, Luther received from Pistorius a pocket watch—a rare gift for which he was grateful; cf. WA Br 4:194.

7. A reference to the castle at Coburg where Luther remained hidden during the Diet of Augsburg.

8. From 1523 to 1532, Luther was engaged in the task of translating the Old Testament from Hebrew into German. Luther's time at the Coburg was a particularly intensive time for this work.

9. Psalm 118 remained Luther's favorite throughout his life. The words from v. 17, "I shall not die, but I shall live, and recount the deeds of the LORD," were, in effect, his personal motto and were sometimes incorporated into his coat of arms. While at the Coburg, Luther had the words of this verse painted on the walls of his room (Brecht 2:372).

even among those who should do better, who honestly say even once in their lifetime to Scripture or to one of the psalms: "You are my beloved book; you must be my very own psalm."

The neglect of Scripture, even by spiritual leaders, is one of the greatest evils in the world.[10] Everything else, arts or literature, is pursued and practiced day and night, and there is no end of labor and effort; but Holy Scripture is neglected as though there were no need of it. Those who condescend to read it want to absorb everything at once. There has never been an art or a book on earth that everyone has so quickly mastered as the Holy Scriptures. But its words are not, as some think, mere words for reading; they are words of life,[11] intended not for speculation and fantasy but for life and action. But why complain? No one pays any attention to our lament. May Christ our Lord help us by his Spirit to love and honor his holy word with all our hearts. Amen. I commit myself to your prayer.

Out of the desert.[12] 1 July 1530. Martin Luther

10. The neglect of Scripture for the sake of other writings was a constant theme in Luther's calls for reform. This also made him reluctant to have his own writings preserved and collected. See *Preface to the Wittenberg Edition of Luther's German Writings* (1539), TAL 4:475–88.

11. Luther is using a word play with the German *Lesewort* and *Lebewort*.

12. Coburg; see n. 7 above.

The Beautiful *Confitemini*

1. O give thanks to the Lord, for he is good;
his steadfast love endures forever!

This psalm is a general statement of thanksgiving for all the kindnesses God daily and unceasingly showers on all people, both good and evil.[13] That is the custom of the holy prophets. When they want to thank and praise God for a particular blessing, they begin with lofty words that are all-inclusive in their praise of every one of his wonders and kindnesses. Since this psalm praises God especially for the greatest benefit he bestowed on the world, namely, for Christ and his kingdom of grace—first promised and now revealed—the writer begins with a general statement of praise: "O give thanks to the Lord; for he is a loving, gracious, good, and compassionate God, who continually does good and abundantly heaps his goodness upon us."

You must not read the words "good" and "his steadfast love" with dull indifference. Nor dare you skim over them "as the nuns read the Psalter,"[14] or as choirmasters and choristers bleat and bellow these fine words in the churches. No, you must bear in

13. That God's goodness is exhibited by divine generosity "to both the good and the evil" is a reference to Jesus's own description of God the Father: ". . . For he makes his sun rise on the evil and on the good, and sends rain on the just and on the unjust (Matt. 5:45); cf. Luke 6:35; Acts 14:16-17. Luther makes this connection already in his very first lectures on the Psalms in 1515 (WA 55/1:759,5), and repeats it again in his glosses on this psalm in 1529 (WA 31/1:49,1). In the exegetical tradition, Augustine also makes a similar point on this verse in his *Ennarationes in Psalmos*: "[God], who not only does not evil for evil, but even returns good for evil."

14. A German saying that means "without understanding." The idea is that the nuns, who were not trained to read Latin, could not understand the psalms that they sung daily.

mind that these are vibrant, significant, and meaningful words; they express and emphasize one theme: God is good, but not as a human being is good; from the very bottom of his heart he is inclined to help and do good continually. He is not given to anger or inclined to punish except where necessary and where persistent, impenitent, and stubborn wickedness compels and drives him to it. A human being would not delay punishment and restrain anger as God does; that person would punish a hundred thousand times sooner and harder than God does.

God abundantly and convincingly proves his friendly and gracious favor by his daily and everlasting goodness, as the psalmist writes: "His steadfast love endures forever"; that is, he unceasingly showers the best upon us. He is the Creator of our bodies and souls, our Protector by day and by night, and the Preserver of our lives. He causes the sun and the moon to shine on us, fire, air, water, and the heavens to serve us. He causes the earth to give food, fodder, wine, grain, clothes, wood, and all necessities. He provides us with gold and silver, house and home, wife and child, cattle, birds, and fish. In short, who can count it all? And all this is bountifully showered upon us every year, every day, every hour, and every minute.[15] Who could measure even this one goodness of God, that he gives and preserves a healthy eye or hand? When we are sick or must get along without one of these, then we begin to realize what a blessing it is to have a healthy hand, foot, leg, nose, or finger; then we begin to realize what a blessing bread, clothing, water, fire, and home are.

If we human beings were not so blind and so smug and indifferent toward the blessings of God, there would not be a man on earth, no matter how wealthy, who would trade an empire or a kingdom for them; for he would surely be robbed in the deal. What is a kingdom compared with a sound body? What is all the money and wealth in the world compared with one sunlit day? Were the sun to stop shining for one day, who would not rather be dead; for what would then be the value of wealth and power? What would the finest wine or malmsey[16] in the world amount to if we had to go without water for one day? What would our magnificent castles, houses, silk, satin, purple, golden jewelry, precious stones, all our pomp and glitter and show help us if we had to do without air for the length of one Our Father?[f]

f For a similar expression, see LW 22:36 n.34.

15. Cf. Luther's similar remarks written the year before in his catechisms on the first article of the Creed and the First Commandment, e.g., "he has given me and still preserves my body and soul: eyes, ears, and all limbs and senses; reason and all mental faculties. In addition, God daily and abundantly provides shoes and clothing, food and drink, house and farm, spouse and children, fields, livestock, and all property—along with all the necessities and nourishment for this body and life. God protects me against all danger and shields me from all evil. And all this is done out of pure, fatherly, and divine goodness and mercy, without any merit or worthiness of mine at all. For all of this I owe it to God to thank and praise, serve and obey him," SC, "Creed," 2; BC, 354-55.

16. An allusion to the increasingly prevalent custom of importing the strong, sweet wines from southern Europe and the Mediterranean into Germany.

These gifts of God are the greatest and also the most despised. Because they are so common, no one thanks God for them. People simply accept and use them daily, as though it had to be so, and we had a perfect right to them and did not even need to thank God. In the meantime they are quick and frantic to do, worry, quarrel, wrangle, strive, and storm after unnecessary money and goods, honor and luxury—in short, after something which cannot hold a candle[17] to the blessings mentioned above. These things are not worth a fraction of the others. Instead, they hinder us in the happy and peaceful enjoyment of the common blessings, so that we can neither recognize them as such nor thank God for them. This is the work of the devil, who will not let us use or recognize the goodness of God and his abundant daily blessings, lest we enjoy too much happiness.

Now, tell me, how many people on earth understand this verse? True, even the worst scoundrel who sings or hears this verse in church imagines that he thoroughly understands its meaning. He feels that he has drained the last drop of meaning from it, even though he has never in his whole life thought much about it or given thanks for the milk he drew from his mother's breast, to say nothing of all the other blessings which, during his whole life, God has immeasurably and unceasingly showered upon him. If God were a usurer and demanded an accounting, his hourly sins of ingratitude would be more numerous than the leaves and grass in the forest.

Therefore this verse should be in the heart and mouth of every man every day and every moment.[18] Every time he eats or drinks, sees, hears, smells, walks, stands; every time he uses his limbs, his body, his possessions, or any creature, he should recall that if God did not give him all this for his use and preserve it for him despite the devil, he would not have it. He should be aroused and trained to thank God for his daily goodness with a joyful heart and cheerful faith and to say to him: "Truly, you are a kind and benevolent God! For your kindness and goodness to me, an unworthy and ungrateful creature, are eternal, that is, unceasing. Praise and thanks are due you!"

This verse also serves to comfort us in all our misfortunes. We are such softies, such sapless sufferers. A pain in the leg or the stirring of a little leaf[19] can cause us to fill heaven and earth with our howls and wails, our grumbling and cursing. We fail to see what a little evil such a small leaf is compared with the

17. The original German saying, "cannot pass the water to something/someone" has the same basic sense as the English idiom in the translation. Cf. LW 22:152 n.118.

18. Luther includes this verse in the *Small Catechism* as part of the prayer for returning thanks after a meal (see SC, "Thanksgiving," 10; BC, 364).

19. Luther refers to this often as an example of how even the harmless and ordinary in creation can terrorize a conscience gripped with fear and guilt before God. Luther gives an extended description of this in his later Genesis lectures (LW 1:170–71).

immeasurable blessings of God that we still have and possess. We are like a king who becomes frantic because he loses one penny. Though he owns half the world, with countless money and possessions, he plays the martyr, throws a tantrum, curses, denounces God, and fulminates against him with other blasphemous language, as today cursing troopers show their manliness by resorting to profanity.

The good God permits such small evils to befall us merely in order to arouse us snorers from our deep sleep and to make us recognize, on the other hand, the incomparable and innumerable benefits we still have. He wants us to consider what would happen if he were to withdraw his goodness from us completely. In that spirit Job said: "Shall we receive good at the hand of God, and shall we not receive evil?" [Job 2:10]. Job, you see, knew very well how to sing this beautiful *Confitemini* and this particular verse; for he said: "As God wills, so let it be; the name of the LORD be praised" [Job 1:21]. He did not simply look at the evil, as we would-be saints do; he kept in sight the goodness and grace of the Lord. With this he comforted himself and overcame evil with patience.[g]

Job pictured in a Byzantine manuscript with Cyclic illustration (c. 1200). Located in Rome at the Biblioteca Apostolica Vaticana.

g Cf. James 5:11.

We also are to look at our misfortunes in no other way than that with them God gives us a light by which we may see and understand his goodness and kindness in countless other ways. Then we conclude that such small misfortunes are barely a drop of water on a big fire or a little spark in the ocean. Then we understand and love the words: "O give thanks to the LORD, for he is good; his steadfast love endures forever!" In translating I did not want to deviate too much from the Hebrew,[20,h] but we Germans would say: "O what a faithful, loving, and good Lord you are! You bestow on me and on all the world goodness and mercy, now and forever. Thanks be to you!"

The Hebrew word חֶסֶד, which was ἐλεημοσύνη to the Greeks and until now "mercy"[i] to the Germans, I translated as "steadfast love";[j] for it really means "goodness in action." Christ himself uses the word when he says: "I desire mercy, and not sacrifice" [Matt. 12:7]. And St. Paul tells Timothy that servants should gladly serve believing masters, for they receive the benefit [1 Tim. 6:2]. Christ says in Matt. 6[:1]: "Beware of practicing your piety." This is what we call "alms," from the Greek ἐλεημοσύνη.[k] Although the word "alms" came to be used incorrectly when referring to a piece of bread for the beggar at our door, it really means ἐλεημοσύνη, חֶסֶד, "goodness in action,"[l] such as God grants us and we, in turn, should show toward others.

"Forever" is not to be understood to mean only the goodness of heaven after this life, when there will be life everlasting.[21] The Hebrew word עוֹלָם means, as we say in German, "continually" or

h For more on the use of Hebrew by Luther and others during the Reformation, see Stephen G. Burnett, *Christian Hebraism in the Reformation Era (1500–1660): Authors, Books, and the Transmission of Jewish Learning* (Leiden: Brill, 2012); Siegfried Raeder, *Grammatica Theologica: Studien zu Luthers Operationes in Psalmos* (Tübingen: J. C. B. Mohr/Paul Siebeck, 1977); Raeder, "The Exegetical and Hermeneutical Work of Martin Luther," in *Hebrew Bible/Old Testament: The History of Its Interpretation*, vol. 2: *From the Renaissance to the Enlightenment*, ed. Magne Saebø and Michael Fishbane (Göttingen: Vandenhoeck & Ruprecht, 2008), 363–406.

i Ger.: *barmherzigkeit*.

j Ger.: *güte*.

k The English and German word *alms* is derived from the postclassical Latin word *alimosina* or *elimosina*, which in turn was derived from the Greek indicated by Luther here.

l Ger.: *wohltat* and *guttat*.

20. Luther began working with Hebrew in his very first lectures on the Psalms, though his knowledge of the language was admittedly rudimentary, largely dependent on Johannes Reuchlin's Hebrew grammar, *De Rudimenta* (1506), and his Hebrew annotations on the seven penitential psalms (1512). The glosses of Nicholas of Lyra (1270–1349) would have given Luther some further insight into Hebrew vocabulary. Later, Luther would consult other works as he continued to strengthen his knowledge of Hebrew, e.g., Pagninus's *Thesaurus linguae sanctae lexicon hebraicum* (1529), Giustiniani's polyglot of the Psalter (1516), the Hebrew concordance of Nathan ben Kalonymous (1447), and the Hebrew grammar of Abraham de Balmes (1523). Luther's Hebrew was continually reinforced by his Wittenberg colleagues, Philip Melanchthon (1497–1560), professor of Hebrew Matthaeus Aurogallus (1490–1543), Caspar Cruciger (1504–1548), and Johannes Bugenhagen (1485–1558), especially as he consulted them for his translation of the Old Testament.

21. Luther's first lectures on the Psalms (1515) interpret this as "in eternity, not temporal mercies," which essentially follows Cassiodorus (c. 490–c. 585) in the *Glossa Ordinaria*: "In this he shows that he is good: because he grants his gifts of mercies in eternity." Luther here disagrees with his earlier view.

"always," be it here or hereafter. For instance, we refer to a restless person by saying: "Why this everlasting running around? Why is he always on the go?" It was necessary for me to explain and to interpret these words in order to understand this verse; for it is used frequently in Scripture, especially in the Psalter. This very verse teaches us which sacrifice pleases God most. We cannot perform a greater or finer deed, or a nobler service to God, than to offer thanks, as God himself tells us in Psalm 50[:23]: "He who brings thanksgiving as his sacrifice honors me, and this is the way I show my salvation." Such an offering pleases him beyond all gifts, endowments, monasteries, or whatever. He says in Ps. 69[:30-31]: "I will praise the name of God with a song; I will magnify him with thanksgiving."[m] This will please the Lord more than a bullock with horns and hooves.

By the same token, while praise and gratitude to God are the believer's highest service both on earth and in heaven, ingratitude is the most shameful vice and the greatest contempt of God; yet this world is full, full, full of it to high heaven. Nevertheless, God is such a gracious Lord, as this verse declares, that in spite of this ingratitude he does not cease doing good. He says in our psalm: "His steadfast love endures forever." His sun rises on both good and evil; his rain falls on the grateful and the ungrateful.[n] He gives as much wealth, power, and as many children to scoundrels as he does to the saints, in fact, much more. He guards against war, pestilence, famine, and all the plagues of the devil. This is divine goodness, which never grows slack or weary in the face of wickedness. No person could ever be so kind, for people cannot stand ingratitude. Ingratitude has driven people mad, crazy, and insane, as the story of Timon shows.[22] It is too much for human nature to do good and to receive nothing but evil in return.

2. Let Israel say: His steadfast love endures forever.

Here the psalmist gives thanks for temporal government and blessed peace, both of which are gifts of God and surely the greatest of temporal gifts.[23] If there were no government or peace, we

22. Timon of Athens (not the philosopher Timon of Phlius), a legendary misanthrope who is referred to in several classical authors, including Plutarch, Cicero, and Lucian. Cf. Shakespeare's play *Timon of Athens* (1623).

23. This interpretation of "Israel" as an indication of temporal government is quite unique. Luther had a similarly unique political interpretation of Song of Songs from lectures given in the same year, which he argued is a dialogue between a prince and his people (see LW 15:191–93).

m In the original Luther uses the numbering of the Vulgate, namely Psalm 49 and Psalm 68.

n Matt. 5:45; Luke 6:35.

could not exist. Israel was the kingdom founded by God and entrusted to King David, as Ps. 78[:70-71] says: "He chose David, his servant, to be the shepherd of Israel, his people."[o] Accordingly, he thanks God for this kingdom and urges everyone to join him in thanksgiving. He also gives an example and a precept for all kings, princes, lords, lands, people, and subjects, to praise and thank God for government and peace in their respective countries and nations, each community, as an Israel, for its own.

The absence of continual war, discord, famine, bloodshed, sedition, murder, and misery in countries, cities, and villages, as well as the continued presence of trades, commerce, and professions—this is just as great a miracle and just as great a proof of the power of God as the creation of the world out of nothing and its continued preservation. For the world is full of devils, and, as we see daily, there are many wanton scoundrels among peasants, townsmen, nobles, lords, and princes. They delight in stealing, robbing, lying, cheating, war, destruction, and disaster. If a powerful God did not check and restrain the devil, human ingenuity and might could not keep the peace and maintain government and authority for a single day. It is, therefore, not without reason that holy David urges people to thank God for temporal peace, authority, and government.

Here lords and princes, as well as subjects, should learn that the government of a land and the obedience of the people are a gift of God—a gift bestowed out of nothing but his pure goodness. Our sword and human wisdom are of no avail, even though some mad princes and lords presumptuously claim that they rule land and people with their power and govern them by their reason. Especially the haughty bigwigs among the nobility and the smart alecks in the cities imagine that they run everything, as though God could not get along without them. But sensible lords and nobles know better. And David, the foremost of all kings and princes, also declares otherwise. Whoever will not believe, let him read history, in Scripture as well as in Roman and pagan literature. There is abundant evidence.

Certainly in the recent insurrection God demonstrated clearly that neither human power nor skill, but he alone, governs the world.[24] For these very same bigwigs who would rob God of

o The original follows the Vulgate numbering, Psalm 77.

24. Luther is referring to the Peasants' War of 1525. See also *Admonition to Peace: A Reply to the Twelve Articles of the Peasants of Swabia*, TAL 5:281–333.

In this scene depicting the Peasants' War, a knight is surrounded by peasant soldiers. Woodcut by Hans Leonhard Schäufelein (c. 1480–1540).

his honor by bragging and boasting of their role in suppressing the insurrection were at that time the most fear-stricken wretches I have ever seen. Now they forget the God who rescued them when in sheer fright they shit their pants. We still smell the stench whenever one of these bigwigs is near. Unfortunately, in those days knighthood had neither heart nor courage. Its impudence and pride lead me to believe that they defy and tempt God to send a new insurrection, that he could show them once more whether the bigwig or God's goodness and power holds the mob in leash. Well, if someone were to shake the tree, the bigwigs would come tumbling down. For they are overripe, and they are pained no end by the momentary peace which God is graciously maintaining, apparently by force and with great difficulty.

So far as I am concerned, I like to see them strut and brag; for it serves to remind me how valiantly they fled in fear before the wretched peasants in the insurrection. Otherwise I would need to have the story engraved in stone or written in a book for a perpetual remembrance. Now I am spared the expense and effort; for whenever one hears or sees one of these bigwigs, the insurrection is painted on him in lurid colors. One is always forced to ask: "Say, isn't this one of those who defied the emperor? Didn't he give up his strong castle for a piece of straw and a log? Isn't he one of those undaunted heroes and brave fire-eaters who now thunder out oaths by St. Velten, Potz macht, St. Quirinius, St. Anthony,[25] although during the insurrection they could only sing woe and lament?"

Scripture declares that God established the states of masters and subjects, and that temporal government is his, as David testifies in Ps. 18[:40]: "Thou didst make my enemies turn their backs to me." And of his own people he says in Ps. 144[:2]: "He subdues my people under me."[p] Here we find little pride in David, as though he could govern his people with power or wisdom. Although he had the finest laws and customs, established by

25. St. Velten (a German form of St. Valentine, d. 269), St. Quirinius (of Neuss, d. 116), and St. Anthony (the Great, d. 356) were very popular saints in the fifteenth and sixteenth centuries and were often invoked together. The latter two were also often paired with St. Hubertus (d. 727) and St. Cornelius (d. 253) to comprise the *Vier Marschälle Gottes*, "the Four Marshals of God," a group especially venerated in the Rhineland in times of distress. "*Potz macht*" is part of a common German curse, "*Potz Velten!*"

p The original follows the Vulgate numbering, Psalm 17 and Psalm 143.

God through Moses, to aid him, together with the prophets who had anointed and confirmed him as king by God's command, he had learned by experience what the power and wisdom of kings and princes can do in a nation if God does not lend a hand. Absalom, his own son, and later Bichri[26] taught him who was king in the land. Likewise Daniel declares in 4[:17] and 5[:21]: "The most high God rules over the kingdom of mortals and sets over it whom HE WILL,"[q] not whom we will or think. Daniel is simply saying that temporal government is purely and solely a gift and grace of God, which no man can establish or maintain by his own wisdom or strength.

26. Luther is thinking of Sheba, son of Bichri (1 Sam. 20:1f.), who opposed David's kingship.

It is futile to expect to subdue subjects, be they peasants or townsmen, by swaggering. A peasant can draw a knife and kill as well as a noble bigwig does. God must do it, and he tells them in Rom. 13[:2]: "Therefore he who resists government will be punished." Such words are the answer; for God insists on it, and his threats will be fulfilled. When subjects are ripe for it, as the peasants were in the revolt, God sentences them to rebellion or disobedience, that they may get a good beating.[r] The masters also are punished by such an insurrection because they lack gratitude for his goodness and benefits and fail to give honor to him who continually maintains and protects peace, obedience, law, and government. This verse counsels Israel to thank God and to confess that his steadfast love endures forever. He always maintains peace and preserves government, no matter how ungrateful and unworthy we may be. Without him there would be murder and war in the country, and revolt and lawlessness in the cities.

Particularly in Germany does he now maintain peace with a special show of power, though there is precious little of it. It is evident that at the present time there is not a single soul in Germany who would preserve law and order in the face of these lawless and robbing nobles or protect government from such faithless and thievish subjects. Robbery and stealing abound; assassins follow their singular practices; people plot and rage. Yet no one's conscience is pricked by these sins against God. I am

q In the original handwritten and printed version "he will" is capitalized for emphasis.

r See Luther's various treatises written during the Peasants' War: *Admonition to Peace* (1525), TAL 5:281–333; LW 46:3–43; *Against the Robbing and Murdering Hordes of Peasants* (1525), LW 46:45–55; and *An Open Letter on the Harsh Book against the Peasants* (1525), LW 46:57–85.

of the opinion that our present peace hangs by a silk thread; in fact, it is solely in God's hands, above and beyond our will and despite the fuming and the raving of all the devils. If human wisdom and the power of man were governing Germany today, she would be lying in ruins tomorrow. Let us, therefore, thank God and pray that his goodness, as in the past, may remain with Israel forever.

3. Let the house of Aaron say: His steadfast love endures forever.

This is a prayer of thanksgiving for a particular gift of God, namely, spiritual government, including priests, preachers, teachers, in short, the precious word of God and the holy Christian church.[27] The greatness of this gift is beyond the grasp and imagination of any person. Only the grace and benevolence of God, not the power and wisdom of men, have prevented the triumph of error, schism, sects, and heresy in the world, and have preserved the word, faith, the Spirit, Baptism, the Holy Scriptures, the Sacrament, and Christians. Without this the devil would overthrow and destroy it all, as he did with the Turk and the pope, as he is doing with the sectarians,[28] and as he did in the past with the heretics. God himself must preserve the church. Our flesh soon tires of the struggle, and the world cannot stand the strain.

Aaron was the high priest entrusted with the ministry. He was to teach the law of Moses and to govern the kingdom of Israel spiritually, before God, just as David was to rule over life and living outwardly, before the world. But as little as David could by his own power and wisdom conduct his earthly office, so little, and still less, could Aaron by his own might and wisdom rule spiritually over heart and soul, even though he had the advantage of the law of Moses, which clearly outlined what he should teach and how he should govern. The Holy Spirit had to help him in his spiritual housekeeping, as he learned by his own experience when Korah tried to usurp the priesthood and incited all the people against him and Moses [Num. 16:1ff.].

This shows you the great cunning of the pope and his vermin. They want to build and maintain the Christian church with their wisdom, with outward regulations, with excommunications, without the word of God, and without praying and preaching—and then defend it by temporal power, fire, sword,

27. Like the previous verse, Luther's interpretation of the "house of Aaron" as the spiritual government in contrast to "Israel," the temporal government, is unique in the exegetical tradition.

28. Literally, "red spirits." A favorite word of Luther's to describe those creating divisions in the church.

and persecution. They do not need the goodness of God, but make this verse read: "Thank our excommunications and our sword, for their power endures forever."

True Christendom preaches the word of God; it forces itself on no one. If anyone will not believe, it lets him be and separates itself from him, as Christ teaches in Matt. 10[:14] and 18[:17], and as Paul consistently does in the book of Acts. The unbeliever is left to God's judgment. But our bloodhounds and murderers suppress the word of God and devise their own articles of faith. Whoever refuses to accept them must burn. We have a frail, new Christendom, of which God and Scripture are ignorant.

Korah, Abiram, Dathan, and their followers and family are swallowed by the earth for revolting against Moses (Numbers 16). From an illustrated version of Luther's German Old Testament (1523).

Ignore those filthy fellows! They are not worthy of our thoughts in this wonderful psalm. In this verse we should thank God for giving us his word and holy kingdom, and for preserving it to us in spite of the devil, the flesh, and the world, out of pure grace and goodness. We have treated it with ingratitude, laziness, indifference, and contempt; and we are utterly unworthy of this great treasure of eternal life. Christ himself brought us the word; we did not invent it. He must preserve it, for we cannot do so with our might and skill. Christ instituted, founded, and built Christendom. He must also protect and promote it.[29] Our wisdom and might will not do it; neither will sword and fire, as Paul says in 1 Cor. 3[:5-9]: "You are God's field, God's building. We are the servants; but neither he who plants is anything, nor he who waters, but God who gives the growth."

4. Let those who fear the Lord *say:*
His steadfast love endures forever.

This fourth prayer of thanksgiving is for the true assembly, namely, for the elect children of God and all the saints on earth,

29. Luther also communicates this same sentiment to an anxious Melanchthon at the Diet of Augsburg, on 3 July 1530 (WA Br 5:435–36).

the genuine Christians. For them this psalm was especially written, and of them it speaks to the very end. In the previous three groups—as, first, in the spiritual government or ministry—there are many who abuse it to satisfy their avarice, pleasure, and honor. Consider the heretics, the sectarians, and our present priesthood. Yet the order is nonetheless good and holy and a divine gift, not to be condemned because of its abuse. Just so the whole world shamefully abuses the holy name of God, Baptism, the Sacrament, and the gospel, in fact, God himself and all his gifts. It does not fear God above all things.

It is also true that in the second group, the temporal rulers, the majority use that which has been entrusted to them for pride, vanity, pleasure, mischief, and all manner of wantonness, without any awe or fear of God. Nevertheless, government remains God's good and useful gift and is a blessing in itself. And in the third category, among the common people generally, there is almost nothing but out-and-out abuse, since everyone uses his position, trade, skill, money, and possessions against his neighbor. At least he does not use them for the good and welfare of his neighbor, as God intends when he gives and preserves all things. There is no fear of God or respect of people. Yet God preserves them all, and for this he is to be praised and thanked.

This little group fears God and is pious. Its membership is gleaned from the three groups mentioned above.[30] For there are still to be found pious, God-fearing, faithful bishops, ministers, preachers, and pastors. One also finds pious and godly princes, lords, nobles, aldermen, and judges, and many pious and God-fearing artisans, farmers, servants, and maids, though they are rare. Because of them God preserves the three groups listed above and bestows so much good on them. Were it not for these, the world would pass away this very hour, as Sodom and Gomorrah did.[31]

The holy prophet David clearly separates this group from the other three, thereby indicating that the others do not honor, fear, or serve God. They serve themselves and seek and have their enjoyment in this life. They even persecute this little group incessantly and vehemently, and refuse to tolerate them, solely because these fear and trust God. They honor and teach the word of God, which the others have no desire to hear or see. In Hebrew "to fear God" really means "to serve God." The fear of God is the service of God. Now we cannot serve him bodily and

30. These three groups correspond to the three medieval estates of the clergy, the nobility, and the common citizen.

31. The idea that God preserves the world for the sake of the church or the elect is rooted in the Scriptures (e.g., Rom. 13:4), but finds expression throughout the tradition. For example, already in the second century Justin Martyr (100–165) wrote, "Therefore God postpones the collapse and dissolution of the universe . . . because of the Christian seed, which he knows to be the cause in nature [of the world's preservation]. If such were not the case, it would be impossible for you to do the [awful] things you do [to us]" (*Apologiae* 2, 7). But most influential, especially for Luther, was Augustine's book *The City of God*, which contrasts the love and peace of the city of man with that of God's eternal city.

visibly here on earth, for he is invisible. We can serve him spiritually by honoring, teaching, and confessing his word and by living according to it. Of course, crosses, suffering, and affliction from the devil, the world, and our flesh are the results.

Now tell me, for what kind of gift may these people be expected to give thanks to God? It cannot be a place in a religious order, for God gives this to one of the other groups. Neither can it be temporal glory, honor, might, peace, or the obedience of others; for these are given to the second group. Nor can it be money, possessions, house, home, health, wife, or child; for all these God gives to those in the first group. It must be something higher and nobler, far surpassing these gifts of our temporal and transient life. David devotes the rest of the psalm to this gift, while he reserves only the first three verses for the other three groups. What is it? He himself will discuss it fully. It is COMFORT and HELP[s] in every kind of suffering, want, and trouble. This is nothing less than the beginning of everlasting life. The world in the three groups mentioned above—the God-fearing excepted—with all its goods, might, and skill, could not give a single drop of this. For when a man is in peril of death, there is small comfort in singing about dancing, pleasure, possessions, honor, power, skill, wife, and children.

As these would now honor God's word and serve him, they must truly suffer and endure mockery, shame, hurt, hatred, envy, defamation, fire, sword, death, and every other calamity from the other three groups, besides much evil, dangerous, and wicked treachery from the devil and his angels, and sin, unrest, and heartache from their own flesh. Paul says, "All who want to live a godly life in Christ Jesus will be persecuted" [2 Tim. 3:12]. And Christ himself says, "If any man would come after me, let him take up his cross" [Luke 9:23]. In Acts 14[:22] we read, "It is through many persecutions that we must enter the kingdom of God." And the wise man, Ecclesiasticus 2[:1] tells us, "My child, if you want to serve God, prepare yourself for testing."[32,t]

Thus, the favor bestowed by God on this little group is completely hidden from the world and appears to be nothing but eternal wrath, punishment, and torment from God himself. By

s In the original handwritten and printed version "comfort" and "help" are capitalized for emphasis.

t Luther uses the word *Anfechtung* here.

32. Ecclesiasticus, also known as the "Wisdom of Sirach" or "Sirach," was likely written by the Jewish scribe Joshua ben Sirach early in the second century BCE. While there never was consensus on the canonical status of the book, it was highly regarded by many in the church, including Luther who called it a "proper spiritual discipline." In Erasmus's debate with Luther over free will, Ecclus. 15:14-17 is a major focus of interpretation and debate; see LW 33:117–25; WA 18:671–76. See also Luther's preface to his translation of the book (LW 35:347–48).

contrast, the ungodly in the three groups seem to be the very children of God, because they are so fully and richly endowed with the visible, temporal, and manifest blessings of God. Therefore it demands skill and grace to discern this secret and hidden blessing, especially since the psalmist praises its eternal character and devotes so many lavish words to it, as we shall hear. Though the spirit is willing and ready, the poor flesh is weak and unwilling [Matt. 26:41]. The flesh would rather have evident, temporal consolation and help, and be above anxiety and need. But it must not and cannot be otherwise. There is no other way to life eternal than this narrow path, which so few come upon (Matt. 7[:14]) and only this small band finds. In short, the blessing of the three groups is this temporal life and being; the blessing of the small group is everlasting life. Therein lies the real difference.

5. Out of my distress I called on the LORD;
the LORD answered me and set me in a broad place.

Here we see where this small band is. It does not move in manifest joy before the world. Distress is its abode. The psalmist pictures himself and his condition, namely, his many troubles. As is proper when one begins to talk about something, he is brief; he sums up all kinds of troubles and calls them "distress." Later he will say and explain more. Thus, I may say: "Oh, how much Paul suffered!" This does not yet explain his sufferings; it merely indicates in a general way that he suffered, but not what he suffered. So the psalmist indicates also the comfort and help of God generally and briefly when he says: "The LORD answered me." As if he were saying: "I must always suffer, but I am always comforted." He will soon describe how this happens and wherein his comfort consists.

In Hebrew the word *distress* means "something narrow." I surmise that the German noun for distress is also derived from an adjective meaning narrow.[u] It implies fear and pain, as in a process of clamping, squeezing, and pressing. Trials and misfortunes do squeeze and press, as is indicated by the proverb: "The great wide world is too narrow for me." In Hebrew, as it is used

u The German word *Angst* sounds similar to the German adjective *eng* ("narrow"), as in the phrase "dire straights." See also LW 13:7 n.6.

here, "in a large place" is contrasted with "distress."[v] "Distress" means tribulation and need; "in a large place" denotes consolation and help. Accordingly, this verse really says: "I called upon the Lord in my trouble; he heard me and helped me by comforting me." Just as distress is a narrow place, which casts us down and cramps us, so God's help is our large place, which makes us free and happy.

Note the great art and wisdom of faith. It does not run to and fro in the face of trouble. It does not cry on everybody's shoulder, nor does it curse and scold its enemies. It does not murmur against God by asking: "Why does God do this to me? Why not to others, who are worse than I am?" Faith does not despair of the God who sends trouble. Faith does not consider him angry or an enemy, as the flesh, the world, and the devil strongly suggest. Faith rises above all this and sees God's fatherly heart behind his unfriendly exterior. Faith sees the sun shining through these thick, dark clouds and this gloomy weather. Faith has the courage to call with confidence to him who smites it and looks at it with such a sour face.[33]

33. Luther's description of faith here echoes his famous sermon on Matt. 15:21-28, first published in 1525, in which the Syro-Phoenician woman continues to trust Jesus in spite of his rebukes. Luther describes this as one who "lays hold of and retains the deep spiritual 'yea' under and above the 'nay' with a firm faith in God's word." See LW 76:378-83.

That is skill above all skills. It is the work of the Holy Spirit alone and is known only by pious and true Christians. The self-righteous are ignorant of it. They prate about good works, although they have never known or performed any. Nor can they perform them, because human nature cannot acquire this skill. As soon as God touches it with a little trouble, it is frightened and filled with despair, and can only think that grace is at an end and that God has nothing but wrath toward it. The devil also adds his power and trickery, in order to drown it in doubt and despondency. The situation is aggravated by the provoking sight of God showering abundant blessings on the other three groups. Then human nature begins to think that the others have only the grace of God and none of his anger. Then the poor conscience becomes weak; it would collapse were it not for the help and comfort that come from God, through pious pastors, or by some good Christian's counsel.[34] Some there are who hang, drown, or stab themselves, or otherwise perish, shrivel, and wither.

34. Compare the *Smalcald Articles* (SA III, 4; BC, 319) in which Luther includes, along with the power of the keys, "the mutual conversation and consolation of brothers and sisters" as that which conveys the gospel.

Whoever can learn, let him learn. Let everyone become a falcon and soar above distress. Let everyone know most assuredly and not doubt that God does not send him this distress to

v The Hebrew term is בַּמָּרְחָב.

destroy him, as we shall see in verse eighteen. He wants to drive him to pray, to implore, to fight, to exercise his faith, to learn another aspect of God's person than before, to accustom himself to do battle even with the devil and with sin, and by the grace of God to be victorious. Without this experience we could never learn the meaning of faith, the word, Spirit, grace, sin, death, or the devil. Were there only peace and no trials,[w] we would never learn to know God. In short, we could never be or remain true Christians. Trouble and distress constrain us and keep us within Christendom. Crosses and troubles, therefore, are as necessary for us as life itself, and much more necessary and useful than all the possessions and honor in the world.[35]

35. At Coburg castle, before the princes left for the Diet of Augsburg to present their confession before the emperor, Luther preached a sermon on the Christian cross and suffering which makes many similar points. It was later published that same year, 1530. See TAL 4:66–78; LW 51:197–208.

We read: "I called upon the Lord." You must learn to call. Do not sit by yourself or lie on a couch, hanging and shaking your head. Do not destroy yourself with your own thoughts by worrying. Do not strive and struggle to free yourself, and do not brood on your wretchedness, suffering, and misery. Say to yourself: "Come on, you lazy bum; fall on your knees, and lift your eyes and hands toward heaven!" Read a psalm or the *Our Father*, call on God, and tearfully lay your troubles before him. Mourn and pray, as this verse teaches, and also Ps. 142[:2]: "I pour out my complaint before him, I tell my trouble before him." Likewise Ps. 141[:2]: "Let my prayer be counted as incense before you, and the lifting up of my hands as an evening sacrifice!" Here you learn that praying, reciting your troubles, and lifting up your hands are sacrifices most pleasing to God. It is his desire and will that you lay your troubles before him. He does not want you to multiply your troubles by burdening and torturing yourself. He wants you to be too weak to bear and overcome such troubles; he wants you to grow strong in him.[x] By his strength he is glorified in you. Out of such experiences people become real Christians. Otherwise, people are mere babblers, who prate about faith and spirit but are ignorant of what it is all about or of what they themselves are saying.

You must never doubt that God is aware of your distress and hears your prayer. You must not pray haphazardly or simply shout into the wind. Then you would mock and tempt God. It would be better not to pray at all than to pray like the priests and

w Ger.: *Anfechtungen*.

x Cf. 2 Cor. 12:10.

monks. It is important that you learn to praise also this point in this verse: "The Lord answered me and set me free." The psalmist declares that he prayed and cried out, and that he was certainly heard. If the devil puts it into your head that you lack the holiness, piety, and worthiness of David and for this reason cannot be sure that God will hear you, make the sign of the cross, and say to yourself: "Let those be pious and worthy who will! I know for certain that I am a creature of the same God who made David. And David, regardless of his holiness, has no better or greater God than I have."

Jesus teaches about prayer (Matthew 6). Woodcut from Luther's interpretation of the epistles and gospels from Easter to Advent, published 1544.

There is only one God, of saint and sinner, worthy and unworthy, great and small. Regardless of the inequalities among us, he is the one and equal God of us all, who wants to be honored, called on, and prayed to by all. Before they became holy and worthy, what did the saints and the deserving souls have that I do not possess? Did they perhaps become holy and worthy by themselves? As unworthy sinners, did they not receive it from the same God from whom I seek to receive it, as a poor, unworthy sinner? He who gave it to David has promised it also to me. He has commanded me to demand, seek, pray, and knock (Matt. 7[:7]). At his command and promise I kneel down, raise my eyes to heaven, and beg for comfort and help. Thereby he is honored as the true God, from whom I implore help and comfort, as a true God deserves. Thus, he regards me as worthy, and he will prove himself to be what he sees that I think he is, a true God. He will not place his divine honor and name in jeopardy for my sake. Of this I am sure. He who does not call on God or pray to him in trouble certainly does not consider him to be God. Nor does he give him the divine honor which we as creatures owe him. Much is said about this elsewhere.[36]

36. Cf. Luther's definition of God vis-à-vis faith in the *Large Catechism* on the First Commandment, written the year before: "If you have the sort of heart that expects from him nothing but good, especially in distress and need . . . then you have the one, true God" (LC, "Ten Commandments," 28; BC, 390). See also LW 13:6 n.4.

6. With the Lord *on my side I do not fear.*
What can mortals do to me?

Leaping with spiritual and eternal joy, the psalmist here shows us what happens when his prayer is heard. He says: "First, God plants this comfort in my heart. This is the subject of this verse, and later of verse eighteen. Next, he also supplies help externally and rescues me from trouble, of which the next verse speaks." Concerning comfort he says: "The Lord is on my side; that is, my cry has been heard. Although troubles still continue, I now have a mighty, strong, powerful Defender, who is with me and supports me. This makes it pleasant and easy to bear my yoke (Matt. 11[:30]). Who is this? It is the Lord himself upon whom I called. In my sore distress he came to me through his eternal word and Spirit. I scarcely know that I have been troubled." We must not, as the sectarians do, imagine that God comforts us immediately, without his word. Comfort does not come to us without the word, which the Holy Spirit effectively calls to mind and enkindles in our hearts, even though it has not been heard for ten years.[37]

37. For Luther's critique of those who teach that the Spirit is received immediately, without the word, see especially the second part of his treatise *Against the Heavenly Prophets* (1525), TAL 2:39–125; LW 40:79–223.

Note how bold and courageous the psalmist has become as a result of this comfort. He has the courage to rise and boast: "I am not afraid; I am not downhearted; I am of good cheer and refuse to worry. It is true that misery and sorrow are with me; they scowl at me and try to frighten me into begging for mercy. But I thumb my nose at them and say: 'Please, Mr. Bogeyman, don't eat me up! You look horrible enough to scare anyone who wants to be frightened. But I have another, lovelier vision, to light my way, like the sun, into eternal life. And so I ignore you, feeble and temporary dark cloud and angry little wind that you are!'"

Then in his God-given comfort he proudly and disdainfully defies the whole world and says: "What can man do to me?" This is meeting defiance with defiance. This could well drive kings, princes, and lords mad, to think that a poor sinner so despises and overwhelms them! He walks over them as though they were straw in the road and tauntingly asks: "Who is lying there?" Or don't you know what "man" means? This word includes every human being, be he Turk, Tartar, Roman emperor, pope, king, prince, bishop, or lord, with all their might, wisdom, wealth, land, and people. In short, it includes all the world, plus its god, the devil, and his angels. Cruel as they are, a poor, forlorn human being should surely be terrified by them. Nevertheless, the psalmist defiantly asks: "What can they do to me?"

"They can murder you!" "Then what? Can they revive me and kill me again? Or perhaps devour my body like a tasty morsel? They can't and won't kill me unless my Lord permits it and tells me so. Without his permission they may plot for a year and a day, draw their knives, gnash their teeth, bite their lips, and scowl. Still they must hear the truth of Ps. 112[:10]: 'The wicked see it and are angry; they gnash their teeth and melt away; the desire of the wicked comes to nothing.'[y] Power and pride are their god and boast. My boast, however, is the Lord. Let them fight with him. They will come to grief and dash against that Cornerstone until they stagger and are crushed.[z] In the meantime I shall continue to sing: 'What can man do to me?'"

Finally, what can an emperor, a pope, a king, a prince, or the entire world do against God? Isaiah says that they are כְּאַיִן [Isa. 40:17], a snap of the fingers. Again he says [33:11]: "You conceive chaff, you bring forth stubble." Great and imposing are their threats. Their bellies are swollen as though they were about to give birth to mountains, a sight to behold; and yet it is only straw, fit for the fire. When it is born, it turns out to be chaff. So is their anger and the result of their threats, chaff which the wind drives away.[a] As long as the Lord remains with us, we shall stand, though they slay us. They have not killed the Lord who is with us; as long as he remains, and wherever he remains, we shall be with him, as he says in John 14[:19]: "Because I live, you shall live also." We shall watch with joy how he disposes of the straw-bellies and their chaff on the day of his great fire. Then we shall learn what this really means: "What can man do to me?"

7. The Lord is on my side to help me;
I shall look in triumph on those who hate me.

What a wonderful God we have! He not only stands by us in trouble, strengthening and comforting us by his word and Spirit so that we survive—he also helps us win and conquer. In the end we have a greater revenge on our enemies than we could wish

y The original follows the Vulgate numbering, Psalm 111.

z Ps. 118:22; Luke 20:17–18.

a Ps. 1:4.

or ask for in the hour of trouble. This happens in one of two ways. One is the gracious way, that they who are hostile and bitter toward us and, as this text says, hate us are converted and become our friends. This brings the greatest pleasure and joy to all the saints on earth. Secondly, those who will not change graciously and in God's name come under wrath and perish in the devil's name, while the Christians survive in spite of them. This fate befell the Jews, the Romans, the heathen, King Pharaoh, and the enemies of the children of Israel. This fate has, thank God, befallen many in our day who thought they could devour us in three weeks. We are still alive, and they rot among the worms. And the same thing will happen to those princes, bishops, priests, and their ilk who still rage against us. They will perish, while our doctrine will survive.

If our teaching is the word of God, this verse belongs to us. Whoever regards it as God's word should never doubt that our enemies will not reach their goal, as we shall see. If anyone doubts that it is God's word, it is of little consequence what he does or does not experience. From the very beginning of Christendom the world, emperors, kings, lords, the cunning, and the wise have devised ever so many plots. This verse, however, has outlasted them all and has held the field while it mocks them joyously and unafraid. "I shall look in triumph upon my enemies." The enemies, where are they? Where is their wrath? What has happened to their evil designs? Why have they not expunged this verse? What has happened to all the plots which the pope and his clergy have bungled during the past ten years?[38] It is a good thing that they have thick skulls; hence, it does not bother them that they failed so often and boasted and cheered for nothing. Finally, in their hardened hearts they will completely fulfill this verse and be destroyed, as the Psalter so abundantly declares.

38. Perhaps a reference to the time since *Exsurge Domini* (1520), the papal bull that threatened Luther with excommunication.

8. It is better to take refuge in the L*ORD*
than to put confidence in mortals.
9. It is better to take refuge in the L*ORD*
than to put confidence in princes.

In the two previous verses the psalmist spoke of God-given comfort and help. Here he speaks of the comfort and aid given by others. He makes fun of such help; in fact, it is as if he had pity for those poor souls who have no God but rely on human comfort and aid. It is a miserable and uncertain comfort, which rests on people who themselves are not sure of their lives for a moment, as Isaiah testifies.[b] And David says in Psalm 146[:3-4]: "Put not your trust in princes, in a son of man, in whom there is no help. When his breath departs, he returns to his earth; on that very day his plans perish." This statement is entirely true. One cannot rely even on holy people or pious princes, much less on tyrants and barbarians. God frequently takes pious people to himself at an early age, and any plans and confidence based on them also perish. God extends the life of tyrants, as Solomon says,[c] so that those who abandon God become the more persistent in their trust in mortals.

While Duke Frederick of Saxony, the pious prince whom we should never forget, was alive, both temporal and spiritual tyrants looked forward to his death.[39] They said: "Luther's heresy is dependent on two eyes; when those are closed, his heresy will die." They were sure that this prophecy of theirs was true. It was an open-and-shut case: "Luther's doctrine rests on Duke Frederick. His trust and help rest on people and princes." They judged others by themselves. Just as they in their despair and in their defection from God placed their trust in princes and lords, so they concluded that we had done likewise, since they knew no other aid or comfort. I have never heard one of them indicate that he trusted in God. In all their shouting, pride, boasting, and defiance they have relied on the emperor, the princes, and the lords. And they brazenly and publicly admit it as though it were a praiseworthy confession of their holy faith in God, while it is just the opposite.

But they go on in their confidence. Day and night their thoughts, words, counsels, and plots are aimed at nothing else but how they may suppress us by force. Their greatest trust lies in the fact that they are many and we are few. It never occurs to them to call on God and pray for help.

39. Frederick III, the duke and elector of Saxony (1486-1525), also known as Frederick the Wise, was Luther's prince and protector during Luther's case with Rome. Frederick's protection of Luther is well known, from keeping Luther from being sent to Rome to his "kidnapping" to the Wartburg. For more on Frederick, see Ingetraut Ludolphy, *Friedrich der Weise: Kurfürst von Sachsen 1463–1525* (Göttingen: Vandenhoeck & Ruprecht, 1997); Sam Wellman, *Frederick the Wise: Seen and Unseen Lives of Martin Luther's Protector* (St. Louis: Concordia, 2005).

Portrait of Elector Frederick III (the Wise) (c. 1490s) by Albrecht Dürer

b Isa. 2:22.

c Eccl. 7:15.

They do not need him and can get along without him! It is enough that they decide to do things thus and so! They are confident that they will not fail. For how could God cause so many mighty and wise people to fail? Of course, it is impossible! They are much too strong and too smart for him. When King Pharaoh pursued the children of Israel to the Red Sea, he did not look to God or ever once pray: "Lord God, give me counsel and help." No, he said: "Just as soon as I draw my sword, they are dead." Alas, he did not miss it by a hair, but planned so perfectly that the next morning he and his people lay drowned in the Red Sea! This is the fate of those who despise God's comfort and aid and rely on human consolation and the help of princes.

For this reason the psalmist declares twice: "It is better to take refuge in the LORD." He is telling us that people cannot comfort and advise us, and that princes cannot come to our rescue. For people do not have the right word or spirit to comfort and uphold a sorrowful heart. Nor do princes have a fist strong enough to help a wretched person and to suppress his enemies. God alone has the word of comfort and the fist for help, regardless of the size and the number of troubles and enemies. Experience substantiates this. When a person is really downcast, how, pray tell me, can all the emperors, kings, princes, and all the power, skill, possessions, and honor of the whole world comfort him? They are all less than nothing, even in the trouble caused by one little everyday sin, unless God's word gives counsel and comfort.

When one has a fatal disease or stands at death's door, what good can the power and might of this world do? If the children of the world were able to help, of what value would it be? Life is uncertain; they die daily, and their comfort and help must give place to death. As plain as this is, the devil is still mighty and will not let us believe it. It remains a rare and remarkable skill not to trust in people or princes. The world is and remains the same and trusts and relies on people and princes, and thus it rejects God and tramples his First Commandment underfoot. People are willing to trust all sorts of false gods, but not the one true and faithful God. Therefore the prophet not only consoles us in these two verses but also laments the opposite, that there are such poor, miserable souls, and that they have no god. Emperors and princes, who cannot be sure of their lives for one moment, are the gods in whom their hearts rely and trust, exult and boast.

Openly and brazenly they boast of their infamous idolatry, as the feeble-minded Philistines boasted of their mutilated Dagon, of whom they should have been ashamed. But they get what they have coming and what they ask for; and, like the Philistines, they are forever disgraced.[d]

This is the time and place to list a few texts and examples from the Bible and other sources, to show that those who trusted in people always perished and crashed miserably. Remember how the dear prophets repeatedly preached and protested against the children of Israel, who again and again made alliances, now with the Egyptians, then with the Assyrians, now with one king, then with another, just so they did not have to trust in God but could trust in people. But they were always badly whipped in this business. The heathen themselves talk about it in their stories, fables, and records. And out of my own lifetime I could give you a sack full of examples from the German lands alone. In high as well as low society I have seen the result of pacts, alliances, and trust in man, and what shameful failure ensued. This verse remains true: "It is better to take refuge in the LORD than to put confidence in man." And again in Ps. 146[:3]: "Put not your trust in princes, in a son of man, in whom there is no help." The wise man also says,[40] Ecclesiasticus 2[:18]: "He who trusts in man shall fail." God does not, should not, and cannot tolerate it. It is idolatry that would rob God of his divinity.

If anyone wants to undertake something that is good, let him by all means begin it with God's help and wager on his goodness, never on human help and comfort. Nor should he fear others, not even the whole world; for this verse does not lie: "It is better to take refuge in the LORD." The wise man has said, Ecclus. 2[:10-11]: "Look at the generations of antiquity, and see. Who that put his trust in the LORD was ever put to shame?" And in Ps. 25[:3] we read: "Yea, let none that wait for Thee be put to shame." Whoever cannot or will not wager on God and trust him should give up and not undertake anything godly or wholesome with confidence in people. When I attacked indulgences for the first time, all the world was shocked and thought I had overreached myself.[41] My prior and my subprior, moved by the hue and cry, came to me fearfully and begged me not to bring disgrace upon our order;[42] for the other orders, especially the preachers,[43] were

40. See n. 32, p. 265.

41. A reference to the beginning of the indulgence controversy initiated by Luther's *95 Theses against Indulgences* (1517); see TAL 1:13–46.

42. This is the only source for this particular autobiographical note about the early Augustinian reactions to Luther's theses against indulgences. The prior at the time was Jacob Probst of Ypres [1486–1562] (Brecht 1:204).

43. The "preachers," or *ordo praedicatorum*, refers to the Dominicans, traditional rivals of the Augustinian Order. Johann Tetzel (1465–1519), the original opponent in the indulgence controversy, was a Dominican.

d 1 Sam. 5:6; Ps. 78:66.

jubilant that the Augustinians would now share their scorching and shameful disgrace. I replied: "Dear fathers, if this work has not been begun in God's name, then it will soon fail. But if it has been undertaken in his name, then leave it to him."[e] They had nothing more to say. The work continues and, please God, will continue even better until the end. Amen.

I have heard a story about that noble bishop, Frederick of Magdeburg, who was also Count of Beichlingen not long ago.[44] Duke Frederick of Saxony, his sworn enemy, was preparing to fight against him. He sent a spy to the bishop's court for the purpose of learning about his defense operations. The spy returned jubilantly to the Saxon prince and informed him that the bishop was making no preparations and that the victory was theirs. The prince asked: "What does the bishop say about the war?" The spy replied: "He says nothing more than this, that he is interested in discharging his duties, visiting the cloisters, and hearing the cases of the poor. He would let God fight for him, since God would take good care of the war." When the prince heard this, he said: "If this is what the bishop says, then let the devil fight him in my stead!" He gave up the war, for he was afraid to fight against God. Now who was it who helped the bishop so quickly and easily, and so completely changed the mind of the prince? Only the name of the Lord. The insignificant and the little word "God" accomplishes such great things so quickly, so powerfully, and so easily. I shall not list the many examples of the enemies who were destroyed because they trusted in people. We see altogether too much of this every day.

44. Frederick III of Beichlingen was bishop of Magdeburg from 1445 to 1464. Luther recounts this story in several other places, e.g., his lectures on Isaiah, 1527–1529 (LW 16 and 17; WA 25:203).

Now our Lord is a God who permits the faithful to suffer and the ungodly to rage, but still does not forsake the pious in their need, and finally overthrows the monsters and rescues his own. In these verses, therefore, the psalmist would use his own example and experience to admonish and encourage us to trust and hope in God, as the First Commandment teaches.[45] Such trust is good, noble, and wholesome here in time and hereafter in eternity. It is the most acceptable offering to God and the finest service and honor we can render him. Furthermore, the psalmist wants to deter us; he wants to warn us in a straightforward manner against placing our trust, hope, boast, and reliance in people and princes, as the children and servants of the world and

45. See n. 36, p. 269.

e Cf. Acts 5:38-39.

the devil do, who despise and reject God and violate the First Commandment. This is evil, shameful, and destructive, here in time and hereafter in eternity. Besides, it is the greatest dishonor, contempt, and robbery of God.

But let no sectarian presume to draw from this beautiful rose of the holy prophet the poisonous teaching[46] that we should kill princes and despise or disobey government. Here David teaches that we should not place our confidence even in pious princes, whom he calls נְדִיבִים, which Christ translates as "benefactors."[f] In their office of doing much good they have been ordained by God, as is abundantly shown elsewhere. We should use and enjoy the princely office and temporal government for food, protection, and peace on earth, as God instituted it. But we should not rely, trust, hope, and boast in them. We must use other temporal goods, money, cattle, houses, homes; but we must not place our trust, hope, and confidence in them. To trust and to use are two different things. The former is appropriate to God; the latter is appropriate to creatures.[47]

46. A German saying that Luther was fond of; namely, that while bees draw honey from a rose, spiders draw only poison, i.e., wicked people produce only evil, and corrupt even the good and beautiful.

47. Luther's distinction seems to be an adaptation of Augustine's famous distinction between *uti* and *frui*, to "use" and to "enjoy." The former is proper with created things, but the latter only for God. For Augustine's use of the pair, see *On Christian Doctrine*, Book 1.

10. All nations surrounded me; in the name of the LORD I cut them off!
11. They surrounded me, surrounded me on every side;
in the name of the LORD I cut them off!
12. They surrounded me like bees; they were extinguished
like a fire of thorns; in the name of the LORD I cut them off!
13. I was pushed hard, so that I was falling; but the LORD helped me.

In these four verses the psalmist relates who it is that persecutes him and from what source the trouble comes to which he has referred above. By his own example he wants to show convincingly the fine teaching and admonition by which he calls on us to put our confidence in God and not in people. It is as if he were saying: "I want to show you by my own example and experience, so that you may see how good it is to trust in God and beware of trusting in people. All the heathen, with their great power, zeal, wrath, fury, cunning, and treachery, have attacked me from all sides. But in spite of their raging fury they have accomplished nothing. It has served only to prove and confirm that God comforts, sustains, and strengthens the faithful in all

f Luke 22:25.

their troubles by his word and Spirit, and does not forsake them. He smashes and destroys the adversaries and thus finally helps us out of trouble and rescues us."

Whether the prophet is speaking here of himself personally or of Christendom—as some claim because he says: "All nations surrounded me"—in general, is of no concern to me.[48] His example applies to all the saints, whether before or after Christ. However, I assume that he refers to himself and to his people, since at the beginning of the psalm he speaks of Israel and Aaron. All the

This woodcut is from "The Seven-Headed Luther" (1529), Johann Cochlaeus's polemic against Martin Luther. This representation of the reformer with seven heads illustrates the contradictory nature of heretics, as well as some of the more destructive aspects of the reformer's work. Cochlaeus was one of Luther's most vigorous Roman Catholic opponents.

48. The *Glossa Ordinaria* reflects a variety of interpretations, from the particular trials during David's reign, to more broadly corporate interpretations, e.g., the nation of Israel/church over against the heathen. Nicholas of Lyra even cites the example of the slaying of Thomas Becket (c. 1118–1170) by King Henry II (1133–1189) in 1170 as indicative of the antagonism of temporal lords over against the church. Luther would have had both the *Glossa* and Lyra available to him. In his first lectures on this psalm (1515), WA 55/1:730, Luther applied this text to both Christ and to the church, following the principle of Augustine (derived from Tyconius [d. c. 390]) indicated in book 3 of *On Christian Doctrine*, that what Scripture says regarding Christ, the head, can be said of the church, his body. Augustine also followed this method in his own interpretation of this verse in his *Ennarationes in Psalmos*.

surrounding heathen hated the Jewish kingdom beyond measure. They attacked and tormented it wherever possible from all sides, especially in the days of David. However, David did not fail but confidently went on the attack and valiantly fought them, until by God's command and with God's help he overcame and defeated them. Thus, he says: "In the name of the LORD I cut them off!" He is an example for all believers, who also suffer and finally conquer, no longer by the sword but by the word of God; for Christendom does not fight with a physical sword.[49]

49. Luther's views on temporal and spiritual coercion and power are expressed in several of his works, especially *On Secular Authority* (1523), TAL 5:79–130. In *Exsurge Domine,* the papal bull threatening Luther with excommunication in 1520, proposition 33 condemned Luther for teaching that it is against the will of the Holy Spirit for the church to burn heretics.

How great the danger is, and how numerous the enemy! He says first, that "all nations," with their mighty host, are arrayed against this small group. Thus, it must be, that all must combine against God and his word, in order to show conclusively that trust in, and reliance on, humanity is nothing before God. Ps. 2[:2] says: "The kings of the earth set themselves, and the rulers take counsel together, against the LORD and his anointed." Humanity can tolerate unopposed other doctrines and gods, and no land or nation will object. But let the word of God appear, and all the world is up in arms. Then there is rage and fury from all sides, and this is true: "They surrounded me, only me. I, I alone, am the one to be surrounded." The Romans could bear their several hundred gods; only Christ they could not tolerate.[g] In our day the people tolerated all the teachings of the monks and the priests, no matter how infamous, even though they sucked the world dry and were a pain and torture for body and soul. But when the word of God comes and teaches only grace and peace and delivers from oppression, everybody resorts to attack, blasphemy, and persecution. Why? The psalmist says: "They have nothing else to do than to surround me, me, because I have the word. The devil must turn against me." It is as Christ says, in John 15[:19]: "If you were of the world, the world would love its own; but because you are not of the world, but I chose you out of the world, therefore the world hates you."

In the second place, the enemies are not only numerous; but they also use their power with all their might, persistency, diligence, and effort. Twice in verse eleven the psalmist says: "They surrounded me; they surrounded me." He shows by these words how they persist and press forward, never relenting or growing

g Cf. Augustine, *The City of God*, III, 12.

tired. They drive themselves incessantly, until they ruin themselves. Though they frequently fail, they are not concerned. They try one plot after another, one undertaking after another. Their god, the devil, goads them on and does not let them rest or relax as long as they can move. The devil instigates all heathen attacks against Christ and his word. Were such attacks a mere human undertaking, the enemies would soon tire and give up in disgust, especially when they realized that they had often attacked only to fail and be disgraced, as always happens to such persecutors.

Thirdly, they are not only serious, active, and restless but most vehement, bitter, hateful, and malicious; and this makes them still more restless. Again, their wasted commotion and vain fury, the fact they do not accomplish as much as quickly as they like but often fail and must give up many a plan and project makes them the more furious and vehement. The more they fail, and the longer the delay, the more frantic they become. Although failure should lead them to repentance, one vice whets another, and one transgression sharpens another. Restlessness makes them furious, and fury makes them restless. As the devil goads and drives them on, they scramble and storm and bluster in his service. They cannot cease or pause. For this reason the psalmist says here: "They surrounded me like bees." A bee is an angry and impetuous little insect. When a bee is angry, it sinks its sting into its enemy and leaves it there, without considering that it dies by this act or can never make any more honey. For if a bee loses its sting, it stops making honey, even if it survives. Because of its anger and its vengeful spirit it loses, in a shameful way, its noble, sweet trade. Henceforth it must be a water carrier for the other bees. Otherwise it could not eat with them. Among the other bees it is now a servant in the house.[50]

The enemies of Christ are equally vindictive and spiteful. They would rather perish than fail to do damage or get revenge. They lose forever all grace to do good and to become true Christians. Their wings buzz and whirr as they plunge their sting into Christ. They cool their fury with their own eternal harm and destruction. Ps. 8[:2] calls them avengers and says: "By the mouths of babes and infants you have founded a bulwark because of your foes, to still the enemy and the avenger." It is a strange and inhuman revenge, simply devilish because it is so unreasonable. The word of God does them no harm but rather brings and offers them every good, grace, peace, welfare, life,

50. Such information would have been available to Luther in Pliny's *Natural History*, XI, 57–60.

and salvation. However, as said before, such lust for revenge is provoked by their failure and inability to do what they want to do and to do it when and how they please. This frustrated and blocked restlessness and wickedness inflames them to such devilish revenge.

In the fourth place, since they must be deeply ashamed at their repeated failure and realize that they have no reason for being angry, furious, and vindictive, they mask and camouflage themselves. They forge a case, and argue that the word of God causes sedition and is detrimental to the peace of the community. Having covered their shame, they no longer feel disgraced in the face of repeated failure and futility. Now they boastfully claim that the devil hinders them in their godly and pious undertaking. Now, as true children of God, they have an important and honest reason for anger, fury, murder, and revenge. They do God a great service when they maintain peace and unity and punish the rebels and the blasphemers. In such a manner poor Christ is shamefully and wickedly betrayed. How can he penetrate their masquerade and see that they are rascals and scoundrels at heart, especially since they put on such a fine front? Surely, he must canonize them! Without a doubt he is so naïve and simple compared with these eminently wise people! The members of the council in Jerusalem acted in a similar manner when they had determined to kill the Son of God. They had often failed, had grown more and more furious, and still had no reason for their anger or their plot. Then Mr. Caiaphas, the high priest, attempted to trick God by saying: "You know nothing at all; you do not understand that it is expedient for you that one man should die for the people, and that the whole nation should not perish" [John 11:49-50]. What was God, the poor soul, to do? He simply had to go along with the masquerade and believe Caiaphas. It was only proper for God to crucify his innocent Son that peace and unity might continue and his people might not perish, as Mr. Caiaphas thundered and prophesied.

Therefore the psalmist states in verse twelve: "They were extinguished like a fire of thorns." When the hedges or fences in a field catch fire, everyone must run to help extinguish, quench, and save, as in an epidemic and a public calamity, lest the fire attack the grain in the field, the vineyard and gardens, and destroy the land and its people. Moses gave the Jews specific legislation regarding the punishment and fine of one guilty of

Jesus on trial before Caiaphas (Matthew 26). Woodcut by Albrecht Dürer.

starting a fire in a hedge of thorns around fields, vineyards, and gardens (Exod. 22:6). This applies also to a fire in the forest, on the prairie, or on a wood lot; and whoever runs to put it out does a good and praiseworthy deed. Now the psalmist says that God's enemies compare their ranting and raving to this running to a fire. When anyone teaches the word of God, he has, as we say in German, set fire to the Rhine; or, as the Hebrew puts it, he has set fire to the fences and the hedges. When this happens, everyone must come running to quench the fire, to kill the heretics and the rebels, to defend and save God's honor and people. This supplies a good and even an honorable and laudable reason for murder and for raging against God. If they fail, they have the double distinction of being holy martyrs in a good work and of suffering great opposition on the part of the devil. What an excellent recipe for hardening a heart and making it impenitent!

Now you can see who throws fear into the faithful and creates affliction for them so that it is necessary for them to call upon the Lord.

1. Their number is large; it embraces all the heathen and all their might, the world and all the devils.
2. They are vehement, determined, and restless, not lazy or sluggish.
3. They are bitter, hateful, and furious; and they leave no hope of grace or reconciliation.
4. Finally, they are the greatest saints in heaven and the most pious people on earth.

Now what did the artist who thus painted these persecutors possibly omit? Which one of these four points would not be enough by itself to harm Christians and fill them with fear? With Christians the opposite is true on all four counts. First, they are alone and few; secondly, they are weak and feeble; thirdly, they are gentle and patient; fourthly, they are the worst heretics in hell and the most dangerous people on earth.

How can a Christian resist such enemies? Where is the victory for which he may hope? All appears to be lost, for they are superior. Our victory, however, lies here: "In the name of the Lord I cut them off." That is the Christian's reply to the four points. With one weapon he will meet them all. Now this is simply too much! This proud soul not only wants to be defended and rescued, but he also wants to subdue the whole world, with its power, wrath, and holiness! Subdue? No, he wants to crush the world with one weapon! If the devil and all his angry underlings only knew this, they would really be worried! What kind of gun or sword will you, sorry pride, use for this feat? I would like to hear this cannon or songstress! It must be a powerful piece! He says: I will tell you. It is called THE NAME OF THE LORD.[h] "Oh, this is a paper cannon, a paper bag," says the boaster. "Then let it be paper; you'll see!" "How do you load it? How do you discharge it? What makes it shoot? What kind of ammunition does it use?"

In the first place, we know that God is almighty and that, compared with him, all the heathen are nothing, as the First Commandment shows. This is the first point. Secondly, he would no more permit his name to remain in disgrace than he would forfeit his divinity. In the Second Commandment he has declared that he will not let his name be used in vain or let this sin go unpunished. This is the second point. When we now honor his name and call upon it, and our enemies malign us on this account, whom are they really persecuting and maligning? Is it not God Almighty himself, and his name? Do you not see the gun being loaded? Since God will not suffer his name to be blasphemed, and we still pray and ask that it be hallowed and honored, don't you believe that this prayer will discharge the gun? And the bullet? Perhaps it will be the Turk or some other sentence or plague of God, bringing death and destruction. The explosion will cause princes, bishops, lords, priests, lackeys, and monks to lie down and scream so that it will re-echo in heaven and resound on earth. They are asking for it. He shot the obstinate Jews with the Romans, the Romans with the Goths and the Wends, the Chaldeans with the Persians, and the Greeks with the Turks.[51] He will also find a bullet for us Germans, to hit us and not miss; for we have pushed things too far and still refuse to quit.

This means that we Christians crush the heathen through our prayers, while God actually does it for the sake of his name, which we use and honor. Whenever we do anything as a result of someone else's advice, command, or request, it is actually done by him who advised, commanded, or requested it; this is a uni-

51. The notion that nations and kingdoms are God's instruments of punishment is especially clear in the prophets, e.g. Isa. 5:10, "Woe to Assyria, the rod of my anger; the staff in their hands is my fury!"

h These words are capitalized in both the original and print version.

52. Luther is referring to the legal principle of agency, *quod facit per alium facit per se*, "whoever acts through another does the act himself."

versal rule.[52] Therefore we can say in good conscience: "I shall crush the world"; that is, I will confidently ask God to hallow his name. Then I have already done it, for he will hear me, as this psalm says [v. 5]: "The LORD answered me." Thus, David, who slew his enemies with a physical sword, did not do this with the power of the sword, as he testifies in Psalm 18 and elsewhere. When he honored, hallowed, and invoked the name of God and prayed for the sake of God's glory, his sword became more than a hundred thousand swords. The name of the Lord is effective if we honor and call upon it. And even though we fail to call upon his name, it is still effective. Of course, there will be no benefit or meaning for us, since we are not interested and do not call upon it. He punishes the heathen, even though this brings no deliverance to the faithful, as the Romans destroyed one another and thereby carried out his sentence.

You say that you praise the name of the Lord. But the other side also claims to honor God's name and serve him, as already said. Here is the crucial issue. Who uses the name of God properly? Your words alone mean nothing. First, listen to your conscience; it cannot deceive God. Next, to guard against deceiving people, consider the fruits; and then you can judge if the tree is good.[i] We, on our side, have no confidence in people, nor can we have; for we are too little, too few, and too weak. We must walk in fear, anxiety, and danger. We must humbly plead with God and mortals. We murder no one because of his doctrine, nor do we rob anyone; but we permit him to believe what he pleases. We do not use force or compulsion, but we let the government judge and punish insurrection, strife, and dissension. We do not scheme and plot harm against anyone, but we prevent this where we can. We diligently keep and promote peace; and we suffer murder, bloodshed, poverty, and persecution. All this is evidence of the proper spirit and is in harmony with this psalm and with all Scripture.

Our opponents, however, trust and rely on people and their help, on emperors and princes. They feel secure, free from care and danger, afraid neither of us nor of any person. They do not call on God, much less humble themselves before others. They are proud, secure, and arrogant; and they force and drive people to believe what they demand. They resort to murder, torture,

i Matt. 12:33.

robbery, and exile without measure. They plot and plan most zealously by day and night how they may inflict hurt and harm, cause damage and create unrest. It is obvious that they neither can nor will have peace. Such behavior cannot be the fruit of a proper spirit; it is contrary to all Scripture. You can never prove that a Christian should commit murder, or even kill by law, or aid and abet such a thing. This is the function of the temporal government and belongs to earthly affairs, as even the pagan Gallio admitted, Acts 18[:14-15]. Christians have another law, judgment, and punishment (Matt. 18[:15-17]).

Moreover, we are concerned that unchastity and disorderly conduct be rebuked and not tolerated. Concubinage, fornication, blasphemy, and cursing are, praise God, decreasing. Marriage is honored, and our beloved youth are being trained well and with all diligence in the word of God and Christian discipline.[53] Among the papists, however, we see the most shameful, licentious, and disgraceful avarice and pride, an offense to all the world. It is worst among the upper classes, where there is no shame or punishment. Precious young people are neglected and allowed to go to rack and ruin. They are taught neither to believe nor to pray. Their teachers do not know how themselves and are ashamed to accept our instruction or example. Therefore it remains undone.

But now comes the crowning sin. We are not ashamed to confess, to the glory of God, our former errors of unbelief and abuse of God's word; and we neither hide nor disguise our sin. They, however, only conceal, mask, camouflage, and gild theirs. By their ranting, arrogance, and blasphemy against us they try to make us blind to the logs in their eyes and aware and critical of the specks that are in ours.[j] They know and believe that in many things our teachings are superior to theirs. They are well aware of their shameful commercializing of the Mass. They know how abominably popes, cardinals, bishops, canons, and priests have infested the world with vice, avarice, fornication, and pride, with their false teachings of indulgences, purgatory, pilgrimages, and similar flagrant abominations. All this they cover up, and not one of them would confess his error and reject it to the honor of God. We have the example of the preaching monks at Bern;[54] they go on in their smug impenitence and entertain no

j Matt. 7:3.

53. In 1524, Luther published a treatise, *To the Councilmen of All Cities in Germany That They Establish and Maintain Christian Schools* (see TAL 5:235–79), to encourage magistrates to provide for the broad education of both boys and girls. In 1529, Luther wrote a preface for a book by Justus Menius (1499–1558) entitled *Oeconomia Christiana,* "The Christian Household," emphasizing the importance of the family and the education of children. In the summer of 1530, a few months before writing this commentary, Luther wrote *A Sermon on Keeping Children* (LW 46:209–58) to encourage families and magistrates in Nuremberg and elsewhere toward such educational goals.

54. Luther is referring to the so-called Jetzer affair in Bern in 1509, in which a lay brother of the Bern Dominican house faked apparitions of the Virgin Mary to make a case for a maculate, as opposed to immaculate, conception. See "The Jetzer Affair," Rudolf Dellsperger, in Religion Past and Present (RPP) (BrillOnline *Reference Works*), the English translation of Religion in Geschichte and Gegenwart (RGG), 4th edition. Hans Dieter Betz, Don S. Browning, Bernd Janowski, Eberhard Jungel, eds.

thought of repentance or improvement but are inflamed against us. [They suggest that] we should die, and their shameful, false, and wicked life survive and be vindicated. That is sin against the Holy Spirit. Everyone can see from their fruits how seriously they take God's name. So much on verses ten, eleven, and twelve.

Verse thirteen now describes what these numerous, powerful, angry, and holy heathen accomplish with their siege and persecution, and how far they actually get: "I was pushed hard, so that I was falling." That is to say: "They want to do me in and destroy me, so that nothing remains. They want to exterminate me root and stem, as Jeremiah threatens his people, Jer. 11[:19]. Well, that they push me around and exile me is a matter of force, and this they can do. But still God preserves me from their designs and limits them, so that they cannot do what they intend. They can push, but they cannot knock down. They can use torture, but they cannot exterminate. They can put me in stocks, but they cannot compel. They can hinder, but they cannot prevent. They can show their teeth, but they cannot devour. They can murder by burning, hanging, and drowning; but they cannot subdue. They can exile, rob, and pillage; but they cannot silence. In short, they shall do something, but their heart's desire they shall not accomplish." They are limited by these words: "The Lord helped me." Who can succeed against the Lord? This will stand: God's word endures forever,[55] unless God and his name no longer abide. Let them rage and rave.

55. Isa. 40:8; 1 Pet. 1:25. The Latin text, *Verbum Domini manet in aeternum,* became the motto of the court of Frederick the Wise in 1522, and then of his successors. Philip of Hesse (1504–1567) would incorporate it into his livery at the Diet of Speyer in 1526. Later in 1531, the Schmalkaldic League took up the verse as its motto.

14. The Lord is my strength and my might;[k]
he has become my Salvation.

Having listed the miracles with which God comforts and helps his people, the psalmist joyfully breaks into a short but

k The Hebrew word here, זִמְרָת, found also in Exod. 15:2, is traditionally translated as "song." One sees this reflected in both the Vulgate, "*laudatio mea,*" and in Luther's translation, "*mein Psalm.*" It is this sense on which Luther comments. However, more recent scholarship has found that in other ancient semitic languages the root word, זמר, has the sense of "protect" as a soldier or husband. If this is the correct cognate, then the sense is a semantic doubling, i.e., "strength" and "protection" or "might"—a common feature in Hebrew poetry. See Ludwig Koehler and Walter Baumgartner, *The Hebrew and Aramaic Lexicon of the Old Testament*, vol. 1, trans. M. E. J. Richardson (Leiden: Brill, 1994), 274: זמר, III; זִמְרָת, II.

beautiful song of praise and thanksgiving to spite, mock, and scorn his persecutors and to glorify and honor God. Whether they want to or not, they must hear that he and his God remain and survive despite their raging and blustering. It is the same song that Moses sings, in Exod. 15[:2], in defiance of the drowned Pharaoh. Isaiah in 12[:2] also sings it. Apparently this was a common song and proverb among the children of Israel. Surely it deserves to be a common song and formula of praise among us also whenever we are delivered from troubles. While we have often sung it after deliverance in the past, we shall sing it more frequently in the future, even to the end. Amen.

Note the fine, threefold summary of the psalmist: The Lord is "my Strength," "my Song," "my Salvation." The first indicates that he trusts wholly and completely in God, that God does, speaks, and quickens everything in him; and he will not boast of his own power, ability, knowledge, wisdom, holiness, or deeds. He will be nothing; in him God will be all and do all. What a sublime song and how rare in this world! He trusts and relies on no person or prince, on none of this world's power, wealth, friends, alliances, support, wisdom, deeds, comfort, or help. He trusts in God alone, in contrast to himself and all the world's might, wisdom, and holiness. This is expressed even more impressively in the song: God alone shall be his strength, trust, and defiance. Next, the psalmist cannot keep still about this. He turns it into a psalm and sings; he preaches, teaches, confesses, and declares what he believes about God. Faith cannot do otherwise; it always confesses what it believes, Rom. 10[:10]. The world cannot bear to hear that its power and wisdom, its holiness and piety, its counsel and deeds, are condemned and rejected, that the help and trust of people and princes should be cast out and despised, and their teaching be held vain and false. The singer of this psalm is taken to task because, as is said, his psalm does not praise God, his preaching does not honor God, his confession does not declare the truth; but that it is all blasphemy, heresy, error, lies, rebellion, and a delusion of the world, the most shameful song on earth and the most dangerous teaching under the sun. To the dungeon with him! Burn him, exile him, curse and damn him! Kill, burn, drown, hang, murder, and confound him as a great service to God! In the third place, God is his salvation and will not utterly abandon the singer and his song. God helps him in life and death and grants him victory. Though all the gates of hell and the whole world rage and rave, God, in the end, will be our salvation; we and our psalm and teaching shall survive, and all the adversaries shall founder. The word of God abides forever. No amount of raging, blustering, blasphemy, or cursing will change this.

The psalmist, therefore, draws a fine contrast. It is like this: "The strength of the enemies lies in themselves; it is the strength of people and princes, in whom they trust, as said before. But my strength, in which I trust, is the Lord. He who is the source of strength deserves the psalm, the praise and thanks, glory and honor. They must praise, honor, and glorify their gods, namely, themselves, people and princes. This they do, openly and unabashed. Their noblest work and worship is to rob and deprive God of the sacrifice of praise and blasphemously to divert and offer it to miserable mortals. O let us really heap scorn on those wretched and obstinate souls who have such miserable gods and must worship a sack of maggots[56] and a stinkpot without a chance of help. Just as their strength and their song, that is, their trust and boast, go down in defeat, so there is no help or victory for them, but only failure and destruction. Psalm 146 tells us that help is never found in people. My victory and salvation lie in the Lord, who can and does help. Here salvation is to be taken as victory or help. In his name and word God lets us gain ultimate victory. He helps us overcome and hold the field, while our persecutors perish and go down in disgrace.

15. There are glad songs of victory in the tents of the righteous:
The right hand of the LORD does valiantly.

The psalmist has finished speaking and singing about his own example, about God's help in his life. He now proceeds to the common example of all the saints. He says that all the righteous are persecuted for the sake of God and his word. Because they trust in God and do not depend on people, God helps them, so that they also sing such a song and praise him. Thus, Moses and the children of Israel sang, Exodus 15; likewise Deborah, Judges 5, and Hannah, 1 Samuel 2, and all the rest. It is a unanimous chorus. When I look at all the saints, especially in the New Testament, the story is the same. I can hear voices of rejoicing in their tabernacles, joyous songs and hymns of salvation and victory, of the help of God. And we sing along and join in the praise

56. One of Luther's favorite epitaphs for himself and the human body, indicating both its mortality and its futility before the resurrection of the flesh. Perhaps the best known occurs in his *Sincere Admonition to All Christians* (1521), LW 45:70: "I plead that everyone should ignore my name and not call himself Lutheran, but Christian. What is Luther? The teaching is certainly not mine. In the same way I was not crucified for anyone. St. Paul, in 1 Corinthians 3, would not allow it that the Christians [in Corinth] be named Pauliners or Peterans, but Christian. How comes it then that I, a poor, stinking, sack of maggots at that, should have someone call the children of Christ by my awful name? Not so, dear friend. Let us erase partisan names and be called Christians, whose teaching we have."

and thanks, just as we are one in our faith and trust in God and also share in suffering. St. Peter comforts us, 1 Pet. 5[:9]: "for you know that your brothers and sisters in all the world are undergoing the same kinds of suffering."

Were it not a special consolation to know and observe that this is the lot of all the saints, St. Peter would not have made this application, and this psalm would not have spoken of it so emphatically. It must comfort and strengthen my heart when I see that St. Paul and the apostles had the same word, God, faith, and cross as I do. As the saying goes: *Gaudium est miseris socios habere penarum*—"it is a comfort to the poor if they do not suffer alone."[57] This is, for one thing, an excellent proverb if it is used properly and applied to Christians. It is frightening for one with a special affliction to feel marked out for this distinctive suffering before all other people. Again, it is comforting when many suffer the same thing; for then that person does not get the horrible thought that he alone has been winnowed out and rejected. But still more comforting is it when all suffer the same and no one is exempt, as is the case among Christians.[58]

This psalm, however, does not speak here of the suffering of the righteous but of victory and rejoicing, for the purpose of increasing our comfort as we see before us the happy picture of the redeemed and are confident that in the end we shall be able to sing as joyously as they. Nevertheless, the psalmist indicates the sufferings of the righteous with the word "salvation" and subsequently with other words, pointing out that the righteous have suffered sorely and fought valiantly in the fight of faith. Otherwise there would be no talk of salvation and victory, or such a song of joy. But now, as suffering abounds—and Paul tells us that the sufferings of Christ in us are many[l]—there is a great deal of salvation and victory, singing and rejoicing, praise and thanks among the righteous. Therefore I hold that it must be apparent to all that in Scripture "the righteous" are the believers who trust in God. "The righteous live by their faith," Rom. 1[:17]. On the other hand, the one who trusts princes and people is wicked and an unbeliever. Therefore in their tabernacles there is no joyful song of salvation and victory, but crying, reviling, blaspheming, and cursing God, followed by howling, wailing,

l 2 Cor. 1:5.

57. Luther is citing one of the various forms of this common proverb in the original Latin. The most common English form is "Misery loves company."

58. Cf. Luther's preface to his German translation of the Psalms from 1524: "Hence, it is that the Psalter is the book of all saints; and everyone, in whatever situation that person may be, finds in the psalms words that fit his or her case or situation—that suit him or her as if they were put there just for his or her sake . . . when these words please a person and suit her or his case, this person becomes sure that they are in the communion of saints, and that it has gone with all the saints as it goes with him or her self, since they all sing with this person one little song" (see this volume, p. 210; LW 35:256).

and the gnashing of teeth in hell.[m] And what song of joy and praise do the righteous sing in their tabernacles? It is this: "The right hand of the LORD does valiantly."

16. The right hand of the LORD is exalted,
the right hand of the LORD does valiantly!
17. I shall not die, but I shall live,
and recount the deeds of the LORD.
18. The LORD has punished me severely,
but he did not give me over to death.

This is the joyful song of the righteous. It is sung by all the saints in their tabernacles, that is, where they gather and dwell. The psalmist refers especially to the righteous in the New Testament,[n] where throughout the churches the gospel of Christ's great miracles is preached. Mark well, this is a song of the righteous, of the believers, not of the godless. For those who do not believe but put their trust in people cannot sing this song; nor can they understand a word of it, though they may prattle it in cathedrals and cloisters, where Sunday after Sunday this beautiful song is shamefully mistreated and mutilated. The godless sing in their hearts: "The right hand of man does valiantly; the right hand of princes is exalted." For they must "sing as their beak has grown." "Kind does not forsake kind."[59]

Under "singing" I include not only making melody or shouting but also every sermon or public confession by which God's work, counsel, grace, help, comfort, victory, and salvation are glorified before the world. The Holy Spirit refers to such singing wherever in the Psalter and the Scriptures songs, hymns, and psalms are mentioned.[60] As verse fourteen puts it: "The LORD is my Strength and my Song; he has become my Salvation." God wants to be praised, glorified, honored, and confessed by us in his works and wonders. Faith does this, for faith cannot be silent but must say and teach what it believes and knows about God, to the glory of God and the instruction of humankind, as Ps. 116[:10] says: "I believed, therefore have I spoken."[o] If faith did not break

59. Common German sayings, meaning "they must sing as they have been taught" and something like "birds of a feather flock together."

60. Cf. Eph. 5:19, "be filled with the Spirit, as you sing psalms and hymns and spiritual songs among yourselves."

m Matt. 22:13.

n See the introduction, pp. 247–48.

o The original follows the Vulgate numbering, Psalm 115.

forth, speak up, and confess, it would not be a true faith, even though it has to suffer and be cursed and persecuted, as the same psalm continues: "I was greatly afflicted." But faith has a Helper who is its Salvation. Verse fourteen teaches that such persecution does not harm our salvation but must promote it; for it defies and blasphemes God, so that he is driven to help, and the righteous are compelled to call on God and to pray to him. Thus, everything turns out just fine.

Woodcut depicting choral singing with instruments (mid-sixteenth century, Germany)

On the basis of verse fourteen, which we explained above, we can thoroughly understand the whole song of the righteous; for it is in complete harmony with this verse. In their assembly the righteous do not sing, teach, preach, confess, or glorify human works, holiness, and wisdom, or the power, consolation, and help of princes, as the hypocrites, the proud, the self-sufficient saints, and the godless, apostate Christians do in their assembly. They reject and despise such stinking self-righteousness and such ineffective help and consolation of people, princes, and the world. They praise only God's grace, works, words, and power as they are revealed to them in Christ. This is their sermon and song, their hymn of praise. This verse distinctly sets "the right hand of God" in contrast with "the right hand of man," in order that we may know that nothing that the hand of mortals can accomplish avails before God. The human work contributes nothing to righteousness, does not remove sin or produce a good work, knows and understands nothing of the truth and the real nature of salvation. Much less can it counsel and help in trouble, danger, death, and hell. It cannot give life and salvation.

The right hand of God, however, does this. First, it does valiantly. This strength and its comfort were explained above, but it requires a little more explaining here. This is the power of God, that whoever believes and trusts in him is thereby delivered from all sins, from a guilty conscience, a sorrowing heart, error, lies, deception, darkness, and all the power of the devil, and is led to grace, righteousness, truth, understanding, consolation, and the true light. As a result, God is our power.[61] We do not live in ourselves but in him, and he acts and speaks all things in us. These are all great, mighty, divine works and miracles, none of which human reason, power, and might can comprehend, much less help to accomplish. As a result, they are led astray by false comfort, preaching, and promises. And the longer it goes on, the deeper they are driven into error, although before the world their case looks good and gives the appearance of being real power and of quickly bringing them to heaven. He, however, who believes in the power of God recognizes it as nothing but the work of humankind, a rotten, ineffective, and vain delusion. Whoever relies on this builds himself a hell.

Secondly, the right hand is exalted, soars high, overcomes, and always gains the victory. That is to say: Believers not only have this consolation from God, that they are rid of their sins and righteous before him; they also receive help from him, so that they finally overcome the devil, humanity, and the world, and are thus delivered from death, hell, and every evil. They do not need the help of people or princes; for this is unnecessary, nor could it perform such great works and miracles. The great and glorious hand of God performs such exalted miracles and helps us in every need. And if we die, his hand will really lead us to a life that has no end. God's right hand is so exalted that neither tribulation nor distress, neither sword nor famine, neither angels nor princes can pull it down, Rom. 8[:35-39]. If we cling to it with a firm faith, as all the righteous do, we are just as exalted; and neither tribulation nor distress, nor prince, nor devil, neither fire nor water nor any other creature can subdue us. Victory will be ours. But whoever relies on the arm of people and puts his confidence in the hand of princes must plunge into the abyss of hell, though they were sailing above the clouds or sitting in heaven.

Thirdly, the psalmist restates his first point and says: "The right hand of the LORD does valiantly!" A good song is worth singing twice. It is customary for people, when they are really happy or joyful, to repeat a word two or three times. They cannot say it often enough, and whoever meets them must hear it. This is the case here, that the dear saints are so happy and joyful over the miracles God does for them when he delivers them from sin and death, that is, from every evil of body and soul, that out of

61. Cf. Luther's preface to his Latin writings, where he recalls his new view of the Scriptures after coming to a new understanding of the "righteousness of God": "At this point I felt that I had been completely born again and had entered paradise itself through wide open doors. There a completely different face of the entire Scripture appeared to me. At that, I ran through the Scriptures as I had them in my memory, and I gathered together in other words parallel expressions, such as 'work of God,' that is what God effects in us, 'power of God,' by which he makes us powerful, 'wisdom of God,' by which he makes us wise, 'strength of God,' 'salvation of God,' 'glory of God'" (TAL 4:502; cf. LW 34:337).

sheer joy they sing their song over and over again: "The hand of the Lord does valiantly; indeed, valiantly does the hand of the Lord. Nothing but the right hand of God can help or comfort." Oh, what can the ungodly do, who rely on themselves, trust in their own work and wisdom, and build and rest on the comfort and help of people and princes?

Whoever will, let him apply these three points to the threefold work of Christ, in that he redeems us from the law, from sin, and from death. This threefold redemption is enumerated in Isa. 9[:4] and in 1 Cor. 15[:56-57].[62] As I have said, however, the important thing is to realize that these words are wholly spiritual and must be heard, sung, and understood by faith. He who gapes at these words open-mouthed and uses his reason and natural eyes will take offense and will consider only the opposite in the righteous and the holy. In the eyes of the world, they are nothing but the devil's own; no one is less righteous and holy, no one a greater sinner and heretic, no one damned deeper into hell, than the righteous. In the eyes of the unbeliever the devil's right hand is the right hand of the righteous. But those on the opposite side—they alone are holy and blessed. For them the right hand of God does valiantly, soars high, is victorious and exalted. For they are the children of God, and no one else.

Verse seventeen of the psalm—"I shall not die, but I shall live"—touches and states the trouble out of which God's hand delivers the righteous, namely, death. The righteous surely feel death when they are in mortal danger. Meeting death eye to eye is not a pleasant draught for the flesh. Death always appears in the company of sin and the law. One readily understands that the saints are really martyrs, for they must live under the threat of death and wrestle and fight with death. If it does not involve tyrants and the ungodly, with fire, sword, prison, and similar persecutions, it involves the devil himself. He can tolerate neither the word of God nor those who keep and teach it. He besets them in life and in death. While the faithful are alive, he uses great attacks on their faith, hope, and love toward God. He beleaguers and storms a heart with fear, doubt, and despair until it shies away from God, hates and blasphemes him, and the wretched conscience believes that God, the devil, death, sin, hell, and all creatures are one and have united as its eternal and relentless enemy. Neither the Turk[63] nor the emperor can ever storm a city with such power as the devil uses in attacking a conscience.

62. Isa. 9:4: "For the yoke of their burden, and the bar across their shoulders, the rod of their oppressor, you have broken as on the day of Midian"; 1 Cor. 15:56-57 (which Luther mistakenly cites as 1 Corinthians 13 in the original): "The sting of death is sin, and the power of sin is the law. But thanks be to God, who gives us the victory through our Lord Jesus Christ." In Luther's *Sermon on Preparing to Die* (1519), he interprets Isa. 9:4 along these lines. The "yoke of their burden" is sin which burdens the conscience, death is the "bar across the shoulders" laid upon us as punishment, and "the rod of the oppressor" signifies hell and its eternal punishments. Christ on the cross "prepared himself as a threefold picture for us, to be held before the eyes of our faith against the three evil pictures with which the evil spirit and our nature would assail us to rob us of this faith" (TAL 4:297; cf. LW 42:106).

63. Luther used the term *Turk* as representative of all Muslims. During Luther's adult lifetime, armies of Islamic soldiers threatened several cities of Europe; see *On War against the Turk* (TAL 5:335–89).

If God permits, the devil can do this also in death or on the deathbed.[p] There he is a master at puffing up sin and pointing to God's wrath. He is a strange and powerful creature who out of one sin can foment such fear and conjure up such a hell. It is true that no human being ever sees his real sins, namely, unbelief, contempt of God's word, the failure to fear, love, and trust God as he should, and similar sins of the heart, which are the chief transgressions. Nor would it be good for him to see them, for I do not know if there is a faith on earth that could endure it without falling and despairing.[64] For this reason God lets the devil operate with our sins of commission. He easily creates hell and damnation for you because you take one drink too many or sleep too long, and soon you become sick with conscience scruples and despondency and practically die of grief.

64. Cf. Luther's earlier devotional writing, *Fourteen Consolations* (1519): "It is, as I have said, so ordered by God, that we may not perish on seeing the evils hidden in the depths of our hearts. For God keeps them hidden, and would have us discern them only by faith, when he points them out to us by means of the evil that we feel. Therefore, 'In the day of evil be mindful of the good' (Ecclus. 11:27). Behold, how great a good it is, not to know the whole of our evil! Be mindful of this good, and the evil that you feel will press you less cruelly."

What is worse, the devil takes your best works and drives and plunges them into your conscience as worthless and condemned, so that all your sins do not frighten you as much as your best works, which are really quite good, and you wish you had done nothing but great sins instead of these works. He wants you to disown them as not having been done by God, and thus to blaspheme God as well. Then death and hell are not far away. But who can list all the tricks by which the devil invokes sin, death, and hell? This is his trade. He has been at it for more than five thousand years, and he is a past master at it. That long he has been the prince of death. He has experimented and practiced thoroughly how to give a poor conscience the foretaste of death. The prophets, especially our dear David, have felt and tasted his power. For they certainly complain, teach, and talk about it as if they had often been there, speaking now of the gates of death, now of hell, now of the wrath of God.

Well, no matter when or how it happens, we learn here that the saints must wrestle with the devil and fight with death, whether by persecution or pestilence or other sickness and mortal danger. In that conflict nothing is better and more vital for victory than learning to sing this little song of the saints, that is, to look away from self and to cling to the hand of God. Thus, the devil is defrauded and made "to find straw to thresh."[65] It works

65. A German saying that means that one has come too late, i.e., the wheat has already been threshed and all that is left is straw.

p For the early Reformation approach to preparation for death, see Austra Reinis, *Reforming the Art of Dying: The* Ars Moriendi *in the German Reformation (1519–1528)* (Burlington, VT: Ashgate , 2007).

like this: I am nothing. The Lord is all my strength, as stated above. I am stripped of everything, of myself and all that is mine. I can say: "Devil, what are you fighting? If you try to denounce my good works and my holiness before God, why, I have none. My strength is not my own; the Lord is my Strength. You can't squeeze blood out of a turnip![66] If you try to prosecute my sins, I have none of those either. Here is God's strength—prosecute it until you have had enough. I know absolutely nothing about either sins or holiness in me. I know nothing whatever except God's power in me."

It would be fine, I hold, if a man could forget about himself and mock the devil with an empty pocket as a certain poor householder mocked a thief whom he caught in his home one night. He said: "You silly thief, do you expect to find something here in the dark when I can't find anything in broad daylight?" What can the devil do when he finds a soul so naked that it can respond neither to sin nor to holiness? He must give up all his skill, both to puff up sin and to decry good works. He is referred to the right hand of God, and he must by all means let it alone. But if you forget this prescription and he seizes you in your sins and good works, and you begin to argue with him, to observe and hear him, then he will shape you to suit himself; and you will forget and forfeit God, his right hand, and everything.

As we have heard, it is an art to forget self. We must keep learning this lesson as long as we live, even as all the saints before us, with us, and after us must do. Just as we still feel sin, we must also feel death. Just as we must fight to rid ourselves of sin by clinging to God's right hand as his word offers it to us, so we must also battle with death and death's prince or chief, the devil, until we are free. See how this verse presents the conflict. The devil, or pursuer, presses in on the saints with death. How do they react? They turn away their eyes, yes, their entire bodies. Emptying themselves, they cling to God's hand and say: "Devil and tyrant, I shall not die, as you pretend. You lie! I shall live, for I will not speak of my own works or those of any person. I know nothing about myself or my own holiness. I have before me only the works of the Lord. Of them I will speak; them I will glorify; on them I will rely. He it is who delivers from sin and death. If you can overthrow his works, you have overthrown me, too."

This verse then emphasizes the two points mentioned above in verses six and seven: comfort and help, with which God blesses

66. The actual sayings that Luther uses here (*"Lieber reuff mich inn der hand odder zele gelt aus ledigem beutel"*) do not translate directly into an equivalent English idiom. The sense is that one can't demand something from that which is empty.

the pious and the righteous. Here you see how the right hand of God mightily lifts the heart and comforts it in the midst of death, so that it can say: "Though I die, I die not. Though I suffer, I suffer not. Though I fall, I am not down. Though I am disgraced, I am not dishonored." This is the consolation. Furthermore, the psalmist says of the help: "I shall live." Isn't this an amazing help? The dying live; the suffering rejoice; the fallen rise; the disgraced are honored. It is as Christ says: "He who believes in me, though he die, yet shall he live," John 11[:25]. Paul speaks in a similar manner: "We are afflicted in every way, but not crushed; perplexed, but not driven to despair," 2 Cor. 4[:8]. These are all words that no human heart can comprehend.

And here you see that this comfort and help are eternal life, which is the true, everlasting blessing of God. The entire psalm has this theme. Since the psalmist separates the pious from the other three groups[q] and yet gives to those groups everything belonging to this life on earth—temporal government and spiritual rule, the goods, benefit, and use of every creature—therefore of necessity the blessings of this small and pious group must be another life, namely, eternal life. Since the three groups begrudge and deny them their blessings in this life, their consolation must be eternal, and their help everlasting. How else can it be, since the psalmist glories in the Lord himself over and above all the possessions of people and princes which the other groups have? The Lord is an eternal possession; therefore everyone can conclude that where the heart recognizes a gracious God, there must be forgiveness of sins. If sins are forgiven, death is gone. And without fail there must be the comfort and confidence of eternal righteousness and everlasting life.[67]

We should recognize this verse as a masterpiece.[68] How mightily the psalmist banishes death out of sight! He will know nothing of dying and of sin. At the same time he visualizes life most vividly and will hear of nothing but life. But whoever will not see death lives forever, as Christ says: "If anyone keeps my word, he will never see death," John 8[:51]. He so immerses himself in life that death is swallowed up by life[r] and disappears completely, because he clings with a firm faith to the right hand of God. Thus, all the saints have sung this verse and will con-

q See n. 30, p. 264 above.

r 1 Cor. 15:55.

67. Cf. the *Small Catechism*, "where there is the forgiveness of sins, there is also life and salvation" (SC, "Sacrament of the Altar," 5-6; BC, 362).

68. See n. 9, p. 252. While at the Coburg, Luther sent a letter to the Swiss composer Ludwig Senfl (c. 1486–1543), asking him for a polyphonic arrangement of *in pace in id ipsum dormiam* (Ps. 4:8, "In peace I will both lie down and sleep"), his favorite antiphon. Senfl fulfilled this request at a later date, but his immediate response was a motet on this verse, "I shall not die, but live."

tinue to sing it to the end. We note this especially in the case of the martyrs. So far as the world is concerned, they die. Yet their hearts say with a firm faith: "I shall not die, but live."

At this point we should learn the rule that whenever in the Psalter and Holy Scripture the saints deal with God concerning comfort and help in their need, eternal life and the resurrection of the dead are involved.[69] All such texts belong to the doctrine of the resurrection and eternal life, in fact, to the whole Third Article of the Creed with the doctrines of the Holy Spirit, the holy Christian church, the forgiveness of sins, the resurrection, and everlasting life. And it all flows out of the First Commandment, where God says: "I am your God, etc."[s] This the Third Article of the Creed emphasizes insistently. While Christians deplore the fact that they suffer and die in this life, they comfort themselves with another life than this, namely, that of God, who is above and beyond this life. It is not possible that they should totally die and not live again in eternity. For one thing, the God on whom they rely and in whom they find their consolation cannot die, and thus they must live in him. Besides, as Christ says, "He is a God of the living, not of the dead" and of those who are no more.[t] Therefore Christians must live forever; otherwise he would not be their God, nor could they depend on him unless they live. For this little group, therefore, death remains no more than a sleep.[u]

But if it is true that they live in God, then it must first be true that they have forgiveness of sin. If they have no sin, they surely have the Holy Spirit, who makes them holy. If they are holy, they are the true holy Christian church, the little flock; and they rule over all the power of the devil. Then one day they will rise again and live forever. These are the great and lofty works of the right hand of the Lord. Compared with them, what are the deeds of people and princes on which the entire world relies and of which it boasts? Isaiah calls them spider webs,[v] fit neither to clothe nor to adorn anything. Only aimless and foolish gnats and flies, the frivolous souls, are caught by them and killed forever.

69. Luther derives this axiom from Jesus's own method of reading the Old Testament exhibited in Matt. 22:23-33. See his comments regarding the same in his commentary on Psalm 90 (LW 13:81-82).

Portrait of Ludwig Senfl (c. 1519) attributed to Hans Schwarz

s Exod. 20:2.

t Matt. 22:32.

u John 11:11-14; 1 Cor. 15:20; 1 Thess. 4:13-15.

v Isa. 59:5.

Now saints live not only in the life to come; they begin life now, by faith. And wherever there is faith, everlasting life has begun. And the texts in Scripture regarding faith also belong to all the doctrines listed above. The three groups we have discussed have no need of faith for this life, since the ungodly have this life most of all. Nor can faith attach itself or cling to anything that counts in this life; it breaks away and clings to that which is above and beyond this life, that is, to God. This verse teaches that the saints begin this eternal life here and live even while dying: "I shall recount the deeds of the LORD." Whoever would tell of the Lord's work must certainly be alive. Though they are dead, their spirit and blood preach, even as Abel's blood cries out against Cain, Gen. 4[:10]. And in Heb. 11[:4] we read that the departed Abel still speaks through his faith.

This is the worst and most discouraging text for tyrants and for murderers of the saints. I hardly know of another verse in Scripture to the effect that the saints, whom they believe to be silenced and suppressed, are just beginning to live and to speak. "What the devil![w] There is no use in arguing with the saints if after death they begin really to do that for which they were killed! They will never cease or desist. They remain un-killed and un-silenced, and proclaim forever the works of the Lord." The pope burned Jan Hus and many other saints, only recently Leonhard Kaiser and many others.[70] But he was so successful in silencing them that their blood now cries out against him until he has lost all his power. Now he must go begging and call on other powers, such as emperors and princes, whom he once arbitrarily trod underfoot. If it were not for them, the poor beggar would have been eaten by moths long ago; and even now such help avails him little and will eventually fail him. He must concede that Jan Hus is his master.

The eighteenth verse in this song is also a masterpiece. It uses the rhetorical devices of confutation, understatement, and interpretation.[x] It declares: "The LORD has chastened me sorely, but he has not given me over to death." What does this mean? He has boasted that he will not die, but live. Thereupon the

70. Jan Hus (d. 1415) was executed at the Council of Constance for his teachings on the church, the papacy, and the sacraments. The significance of Hus for Luther was first at the Leipzig Debate (1519), when Luther admitted that the Council of Constance erred in condemning Hus. Later Hus was largely seen as an image of the innocent martyr who suffered for the sake of God's word. Leonhard Kaiser (d. 1527) was a Lutheran pastor in Waizenkirchen, Austria, who was forced out of his position in 1524. After residing in Wittenberg, he returned home in 1527 to bury his father and attend to his family. During this time he was arrested by authorities and interrogated by Johann Eck (1486–1543). Condemned as a heretic, appeals from Luther and John, the elector of Saxony, did not avail. He was burned 15 August 1527.

w The German phrase here is *Kroden teufel*.

x Luther is referring to devices denoted in Aristotle's *Rhetorica ad Alexandrum*, ch. 36. For Luther's understanding and use of rhetoric see Helmar Junghans, *Martin Luther und die Rhetorik* (Leipzig: Verlag der Sächsischen Akademie der Wissenschaft zu Leipzig, 1998).

flesh, world, people, and princes speak up and would weaken and discourage him: "Is it not death if you are burned, beheaded, drowned, strangled, condemned, and exiled? I would think that you could tell whether this can be called life. Where is your God? Let him help you! Of course, Elias will come and take you down!"[y] To this he replies unshaken, and he comforts himself thus: "On the contrary, this dying is nothing. It is only a fatherly rod, not wrath. It is only a foxtail, nothing serious. God is only chastising me as a dear father chastises his dear child.[z] It may hurt a little, and it is not sugar; it is a rod. However, it does not kill, but rather helps me live." This is surely a good interpretation and an effective confutation, to make a benevolent rod out of the word "death." Only the Holy Spirit and the right hand of God can teach this art. It hurts beyond measure when to suffering there are added blasphemy, mockery, wagging of the head, and hostility, as the Jews did to Christ on the cross. Flesh and blood would do the opposite and turn a benevolent rod into death and hell, for it is ready to give up and despair if it lacks as much as a loaf of bread. This is a poor interpretation.

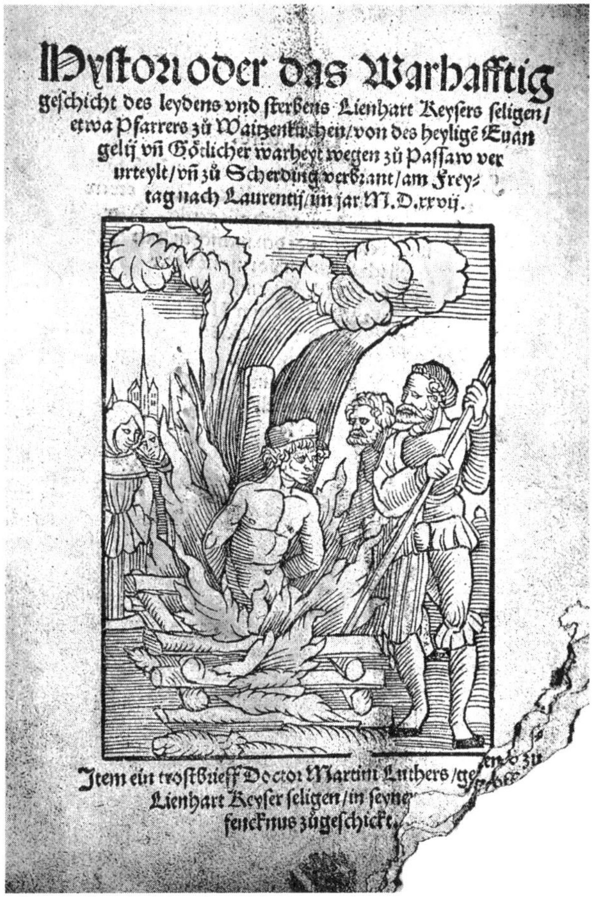

Woodcut depicting the 1527 burning of Pastor Leonhard Kaiser (mid-sixteenth century)

It is a much greater art to be able to sing this verse when the devil, as he did to Job and many other saints, becomes so hostile that death appears. He can give the heart a most forceful picture of death. He does not simply say, as people would: "You shall be burned or drowned." He magnifies what a horrible, abominable, eternal thing death is, and raps out the wrath of God. With overwhelming thoughts he drives and presses into the heart until it becomes unbearable and unendurable. Here a good interpreter is needed, one who can outshout the devil and overcome him by saying: "This is still not death, nor is it God's wrath. It is gracious chastisement and

y Matt. 27:49.
z Heb. 12:5-11.

fatherly punishment. I still know that he will not turn me over to death. I will not believe it is wrath, even though all the devils of hell were to affirm it in chorus. Were an angel from heaven to say this, let him be accursed.[a] Were God himself to say it, I would still believe that he was trying me as he tried Abraham, merely feigning wrath, and not in earnest. For he does not take back his promise. Here is the truth: He chastises me, but he will not kill me. I insist on this and will not let anyone take it from me or explain, interpret, or expound it differently."

He feels death, and yet he refuses to feel it or call it death but clings to the gracious right hand of God. He does not deny that God sends him death, but he and God have an understanding. Neither will call it death or let it be death; it is a father's rod and a child's chastisement. These are all lofty words that are not found in the hearts of people and princes; neither can they enter there, as St. Paul says: "We impart a secret and hidden wisdom of God. . . . None of the rulers of this age understood this," 1 Cor. 2[:7-8]. Let these words on this beautiful song of the dear saints suffice for the moment. Next:

19. Open to me the gates of righteousness,
that I may enter through them and give thanks to the Lord.

What? Has he not already thanked throughout the whole psalm, in one continuous thanksgiving? Why does he now ask that the gates be opened in order that he may give thanks? This is said in the spirit of the dear fathers in the Old Testament, who longed with all their hearts for the kingdom of Christ and the revelation of the gospel, as his previous hymn prophesied. He is actually praying: "O Lord God, would that I might be among the throng which shall sing such a song of the works and blessings of Christ, and that I could join in the thanking, praising, and preaching! How happy I would be! Who will open the gate for me and help me enter the place where the true, free, and joyful thanks and praise will really begin?" But now it is all still closed, and the gospel and Christendom are not yet revealed, as Ps. 42[:4] says: "I went with the throng and led them in procession into the house of God, with glad shouts and songs of thanksgiving, a multitude keeping festival."

a Gal. 1:8.

Christ also tells his disciples: "Blessed are the eyes which see what you see! For I tell you that many prophets and kings desire to see what you see, and did not see it, and to hear what you hear, and did not hear it" [Luke 10:23-24].

This verse of the psalm is a heartfelt prayer for the gospel and the kingdom of Christ. It asks for the removal of the burden of the law of Moses, of which Peter says in Acts 15[:10] that neither our fathers nor we were able to bear it. The psalmist calls the New Testament "gates of righteousness" in the Hebrew sense; for there "gates" meant town halls, schools, synagogues, courthouses, or similar public places where public matters are handled in open assembly, as in Prov. 31[:23]: "Her husband is known in the gates, when he sits among the elders of the land." The word is often used like this here and there in the Old Testament. Accordingly, the gates of righteousness are nothing else than the parish or bishopric where the ministry of the church—preaching, praising God, thanksgiving, singing, baptizing, distributing and receiving the Sacrament, admonishing, comforting, praying, and whatever else pertains to salvation—is publicly exercised. There sit the councilors of the spiritual kingdom of Christ, pastors, preachers, bishops, teachers, and the rest of the clergy.

He calls the New Testament, in contradistinction to the Old, "gates of righteousness." For in the New Testament[71] there is nothing but the doctrine of the forgiveness of sins, of grace, of justifying and sanctifying faith, and nothing about the works of the law or our own works. But the law, in its administration and treatment, aims at works, creates sinners, and multiplies sin and wrath, as St. Paul says in Romans and in Galatians. It cannot contribute to righteousness. Therefore it may be called "gates of sin or of unrighteousness." The law is not grace. Since grace alone justifies, it is impossible for the law to justify. It must make people sinners and incite wrath, Rom. 4[:15]. For this reason Paul boldly calls the law of Moses "the dispensation of condemnation," 2 Corinthians 4.[b] Again, he calls it "an agent of sin," Gal. 2[:17]. Furthermore, he says that "the sting of death is sin, and the power of sin is the law," 1 Cor. 15[:56]. Our present exponents of works—of whom the world is full—almost all bishops and clergy, belong to the Old Testament.[72] They have closed these

71. Luther is using "New Testament" primarily as a theological category here, rather than a designation for a salvation-historical epoch or, even less, a collection of books. By 1515, in his lectures on Romans, Luther begins to sharply distinguish the concepts of gospel/New Testament and law/Old Testament from their traditional salvation-historical designations. One sees this even more clearly in his lectures on Hebrews in 1518. See Kenneth Hagen, *A Theology of Testament in the Young Luther: The Lectures on Hebrews* (Leiden: Brill, 1974).

72. Cf. n. 71 above.

b Luther intended to cite 2 Cor. 3:9.

gates of righteousness and have converted them into gates of sin. They can do nothing so well as, by purely human ordinances, to load and perplex consciences with false, unnecessary, imaginary sins, as Christ and the apostles foretold of them.[73] Nevertheless, a few gates of righteousness remain.

20. This is the gate of the Lord;
the righteous shall enter through it.

Just as in the preceding verse he separated the Old Testament from the New and abolished it so far as doctrine and preaching are concerned, so here he separates the one from the other in the matter of public worship. The Jews took inordinate pride in their worship and gloried in nothing but their holy temple and their sacrifices and incense, for which the whole priestly tribe of Levi had been appointed. Here, they said, here at Jerusalem is the Lord's temple; this is the true gate, where one must come before the Lord, sacrifice, burn incense, serve God, and become pious. The psalmist does not simply say "gates," but "gate of the Lord," the singular. He means the gate of the temple, where the Lord has his special residence as in a castle or town hall. Here the service of God is cultivated most thoroughly and frequently. But this is not the real temple, incense, and sacrifice. Here is the true temple, the true gate, the service of God, the true sacrifice, namely, the sacrifice of thanksgiving, of which he speaks in the next verse and again later.

Furthermore, hypocrites, scoundrels, and sinners entered the gate of that temple; but only the righteous and the saints enter this gate of the Lord in order to serve him. For no one can enter the Christian congregation or be a member of Christendom unless he is a believer, that is, righteous and holy, as the article of the Creed says: "I believe in the holy Christian church." Whoever does not believe and is not holy and righteous does not belong to the holy Christian church. They cannot enter this gate, cannot pray, offer thanks, praise, or serve God, and do not know God, even though they live among Christians and may hold an office among Christians, such as pastor, preacher, or bishop, or outwardly partake of the Sacrament. 1 John 3[:6] says: "No one who abides in him sins; no one who sins has either seen him or known him." And again in 1 John 3[:8]: "He who commits sin is of the devil."

73. E.g., 1 Tim. 4:13, "Now the Spirit expressly says that in later times some will renounce the faith by paying attention to deceitful spirits and teachings of demons, through the hypocrisy of liars whose consciences are seared with a hot iron. They forbid marriage and demand abstinence from foods, which God created to be received with thanksgiving by those who believe and know the truth."

This article was condemned at the estimable Council of Constance, together with this verse and all Holy Scriptures.[c] For at that time Jan Hus confessed that there is one holy Christian church and that if the pope were not pious and holy, he could not be a member of that holy church, much less its head, even though he might hold that office.[74] For this Hus was burned and cursed as a heretic. Even more so is St. Peter cursed, for he calls such people "a blot and blemish" on the holy church, 2 Pet. 2[:13]. If he were still alive, the devil would detect him in these murders of the saints, and St. John likewise; for he plainly says: "He who commits sin is of the devil" [1 John 3:8]. The unrighteous counter by saying: "Although the pope, bishops, and others sin grievously, they do not belong to the devil and his synagogue.[d] They belong to Christ and to God and are members and heads of holy Christendom." Verily, they are members of the church, just as spittle, snot, pus, sweat, shit, urine, stench, mange, smallpox, boils, syphilis, and all diseases are members of the body. They are in and on the body, like blemishes and filth, which the body must bear with great danger, trouble, and unwillingness.

74. Luther is referring to Jan Hus's treatise on the church, *De Ecclesia*, which Luther studied shortly after the Leipzig debate in 1520.

Painting of Jan Hus at the Council of Constance by Václav Brožík (1851–1901)

I hope that by this time almost everybody knows that whoever prides himself on being a Christian must also take pride in being holy and righteous. Since Christendom is holy, a Christian must also be righteous and holy, or he is not a Christian. All Scripture calls Christians holy and righteous, as does this verse, and as they are often called in Daniel, chapter 7. This is not boastfulness; it is a necessary confession and an article of faith. The papal hypocrites, with their false and blasphemous humility, glory in being sinners and do not want to be called holy. Nevertheless, they boast that their order, their rank, their rule, and their life are holy. Moreover, they represent their works as something sacred. They do not lie when they say they

c See n. 70, p. 298 above.

d Rev. 2:9.

are sinners—if only they were serious and sincere; but they are not. They lie to themselves; they are sinners before God; their whole position is false. However, they will not admit it but pretend to be holy, while with their mouths they humble themselves as sinners. That is a double lie as well as blasphemy against God.

We must realize that in our persons as children of Adam we are damned sinners, without any righteousness or holiness of our own. However, since we are baptized and believe in Christ, we are holy and righteous in Christ and with Christ. He has taken our sin from us and has graced, clothed, and adorned us with his holiness. Thus, the whole Christian church is holy, not by itself or by its own work but in Christ and through Christ's holiness, as St. Paul says in Ephesians 3: "He has cleansed her by the washing of water with the word."[e] Anyone who hesitates to boast and confess that he is holy and righteous is actually saying: "I am not baptized. I am not a Christian. I do not believe in Christ. I do not believe that Christ died for me. I do not believe that he took away my sins. I do not believe that his blood has cleansed me, or that it can cleanse me. In short, I do not believe a word of what God has declared of Christ and all Scripture testifies." What kind of person thinks or says such things? What Turk or Jew is such a desperately wicked being? Now those who would be pious and saved by their works, such as the monks and priests and all popery, certainly think and believe thus. They deny Christ, as Peter says in 2 Pet. 2[:1] and Paul in Gal. 6[:12].

The psalmist also refers to all other outward partiality, to the effect that in the Christian church there is no respect of persons. Whoever believes and is righteous enters this gate, whether Jew or Greek, man or woman, virgin or married, servant or maid, rich or poor, king or prince or nobleman, townsman or peasant, strong or weak. The Jews prided themselves on being the seed of Abraham and on having the law. They believed that this made them God's favorites, just as today our clergy claim to be the best, and the nuns think they are special brides of Christ. But here it is stated that the righteous enter. Monks and nuns do not enter unless they first become righteous and Christian. Christ says that his kingdom does not consist of external ways and behavior, Luke 17[:20]. We cannot say: "It is here; it is there."

e Luther intended to cite Eph. 5[:26].

It is found in the heart. But it is hard to believe this is true; and that is one of the doctrines of the damned heretics.

*21. I thank you that you have answered me
and have become my Salvation.*

These are the sacrifices and the divine services that are performed by the righteous and by Christians in the gates of the Lord in the New Testament. They thank God and praise him with preaching, teaching, singing, and confessing. These sacrifices are twofold. The one is our humility, of which David speaks in Ps. 51[:17]: "The sacrifice acceptable to God is the broken spirit; a broken and contrite heart, O God, you will not despise." This is a great, broad, long, daily, and unending sacrifice. Here God corrects us through his word in all our works and reduces our holiness, wisdom, and strength to nothing, so that before him we are guilty sinners (Rom. 3:23). He gives his word impressive power, frightens our conscience, and afflicts us with all kinds of troubles, so that our sinful old Adam[75] becomes mellow and soft. Finally, by the time we die, our pride, trust, and confidence in our own efforts and knowledge are dead. Whoever can suffer and endure this and remain constant and persevere, and at the same time thank and praise God as one who sincerely means well, he it is who can sing this verse: "I thank you that you humble me." He does not say: "The devil humbles me," but: "You, you, are the one. It is your gracious will for my good. Without your will the devil could not do it."

The other sacrifice is this, that when God again comforts and helps us, the Spirit and the new man gain as the flesh and the old man wane. As time goes on, God gives us an ever greater and richer gift and helps us overcome and win, so that we rejoice before him and in him, as he says in Ps. 50[:15, 14]: "Call upon me in the day of trouble; I will deliver you, and you shall glorify me. Offer to God a sacrifice of thanksgiving, and pay your vows to the Most High."[f] Whoever does so sings this verse: "I thank you that you are my Salvation, my Helper and Savior." This also is an unending, great, and daily sacrifice of the righteous in the gate of the Lord. Here God rejects and discontinues all the sacrifices

75. Luther's use of the term "old Adam" is derived first and foremost from the biblical "old man" of Eph. 4:22; Col. 3:9; and Rom. 6:6: "We know that our *old man* was crucified with [Christ] so that the body of sin might be destroyed, and we might no longer be enslaved to sin." This designation of one's sinful nature inherited from Adam's first transgression continues on in the life of the baptized, and, according to Luther, must be continually overcome by the "new man" whose identity remains in Christ and lives by the power of his Spirit. It is roughly equivalent to Paul's common use of the term "flesh."

f Luther cites the Vulgate numbering here, Psalm 49.

of the Old Testament, which were images and symbols of these thank offerings and which could be offered by both the pious and the wicked. These thank offerings, however, can be offered by no one except the pious and the righteous, or Christians. This is clear from history, when the Jews raged in the days of the apostles just as do the work-righteous of today, when their works and wisdom are rejected. They refuse to be humble, and they blaspheme instead of thanking. They revile, persecute, and murder, under the impression that their service must be a most acceptable offering to God as in John 16[:2].

This is a happy verse, singing out of pure joy: "Are you not a wonderful and delightful God, to govern us so amazingly and so kindly? You exalt us when you humble us. You make us righteous when you make us sinners. You lead us to heaven when you cast us into hell. You grant us the victory when you cause us to be defeated. You give us life when you permit us to be killed. You comfort us when you cause us to mourn. You make us to rejoice when you permit us to weep. You make us to sing when you cause us to cry. You make us strong when we suffer. You make us wise when you make fools of us. You make us rich when you send us poverty. You make us masters when you permit us to serve." Innumerable are the wonders included in this verse; and all Christendom together praises God for them in these few short words: "I thank you that you have humbled me, and have helped me again."

22. The stone which the builders rejected
has become the chief cornerstone.

Now the psalmist turns to the head of holy Christendom and presents him as an example. Since he was humbled and exalted as much as and more than all the saints, we should not deem it odd or strange if we also suffer tribulation and affliction. "If they have called the master of the house Beelzebul, how much more will they malign those of his household? The servant is not better than his Master" [Matt. 10:24-25]. In the verse before us the psalmist summarizes the sufferings and resurrection of Christ.[76] By using the word "rejected" he indicates the suffering, death, disgrace, and reproach to which Christ was subjected. By using "the chief Cornerstone" he indicates his resurrection, life, and eternal dominion. He uses the parable of a building. When

76. Jesus quotes verse 22 in Matt. 21:42. Luther knew this and therefore immediately reads this verse christologically.

a stone does not fit into the wall or match the others, but disfigures the whole building and is an unfit, useless stone, it must be rejected. Then another builder, a stranger, comes along. He knows well how to use the stone and cries: "Stop, you big fools, are you really builders and still do not want that stone? I can use it, not merely to plug a hole or for fill, nor as a common, ordinary stone, but as a cornerstone in the foundation. It shall bear not one but two walls, and it shall do more than all the other stones in the whole building."

Thus, Christ would not fit the ways and holiness of the Pharisees, or the whole world itself. They could not stand him. He disfigured their building. He reprimanded and rebuked their outwardly fine and holy behavior. Then they became angry and condemned and rejected him, for they did not know how to use him. Then God, the real Builder, chose him and made him the Cornerstone of the foundation on which the whole Christian church, made up of Jews and Gentiles, stands. It is no different today. The stone is rejected and stays rejected. Nonetheless, with the believing righteous, who build, not on their human works or on the might of princes but on this stone, he remains precious, noble, and valuable.[g]

Note who they are who reject this stone. They are not simple folk, but the best, that is, the holiest, wisest, most learned, greatest, and noblest. These are offended. The poor, miserable sinners, the downcast, the wanderers, the despised, the little people, and the unlearned accept him joyfully and gladly. Those others are called builders, that is, they edify, improve, and govern for the good of the people by preaching and teaching. They are not called destroyers, wreckers, or bunglers. They are builders, the most necessary, most useful, and best people on earth. Were it not for them, the skies would cave in before nightfall, and land and people would be destroyed. These are the rulers of the spiritual and temporal estates, whose laws govern land and people, and who would also teach God. Among the Jewish people they were the high priests and princes of Jerusalem, Pilate of Rome, and Herod of Galilee. They rejected this Stone and could not tolerate it in their building or government. They knew better.

So, then, if kings, princes, bishops, lords, saints, the wise, the prudent, the rich, and the learned persecute the gospel, this is

g Cf. Isa. 28:18 and 1 Pet. 2:6-7.

not surprising. Who else would do it? No one else can. If there is to be persecution, they must do it; for they are the "builders." They do it also for the sake of their office; for they must see to it that their building has no crack, rent, or disfiguration. Therefore they cannot tolerate the word of God or those who declare it, for such a person disfigures their building by causing cracks and rents in it. He is a rabble rouser who misleads the people whom they have so beautifully edified, ordered, and organized. His way of doing things is entirely different from theirs.

But note for your great comfort that here two buildings oppose each other. The one rejects the other. The rejected building, however, has a mighty Builder, who on one Stone erects two strong and everlasting walls. What becomes of the building and of the builders who reject this building? Nothing is said of them here; God knows nothing of them. This is a sign that they and their building have come to naught. He speaks only of the rejected Stone and building; this is his concern. Be careful, therefore, lest you be found in the building which delights in condemning, rejecting, and riding high. Do not be afraid to be in the structure which is rejected, for God will remove your rejection. He will not recognize those who reject you. They will perish, and you will abide forever. No righteousness, no works, no holiness will endure save that which is Christ, the Cornerstone. There is no other Cornerstone. Our own works, though we labor forever, can never be the cornerstone; they will be chaff in the wind.[h] It can never be otherwise. We read that this rejected Stone is the Cornerstone or Foundation, as in 1 Cor. 3[:11-13].

23. *This is the* L*ORD's doing; it is marvelous in our eyes.*

The psalmist says that the Lord himself is this amazing Builder who will make fools of all other builders, the wise of this world. He chooses and exalts that which they have rejected, as St. Paul says in 1 Cor. 1[:27]: "God chose what is foolish in the world to shame the wise." We also read in Hab. 1[:5]: "Look among the nations, and see; wonder and be astounded. For I am doing a work in your days that you would not believe if told." As the verse before us says, God always performs works which unbelievers do not think he can perform. He makes fools of them. And yet this is a particularly great work in which he makes the rejected Stone

h Cf. Ps. 1:4; 1 Cor. 3:11-13.

the selected Cornerstone. This is such a great and amazing work that not only the heathen with all their understanding and wisdom made fools of themselves but also His own people, the Jews, so stumbled and took offense at it that they utterly destroyed themselves.[77] They lost kingdom and priesthood, heaven and earth. And by no miracles, no matter how great and substantial, could they be preserved; nor can they now be restored, even by much plague and punishment.

What is the cause of so much dissension among Christians today, of so many heresies and sects? Why is the papacy now so rabid, furious, blind, mad, and foolish that it cannot tolerate the teaching that faith without works makes people pious, blessed, alive, and free from sin, death, and the devil? As long as they confess with the mouth that Christ is the Cornerstone, first rejected and then elected, why do they refuse to let him be effective or actually to acknowledge him as such? Is there any wonder that carnal-minded people and false hypocrites take offense at this? David says that this is marvelous in our own eyes. Even though the dear saints and Christians take no offense, it is still amazing to their hearts and difficult to believe; they must study it all their lives to believe it. What others feel, that they know best. I consider myself a Christian, but I know full well how hard it was, still is, to grasp and hold this Cornerstone. People may call me a Lutheran, but they misjudge me; or at best I am a poor and weak Lutheran.[i] May God strengthen me!

We learn quickly to say: "Christ is our Salvation. He is our Righteousness. Our works cannot free us from sin and death. The rejected Cornerstone must do it." My little books show and testify how well and thoroughly I know this. But when I enter the battle and must come to grips with the devil, sin, death, trouble, and the world; when there is no help, counsel, and consolation except this Cornerstone, then I understand how little I can do and what an art it is to believe in Christ. Then I understand well what David means when he says: "It is marvelous in our eyes." To be sure, to us it seems to be challenging and almost vexatious—absolutely nothing more. But my papists—they sing: "In our eyes it is not worth mentioning; it is trifling." "Faith? Faith?" they say. "What do you mean? Do you think we are heathen or Jews?" Before anyone can recite this verse, they have believed it fully in

i See Luther's remarks on the name "Lutheran" (n. 56, p. 288).

77. 1 Cor. 1:22-24: "For Jews demand signs and Greeks desire wisdom, but we proclaim Christ crucified, a stumbling block to Jews and foolishness to Gentiles, but to those who are called, both Jews and Greeks, Christ the power of God and the wisdom of God."

the twinkling of an eye—so fully, unfortunately, that they have left nothing of it either for us or for anybody else.

Even though all Scripture says that God is marvelous in all his works, and calls him a worker of miracles, the world does not believe this until it experiences it personally. Everyone in his own heart pictures God as he thinks God ought to act. They prescribe for him all the words and deeds that he must follow. No one considers: "Why, if he were to act according to my thoughts and understanding, there would be nothing amazing about his works. What if his actions transcend, and differ from, my ideas?" But this does not happen, says Isaiah. They will not quit their fantasizing. They make and shape a god according to their own likes.[j] A monk makes a god who sits on high and thinks: "Whoever observes the rules of Saint Francis, I will save."[78] A nun imagines: "If I am a virgin, God is my bridegroom." A priest: "God gives heaven to everyone who offers Mass and prays his hours." No one realizes that God chooses only the rejected Cornerstone and condemns all their making and building. God must suffer himself to be made, corrected, and formed, from the beginning of the world to its end. No one has any use for the Cornerstone on which he builds and forms us.

78. St. Francis (c. 1181–1226), founder of the mendicant order named after him, was the ideal ascetic in the Middle Ages. His rule required an absolute denial of any and all possessions, which he regarded as the true apostolic life. In spite of Francis's own well-attested humility, Luther will often use those who boast in following St. Francis as a prime example of one who exhibits a piety of works righteousness.

24. This is the day which the L*ORD* *has made;*
let us rejoice and be glad in it.

This is the time of the New Testament, a different day from that which the good sun daily makes. Here the Lord himself is the Sun; he creates this day with its light and splendor. This day is not followed by night, nor does its light shine into the eyes of the body; it shines into the heart. Nor is this the light of reason, which also is a sun, outwardly showing and teaching works and righteousness before the world. This light teaches grace, peace, and forgiveness of sins before God, of which reason knows nothing. Thus, Christ is called the Sun of Righteousness in Mal. 3: "But for you who fear my name the Sun of Righteousness shall rise, with healing in Its wings."[k] This Sun is to bring righteousness to light, that is, to deliver from sin and make righteous all who believe in him. It is to give salvation and save from death

j Isa. 44:9-17.

k Luther intended to cite Mal. 4:2.

all those who take refuge under his wings or in his light. This brightness is nothing else but the light and revelation of the gospel in all the world, which proceeds from Christ and illumines and enlightens the hearts of the believers, just as the light of the sun goes forth and enlightens the eyes of our bodies and the visible world.

This is a happy day, as the psalmist here rejoices and says: "Let us be glad!" The light and teaching of grace gives the heart peace, rest, and joy in Christ. It realizes that its sins are without merit, that it is delivered from death, and that in God it forever has a gracious Father through Christ, as St. Paul says in Rom. 5[:1]: "Therefore since we are justified by faith, we have peace with God through our Lord Jesus Christ." And then he further describes this peace and joy as something that endures in tribulation and gives courage. No unbeliever can know anything of this joy and peace, nor can those who by their works endeavor to be pious and wipe out their sins. Though they bellow this verse ever so much, especially on Easter Day,[79] they have no understanding of it except as a material, external Easter at which they rejoice in the eating of cake and not in the grace and redemption of Christ.

It is necessary for the prophet to praise this day so emphatically as the Lord's own day, and to admonish us to rejoice. To all outward appearances the day is gloomy and shines like filth in a lantern.[80] So far as the world is concerned, it is darkness, error, heresy, and the devil's own night, to be rejected as its Sun, the noble Cornerstone, is rejected, from whom it receives its light. Therefore the joy and peace of which he sings are more tribulation, discord, and every misfortune, since he is shamefully hated and persecuted by the world, as Christ, the precious Sun, says in Matt. 10[:22]: "And you will be hated by all for my name's sake." Accordingly, just as the light of this day is secret and hidden from the world, so its joy is spiritual and unknown to the flesh, although it is the noblest joy and the supreme light. What could be more precious and nobler than an enlightened heart, a heart that knows God and all things, a heart that can judge rightly and speak truly in all things before God? Where could there be a higher or greater joy than in a happy, secure, and fearless conscience, a conscience that trusts in God and fears neither the world nor the devil? On the other hand, where is there greater melancholy and a heavier heart than in an evil, despairing, and

79. Psalm 118 was the appointed psalm for Easter and, according to many early Christian sources, was sung then already by the fourth and fifth centuries.

80. A German saying that plays off the irony of something that appears the opposite of what it ought.

guilty conscience? What is more wretched and miserable than an erring and uncertain heart which can judge nothing properly?

25. Save us, we beseech you, O L*ORD!*
O L*ORD, we beseech you, give us success!*

Here we have the *Hosia Na* which the people sang for the Savior when he rode into Jerusalem on Palm Sunday.[l] This verse and the following were taken from this psalm on that occasion. Apparently this psalm was well known to the people. הוֹשִׁיעָה means "help" or "do help."[m] The נָא added to it sounds a prayer and indicates the heart's desire. We would say in German: "Help, O dear one, help, do help!" As the "O" and the "do" indicate our hearts desire to persuade him whom we beg, so the נָא functions in the same way in Hebrew. When it is added to הוֹשִׁיעָה and becomes הוֹשִׁיעָה נָא, it means "O LORD, help" or "O dear LORD, help." The name "Jesus" is derived from the same Hebrew word. It means Helper or Savior, as the angel says to Joseph (Matt. 1:21): "You shall call his name Jesus, for he will save his people from their sins." הוֹשִׁיעָה, "Joshua," and "Jesus" sound almost alike; and Joshua is the same name as Jesus. In the course of time the word הוֹשִׁיעָה נָא was changed to "Osanna." Finally, even women and bells were baptized and called "Osanna."[81]

This verse is a prayer or a wish of joy, as when we wish someone good luck and success as he undertakes a new venture or receives something good. Elizabeth, the mother of St. John, received the good wishes of the women regarding her young son, Luke 1[:58]. She herself also joyfully extended good wishes to the Virgin Mary when Mary visited her.[n] Here, too, as the glad day of the gospel

81. While bells were not "baptized" in a sacramental sense, they were consecrated with rites that overlapped those in Baptism, e.g., anointing with oil and water, mini-exorcisms, and naming. Luther is critical of the practice as a foolish human invention that makes a mockery of the Sacrament of Baptism, e.g., SA III, 15, 4; BC, 326.

Jesus rides into Jerusalem on a donkey to the waving of palm branches (Matthew 21). Woodcut from a book of Luther's commentary on the epistles and gosepels from Advent to Easter (1530).

l Matt. 21:9.

m For Luther's knowledge and use of Hebrew, see n. 20, p. 257.

n Luke 1:42.

dawns and the kingdom of grace begins, in which sin and death end and righteousness lives and rules, the psalmist leaps for joy and pours out his heart saying: "*Hosia Na*, Lord; God grant it; God be praised! Happy and blessed is the day on which this light breaks. Heaven and earth and everything in them rejoice with us that we have lived to see this day." At the same time he desires and asks that it may continue as it began. He prays: "O LORD, Give us success," as we often do in such a joyful wish: "God grant that this may abide and continue, that it may succeed and never end!"

The kingdom of Christ must suffer much adversity from the devil, the world, and the flesh, and always stands as if it were about to fall and perish, as the fierce tyrants gain the upper hand. Against these attacks, however, these words stand firm: הוֹשִׁיעָה, הוֹשִׁיעָה, הוֹשִׁיעָה! "Help, help, help!" And הַצְלִיחָה, הַצְלִיחָה, הַצְלִיחָה! "Give us success, give us success, give us success!" These words stand firm, and the wish of joy must endure and gain the victory. We may well sing the *Hosia Na* against our papists, Turks, and factions. No one else will sing it for us. They need no *Hosia* or Jesus. They have their own might and strength. They prefer to sing: "Aha! Aha!" Ps. 35[:21].[82] They cry: "Down with the heretics!" Let them rejoice! I have not lived very long, but I have heard many such shouts of joy turned into howls, while the *Hosia Na* survived with honor.

82. Luther continues with several other expletives, "*Euge, Euge, Da, Da, Heha, Heha!*"

26. Blessed be the one who comes in the name of the LORD.
We bless you from the house of the LORD.

This still belongs to the joyful wish that Christ, the King of Grace, enter through his gospel and come in the name of the Lord. Again, there is need of such a joyous wish. For there are many who roam about in their own name and bring, not the word of grace but a doctrine of works and the phantasies of their own minds. They, with all the rest of the world, receive this King by saying: "Cursed is he that comes in the name of all the devils; death to him!" as the Jews did when they cried: "Away with him; crucify him at once!" He must be the rejected and condemned Cornerstone, and his word an accursed heresy of the devil. This is the song of the cathedrals and cloisters. Only believers sing: "Praised and blessed be he that comes in the name of the Lord!"[83]

83. Luther is exploiting the irony that these verses are a central part of the liturgy and are thus sung at every Mass in the cathedrals and cloisters.

Then these singers also experience the next thing: "We bless you from the house of the LORD." These words teach that this joyous wish is not only for the King but also for all you who are in his household, who believe in him and accept him. Praised, happy, blessed, and full of all grace and joy are you because you are of the house of the King! "You are not strangers and sojourners, but members of the household of God."[o] You are built on the rejected Cornerstone. Although you are rejected and must be called the devil's household, it does not matter. Let them blaspheme and curse. Be content that we bless you and call you blessed and rich. Our testimony is the testimony of God and of all the angels, all the saints, and all the creatures of God. Why are you concerned about the devil and the world?

I think everyone knows that "God's house" means where he dwells, and that he dwells where his word is, be it in the field, in church, or on the sea. On the other hand, where his word is absent, he is absent, nor is his house there; but there the devil dwells, though it be a church of gold blessed by all the bishops. But where God's house is, there is pure blessing, grace, and life, as the psalmist says: "We bless you from the house of the LORD." You are blessed, because you are in the Lord's house. God says in Exod. 20[:24]: "In every place where I cause my name (that is, my word) to be remembered, I will come to you and bless you." In this passage this verse in the psalm had its origin. Wherever God sends out his word, by which his name and work and not our name and work are praised, there he also comes with pure grace and every blessing, as Moses declares. But wherever the devil sends out his word and it is accepted, he follows with his curse and eternal destruction. The world, however, does not believe this and considers and praises the devil as God, his curse as a blessing, and his lies as truth.

27. The LORD is God, and he has given us light.
Bind the festal procession with branches,
up to the horns of the altar.

Here the psalmist names the child, and specifically states who the king is who rides in the name of the Lord. He says: It is God, the Lord himself, who appears and shows us his light. He

o Eph. 2:19.

may be a rejected stone, but he is still God; for he refers to him who has appeared and enlightened us, whose gospel and light we feel in our hearts. It is the Lord God himself, and there is no other God. Why else would he use such lofty praise, "The LORD is God"? For no Jew would doubt this if it did not mean a man. But this calls for faith, when it is said that the rejected Cornerstone, which enlightens the world with a new day, is God and Lord. If he were not a man, he could not be the rejected Cornerstone; for God cannot be rejected. And yet he is not only a man but also God himself. At this point the psalmist faces the loathing and offense of the Jews and of all those to whom it is an abomination to hear that a man is true God. They fear some form of idolatry. For this reason he would say: "Do not be alarmed; there is no danger of idolatry. This is the true God himself, for no one else can grant release from sin and death or enlighten hearts except God. His works prove that he is God."

Then [the psalmist] commands that the festival and the new day be bound with branches. Thereby he abolishes the Old Testament. The Jews had a festival called the Feast of the Tabernacles, or *Succoth*, which they celebrated for eight days in memory of the forty years during which the children of Israel had lived in tents in the wilderness, Lev. 23[:33-43]. To this he refers and would say: "Why do you still make a show with your branches and tabernacles? Something new has come, and your custom is done. This is another day, another house of God, another altar, another festival, another life. Now come here and celebrate this new festival with branches, since our new King and God rides in with grace and blessing and appears to the whole world in his word. Put your branches here in the house of the Lord, not in the field or in your yards. Put them even on the horns or corners of the altar, that everything may be full of branches and merriment. There is no longer any difference between the Levites and the people. Everyone who believes may approach the altar, a privilege not granted in the law."[84]

In addition, he explains what the branches and leaves symbolize, namely, that people should adorn, praise, beautify, and exalt the name of God with joyful, fresh, green, and beautiful preaching and singing. These are the branches cut from beautiful trees, that is, taken from the prophets. And when he speaks of the place or corners called the horns of the altar, he means the altar of thanksgiving.[85] There those branches are offered as

Woodcut from a 1662 publication depicting the Succoth custom of building booths from branches

84. Cf. 1 Pet. 2:9: "But you are a chosen race, a *royal priesthood*, a holy nation, God's own people, in order that you may proclaim the mighty acts of him who called you out of darkness into his marvelous light."

85. Similarly, Augustine interprets this verse as the "inner house of God" in which the spiritual sacrifice of praise is offered.

thank offerings; and no longer are calves, sheep, birds, and the like to be slaughtered. Now everything that formerly was outwardly performed by the Levites is done by thanks and praise, preaching and teaching.

28. You are my God, and I will
give thanks to you; you are my God; I will extol you.

The psalmist now concludes this psalm with a strong declaration and denunciation against all offenses and examples of the unbelievers. He would say: "They will not accept you as God. You are the rejected stone, a malefactor crucified among malefactors. Your word and service are held to be the devil's word and service. For this I must suffer all manner of disgrace and danger. But let it pass; you are nevertheless my God. I will still believe in you, and I know for a certainty that you are my God. Let the law, temple, altar, and all services at Jerusalem be gone. Let friend and foe pass away. Let there be no more wisdom, holiness, strength, goods, honor, and whatever else will pass away. I desire you alone; in place of all these you will be more than enough. I shall be your poor little parson and priest and offer true sacrifices and services of God, namely, the thank offering and the hymns of praise. This will be my priestly office, my feast of the tabernacles, that I preach or praise nothing but you, the rejected Cornerstone, the crucified God. This is my resolution. By this I will abide. This shall be the long and short of it. This is what I sought and meant with this psalm. Let no one tell me anything else. Let me not be confused. As St. Paul says in Gal. 6[:17], 'I bear on my body the marks of Jesus.'" Amen. *Hosia Na.* Amen.

29. O give thanks to the Lord, for he is good;
for his steadfast love endures forever!

We often sing a good song over again from the beginning, especially one we have sung with pleasure and joy. Thus, a bride prepares a wreath for her groom, bringing the two ends together to make it a beautiful decoration for her head. That is what David does in this psalm. After he has ended his song to all the blessings of God and has especially praised the last, his eternal grace, he says: "Oh, who can ever thank God enough for his goodness! It is as I said at the beginning of this psalm: 'His steadfast love endures forever. Especially does it endure for that poor little fourth group.'[p] If only people would believe this!" People also do good deeds, but no good deed lasts forever. Human nature cannot stand ingratitude. Nor does humanity do good for God's sake or for the sake of virtue, but only for their own sake.

This you can see if you observe a man who has done good deeds for a number of people. If they later are ungrateful or say or do something that provokes him, you will see how he flares up, scolds, judges, and says reproachfully: "Well, I helped him once or twice; now that's all. He need not come to me again!" And if the occasion ever arises when he can get revenge or sees that his help is needed, he will act like a block of wood or a balky horse. If he can do no more, he resists wherever he can and leaves the good undone. Yet he thinks he is pious and does the right thing, without any compunctions of conscience. He cannot rise to the point where he would think: "Well, I did not do that good deed for him because of his wickedness, nor shall I stop on this account. God bestows much good on me daily, though all my life I have done nothing but grieve him." No, he does not draw such thoughts from the example of his ungrateful neighbor, which ought to lead him to sweep before his own door and consider his own ingratitude.

Basically, what is human kindness but a threefold misdeed? With it people seek thanks and honor, yes, even mastery over those to whom they do good. It is a proud, boastful, vindictive, and selfish kindness, one that later turns to anger and everlastingly hurts and damages wherever it can. About mortals this verse might well be changed to read: "Shame on mortals for being so wicked, for the harm they do endures forever. Their kindness is brief and temporary, it is done only to those who adore and honor them. They hate to lose a blessing or have it fail to yield dividends." But God and his children do good without returns. They gladly waste their kindness on the ungrateful, as it is written, Prov. 16[:4]: "The Lord has made everything for its purpose." Therefore he does not stop doing good because of the wickedness of people. Thus, he proves that he is good by nature, and that his goodness does not stand or fall by the vice or virtue of another, as human goodness may stand on the virtue of one and fall by the vice of another and even become worse than he

p See Luther's comments on v. 4, pp. 263–66.

is. The entire thirty-seventh Psalm speaks of this,[q] and the verse before us is explained sufficiently for the time being. May Christ, our Lord, make us human beings true, perfect Christians. To him be praise and thanks forever! Amen.

q Luther cites the Vulgate numbering, Psalm 36.

Preface to the Prophets

1545 (1532)

BROOKS SCHRAMM

INTRODUCTION

Luther's translation of the Bible into German spanned the years 1522–1534.[a] The project initially proceeded in rapid fashion, with the New Testament and the Old Testament books of Genesis through Song of Songs already in print by the autumn of 1524. The Prophets, however, and the Apocrypha would not appear until 1532 and 1534, respectively. As was the case with Job, the Prophets proved difficult to translate, and this, coupled with Luther's illnesses and the manifold demands on his time and attention, accounted for the delays in their completion.[b] During this same time, Luther was lecturing on a number of the prophetic books (Minor Prophets [Hosea through Malachi], 1524–1526; Isaiah, 1528–1530), and the lectures and translations were mutually related and informing. In 1526, translations of Jonah and Habakkuk, together with commentary, were published; in 1527, the translation of Zechariah, also with commentary, and in 1528, the translation of Isaiah were published.

a For further detail on Luther's German Bible, see the introduction to *Preface to the Old Testament*, this volume, pp. 41–44.

b See Brecht 3:95.

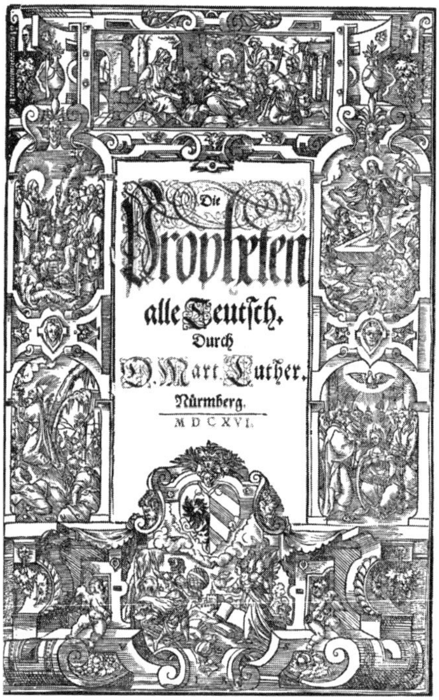

This title page, to "The Prophets" section of a 1616 printing of Luther's German Bible, depicts scenes from the life of Jesus, including his birth, preaching, praying in the Garden of Gethsemane, crucifixion, and resurrection, and the Holy Spirit descending on Pentecost.

The translation of Daniel, on which Luther had not lectured, appeared in 1530.[c] The remaining prophetic books were finished by the autumn of 1531, and the complete group of the Prophets appeared in March 1532 under the title *Die Propheten alle Deudsch* (Wittenberg: Hans Lufft).[d] Luther's German translation of the Prophets was preceded by that of the Anabaptist scholars Ludwig Haetzer and Hans Denck,[1] which had appeared in 1527 (Worms: Peter Schoeffer), the so-called *Wormser Propheten* ("Prophets of Worms").[e] Luther both utilized and criticized this

1. Ludwig Haetzer (1500–1529) was beheaded in Konstanz, Germany, for his Anabaptist radicalism, though the charge was adultery. Hans Denck (1495–1527), a fierce opponent of the reformers, died of bubonic plague in Basel.

A seventeenth-century engraving of Ludwig Haetzer

c See *Preface to the Prophet Daniel* in this volume, pp. 375–410.

d See the image above.

e The actual title was *Alle Propheten nach Hebräischer Sprach verteutschet* ("All of the Prophets Translated into German from the Hebrew Language"). This was the first Protestant translation of the Prophets into German.

Title page of *Alle Propheten* (Augsburg edition, 1528)

translation,[2] and in the end he was convinced that his translation was superior.[3]

The *Preface to the Prophets* was composed while Luther was visiting his mortally ill Elector John,[4] in February 1532. Luther's own health was so poor at the time that he wrote to Philip Melanchthon (1497–1560) that the latter may have to use his skill and eloquence to finish the preface if Luther himself died before having completed it.[f] More so than *Preface to the Old Testament*, the *Preface to the Prophets* reflects the pressure and impact of contemporary events: the aftermath of the Peasants' War; the fear of the looming threat of the Turks;[5] and the growing conviction that contemporary idolatry, whether that of the pope or of the "left-wingers," is a repristination of ancient Israel's primary idolatry, which was the attempt to worship the true God but apart from God's command. Luther thus locates idolatry precisely in good

f See Brecht 3:97 and WA Br 6:269,14–18.

2. In a May 1527 letter (LW 49:165) to his old friend Wenceslaus Linck (1483–1547), Luther commented on the *Wormser Propheten*: "I do not condemn the German translation of the prophets published in Worms, except that the German is quite confusing, perhaps due to the local dialect. The translators were diligent, but who can manage to do everything? I myself am now getting ready to translate the prophets into German, and at the same time I shall lecture on Isaiah, so that I may not be idle. Pray to the Lord for me, and for his church!" (See Brecht 3:95; Raeder 2:398).

3. Luther's high estimate of his Prophets translation is reflected in a Table Talk from early 1532: "By the grace of God the Psalter and the Prophets have now been composed in the best translation, so that we might learn more from the bare text than from the lengthy commentaries of others" (WA Br 2:40,19–22; #1317; LW 54:135).

4. John the Steadfast (1468–1532), who served as elector of Saxony from 1525 to 1532, was the brother of Frederick the Wise (1463–1525). Frederick served as elector of Saxony from 1486 to 1525 and was Luther's protector.

5. In Luther's lengthy 1530 *Preface to the Prophet Daniel* (LW 35:294–316), and especially in his treatment of Dan. 7:24-26, he finds the Turks prophesied as the final anti-godly kingdom. In that same year, while he was at the Coburg during the Diet of Augsburg, Luther published a special preface to his translation of Ezekiel 38–39 in which he identified the biblical "Gog" with the Turks (WA 30/2:223–26).

human intentions, and he even grants that the Turk intends to worship the one true God.

It is well known that Luther rejected the canonical status of those Old Testament books known as Apocrypha, although these books were translated and included in the complete Luther Bible at the end of the Old Testament as a kind of appendix.[6] In practice, therefore, Luther's Old Testament regarded as canonical the same books as did the synagogue (that is, the books contained in the Hebrew Bible), as opposed to the longer collection contained in the Greek Bible (Septuagint) and the Latin Vulgate Bible, for which no Hebrew [or Aramaic] originals were known. But Luther continued the traditional Christian practice of placing the Prophets at the end of the Old Testament, rather than in the middle, where they are in the Hebrew Bible. The result was a novum: a shorter Old Testament than the church had ever used, but one that nevertheless placed the Prophets as close as possible to the New Testament.[7]

Outline of *Preface to the Prophets*

- Appeal for the relevance of the Prophets for Christians
- Central aspects of the message of the Prophets
    - 1. The Prophets proclaim the kingdom of Christ
        - The Christian must suffer before entering the kingdom
    - 2. The Prophets provide examples and experiences of the First Commandment
        - These lead the Christian to fear of God and to faith
        - Why the Prophets contain more threat than comfort
    - 3. The Prophets cry out most of all against idolatry
        - Idolatry defined as worship of the true God, but without God's commandment
        - Idolatry among the Jews
        - Idolaters among the Christians

6. Prefaces were composed for the Apocryphal books as well, but in the table of contents these books, placed at the end, were not numbered along with the other thirty-nine canonical books of the Old Testament; the same practice was followed with Hebrews, James, Jude, and Revelation in the New Testament, where only twenty-three books were numbered. The heading for the Apocryphal books was as follows: "APOCRYPHA: These books are not to be regarded as equal to sacred Scripture, but it is nevertheless beneficial and good to read them" (Hans Volz, ed., *D. Martin Luther: Die gantze Heilige Schrifft Deudsch, Wittenberg 1545* [Munich: Rogner & Bernhard, 1972]), 1674.

7. The Hebrew Bible is divided into three sections: Law (Torah), Prophets, and Writings, with Daniel included as part of the Writings. Luther maintained Christian tradition in counting Daniel as one of the Prophets and locating the book immediately after Ezekiel.

The Translation

The translation presented here is a revision of LW 35:265–73 and is based on the *Preface to the Prophets* in the 1545 Luther Bible, WA DB 11/1:3–15 (odd numbers). This 1545 preface was virtually unchanged from the original 1532 version. Luther's biblical quotes and allusions have been translated directly, and thus may at times differ from the biblical versions used in LW. The translation is also informed by the modern German versions of the preface presented by Bornkamm and Aland.[g]

PREFACE TO THE PROPHETS

TO[h] HUMAN REASON the prophets seem to be a very minor thing, as if there is little of use to be found in them.[8] This is especially so when Mr. Know-it-all[i] comes along, the one who knows sacred Scripture by heart and right down to the minutest detail. Out of the great riches of his spirit he regards it as a matter of purely worthless and dead idle talk. As a result the events[j] and the works are now no longer noticed, and only the words or stories[k] are heard.[9] This should come as no surprise, since at present God's word is despised, even though each day the signs and events,[10] and the kingdom of Christ as well, are powerfully before our eyes and

8. In a manner similar to the beginning of *Preface to the Old Testament*, Luther begins with an appeal for the relevance of the Prophets for Christians.

9. The distinction that Luther is making here appears to be that between mere stories, on the one hand, and actual historical events, on the other.

10. At the time of the writing of this preface, the Turks had begun a cautious advance into Hungary. "Luther associated the threat from the Turks with the end of history" (Brecht 3:351).

g Heinrich Bornkamm, ed., *Luthers Vorreden zur Bibel*, 3d ed. (Göttingen: Vandenhoeck & Ruprecht, 1989), 81–91; Kurt Aland, ed., *Luther Deutsch: Die Werke Martin Luthers in neuer Auswahl für die Gegenwart*, vol. 5: *Die Schriftauslegung*, 2d ed. (Stuttgart: Ehrenfried Klotz; Göttingen: Vandenhoeck & Ruprecht, 1963), 23–32.

h WA DB 11/1:3; LW 35:265.

i *Meister Kluegel*, or more commonly, *Meyster Klüglin(g)*, is a favorite term of Luther's for the one who always knows better than everyone else.

j Ger.: *die Geschichte.*

k Ger.: *die Historien.*

operative. How much more would it be despised if the events and deeds were no longer present? For just so did the children of Israel despise God and God's word even when they still had before their eyes the bread from heaven, the fiery pillar, the bright clouds, and the priesthood and principality as well.

Therefore we Christians should not be such shameful, scornful, ungrateful know-it-alls,[l] but rather read and use the prophets earnestly and beneficially. For, in the first place, they proclaim and bear witness to Christ's kingdom in which we now live, and in which all believers in Christ have heretofore lived, and will live until the end of the world.[11] It is a strong comfort—and a comforting strength—for us to have such mighty and ancient witnesses for our Christian life. Through them our Christian faith is supremely comforted to the effect that it[m] is the right station[n] before God, over against all other wrong, false, human saintliness and factions.[12] These factions—because of their great appearance and their multitude of adherents, and in turn because of the cross[o] and the few who cling to Christian faith—greatly provoke and assail[13] a weak heart. So, at present, the Turk,[14] the pope,[15] and other factions are great and powerful stumbling blocks for us.

For that reason, then, the prophets are beneficial for us, as St. Peter boasts in 1 Pet. 1[:11-12] that it was not to themselves that the prophets made known what was revealed to them but rather to us. It was to us (he says) that they made it known. For they have served us thus with their prophesying in order that whoever would be in Christ's kingdom should know, and prepare themselves accordingly, that they must first suffer many things before they come to glory.[16] By this we become certain of two things: that the great glory of the kingdom[p] of Christ is surely ours and that it will come hereafter; and that it is nevertheless preceded by the cross, disgrace, misery, contempt, and all kinds of suffering on account of Christ. The purpose is so that we will not become disheartened through impatience or unbelief, or

l Ger.: *Klueglinge*.

m I.e., our Christian faith.

n Ger.: *Stand*.

o LW 35:266.

p WA DB 11/1:5.

11. Luther always regarded the messianic/christological aspect of the Old Testament as primary and most important to recognize. But as will be seen from his treatment of the First Commandment and of idolatry below, he did not read the Old Testament in an exclusively christological manner.

12. The term *Rotten* and the related *Rottengeister* admit different translations. In his Latin writings, Luther uses *sectarii* and *sectarii spiritus*, from which our English translations "sects," "factions," "sectarians," "sectarian spirits," and "factious spirits" are derived. The German terms imply "gangs," "hordes," and "mobs," and specifically activity that is illegal and forceful, which can be clearly seen in the title of Luther's pamphlet, *Against the Robbing and Murdering Hordes of Peasants* (1525), LW 46:49-55, where "hordes" renders *Rotten* (see Brecht 2:137-38). In this translation, *Rotten* is rendered with "factions" and *Rottengeister* with "factious spirits."

13. The verb *anfechten*, used here, and the related noun, *Anfechtung*, have no precise equivalents in English. In Luther, the terms often render the Latin *tentare* (to tempt, test, try) and *tentatio* (temptation), but they are not interchangeable. E.g., Luther does not use *Anfechtung* in the sixth petition of the Lord's Prayer, and the term occurs rather sparingly in his Bible translation. Martin O. Dietrich defines *Anfechtung* as "an assault on either the body, mind, or soul, involving fear, conscience, sin, or guilt, and is always a test of one's faith. *Anfechtung* can stem from the devil, or from the hidden God" (LW 42:181). See *Comfort When Facing Grave Temptations* [*Anfechtungen*] (1521), LW 42:183-86; Denis R. Janz, "To Hell (and Back) with

Engraved portrait of Sultan Suleiman the Magnificent (1562) by Melchior Lorck (1526–1598)

despair of that future glory, which will be so great that even the angels desire to see it.[q]

In the second place, the prophets show us many great examples and experiences of the First Commandment.[17] They explicate it in masterly fashion, both in words and examples, so as to drive us powerfully to the fear of God and to faith, and to preserve us in them. For after they have prophesied of Christ's kingdom, all the rest is nothing but examples of how God has so strictly and severely confirmed God's First Commandment. So to read or hear the prophets is surely nothing else than to read and hear how God threatens and comforts. God threatens the

q See 1 Pet. 1:12.

Luther: The Dialectic of *Anfechtung* and Faith," SRR 13 (Spring 2011): 41–55.

14. Suleiman I, "the Magnificent" (1494–1566), was the longest-reigning sultan of the Ottoman Empire (1520–1566). On Luther and the Turks, see *On War against the Turk* (1529), TAL 5:335–89; LW 46:161–205; *Appeal for Prayer against the Turks* (1541), LW 43:219–41; Brecht 2:363–68; 3:351–57.

15. Clement VII (r. 1523–1534); Paul III (r. 1534–1549).

16. Luther's marginal gloss at this point reads simply: "Whoever wants to be in Christ's kingdom must first suffer" (WA DB 11/1:3,27ff.).

17. Luther is known as the theologian of justification by faith, which he certainly was. But his theology is not adequately presented unless one reckons with the central and fundamental role that the First Commandment plays in his thought. In his conception, it is the First Commandment that binds the two volumes of the Christian Bible together as a theological unity. Especially revealing of its centrality is a comment Luther made in the early 1530s: "In the future life all commandments will cease—except the first" (WA TR 1:159,31–32 [no. 369]).

godless, who are secure and proud. And if threatening does not help, God reinforces it with punishments, pestilence, famine, and war, until they perish. In this way God makes good on God's threat in the First Commandment.[r] But God comforts the God-fearing, who are in all sorts of distress, and also reinforces it with assistance and counsel, through all kinds of wonders and signs, against all the might of the Devil and the world. In this way God makes good on God's comfort in the First Commandment.[s]

With sermons and examples like these the prophets once again serve us more than abundantly. They do this so that we will not be provoked when we see how securely and proudly the godless despise[t] God's word and care absolutely nothing about God's threats,[u] as though God were some kind of nonentity. For in the prophets we see that things have never turned out well for anyone who has despised God's threats, even though they were the mightiest emperors and kings or the most saintly and learned people on whom the sun has ever shone. On the other hand, we see that no one has ever been forsaken who has dared to rely upon God's comforts and promises, even though they were the most miserable and poorest sinners and beggars that were ever on earth; indeed, even if they were a slain Abel[v] or a swallowed Jonah.[w] By this the prophets illustrate for us that God holds fast to God's First Commandment and wills to be a gracious father to the poor and believing, and that for God no one is too lowly or too despised. On the other hand, God wills to be an angry judge to the godless and the proud. No one is too great, too mighty, too wise, or too saintly for God, be it the emperor, the pope, the Turk, or even the Devil.[18]

For this reason, it is beneficial and necessary for us today to read the dear prophets, so that we may be strengthened and comforted by these examples and sermons against the unspeakable, innumerable, and (if God so will) ultimate provocations of

18. This paragraph reinforces a major point made in the *Large Catechism*: "Thus, [God] demands that all our actions proceed from a heart that fears God, looks to him alone, and because of this fear avoids all that is contrary to his will, lest he be moved to wrath. Conversely, he demands that our actions proceed from a heart that trusts in him alone and for his sake does all that he asks of us, because he reveals himself as a kind father and offers us every grace and blessing. This is exactly the meaning and the right interpretation of the first and chief commandment, from which all others proceed" ("Conclusion of the Ten Commandments," *Large Catechism*, BC, 324).

r See Exod. 20:5; Deut. 5:9.

s See Exod. 20:6; Deut. 5:10. On this and the previous point, see also "Explanation of the Appendix to the First Commandment," BC, 390–92.

t LW 35:267.

u Ger.: *vnd so gar nicht vmb sein drewen geben.*

v See Gen. 4:1-16.

w See Jonah 1–2.

the damned world. How the Turk[x] regards our LOrd Jesus Christ and his kingdom as if it were some kind of nonentity compared[y] to himself and his Mohammed![19] And how greatly the dear, poor gospel and word of God are despised on this side, among us and under the papacy, compared with the glorious pretense and riches of human commandments and saintliness! With what utter certitude the factious spirits,[z] the Epicureans,[20] and others like them follow their own presumptions, contrary to sacred Scripture! What an utterly audacious and wild life everyone now lives, following their own wantonness, and contrary to the clear truth which is now as plain as day![a] Thus, it appears as if neither God nor Christ amounts to anything, and this is not even to mention the severity of God's First Commandment![b]

But they say, "Wait, wait! What if the prophets are lying and[c] deceiving us with their stories[d] and sermons?" There have been mightier and more numerous kings—worse scoundrels, too—who have perished, and these[21] will not escape either. On the other hand, there have been needier and more miserable people who have nevertheless been gloriously helped, and we[22] shall not be forsaken either. Just as they are not the first to have been defiant and boastful, so are we not the first to have suffered and been stricken.[e] See, this is the way we make the prophets beneficial to us, and, thus, the reading of them becomes fruitful.

But it is good to consider the reason why there is more threatening and punishing in the prophets than comforting and promising. Because the godless outnumber the pious[f] at all times, one must always inculcate the law much more than the promises. For the godless are secure anyway, and they are quite nimble in applying the divine comforts and promises to themselves while

x See n. 33, p. 331 below.

y WA DB 11/1:7.

z Ger.: *Rottengeister.*

a Ger.: *so jtzt am tage.*

b Ger.: *Schweige das Gottes erste Gebot solt so strenge sein.*

c LW 35:268.

d Ger.: *Historien.*

e This last phrase, "so are we not the first to have suffered and been stricken," was left untranslated in LW 35:268.

f Ger.: *die Fromen* (*Frommen*). Luther's standard translation for Hebrew ישרים (*yesharim*), "the upright."

19. The Prophet Mohammed (570–632), founder of Islam and author of the Qur'an. In Luther's new *Preface to the Revelation of St. John* (1530), he identifies the sixth evil angel of Revelation 10 with Mohammed: "The second woe is the sixth angel, the shameful Mohammed with his companions, the Saracens, who inflicted great plagues on Christendom, with his doctrines and with the sword" (LW 35:404). Luther was a proponent of publishing translations of the Qur'an, so that Christians would be properly informed about what they were facing and be prepared to refute it. In 1542, he published his own paraphrased translation of the thirteenth-century treatise "Refutation of the Alcoran by Brother Richard, Dominican" (*Verlegung des Alcoran Bruder Richardi, Prediger Ordens*; WA 53:272–388) with copious polemical marginal glosses. In 1543, he also wrote a preface to the scholarly Latin translation of the Qur'an by the Zurich theologian Theodore Bibliander (1509–1564) (*Vorrede zu Theodor Biblianders Koranausgabe*; WA 53:561–72).

20. Luther uses the term to refer to contemporaries—such as Erasmus (1466–1536) and other humanists—whom he regards as counterparts to the ancient Athenian philosopher Epicurus (342–270 BCE), and whose characteristic was an excessive this-worldly orientation.

21. The antecedent is the factious spirits and Epicureans, that is, the ones described immediately above, who follow their own wantonness.

22. That is, we who at present hold fast to the First Commandment.

applying the threats and punishments to others. And there is no way to turn them away from this perverse notion and false hope. For their motto[g] is, "PEACE AND SECURITY;[23] all is well."[h] They stick to that and take it with them to destruction, as St. Paul says, "Destruction comes upon them suddenly."[24]

23. Luther here uses the Latin phrase, *PAX ET SECURITAS*, which is the Vulgate's rendering in 1 Thess. 5:3.

24. A paraphrase of 1 Thess. 5:3.

25. This heading and the one below were not in the original 1532 preface.

Idolatry[i] among the Jews[25]

Moreover, since the prophets cry out most of all against idolatry, it is necessary to know the form which this idolatry took.[j] Among us under the papacy, many flatter themselves greatly and think[k] that they are not idolaters like the children of Israel were. This is also why they regard the prophets disparagingly—especially in the part of their message where they speak of punishment for idolatry—as not being applicable to them. They are far too pure and also too saintly to commit idolatry, and it would be ludicrous for them to be afraid or terrified in the face of threats and reprimands concerning idolatry. But that is exactly what the people of Israel did. They simply would not believe that they were idolatrous. Therefore the threats of the prophets had to be lies and the prophets themselves damned as heretics.

Now, the[l] children of Israel were not such mad saints as to worship mere wood and stone. This was especially true of the kings, princes, priests, and prophets, and yet they were the most idolatrous of all. Their idolatry, however, consisted in letting go of the divine worship which had been instituted and organized in Jerusalem—and wherever else God would have it—and improving on it, instituting it, and setting it up elsewhere, according to

g Ger.: *Reim.*

h Ger.: *Es hat nicht not* is a paraphrase of the same portion of 1 Thess. 5:3. Cf. Luther's rendering in his New Testament: *es ist friede, es hat keine fahr* (WA DB 7:247,3).

i Ger.: *Abgoetterey.*

j WA DB 11/1:9.

k From here to the end of the preface, the verb *meinen* (perceive, understand, discern, sense, feel, consider, ponder, think, intend, mean) occurs numerous times. It is difficult if not impossible to render consistently in English.

l LW 35:269.

their own conceit and presumption,[m] without God's command, and making up new forms and persons and times for it. This was despite the fact that Moses had strictly forbidden it, especially in Deuteronomy 12,[26] and had pointed them to the place that God had chosen for God's tent and dwelling.[n, o] This false conceit was their idolatry. Yet they regarded it as of great value and relied upon it as if they had arranged it well, though it was pure disobedience and apostasy from God and God's command.

So we read in 1 Kgs. 12[:28-33] that Jeroboam[27] not only set up the two calves, but he also had it preached to the people, "You shall no longer go up to Jerusalem; rather see, O Israel, here is your God, who brought you out of Egypt."[p] He does not say, "See, O Israel, here is a calf," but, "Here is your God who brought you out of Egypt." He freely confesses that the God of Israel is the true God[q] who brought them out of Egypt; yet one need not run after God to Jerusalem but rather one can find God just as well here at Dan and Beersheba,[28] where the golden calves are. Thus, his opinion was that one can sacrifice to and worship God just as well before the golden calves—as before a sacred symbol of God—as God was sacrificed to and worshiped before the golden ark at Jerusalem. See, this then means to abandon the divine worship in Jerusalem and thereby to deny God who commanded such divine worship, as if God had not commanded it.

26. Deuteronomy 12 contains what is known as the law of cultic centralization, that is, the restricting of the locus of legitimate sacrifice to one and only one sanctuary.

27. King Jeroboam I, the first king of the Northern Kingdom of Israel, who began to rule after the death of Solomon, c. 920 BCE.

28. See 1 Kgs. 12:30-33. Jeroboam's two temples were established at Dan and Bethel, not Dan and Beersheba.

Jeroboam I sets up two golden calves, one at Bethel and the other at Dan. Illustration by Pierre Eskrich (c. 1550–c. 1590).

m Ger.: *aus eigener andacht vnd gut duenckel.* The meaning of *Andacht* as "devotion" is a post-Luther linguistic development.

n *Hütte* (tent) and *Wohnung* (dwelling) are Luther's standard translations for the "Tent of Meeting" and the "Tabernacle" in Exodus 25–40.

o See Deut. 12:5, 11, 13-14, 17-18, 21, 26.

p Luther is following here his 1524 translation of 1 Kgs. 12:28. In later editions of his Bible translation, he follows the plural reading of the Hebrew text: *Sihe, Da sind deine Goetter Jsrael, die dich aus Egyptenlande gefuert haben* ["See, here are your *gods*, O Israel, who brought you out of the land of Egypt" (emphasis original)] (WA DB 9/1:449,28).

q Ger.: *der rechte Gott.*

Thus, the people of Israel built on their own works and conceit, and not purely on God alone. With this conceit they subsequently filled the land with idolatry; on all the hills, in all the valleys, under all the trees, they built[r] altars, offered sacrifice, and burned incense. And all this had to be called worshiping the God of Israel. Whoever said otherwise was considered a heretic and a false prophet. For this is what committing idolatry really means: the setting[s] up of divine worship out of one's own conceit, without God's bidding. For God will not be taught by us how God is to be worshiped. God wants to teach us and specify that God's word is supposed to be there, which will enlighten and guide us. Without God's word everything is idolatry and pure lies, no matter how devout and beautiful it may be. We have often written about this.[29]

29. It is not clear precisely which texts Luther is referring to here, but see, e.g., *Treatise on Good Works* (1520), TAL 1:257–367; LW 44:21–114; *Against the Heavenly Prophets* (1525), TAL 2:39–125; LW 40:79–223; explanation of the First Commandment in the *Large Catechism*, BC, 386–92.

Idolators[t] among the Christians

From this it follows that among us Christians all those are idolatrous—and the prophets' reprimands truly apply to them—who have invented or are maintaining new forms of divine worship, without God's order or command, out of their own conceit and, as they say, good intentions.[30,u] They are thereby certainly putting their trust in their own self-chosen works, and not simply and purely in Jesus Christ. For in the prophets, such people are called adulteresses;[v] they are not content with their own husband, Christ, but run after others as well, as though Christ alone could be of no help without us and our works, or as though Christ alone had not redeemed us and we would have to do something toward it ourselves. Still we know very well that we did absolutely nothing toward having Christ die for us, taking our sins upon himself and bearing them on the cross, not only before the whole world could even think of any such thing, but also before we were even born. Just as little, indeed even less, did

30. Luther's marginal gloss at this point reads: "Those who invent or maintain new forms of divine worship, apart from God's command, are idolators" (WA DB 11/1:11,10ff.).

r WA DB 11/1:11.

s LW 35:270.

t Ger.: *Abgoettische.*

u Ger.: *aus eigener andacht, vnd (wie man spricht) guter meinung.* A likely allusion to the Scholastic phrase *bona intentio.*

v See Ezek. 16:32, 38; 23:45; Hos. 2:2ff.

the children of Israel do toward bringing the plagues upon Egypt and Pharaoh,[w] and toward setting themselves free through the death of the firstborn of Egypt.[x] God did this completely alone, and they did nothing at all.

"Of course," they say, "with their divine worship the children of Israel worshiped idols and not the true God; but in our churches we worship the true God and the one LOrd Jesus Christ. For we have nothing to do with idols."[y] I answer: That is exactly what the children of Israel said. They all declared that their entire divine worship was directed to the true God, and they certainly would not allow anyone to call it the worshiping of idols any more than our clergy[z] would allow it. For this reason, they killed and persecuted all the true prophets.[a] For they, too, would truly have nothing to do with idols, as the histories[b] tell us.

For thus we read in Judg. 17[:2-3] that the mother of Micah, when he had taken the eleven hundred pieces of silver from her and again returned them, said to him, "May my son be blessed by the LORD. I vowed this silver to the LORD, that my son should take the silver and have an idol and an image[c] made[d] of it," etc. Here one learns clearly and distinctly that the mother is thinking of the true God, to whom she has vowed the silver, out of which an idol and an image would be made. For she does not say, "I have vowed this silver to an idol,"[e] but "to the LORD," a word which is known among all the Jews to mean the one true God.[31] The Turk also does the same thing; in his divine worship he names and thinks of the true God who created heaven and earth.[32] The Jews, Tartars,[33] and now all unbelievers do the same. Nevertheless with them it is all pure idolatry.

Also, how strangely did that wondrous and great man Gideon fall, in Judg. 8[:22-27]. To the children of Israel who desired that he and his children should be their Lord, he said, "Neither I nor

w See Exodus 7–10.

x See Exodus 11–12.

y Ger.: *Denn wir wissen von keinem Abgott.*

z Ger.: *vnser Geistlichen.*

a LW 35:271.

b Ger.: *die Historien.*

c Ger.: *ein Goetzen vnd Bilde.*

d WA DB 11/1:13.

e Ger.: *Abgott.*

31. It was Luther's consistent practice in his Bible translation to render the four-letter name of God in the Hebrew Bible (the Tetragrammaton), יהוה (Y-H-W-H), in all-capital letters as *HERR* (LORD), and the generic Hebrew word for "lord," אדני ('Adonai) as *HErr* (LOrd) in half-capitals when it refers to God. In this example, Micah's mother explicitly uses the Tetragrammaton twice, which is integral to Luther's argument. LW 35:271, however, simply renders with "Lord," thus obscuring the point that Luther is making. (For further detail on Luther and the Tetragrammaton, see the original 1523 *Preface to the Old Testament*, this volume, pp. 62–63.)

32. Luther's marginal gloss at this point reads: "The divine worship services of the Turks, Jews, and all unbelievers are pure idolatry" (WA DB 11/1:13,1ff.). On the question of Luther's understanding of other religions and other forms of worship, see Heinrich Bornkamm, "The God of the Old Testament," in *Luther and the Old Testament*, ed. Victor I. Gruhn, trans. Eric W. and Ruth C. Gritsch (Mifflintown, PA: Sigler Press, 1997), 45–80.

33. "Tartars" is Luther's term for the Asian forebears of the contemporary Turks. He also refers to the same people as "the red Jews" (*die roten Jüden*). See, e.g., *Preface to the Revelation of St. John*, LW 35:409. On the red Jews, see Andrew Colin Gow, *The Red Jews: Antisemitism in an Apocalyptic Age 1200–1600*, SMRT 55 (Leiden: Brill, 1995). In the 1546 Luther Bible, published after his death, Luther's final marginal gloss on Rev. 20:8 reads: "Gog: this refers to the Turks, who are descendants of the Tartars who are called the red Jews" (WA DB 7:471,8).

my children will be your Lord, rather the LORD[34] (that is, the true God) will be your LOrd."[35] To be sure, he took the jewels that they gave him, but he made of them, not an image or an altar, but only a priest's garment.[36] Out of his conceit he also wanted to have divine worship in his own city. Nevertheless, Scripture says that thereby all Israel committed whoredom, and his house perished because of it. Now, this great and saintly man was not thinking of any idol[f] but of the one true God, as his fine words—so rich in spirit—testify, when he says, "The LORD will rule over you, not I, etc." By these words[g] he plainly gives glory to God alone; he confesses the true God and will have only the true God held as God and LORD.

Likewise, we heard above that King Jeroboam in 1 Kgs. 12[:28] does not call his golden calves "idols" either, but rather "the God of Israel, who brought them out of Egypt." This is of course the one true God, for no idol brought them out of Egypt. Nor was it his intention to worship idols. Rather, because he feared (as the text says)[h] that his people would fall away from him to the king of Judah if they were to maintain divine worship only in Jerusalem, he invented his own divine worship in order to keep them to himself. Nevertheless, he thereby intended the true God who dwelt in Jerusalem, with the exception that it would not be necessary to worship God only in Jerusalem.

But why expend so many words on it? It is God who confesses that with their divine worship the children of Israel intended no idol, but rather God alone. For God says so in Hos. 2[:16-17], "Then, says the LORD, you will call me 'my husband,' and no longer will you call me 'my Baal.' For I will put aside the names of the Baals from her mouth, and the names of the Baals will be remembered no more." Here one must confess that it is true: with their divine worship the children of Israel intended no idol but rather the one true God, as God plainly says here in Hosea, "You will no longer call me 'my Baal.'" Now among[i] the people of Israel, Baal[j] was the greatest, most common, and most glorious divine worship; yet it was pure idolatry, despite the fact that by it they intended the true God.

f Ger.: *Abgott.*

g LW 35:272.

h 1 Kgs. 12:26-27.

i WA DB 11/1:15.

j That is, Baal worship.

34. As in the previous example, the key is Gideon's explicit use of the Tetragrammaton in Judg. 8:23.

35. The Hebrew text of Judg. 8:22-23 literally reads: "The men of Israel said to Gideon, 'Rule over us, you, your son, and your son's son, for you have saved us from the hand of Midian.' But Gideon said, 'Neither I nor my son will rule over you, rather YHWH will rule over you.'" Luther's dynamic translation of the text, which is also reflected here in the preface, is: "Then some in Israel said to Gideon, 'Be Lord over us, you and your son and your son's son, because you have redeemed us from the hand of the Midianites.' But Gideon said to them, 'I will not be Lord over you, and neither will my son be Lord over you, rather the LORD will be Lord over you'" (WA DB 9/1:115,22-23).

36. *Priesterkleider* is a reference to the priestly *ephod* in Judg. 8:27, a garment which Luther normally translates as *Leibrock* ("robe"). The root meaning of the Hebrew word *ephod* is unknown.

Therefore it does not help our clergy at all to pretend that in their churches and religious foundations they do not worship idols, but only God, the true LORD. For here you learn that it is not enough to say or think, "I am doing it to honor God; I intend the true God. Also, I want to worship the one God." For all idolaters say and intend the very same thing. It is not the intending or the thinking that counts, otherwise those who martyred the apostles and Christians would also have been worshipers of God. For, as Christ says in John 16[:2], they intended to offer worship to God. And in Rom. 10[:2] St. Paul testifies to the Jews that they have zeal for God. And in Acts 26[:7] he says that with their divine worship day and night they hope to attain to the promisesd salvation.

On[k] the contrary, let everyone see to it that they are certain that their divine worship has been instituted through God's word, and not invented out of their own devotion or good intentions.[37] For whoever maintains divine worship that does not have God's testimony should know that they are not worshiping the true God but rather their own made-up idol; that is, their own pretense[l] and false thoughts. Thereby they are worshiping the Devil himself, and all the words of the prophets are against them. For such a God who would have us institute divine worship according to our own choice and conceit—without God's command and word—is nowhere to be found. There is only one God, who through God's word has abundantly instituted and commanded all the various stations of life[m] and the divine worship by which God wills to be worshiped.

We should abide by this and not turn aside from it either to the right or to the left,[n] doing neither more nor less, making it neither worse nor better. Otherwise there will be no end of idolatry, and there will be no difference between true divine worship and idolatry, since all intend the true God, and all use God's true name. To this same one God be thanks and praise, through Jesus Christ, God's Son, our LOrd, who is blessed forever. AMEN.

37. Luther's marginal gloss at this point reads: "Divine worship apart from God's word is worship of the Devil" (WA DB 11/1:15,13ff.).

k LW 35:273.

l Ger.: *duenckel.*

m Ger.: *Stende.*

n See, e.g., Deut. 5:32; 28:14; Josh. 1:7; Prov. 4:27.

Der Prophet Jesaia
Deudsch.
Wittemberg. 1 5 2 8.

The title page of *Der Prophet Jesaia Deudsch* (Wittenberg, 1528), which depicts Isaiah's vision of the heavenly throne room above the temple of Jerusalem. An angel touches a hot coal to Isaiah's lips with a pair of tongs.

Preface to the Prophet Isaiah

1545 (1528)

BROOKS SCHRAMM

INTRODUCTION

Luther began his translation of Isaiah in February 1527.[1] The difficulty of the task is indicated by a remark in a 14 June 1528 letter to Wenceslas Linck (1483–1547): "We are sweating over the work of putting the Prophets into German. God, how much of it there is, and how hard it is to make these Hebrew writers talk German! They resist us, and do not want to leave their Hebrew and imitate our German barbarisms. It is like making a nightingale leave her own sweet song and imitate the monotonous voice of a cuckoo, which she detests."[a] Progress on Isaiah was further delayed by Luther's illness in the summer of 1527,[b] as well as by the plague that struck Wittenberg in the late summer, forcing the university to move to Jena for eight months and depriving Luther (who remained behind) of his collaborators, Philip Melanchthon (1497–1560) and Matthaeus Aurogallus (1490–1543).[2] After the return of the university to Wittenberg in spring 1528, the translation was resumed and the decision made to publish Isaiah separately rather than waiting for all of the Prophets to be complete. *Der Prophet Jesaia Deudsch* (Wittenberg: Hans Lufft),

1. Reflecting on the interruption of the Old Testament translation project caused by the Peasants' War and its aftermath, Luther wrote to Johann Lang (c. 1487–1548) on 4 February 1527 that he was turning again to the translation of the Prophets, "which this barbarous and animalistic nation has taken from me" (Brecht 3:95; WA Br 4:168,7–9).

2. Matthaeus Goldhahn (Aurogallus) taught Hebrew at the University of Wittenberg from 1521 to 1543. Luther relied closely on him in matters of Hebrew grammar.

a LW 35:229; WA Br 4:484,19–23.

b On Luther's illness, see Brecht 2:205–7.

together with this preface, appeared in October 1528.[c] The translation of Isaiah was foundational for Luther's *Lectures on Isaiah*, which he delivered from 18 May 1528 through 22 February 1530.[d]

As a precritical interpreter, Luther regards all of the material in Isaiah as stemming from the lifetime of Isaiah of Jerusalem in the late-eighth and early-seventh centuries BCE, and he emphasizes the necessity of interpreting the book's central themes—(1) chastisement for idolatry and proclamation of the coming kingdom of Christ; (2) the Assyrian king Sennacherib's siege of Jerusalem; (3) and prophecy of the coming Babylonian Exile and return to the land—against that specific historical background. At the same time, he acknowledges that Isaiah may not have been the actual author of the book named for him. The provocative character of this acknowledgment is noted by Heinrich Bornkamm: "In his prefaces to the Bible translations of the individual prophets [Luther] openly expressed his doubts regarding the writing of the books by these prophets themselves. His prefaces have disappeared from later editions of the [Luther] Bible probably partly because of this."[e]

The Translation

The translation presented here is a revision of LW 35:273–78 and is based on the *Preface to the Prophet Isaiah* in the 1545 Luther Bible, WA DB 11/1:17–25 (odd numbers). This 1545 preface was virtually unchanged from the original 1528 version. Luther's biblical quotes and allusions have been translated directly, and thus may at times differ from the biblical versions used in LW. Insofar as possible, Luther's terminology has been rendered consistently throughout. The translation is also informed by the modern German versions of the preface presented by Borcherdt/Merz and Bornkamm.[f]

c See the image on p. 334 above.

d See LW 16 and 17; Raeder 2:379–80.

e Heinrich Bornkamm, *Luther and the Old Testament*, ed. Victor I. Gruhn, trans. Eric W. and Ruth C. Gritsch (Mifflintown, PA: Sigler Press, 1997), 192.

f H. H. Borcherdt and Georg Merz, eds., *Martin Luther: Ausgewählte Werke*, 3d ed., vol. 6: *Bibelübersetzung, Schriftauslegung, Predigt* (Munich: Chr.

PREFACE TO THE PROPHET ISAIAH

THOSE[g] WHO WOULD BENEFIT from reading the holy prophet Isaiah and understand him better should not despise this counsel and advice of mine, unless they have better advice or are themselves better informed. In the first place, they should not skip over the title or beginning of this book,[3] but rather learn to understand it as thoroughly as possible. Otherwise they might think that they understand Isaiah very well and then have to face the charge that they have not even understood the[h] title or first line, not to mention the entire prophet. For this title should really be regarded as a gloss and a light on the entire book, and Isaiah himself, as with his finger, points his readers to it as the introduction and basis of his book. But to those who despise the title or do not understand it, I say that they should leave the prophet Isaiah alone, or at least that they will not understand him thoroughly. For it is impossible to grasp or perceive the prophet's words and meaning properly and clearly without this thorough knowledge of the title.[i]

When I speak of the title, I do not mean only that you should read or understand the words "Uzziah, Jotham, Ahaz, Hezekiah, the kings of Judah," etc., but that you should take for yourself

3. See Isa. 1:1, according to Luther's translation: "This is the vision of Isaiah, the son of Amoz, which he saw concerning Judah and Jerusalem at the time of Uzziah, Jotham, Ahaz, and Hezekiah, the kings of Judah."

Kaiser, 1958), 51–55; Heinrich Bornkamm, ed., *Luthers Vorreden zur Bibel*, 3d ed. (Göttingen: Vandenhoeck & Ruprecht, 1989), 91–97.

g WA DB 11/1:17; LW 35:273.

h LW 35:274.

i On Isaiah in the history of Christian thought, see John F. A. Sawyer, *The Fifth Gospel: Isaiah in the History of Christianity* (Cambridge, UK: Cambridge University Press, 1996). On Luther's Old Testament hermeneutics in general and his specific approach to Isaiah in particular, see Brevard S. Childs, "Martin Luther," in *The Struggle to Understand Isaiah as Christian Scripture* (Grand Rapids: Eerdmans, 2004), 181–206.

the last book of Kings and the last book of Chronicles and take hold of them well, especially the stories,[j] the speeches, and the events[k] that occurred under the kings named in the title, clear to the end of those same books.[l] For if one would understand the prophecies, it is necessary that one know how things were in the country, how matters lay, what was in the mind of the people, and what kinds of plans they had with or against their neighbors, friends, and enemies, and especially whether in their country they followed God—and the prophet and his word and divine worship—or idolatry.[4]

4. The relationship between the historical and the christological in Luther's interpretation of Isaiah is captured nicely by Siegfried Raeder: "In the book of Isaiah Luther found more detailed prophecies about Christ and his kingdom than in any other scripture of the Old Testament. Nevertheless, besides the christological exposition, he did not neglect the historical interpretation" (Raeder 2:380).

5. These section headings appeared neither in the original 1528 preface nor in the complete German Bible of 1534.

Countries Located around Jerusalem and Judah[5]

In addition, one would also do well to know how these countries were located with reference to one another, so that the foreign, unfamiliar words and names might not make reading unpleasant and obscure or impede understanding. In order to do my simple Germans[m] a service, I will briefly point out the territory located around Jerusalem or Judah, where Isaiah[n] lived and preached, so that they may so much the better see in what direction the prophet turned when he prophesied toward the south or the north[o] etc.

Toward the east,[p] the nearest thing to Jerusalem or Judah is the Dead Sea, where Sodom and Gomorrah stood ages ago.[q] Beyond[r] the Dead Sea lies the country of Moab, and of the children of Ammon. Further beyond lies Babylon or Chaldea, and

j Ger.: *die Geschicht.*

k Ger.: *zufelle.*

l See 2 Kings 15–20; 2 Chronicles 26–32.

m Ger.: *meinen einfeltigen Deudschen.*

n WA DB 11/1:19.

o Ger.: *gegen Mittage, oder Mitternacht.* In the following geographical descriptions, Luther uses the main hours of the day (morning, afternoon, evening, midnight) to represent the four cardinal directions.

p Ger.: *Gegen Morgen.*

q See Genesis 18–19.

r LW 35:275.

further still the country of the Persians, about which Isaiah speaks so much.

Toward the north[s] lies Mount Lebanon, and across from it Damascus and Syria. Further on eastward lies Assyria, with which Isaiah also deals extensively.

Toward the west[t] lie the Philistines along the Great Sea,[6] the worst enemies of the Jews. Along the Sea to the north of them lie Sidon and Tyre, which border on Galilee.

6. I.e., the Mediterranean.

Toward the south[u] there are many countries. For example: Egypt, the country of the Moors,[v] Arabia, the Red Sea, Edom and Midian, such that Egypt lies to the southwest[w] [of Judah and Jerusalem].

These are some of the lands and names about which Isaiah prophesies, the neighbors—enemies and friends—surrounding the land of Judah like wolves around a sheepfold. From time to time they made alliances and counteralliances with some of them, but it did not help them at all.

What the Prophet Isaiah Deals With

Thereafter, you must divide the prophet Isaiah into three parts. In the first part, just like the other prophets, he treats two things. First, he preaches a good deal to his people and chastises them for their various sins, but especially for the manifold idolatry which had gotten the upper hand among the people (as pious preachers now and always do and must do with their people). He keeps them in line[x] with threats of punishment and promises of good.[7] Second, he disposes and prepares them to await the coming kingdom of Christ, about which he prophecies more clearly and more diversely than any other prophet. In chapter 7 he even describes the mother of Christ, the Virgin Mary, and how she is

7. In his *Preface to the Old Testament*, Luther identifies the polemic against idolatry as the central Old Testament theme (see this volume, pp. 51–52).

s Ger.: *Gegen Mitternacht.*

t Ger.: *Gegen Abend.*

u Ger.: *Gegen Mittage.*

v Ger.: *Morenland* (*Mohrenland*), known as "Cush" in the Hebrew Old Testament and "Ethiopia" in the Greek New Testament.

w Ger.: *Also das Egypten gegen Abend im mittag ligt.*

x Ger.: *Vnd behelt sie in der zucht.*

to conceive and bear him with her virginity intact.[8,y] In chapter 53 he describes Christ's passion together with his resurrection from the dead, proclaiming his kingdom as powerfully and plainly[z] as if it had just happened,[a] already at that time.[9] This must have been a splendid and highly enlightened prophet. For

The Virgin and the Child under the Apple Tree (1530s) by Lucas Cranach the Elder. The Child Christ holds bread and apple in his hands. The apple symbolizes original sin, the bread (the body of Christ) the redemption. The Virgin is considered to be the second Eve, redeeming the sin of the first.

y Ger.: *mit vnuerserter Jungfrawschafft*. Literally, "with undamaged virginity."

z Ger.: *duerre*. Literally, "dryly."

a LW 35:276.

8. Isaiah 7:14 is a traditional interpretive crux. The Hebrew text [MT] uses עלמה (*'almah*; a young woman biologically fit for marriage), while the Greek OT [LXX] and Matt. 1:23 use παρθένος (*parthenos*; virgin). Luther always translated this passage with *Jungfrau* (virgin). Throughout his life, Luther held to the *virginitas perpetua* (perpetual virginity) of Mary, and it was normal for him to refer to her as *semper virgo* (ever virgin). See, e.g., the Latin text of the *Smalcald Articles*, Part 1 (as noted in BC, 300). As a logical corollary, Mary could not have had any other biological children. See, e.g., *Sermons on the Gospel of St. John* (LW 22:214–15). On the manifold significance of Mary, see Jaroslav Pelikan, *Mary through the Ages: Her Place in the History of Culture* (New Haven: Yale University Press, 1996).

9. During Lent of 1544, Luther gave a special lecture on Isaiah 53, which was characterized by intense polemic against Jewish interpretations of the passage (*Enarratio 53. capitis Esaiae*, WA 40/3:685–746). This lecture is scheduled for translation into English in the new series of the American edition of *Luther's Works*, ed. Christopher B. Brown (St. Louis: Concordia, 2009–).

all the prophets do the same thing: they teach and chastise the people of their time, and in addition they proclaim Christ's coming and kingdom, directing and pointing the people to Christ as the common Savior of both those who have gone before and those who are yet to come.[b] Some do this more than the others, and some more extensively than the others, but Isaiah does this the most and the most extensively of all of them.

In[c] the second part, he has to do especially with the empire of Assyria and the emperor Sennacherib. He also prophesies more and at greater length about this than does any other prophet, namely, about how that emperor would conquer all neighboring countries, including the kingdom of Israel, and also inflict much misfortune on the kingdom of Judah.[10] But there he stands like a rock, with his promise that Jerusalem shall be defended and delivered by him.[d, e] And this is one of the greatest miracles to be found in Scripture, not only because of the event,[f] that such a mighty emperor should be defeated before Jerusalem, but also because of the faith to believe it.[g] It is a miracle, I say, that anyone at Jerusalem could have believed him in such an impossible thing. Without doubt, Isaiah must have often heard many bad words from the unbelievers. Yet he did it; he defeated the emperor and defended the city. Therefore, he must have been well regarded by God as a precious man.

This illustration from the *Nuremberg Chronicle* (1493) depicts the Jewish people being expelled from Jerusalem by the forces of Babylonian King Nebuchadnezzar.

In the third part, he has to do with the empire of Babylon. Here he prophesies of the Babylonian captivity, whereby the people were to be punished and Jerusalem destroyed by the emperor

10. The Northern Kingdom of Israel fell to the Assyrians in 722 BCE. On Assyrian King Sennacherib's siege of Jerusalem, see John J. Collins, *Introduction to the Hebrew Bible and Deutero-Canonical Books*, 2d ed. (Minneapolis: Fortress Press, 2014), 291–94.

b On Christ as the savior of certain Old Testament characters even in Old Testament times, see MLBJP, 12–14.

c WA DB 11/1:21,1.

d I.e., by Isaiah himself.

e See Isaiah 36–39; 2 Kings 18–20; 2 Chronicles 29–32.

f Ger.: *Nicht allein der Geschicht halben.*

g Ger.: *Sondern auch des glaubens halben, das [=dass] mans hat gegleubt.*

of Babylon. But here is his greatest difficulty:[h] comforting and preserving his people yet to be in this destruction and captivity yet to come, so that they might not despair, as if it were all over for them and Christ's kingdom would not be coming and all prophecy were false and of no effect.[i]

What rich and full sermons he gives here: Babylon shall in turn be destroyed, and the Jews will be released and return again to Jerusalem.[11] With proud defiance against Babylon, he also indicates the names of the kings who shall destroy Babylon, namely, the Medes and Elamites, or Persians, and especially the king who shall release the Jews and help them back to Jerusalem, namely, Cyrus,[j] whom Isaiah calls "God's anointed."[12,k] He does all of this long before there was a kingdom in Persia. Because for him everything has to do with the Christ,[l] so that his future coming and the promised kingdom of grace and salvation would not be despised or of no effect because of unbelief and great misfortune and impatience among his people. This would all be in vain, unless they awaited it and believed confidently that it would come. These are the three things that Isaiah deals with.

11. Luther does not spiritualize the captivity and return, for Christ's future coming was contingent upon the actual historical return of Israel from Babylon. See *Lectures on Isaiah* (LW 17:3), where he distinguishes between "external" prophecy (i.e., prophecy that concerns purely temporal matters) and "spiritual" prophecy (i.e., prophecy concerning Christ and the kingdom of Christ).

12. Cyrus II (the Great), was king of Persia from 559 to 530 BCE. He is mentioned by name in Isa. 44:28 and 45:1.

The Order of the Book of Isaiah

But the order in which he treats things is not such that he subsumes each one under its own place, with its own chapters and pages. Rather, it is almost completely blended together, such that he introduces much of the first theme[m] under the second and third themes, and he even deals with the third theme before the second.[13] Now, whether[n] this took place at the hands of those who collected and wrote down the prophecies (as is thought to have happened with the Psalter),[14] or whether he himself arranged it this way as time, occasion, and persons suggested he speak about

13. Luther may have in mind here Isaiah 13–14, the long oracle against Babylon that occurs early in the book.

14. See Luther's 1528 *Preface to the Psalter* (LW 35:253–57). In his 1524 *Preface to Solomon's "The Preacher"* (i.e., Ecclesiastes), Luther grants that Solomon's words were collected by others and, thus, that Solomon was not the actual author (LW 35:263–64).

h With Bornkamm, *Luthers Vorreden zur Bibel*, 95, taking *erbeit* (*Arbeit*) in the sense of *Mühe*.

i Ger.: *falsch vnd verloren sein*.

j LW 35:277.

k Ger.: *den Gesalbeten Gottes*.

l Ger.: *Denn es ist jm alles vmb den Christum zu thun*.

m Ger.: *stueck*.

n WA DB 11/1:23,1.

each part—these times and occasions not being alike and not having a specific order—this I do not know.[15]

But he at least treats things in such an order that he deals with the first theme as the most excellent and inculcates it from beginning to end, all the way through the second and third themes. This is what we are also supposed to do in our sermons. The two parts of our most excellent theme—chastising the people and preaching about Christ—should always run concurrently, although as occasion arises we may at times undertake to preach on other topics, such as the Turk or the emperor, etc.

From this, anyone can easily understand the prophet and be at home in him,[o] such that the order will not confuse or weary them, as may happen to the inexperienced. We have really done our best to make Isaiah speak good, clear German, although he has not lent himself easily to it and has strongly resisted it.[16] Those who know German and Hebrew well will readily see that, and most of all the smart alecks[p] who imagine[q] that they know everything. Isaiah was really so eloquent in Hebrew that the awkward German tongue did not sit well with him.[r] [This is what occasioned our publishing of Isaiah separately,[17] to see how in this desolate, wild, and ungrateful time he would fare among the people, in order that, God willing, we might with greater assurance let the other prophets follow after.][18]

What benefit there may be for those who read Isaiah, I prefer to let the readers experience for themselves, rather than describe it for them. For those who do not, or will not, experience it for themselves, there is no benefit in making much of it. He is truly full of living, comforting, tender sayings for all poor consciences and miserable, sorrowful hearts. Likewise, there are also plenty of words of threatening and terror in it against the stubborn, proud, hard heads of the godless—if that may be of any help.

But you should view Isaiah among the Jewish people as nothing other than a despised man, indeed as a fool and a crazy person. For they did not regard him as we regard him now. Rather, as he himself testifies in chapter 58,[s] they stuck out their tongues

o Ger.: *vnd sich drein schicken.*

p Ger.: *die Duenckelmeister.*

q LW 35:278.

r Ger.: *das jn die vngelencke Deudsche zunge sawr ankomen ist.*

s The proper reference is Isa. 57:4; cf. 58:9.

15. In his 1532 *Preface to the Prophet Jeremiah,* Luther draws a similar conclusion regarding the lack of chronological order in Jeremiah: "So it seems as though Jeremiah did not compose this book himself, but that the parts were taken piecemeal from his utterances and written into a book. For this reason one must not worry about the order or be hindered by the lack of it" (LW 35:280–81).

16. On the difficulty of translating the Prophets in general and Isaiah in particular, see the introduction, p. 335.

17. A reference to the 1528 first edition of the Isaiah translation. See the introduction, pp. 335–36.

18. This bracketed sentence appeared in the 1528 edition but was dropped in 1532 and later editions.

at him, and pointed their fingers at him, and regarded all of his sermons as foolishness. This was the case for all but a few pious children of God in the crowd, such as King Hezekiah.[19] For it was the custom among the people to mock the prophets and regard them as crazy (2 Kgs. 9[:11])—as has always happened to all servants of God and preachers, is happening every day, and will continue to happen.

One[t] can also note that the thing for which Isaiah chastises the people most of all is idolatry. The other vices, such as self-indulgence, drunkenness, and greed, he hardly touches on three times. But all the way through he chastises the presumption regarding their self-chosen worship of idols[20] and their own works, or their comfort with kings and alliances. This was intolerable[u] to the people, for they wanted what they were doing to be regarded as right. Because of this, too, he is finally supposed to have been killed by King Manasseh[21] for being a heretic and seducer, and, as the Jews say, to have been cut in two with a saw.[22]

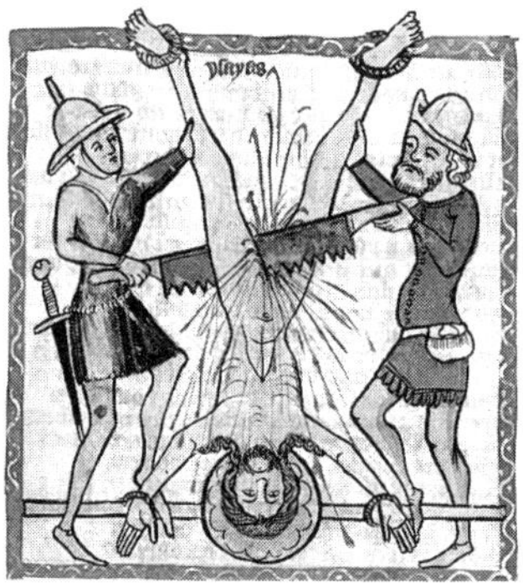

This image from *Speculum humanae salvationis* (c. 1360) depicts the prophet Isaiah being executed by sawing, as detailed in chapter 5 of the third-century Christian pseudepigraphical work *Ascension of Isaiah* (Isa. 5:1-14).

19. Hezekiah, king of Judah (c. 715–c. 686 BCE) was the reigning monarch during Assyrian King Sennacherib's siege of Jerusalem in 701 BCE.

20. Defining idolatry as "self-chosen worship" is the most prominent theme in Luther's *Preface to the Prophets* (see this volume, pp. 338ff).

21. Manasseh, king of Judah (c. 686–c. 642 BCE).

22. That Isaiah was martyred at the hands of Manasseh, whom 2 Kgs. 21:16 and 24:3-4 charge with shedding innocent blood, is a postbiblical Jewish tradition and dates to the second century BCE. Both the Babylonian and Jerusalem Talmuds know the tradition (*b. Yebam.* 49b; *y. Sanh.* 10). On the Christian side, it is likely reflected in Heb. 11:37 and was known already by Justin Martyr (c. 100–167 CE) and Tertullian (c. 160–c. 220 CE). The visual representation of Isaiah's martyrdom was common in Luther's world. See M. A. Knibb, "Martyrdom and Ascension of Isaiah," in *The Old Testament Pseudepigrapha*, ed. James H. Charlesworth, 2 vols. (Garden City, NY: Doubleday, 1983, 1985), 2:143–76. For other Luther references to this tradition, see WA TR 1:376,12–19, #796; 3:155,25–29, #3044.

t WA DB 11/1:25,1.

u Ger.: *vnleidlich*.

Lectures on Isaiah 53

1528–1530

BROOKS SCHRAMM

INTRODUCTION

From the summer of 1524 through the summer of 1526 Luther lectured on the twelve minor (or shorter) prophetic books. Of the three major (or longer) prophetic books—Isaiah, Jeremiah, and Ezekiel—Luther only ever lectured on Isaiah.[1] Although he was convinced that all of the prophets spoke about Christ and his coming kingdom, it was in Isaiah that Luther found the majority of these references, and this may account in part for the special focus on Isaiah.[a] In a letter to Wenceslas Linck[2] on 4 May 1527, Luther announced his intention to lecture on Isaiah: "I myself am now getting ready to translate the prophets into German, and at the same time I shall lecture on Isaiah, so that I may not be idle."[b] It was long thought that Luther began the Isaiah lectures in the summer of 1527, but because of his own significant illness that summer, as well as the onset of the plague in Wittenberg and the subsequent moving of the university to Jena, the lectures were not begun until the following year. The dates

1. All of Luther's biblical lectures delivered at the University of Wittenberg were given in Latin.

2. Like Luther, Wenceslaus Linck (1483–1547) was an Augustinian monk who gained his doctorate in theology in 1511 and was dean of the theological faculty at Wittenberg when Luther was graduated as doctor in 1512. In 1520, Linck succeeded Johann von Staupitz as vicar general of the Augustinian Order in Germany; on 28 January 1523, he resigned the Augustinian Order and became a Protestant preacher in Altenburg. Linck was one of Luther's oldest friends.

a See Luther's *Preface to the Prophet Isaiah*, this volume, pp. 335; and Heinrich Bornkamm, *Luther in Mid-Career 1521–1530*, ed. Karin Bornkamm, trans. E. Theodore Bachmann (Philadelphia: Fortress Press, 1983), 575–76.

b LW 49:165.

for these approximately 150 Isaiah lectures are now established as 18 May 1528–22 February 1530.[c] The bulk of the lectures were delivered during 1529, with the lectures on Isaiah 53 falling in the summer of that year.

Not all of Luther's sources for the Isaiah lectures can be established, but several are clearly evident. He had Jerome's[3] Isaiah commentary (*Commentaria in Isaiam prophetam*, c. 410) before him, and he alludes to it frequently. Nicholas of Lyra's[4] commentary on the Bible (*Postilla litteralis super Bibliam*, 1322–1331) served as Luther's initial conduit into the world of medieval Jewish biblical interpretation, primarily that of Rashi.[5] Luther's Wittenberg colleague Johannes Bugenhagen had lectured on Isaiah in 1523–1524 utilizing Luther's theological insights, but Luther apparently did not have access to a copy of Bugenhagen's lectures.[d] He did, however, make significant use of the new Isaiah commentary by the Basel Hebraist, Johannes Oecolampadius[e] (*In Iesaiam prophetam Hypomnematon, hoc est, Commentariorum, Ioannis Oecolampadii Libri VI* [Basel, 1525]). This Latin commentary was of great interest to Luther, because it was based on the Hebrew text of Isaiah.[6] Finally, Luther consulted the new German translation of Isaiah by the Anabaptist scholars Ludwig Haetzer and Hans Denck, which appeared in 1527 as part of their translation of all of the prophetic books.[f]

As a precritical interpreter of Isaiah, Luther regarded the entire book as stemming from the lifetime of Isaiah of Jerusa-

3. St. Jerome (c. 347–420), the translator of the Latin Vulgate Bible.

4. Nicholas of Lyra (c. 1270–1349), French Franciscan. His biblical commentaries were second only to the twelfth-century *Glossa ordinaria* in terms of influence on medieval Christian biblical interpretation. See Deeana Copeland Klepper, *The Insight of Unbelievers: Nicholas of Lyra and Christian Reading of Jewish Text in the Later Middle Ages* (Philadelphia: University of Pennsylvania Press, 2007).

5. "Rashi" (1040–1105), Rabbi Shlomo ben Yitzchaq [Rabbi Solomon son of Isaac], Troyes, France, was the most prolific and influential of the medieval Jewish biblical commentators. Still valuable for the study of Rashi is Herman Hailperin, *Rashi and the Christian Scholars* (Pittsburgh: University of Pittsburgh Press, 1963).

6. Luther makes explicit reference to this commentary in his preface to the *Lectures on Isaiah* (LW 16:4): "Oecolampadius has translated Isaiah with adequate care" ("*Oecolampadius satis diligenter transtulit Esaiam*," WA 31/2:2,15). Being part of the same circle of Christian Hebraists along with Konrad Pellikan (1478–1556) and Sebastian Münster (1489–1552), Oecolampadius brought to Luther's attention significantly more of the Jewish interpretive tradition than was available via Lyra. In 1534/1535, Münster would publish his master work, *Biblia hebraica latina*, a Latin translation of the Hebrew Bible together with footnotes and annotations containing numerous references to a plethora of medieval Jewish biblical commentators. This publication would be indispensable for Luther in his later anti-Jewish exegetical polemics.

c These dates were established by Dietrich Thyen, *Untersuchungen zu Luthers Jesaja-Vorlesung* (theol. Diss. Heidelberg, 1964). The significance of Thyen's dissertation is discussed in Bornkamm, *Luther in Mid-Career*, 575–76; and Brecht 2:498–99 n.23.

d See Bornkamm, *Luther in Mid-Career*, 576–77. On Johannes Bugenhagen (1485–1558), see Kurt K. Hendel, *Johannes Bugenhagen: Selected Writings*, 2 vols. (Minneapolis: Fortress Press, 2015).

e Johannes Oecolampadius (1482–1531). On his biblical interpretation in general and on Isaiah in particular, see Peter Opitz, "The Exegetical and Hermeneutical Work of John Oecolampadius, Huldrych Zwingli, and John Calvin," in *Hebrew Bible/Old Testament: The History of Its Interpretation*, vol. 2: *From the Renaissance to the Enlightenment*, ed. Magne Sæbo (Göttingen: Vandenhoeck & Ruprecht, 2008), 407–13.

f On Haetzer and Denck and the *Wormser Propheten*, see the introduction to *Preface to the Prophets* in this volume, pp. 320.

lem in the late-eighth and early-seventh centuries BCE.[g] When he reads Isaiah, he consistently distinguishes between those prophecies that are strictly historical (or "external"), that is, those that applied to the situation of historical Israel prior to the coming of Christ, and those "spiritual" prophecies that apply to Christ and his coming kingdom. Examples of prophecies that fall into the former category would be those concerning Sennacherib's siege of Jerusalem, the Babylonian captivity, the figure of the Persian king Cyrus, and the return from Babylon. But, in a move that anticipates contemporary Isaiah scholarship, Luther also sees a major structural division in the book beginning at chapter 40, and he titles the chapters 40–66 "The Second Book of Isaiah":

Portrait of Johannes Oecolampadius by Hans Asper (1499–1571)

> We rightly divide Isaiah into two volumes. We have heard the first one, in which the prophet has functioned as a historical prophet and leader of the army, because so far he has prophesied concerning Christ and concerning the defeat of the king of Assyria. Then he has both comforted and reproved the people. In the following book the prophet treats two matters: Prophecies concerning Christ the king and then concerning Cyrus, the king of Persia, and concerning the Babylonian captivity. This second book is nothing but prophecy, first external, concerning King Cyrus, and then spiritual, concerning Christ. And here the prophet is the most joyful of all, fairly dancing with promises.[h]

Luther sees another significant structural division at chapter 49, arguing that the prophecies from that point forward are all christological in character: "From this chapter to the end there is

g See the introduction to *Preface to the Prophet Isaiah*, this volume, p. 336.

h LW 17:3.

nothing but Christ, and although the prophet at the same time occasionally corrects and rebukes, the scope of this treatise [i.e., chaps. 49–66] has to do with Christ, with the calling of the Gentiles, and with the rejection of the Jews."[i]

Of the manifold prophecies throughout the book that are regarded as expressly christological, Isaiah 53 is, to be sure, the central text for Luther. He reads Isaiah 53 completely in terms of the suffering, death, and resurrection of Christ. The prophecy has no historical or external component in the sense that it could have at one time applied to events in the time of Isaiah, or Cyrus, or to the restoration after the Babylonian Exile. In the way in which the text portrays the fate of the anonymous "servant," Luther sees the primary Pauline concepts of "the righteousness of God" and "the justification of the sinner" both explained and proclaimed. It is, thus, "the pure gospel"[j] and "the preeminent article of our faith and our confession, which is dealt with extensively by Paul."[k]

Because Luther accorded so much theological weight to Isaiah 53, and because his interpretation ruled out any other understanding of the passage, he was inexorably drawn to refute Jewish readings that contradicted his Christian reading.[l] In his treatment of Isaiah 53 in the *Lectures on Isaiah*, the anti-Jewish arguments are generally subsumed under the claim that Jews refuse to accept a Christ, or a Messiah, who suffers. During the seasons of Lent and Easter of 1544, however, Luther would lecture directly on Isaiah 53, and there his engagement with the Jewish interpretive tradition is more far reaching.[m]

i LW 17:169.

j *A Brief Instruction on What to Look For and Expect in the Gospels* (1521), TAL 2:30; LW 35:118.

k *Lecture on Isa. Chap. 53* (1544) WA 40/3:687,9–11. See immediately below.

l On Luther's anti-Jewish polemics as being primarily based in debates over proper interpretation of the Old Testament, see MLBJP, 3–16.

m See *Enarratio 53. capitis Esaiae* (1544), WA 40/3:685–746. This crucial Luther document is scheduled to be translated as part of the new series of Luther's works: *Luther's Works: American Edition, New Series*, ed. Christopher B. Brown (St. Louis: Concordia, 2009–). In the preface to those lectures, Luther states: "It is simply amazing that Isaiah had so much light that he was able to depict the mysteries concerning Christ so eloquently and properly, more properly even than the Evangelists, with the exception of Paul who is the chosen instrument" (WA 40/3:685,27–30). Also to be translated in the same series is the

The Translation

The translation presented here is a revision of LW 17:215–32 and is based on Anton Lauterbach's[7] student lecture notes published in WA 31/2:428–41. Luther's treatment of Isaiah 53 contains numerous direct quotes from and allusions to the Latin Vulgate Bible. These have been translated directly in order to facilitate the reader's understanding of the point(s) that Luther is making with the biblical reference. Insofar as possible, Luther's terminology has been rendered consistently throughout.

7. Anton Lauterbach (1502–1569), theological student at the University of Wittenberg and well-known recorder of many of Luther's sermons and table talks.

LECTURES ON ISAIAH 53[n]

52:13. "Behold, my servant will understand and be exalted and lifted up."

WE THUS DIVIDE THIS CHAPTER, which indicates the manner in which that king will liberate us. "*Behold, my servant will understand.*" Here we begin chapter 53.[8] Until now you have heard the kingdom of Christ described in the cross, in such a way that it is propagated by faith and the word alone. Yet in that leading of faith, of the word, and of the cross, liberation and protection

8. The Luther Bible also followed the practice of beginning chapter 53 at this point rather than three verses later. Modern critical scholarship regards 52:13—53:12 as a single unit.

closely related special lecture on Isaiah 9, which Luther delivered during Advent and Christmas of 1543 (*Enarratio capitis noni Esaiae*, WA 40/3:597–682). These two lectures can be regarded as capstones to Luther's three major anti-Jewish treatises of 1543: *On the Jews and Their Lies* (TAL 5:441–607; LW 47:137–306); *On the* Schem Hamphoras *and On the Lineage of Christ* (TAL 5:609–65); and *On the Last Words of David* (LW 15:265–352).

n WA 31/2:428,3; LW 17:215. In the *Scholia*, the published version of Luther's *Lectures on Isaiah* which appeared in 1532 (rev. 1534), and which was not edited by Luther himself, this chapter heading is

are not lacking. In this chapter he[o] primarily treats the head of the kingdom, as he treats the person of the king and the manner of his liberation. This is the foremost passage[p] on the suffering and resurrection of Christ, and there is scarcely another like it.[9] Therefore we must memorize this passage, for it strongly drives out the obstinacy of the Jews.[q] For the Jews cannot deny that it speaks about Christ. The Jews indeed concede the glories of Christ in this chapter, but they refuse to concede the cross and sufferings.[10] Yet this is what the text says: This king will be glorious, but only after death. This indicates that this king is different from a bodily[r] one, because he will begin [to reign] after death. "*Behold, the understanding servant.*" He calls him a servant, as above [Isa. 42:2]: he will not strain, he will not cry out in the streets. There he is not the type of servant imagined by the monks, rather he is a servant, that is, a minister of the word, an apostle, and an ambassador. What will this servant do? "*He will understand.*"[s] The Hebrew word *Maschin*[t] means he will act wisely, he will be able to deal circumspectly with a matter.[u] They are said to act wisely who carry an important and extremely dangerous matter through to its conclusion in such a way that they nowhere do violence to it. The political official needs this wisdom to take note of all dangers, beware of all snares, and bring everything to a successful conclusion.[v] So Matt. 10[:16] reads: "Be wise as serpents." Now, the serpent is a shrewd animal, involving itself in violence and snares. Summary: The office of a wise person[w] requires not ruling by violence, not ramming one's head through,[x] but even in the midst of a desperate matter to see

followed by the title: "*De Christi passione et glorificatione*" ("On the Suffering and Glorification of Christ"), WA 25:325,32.

o I.e., the prophet.

p Lat.: *locus.*

q Lat.: *Iudeorum obstinaciam.*

r Lat.: *corporalem.* LW 17 had translated "ordinary."

s The Latin verb *intelleget* is a direct translation from LXX (the Greek OT), συνήσει (*sunesei*). As Luther will show, the Hebrew verb is more malleable.

t *Maschin* is an error for מַשְׂכִּיל (*maskil*). The correct term is יַשְׂכִּיל (*yaskil*).

u The last phrase is in German: *kan sewberlich myt eynem dynck umb gehen.*

v The last phrase is in German: *und brengets uberal feyn erdurch.*

w LW 17:216.

x The phrase is in German: *nicht myt dem kopp erdurch.*

9. From antiquity to the present day, Isaiah 53 stands as one of the most commented-upon Old Testament passages in all of Christian history. For a concise selection of pre-Reformation Christian interpretations of the passage, see Robert Louis Wilken, ed., *The Church's Bible, Isaiah: Interpreted by Early Christian and Medieval Commentators* (Grand Rapids: Eerdmans, 2007), 412–30. For contemporary critical approaches, see Bernd Janowski and Peter Stuhlmacher, eds., *The Suffering Servant: Isaiah 53 in Jewish and Christian Sources*, trans. Daniel P. Bailey (Grand Rapids: Eerdmans, 2004).

10. In Jewish tradition, the explicit messianic interpretation of Isaiah 53 is known from the Targum (the Aramaic translation of the Hebrew Bible) to Isaiah, where Isa. 52:13 is rendered: "Look, my servant, *the Messiah*, will prosper, he will be exalted and increase, and will be very strong" (emphasis added). On Luther's use of the Targum, see Hans-Martin Kirn, "Traces of Targum Reception in the Work of Martin Luther," in *A Jewish Targum in a Christian World*, ed. Alberdina Houtman, E. van Staalduine-Sulman, and Hans-Martin Kirn (Leiden: Brill, 2014), 266–88. For the Targums in English translation, see Martin McNamara, et al., eds., *The Aramaic Bible: The Targums*, 19 vols. (Wilmington, DE: Michael Glazier, 1987–).

the matter through gently, and bring everything to an orderly conclusion.[y] Thus, Christ will meet with a most intricate matter. This affair will be imposed on him in such a way that he will have an entirely impossible office, and yet he will handle it so well that he will dispose of the cause without force and without danger. He has accomplished it wisely and without tumult. This is what "*my servant will act wisely*" means.[z] Previously no such person was found, although David[a] is called a "*zechen*"[b] man, that is, one who is wise in the Scriptures [1 Chron. 22:12]. Summary: My servant will not be tumultuous, as you have thus far acted with violence under the law, but his ministry is most pleasant and delightful, and he handles everything in the most pleasant manner, neither offending nor hurting anyone. But this wisdom is the antithesis of every kind of force and tyranny on the part of the authorities. Then, when his first office and ministry have been accomplished, he will be in glory. He will bring it about that even in this life he will arrive at glory after many people have attacked [him].[c] But I understand it simply in this way: Here, in the time of [his] life, he will be a servant. After death he will be Lord. In this life he will be the wisest servant.

[52:14]. "As they were stupefied."

He describes the person. But this is the way it will be.[d] The ministry and glorification of Christ will assume such a form that the whole world will take offense at him. This glorious king will be in such a form that many will be stupefied. I read it thus: "Many take offense at him." [The Hebrew verb] *shamon*[e] means to be appalled,[f] to be disturbed.[g] The word describes the posture of one who is nauseated and full of revulsion, because his

y The final phrase is in German: *feyn sewberlich erdurch gehen.*

z These two sentences are a mixture of German and Latin: *Er hats prudenter sine tumultu verbracht. Das heyst: servus meus prudenter aget.*

a WA 31/2:429,1.

b "*Zechen*" is an erroneous transliteration of Hebrew שׂכל (*sekhel*; "insightful or understanding").

c Lat.: *accesso populo multo.*

d The phrase is in German: *Aber es gehet alſʒo zw.*

e Erroneous for *shamam* (שׁמם).

f The word is in German: *Entseczen.*

g The word is in German: *vorstellen.* The translation is only a guess.

appearance will be so repulsive that many will be nauseated and offended. "*At him.*" What is the reason for this?

"Because his appearance was marred in comparison to others."

(He looks ugly in comparison to other people.)[h] Here you see the glorious king described with the foulest appearance, against the Jews who look for him in glorious form.[11] It follows therefore that the Messiah is not to be expected in a bodily kingdom,[i] because his appearance is so extremely spoiled. He is reckoned with the unrighteous, crucified as[j] seditious, killed by his own people in supreme disgrace, and [regarded as] the absolute least of all.[k] [Nevertheless,] his public appearance, as of one doing nothing, possesses majesty. Note, therefore, that this minister will be more disgraceful before the eyes of others than anyone else. For this reason the Jews ought to receive him, yet many take offense at him, because his appearance will be so offensive.

11. The Targum to Isaiah 53, mentioned above, systematically eliminates all suffering on the part of the Messiah. For example, in the Targum's translation of 52:14, the people of Israel suffer, but not the Messiah: "Just as the house of Israel hoped for him for many days—*their* appearances were so dark among the peoples, and *their* aspect beyond that of human beings—" (emphasis added).

"And his beauty beyond that of other human beings."

This repeats what was said above, that his form is more despised than that of other human beings. No one is despised as much as he is.

[52:15]. "Thus he will sprinkle[l] the nations."

Here the glory appears again.[m] He proceeds with two parts. He says that this minister is wise and glorious, but another part follows. He will be without glory and despised. Then follows:[n] and his glory will nevertheless be such that he will sprinkle the nations, and kings will shut their mouths. That is, all kings will be ashamed and will know that he is a supreme king, and hence

h The sentence is in German: *Er hat gar eyn ungestalt gegen andern lewthen.*

i Lat.: *in regno corporali.*

j LW 17:217.

k Lat.: *et extremissimus hominum.*

l A literal translation in Jerome's Vulgate for Hebrew יזה (*yazzeh*), which is likely corrupt.

m The phrase is in German: *Do kumpt wider die gloria.*

n The phrase is in German: *Und folgt darnach.*

they will shut their mouths. They will all humble themselves.[o] Reconcile this contradiction:[p] all kings regarded themselves as servants in relation to him, and yet he will be despised and without glory. Thus, it is certain that Christ's kingdom is spiritual and ultimately beyond death.[12]

"*Sprinkle.*"[q] This is a Hebraism for "it will be preached." Sprinkling in the law signifies preaching, as if to say: "After Christ will have suffered, he will be preached not only among the Jews but also among the Gentiles as water is scattered and sprinkled on people." Thus, Peter states [1 Pet. 1:2]: "in the sprinkling of the blood of Christ," that is, in the preaching of the blood of Christ. So then Christ is preached as both glorious and despised. Accordingly, Paul preaches Christ alone as deformed and crucified. He must always be preached in this way, yet nonetheless he will be received even by kings. This is an effective text against the Jews,[r] which they can preach with respect to no other king but Christ.[13]

"For that which has not been told."

Paul treats this passage in Rom. 15[:22-24] when he says that he has not come to Rome because he was kept from it by his preaching in a new place. That passage deals with the propagation of the word, so that his[s] word might resound everywhere to kings who shut their mouths. Thus, Christ[t] is described as being preached even among the Gentiles. Here you plainly see a spiritual kingdom described, one that does not go forward with weapons but with word and narration.[u] Thus, this kingdom of Christ's suffering and Christ's resurrection was propagated in the church by preaching alone.

o The phrase is in German: *Sie zcihen alle yre pfeyffen eyn.*

p The phrase is in German: *Leympts zusammen.* WA 31/2:429 n.5 suggests *Reimt's* for *Leympts.*

q WA 31/2:430,1.

r Lat.: *Efficax est textus contra Iudeos.*

s The antecedent is unclear.

t LW 17:218.

u Lat.: *sed verbo et narracione.*

12. That Christ's kingdom is spiritual, and not corporeal/physical/earthly/this-worldly, is a fundamental teaching of Luther's. On the "two kingdoms" in Luther's thought, see Bernhard Lohse, *Martin Luther's Theology: Its Historical and Systematic Development*, trans. Roy A. Harrisville (Minneapolis: Fortress Press, 1999), 151–59, 314–24.

13. The interpretive history of Isaiah 53 within Jewish tradition is highly diverse, but there is a general tendency to understand the servant figure in corporate terms, that is, as a reference to the people of Israel. See esp. Adolf Neubauer and S. R. Driver, eds., *The Fifty-Third Chapter of Isaiah According to the Jewish Interpreters*, 2 vols. (New York: KTAV, 1969). Luther gained awareness of this corporate interpretation, but he regarded it as impossible: the Jews "do not interpret this passage with respect to the son of God or to 'the arm of the Lord,' the Messiah, but rather with respect to themselves, who are now oppressed by the Romans, downtrodden and carried into Roman captivity. They do this with horrible blasphemy, and in no other passage is their delirium greater and more foolish than in this fifty-third chapter" (*Lecture on Isa. Chap. 53* [1544], WA 40/3:688,7-11).

[53:1].[v] *"Who has believed what we have heard?"*[14]

Seeing the greatness of Christ, the prophet considers his Jews, how few there will be who will believe this. He had said of this that almost all will regard him as an offense. Many Gentiles will receive him but only a few Jews.[15] Thus, he says here, "Who will ever believe this?"[w] The Jews were indeed nauseated, as we see in the accounts of the gospels and the Acts of the Apostles. This is what the prophet is lamenting here, that so offensive an appearance of Christ is to be received and honored by kings. This reception is effected not by reason and its investigations but through the Holy Spirit and the word alone. For to believe that Christ, so exceedingly repulsive and killed between robbers,[x] is the savior—this no reason can believe. For no fouler kind of death can be read about than that about Christ, and to believe that under that form he is the Messiah, and to die in that faith—that is the office of the Holy Spirit.[16,y]

So far he has completed one paragraph concerning Christ as the servant hanging [on the cross], and his completely absurd appearance, and his sublime kingdom, so that the kings will shut their mouths. Therefore I conclude that Christ will have an eternal kingdom after his death. A second paragraph:

[53:2]. "He grew up like a bush."[z]

Then the prophet persists with his prophecy concerning the suffering of Christ. He springs up *"like a bush and like a root."* This is wonderful.[a] *"Before him,"* he says. He indeed grows up before God,[b] but not before the world. This is a metaphor, as if to say, a root does not spring up in dry[c] ground. It strikes me as if a lovely

14. The Luther Bible translates this phrase as: *"Aber wer gleubt vnser Predigt?"* ("But who believes our sermon?"), WA DB 11/1:157,1.

15. Luther dealt with the question of Jewish conversion at various stages of his career, and he was never optimistic in this regard. The position stated here was already articulated in his early *Lectures on Romans* (1515–1516), when he glossed Paul's statement in Rom. 9:6, "Not all who are from Israel are Israel," with "Not all *but only a few* who are from Israel are Israel" (LW 25:80). On the other hand, he remained insistent throughout his career that the Jews "are the first people and the chief part of the church" (LW 16:33).

16. On the inextricable relation between the Spirit and faith in the thought of Luther and his closest associates, see Melanchthon's formulation in the *Augsburg Confession*, Art. 5 (BC, 40–41).

v LW 17:219.

w The phrase is in German: *Wer wyl das ummer meher glewben?*

x See Matt. 27:38; Luke 23:33.

y Lat.: *Nam nulla fedior species mortis legi potest quam in Christo et sub illa forma credere illum esse Messiam et in illa fide mori, illud est officium spiritus sancti.*

z The Vulgate uses the same term, *virgultum*, in Gen. 2:5.

a A mixed German/Latin phrase: *das ist mirabile.*

b The phrase is in German: *vor got wechst er wol.*

c WA 31/1:431,1.

sprout were to grow up out of dry ground,[d] that is, it is impossible for an arid Christ to effect anything good. Trying to draw water from a rock and oil from iron is just as believable as saying that Christ must be splendid and glorious.

"He[e] has neither splendor nor elegance."

Not having splendor or elegance simply deprives him of everything, since no robber was completely without splendor. But here there is to be no form or adornment whatsoever.[f]

"That we might indeed look at him," because he was crucified publicly.

"And there was no appearance, which we might desire," in which we might take pleasure,[g] which we could desire. Everything about him was abominable." See how the prophet labors in describing his contemptible appearance. It is as if he were saying, "The people treated him in the most horrible way."[h]

[53:3]. "Held in contempt and regarded as least of all; a man full of pain and experienced with weakness."

"Regarded as least of all" is *Hadal*[i] in Hebrew, one whom nobody pays any attention to,[j] one from whom all turn away. This is no easy suffering. These words cannot be understood as referring to the glory of the kingdom, nor do they speak of a simple and spiritual suffering. They speak rather of an external, manifest, and extremely repulsive suffering. Away with the Jews who refuse to admit that this refers to Christ. For they imagine two Messiahs.[17] They say that one has already come and is walking around in the world in beggar's clothing and that a second one is to come in temporal glory.[18,k] Thus, this text compelled them.

d The phrase is in German: *Es gemanet mich eben, als eyn schoen sproesleyn solde wachsen aus eyner durren erden.*

e LW 17:220.

f The sentence is in German: *Hie sol gar keyne gestalt seyn noch schmuck.*

g The phrase is in German: *do wyr hetten lust mugen zuhaben.*

h The phrase is in German: *Man hat uffs grewlichst myt ym umbgangen.*

i Heb.: חדל (*ḥadal*).

j The phrase is in German: *des man sich gar nicht annympt.*

k Lat.: *in temporali gloria.*

17. Rabbinic Judaism does in fact have a tradition of dual Messiahs, in which the "Messiah son of Joseph" (or Ephraim) will die in battle against the enemies of Israel prior to the coming of the "Messiah son of David," who will then usher in the messianic kingdom. See Ephraim E. Urbach, *The Sages: Their Concepts and Beliefs*, trans. Israel Abrahams, 2 vols. (Jerusalem: Magnes Press, Hebrew University, 1975), 1:649–92; 2:990–1009. Another tradition, dating to the late Second Temple period, regarding a priestly Messiah, the "Messiah of Aaron," and a political Messiah, the "Messiah of Israel," is now known from the Dead Sea Scrolls. The author of the NT book of Hebrews was clearly influenced by this concept of the priestly Messiah. On Jewish messianic beliefs in the late Second Temple period, see John J. Collins, *The Scepter and the Star: Messianism in Light of the Dead Sea Scrolls*, 2d ed. (Grand Rapids: Eerdmans, 2010).

18. The odd tradition of the Messiah living among lepers at the gates of Rome is known from the Babylonian Talmud, *b. Sanh.* 98a. Luther will refer to it again in *On the Jews and Their Lies* (1543): "[The Jews] confess that the Messiah came at the time when Jerusalem was destroyed, but that he is in the world secretly, sitting among the beggars in Rome and doing penance for the Jews, until the time when he will break forth. These are neither Jewish nor human words but the words of the arrogant, mocking Devil, who, through the Jews, mocks us Christians together with our Christ in the bitterest and most poisonous fashion. It is as if he were saying: 'The Christians brag a lot about their Christ, but they have to submit to the Romans, be martyred, and be beggars in the world. And not

"He is a man full of pain."

This does not signify weaknesses but many sicknesses and pains; a wounded, stricken person, as the following text shows.

"And thus held in contempt, such that others turn away their countenance from him."

The Hebrew is *Mimemmon.*[l] "*Countenance*" refers to others who saw him; as if to say, Christ, as often as they saw him, they turned away from his miserable face. There was a nausea [caused] by seeing. These are two paragraphs[m] in which he describes the glory and the dishonor and the suffering of Christ. Now follows a third paragraph which describes what Christ would accomplish.

We have heard[19] that in these paragraphs there was a description of Christ's person with respect to his suffering and his glorification. The article of the church, that the kingdom of Christ is not of this world,[n] is founded on this passage.[20] Now follows what he would accomplish by his suffering, whether he suffered on his own account or on account of others. And this is the second part of our understanding and justification, to know that Christ suffered and was cursed and killed,[o] but FOR US.[p] It is not enough to know the matter, namely, the suffering, but[q] it is necessary to know its use.[r] The pope retained the matter but denied the use. The Anabaptists[s] deny both.[21] Of this he speaks as follows:[t]

l Heb.: ממנו (*mimmennu*; "from him").

m The phrase is in German and Lat.: *Das sindt duo paragraphi.*

n Lat.: *non esse mundanum.*

o LW 17:221.

p Lat.: *sed PRO NOBIS.*

q WA 31/2:432,1.

r Lat.: *Non satis est scire rem, scilicet passionem, sed usum eius scire necesse.*

s Lat.: *Anabaptistae.*

t The phrase is in German: *Dorvon redet er alßo.*

only at the time of the Emperor but also at the time of the pope. They, however, achieve nothing in my kingdom in the world. I will surely remain their Lord.' Yes, mock on, you wretched Devil, and laugh about it. You will tremble enough for having done so" (WA 53:461,6–16; cf. TAL 5:503; LW 47:190–91 [192]).

19. A new lecture begins at this point.

20. Luther likely has Jesus's words to Pilate in John 18:36 in mind, which is rendered in the Luther Bible: "Jesus replied: 'My kingdom is not from this world. If my kingdom were from this world, my servants would fight for it, so that I might not be handed over to the Jews. But my kingdom is not from here.'"

21. Despite Luther's statement at the end of his 1535 preface to the *Lectures on Galatians* that he intended to address the Anabaptist question more fully (LW 26:149), the only treatise he ever wrote on the subject was *Concerning Rebaptism* (1528), LW 40:229–62. Luther initially opposed the execution of Anabaptists but later changed his mind, on the grounds of public blasphemy. See *Commentary on Psalm 82* (1530), LW 13:61–62. On Luther and the Anabaptists, see Brecht, 2:334–39, who argues that Luther's precise knowledge of Anabaptist teachings was limited. For example, Balthasar Hubmaier (c. 1480–1528), Anabaptist pastor and theologian (see image), was burned at the stake as a heretic in Vienna on 10 March 1528. He was known for including the phrase "The truth is immortal" in several of his writings.

Engraving of Anabaptist Balthasar Hubmaier by Christoffel van Sichem (1581–1658)

[53:4]. "Truly he has borne our weaknesses," etc., "yet we reckoned him as if wounded,[u] *stricken by God."*[22]

This is the use of the suffering of Christ.[v] It was not for himself and his sins but for our sins, our pains. What we ourselves should have suffered is what he bore. Here you see the fountain from which St. Paul derives innumerable streams of the suffering and merits of Christ, while damning all the religions, merits, and endeavors in the whole world by which salvation is sought.[23] Note the innumerable sects who to this day are laboring for salvation. But here he says, "He for us."[w] It is difficult for the flesh to resign all its [resources], to go beyond itself, and to be transferred into Christ.[x] We who have merited nothing should not have regard for our merits but simply hold fast to the word [as though suspended] between heaven and earth, even though we do not feel it. Unless we have been divinely imbued, we will not understand this. Therefore I delight in this text as if it were in

u The Vulgate reads at this point: *quasi leprosum* ("as if he were a leper").

v Lat.: *Hic est usus passionis Christi.*

w Lat.: *Ipse pro nobis.*

x Lat.: *in Christum transferri.*

22. When Luther was convinced that an Old Testament text referred specifically to Christ, he tried to make that as transparent as possible via translational subtlety. A classic example is this particular verse, which is rendered in the Luther Bible as follows: "Truly he bore our illness and carried our pains upon himself; but we regarded him as *the one* who was plagued and stricken and martyred by God" (WA DB 11/1:157,4; emphasis added). For a concise treatment of Luther's Old Testament translation techniques, see "Luther's Christian Translation of the Old Testament," in Heinrich Bornkamm, *Luther and the Old Testament*, ed. Victor I. Gruhn, trans. Eric W. and Ruth C. Gritsch (Mifflintown, PA: Sigler Press, 1997), 219–46.

23. This is not a mere rhetorical flourish on Luther's part. He is convinced, and not without warrant, that Paul's theology of atonement is derived from a concrete Old Testament text, namely, Isaiah 53. On the influence of Isaiah 40–55, and especially Isaiah 53, on Paul, see Joseph Blenkinsopp, *Isaiah 40–55: A New Translation with Introduction and Commentary*, AB 19A (New York: Doubleday, 2002), 87–92.

the New Testament.[24,y] This new doctrine, which strikes down the righteousness of the law, appeared plainly absurd to the Jews. For that reason the apostles needed the Scripture: *"Surely [our] weaknesses."* His suffering was nothing else than our sin. These words, OUR, US, [FOR] US,[z] should be written in gold letters. Whoever does not believe this is not a Christian.[a] *"And we imagined"*: as if to say, we imagined that he was suffering because of his own transgression. Before the world and before the flesh,[b] Christ does not suffer for us, because he appeared to have merited it. This is what the prophet says here, too, that he was judged guilty before the world. Therefore it is difficult to believe that such a one suffered for us. For the law is that one dies for one's own sin. According to both natural and divine reason, one bears one's own sin. But here he is stricken contrary to all law and customs. Hence, reason concludes that he was stricken by God on his own account. Therefore here he[c] forces the suffering of Christ upon us so diligently, beyond all righteousness and our rational capacity, namely, that all that Christ has is mine.[d] This is the preaching of the whole gospel, to demonstrate to us that Christ suffered for us contrary to law, rights, and[e] precedent. He explains clearly what [it means] to suffer for us.

[53:5]. "He was wounded."

The prophet describes the suffering of Christ in copious fashion. Word by word he explains it against the hardened Jews.[25,f] Do you want to know what it is to bear our sins, that is, [what it means that] *"He was wounded"*? Here you have the definition of Christ perfectly and absolutely, because this chapter speaks about him.[g] Christ is a human being, a minister of the word,

24. It is a distinctive teaching of Luther's that the "Old Testament" is not to be directly equated with the "old covenant" and "law"; the OT is also "gospel" in that it proclaims Christ and inculcates faith. A corollary is, therefore, that the faith of the Old Testament and the faith of the New Testament are the same. "The ancestors [in the Old Testament] believed the same as we do. There is only one faith, even though, it may have been less clear then" (*Lectures on Romans* [1515–1516], LW 25:153).

25. The image of the hardened Jew is common in Luther's writings and becomes more prevalent in the latter half of his career as he realizes that Jews are not persuaded by his christological interpretations of the Old Testament. The image is central in *On the Jews and Their Lies* (1543), TAL 5:441–607; LW 47:137–306.

y Lat.: *Ideo delector in hoc textu quasi novi testamenti.*

z Lat.: *NOSTRUM, NOS, NOBIS.*

a Lat.: *Qui haec non credit, non est Christianus.*

b Lat.: *Coram mundo et coram carne.*

c I.e., the prophet.

d Lat.: *scilicet ut eius omnia sint mea.*

e LW 17:222.

f Lat.: *contra obduratos Iudeos.*

g Lat.: *Hic habes definicionem Christi perfecte et absolute, quia hoc Caput loquitur de illo.*

who by means of suffering bore our sins. How will the unbridled Jew[h] respond to this definition? From this you will conclude how alien the doctrines of Paul and the pope are [to one another]. Paul holds fast to this Christ alone[i] as the bearer [of sin]. By means of this singular word, "the lamb of God" [John 1:29], John the Baptist understands this Levitical sacrifice, which he suffered for the sins of all. The consequence follows: therefore the law and merits do not justify. Away with the Antichrist pope and his traditions, because Christ has borne all these things.[j] I am amazed that this text has been obscured in the church for so long. They indeed see the dispute of Scripture that faith without works is dead [Jas. 2:26], and we say the same thing. In public dispute, however, we say that works are necessary, but they do not justify.[k] Thus, anyone may conclude in private: "It is all the same whether I have sinned or whether I have done well." This is difficult for the conscience to believe, that it is the same, and [that it is] plainly angelic and divine. Therefore this text truly concludes with this consequence: "Christ alone bears our sins. Our works are not Christ. Therefore there is no righteousness of works." When viewing Scripture as a whole,[26,l] surely none of the papists can evade [the fact] that Christ has accomplished everything for justification, and therefore we do not [accomplish anything]. Appeal to works, rewards, and merits and make much of them[m] with regard to external remuneration.

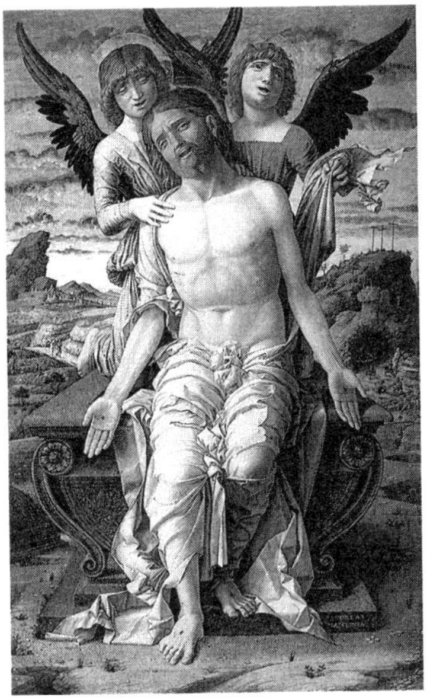

Portrait of Jesus as the Man of Sorrows by Andrea Mantegna (1431–1506)

26. In terms of biblical interpretation, Luther consistently argued that the "meaning of the whole" constrains the "meaning of the parts." That "whole" was the two-volume Christian Bible and its "meaning" was the saving work of God in Jesus Christ on behalf of sinful humanity, understood via a Pauline lens. A classic example is the way in which Luther used the "whole" to constrain the meaning of James: "That epistle of James gives us much trouble, for the papists embrace it alone and leave out all the rest. Up to this point I have been accustomed just to deal with and interpret it according to the sense of the rest of Scriptures. For you will judge that none of it must be set forth contrary to manifest Holy Scripture" (*The Licentiate Examination of Heinrich Schmedenstede* [1542], LW 34:17).

h Lat.: *Iudeus effrenis*.

i WA 31/2:433,1.

j On the pope as Antichrist in Luther's thought, see, e.g., Volker Leppin, "Luther on the Devil," SRR 16, no. 2 (2014): 13–27; Brecht 3:357–67; Scott H. Hendrix, *Luther and the Papacy: Stages in a Reformation Conflict* (Philadelphia: Fortress Press, 1981), esp. 150–52. Luther's own final statement on the matter is *Against the Roman Papacy, an Institution of the Devil* (1545), LW 41:263–376).

k Lat.: *Sed publica contencione dicimus opera necesse esse, sed non iustificancia*.

l Lat.: *videns scripturam totam*.

m The phrase is in German: *und hebe sie hoch*.

Only do not attribute justification and the forgiveness of sins to them. We can preach and examine this passage in public, but it is difficult to believe it in private. Because I preserve this article, "Jesus Christ is the Savior," then all of the other articles concerning the Holy Spirit and the church and Scripture are preserved. Thus, Satan attacks no article so much as this one.[27] That person alone is a Christian who believes that Christ labors for us and that he is the lamb of God killed for our sins.[n] When this [article] stands, all monasteries of righteousness, etc., are struck down by a thunderbolt. Read all of the epistles of Paul concerning redemption, salvation, and liberation in a manner that is consistent with this[o] text, because they are derived from this fountain.[p] A blind papacy read and chanted these and similar words as in a dream, but no one really paid attention. If they had, they would have cast off all of their own righteousness from themselves. Therefore it is not enough to know and hold fast to the matter, rather the use and the power of the matter [are also required]. When this is the case, we stand invincible on the royal road, where the Holy Spirit is present against all sects and deceptions. When this doctrine is preserved, we can firmly resist all people, but when it is lost, we proceed from one error to the next, as we see with the babbling Fanatics[q] and Erasmus.[28] Our nature fights against the use and the power of [Christ's] suffering. Both the pope and the Turk believe and preach the matter, but they do not have the use. But as for you, lift up this article and extol it above every law and righteousness, and let it be to you an immense sea over against a little spark. Christ who has suffered is the sea. Your works and righteousness are the little spark. Therefore, when you place your sins on your conscience, take heed not to be frightened, but freely place them on Christ, as this text[r] says, *"He has borne our iniquities."* It is plainly neces-

27. Luther repeatedly emphasizes the centrality of the Second Article of the Creed for his teaching on justification, a teaching which he regarded as non-negotiable: "Nothing in this article [i.e., the article on justification] can be conceded or given up. . . . On this article stands all that we teach and practice against the pope, the devil, and the world" (*Smalcald Articles* [1537], in BC, 301). The distinctiveness of Luther's position can be described as follows: "It was the first time in all the history of theology and dogma that the decisive truth of Christian faith was concentrated in such fashion on one specific article. . . . Prior to the sixteenth century, the doctrine of justification never assumed a significance even remotely comparable to that in Luther" (Lohse, *Martin Luther's Theology*, 259).

28. Desiderius Erasmus of Rotterdam (1466–1536), Catholic priest and leading European humanist. After their literary debate over free will in 1524–1525, Luther rarely, if ever, said anything positive about him. As can be seen here, Luther regularly lumped together various diverse groups and persons, on the grounds that they commit a common fundamental theological error and are thus various expressions of the same kind of religious thought.

n Lat.: *Christianus solus est ille, qui credit Christum laborantem pro nobis et agnum dei pro peccatis nostris occisum.*

o LW 17:223.

p Lat.: *Ad hunc textum lege omnes Pauli epistolas de redempcione, salvacione et liberacione, quae derivantur ex hoc fonte.*

q Lat.: *in blaterantibus Schuermeriis.* The final term is a transliteration of German *Schwärmer.* In his Latin writings, Luther normally uses the term *fanatici.* See *Against the Heavenly Prophets in the Matter of Images and Sacraments*, TAL 2:39–125.

r WA 31/1:434,1.

sary for us to entrust our sins to Christ. If you want to regard your sin as resting on you,[s] then the thought in your heart does not come from God but from Satan himself, contrary to Scripture, which by God's will places it on Christ. Say therefore: "I see my sin on Christ, therefore my sin is not mine but another's. I see it on Christ." It is a great matter to say confidently: "My sin is not mine." However, it is a supreme battle against a most powerful beast, which here becomes most powerful.[29,t] "I observe sins gathered together onto Christ." Thus, a certain hermit who was extremely agitated by Satan but who was unable to evade him, said: "I have not sinned. Everyone should regard their conscience as free." He did not answer well, because he did have sin. This is what he should have said: "My sins have been transferred to Christ; he has them."[u] This is the transplanting of the wild olive into the olive tree.[30] It is not without purpose that [the prophet] uses so many words in this article, because it is necessary for Christians to know that these are their own sins, whatever sins there are, because they have been borne by Christ, by whom we have been redeemed and saved. This is the Savior, etc., from eternity,[v] from death and sin. Thus, by this thunderbolt the law and its righteousness[w] are struck down, just as you see Paul treat the issue in great detail.

Something further must be noted, lest those despair who do not feel this. There Satan can turn the antidote into poison and hope into despair. For when Christians hear these supreme consolations and then see how weak they are with regard to their faith in them, they soon suppose that they do not pertain to them. In this way Satan is able to turn consolation into confusion.

29. Luther often described the experience of justification in highly existential terms, as a life and death struggle within the believer. See his extended explication of the issue in his interpretation of Gal. 3:23-25 in the *Lectures on Galatians* (1535) LW 26:335–51.

30. The image is drawn from Rom. 11:13-24.

Portrait of Desiderius Erasmus (1526) by Albrecht Dürer

s The phrase is in German: *Wiltu deyne ßunde yn dyr sehen.*

t Lat.: *sed summa pugna contra potentissimam bestiam, quae fit hic potentissima.*

u Lat.: *Mea peccata translata in Christum. Ille haec habet.*

v *Ab eterno* in this context is a possible allusion to Prov. 8:23.

w LW 17:224.

But as for you, however weak you may be, know that you are a Christian, whether you believe perfectly or imperfectly, even while feebleness remains in you—that feeling of death and sin.[31] To such a one it is said: "Friend,[x] your situation is not desperate, but pray with the apostles for the perfection of [your] faith." Paul also labored with this and was anxious. For a Christian is not so much perfect, but rather that one is a Christian who has, that is, who begins to have, the righteousness of God.[32] I say this on account of the weak, so that they might not despair when they feel the bite of sin within themselves. For they should not yet be masters and doctors but rather disciples of Christ, people who learn Christ, not perfect doctors. Let it suffice for us to remain with that word as learners. Therefore, however perfect and absolute the doctrine of Christ is which affirms that all our sins belong to Christ, it is nevertheless not perfect in our life.[y] It is enough for us to have begun and to be reaching out for what is before us. Therefore a Christian human being must be especially vexed in their conscience and heart by Satan, and yet must remain with the word and not seek peace anywhere else than in Christ. It is not necessary to make a tree trunk or a stone out of a Christian, as one who does not feel sin in themselves, in the manner of the exceedingly spiritual Fanatics.[z]

"The[a] discipline of peace."

Peter treats this passage [1 Pet. 2:24]. Christ the person is not a judge and an angry God but rather one who bears and carries our sins, a mediator. Away with the papists, who have set Christ before us as a terrible judge and have turned the saints into intercessors. There they have added fuel[b] to the fire. For by our own nature we are [already] afraid of God. Therefore blessed are those who as uncorrupted young people arrived at this understanding, that they are able to say: "I have only known Jesus Christ as the bearer of my sins." Then the name of Christ is most delight-

31. The paragraph to this point is a description of what Luther elsewhere refers to as the experience of *Anfechtung*. The term is related to but not synonymous with the Latin term *tentatio* ("temptation, trial"). It implies a spiritual assault on the conscience and soul of the believer that places the faith of the believer in extreme doubt. Luther uses the term only rarely in his Bible translation. Interestingly, however, in one text he uses it of Christ himself: "You are the ones who have stayed with me in my *Anfechtungen*" (Luke 22:28). For the basic idea, see *Comfort When Facing Grave Temptations [Anfechtungen]* (1521), LW 42:183–86.

32. The language of "beginning" and "becoming" rather than "being" and "arriving" is characteristic of Luther's thought regarding justification. It is also implicit in Luther's famous formulation of Christian existence as *simul peccator et iustus* ("at the same time sinner and righteous"), which he used for the first time in the *Lectures on Romans* (1515–1516), LW 25:260; cf. *Disputation Concerning Justification*, LW 34:152, 167. See Lohse, *Martin Luther's Theology*, 74–78.

x Lat.: *frater.*

y Lat.: *Ergo quamvis doctrina Christi est perfecta et absoluta, quae omnia nostra peccata Christi esse affirmat, Sed in vita nostra non est perfecta.*

z Lat.: *ut suermerii spiritualissimi sunt*. See n. *q*, p. 360 above.

a WA 31/1:435,1.

b Lat.: *oleum*, literally "olive oil."

ful.[33] "*The discipline,* or chastisement, *of our peace,*" that is, his discipline is the remedy that pacifies our conscience. For prior to Christ there is nothing but confusion.[c] But he was disciplined on account of our peace.[d] Note the wonderful exchange:[34,e] one sins, another pays the penalty; one deserves peace, the other has it. The one who deserves peace has discipline, while the one who deserves discipline has peace. It is an arduous matter to know what Christ is. Would that our Fanatics[f] could perceive this properly.

"And by his bruise we are healed."

See how pleasantly he[g] sets Christ before us. It is a wonderful plaster. His bruises are our healings. The bruises should be ours and the health should be in Christ. Therefore this is what is to be said to a Christian: "If you want to be healed, do not look at your own wounds, but look upon Christ."

[53:6]. "All we like sheep have gone astray."

This is the conclusion and confutation of the preceding. There he calls all our labors and endeavors errors. Christ alone was without sin.[35] All the apostles have attacked the religions and the law itself with this text: "*We all have gone astray.*" By means of their own [rules] and their own way, they want to place our sins on us, saying, "If you will observe these things, you will be free from your sins." Yet he[h] says that "our sins" and the sins "of all" have been gathered together onto that Christ.

"All we like sheep have gone astray."

As I said yesterday:[36] This is the supreme and chief article of faith,[i] that our sins, placed on Christ, are not ours; again, that

33. In the popular piety of the late Middle Ages, the image of Christ as judge was strongly emphasized, while the compassionate, forgiving side of the divine was often focused on the Blessed Virgin Mother. At the heart of Luther's work was the attempt to recover the central image of Christ the bearer of human sins. See *Commentary on the Magnificat* (1521), TAL 4:307–83; LW 21:295–358.

34. The Latin here is functionally equivalent to the phrase used by Luther in the German version of *The Freedom of a Christian* (1520) ("der froelich wechßel und streytt"; "the joyful exchange and struggle" [WA 7:25, 34]). There he develops this traditional Christian idea in the direction of faith as that which binds the soul of the believer to Christ in marriage. See Philip D. W. Krey and Peter D. S. Krey, *Luther's Spirituality*, The Classics of Western Spirituality (New York: Paulist, 2007), 69–70, 75–76.

35. This is a direct allusion to Heb. 4:15, the only explicit statement in the New Testament regarding the sinlessness of Christ.

36. A new lecture begins at this point.

c The Latin term is plural: *turbaciones*.

d LW 17:225.

e Lat.: *Vide mirabilem mutuacionem*.

f Lat.: *nostri suermerii*. See n. *q*, p. 360 above.

g I.e., the prophet.

h I.e., the prophet.

i Lat.: *Iste est summus et maximus fidei articulus*.

the peace is not Christ's but ours. Once this foundation is established, everything that is built upon it will be well. If we do not push against this stone, the other doctrines will not harm us. Satan cannot but attack this article alone by means of tyrants and sects. The whole world can put up with[j] every sectarian doctrine and even support them in peace, but it cannot bear this faith and the rejection of all works and merits. Because self-glory is brought to naught, it likes to hear about its own glory and is, therefore, not willing to reject its own. Summary: The head of self-righteousness must be cut off. I grant that the works of the godly are good and just, but they do not justify.[k] Satan[l] cannot bear this, and on account of this we are persecuted and we suffer to the present day, because we have taught all things in peace, tranquillity, patience, and purity, more than he[m] has, at least. By this text we have overthrown every alien righteousness[n] and hypocrisy.[37] Therefore write this text on the foundation in gold letters or in your own blood. That is why he says "*All we*," and no one is excepted.[38]

"*Each*[o] *one of us all*," because Christ has nothing from us but death and labor (see chap. 43 above),[39] and we have righteousness and life from him.

"And the Lord has placed."

This strengthens our conscience that Christ did not take up our sins by his own will but by the will of the Father who had mercy on us. "*On him*," not on us, contrary to every law and government,[p] where whoever sins is punished. Here, however, we have the punishment of our sins on Christ himself. In public

37. Luther is using the phrase "alien righteousness" here generically and not in the technical sense that he first develops in *Sermon on Two Kinds of Righteousness* (1519), TAL 2:9–24; LW 31:297–306. On the technical usage, see Robert Kolb, "Luther on the Two Kinds of Righteousness: Reflections on His Two-Dimensional Definition of Humanity at the Heart of His Theology," *Lutheran Quarterly* 13, no. 4 (1999): 449–66.

38. Although he does not use the explicit terminology here, this passage for Luther is a central proof-text for the doctrine of original sin, similar in significance to the chief proof-text, Ps. 51:7, which reads in the Luther Bible: "Look, I was begotten from sinful seed, and my mother conceived me in sin" (WA DB 10/1:265b,7). For a programmatic statement from Luther on original sin, see *Confession Concerning Christ's Supper* (1528), LW 37:362–63.

39. At Isa. 43:24, "But [by your sins] you have made me serve," Luther states: "This toil has been shifted to Christ. . . . This, then, is the Christian religion: one has sinned, another has made satisfaction. The sinner does not make satisfaction; the satisfier does not sin. This is an astounding doctrine" (LW 17:99).

j The phrase is in German: *Die gancze weldt kan leyden.*

k Lat.: *Concedo quidem opera piorum esse bona, iusta, sed non iustificancia.*

l WA 31/2:436,1.

m I.e., Satan.

n Lat.: *omnem iusticiam alienam.*

o LW 17:226.

p Lat.: *politia.*

life,[q] however, if anyone sins before the world, let them be punished by the civil authority.[r]

Another Paragraph[s]

[53:7]. "He was offered up because he wanted to be."[40, t]

This is noted and chanted everywhere[41] against the offense of the cross over against Jews and Gentiles who say, "How can he hope to save others when he could not save himself?"[u] For that reason this text responds to this slander: *"Because he himself wanted to be."* This is a good sentiment, but it is different in Hebrew:[v] *"He was beaten and humiliated,"*[w] *yet he opened not his mouth; he was like a lamb."* This text about his suffering is treated by Peter in this way: "When he suffered, he did not resist." [1 Pet. 2:23].

Summary: This paragraph expresses the will and the patience of the suffering Christ, that he does not even think of vengeance. For this is the way for Christians to suffer, that they suffer most patiently without threats and curses, yes, that they even pray for and bless those who do them harm.[x] Therefore, in a most felicitous way, he describes Christ's patience by comparing him to a sheep. This is the force[y] of that crucifixion, that such a Christ will suffer who is described[z] as overflowing in suffering like that of sheep, with his whole heart filled with love.

"Which is led to the sacrifice."

For the sheep that is to be shorn and sacrificed is silent. So Christ, keeping silence, always has compassion on their malice.

q Lat.: *Foris.*
r Lat.: *a magistratu.*
s This heading appeared in Luther's manuscript.
t Lat.: *"Oblatus est, quia ipse voluit."*
u Cf. Matt. 27:42; Mark 15:31; Luke 23:35.
v Lat.: *Bona est sententia, sed in hebreo aliter est.*
w "He was beaten and humiliated" is Luther's direct translation from the Hebrew.
x See Luke 6:27-28.
y Lat.: *epithesis*, from Greek: ἐπίθεσις (*epithesis*).
z With LW 17:226 n.3, emending *describit* to *describitur.*

40. This is a direct quote from the Vulgate, but Jerome's translation, agreeing with neither the Hebrew (MT) nor the Greek text (LXX), manifests strong overtones of the Gospel of John. Luther addresses this issue immediately below.

41. A reference to the Gregorian chant based on this passage: *"Oblatus est quia ipse voluit, et peccata nostra ipse portavit"* ("He was offered up because he wanted to be, and he bore our sins").

Thus, you have Christ undergoing the most disgraceful suffering in his person and yet [undergoing it] with a most patient heart. Having completed the first part, he[a] [now] begins the second one, concerning the resurrection.

[53:8]. "He was taken away from anguish and judgment."[42]

42. The Hebrew phrase מעצר וממשפט לקח (*me-'otzer u-mimmishpaṭ luqqaḥ*) is difficult. Modern critical translations tend to construe the Hebrew prepositions as instrumental, and thus render: "By a perversion of justice (or, 'by oppressive judgment') he was taken away."

Now he begins to deal with his glorification. Look, here he confesses that the one whom[b] he had until now described as a sheep to be killed and whom he had defined as destined for a most repulsive death for the sins of others[c] is to be resurrected. Now he describes him again. He is not dead but taken away from anguish. Here he says: his anguish *"and judgment"* are ended. This cannot be said of a dead person remaining in the grave but of one liberated and resurrected. The text says that he was anguished and in judgment, but has now been taken away from them, hence resurrected.

"Who will explain his generation?"

Who can explain its duration, because his life and duration are eternal? Note the two contrary statements: someone dying and yet enduring eternally. "*Generation*" properly signifies age,[d] time,[e] lifetime.[f] It is a proverbial statement that "a generation goes, and a generation comes, but the earth remains" [Eccl. 1:4]. This must be understood as referring not to generation but to age. Here, then, he places Christ in an eternal age, something that cannot be uttered, namely, that he has been transferred into eternal life.[g] Peter expounds on it in Acts [2:24]: "God raised him up, the pains of death having been loosened, because it was not possible for him to be held by it," and led him into generation, that is, into length [of life] and eternity. For Christ has such

a I.e., the prophet.

b LW 17:227.

c WA 31/1:437,1.

d Lat.: *etatem.*

e Lat.: *seculum.*

f The word is in German: *Manßczeyt.*

g Lat.: *scilicet in vitam eternam transpositum.*

length of life that it cannot be explained. Unless we believe it by faith, eternity is ineffable.[h]

"For he was cut off from the land of the living
on account of the transgressions of my people."

Again[i] he says: when Christ was stricken "*on account of the transgressions of my people.*" Over and over he says "*on account of the sins of my people.*" Let us not simply pass over Christ's suffering; we must always consider its use, that it was on account of our sins. He says that he was separated into another life,[j] something no one understands from the perspective of this life. Therefore the Jews are in error when they hope that he[k] will reign in this life. No, in this life he served, preached, suffered, and then he passed from [this] world to another place.[l]

"*From the land of the living,*" from this time where we live. Through this suffering he was transferred from a mortal life to an immortal one.[m]

[53:9]. "And he will make the godless for his grave."[43,n]

If the Jews and we, in our weakness, should still be in doubt about Christ having suffered, the following proves it even more, as if to say, "He[o] not only died, but he was also buried." "*His grave will be made with the godless and with a rich person in his death.*" It is clearly evident that Christ was buried and dead. The Jews propose "lifted up" instead of "buried." Here, however, the text clearly states that he was buried. No one is said to be buried unless they are dead, and so he was buried as a godless person. Thus, this text refutes the slanders which deny that Christ died,[44] and it is a confirmation of our faith.

43. The Latin is a highly literalistic translation of the Hebrew. Luther clarifies below. The translation in Luther's German Bible is: "And he was buried like the godless and died like a rich person."

44. An allusion to various forms of Docetism, an early Christian teaching, subsequently identified as heretical and condemned, that Christ only seemed to suffer and die.

h Lat.: *Nam nisi fide credamus, eternitas est ineffabilis.*
i The phrase is in German: *Aber mal.*
j Lat.: *Dicit eum separatum in aliam vitam.*
k I.e., the Messiah.
l Lat.: *et deinde ex mundo transivit in alium locum.*
m Lat.: *Per hanc passionem translatus de mortali vita ad immortalem.*
n Lat.: "*Et dabit impios pro sepulture.*"
o LW 17:228.

We will now examine the grammar. [We are dealing with] a Hebraism. In Scripture "rich person" is used for "godless" as a kind of trope or figure, because it frequently happens that the rich of [this] world[p] are godless and their riches are often used for godless purposes. Therefore he says here that he died like a godless person and was buried like a rich person, just as the gospel states that he was done away with for being seditious and was buried along with this name and disgrace. The Jews, who might contend here against Christ being a king, cannot quibble, since he was to die in this way according to Scripture.[45]

45. A reference to 1 Cor. 15:3: "that Christ died for our sins according to the Scriptures."

"Although he had done wrong to no one, and there was never any deceit in his mouth." The most innocent Christ was judged by the Jews to be the most guilty, one who was most innocent and guiltless in doctrine and in life. They had not a word to say to him.[q] Although he was innocent, yet the Lord willed that he should submit to being the most criminal of all human beings. Therefore he compares him to all other human beings, who, even though they be very holy, are guilty. This single Christ is the exception, who alone is righteous and holy. For that reason death could not hold him.

Another Paragraph[r]

[53:10]. "If he gave his soul as the measure."

You now have the suffering person, described in terms of suffering and resurrection. Now he describes the fruit of his suffering, and this is its fruit, that he will have a succeeding kingdom according to the statement: "He sits at the right hand of the Father, whence he will come."[46] *"If he gave his soul,"* that is, he himself gave his own life as a sacrifice for transgression. "Transgression" is properly called "guilt" in Ps. 32[:5].[s] "And they will not commit offense" [Ps. 34:23].[t] "To commit offense" properly means that someone has done something and continues to be

46. A direct quotation from the conclusion to the Second Article of the Apostles' Creed.

p WA 31/2:438,1.

q The phrase is in German: *Man hat nicht eyn wortleyn zw yhm gehat.*

r This heading appeared in Luther's original manuscript.

s The term *reatus* ("guilt") does not actually occur in this passage.

t This phrase is not recognized as a direct biblical quote in WA 31/2:438,20.

guilty.[u] Thus, we are unable to erase our guilt. Therefore only Christ [can do it].

Because, therefore, *"he gave his soul for transgression,"* it follows that *"he will see [his] seed, he will be prolonged,"* etc. Thus, he wants to say: "We hope that the Messiah, of whom you say that he is dead, will be the completely invincible king." And we say to them: "A king both ancient and eternal marches out, and he will see his seed for a long time. None of your kings will forever and eternally see their seed, as he will." For a king of the world does not see his seed for a long time. In fact, when he dies, he leaves them behind. Here you see what *"the will of the Lord"* is. The Lord placed all our iniquities upon him, liberating us from death and giving us eternal life. This is *"the will of God."*

[53:11]. "[For] this, for which his soul labored."

So far he has expressed more about his soul being in labor, in misfortune.[v] Thus, he must receive his reward. Thus, *"he will see and be satisfied."* He will see his delight[w] in all things and have a full measure of pleasures. Everything will go just as he wants it.[x]

"By his knowledge he will justify."[y]

As to the means by which the course of the kingdom[z] will proceed, how will this king be propagated? This will be the means: *"Through his knowledge."*[a] This is a very beautiful text. *"Through the knowing of him*[47] *he will justify many, because [he will bear] their iniquities."* Those who acknowledge that their sins have been borne by him are righteous. The definition of righteousness is wonderful. The sophists[b] say that righteousness is the fixed will of one rendering to each their own. But here he says that righteousness

47. Lat.: *"Ipse per noticiam sui."* Through a suble translational shift, Luther is bringing out the distinction between "Christ's knowledge" (a subjective genitive) and "knowing Christ" (an objective genitive).

u LW 17:229.

v The phrase is in German: *ym unglug.*

w The phrase is in German: *Er sol seyn lust sehen.*

x The sentence is in German: *Es wyrt ym noch allem seynem wyllen gehen.*

y Lat.: *"In sciencia sua iustificabit."*

z WA 31/2:439,1.

a Lat.: *"Per scienciam suam."*

b Lat.: *Zophistae.* The term is commonly used by Luther to refer to Scholastic theologians.

is the knowledge of Christ, who bears our iniquities.[c] Therefore whoever will know and believe [in] Christ as the one bearing their sins will be righteous.

"Many servants."

Thus, the gospel is the means or vehicle through which the knowledge of God[d] comes to us. Therefore the kingdom of Christ does not consist in works or endeavors, because no rule and no law, not even Mosaic law, can lead us to that knowledge, but we come to it by means of the gospel. For a Christian cannot come to this knowledge by means of laws, either moral or civil, but must ascend to heaven through the gospel. Thus, he says here, "*through the knowledge of him.*"[e] There is no other method[f] or means of [obtaining] liberty than the knowledge of Christ. Thus, Peter and Paul always say that we must increase in this knowledge,[g] because we can never be perfect in it.[h] The knowledge of Christ is to be taken passively, as that by which he is known, namely, by the preaching of his suffering and death.[48,i] Therefore note this new definition of righteousness. Righteousness is the knowledge of Christ.[j] What is Christ? He is the person who bears all our sins. These are indescribable gifts and hidden and ineffable kinds of wisdom.

We have heard[49] this remarkable passage "*by his knowledge*" and "*iniquities.*" I have said that the individual words must be examined in supreme faith, and they must be read and considered with the most watchful eyes, so that it is not simply any kind of knowledge or knowing but a justifying knowledge, in opposition to other kinds of knowledge. Thus, you see this wonderful definition of righteousness through the knowledge

48. The interpretation of the "knowledge of Christ" and the "righteousness of God" in terms of passivity on the part of the believer is one of Luther's most seminal teachings. See esp. *Lectures on Romans* (1515–1516), LW 25:8–9; 32; 151–53; *Lectures on Isaiah* (1528–1530), LW 17:176; *Lectures on Galatians* (1535), LW 26:4–12; *Preface to the Complete Edition of Luther's Latin Writings* (1545), TAL 4:500–502; LW 34:336–38.

49. A new lecture begins at this point.

c Lat.: *Hic dicit iusticiam esse cognicionem Christi portantis iniquitates nostras.*

d Lat.: *cognicio dei.*

e Lat.: "*per cognicionem sui.*"

f Lat.: *ratio.*

g LW 17:230.

h See 2 Pet. 3:18; Col. 1:10.

i Lat.: *Sciencia Christi passive sumenda, qua ipse cognoscitur, scilicet praedicacione passionis et mortis eius.*

j Lat.: *Iusticia est cognicio Christi.*

of God. It sounds ridiculous[k] to call[l] righteousness a speculative knowledge. Thus, it is said in Jer. 9[:24]: "But let them glory [in this], that they know me." Therefore this knowledge is the formal and substantial righteousness of Christians, [that is,] faith in Christ, which I apprehend through the word. I indeed apprehend the word by the intellect, but to assent to that word is the work of the Holy Spirit."[m] It is not the work of reason, which always seeks its own kinds of righteousness. The word, however, sets forth another righteousness through the reckoning and the promises of Scripture, which cause this faith to be reckoned for righteousness.[n] This is our glory that we know with certainty that our righteousness is divine, in that God does not reckon our sins. Therefore our righteousness is nothing else than God's reckoning. Let the Christian who has been persuaded by these words cling firmly[o] to them, and not be deceived by any pretense of works[p] or by one's own suffering, but rather say: It is written that the knowledge of God is our righteousness, and therefore no monk, no celibate, etc., is justified.

"And he bore their iniquities."

Here he repeats, as it were, the foundation. For to receive Christ is righteousness.[q] The other part is, Who is Christ? He answers: "Christ is not a judge, a tormentor, or a tyrant, as reason apart from the word fashions him, but he is the bearer of our iniquities." Yet he will become a judge and a tyrant to those who

Jesus is flogged in this woodcut published in a 1537 volume of homilies by Johann Eck.

k The phrase is in German: *Es lauth lecherlich.*

l With WA 31/2:439 n.2, reading *appellari* for *appellacionem.*

m Lat.: *Est ergo formalis et substancialis iusticia Christianorum ipsa cognicio, fides in Christum, quam apprehendo per verbum. Verbum apprehendo quidem intellectu, sed assentiri illi verbo est opus spiritus sancti.*

n Variations of the Latin verb *reputare* have been translated consistently with forms of "to reckon" in order to bring out the linkage that Luther is making with Gen. 15:6: "[Abram] believed the LORD, and it was reckoned to him as righteousness."

o WA 31/2:440,1.

p Lat.: *alio fuco operum.*

q Lat.: *Nam ferre Christum est iusticia.* The verb *ferre* literally means "to bear or carry," but the idea of a Christian bearing Christ seems clearly out of place here. Thus, a secondary meaning of the verb—"to get, obtain, acquire, receive"—has been adopted.

50. A reference to the final judgment.

refused to believe in him.[50] It is, however, the[r] office of Christ to bear our sins. Therefore we must conclude from this text: "If Christ bears my iniquities, then I do not bear them." And all doctrines which teach that our sins must be borne by us are godless. Thus, from such a text innumerable thunderbolts have come forth against godless self-righteousness. Thus, Paul by this article of justification struck down every kind of self-righteousness. Therefore we must diligently [observe][s] this article. For I see that very many snorers treat this article. They are the ones who consider these words as though looking at their face in a mirror (as

The Last Judgment in the Sistine Chapel (completed 1541) by Michelangelo

r LW 17:231.

s The Weimar text has an incomplete sentence.

James says [1:23-24]). When they soon come upon another object or obligation,[t] they are overwhelmed, and they forget the grace of God. Thus, you must consider this article most diligently and not be seduced by other doctrines, difficulties,[u] or persecutions.

[53:12]. "Therefore I will distribute very much to him, and I will divide the spoils of the mighty and strong ones."

Here he repeats as if by an exclamation.[v] Since "*he handed over his soul in death*" and was not simply dead but "*he was reckoned with the criminals*," in these words he repeats the suffering of Christ. Here he says: "*He handed over . . . to death.*" With that battering ram he hammers the stubbornness of the Jews,[w] who refuse to hear about that Christ who dies but who expect rather an immortal Christ. Here he describes the manner of his death in a very simple and expressive way. He says he will die and then points with his fingers, "*He will be reckoned with the worst*," as if to say, "You Jews want to acknowledge your Christ. He will appear in such a form that he will die the most contemptible death between robbers." The Jews refused to see this text, because they expect a glorious Christ before they would believe in a crucified one.[51] This is the way it happens to us who are blind, but let us all the more believe [in] the crucified one.

"Yet he [bore] the sins of many."

He has described [his] death. Now he delineates the efficacy and power of his sufferings. He says, "He did not die in vain, but all the promises of Scripture are completed,[x] and all our sins have been taken away. He did not labor in vain by his death, but [he labored] to fulfill the promises[y] and liberate us.

51. A recurring polemic in the *Lectures on Isaiah* is that Jews habitually construe the Messiah in a this-worldly, triumphant manner, e.g., "They look for a stately and triumphant king, surrounded by a countless army of fighting angels" (LW 17:192); "This is very clear in opposition to the Jews, who are hoping for a Christ who will reign and rule over a worldly empire" (LW 17:330); "And this is a clear passage in opposition to the boasting of the Jews that the Messiah should walk in splendor" (LW 17:333); etc.

t Lat.: *officium*.

u Lat.: *negociis*.

v Lat.: *epiphonema*, from Greek: ἐπιφώνημα.

w Lat.: *pertinaciam Iudeorum*.

x Lat.: *absolutae*.

y Lat.: *pro absolvendis promissionibus*.

Fourth:[z] *"And he interceded for the transgressors."* There he commends[a] his patience to us. He was sincerely glad to do it.[b] First he describes the suffering, second, the kind of suffering, third, the efficacy of the suffering, and fourth, his patience. Thus, he compassionately prayed for transgressors and crucifiers and wept for them, and he did not deal with them with threats. Who can place the Christ thus depicted in love into their heart, as he is here described? Oh, we would be such blessed people[c] if we could thus believe this most noble text, which must be magnified.[d] I would wish it to be celebrated in the church, so that we might accustom ourselves to an alert investigation of it, that we might conceive of Christ as none other than the one who bears and shoulders the burden of our sins. This figure is a solace to the afflicted, but to snoring readers they are nothing but empty words.

z WA 31/2:441,1.

a LW 17:232.

b The phrase is in German: *Er hats von herczen gerne gethan.*

c The phrase is in German: *O wyr weren ßelige lewthe.*

d The phrase is in German: *der do gros werden sol.*

Preface to Daniel

1530

EUAN K. CAMERON

INTRODUCTION

Martin Luther's prefaces to books of the Bible played a vital role in his presentation of the Scriptures to the German people in their own language. At the very beginning of his New Testament preface of 1522 Luther wrote that he had wished to send the Scriptures out unadorned, but so many erroneous interpretations were around that explanatory prefaces were needed for ordinary people.[a] Yet the prefaces were vastly different one from another. Some were just brief summaries of the book concerned. The preface prepared for Romans[b] presented a virtual synopsis of Luther's core theological claims. The preface to Daniel, first issued in 1530, offered a vision of God's work in history through the exegesis of a supposedly prophetic text.

After racing through the New Testament, the Pentateuch, the historical books, and some of the poetic books of Hebrew Scripture between 1522 and 1524, Luther rather stalled over translating the prophets (not surprisingly, given his many other concerns in the later 1520s). He began to issue the prophetic books in installments (Isaiah, for instance, appeared in 1528)

a WA DB 6/2; LW 35:357; this volume, p. 416.

b See this volume, pp. 457–79.

until the complete edition of the prophetic books appeared in 1532. As part of this process Luther published *The Prophet Daniel in German* as a separate pamphlet in 1530. It was treated as a separate work, and supplied with a dedication to Johann Friedrich of Saxony (1503–1554).[c] Annexed to this translation was the first version of the preface, which is here edited. In subsequent versions (1541, and then 1545), this preface would be considerably expanded with further chronological calculations and ever-fiercer anti-papal rhetoric. The definitive edition of the Daniel prefaces, with parallel texts allowing comparison of the different editions and an exhaustive critical apparatus, was published in the WA Deutsche Bibel series.[d] This edition appeared in 1960 and could not be taken into account in the corresponding volume 35 of the LW edition, which also appeared in 1960. This annotated version of the preface incorporates (much abridged) highlights of the exhaustive apparatus in WA DB.

It is not easy to re-create for modern readers just how important the book of Daniel was to medieval and early modern religious thought. At present, biblical scholars regard it as a very late, fragmented, mostly postexilic combination of miracle stories and poetic visions, combined with a coded narrative of the wars of the Seleucids and the Ptolemies in late antiquity. In the Tanakh it belongs with the "writings" (*Ketuvim*: כְּתוּבִים, "Writings") rather than the prophetic books (*Nevi'im*: נְבִיאִים, "Prophets"). Most scholars would agree that the last six chapters (at least) date from around the same time as the book of Maccabees in the second century BCE and describe retrospectively the events that they "foretell."[e] The book was viewed very differently in Luther's time. Thanks in part to the early Christian exegetical tradition, Daniel was believed to be an authentically prophetic writing that foretold historical events in exceptional detail. It was used as a key for understanding world history. In particular, one passage (9:24-27) was believed to present a specific foretelling of the time of the coming of the Messiah that related directly to the ministry of Jesus. For many commentators, including

c Martin Luther, *Der Prophet Daniel Deudsch* (Wittenberg: Hans Lufft, 1530).

d WA DB 11/2:2–131.

e James L. Kugel, *How to Read the Bible: A Guide to Scripture, Then and Now* (New York: Free Press, 2007), 650–59; John J. Collins, *Introduction to the Hebrew Bible* (Minneapolis: Fortress Press, 2004), 553–80.

Luther, it also contained a message of comfort for the future, reassuring Christians that God was in control of the continuing process of world history.

The context in which Luther wrote this preface was vitally important. The Ottoman Empire had embarked on a campaign of expansion both on land in east-central Europe and at sea in the Mediterranean. In the decisive battle of Mohács (29 August 1526), Suleiman I (1494–1566) defeated the Hungarian and allied armies and inaugurated an era in which Hungary and the Balkans would constitute a frontier zone fought over by Turks and Habsburgs for nearly two centuries. By 1529, the Ottomans were besieging Vienna, and the city could potentially have fallen. In this climate Luther wrote his fervent and in places apocalyptic pamphlet *On War against the Turk*.[f] Already in 1527, Philip Melanchthon (1497–1560) had seen the advance of the Turks as fulfilling the prophecies of Daniel: he and Justus Jonas (1493–1555) would work on the text before Luther did.[g] In 1530, Luther would revise his preface to Revelation, applying it to the events of his own time.[h]

This Turkish sixteenth-century miniature painting by an unknown artist depicts a duel before the Battle of Mohács.

So the preface of Daniel was written in the light of what Luther saw as an increasingly polarized cosmic struggle between the forces of the gospel and the forces of Antichrist. The text, therefore, was to be read for its spiritual comfort and the divine promises contained in it. Luther affirmed that the preface was intended for the "simple, who do not know and cannot read history." The preface presented, on the face of it, a simple chapter-by-chapter synopsis of the contents of the book. However, Luther distributed his attention very unevenly, and intentionally so. He spent most of his time expounding on five distinct passages in Daniel: the famous vision of the statue of descending qualities of material in Nebuchadnezzar's dream, in chapter 2; the vision of the four

f See TAL 5:335–89; LW 46:155–204; WA 30/2:160–97.

g WA DB 11/2:xxvi–xl.

h WA DB 7:406–21; LW 35:399–411.

beasts in Daniel's vision in chapter 7 (which was interpreted to make essentially the same point); the historical prophecies of the battles between the Hellenistic rulers in chapter 8; the prophecy of the coming of the Messiah after "seventy weeks" in chapter 9 (vv. 24-27); and the very detailed coded history of the intrigues and warfare of the Seleucid and Ptolemaic kingdoms in chapter 11.

Conversely, Luther showed remarkably little interest—at least as far as the preface was concerned—in some of the miraculous stories and even some of the mysterious prophecies that would preoccupy later exegetes. He does not analyze the miracle in chapter 1, where Daniel and his companions were shown to be in perfect health despite eating their choice of simple food rather than the luxuries of the Babylonians (1:5-15). He passes quickly over the deliverance of the three young men from the fiery furnace (3:19-30) and even Daniel's survival in the den of lions in the time of Darius (6:6-24). The mysterious reference to "time, times, and half a time" in 12:7[i] is passed over without comment. Luther was writing a preface, not a commentary, so was, of course, under no obligation to discuss these elements.

Luther's choices suggest that he viewed Daniel as valuable for its pastoral lessons, at least as far as the ordinary readers were concerned. When Jewish people were suffering military defeat and living in exile, God comforted them with superior wisdom, and brought them to places of honor. The elevation of Daniel demonstrated God's favor in an outstanding way: "Behold how God is able to console and to honor his captive Jews, by taking the son of a townsman from destroyed Jerusalem and making him a twofold emperor, in Babylon and Persia."[j] Moreover, Luther regarded the prophecies of Daniel as some of the most positive and specific foretellings of Jesus Christ in the whole of the Old Testament. The text had a particular value in confuting rabbinic claims that the Messiah was not yet come. In 1541, Luther would place considerable weight on this prophecy in his chronological table, *Supputation of the Years of the World*.[k] In his later writings on Judaism, Luther would return again and again to the foretellings of the Messiah in Daniel 9 as testimonies to Jesus that were so

i Vulgate: "*in tempus, et tempora, et dimidium temporis*."

j See p. 409 below.

k See WA 53:1-184.

clear that (he argued) only the utterly obstinate could fail to see them.[l] Finally, Luther returned again and again to God's judgment on tyrants. For someone so casually denounced for selling out to princes, Luther would write repeatedly that God meted out exemplary punishments to those who governed badly.

Portrait of Johann Carion by Lucas Cranach the Elder (c. 1530)

Almost uniquely of Luther's Bible prefaces, Luther's preface to Daniel requires some investigation of its sources and intellectual context.[m] It was not a freely or spontaneously written piece: rather, it displays some care in the selection of sources. First, it appears likely that Luther was heavily influenced by the researches into world history being conducted by Philip Melanchthon and his friends, especially the astrologer-turned-historian Johann Carion (d. 1537), whose German *Chronica* would first appear in 1531, and would later receive a thorough rewriting in Latin from Melanchthon and Caspar Peucer (1525–1602).[n] In certain details Luther followed the views of the Melanchthon-Carion group against the opinions of earlier writers (for example, in the debates over the "second year of Longimanus"). However, Luther also researched and drew selectively from a range of antique and medieval sources, which be blended into a personal synthesis. First, Luther used the book of Maccabees (which he would issue in translation in 1533) as a source for the Maccabean revolt against Antiochus IV (d. 164 BCE). Second, Luther used Jerome's (c. 347–419) commentary, the fullest and most widely used commentary on Daniel from Christian antiquity.[o] He also drew upon Nicholas of Lyra's (c. 1270–1349) postils on Daniel for many details—including the family tree of the Seleucids and Ptolemies that he included in the preface—though he modified

l See Luther's texts on Judaism in TAL 5, especially 429–36, 533–58, 659–63; see also, e.g., LW 47:246.

m WA DB 11/2:xlii.

n [Johannes Carion], *Chronica, durch Magistrum Johan Carion, vleissig zusamen gezogen, meniglich nützlich zu lesen* (Wittenberg: Rhaw, 1531) (further editions in 1533 and subsequently); [Johannes Carion, ed. Philip Melanchthon and Caspar Peucer], *Chronicon Carionis expositum et auctum multis et veteribus et recentibus historiis . . . ab exordio mundi usque ad Carolum Quintum imperatorem, a Philippo Melanthone et Casparo Peucero: Adjecta est narratio historica de electione et coronatione Caroli V imperatoris . . .* (Wittenberg: J. Crato, 1572).

o [St. Jerome], *Jerome's Commentary on Daniel*, trans. Gleason L. Archer Jr. (Grand Rapids: Baker, 1958).

Lyra's material in multiple ways.[p] For the theme of the "translation of the empire" from the Greeks to the Romans, and from the Romans to the Franks and Germans, Luther probably drew on the twelfth-century bishop and historian Otto of Freising (c. 1114–1158), whose work had been edited some fifteen years earlier by Johannes Cuspinian (1473–1529).[q] It is also possible that Luther may have made some use of the chronological forgeries of Annius of Viterbo (c. 1432–1502), which purported to provide evidence linking biblical to classical chronology and which were taken seriously in Wittenberg at this time.[r]

Daniel's dream of the four beasts: a lion with wings, a bear, a leopard with wings and four heads, and a beast with ten horns and one eye. Note that an army is amassed on the border of Asia and Europe. The woodcuts in this 1533 printing of the Luther Bible are the work of the German artist Erhard Altdorfer (d. 1561).

The impact of Luther's preface was considerable. Even the illustrations in the 1530 edition—showing the statue of Nebuchadnezzar's dream and a schematic world map with the symbolic beasts of Daniel 7 (known subsequently as "Daniel's Dream Map")—would be endlessly imitated and copied through multiple editions of the Luther Bible. In the following decades nearly every major reformer would prepare an extensive and detailed commentary on the book of Daniel from both a historical and pastoral-theological perspective. The most important for the Lutheran church would be

p For an example of an edition of Lyra available to Luther, see *Textus biblie cum glosa ordinaria: Nicolai de Lyra postilla, moralitatibus eiusdem, Pauli Burgensis additionibus, Matthie Thoring replicis*, ed. Conradus Leontorius, 7 vols. (Basel: Johannes Petri et Johannes Frobenius, 1506–1508).

q Otto, Bishop of Freising, *Ottonis Phrisingensis Episcopi, viri clarissimi, Rerum ab origine mundi ad ipsius usque tempora gestarum libri octo*, ed. Johannes Cuspinianus (Strassburg: Matthias Schürer, 1515).

r On Annius and the debates around him see, e.g., Anthony Grafton, *Forgers and Critics* (Princeton: Princeton University Press, 1990), and several other works by the same author.

Philip Melanchthon's commentary, issued in 1543.[s] To a degree that is hard to imagine now outside fringe apocalyptic Protestantism, the book of Daniel gave the churches of the Reformation comfort that God was in control of history, and that the purposes of salvation were being worked out in and through history, despite all evidence to the contrary. Daniel, as understood in the Reformation, fused salvation history, apocalyptic, and the visions of Antichrist in a way that helped embattled Lutherans and reformed Protestants to see their predicament in biblical terms.

This revision of the text in LW 35:294–316 takes into account the 1530 printed edition and also the text in WA DB 11/2:2–130. The WA DB edition offers parallel texts of all the different versions of this preface, which grew greatly through revisions in 1541 and 1545. At the urging of Georg Rörer (1492–1557), Luther prepared early in 1541 an extensive polemical commentary on Daniel 12, which in the 1541 edition of the complete Bible he then appended to his 1530 preface.[t] These additions are omitted here.

s Philip Melanchthon, *In Danielem Prophetam Commentarius* (Leipzig: Nicolaus Wolrab, 1543); important commentaries on Daniel were also published by Joannes Oecolampadius (1482–1531), Heinrich Bullinger (1504–1575), and John Calvin (1509–1564).

t WA DB 6/2:lxxxix.

PREFACE TO DANIEL[u]

IN THIS PREFACE I desire to provide a short instruction on this book of St. Daniel in order that the simple people and those who do not know and cannot read the histories may nevertheless get the gist of its meaning. Before proceeding, let me point out that Daniel came to Babylon some years before the destruction of Jerusalem, during the reign of King Jehoiakim. King Nebuchadnezzar had had Jehoiakim captured and bound, and would have brought him to Babylon, too, had he not changed his mind and let him remain. As it was, Nebuchadnezzar brought some of the best people back with him (including Daniel) as well as vessels from the temple in Jerusalem. We can read all about this in 2 Kings 24, and in 2 Chronicles 36.[v]

The first chapter brings us a fine example from Daniel's life. We see how holy, how God-fearing, and how possessed he was of a great and noble faith in God;[1] and all this in the very midst of the wild and pagan life and the abominable offenses which he had to listen to and look upon every day at Babylon. In spite of it all, he remained firm and steadfast, and conquered all these temptations in his heart. For this reason there follows almost immediately [the account of] how God showed him great mercy, first highly honoring him in things of the spirit by granting him wisdom and understanding beyond that of other men, and then //[w] by elevating him also in worldly affairs and doing nothing but great and mighty deeds and miracles through him. God did this to show us all how much he loves and cherishes those who fear and trust in him; with such an impressive example he prods us in a kindly way to faith and the fear of God.

1. Faith is a theme that runs through multiple Reformation commentaries on Daniel, especially Melanchthon's commentary (1543; see n.18, pp. 98–100, also 152–64). It is remarkable, however, that Luther says nothing about the miracle in chapter 1, where the Israelites were made to appear healthier than others despite eating simple food and rejecting the Babylonians' food. A focus on food taboos would have been entirely unhelpful for Luther given his objection to Catholic food restrictions; so here he steers the point of the story away from the details of food choices to the more comfortable issue of faith and trust in God.

u WA DB 11/2:2–3; *Der Prophet Daniel Deudsch* (1530), sig. Bi r.

v Cf. Dan. 1:20.

w *Der Prophet Daniel Deudsch* (1530), sig. Bi v. For ease of comparison between the different editions of the text, this symbol (//) indicates where a new page begins in the Weimar Deutsche Bible edition, also in the original first edition of the preface published separately in 1530.

In the second chapter the honoring of Daniel begins; it is occasioned by the king's dream which Daniel, with the help of divine revelation, discerns and interprets. As a result, Daniel becomes a ruler of the entire Babylonian realm and a bishop or chief prefect over all the priests and learned men. This takes place also for the comforting of the whole Jewish community, that despite their wretched condition they should neither despair //[x] nor grow impatient, as if God had abandoned them or withdrawn his promise of Christ. This is why a captured Jew must rule in such a great kingdom, while no Babylonian can enjoy similar honor. It is just as though Daniel had been led away captive for the express purpose of being made a great ruler, even over those who had captured him and were now holding him.[2] So wondrously does God lead his faithful ones; he bestows upon them far more than anyone could wish.

2. The theme of divine providence runs through the Reformation concept of history and the Reformation understanding of God's actions in general.

Nebuchadnezzar had a dream of a great statue (Daniel 2), which the king ordered Daniel to interpret. The woodcuts in this 1533 printing of the Luther Bible are the work of the German artist Erhard Altdorfer (d. 1561). The Altdorfer version of the world map (p. 380) and this image both rework the original versions found in in the first edition of Luther's translation of Daniel, from 1530.

x WA DB 11/2:4,5.

The dream, however, and the image are clearly interpreted in the text by Daniel himself in terms of the four kingdoms. The first kingdom is that of the Assyrians or Babylonians; the second, that of the Medes and Persians; the third, that of Alexander the Great and the Greeks; the fourth, that of the Romans. Everyone agrees on this view and interpretation; //[y] subsequent events and the histories prove it conclusively.[3] Daniel has most to say about the Roman Empire. Therefore we must pay close attention. At the end [2:41-45], where the iron legs begin to divide into the toes of the feet, Daniel points out three things about the Roman Empire.[z]

The first is that the toes are divided, although they retain their origin in the iron foot.[4] Just as in the human body the toes separate while projecting from and belonging to the foot, so also was the Roman Empire split, as Spain, France, England, and other parts came out of it. Nevertheless it has continued to grow and, like a plant, has been transplanted or (as they say) transferred [*translatum*] from the Greeks to the Germans.[5] Yet this has occurred in such a way that its nature as iron was retained, for the empire still has its estates, offices, laws, and statutes as of old. Therefore Daniel says here that even though it will be a divided kingdom the root, plant, or trunk of iron will nevertheless be in it.

The second thing—that these divided toes are dissimilar, partly iron and partly clay—Daniel himself interprets in terms of this divided kingdom: now it is mighty, now weak. This, too, has come to pass. Often there have been numerous brave emper-

3. This interpretation of the four parts of the statue as representing the four monarchies of the Assyrians/Babylonians, the Medes/Persians, the Hellenistic kingdoms, and the Romans was made popular by Jerome's commentary on Daniel as it relates to 2:31-43; see Jerome's commentary edited by Gleason Archer (see n. *o*, p. 379 above). This interpretation of the vision was nearly universal in Luther's time, though later in the sixteenth century other readings of the vision would emerge.

4. This passage does not follow Jerome, and appears to be Luther's own interpretation. The division of the Roman Empire into separate kingdoms, of course, occurred long after Jerome's time. Melanchthon's 1543 commentary (27) reads the division of the statue's feet in the same way.

5. This concept of *translatio imperii* was articulated most fully in the Middle Ages by Otto of Freising, whose histories were re-edited in Luther's lifetime and would have been known to him. See Otto, Bishop of Freising, *The Two Cities: A Chronicle of Universal History to the Year 1146 A.D.*, trans. Charles Christopher Mierow, ed. Austin P. Evans and Charles Knapp (New York: Octagon Books, 1966), 94, 114, 117, 353.

y *Der Prophet Daniel Deudsch* (1530), sig. Bii r.

z For this section compare Jerome's commentary on 2:41-45.

ors like Charlemagne,[6] the three Ottos,[7] and others, //[a] who were //[b] unconquerable; and in turn there have often been weak and unfortunate emperors who were frequently defeated. All this is said, however, in order that we might know that the Roman

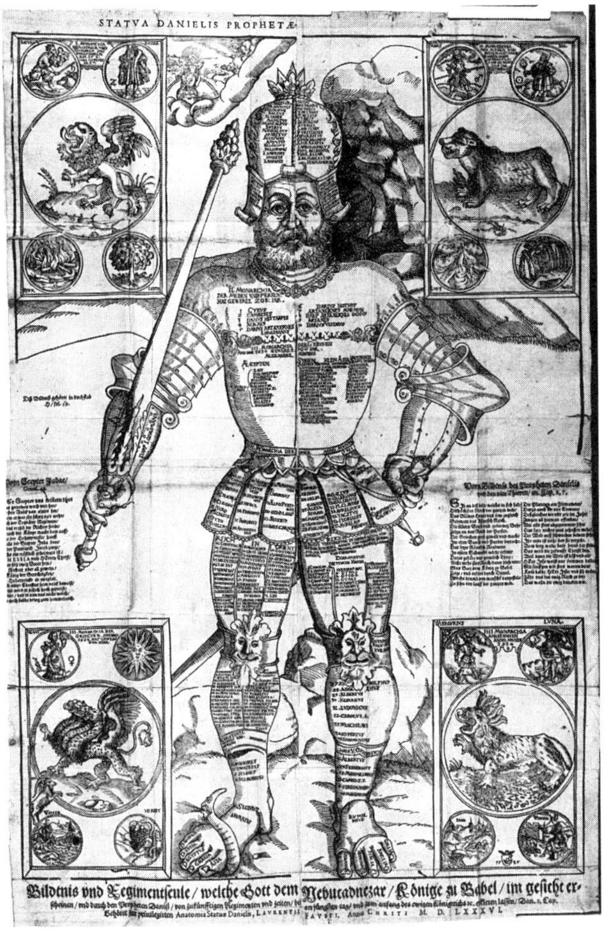

Woodcut of the statue described by the prophet Daniel, from Lorenz Faust's *Anatomia statuae Danielis* ("An anatomy of Daniel's statue," Leipzig: Johann Steinman, 1585)

6. Charlemagne (c. 747–814), also known as Charles I, was king of the Franks, king of the Lombards. His "imperial" coronation in 800 began the process by which the German lands became known as the "Holy Roman Empire of the German Nation," though Charlemagne's collection of territories disintegrated soon after his death. Again, this reflection on strong and weak emperors is probably original to Luther.

7. Luther refers to Otto I, "the Great" (r. 936–973); Otto II (r. 973–983); Otto III (r. 983–1002).

a WA DB 11/2:6,7.

b *Der Prophet Daniel Deudsch* (1530), sig. Bii^{v}.

Empire is to be the last, and that no one will be able to destroy it save Christ alone and his kingdom. Therefore, even though many monarchs may have risen against the German Empire and the Turks may rage against it, and even though all such enemies may perhaps win an occasional battle, they are nevertheless unable to conquer an iron root or plant like this, or to destroy it.[c] It must remain until the last day, no matter how weak it may be. For Daniel does not lie, and up until now experience—with respect to both the popes themselves and the kings—has borne this out.

The third thing—that such divided and dissimilar toes are mixed or interchanged—Daniel himself interprets in terms of this weak kingdom seeking strength and support by means of alliances and intermarriages here and there among other kings.[8] But this will not help, neither will it secure peace and concord. If the kingdom is to endure, it must find its strength and victory in God's providence alone.

8. This observation presumably refers to Dan. 2:43.

The mountain, from which the stone is cut without human hands [2:45], is interpreted by some as signifying the blessed Virgin Mary, from whom Christ was born without human cooperation. This is not an un-Christian interpretation. Yet it may also be that the mountain signifies the whole Jewish people from whom Christ //[d] sprang. He is their flesh and blood but has been torn from them and has come among the Gentiles. Among the Gentiles he has become a Lord in all the world—in all four of these kingdoms—and will so remain.

In the third chapter Daniel again records a great miracle of faith. There the three men are preserved in the fiery furnace, so that God is confessed and praised by the king [Nebuchadnezzar] throughout the entire realm, even in writing.[9] This, too, happened for the consolation of the Jews who, along with their God, were despised nobodies at Babylon under the tyrants and false gods. But now their God is highly honored above all gods, in order that they may firmly believe that at the proper time he can and will indeed save them, and meanwhile hold fast to and console themselves with this honor he receives and this miracle he performs. //[e]

9. Luther's discussion of this theme in the preface is far less extensive than that of Jerome, who served as one of Luther's sources. Luther was really not much interested in the miraculous aspects of the story.

c See the notes of the Weimar editors in WA DB 11/2:xxviff. concerning the Turkish threat at the time when Luther was writing this preface.

d *Der Prophet Daniel Deudsch* (1530), sig. Biii r.

e WA DB 11/2:8,9.

Nebuchadnezzar has Shadrach, Meshach, and Abedneggo thrown into the fiery furnace for not bowing to the idol, but an angel appears with them to protect them (Daniel 3). Image from a Bible printed in 1550.

In the fourth chapter a pointed example is directed against the bloodthirsty and the tyrants.[10] For the great and mighty king [Nebuchadnezzar] is here robbed of his reason. He becomes so raving mad that he has to be treated like a mad dog, chained and put out in the field because people cannot stand his presence. Today, because we simply read this in a book, it may appear as a minor matter. If we had been present, however, and seen something like this, we would have been witnessing a terrifying and horrible judgment of God. Everyone would have been moved with compassion //[f] for all the overlords and evil tyrants, that they have to expect such gruesome judgment when they abuse their position as rulers.

This, too, however, happened for purposes of consolation—at that time the consolation of the wretched captive Jews, today and evermore the consolation of those who are plagued by tyrants or who suffer injustice—that all may see how God intends and is able to avenge us against our enemies even more fully than we dare to dream.[11] As Psalm 58[:10] declares,[g] "The righteous will rejoice when he sees the vengeance; he will bathe his feet in the blood of the wicked." For this reason we should not only put up

10. Despite the image that is sometimes presented of Luther as the supporter of princes, in his prophetic writings Luther characteristically warned against tyrannical rulers. Even five years after the disasters of the 1525 Peasants' War, Luther was still ready to write inflammatory things about bad governments.

11. This kind of moral application of a biblical story is typical of sixteenth-century biblical commentary, and distinguishes it from modern historical-critical readings. Calvin, when he wrote his commentary on Daniel, would engage in copious amounts of the same kind of moral exhortation based on the text.

f *Der Prophet Daniel Deudsch* (1530), sig. Biii v.

g In this case Luther's numbering of the psalms and the modern numbering coincide.

patiently with such tyrants but also pity them for the judgment that they have coming to them, and pray for them earnestly just as the righteous Daniel does here. For Daniel is troubled that things were to go so badly for the king (who, after all, had captured the Jews and destroyed their land); Daniel wished such evil rather upon the king's enemies.

However, for the righteous lords and princes this is also a comforting and lovely image, that God the Lord depicts even this tyrannical king as a beautiful tree which nourishes all the beasts and lets them rest in its shade. Hereby God makes it clear that through civil authority [*Oberkeit*] he provides and maintains peace and tranquility, protection and defense, sustenance and possessions, and this entire temporal life, and that it is pleasing to him wherever a lord or prince practices his office conscientiously.[12] For these are fine fruits, fine leaves, fine foliage, //[h] Daniel [4:21-22] says; that is, these are precious, noble, good works. Because it is so pleasing to God himself that he thus portrays, praises, and adorns it, a lord should indeed exercise his office with all eagerness and delight, even though it be full of toil and trouble. By the same token, we, too, ought not to pay attention to how evil the tyrants may be but to how precious and useful is the office which they have from God, instituted for our benefit and welfare.

12. This passage shows the other side of Luther's views on politics: the rulers may set a poor example, but the institution of government is a divine ordinance intended for human good. See Luther's *On Secular [Temporal] Authority: To What Extent It Should Be Obeyed*, TAL 5:79–129; LW 45:75–130.

In the fifth chapter, however, comes another example against the tyrants. The example in the previous chapter is still bearable because the king permits himself to be rebuked and then turns to God with proper repentance, humility, and confession; so that, undoubtedly, this is a case of a tyrant becoming a great saint. But here [in this fifth chapter] the hardened //[i] and unrepentant tyrant [Belshazzar] is punished mercilessly for his evil. At one blow he loses everything, land, people, and his own life. This is surely written to terrify all similar tyrants.

The sixth chapter brings us the fine and precious example of a good and righteous king [Darius] who loved Daniel. As far as the other big shots[j] were concerned, Daniel had to pay for this favor [he enjoyed with the king]; they prove him guilty of a petty

h *Der Prophet Daniel Deudsch* (1530), sig. Biv ʳ.

i WA DB 11/2:10,11.

j *Grossen Hansen* (see p. 211 n.9).

intrigue and he is finally thrown into the den of lions.[13] Once again the captive and wretched Jews were undoubtedly grieved. But once again God proves himself righteous and comforting; for he so marvelously reverses the plot that that which Daniel's enemies had prepared for him they had to swallow themselves. //[k] This is just as Ps. 7[:14, 16][l] declares, "[The wicked] are pregnant with mischief and bring forth lies. Their mischief returns upon their own head, and on their own pate their violence descends." Thus, Daniel's life is nothing but a fine, clear mirror. In it we see the conflict and victory of faith, which, by the grace of God, triumphs over all mortals and devils; we see, too, the great fruit and use of faith, which it produces through patience and cross-bearing, before both God and the world.[14]

In the seventh chapter begin the visions and prophecies of the future kingdoms, especially of the kingdom of Christ, for whose sake all these visions came to pass. To begin with, the four kingdoms, which he pointed out above in chapter 2[:31-43] in the great image, he now sees again in another form, namely, in the four beasts. Most of his attention centers on the fourth beast, the Roman Empire, about which he wants to say something more. For under that very Roman Empire the greatest event on earth was supposed to take place, namely, that Christ should come and redeem humanity, and the world should come to its end.

So, then, the first beast is here the kingdom of Assyria and Babylon, which is the lion[15] with the two wings of an eagle; for this is the noblest and best of all, the golden kingdom, as was said above.[m] The two wings are the two parts of the kingdom, Assyria and Babylon. To it is given a human heart, and it stands upon its feet. The other kingdoms had //[n] no such king [as Nebuchadnezzar], who came so wondrously to the knowledge of God; neither did the others have so many great, holy, and wise men at court as did this kingdom.[o]

13. Again, Luther's summary of one of the most famous miracle stories is intentionally simple and undeveloped.

14. Luther's point here would be taken up and amplified in Melanchthon, *In Danielem Prophetam Commentarius*, 98–100, 162–64.

15. Interestingly, here Luther does not follow Jerome, who described the lion of this text as a lioness (as is found in some readings of the Hebrew and the Septuagint).

k *Der Prophet Daniel Deudsch* (1530), sig. Biv v.

l In the NRSV this is v. 14; it is v. 15 in the numbering of the *Book of Common Prayer*.

m See p. 384 above.

n *Der Prophet Daniel Deudsch* (1530), sig. Ci r.

o This paragraph break is not found in the 1530 text or in the WA DB edition.

Engraving of *Daniel's Vision of the Four Beasts* by Matthäus Merian (1630)

The second beast, the bear, is the kingdom in Persia and Media, which destroyed the preceding kingdom of Babylon and tore out its //[p] wings. Among its teeth it has three ribs, that is, three big and long teeth. These are the foremost kings, Cyrus, Darius, and Xerxes,[16] who accomplished the most in this kingdom and devoured much flesh, that is to say, won great lands.[q]

16. Jerome, like Luther, confronted the fact that there were three teeth in the prophecy and more than three kings of Persia. The Persian Empire had ten kings: Cyrus (538–529), Cambyses (529–522), Darius I Hystapsis (522–486), Xerxes I (485–465), Artaxerxes I Longimanus (464–424), Xerxes II (a few months in 424–423), Darius II Nothus (423–404), Artaxerxes II Mnemon (404–359), Artaxerxes III Ochus (359–338), and Darius III Codomannus (338–331). W. O. E. Oesterley, *A History of Israel* (Oxford: Clarendon, 1932), II:466. Luther assumed that only the chief kings were referred to. Jerome, in contrast, reasoned that "the three rows in the mouth of the Persian kingdom and between its teeth we must take to be the three kingdoms of the Babylonians, the Medes, and the Persians, all of which were reduced to a single realm" in his commentary on 7:[5].

p WA DB 11/2:12,13.

q This paragraph break is not in the original 1530 edition.

The third beast, the leopard with four wings and four heads, is the kingdom of Alexander the Great in Greece, which later broke up into four kingdoms—as we shall hear in the next chapter.[r]

The fourth beast, with the iron teeth, is now the really guilty one. This is the last, the Roman Empire; with it the world should have an end, as Daniel here has much to say about the final judgment and about the kingdom of the saints that is to follow this one. However, he portrays this Roman Empire in such a way that it should first be broken up into ten kingdoms. These are the ten horns: Syria, Egypt, Asia [Minor], Greece, [North] Africa, Spain, Gaul, Italy, Germany, England, etc.[17] He also indicates that one small horn shall knock off three among the top ten horns—meaning Mohammed[18] or the Turk who now holds Egypt, Asia, and Greece //[s]—and that this same little horn will fight the saints and blaspheme Christ, something that we are all experiencing and seeing before our very eyes.[19] For the Turk has had great victories against the Christians, yet denies Christ while elevating his Mohammed over all. Certainly we have nothing to wait for now except the last day, for the Turk will not knock off more than these three horns.[20]

r See below, eighth chapter.

s *Der Prophet Daniel Deudsch* (1530), sig. Ci v.

17. John Calvin, in his 1561 commentary on Daniel, interpreted this passage quite differently, to refer to individual rulers, and found the attempts to make correspondences with the Roman provinces or subsequent kingdoms a "great mistake."

18. Mohammed (c. 570–629), the founder of the Muslim (Islamic) faith. Luther here followed the practice of contemporary commentators in interpreting the prophecy in relation to the events of his own time. Melanchthon, *In Danielem Prophetam Commentarius*, 111–12, identified the little horn with Islam.

19. The Ottoman Turks captured Constantinople in 1453, and soon held all of Greece. In 1517, under Selim I (c. 1470–1520), they took Egypt. The campaigns of Suleiman the Magnificent (1520–1566) up the Danube valley led to the first—unsuccessful—siege of Vienna in 1529, and instilled in Luther and his central European contemporaries a proverbial dread of the Turk. William L. Langer, ed., *An Encyclopaedia of World History* (Boston: Houghton Mifflin, 1948), 327, 422. Cf. 407 n.89.

20. References to the last days, the end of time, and the second coming featured with particular intensity in Luther's writings at certain periods in his life. One interpretation portrays Luther's image of himself as that of a prophet called to denounce the Antichrist before the second coming. See Heiko A. Oberman, "Martin Luther: Forerunner of the Reformation," in Oberman, *The Reformation: Roots and Ramifications*, trans. A. C. Gow (Edinburgh: T&T Clark, 1994), 21–52. It is somewhat surprising here that Luther does not appear to make use of the prophecies of the "ancient of days" and the "son of Man" (vv. 9-14), although those would appear to have been useful to his purpose. However, he passed over them to the "horns" prophecy, which probably seemed more urgent in the political context.

In the eighth chapter Daniel experiences a special vision. Unlike the former, this one pertains not to the whole world but to his own people, the Jews; it shows how they were to fare prior to the Roman Empire and before the coming of Christ, namely, under the third empire, that of Alexander the Great. Once again the purpose is to console the Jews, that they may not despair amid the wretchedness that is to engulf them, as if Christ would leave them again and not come.[t]

Daniel himself interprets this vision as follows. The ram with the two horns is the king of Media and Persia.[21] The he-goat is Alexander the Great, who defeated Darius [III], the last king of Persia, and took away his kingdom. Daniel also says //[u] that the he-goat flew, so that he did not even touch the ground. For Alexander went so fast that in twelve years he conquered the world; he had begun at the age of twenty and died at the age of thirty-two.[22] Indeed, humanly speaking, no greater person than Alexander has come or will come on this earth.[v] But whatever rises rapidly also falls rapidly;[w] Alexander's empire crumbled as soon as he died, and these four kingdoms came in its place: Syria, Egypt, Asia, Greece.[x]

Now Daniel skips over two of them, Asia and Greece, and centers attention on the two others, Syria and Egypt. For it is between these latter two that the land of the Jews is located. Syria lies to the north and Egypt to the south, and the two stood in perpetual conflict against each other. This is why the Jews were bedeviled from both sides, being caught between two fires.[y] Now they fell to the Egyptians, now to the Syrians, depending on which of these kingdoms was the stronger. So they had to pay dearly for their location, just as always happens in the course of

21. Here Luther once again followed Jerome and the interpretative tradition: see Jerome's commentary on vv. 4-5. Note also the expository passage in the biblical text itself, in 8:20-22.

22. Cf. 1 Macc. 1:1-7. Alexander was born in 356 BCE and succeeded his father, Philip, as ruler of the Macedonian Empire in 337. His twelve years of actual campaigning, 334-323, included an early triumph over Darius III (d. 330) at the Battle of Issus in 333. Langer, *Encyclopaedia of World History*, 65.

t This paragraph break was added by the LW editors and is not found in WA DB 11/2. The 1530 edition has a greater space than usual but not a paragraph break.

u WA DB 11/2:14,15.

v A new paragraph begins here in the 1530 edition: *Der Prophet Daniel Deudsch* (1530), sig. Cii r.

w Cf. Wander, I:223, "*Bald*," nos. 11, 12.

x The new paragraph begins before this sentence rather than after it in WA DB 11/2 and in the 1530 edition.

y *Zwischen Thur und Angel steckten*. See Wander, IV:1200, "*Thür*," no. 221. Luther's point here appears to derive from Nicholas of Lyra: see *Textus biblie cum glosa ordinaria: Nicolai de Lyra postilla*, vol. 4, fol. 322v.

war.[z] This was especially true when that wanton man, whom the histories call Antiochus the Noble, was king of Syria.[23] He manhandled the Jews gruesomely, and raved and raged in their midst like a demon. He abolished the worship of God in Jerusalem, desecrated the temple, plundered its treasures, set up idols and idolatry in it, and chased out and murdered the priests and everyone else whose will was opposed to his own. He was bent on mixing all kinds of faith into a single faith, and this was to be the faith of the Greeks. To that end he had the help of a number of traitorous rascals among the Jews, fellows who could not otherwise get ahead, as we find further in 1 Macc. 1[:41-53].[a] Antiochus, of course, could not carry on this way for long. //[b]

Detail of Alexander the Great on a mosaic (c. 100 BCE) depicting his battle against Darius III of Persia at the Battle of Issus (333 BCE).

Now concerning this Antiochus, Daniel [8:9] says that following Alexander, a small horn would be coming out of one of the four big horns. This is Antiochus the Noble, coming out of the horn of Syria. He was mighty against the south and the east, and against the glorious land, that is, the land of the Jews. By means of treachery and deceit this Antiochus snatched much land and many cities from the king of Egypt, as we shall learn in chapter 11.[c] Thus, he also cast many stars to the ground, so that many saintly people among the Jews were put to death.[24] He devastated and desecrated the worship of the God in heaven in the temple [at Jerusalem] and placed idols in it.[d] Against such a devil God raised up Judas Maccabaeus and his brothers. They fought, and performed valiant and righteous deeds. In five years they had killed some two hundred thousand men, as we read in 2 Maccabees.[25] They cleansed the land and the temple, and

z A new paragraph begins here in the WA DB 11/2 edition.

a See Luther's *Preface to 1 Maccabees* in LW 35:350–53.

b WA DB 11/2:16, 17; *Der Prophet Daniel Deudsch* (1530), sig. Cii v.

c See pp. 398–407.

d A new paragraph follows here in the WA DB 11/2 edition.

23. Antiochus IV Epiphanes (ruled 175–164 or 163 BCE). See the chart below, p. 400. Compare with *Jerome's Commentary on Daniel*, 8:[9-14]. See also Melanchthon, *In Danielem Prophetam Commentarius*, 132. His title "Epiphanes" implied that he was a manifestation of the divine. Luther persistently refers to this ignoble personality as "Antiochus der Edle" with heavy sarcasm.

24. This comment appears to be a reference to Rev. 12:4. It is not entirely clear why Luther introduces this phrase here, save that it shows his conviction that apocalyptic and prophecy were intertwined.

25. This round figure Luther probably attained by totaling those given in 2 Macc. 8:24, 30; 10:17, 23, 31; 11:11; 12:19, 23, 26, 28; 13:15; 15:27.

made everything right again. The text here [Dan. 8:14] tells us that after twenty-three hundred days—which makes six and one-quarter years—the temple would be cleansed. For this length of time Antiochus vented his fury on the Jews, but he died in the seventh year. These figures readily agree, as the book of [1] Maccabees [1:20-24; 6:16] proves.[26]

Therefore the angel here warns that King Antiochus will do great harm, and that he is an impudent and insolent monarch. For he led an immoral and disgraceful life, with a complete absence of discipline,[e] as the histories tell us. However, he shall //[f] be broken, as the angel says [8:25], by no human hand. For since he wanted to go after gold in Persia, he gave orders to his field commander, Lysias, to destroy and wipe out the Jews.[27] But when Antiochus was unable to get any gold, and received the news that Judas Maccabaeus (d. 160 BCE) had defeated and put to rout Lysias and his army, he became ill with rage and impatience because things had not turned out for him as he had planned, and died after intense suffering and misery in a strange land.[28]

This is what must happen to tyrants. For Antiochus is here set up as an example of all evil kings and princes, especially those who rage against God and his word. //[g] It is for this reason that the earlier teachers have designated and interpreted Antiochus as a figure of the Antichrist,[29] and rightly so. For such a wild and filthy fellow, such a raving tyrant, is supposed to be chosen to represent and portray the ultimate abomination, as several words in this chapter [8] and in chapter 12[h] suggest and secretly disclose.

The ninth chapter[30] opens with a splendid prayer in which Daniel prays for his people who are held captive in Babylon, and for the city of Jerusalem and the temple. He prays that the Jews might return to Jerusalem and there resume their worship of

e Ger.: *ynn aller unzucht.*

f *Der Prophet Daniel Deudsch* (1530), sig. Ciii r.

g WA DB 11/2:18,19.

h For Luther, according to the chapter divisions in his translation of the prophet (EA 41:287–94), Dan. 11:2b-35 constitutes the eleventh chapter and Dan. 11:36—12:13 constitutes the twelfth chapter.

26. Luther had been translating 1 Maccabees around the time when the Daniel edition was produced. His translation of the first book appeared in 1533. According to his comments in the prefaces, Luther did not regard the second book of Maccabees as particularly useful. The paragraph break here does not appear in WA DB 11/2.

27. The story of Lysias and Judas Maccabeus is told in detail in 2 Maccabees 11–12.

28. Luther's phrasing here alludes to 1 Macc. 6:8-13: "Behold, I perish through great grief in a strange land." The same phrase is reported in 2 Macc. 9:28. The death of Antiochus is reported in detail in 2 Maccabees 9, though there (unlike 1 Maccabees 6) it is not related to the campaign of Lysias.

29. "Building on the interpretation given already in 2 Thess. 2:3–4, most of the early fathers—Irenaeus, Clement, Tertullian, Origen, Eusebius, Jerome—continued to rely in varying degrees on an apocalyptic rather than an historical exegesis." James A. Montgomery, *A Critical and Exegetical Commentary on the Book of Daniel*, The International Critical Commentary (New York: Scribner's, 1927), 398–99, 469. LW 35:302 n.161.

Luther's phrase here echoes Jerome's *Commentary on Daniel* on 8:[14]: "Most of our commentators refer this passage to the Antichrist, and hold that that which occurred under Antiochus was only by way of a type which shall be fulfilled under Antichrist."

30. There follows from this point a disproportionately long section of the preface, in terms of the number of words devoted to a single chapter. Its importance derives from the calculation of the "weeks," which was regarded as an important prophetic testimony to

God. The prayer is answered, and to Daniel is revealed the number of years until Christ should come and begin his eternal kingdom. Now this is a remarkable and great revelation of Christ //[i] which sets the time so surely and accurately.

These seventy weeks, as decreed by the angel,[31] are unanimously regarded by all teachers as weeks of years and not as weeks of days; that is, one week denotes seven years and not seven days. Experience also demands this interpretation, for seventy weeks of days add up to less than two years, and this would be no remarkable [span of] time for such a glorious revelation. But seventy weeks of years total four hundred and ninety years. This is how long men were still supposed to wait for Christ, and then his kingdom was to begin.[j]

Here, of course, we must inquire as to where and when these seventy weeks begin. The angel explains them; he begins in the year that a command goes out for the rebuilding of Jerusalem. For he speaks thus, "From the going forth of the word to restore and build Jerusalem," etc. [9:25], which some have badly stretched and twisted.[32] But in order that we may proceed correctly in this matter we must begin these seventy weeks with the second year of King Darius, who was called Longimanus.[33] For in that //[k] same year the word of God came through the prophets Haggai [1:1-15] and Zechariah [1:1-17], and Zerubbabel gave orders to build the temple; as we read in the first chapter of both of these prophets.[l] This same Darius commanded the very same thing, and his commandment was executed accordingly, Ezra 6[:6-15].[m]

Now the calculation [of the years] agrees with this. From the commandment or word spoken through Haggai, up to the baptism of Christ when he took up his office and when his kingdom or the New Testament began—//[n] the angel here speaks of him

i *Der Prophet Daniel Deudsch* (1530), sig. Ciii v.

j In WA DB 11/2 the sentence runs on without a break to the next paragraph; likewise in the 1530 edition.

k WA DB 11/2:20,21.

l Cf. LW 35:329–30.

m The paragraph break here in LW breaks a continuous sentence in the original.

n *Der Prophet Daniel Deudsch* (1530), sig. Civ r.

the coming of Christ, and therefore as confirmation that Jesus was indeed the Messiah. Jerome assigned three times as much commentary (including quoting the words of other Christian historians and chronographers) to verses 9:24-27 as to the entire remainder of the chapter. Luther also discusses these verses in detail in his *On the Jews and Their Lies*, TAL 5:550–60.

31. The translation "seventy weeks" (Dan. 9:24) in the KJV and NRSV is literal; the translation "seventy weeks of years" in the RSV represents the interpretation that Luther describes as universal. Jerome's commentary on this passage refers back to one of the earliest Christian chronographers, Julius Africanus (early third century). Compare Sextus Julius Africanus, *Chronographiae: The Extant Fragments*, ed. Martin Wallraff, with Umberto Roberto, et al. (Berlin: W. de Gruyter, 2007), 237, 281ff.

32. Luther's comment here may be an allusion to the quotations from Africanus, Eusebius, Hippolytus, Apollinarius, and others in Jerome's commentary, which all make very intricate calculations on these figures (and all different from each other) based on this point in the text. A paragraph break follows here in WA DB 11/2 and in the 1530 edition.

33. The epithet Longimanus (*Langhand*) was applied historically to Artaxerxes I (464–424 BCE), the grandson of Darius I (522–486). Luther is somewhat unusual in computing the "weeks" from the second year of Artaxerxes Longimanus. The authorities quoted by Jerome on this passage tended to favor the sixth [Eusebius] or the seventh year of his reign. This choice would be echoed (for example) by Heinrich

as a "prince"—is incidentally 483 years.[34] This makes sixty-nine of these weeks, of which the angel says, "Unto Christ, the prince, there shall be seven weeks, and threescore and two weeks," that is, sixty-nine weeks.[35] //[o] The calculation is as follows: from the second year of Darius to Alexander the Great are 145 years, according to Metasthenes; from Alexander to the birth of Christ are 311 years, as the histories attest;[36] and from the birth of Christ to his baptism are thirty years, according to Luke 3[:23]. That makes a total of 486 years; these are the sixty-nine weeks. There is a remainder of three years. These we must ignore in our calculations because it often happens in such calculations and histories that a half-year is called a whole year. It is impossible to account for every day and hour when writing history. It is good enough for us to come this close, especially since we have such specific scriptural information concerning the main items.[37]

This opinion approximates that of those who begin the seventy weeks with the twentieth and last year of Cambyses, the father of Darius, who gave permission to Nehemiah to return and restore Jerusalem, Nehemiah 2,[38] for the twentieth year of Cambyses is actually two years before the second year of Darius.[39] Now when a great event happens within [a matter of] three years, one must really understand it as comprising one year, that is, a single period of time, and say: it happened about such //[p] and such a time. So here one must say: The word of God—that Jerusalem should be restored and built—went forth in the second year of Darius, about the time that Nehemiah came from Cambyses and began to rebuild Jerusalem, etc. For this was a great event, begun by many—and even promoted by angels, as Zech. 1[:7-17] declares—yet not by everybody at once on the same day or at the same hour [Ezra 1-6].[40]

o WA DB 11/2:22,23. A new paragraph begins here in the WA DB edition.

p *Der Prophet Daniel Deudsch* (1530), sig. Civ r.

Bullinger in his *Epitome temporum et rerum ab orbe condito ad excidium . . . ultimum urbis Hierosolymorum sub Imperatore Vespasiano* . . . (Zurich: C. Froschoverus, 1565), fo. 82r. However, Luther appears to share his preference for the *second* year with Johannes Carion, *Chronica* (Augsburg: Steiner, 1533) fo. 64r, to which he probably had access before its publication. Luther's *Supputatio annorum mundi* of 1541, as published in WA 53:107, also begins the weeks with the second year of "Darius" Artaxerxes Longimanus. Melanchthon, *In Danielem Prophetam Commentarius*, 168, follows Carion and Luther on beginning with the second year.

34. Luther appears to follow the calculation embedded in the second extract from Eusebius summarized by Jerome in his commentary, which also includes the 483 years calculation.

35. In Dan. 9:25 Luther follows Jerome's Vulgate (cf. KJV) rather than the Masoretic Text in combining the figures "seven weeks and sixty-two weeks" as one numeral. The RSV and, following it, the NRSV adopt the Masoretic reading: they assign the seven weeks to the coming of an "anointed prince" and then the sixty-two weeks to the rebuilding of the city. Such a reading makes it impossible to use the text as a foretelling of the coming of Jesus.

36. See n. 16, p. 390 and n. 22, p. 392.

37. It is interesting that Luther does not appeal, as Africanus and Jerome did, to the Hebrew counting of lunar months to resolve the problem. See Martin Wallraff, ed., *Iulius Africanus: Chronographiae. The Extant Fragments*, in collaboration with Umberto Roberto, Karl Pinggéra, and William Adler. Die griechischen christlichen Schriftsteller

//[q] Now the angel further divides these seventy weeks into three parts. In the first seven weeks—that is, in forty-nine years—(he says) the wall and streets shall be rebuilt, in troublous times.[41] And he really had trouble, too, because of the intense opposition in the neighboring countries [Neh. 2:10; 4; 6]. This agrees with the statement of the Jews to Christ in John 2[:20], "It has taken forty-six years to build this temple, and will you raise it up in three days?" Then after sixty-two weeks (he says) Christ shall be put to death.[r]

Here he shows what is to happen when these sixty-nine weeks are up, and Christ has begun [his ministry], namely, that Christ shall be crucified (which happened in the fourth year after the sixty-nine weeks and after the beginning [of his ministry]), and that the city of Jerusalem shall therefore finally be destroyed, and Judaism come to an end (which afterward happened at the hands of the Romans). //[s] The one last week—that is, seven years—is the time which follows the sixty-nine weeks, during which (as has been said) Christ was supposed to be put to death. And that took place in this way (as the angel states [9:27]): //[t] He shall make a covenant with many for one week. For the preaching of Christ spread mightily during those seven years, both through Christ himself up into the fourth year, and thereafter through the apostles, proclaiming to the people the promised grace. In the midst of that same week—that is, during the fourth year after his baptism—Christ was put to death. And then the sacrifice ceased; that is, through

An image showing the destruction of the temple after the fall of Jerusalem, and the subsequent looting, with the temple's treasures being taken back to Rome. This image is taken from the inside wall of the Arch of Titus in Rome.

der ersten Jahrhunderte, NF 15, trans. W. Adler. (Berlin and New York: de Gruyter, 2007), 283.

38. According to Neh. 2:1-8 the permission was granted by Artaxerxes, in the twentieth year of his reign.

39. See n. 16, p. 390.

40. At this point a relatively short interpolation begins, first found in the 1541 version of the preface. It explains the delay of forty-six years in building the temple because building had been forbidden by Cambyses.

41. Luther follows the Vulgate in rendering Dan. 9:25 (cf. KJV).

q WA DB 11/2:24,25.

r This paragraph break appears in the LW edition but not in the 1530 original or in the WA DB edition.

s A new paragraph begins here in WA DB 11/2.

t *Der Prophet Daniel Deudsch* (1530), sig. Di[r].

Christ's death, which is the true sacrifice, the Jewish //[u] sacrifice and worship were abolished.[v] Then the Romans under Emperor Caius Caligula[42] placed an idol in the temple (as the angel says here [9:27] as a sign that the temple and Judaism were to be at an end.[43]

//[w] The tenth chapter is a prologue to the eleventh. Yet in it Daniel writes something special about the angels, the like of which we find nowhere else in the Scriptures, namely, that the good angels do battle with the evil angels in defense of men.[x] Besides, Daniel calls also the evil angels princes, as when he speaks of "the prince of Greece" [10:20]. Hence, we may understand why things are so wild and dissolute at the courts of kings and princes, and why they hinder the good and bring on war and unhappiness. For there are devils there, hounding and goading, or hindering to such an extent that nothing goes as it should. For example, though the Jews were supposed to get out of Babylon by the help of the Persian kings, nothing happened despite the willingness of the kings; as a result this [good] angel here says that he has his hands full and must fight against the prince of Persia, //[y] and expresses the concern on departing that the prince of Greece will come in the meanwhile. It is as if he were to say, "Where we parry one misfortune the devil produces another; if you get liberated from Babylon, then the Greeks will bedevil you." Now that is enough on this, for it would require more space and time to speak of it further.

In the eleventh chapter[44] Daniel prophesies to his people, the Jews—almost exactly as he does in the eighth chapter[z]—con-

42. Caligula was the third emperor of Rome (37–41 CE). Given to megalomania, he had himself worshiped as a god, but was foiled in a scheme to place his statue at the temple in Jerusalem by the legate of Syria, Petronius. Caligula died by assassination (LW 35:341 n.12).

43. A new interpolation to the preface followed in the 1541 edition: this comprised further intricate mathematical calculations, which differed slightly from those of 1530 and also from those proposed by Melanchthon in his 1543 commentary. Compare the notes to Luther, *Supputatio*, in WA 53:30–31, which show slightly different calculations in Melanchthon and in Carion, *Chronica*, fo. 64ᵛ.

44. For Luther, according to the chapter divisions in his translation of the prophet (EA 41, 287–94), Dan. 11:2b-35 constitutes the eleventh chapter, and Dan. 11:36—12:13 constitutes the twelfth chapter. One should note that Daniel's text describes all these figures cryptically as the "king of the north," "king of the south," etc. Luther provides the historical account as a key, but omits to mention that no names are typically given in the biblical vision itself.

u WA DB 11/2:26,27.

v Luther, *Supputatio*, in WA 53:125, makes the same computation.

w The WA DB edition of the 1530 text resumes on WA DB 11/2:30, second paragraph.

x On Luther's angelology, see Philip Soergel, "Luther on the Angels," in Peter Marshall and Alexandra Walsham, eds., *Angels in the Early Modern World* (Cambridge/New York: Cambridge University Press, 2006), 64–82.

y *Der Prophet Daniel Deudsch* (1530), sig. Di ᵛ.

z See pp. 392–94 above.

cerning Alexander the Great and the two kingdoms, Syria and Egypt, chiefly on account of Antiochus (called the Noble) who is to plague the Jews. But he describes Antiochus in such a way that //[a] his words ultimately tend under the figure of Antiochus to portray the very Antichrist.[45] And so Daniel is actually referring here to these last times of ours just before the last day.[46] For all teachers are unanimously agreed that these prophecies about Antiochus point to the Antichrist. Daniel's words, too, show compellingly that he does not mean exclusively Antiochus but is actually mixing together Antiochus and the Antichrist, and thus purposely scrambling his otherwise clear and transparent words.

There shall stand up yet (he says [11:2]) three kings in Persia. He does not mean this in the sense in which the Jews interpret it, that Persia should have so few kings; for the Persians have had at least ten kings.[47] Rather, these four are said to be standing up in Persia because they were especially distinguished beyond the others. Thus, after Cyrus came Cambyses, Darius, and Xerxes;[48] and these are the four //[b] most important. Of the four, Xerxes was the richest; he campaigned with innumerable forces against the Greeks, but was disgracefully defeated[49] and barely escaped with his life. After that comes Alexander and his four successors who, however, were neither of his lineage nor blood.

Then come the two kingdoms, Syria and Egypt, and how they fall to tearing and mauling each other. Here we must really set down the names of the kings on a sheet of paper, so that we do not become confused in the histories and in the text before us.[50,c]

a WA DB 11/2:32,33.

b *Der Prophet Daniel Deudsch* (1530), sig. Dii r.

c WA DB 11/2:34,35.

45. See the extensive discussion of this passage as a description of Antichrist in Jerome's commentary, on 11:[24]: "But those of our persuasion believe all these things are spoken prophetically of the Antichrist who is to arise in the end time."

46. In a letter dedicating his translation of the book of Daniel to John Frederick of Saxony (1530), Luther expressed his conviction that the end of the world was near at hand (see EA 41:233–37).

47. See n. 16, p. 390 "At least": there was disagreement on this point. See WA DB 11/2:32–33 n.3 for the variation in the estimates of the number of Persian kings.

48. The identification of these four kings as the most important follows *Jerome's Commentary on Daniel*, on 11:[2].

49. Xerxes I (486–465) was defeated by the Greeks on the sea at Salamis (480) and on the land at Plataea and Mycale (479). Langer, *Encyclopaedia of World History*, 40.

50. Luther adapted the family tree, in places changing many details, from one found in Nicholas of Lyra's commentary. This table was first printed in Koberger's edition of Lyra's postils from 1481, then was included in multiple editions of the *Biblia cum Postillis Lyra*. See *Textus biblie cum glosa ordinaria: Nicolai de Lyra postilla*, vol. 4, fo. 323r. See WA DB 11/2:33 n.8 and subsequent notes for the ways that Luther alters the names in the family tree. (See the chart on page 400.)

Alexander the Great [337–323][d]

King Seleucus [I], Nicator[51] in Syria [311-280]	King Antigonus [I], in Asia [315-307]	King Antipater, in Greece [322-319]	King Ptolemy [I], [Soter I], in Egypt [305-282]
Antiochus [I] Soter [280-261]			Ptolemy [II], Philadelphus [285-246]
Antiochus [II], Theos [261-246]	Berenice [II]	(siblings)	Ptolemy [III], Euergetes [I] [246-221]
Seleucus [II], Kallinikos [246-225]	Antiochus Hierax		
Seleucus [III], Keraunos [225-223]	Antiochus [III] the Great [223-187]		Ptolemy [IV], Philopator [221-203]
			Ptolemy [V], Epiphanes [203-180]
Seleucus [IV], Philopator [187-175]	Antiochus [IV], Epiphanes, the Noble [175-163]	Cleopatra [I]	Ptolemy [VI], Philometor [180-145]

51. Luther in the 1530 edition original has "Seleucus Nicanor," which was the contemporary spelling, rightly or wrongly. While "Nicator" is now the commonly used surname for Seleucus I, Luther and contemporaries typically wrote "Nicanor," which was not necessarily an error but an alternative form. See Matthijs Den Dulk, "Seleucus I Nicator in 4 Maccabees," *Journal of Biblical Literature* 133, no. 1 (Spring 2014):133–40.

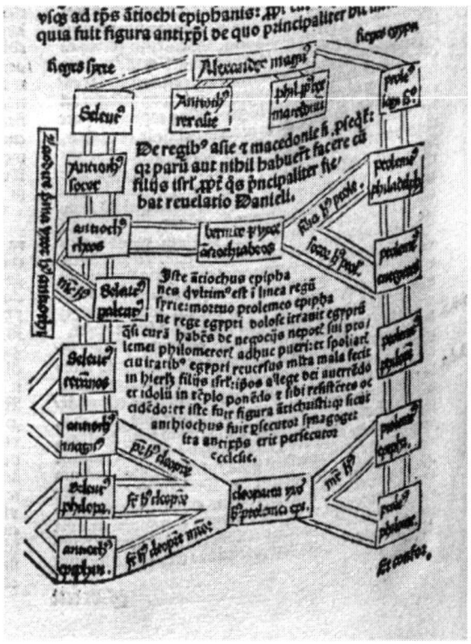

Family tree of Alexander the Great as in *Biblia cum postillis Lyra*. See n. *p*, p. 380 and n. 50, p. 399.

d Dates and titles given in brackets in this table are taken from Oesterly, *History of Israel*, II:466, supplemented as needed by Langer, *Encyclopaedia of World History*, passim.

//[e]After Alexander the kingdom in Egypt became very strong, as Daniel [11:5] here indicates. The same was true of the kingdom in Syria. Neither was able to conquer or subjugate the other, though each of them tried often and would have liked nothing better.[f]

The first war[52] took place between Antiochus [II] //[g] Theos and Ptolemy [II] Philadelphus; after prolonged campaigning they finally reached an accord. Ptolemy [II] Philadelphus was an especially fine king, for he sought peace and patronized the arts. He supported many learned men and gathered a splendid library[53] from all parts of the world. He also did many fine things for the Jews, gloriously adorning the temple and worship in Jerusalem. In fact, I would even count him among the saintly kings.[54] In order to make the peace more secure, he gave his only daughter, Berenice, in marriage to Antiochus Theos; and then he died. Berenice, however, the daughter of a mighty monarch and now herself a powerful queen and lady at court, schemed that her [infant] son should inherit the kingdom of Syria. But the plot failed, for Laodice, the [divorced] former queen of Antiochus Theos, and her two sons, Seleucus Kallinikos and Antiochus Hierax, hated Berenice and her son and desired themselves to inherit the kingdom. Laodice poisoned her lord, Antiochus Theos, and then stirred up her two sons against Berenice, their stepmother. They chased her out and finally murdered not only her but also her child and all her retinue. It is to this situation that Daniel has reference when he says [11:6], "She shall not retain the strength //[h] of her arm, and her offspring shall not endure; but she shall be given into death, with her child, and her attendants, indeed also with her lord king through whom she had become mighty."

e *Der Prophet Daniel Deudsch* (1530), sig. Dii v.

f There is no paragraph break at this point in the 1530 edition.

g WA DB 11/2:36,37.

h *Der Prophet Daniel Deudsch* (1530), sig. Diii r.

52. This detailed narrative has no precise equivalent in the earlier commentators. Luther appears to have compiled it from Jerome, Lyra, and also from the *Philippic Histories* of Marcus Junianus Justinus (second-third centuries), often known simply as Justin and sometimes confused with Justin Martyr. See the discussion in the notes to the edition of this text in WA DB 11/2. In this "Second Syrian War" (260–255) Ptolemy II lost to Antiochus II some of the territory he had taken earlier in the "First Syrian War" (276–272) from Antiochus I. Langer, *Encyclopaedia of World History*, 81, 84.

53. The idea of founding at Alexandria a "Museum"—a temple of the Muses—with library attached was probably first conceived by Demetrius of Phalerum (c. 350–c. 280 BCE) and implemented by Ptolemy I (c. 367–c. 283 BCE). All of the early Ptolemies fostered the enterprise until it became the largest collection of Greek books in the world. Edwyn Bevan, *A History of Egypt under the Ptolemaic Dynasty* (London: Methuen, 1927), 124–25.

54. See Dan. 4:34-37. Luther appears to base his high opinion of Ptolemy II (d. 246 BCE) on the *Letter of Aristeas*, one of the pseudepigraphic writings composed by an Alexandrine Jew sometime between 200 and 93 BCE, but attributed to Aristeas, an officer at the court of Ptolemy Philadelphus (r. 285–246 BCE). This letter contains the famous story of the translation of the Septuagint by the seventy-two translators sent down from Jerusalem to Alexandria at Ptolemy's request, in return for which rich gifts were sent to Jerusalem. It was first printed in a Latin Bible at Rome in 1471 and at Nuremberg in 1475, and in a separate edition at Erfurt in 1483 (see LW 35:308 n.181).

Ptolemy [III] Euergetes, the brother of Berenice, then avenges and punishes this crime by making war on the two brothers, Seleucus [II] and Antiochus [Hierax].[55] He drove them out, plundered //[i] their kingdom, and returned home [to Egypt]. Shortly thereafter, as befits those guilty of matricide, these two brothers finally came to a wretched and miserable end. Daniel speaks about all this here [11:7], saying that the king of the south shall move with an army against the king of the north and shall prevail.

After the death of Ptolemy Euergetes, Seleucus [III] Keraunos and Antiochus the Great, sons of the deceased Seleucus [II] Kallinikos, prepared for war. In the midst of these preparations, however, Seleucus Keraunos died. Consequently, Antiochus [III] had to hurry back from Babylon and direct the campaign which had already begun against Ptolemy [IV] Philopator, the son of Ptolemy Euergetes. Ptolemy, however, defeated Antiochus the Great and his army.[56] This is what Daniel is saying here [11:10-12], that the sons of Kallinikos shall be stirred up[57] and move against Ptolemy Philopator, but Philopator will defeat them, and through his victory become proud. For this same Philopator subsequently fell into vice, and at last, for the sake of a prostitute, murdered his queen Euridice, who was also his sister. //[j]

Following the death of Philopator, however, Antiochus [III] the Great armed himself more powerfully [than before] against Philopator's son, known as Ptolemy [V] Epiphanes, who was still a mere child of four or five years. Now, as often happens when [infant] monarchs must have guardians, other kings—such as Philip of Greece[58]—conspired against him along with Antiochus and were eager to divide among themselves the land of the boy-king, Epiphanes. Moreover, there was also dissension in the country itself, and //[k] the Jews too defected from Epiphanes to Antiochus. For this reason Daniel says here [11:13-16] that King Antiochus shall come again and that many shall turn against the child, Epiphanes, that the forces of the south—that is, the picked troops of Epiphanes which he had in the lands of Phoenicia and Judea, and at Jerusalem—could not stand before him. Instead, Antiochus conquered all these lands, entering also the

55. Ptolemaic power reached its height during this "Third Syrian War" (246–241). Langer, *Encyclopaedia of World History*, 84.

56. Despite initial successes in the "Fourth Syrian War" (221–217) Antiochus III (r. 223–187 BCE) the Great ultimately lost all but one of the cities he had taken from Ptolemy IV (r. 221–203 BCE). Langer, *Encyclopaedia of World History*, 81, 84.

57. Here again, Luther overlooks the coded language of the text and treats it as a transparent reference to the characters in the late antique history.

58. In 203 BCE Philip V of Macedon (r. 221–179) allied himself with Antiochus III against Egypt. The "Fifth Syrian War" (201–195) was decided by Antiochus's victory at Panium in 200. Langer, *Encyclopaedia of World History*, 80–81.

i WA DB 11/2:38,39.

j *Der Prophet Daniel Deudsch* (1530), sig. Diii v.

k WA DB 11/2:40,41.

glorious land of Jerusalem. It was there that the Jews helped him to rout completely the picked troops of Epiphanes. In return for this help, Antiochus highly honored the Jews, giving them ample goods and much freedom.[59]

When, however, Antiochus planned to move on and to capture Egypt itself, Ptolemy Epiphanes called on the Romans [for help]. Thereupon Antiochus had to cancel his plans. He made a treaty with Ptolemy Epiphanes and gave him his daughter, Cleopatra, in marriage—not in good faith, however, but as Daniel says here [11:17], to destroy him. For by means of his daughter, Antiochus thought to take the young man's kingdom away from him. But the queen //[l] [Cleopatra][60] and the Egyptians themselves frustrated these plans.[m]

Next Antiochus waged war against the islands of Asia Minor (as Daniel [11:18-19] relates) and took many of them. But in the process he ran into the Romans, who drove him back and stripped him of a fine cloak—nearly the whole of Asia Minor.[61] After that Antiochus turned back to his home and undertook an expedition to Persia, aiming there to make a big haul of gold from the temple at Elymais [1 Macc. 6:1-3]. But the inhabitants were on the alert and brought death to him and to his army. So he remained in a strange land and was never found. //[n]

Prior to this, however, when the Romans still had him on the run, he had sent his son, Antiochus—later called the Noble, though he was actually the lowest and most contemptible—to Rome as a hostage and pledge [1 Macc. 1:10]. Now that the elder Antiochus [III] was dead, another of his sons, Seleucus [IV] Philopator, became king. But he was quite incompetent and, as Daniel [11:20] says, better fitted to be a constable or bailiff than a king. Actually, he accomplished nothing noble or honest, and soon died.[o]

Thereupon Antiochus [IV] the Noble secretly escaped from Rome. Although he, too, was contemptible and the kingdom was not intended for him (as Daniel [11:21] says), he nevertheless

59. On the friendship of Antiochus for the Jews, see Flavius Josephus, *The Antiquities of the Jews*, XII, iii, 3–4.

60. Arriving in Egypt about 194 BCE, following the peace treaty of 197, Antiochus's daughter found the place to her liking, promoted her husband's cause, supported the Egyptian alliance with Rome, and dashed her father's hopes for the absorption of Egypt into the Syrian realm. She was the first of what became a line of Egyptian Cleopatras. See *The Interpreter's Bible* (New York: Abingdon, 1952–1957), VI:521–22.

61. Antiochus waged war against Rome in 192–189. After a decisive defeat at the hands of the Roman forces at Magnesia (190), he paid a large indemnity, surrendering Asia Minor, which was divided between Rhodes and Pergamum. Langer, *Encyclopaedia of World History*, 81.

l *Der Prophet Daniel Deudsch* (1530), sig. Div r.

m There is no paragraph break at this point in the 1530 edition or in WA DB 11/2.

n WA DB 11/2:42,43.

o There is no paragraph break, only a short space in the line, at this point in the 1530 edition.

sneaked in and made such a good pretense that by craftiness he became king. This is the last king about whom Daniel writes, that noble and pious child who did everything with stealth and craftiness, with lies and deceit, as befits not a king but a wanton scoundrel. His schemes were so boorish, crude, and impudent, that—as we shall see—//[p] he showed not the slightest interest in [maintaining] even the appearance of respectability and honor. It was primarily on account of this knave and wanton fellow that the vision [8:2-14] took place, //[q] as a solace for the Jews whom he was to plague with all sorts of misery.

Ring showing
Ptolemy VI Philometor

Coin of
Antiochus IV Epiphanes

Now, when he had craftily taken over the kingdom, he proceeded with the same cunning to other things. Inasmuch as the king of Egypt, Ptolemy [VI] Philometor (c. 180–145), the son of his sister [Cleopatra], was still too young, Antiochus made a pretense of being a faithful guardian of his nephew; he took over the cities in Syria, Phoenicia, and Judea. When the Egyptian prefects demanded them back, Antiochus refused to withdraw. Then the conflict broke out, of which Daniel here [11:21-22] says that he shall overwhelm like a flood the Egyptian armies (that is, the

p WA DB 11/2:44,45.

q *Der Prophet Daniel Deudsch* (1530), sig. Div v.

prefects and picked troops of Philometor); for Antiochus won the victory.

Not satisfied with that coup, he schemed underhandedly to take over the whole land of Egypt as well. He made an alliance with Philometor's chief officers and pretended that he was doing everything as a faithful guardian in the best interests of the nephew. By means of such deceit (as Daniel here [11:23-24] says) he came to Egypt with a small people; for the Egyptians opened all the gates to this dear kinsman. He seized the crown and made himself king of Egypt. By such deceitfulness he robbed, plundered, and despoiled the entire country (as the text here [11:24] declares), something his forebears had never been able to do by force. And then he returned home.

Meanwhile, since King Philometor had now become of age and assumed the kingship, he was bent on recovering by force what actually belonged to him. The two kings thus began to arm against each other. But when that noble child, //[r] Antiochus, realized that Philometor had probably grown too powerful for him, he resorted again to his innate virtue and used money to arrange treason. Philometor's own people defected to the enemy, and in the ensuing struggle many fell down slain. Yet Antiochus did not succeed in capturing the country. So he made //[s] peace once again with his kinsman. Eating and speaking with Philometor at the table, Antiochus expressed the desire to see Egypt once again; but nobody trusted him anymore. As Daniel here [11:27] declares, each king was bent on the undoing of the other, under the guise of peace. Thus, Antiochus returned home with great substance, and on the way he was admitted into Jerusalem by craftiness and deceit. He shamefully plundered the temple and the city, as 1 Macc. 1[:20-28] reports, and as Daniel says here [11:28] also: he shall set his heart against the holy covenant.

Some two years later, since his lies and skulduggery were no longer effective, Antiochus determined to take Egypt by force. He confronted his nephew no longer as a guardian but as an enemy. But as Daniel [11:29] declares, he was not to succeed as he had before. For the Romans—who had been designated as the guardians and protectors of Ptolemy Philometor by terms of his father's last will and testament—sent to Antiochus with

r *Der Prophet Daniel Deudsch* (1530), sig. Ei[r].

s WA DB 11/2:46,47.

an armed force an ambassador, Marcus Popilius, who gave him orders to get out of Egypt.[62] Artfully as ever, Antiochus tried to put the Romans off with smooth words, pretending that he simply wanted to take counsel with his relatives. Right then and there Marcus Popilius, //[t] with the staff he carried in his hand, drew a circle in the sand[63]—Antiochus was standing by the sea—and declared in the name of the Roman senate, "You do not leave this circle until you answer whether you want peace or war!" In disgrace Antiochus had to withdraw and thus returned home. //[u]

Depiction of Proconsul Caius Popilius Laenas drawing a line in the sand around Antiochus IV by Louis-Jean-François Lagrenée (1725–1805)

Retiring via Jerusalem, he vented his wrath on the temple, the worship, and the people. For he had no other outlet for his defiance than against God and his kingdom. Many scoundrels among the Jews lent him a hand and joined his side, until God raised up against him Judas Maccabaeus and his brothers, as

62. Luther makes a mistake here. The Roman ambassador who prevented Antiochus IV from attacking Egypt was named Caius Popilius Laenas, as is made clear in Polybius's *History*, 27:1. Livy's *History*, 45:12, gives his name simply as Popilius, as does Carion's *Chronica*. However, the *Roman History* of Velleius Paterculus, 10:1, gives his name as Marcus Popilius Laenas, who was a consul in 173 and 158 BCE. Luther was probably misled by Jerome's commentary, which discussed this incident in detail when commenting on 11:[27-30].

63. Some have claimed that this incident is the origin of the common expression about "drawing a line in the sand," though there are other explanations.

t *Der Prophet Daniel Deudsch* (1530), sig. Ei v.

u WA DB 11/2:48,49.

was indicated above in chapter 8,[v] and as Daniel here relates in the text [11:30-35].[64]

The twelfth chapter[65] of Daniel—as all teachers unanimously interpret it—under the name of Antiochus[66] has to do wholly with the Antichrist and with these last times in which we are living.[w] For this reason we do not have to consult the histories any longer at this point. Rather, it is the clear gospel which now indicates and discloses plainly to everyone just who the real Antiochus is. It identifies clearly him who has magnified himself above every god, who has not simply failed to regard the love of women—that is, the estate of marriage—but actually forbidden it, in its place filling the world with the idolatrous worship of his own god[67] and with carnal unchastity, and who has parceled out the treasures and possessions upon earth, etc. [11:36-39]. For the love of women [*Frauenliebe*] does not mean here [11:37] fornication or impure love. It must mean that pure and honorable love of women [*liebe zu Weibern*] which God created and //[x] commanded, namely, married love, since the prophet here reckons among the foremost crimes of the Antichrist that he does not regard the love of women. We shall also drop the matter at this point, for only in experience can this chapter be understood and Antiochus spiritually discerned; and as he says [12:2] the resurrection of the dead and the true redemption shall follow immediately thereafter.[68] //

From this book we see what a splendid, great man Daniel was in the sight of both God and the world. First in the sight of God, he above all other prophets had this special prophecy to give. That is, he not //[y] only prophesies of Christ, like the others, but also reckons, determines, and fixes with certainty the times and years. Moreover, he arranges the kingdoms with their doings so precisely and well, in the right succession down to the fixed time of Christ, that one cannot miss the coming of Christ unless one

v See pp. 392–94 above.

w See n. 46, p. 399.

x *Der Prophet Daniel Deudsch* (1530), sig. Eii r.

y WA DB 11/2:126,127.

64. Luther's detailed narrative does not appear to derive in its entirety from a single source. If his extensive discussion of chapter 11 is indeed original, it shows how important Luther considered this part of Scripture to be.

65. For Luther, according to the chapter divisions in his translation of the prophet (EA 41:287–94), Dan. 11:2b-35 constitutes the eleventh chapter and Dan. 11:36—12:13 constitutes the twelfth chapter.

66. The "name" of Antiochus appears nowhere in the biblical text. Here Luther appears to mean that a story obviously written about the historical king Antiochus can also be understood of the Antichrist. Luther is here reckoning the twelfth chapter to begin with 11:36, as noted above. His comments clearly refer to 11:36-45 in the modern numbering.

67. The Hebrew word is *maozim*, which Luther quoted in the Hebrew in his translation. The word is translated as the "god of fortresses" in the NRSV. However, the word was regarded as a symbol for the Mass in later Protestant exegeses of 11:38, notably in Caspar Peucer's continuation of Melanchthon's reworking of Carion's *Chronica* (1572), 367, 420.

68. Luther does not address the body of Daniel 12, especially the text referring to "times, times and a half," which would be extensively commented on by other exegetes. Nor did he annotate these passages in the translation itself. At this point Luther added another interpolation in later editions, which expanded at much greater length on the sins of the Antichrist (the papacy). The text of the 1530 preface resumes

does it willfully, as do the Jews.[69] In addition, from that point on until the last day, Daniel also depicts the condition and state of the Roman Empire and the affairs of the world in such an ordered way that one cannot miss the last day or have it come upon him unawares, unless one does this, too, willfully, as our Epicureans[70] are doing just now.

Therefore it seems to me that St. Peter had Daniel especially in mind when he says in 1 Pet. 1[:11], "The prophets searched what, and what manner of time the Spirit of Christ did signify," etc. //[z] The "what" means that he definitely reckons and determines the time, how long and how many years it was to be until then. The "what manner" means that he depicts well how things are to be in the world at that time, who is to exercise supreme rule, or where the empire is to be. Thus, Daniel proclaims not only the time but also the activity, shape, and nature of that time. And this strengthens our Christian faith immeasurably and makes us sure and firm in our consciences. For we see in operation before our very eyes that which he described and depicted for us so plainly and correctly in his book so long ago.

For Daniel freely prophesies and plainly declares that the coming of Christ and the beginning of his kingdom (that is, Christ's baptism and preaching ministry) is to happen five hundred and ten years after King Cyrus (Daniel 9),[a]—when the empire of the Persians and of the Greeks is at an end, and the Roman Empire in force (Daniel 7 and 9)[b]—and that therefore Christ assuredly had to come at the time of the Roman Empire, when it was at its height, the empire which was also to destroy Jerusalem and the Temple, since after Rome there is to be no other empire but only the end of the world, as Daniel 2 and 7[c] clearly state.

In the sight of the world, too, Daniel was a splendid and great man. For we see here that he rules the first two kingdoms[d] as their chief prefect. It is as though God were to say, "I must provide leaders [*Leute*] for these kingdoms, even //[e] if I have to let my Jerusalem and my people be destroyed in order to do so." Though

z *Der Prophet Daniel Deudsch* (1530), sig. Eii v.

a Cf. pp. 394–98.

b Cf. pp. 389–91, 394–98.

c Cf. pp. 383–86, 389–91.

d The four kingdoms of Daniel 2 are interpreted on pp. 383–86.

e *Der Prophet Daniel Deudsch* (1530), sig. Eiii r.

at WA DB 11/2:124, near the bottom of the page.

69. Luther would develop this point with ever-greater ferocity in his anti-Jewish writings in the 1540s. See *About the Jews and Their Lies* (1543) and *On the* Schem Hamphoras (1545), TAL 5:441–665.

70. Tradition had long referred to hedonistic ethics as Epicurean. While the Athenian philosopher Epicurus (342–270 BCE) regarded pleasure as the absolute good, he did not thereby mean merely immediate bodily pleasures (sensual gratification) but also those derived from the intellectual and moral faculties.

Daniel was never a king, and never had great wealth or honor out of it, nevertheless, he did //[f] possess and perform the functions, duties, and offices of a king. That is the way the world operates: those who work most about the place have the least, and those who do nothing get the most; in the words of the gospel saying, "One sows and another reaps" (John 4[:37]). Indeed, what is worse, he had to take hatred, envy, perils, and persecution as his reward for it all, for that is the reward with which the world is accustomed to repay all services and benefits.[g]

However, this does not hurt Daniel. He is the dearer to God because of it, and God rewards him all the more bountifully, looking upon Daniel as king in Babylon and Persia. For God reckons and judges according to the deed and fruit, not according to the person and name. Daniel is, therefore, indeed the true king of Babylon and Persia, even though he lacks the royal person and name, and gets out of it no wealth but only unhappiness and all kinds of peril. Behold how God is able to console and to honor his captive Jews, by taking the son of a townsman from destroyed Jerusalem and making him a twofold emperor, in Babylon and Persia.[h] In short, among all the children of Abraham, none was so highly exalted in the world as Daniel. Joseph was indeed great in Egypt with King Pharaoh. David and Solomon were //[i] great in Israel. But they were all little kings and lords compared with the kings of Babylon and Persia; and it was among these that Daniel was the chief ruler. He miraculously converted them to God, and doubtless produced great fruit among the people in both empires; through him they came to a knowledge of God and were saved. This is well indicated by the documents and decrees of these emperors that the God of Daniel was to be honored in every land (Daniel 2 and 6).[j]

This Daniel we commend to the reading of all good Christians, to whom he is comforting and useful in these wretched, last times. But to the wicked he is of no use, as he himself says at the end [12:10], "The wicked shall remain wicked and shall not

f WA DB 11/2:128,129.

g This paragraph break does not occur in the original text, where the sentence continues without a break.

h At this point there is a paragraph break in the WA DB edition.

i *Der Prophet Daniel Deudsch* (1530), sig. Eiii[v].

j Cf. pp. 383–86, 388–89.

Fresco of the prophet Daniel
painted by Michelangelo and assistants
for the Sistine Chapel between 1508 and 1512

understand." For the prophecies of Daniel, and others like them, are not written simply that all may know history and the tribulations that are to come, and thus satisfy their curiosity, as with a news report, but in order that the righteous shall be encouraged and made joyful, and strengthened in faith and hope and patience. For here the righteous see and hear that their misery shall have an end, that they are to be freed from sins, death, the devil, and all evil—a freedom for which they yearn—and be brought into heaven, to Christ, into his blessed, everlasting kingdom. This is how Christ, too, in Luke 21[:28], comforts his own by means of the terrible news, saying, "When you shall see these things, look up and raise your heads, because your redemption is near," etc. //[k] For this reason we see that here, too, Daniel

k WA DB 11/2:130,131; *Der Prophet Daniel Deudsch* (1530), sig. Eiv [r].
A new paragraph begins at this point in the WA DB edition.

always ends all his visions and dreams, however terrible, with joy, namely, with Christ's kingdom and advent. It is on account of this advent, the last and most important thing, that these visions and dreams were given, interpreted, and written.[l]

Whoever would read them with profit must not depend entirely on the histories or stick exclusively to history, but rather refresh and comfort his heart with the promised and certain advent of our Savior Jesus Christ, who is the blessed and joyful redemption from this vale of misery and wretchedness. To this may he help us, our dear Lord and Savior, to whom with the Father and the Holy Spirit be praise for ever and ever. Amen.

l There is no paragraph break at this point in the original editions.

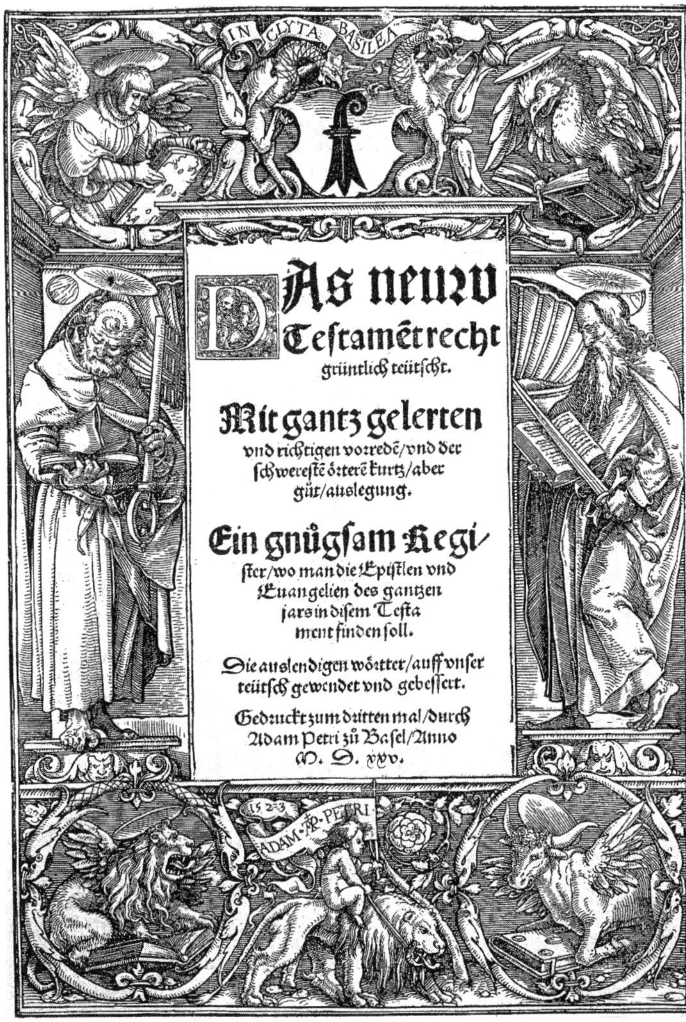
IN CLYTA BASILEA

DAs newv Testamēt recht grüntlich teütscht.

Mit gantz gelerten vnd richtigen vorredē/vnd der schwerestē örterē kurtz/aber güt/auslegung.

Ein gnůgsam Register/wo man die Epistlen vnd Euangelien des gantzen jars in disem Testament finden soll.

Die auslendigen wörtter/auff vnser teütsch gewendet vnd gebessert.

Gedruckt zum dritten mal/durch Adam Petri zů Basel/Anno M. D. xxv.

1523

ADAM PETRI

Title page of Adam Petri's reprint of Martin Luther's translation of the New Testament. From a reproduction of the 1525 edition. Top: the Basel coat of arms framed by basilisks. Sides: Peter and Paul. Bottom: the Christ child riding the lion of Judah—the printer's device of Adam Petri. Woodcut by Hans Lützelburger (1495–1526) after an original design by Hans Holbein the Younger (1497–1543).

Preface to the New Testament

1546

KENNETH G. APPOLD

INTRODUCTION

If one were to identify the single greatest achievement of Martin Luther's career, one would almost certainly pick his translation of the Bible. While not the first translation of the Bible into a vernacular language, nor even the first into German, the Luther Bible had an incomparable impact.[a] Thanks to its powerful language, its timing within the unfolding events of the Reformation, its use of the printing press, and the celebrity of its author, Luther's translated Bible defined an era. Key Reformation concepts such as "*sola scriptura*" or "the priesthood of all believers," each helping to reconfigure religious authority, would not have been realizable without this achievement. Arguably, Luther gave the Bible to the people.

Having the Bible, however, is not the same as being able to read the Bible, much less understand it properly or helpfully. Consequently, Luther found himself writing explanatory guides to Scripture, such as *A Brief Instruction on What to Look For and Expect*

a For more on Luther's Bible translation in its historical context, see Euan Cameron, "The Luther Bible," in *The New Cambridge History of the Bible from 1450 to 1750*, ed. Euan Cameron (Cambridge, UK: Cambridge University Press, 2016), 217–38.

in the Gospels (1521)[b] and a variety of prefaces to both the Old and New Testaments, as well as to individual books of the Bible. The following text, Luther's *Preface to the New Testament*, accompanied the last complete edition of his Bible during his lifetime, published in 1546. It is based on his preface to the first edition of the newly translated New Testament, printed in September of 1522. This preface is notable for its astonishingly uninhibited attitude toward the biblical text. It is the work of a man completely at home and at ease with Scripture, freely identifying his favorite parts (the Gospel of John) and disparaging those he felt to be inadequate (the Epistle of James). The preface also reveals much about Luther's hermeneutical approach to the Bible, and about his understanding of how the word of God works.

Key to Luther's approach to Scripture is his distinction between law and gospel, to which he also refers as commands and promises. The two form a kind of existential dialectic. The law accuses and drives the sinner into the arms of Christ, who promises salvation. This is the gospel message, the "good news" of Christ, "who by his death and resurrection has overcome for us the sin, death, and hell of all who believe in him." Importantly, neither commands nor promises need to be spelled out literally in order to function as such. In this case, Luther is more interested in the performative qualities of Scripture than in its lexical content. In other words, he understands the word of God as a "living voice" that makes the law-gospel dialectic happen. That, more than any of the stories or histories, is what the Bible is about. And as beautiful as some of the early printings of Luther's New Testament appeared, he never saw them as ends in themselves or as commodities. They were instruments.

Luther's heavy reliance on theological categories that, while certainly derived from Scripture, are not always immediately apparent to an uninitiated reader, compelled him to compose these prefaces. He believed the reader needs to be instructed and told "what to look for." To a modern reader that may seem heavy-handed. Indeed, Luther is occasionally accused of "eisegesis"—reading his own theological presuppositions into Scripture. Such concerns overlook two important points: first, Luther's Bible translation was genuinely revolutionary in that it gave an unprecedented number of laypeople access to the Bible; for such

b TAL 2:25–37; LW 35:117–24.

people, reading Scripture (or even having it read to them) constituted an entirely new experience; they both needed and wanted guidance. Second, Luther's theological insights were themselves products of his exegesis. According to his own account, given in another preface, in this case to the complete edition of his Latin works in 1545,[c] Luther came to his understanding of law and gospel while reading and meditating on Rom. 1:17. Rather than "reading into" Scripture, Luther therefore engages in a classic "hermeneutic circle," extracting meaning from the text and applying it to further readings.

Contemporary readers of Luther's preface to the New Testament will also notice his overtly christological readings of the Hebrew Bible. Within the framework of Luther's theological commitments, this christological hermeneutic, while apparently supersessionistic with respect to Judaism, has the virtue of rescuing the Old Testament from the secondary status it might have acquired for Christians if it had only functioned as a source of the law. Luther himself recognizes the problem and aims consciously for a more holistic approach to reading Scripture.

c TAL 4:489–503; LW 34:336–38.

PREFACE TO THE NEW TESTAMENT[d]

[IT WOULD BE RIGHT AND PROPER for this book to go forth without any prefaces or extraneous names attached and simply have its own say under its own name. However, many unfounded (*wilde*) interpretations and prefaces[e] have scattered the thought of Christians to a point where no one any longer knows what is gospel or law, New Testament or Old.[1] Necessity demands, therefore, that there should be a notice or preface, by which the ordinary man can be rescued from his former delusions, set on the right track, and taught what he is to look for in this book, so that he may not seek laws and commandments where he ought to be seeking the gospel and promises of God.

Therefore it should be known, in the first place, that the notion must be given up that there are four gospels and only four evangelists.[2,f] The division of the New Testament books

d The basis of this translation is the text in LW 35:357–62. Many of the fine notes from this edition have also been retained and are identified as such. LW 35:357 n.1: "Prior to the 1534 edition of the complete Bible this preface—intended perhaps as a preface to the entire New Testament or at least to the first part of the New Testament including the Gospels and Acts (see WA, DB 7, xxxi)—carried as a title the single word, 'Preface.' We have based our translation on the version which appeared in the 1546 edition of the complete Bible, noting significant variations from earlier versions, particularly from the first version as it appeared in the September Testament of 1522 WA, DB 6, 2–11. See LW35:227–32 for the general introduction to all of Luther's biblical prefaces."

e LW 35:357 n.2: "On the ancient practice of providing prefaces, see LW35:231. On the prefaces which appeared in early printed German Bibles, including the text of that to the book of Romans in the Mentel Bible—the first printed Bible in High German published by Johann Mentel (c. 1410–1478) in Strassburg about 1466; [see Johann Michael Reu, *Luther's German Bible* (Lutheran Book Concern, 1934), 35 and 305, n. 71.]"

f LW 35:357 n.3: "Limiting the number of Gospels to four was an ancient practice going back at least to Jerome, who based his position on the existence of but four living creatures in Ezekiel 1 and Revelation 4—the man, lion, ox, and eagle. MPL 30, 531–534. WA, DB 6, 536, n. 2, 12. Cf. p. 360, n. 9."

1. Luther quickly introduces his central hermeneutical theme: the ability to identify and distinguish law and gospel.

2. This is not a text-critical statement but, rather, a theological and hermeneutical one. For Luther, there is only one "gospel," understood as a specific kind of message (see below). This insight takes precedence over the external features of the text, such as its division into various books.

into legal, historical, prophetic, and wisdom books is also to be utterly rejected. Some make this division,[g] thinking thereby (I know not how) to compare the New with the Old Testament. On the contrary it is to be held firmly that][h]

Just as the Old Testament is a book in which are written God's laws and commandments, together with the history of those who kept and of those who did not keep them,[i] so the New Testament is a book in which are written the gospel and the promises of God, together with the history of those who believe and of those who do not believe them.[j]

For "gospel" [*euangelium*] is a Greek word and means in Greek a good message, good tidings, good news, a good report, which one sings and tells with gladness.[3] For example, when David overcame the great Goliath, there came among the Jewish people the good report and encouraging news that their terrible enemy had been struck down and that they had been rescued and given joy and peace; and they sang and danced and were glad for it [1 Sam. 18:6].

A page from the Mentelin Bible (1466) showing the beginning of the book of Genesis

g LW 35:357 n.4: "This division had been made, e.g., in the 1509 Vulgate printed at Basel, which Luther had probably used. WA, DB 6, 537, n. 2, 14."

h LW 35:358 n.5: "The portions here set in brackets did not appear in any editions of the complete Bible, nor in editions of the New Testament after 1537. Divergences from the original 1522 text were due primarily to Luther's desire to accommodate the text of the New Testament prefaces to that of the Old Testament prefaces with which they were—in the 1534 complete Bible—to appear for the first time, rather than to criticism on the part of Jerome Emser (1477–1527) or other opponents. That these divergences were not taken into account in the 1534–1537 separate editions of the New Testament was probably due to the carelessness of the printer, Luther having likely given no personal attention to these particular editions. WA, DB 6, 536."

i Cf. LW 35:236.

j LW 35:358 n.7: "The editions prior to the 1534 complete Bible here add, 'Thus one may be sure that there is only one gospel, just as there is only one book—the New Testament—one faith, and one God who gives the promise' (Eph. 4:4-6)."

3. Academic writings in Luther's time often began with an etymological account of their subject.

Thus, this gospel of God or New Testament is a good story and report, sounded forth into all the world by the apostles,[4] telling of a true David who strove with sin, death, and the devil, and overcame them, and thereby rescued all those who were captive in sin, afflicted with death, and overpowered by the devil. Without any merit of their own he made them righteous, gave them life, and saved them, so that they were given peace and brought back to God. For this they sing, and thank and praise God, and are glad forever, if only they believe firmly and remain steadfast in faith.

This report and encouraging tidings, or evangelical and divine news, is also called a New Testament.[5] For it is a testament when a dying man bequeaths his property, after his death, to his legally defined heirs.[k] And Christ, before his death, commanded and ordained that his gospel be preached after his death in all the world [Luke 24:44-47]. Thereby he gave to all who believe, as their possession, everything that he had.[6] This included: his life, in which he swallowed up death; his righteousness, by which he blotted out sin; and his salvation, with which he overcame everlasting damnation. A poor man, dead in sin and consigned to hell, can hear nothing more comforting than this precious and tender message about Christ; from the bottom of his heart he must laugh and be glad over it, if he believes it true.

Now to strengthen this faith, God has promised this gospel and testament in many ways, by the prophets in the Old Testament, as St. Paul says in Rom. 1[:1], "I am set apart to preach the gospel of God which he promised beforehand through his prophets in the holy scriptures, concerning his Son, who was descended from David," etc.

To mention some of these places: God gave the first promise when he said to the serpent, in Gen. 3[:15], "I will put enmity between you and the woman, and between your seed and her seed; he shall bruise your head, and you shall bruise his heel." Christ is this woman's seed, who has bruised the devil's head, that is, sin, death, hell, and all his power. For without this seed, no man can escape sin, death, or hell.

k Cf. LW 35:87-90.

4. Luther's confidence that the gospel has gone out into "all the world" is significant for two reasons: first, in contrast to some other Christian confessions who hold that the gospel is meant only for the elect, Luther and his followers insist on its universal applicability. Second, the notion that God finds ways to make the gospel known throughout the world served as a consolation to later Lutherans who found themselves unable to participate in the mission endeavors of their early-modern Roman Catholic counterparts.

5. Luther understands the term *testament* literally and thereby detaches it from its role of signifying one of the two parts of the Bible. Aspects of Christ's "new testament" can be found throughout the Bible, including in the "Old Testament," as the examples show.

6. Sometimes called the "mystical (or happy) exchange," this aspect is treated more fully in *The Freedom of a Christian* (LW 31:333-77, esp. 351-52; see also TAL 1:499-507).

Again, in Gen. 22[:18], God promised Abraham, "Through your descendant shall all the nations of the earth be blessed." Christ is that descendant of Abraham, says St. Paul in Gal. 3[:16]; he has blessed all the world, through the gospel [Gal. 3:8]. For where Christ is not, there is still the curse that fell upon Adam and his children when he had sinned, so that they all are necessarily guilty and subject to sin, death, and hell. Over against this curse, the gospel now blesses all the world by publicly announcing, "Whoever believes in this descendant of Abraham shall be blessed." That is, he shall be rid of sin, death, and hell, and shall remain righteous, alive, and saved forever, as Christ himself says in John 11[:26], "Whoever believes in me shall never die."

Again, God made this promise to David in 2 Sam. 7[:12-14] when he said, "I will raise up your son after you, who shall build a house for my name, and I will establish the throne of his kingdom forever. I will be his father, and he shall be my son," etc. This is the kingdom of Christ, of which the gospel speaks: an everlasting kingdom, a kingdom of life, salvation, and righteousness, where all those who believe enter in from out of the prison of sin and death.

There are many more such promises of the gospel in the other prophets as well, for example Mic. 5[:2], "But you, O Bethlehem Ephrathah, who are little to be among the clans of Judah, from you shall come forth for me one who is to be ruler in Israel"; and again, Hos. 13[:14], "I shall ransom them from the power of hell and redeem them from death. O death, I will be your plague; O hell, I will be your destruction."

The gospel, then, is nothing but the preaching about Christ, Son of God and of David, true God and man, who by his death and resurrection has overcome for us the sin, death, and hell of all people who believe in him.[7] Thus, the gospel can be either a brief or a lengthy message; one person can write of it briefly, another at length. He writes of it at length, who writes about many words and works of Christ, as do the four evangelists. He writes of it briefly, however, who does not tell of Christ's works, but indicates briefly how by his death and resurrection he has overcome sin, death, and hell for those who believe in him, as do St. Peter and St. Paul.

See to it, therefore, that you do not make a Moses out of Christ, or a book of laws and doctrines out of the gospel, as has been done heretofore and as certain prefaces put it, even those

7. Here is the most complete definition of the gospel in Luther's preface.

of St. Jerome [c. 347–419].[l] For the gospel does not expressly demand works of our own by which we become righteous and are saved; indeed, it condemns such works.[8] Rather, the gospel demands faith in Christ: that he has overcome for us sin, death, and hell, and thus gives us righteousness, life, and salvation not through our works, but through his own works, death, and suffering, in order that we may avail ourselves of his death and victory as though we had done it ourselves.

8. Here Luther simply warns the reader not to confuse law and gospel. For more on Luther's views on Moses, particularly with respect to this set of issues, see *How Christians Should Regard Moses* (TAL 2:127–51; LW 35:161–74).

To be sure, Christ in the gospel, and St. Peter and St. Paul besides, do give many commandments and doctrines, and expound the law. But these are to be counted like all Christ's other works and good deeds. To know his works and the things that happened to him is not yet to know the true gospel, for you do not yet thereby know that he has overcome sin, death, and the devil. So, too, it is not yet knowledge of the gospel when you know these doctrines and commandments, but only when the voice comes that says, "Christ is your own, with his life, teaching, works, death, resurrection, and all that he is, has, does, and can do."

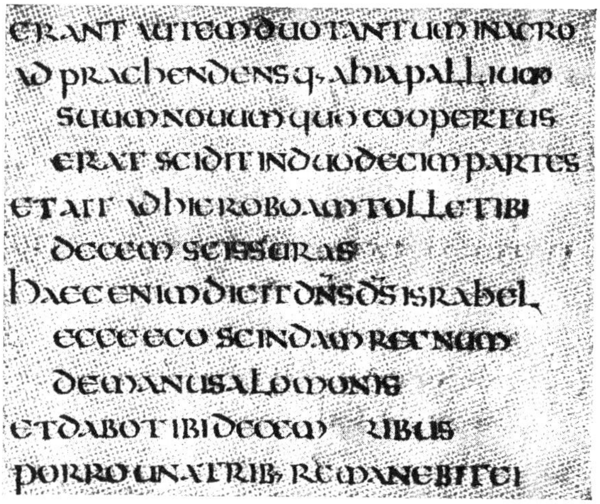

A page from the Vulgate dating to the ninth century. The text is 1 Kgs. 11:30.

Thus, we see also that he does not compel us but invites us kindly and says, "Blessed are the poor," etc. [Matt. 5:3].[m] And the apostles use the words, "I exhort," "I entreat," "I beg," so that one sees on every hand that the gospel is not a book of law, but really a preaching of the benefits of Christ, shown to us and given to us for our own possession, if we believe. But Moses, in his books, drives, compels, threatens, strikes, and rebukes terribly, for he is a lawgiver and driver.

Hence, it comes that to a believer no law is given by which he becomes righteous before God, as St. Paul says in 1 Tim. 1[:9], because he is alive and righteous and saved by faith, and he needs

l LW 35:360 n.9: "Each of the four gospels had its own preface in Jerome's Vulgate. Luther's concern for the 'one gospel' kept him from ever writing four such separate prefaces. Indeed at the beginning it seems likely that he envisioned but one preface for the entire New Testament. WA, DB 6, 537, n. 8, 5; WA, DB 7, xxi. Cf. LW 35:117–24."

m Cf. Luther's commentary on the Sermon on the Mount (LW 21:3–294).

nothing further except to prove his faith by works. Truly, if faith is there, he cannot hold back; he proves himself, breaks out into good works, confesses and teaches this gospel before the people, and stakes his life on it. Everything that he lives and does is directed to his neighbor's profit, in order to help him—not only to the attainment of this grace, but also in body, property, and honor. Seeing that Christ has done this for him, he thus follows Christ's example.

That is what Christ meant when at the last he gave no other commandment than love, by which men were to know who were his disciples [John 13:34-35] and true believers. For where works and love do not break forth, there faith is not right, the gospel does not yet take hold, and Christ is not rightly known. See, then, that you so approach the books of the New Testament as to learn to read them in this way.

[Which are the true and noblest books of the New Testament][n]

[From all this you can now judge all the books and decide among them which are the best. John's Gospel and St. Paul's epistles, especially that to the Romans, and St. Peter's first epistle are the true kernel and marrow of all the books. They ought properly to be the foremost books, and it would be advisable for every Christian to read them first and most, and by daily reading to make them as much his own as his daily bread. For in them you do not find many works and miracles of Christ described, but you do find depicted in masterly fashion how faith in Christ overcomes sin, death, and hell, and gives life, righteousness, and salvation. This is the real nature of the gospel, as you have heard.

If I had to do without one or the other—either the works or the preaching of Christ—I would rather do without the works than without his preaching. For the works do not help me, but his words give life, as he himself says [John 6:63]. Now John writes very little about the works of Christ, but very much about his preaching, while the other evangelists write much about his works and little about his preaching. Therefore John's Gospel is the one, fine, true, and chief Gospel, and is far, far to be preferred over the other three and placed high above them. So, too, the epistles of St. Paul and St. Peter far surpass the other three Gospels, Matthew, Mark, and Luke.

n See LW 35:358 n.5.

In a word, St. John's Gospel and his first epistle, St. Paul's epistles, especially Romans, Galatians, and Ephesians, and St. Peter's first epistle are the books that show you Christ and teach you all that is necessary and salvatory for you to know, even if you were never to see or hear any other book or doctrine. Therefore, St. James' epistle is really an epistle of straw,[o] compared to these others, for it has nothing of the nature of the gospel about it. But more of this in the other prefaces.][p]

o LW 35:362 n.11: "On the term 'straw' cf. Luther's reference on LW 35:395 to 1 Cor. 3:12. Luther's sharp expression may have been in part a reaction against Andreas Karlstadt's excessive praise of the book of James. Cf. WA, DB 6, 537, n. 10, 6–34, and the literature there listed."

p LW 35:362 n.12: "See especially the Preface to James (LW 35:395–98). Cf. also Luther's negative estimate of the book of James already in his 1520 *Babylonian Captivity of the Church* [TAL 3:121; LW 36:118; and in his *Resolutiones* of 1519 in WA 2:425]."

Sermon on the Mount

(Matthew 7:12)

1530–1532

KENNETH G. APPOLD

INTRODUCTION

The following excerpt stems from Luther's commentary on the Sermon on the Mount. Luther had held a series of weekday sermons on the Gospel of Matthew in Wittenberg's *Stadtkirche* between the fall of 1530 and the spring of 1532, from which the section on Matthew 5–7 was transcribed by hearers and published as a commentary. Both the identity of the transcribers and the degree of Luther's involvement in preparing the edition remain unclear. Luther did, however, add a preface to the first printed edition (Wittenberg, 1532), which documents his commitment to the commentary and provides insight into his thoughts on its publication.[a]

Against the backdrop of Luther's larger body of work, the sermons on Matthew 5–7 form an interesting counterpoint. The Beatitudes were a popular subject for medieval Scholastic theologians because they contain one of the most succinct yet challenging summaries of Jesus's moral teaching. Here one could find a "fulfillment" of Jewish law and at the same time what appears

a Cf. WA 32:299–544; LW 21:3–294. For details on the work's provenance and publication, see WA 32:lxxv–lxxvii; LW 21:xx–xxi.

Woodcut depicting the Sermon on the Mount from a 1544 publication of Luther's interpretation of the epistles and gospels from Easter to Advent

to be a "new law" leading to blessedness (Matt. 5:17).[b] Precepts such as those presented in Matt. 5:3-11, emphasizing poverty in spirit, hunger for righteousness, mercy, and peacemaking in the face of worldly persecution, formed a foundation for medieval accounts of Christian virtue. Here, too, were stirring examples of the kinds of works of charity that Christian faith makes possible and, indeed, demands. Progress in such a life, supported by the grace of God, could mark the Christian's ascent toward beatitude.

Luther takes a different approach to the law and its relationship to blessedness. In Luther's theological conception, the law's primary function lies in accusing the sinner and exposing the futility of human moral striving. This in turn drives the sinner into the arms of an unconditionally gracious and forgiving God, cementing a relationship that will have transformative consequences for the believer's moral life. Works of charity, in the reformer's view, flow naturally out of the humbled but restored soul of a person reconciled with God. The law no longer accuses but is written "in the heart" of the believer, who follows its precepts spontaneously and without external prompting.

Next to this "theological" use of the law, Luther also makes room for the law's "civil" use. Because Christians live in mixed societies dominated by un-Christian motives, rulers are called upon to establish and maintain external order. Obeying such laws is an important part of the Christian "external" life, but it has no direct bearing on one's "internal" salvific relationship with God.

b For a brief overview of influential medieval interpretations of Matthew 5–7, and their impact on Luther, see Karin Bornkamm, "Umstrittener 'spiegel eines christlichen Lebens.' Luthers Auslegung der Bergpredigt in seinen Wochenpredigten von 1530 bis 1532," in *Zeitschrift für Theologie und Kirche* 85, no. 4 (December 1988): 409–54, esp. 412–23.

With those theological commitments in mind, it is easy to see why the text of Matthew 5–7 would pose an interesting challenge to Luther. Here he encounters a different kind of law that appears to fulfill the older, accusatory law but, at the same time, introduces new precepts, a "new law" whose function does not align neatly with either the "theological" or "civil" understandings of law found in most previous examples of the reformer's thought.

As is often the case with Luther, pressure prompts polemic, and his preface to the published commentary provides an unusually coarse example of this.[c] He identifies two types of opponents. To "the left" lie the Scholastic theologians who either use Matthew 5–7 as an occasion for semi-Pelagian "works righteousness" or restrict its more difficult precepts to monks and weaken the Sermon's impact on ordinary Christians. To "the right" lurk "enthusiasts" who, ignoring the persistence of sin in the human condition, view the text as a recipe for exaggerated Christian perfectionism. Neither of these targets is more than a straw man, however, and while both appear in various pejorative guises throughout Luther's commentary, they should not distract from the much more profound project at the heart of this work: articulating a positive role for Christ's law in the lives of justified Christian believers.

Nowhere is that project more cogently framed than in the section on Matt. 7:12. Here Luther meditates on a version of Christ's "Golden Rule": "So whatever you wish that others would do to you, do so to them; for this is the law and the prophets." Here, too, the reader encounters Christ as "teacher" and guide to the Christian's conscience.

c WA 32:299–301; LW 21:3–6.

SERMON ON THE MOUNT (MATTHEW 7:12)[d]

12. So whatever you wish that others would do to you, do so to them; for this is the law and the prophets.

WITH THESE WORDS he concludes the teaching he has been giving in these three chapters, and wraps it all up in a little package where it can all be found. Thus, everyone can put it in his bosom and keep it;[1] it is as if he were saying: "Would you like to know what I have been preaching, and what Moses and all the prophets teach you? I shall tell it to you so briefly and put it in such a way that you dare not complain about its being too long or too hard to remember." This is the kind of sermon that can be expanded or contracted; from it all teaching and preaching go forth and are broadcast, and here they come back together. How could it be put more succinctly and clearly than in these words? The trouble is that the world and our old Adam refuse to let us ponder what he says and measure our lives against the standard of this teaching.[2] We let it go in one ear and out the other. If we always measured our lives and actions against this standard, we would not be so coarse and heedless in what we do, but we would always have enough to do. We could become our own teachers, teaching ourselves what we ought to do; and we would not have to chase after holy lives and holy works, nor would we need many lawyers and law books.[3] This is stated briefly and learned easily, if we only were diligent and serious in acting and living according to it.

Let me illustrate it with a somewhat crude example. Surely there is no one who would enjoy being robbed; if he asks his own heart about this, he has to say that he really would not enjoy it at all. Now, why does he fail to draw the conclusion that he should treat others the way he wants to be treated? At a market, you

1. Luther understands the word of God as something living and efficacious (*viva vox evangelii*), which enters and stirs the hearer's heart.

2. According to Luther, Christians retain an aspect of sinfulness after conversion. While defeated formally, sin continues to impinge upon the believer's life in faith. Luther uses the term "old Adam" to refer to that dimension of the Christian experience; he also uses the formula "*simul iustus et peccator*" (simultaneously just and sinner).

3. If Christ took up exclusive residence in our hearts and there were no continuing reality of sin (see "old Adam," above), then we would not be tempted to justify ourselves by means of works, nor would we have need of the law to accuse or restrain us.

d This translation is based on LW 21:235–41, with minor updates.

see everyone marking up his prices as high as he pleases, asking thirty pfennigs for something that is not worth ten.[4] If you ask him, "Friend, would you want to be treated that way?" he must be honest and reasonable enough to say: "I would be willing to pay for it what its market value is and what would be reasonable and proper, so that I am not overcharged." There, you see, your heart is telling you honestly how you would like to be treated. And your conscience is arguing that you should treat others the same way;[5] it can teach you well about your relations with your neighbor in buying and selling and all kinds of business, all things belonging to the Seventh Commandment (Exod. 20:15): "You shall not steal."

An illustration (1520) of the violation of the seventh commandment, "You shall not steal"

It is the same with the other commandments. If you have a wife, a daughter, or a maid, you would not want her to be corrupted or to acquire a bad reputation. You want everyone to respect her, to treat her well, and to speak the best about her. Then why are you so perverse that you yearn for someone else's wife and want to corrupt her yourself? Why do you not help to improve her reputation, instead of finding pleasure in talking behind her back and slandering her? Similarly, you would not want anyone to do you injury or harm, to malign you, or to do anything like that. Then why do you yourself violate the

4. Luther frequently offers critiques of merchants, bankers, and capitalist economic practices. See *Trade and Usury* (1524), TAL 5:131–81; LW 45:245–310; WA 15:293–313,321f.; WA 6:36–60.

5. "Conscience," as the capacity of persons to see themselves from a detached perspective as they stand before God, is a key notion to this commentary. For more on Luther's understanding of conscience, see Randall Zachman, *The Assurance of Faith: Conscience in the Theology of Martin Luther and John Calvin* (Minneapolis: Fortress Press, 1993).

rule and standard that you demand of others and want them to keep? How can you judge, criticize, and condemn someone else if he does not treat you that way? Why do you refuse to obey your own rule? Go through all the commandments of the Second Table this way, and you will find that this is really the summary of all possible sermons, as he himself says here. Thus, this is properly termed a short sermon. But, on the other hand, if it were expanded through all the details it implies, it is such a long sermon that it would be endless, since the things that will be done on earth until the last day are innumerable. It takes a good teacher to condense and summarize such a long, drawn-out sermon in such a way that everyone can carry it home with him, be reminded of it daily, and see what is missing in his whole life; for he has it written in his own heart, in fact, in his whole life and activity, as we shall hear in more detail.

I am convinced, moreover, that it would be influential and productive of fruit if we only got into the habit of remembering it and were not so lazy and inattentive.[6] I do not regard anyone as so coarse or so evil that he would shirk this or be offended at it if he really kept it in mind. It was certainly clever of Christ to state it this way. The only example he sets up is ourselves, and he makes this as intimate as possible by applying it to our heart, our body and life, and all our members. No one has to travel far to get it, or devote much trouble or expense to it. The book is laid into your own bosom, and it is so clear that you do not need glasses to understand Moses and the law. Thus, you are your own Bible, your own teacher, your own theologian, and your own preacher.[7] The way he directs you, you only need one look at them to find out how the book pervades all your works and words and thoughts, your heart and body and soul. Just guide yourself by this, and you will be more wise and learned than all the skill and all the books of the lawyers.

To take a crude example again: If you are a manual laborer, you find that the Bible has been put into your workshop, into your hand, into your heart. It teaches and preaches how you should treat your neighbor. Just look at your tools—at your needle or thimble, your beer barrel, your goods, your scales or yardstick or measure—and you will read this statement inscribed on them. Everywhere you look, it stares at you. Nothing that you handle every day is so tiny that it does not continually tell you this, if you will only listen. Indeed, there is no shortage of preach-

6. Although the German phrase "*gewenet daran zu gedencken*" (WA 32:495) is clearly nontechnical, Luther's choice of words calls to mind the Scholastic notion of intellectual and moral "habits" (*habitus*).

7. This powerful statement reveals much about Luther's hermeneutical approach. Christ establishes such intimacy with the believer that the law's pedagogical force is fully internalized.

ing. You have as many preachers as you have transactions, goods, tools, and other equipment in your house and home. All this is continually crying out to you: "Friend, use me in your relations with your neighbor just as you would want your neighbor to use his property in his relations with you." In this way, you see, this teaching would be inscribed everywhere we look, and engraved upon our entire life, if we only had ears willing to hear it and eyes willing to see it. It is being presented to us in such abundance that no one can give the excuse that he did not know it or that it was not announced and preached to him often enough. But we are like the vipers, which stop up their ears and become deaf when someone tries to trap them.[e] We refuse to see or hear what is inscribed on our own heart and thoughts, and we plunge in recklessly: "Ha! What do I care about somebody else? I may do business with my own possessions as I please, and sell them for as much as I can get for them. Who is going to stop me?" That is what Squire Skinflint and Squire Squeeze[f] do at the market. If someone rebukes and threatens them from the word of God, they simply laugh and mock and become firmer in their wickedness. But we are not preaching to such people, and neither is Christ.[8] He wants to have nothing to do with them and despises them as much as they do him. He will let them go to the devil, so that he and they will have nothing further to do with each other.

Those who want to be pious, who fear God, and who think about how to live and behave, must know that they simply have no right to do business with their property and manage it as they please, as though they themselves were the lords of all. They have the obligation to carry on their business in a proper and orderly way; this is why there is territorial and civil law.[9] That is how everyone would want his neighbor to treat him; therefore he should also treat his neighbor that way, taking and offering only good merchandise. Christ means this commandment seriously, and he will not let it be made free or optional, as though one could obey it or disobey it with impunity. He will enforce it, too, however much the world may take it as an insult and despise it. If you do not obey it, he will deal with you according to your

8. Luther makes clear that his message is directed toward the believers. His exposition of the law, therefore, is not geared toward maintaining civil order in a morally mixed society but, rather, toward the beatitude of believing Christians.

9. Luther refers to the civil, or political, use of the law.

e See LW 21:237 n.16: "Apparently an allusion to Ps. 58:4, 5; see also LW 21:333 n.33."

f See LW 21:237 n.17: "The German titles are, respectively, *Juncker Viltz* and *Knebel*."

own standard and judgment, and it will strike you in your house and home. You will have no blessing from what you have acquired in disobedience to this teaching, but you and your children will have only trouble and sorrow. He wants his commandment to be kept; otherwise you will have neither property nor good fortune.

A rich man takes food and other goods from a poor man. This image was used to illustrate Martin Luther's sermon on usury and ill-gotten gains (1520).

In the second place, Christ not only makes this so intimate, as we have said, that we have to see it in everything we look at, he also portrays it in such a way that everyone has to blush in shame over himself.[10] There is no one who enjoys doing something wrong when other people can see it. No one dares to sin publicly, in the presence of people, with the same freedom as he does privately, where no one can see him. So Christ intends here to appoint us as our own witnesses and to make us afraid of ourselves.[11] Then if we do something wrong, our conscience will stand up against us with this commandment, as an eternal witness, and say: "Look here, what are you doing? According to the usual fair-business practice, you ought to put such and such a price on this. But you are putting on a much higher price. Or the way you are debasing and misrepresenting this merchandise, you would not want to have someone else sell you something like that." How it would annoy you if someone charged you a gulden for something barely worth ten groschen! If you had one drop of honest blood in your body, you would have to be ashamed of yourself. If someone else acted this way, you would call him a thief and a villain. Then why are you not ashamed of yourself, since it is not someone else but yourself who has to make this accusation, and you are condemned by your own conscience? This may be all right for a brazen hardhead, who has no sense of shame before the people or before himself, much less before God. But when someone else treats you that way you can quickly exclaim: "Is it not a sin and a shame and a clever[g] way of robbing my wallet?"

10. Here Luther refers to the theological, or spiritual, use of the law.

11. This is another reference to the conscience.

g See LW 21:239 n.18: "The edition of 1534 has *terrible* instead of *clever.*"

You can quickly recognize a thief and a villain in someone else; but you refuse to see the one working in your own breast, whom you can easily catch and feel.

Oh, how many fellows like this there are in all the businesses and trades![12] They go along, smugly deceiving and cheating the people wherever they can; still they refuse to be called thieves and villains, so long as they do it secretly and adroitly. If everyone had to give back what he has stolen and robbed in his business or job, very few people would be able to keep anything. Yet they go along like pious people, because no one dares to accuse and denounce them publicly. They suppose that they are sinless; yet if they look around, every corner of their house and home is full of theft and, by God, they do not have a single gulden or two in the house that was not stolen. Yet none of this is supposed to be called theft. If it were merely theft, and not murder in addition! Shoddy merchandise or unwholesome food and drink can make people weak and sick. Thus, you deprive them not only of their money but also of their health. Many a person eats and drinks and then gets sick and often dies as a result. My friend, except for the name, is this not as bad as breaking into his house or rifling his treasure chest or striking him dead?

Now, if you were not such a heinous and brazen person, you would be ashamed when your conscience says this to you and reminds you of this saying. It would give you pause. In fact, it would make you so afraid that you would be unable to remain at rest anywhere on account of it. This burden continually oppresses us and drives us. It is an eternal witness against us, always condemning us, so that it becomes unbearable. It would soon teach you that you have to stop this robbing and stealing and whatever else you would not like to have someone else do to you. Get used to looking at this saying once in a while and practicing it on yourself. Thus, in your whole existence, in every task in which you have contact and dealings with your neighbor, you have a daily sermon in your heart.[13] From it you can easily learn to understand all the commandments and the whole law, how to control and conduct yourself personally and socially. On this basis you can easily decide what is right and wrong in the world.

But you may say: "How can he say that the law and the prophets consist in this? Do not the Scriptures of the law and the prophets contain much more than this? They contain the doctrine of faith and promises, which are not mentioned here." The

12. Again, referring to merchants as thieves, Luther avails himself of some of his favorite moral pejoratives: thieving, robbing, and murdering. See *Against the Robbing and Murdering Hordes of Peasants* (1525), LW 46:49–55; WA 18:357–61.

13. Luther appears to describe an internalized pedagogical use of the law.

answer is that here Christ names the law and the prophets in direct contrast to the gospel or the promise. He is not preaching here about the sublime doctrine of faith in Christ but only about good works. These are two distinctive proclamations; both must be preached, but each at its appropriate time. You can tell that plainly from the words in the text where he says: "Whatever you wish that others would do to you, do so to them." By this he indicates that his preaching here does not go beyond the relation that people have with us and we with them, and that it is not talking about the grace of Christ which we receive from God. What he intends to say now is this: "When the time comes to preach about the good life and about the works which we should perform in our relations with our neighbor, you will find nothing in all the law and the prophets except what this saying teaches." He uses the words "others" and "do so to them" to specify that he is discussing only the commandments of the Second Table.

The best thing in the saying is that he does not say, "Other people shall do so to you," but, "You shall do so to other people." Everyone would like to have others do good to him. There are many villains and rascals who have no objection if other people are pious and do good to them, but they refuse to treat anyone else that way. So our peasants nowadays suppose that it is an injustice and a great burden that they are required to give fair measure, and yet they can yell and complain that their taxes are robbery.[h] Such people are simply snakes. Now, some are a little better when they say: "I would be willing to take my turn and to do what I should if other people did it to me first." This saying declares: "You should do what you expect from another." If you want others to do it to you, you begin and be the first. And if they refuse, you do it anyway. If you will not be pious and do good until you see it in someone else, nothing will ever come of it. If others refuse, you are still obliged to do it, on the basis of the law and of what this ordinance declares to be right, since that is how you would like to be treated. Whoever wants to be pious must not let himself be diverted by the example of other people. It is not right for you to say: "He cheated me, and so I have to do him dirt in turn." Because you do not like it, do not

h For more on Luther's conflict with the German peasants, see *Admonition to Peace: A Reply to the Twelve Articles of the Peasants in Swabia* (1525), TAL 5:281–333; LW 46:5–43; WA 18:291–334.

do it to him; begin with the way you would like to be treated. By your example you may prompt other people to do good to you in turn, even those who used to do you damage before. When you do not do good yourself, your reward is that no one does good to you either. And it serves you right, before God and the people.

This painting (1561) on the altarpiece of the Church of Torslunde, Denmark, depicts a Lutheran worship service after the Reformation in 1536.

A Sermon on John 1:14a: "And the Word Became Flesh"

1537

PAUL ROREM

INTRODUCTION

It is true, as often said, that Martin Luther was neither a systematic theologian nor a parish pastor but, rather, a university professor of the Bible, especially the Old Testament. Yet this sermon, among many in a series on the Gospel of John, can illustrate his extensive career as a preacher (see image at left). From relatively late in his long career, namely 1537, this series of sermons reflects his fully developed views of Scripture, of exegesis and preaching, and especially of the incarnation as central to the Christian message. The incarnation was central for Luther not only as history's pivotal event ("the Word became flesh," John 1:14) but also as the key to understanding the relationship of the divine and the human more broadly: in Scripture itself, in the words of absolution and preaching, in the sacraments, and in the church in general.

Portrait of Johannes Bugenhagen (1532) by Lucas Cranach the Elder

Context

When the dust had settled in Wittenberg after Luther's excommunication, the parish had a new pastor, Johannes Bugenhagen (1485–1558).[a] Sometimes called Pomeranus, after his homeland of Pomerania, he had come to Wittenberg as a student and soon emerged as a leader. He was the pastor of the Wittenberg city church, St. Mary, from 1523 until his death in 1558. Pastor Bugenhagen was Luther's own pastor, both for pastoral acts, such as presiding at Luther's 1525 wedding and his 1546 funeral, and also for many occasions of pastoral care, especially during serious illnesses and Luther's near-death experience in 1527.[b] He was also a remarkable organizer and churchman in his own right. Precisely for these administrative gifts he was sometimes called away from Wittenberg to help organize the Evangelical reform of a church elsewhere. His "church orders" (guidance for parish life, including schools and care for the poor) had already helped establish Evangelical foundations in Braunschweig (1528), Hamburg (1529), Lubeck (1531), and his native Pomerania (1534). During such trips, Luther sometimes filled in for him as preacher.

On this occasion, Bugenhagen was called to Denmark in the summer of 1537 to help organize the Evangelical cause there and stayed two full years. Luther, although recovering from an illness, was immensely loyal to his own dear pastoral friend and started filling in for "our pastor, Dr. Pomeranus,"[c] in July of 1537. The present sermon, well along in the prologue to the Gospel of John, is dated 1 September 1537, as the seventh in the series. Of course, Luther had written and preached often on the Fourth Gospel before this. In fact, his earliest known sermon was on the Gospel of John, to his Augustinian community at Christmas time in 1514.[d] Christmas alone provided many occasions for preaching on John's prologue, as when Luther's 1522 Christmas postil called John 1:12 the point of the entire gospel message.[e] This particular sermon is one of fifty-three sermons

a For more on Bugenhagen and his importance to the Lutheran Reformation, see the recent two-volume set of his writings, introduced and edited by Kurt Hendel, *Johannes Bugenhagen: Selected Writings* (Minneapolis: Fortress Press, 2015).

b Martin Lohrmann, "Bugenhagen's Pastoral Care of Martin Luther," *Lutheran Quarterly* 24 (2010): 125–36.

c LW 22:5.

d LW 22:ix.

e Timothy J. Wengert, *Reading the Bible with Martin Luther* (Grand Rapids: Baker Academic, 2013), 65.

on John, chapters one into four, from July 1537 to September of 1540, since Luther kept preaching occasionally on John even after Bugenhagen returned from his long stay in Denmark.[f]

Contents

Preaching on the prologue to the Gospel of John gave Luther ample opportunities to emphasize the theological centrality of the incarnation, both as pivotal event and also as a motif or paradigm for the overall relationship of the divine and the human in several related spheres such as Scripture and the sacraments. Salvation itself was anchored in the incarnation insofar as mortality and death were not only entailed in the human condition assumed by God the Son but also overcome in the resurrection. Early on, Luther's influential *Freedom of a Christian*[g] emphasized the "happy exchange" of Christ and the sinner, only possible because Christ had taken on the sinner's incarnate existence. All of this is articulated early on in Luther's sermon series, for example, in the start of the fifth sermon just two weeks earlier (18 August 1537):

> This means that he ate, drank, slept, awakened, was tired, sad, and happy. He wept and laughed, hungered, thirsted, froze, and perspired. He chatted, worked, and prayed. In brief, he required the same things for life's sustenance and preservation that any other human being does. He labored and suffered as anyone else does. He experienced both fortune and misfortune. The only difference between him and all others was that he was sinless. Since he was also very God, he was free of sin.[h]

Toward the end of this preaching sequence, in 1540, Luther also conducted an academic exercise on the subject of the incarnation, a "disputation" concerning the divinity and humanity of Christ, against Caspar Schwenckfeld's denial that Christ ever

f All included in LW 22.

g See TAL 1:467–538.

h LW 22:73.

was such a human creature.[1] In that formal context of careful definitions of concrete and abstract terminology, Luther's enduring commitment to the centrality of the incarnation (fully divine, fully human) finds another expression.

1. Caspar Schwenckfeld (1489–1561) was a Silesian nobleman who championed a "spiritualist" view about Christ's "heavenly flesh." See FC, SD XII, 658f. Luther's disputation is translated from WA 39/2:92–121 by Mitchell Tolpingrud as "Luther's Disputation Concerning the Divinity and the Humanity of Christ," *Lutheran Quarterly* 10 (1996): 151–78.

A SERMON ON JOHN 1:14A: "AND THE WORD BECAME FLESH"[i]

IN OUR TEXT the Word gets a new name. Earlier in our chapter the evangelist called the Word God, then a Light which came into the world and created the world and yet was not accepted by the world. Now he uses the term "flesh." He condescends to assume my flesh and blood, my body and soul. He does not become an angel or another magnificent creature; he becomes human. This is a token of God's mercy to wretched human beings; the human heart cannot grasp or understand, let alone express it. However, we Christians can at least learn to prize and esteem these words; they were acknowledged and preserved even in the papacy. Although the Antichrist in Rome and the devil frightfully mutilated and perverted all that is divine in the church, God nevertheless miraculously preserved Holy Scripture—even though it was darkened and dimmed under the pope's accursed rule—and passed it down to our day. Thus, God also preserved these words of the gospel, which were read from the pulpit every Sunday, although without the proper understanding. Also the words of the Decalogue,[2] the Creed, and the Lord's

2. The Ten Commandments.

i The translation is based on LW 22:102–17, with a few subheadings early on added in brackets.

Prayer, as well as Baptism and one kind in the Sacrament have survived under the pope's devilish regime. God restrained him from destroying and treading everything underfoot. Although the gospel was obscured and the proper understanding of it was hidden, God still kept it for the salvation of his own. These words, too, "And the Word became flesh," were held in reverence. They were sung daily in every Mass in a slow tempo and were set to a special melody, different from that for the other words.[3] And when the congregation came to the words "from the Virgin Mary, and was made human," everyone genuflected and removed his hat. It would still be proper and appropriate to kneel at the words "and was made human," to sing them with long notes as formerly, to listen with happy hearts to the message that the Divine Majesty abased himself and became like us poor bags of worms, and to thank God for the ineffable mercy and compassion reflected in the incarnation of the Deity. But who can ever do justice to that theme?

Painting (1590) of the Council of Nicea (325) in the Sistine Chapel, Vatican

3. Luther is here quite naturally associating the Johannine phrase "the Word became flesh" with the double Nicene expression: he "was incarnate" and "became truly human." The Nicene Creed, actually the "Nicene-Constantinopolitan Creed" from the Councils of Nicaea (325) and Constantinople (381) and originally for baptisms only, had been part of the Latin Mass for centuries by Luther's time. His own 1523 revision of the Mass (*Formula Missae*) retained the Creed and the practice of singing it, and even, as he says here, the (optional) bowing or kneeling at these crucial words signaling the incarnation. As evident throughout this sermon, as well as in Luther's hymnic paraphrase of the Creed (LW 53:271), his emphasis is on the (divine) Word becoming human and thus mortal flesh, as the center of the Christian faith.

[Father Bernard][j]

The dear church fathers took particular delight in these words; they set great store by them, and they praised God, as we read here and there in their books, for the great honor conferred on us when he humbled himself and assumed our flesh and blood. In Heb. 2:16 we hear: "He did not take on himself the nature of angels, but humbled himself and he took on the seed of Abraham." He became our flesh and blood. Who can express this adequately? The angels are much holier than we poor sinners, and yet he adopted our nature and became incarnate from the flesh and blood of the Virgin Mary.

Vision of St. Bernard with St. Benedict and John the Evangelist (on right) (1504), by Fra Bartolomeo

This fact elicited the awe of St. Bernard[k] and gave rise to many fine thoughts, found especially in his devotions. He gave it as his opinion that this had caused the archfiend Lucifer's fall and eviction from heaven. Perhaps Lucifer, so St. Bernard supposed, had foreknowledge of God's eternal resolution to become a human in time, and not an angel. This provoked his insolence against God. He was aware, of course, that he was a creature more beautiful and excellent in appearance than a human. This also aroused his envy of humankind; he begrudged humanity the high honor of God's assumption of human nature. This vexed him and his companions. They became envious when they learned that God would despise them and assume human nature. Therefore, Lucifer and his hosts fell and were driven out of heaven.

For if an emperor were to place a beggar at the head of his table and were to assign the seats at the lower end to great and

j This heading and others in brackets were not in the original text. They have been added to aid the reader.

k For more on Bernard of Clairvaux, see n. 4 below.

mighty lords, kings, princes, to learned scholars and wise counselors, they would certainly be amazed and humiliated by this act. We human beings on earth cannot do better than the elder son, of whom we read in Luke 15:25-30. His brother, the prodigal son, the reveler and rake, was now reduced to begging and had returned. In welcome, his father had butchered a fatted calf for this spoiled son, who had devoured his living with harlots and knaves, whereas the father had never given even a kid to him who always obeyed his commands. When the elder brother heard all this, he became angry and jealous.

St. Bernard thought that Lucifer and his company were similarly affected when they learned that God was to become a human and not an angel. And if we really ponder the matter, we cannot but conclude that it would have been far more reasonable and honorable for God to adopt the nature of his noblest creatures, the angels, than that of sinful human nature, which had imbibed the poison of the old serpent, the devil, in Paradise. God's assumption of human nature and the union of God and humanity in the person of Christ are comparable to placing a filthy sow at table and chasing away holy and pious people.

Furthermore, St. Bernard said that the good angels rejoiced at the time and said: "If this arrangement is pleasing to God, our Lord and Creator, then it is also pleasing to us." And they remained in heaven and recognized Christ as their Lord and God. This is verified in Matt. 28:6, where the angel says to Mary Magdalene and to other women: "Come, see the place where the Lord lay."

Although these ideas expressed by St. Bernard do not constitute an article of faith, they do sound plausible. It is indeed annoying to our nature to see God himself take on this poor, feeble, and corrupt human nature, and disdain the holy, glorious, angelic nature. Thus, St. Bernard's heart and mind gave free play to his reflections on the words of our text, and his meditations betoken his wondering delight over them. That is also what he wants to convey to and impress on us.[4]

The dear fathers, I say, were amazed that the divine majesty assumed every aspect of this bag of worms, our human nature, except sin and guiltiness of death. He ate, drank, slept, waked, etc.; but he was not born in sin as we were. To be sure, this is so indescribable and inexplicable that anyone who really believes it must needs wonder. Yes, heaven, earth, and every creature must

4. That Luther so valued "the fathers" and that he numbered St. Bernard of Clairvaux (1090–1153) among them may seem doubly surprising. But Luther consistently cited and appreciated the "church fathers," meaning especially St. Augustine (354–430) from the early church, and he used the traditional definition of "father" to include Bernard (and other twelfth-century authors) since they preceded the "Scholastics" or schoolmen of the thirteenth century such as Thomas Aquinas (1225–1274). In fact, Luther held Bernard in consistently high regard exactly for this emphasis on Christ and the incarnation. An earlier sermon in this series had quoted Bernard quite fully on Christ's "holy suffering and death" (LW 22:52).

be awe-stricken at the thought that God should regard humanity dearer and nobler than an angel, although a human is really a wretched creature by comparison. God's preference for the human nature over the angelic might well arouse envy. But all this should make us meditate on the great glory that is ours. For the angels in heaven rejoice over the incarnation. This is why they constantly surround the Lord and serve him. This is why they were about his grave when he arose from the dead.

Therefore, the holy fathers had good reason to contemplate these words so much: "And was made human." It would not be out of place for us still to weep for joy. Even if I should never be saved—which God forbid!—this thought would still fill me with joy: that Christ, who is of my flesh, blood, and soul, is sitting in heaven at the right hand of God the Father, and that such an honor has been conferred on my frame, flesh, and blood. As St. Bernard further deliberated on these words, he derived some very comforting thoughts from them. He said: "Now I can see that God my Lord is not angry with me; for he is my flesh and blood and sits at the right hand of the heavenly Father as Lord over all creatures. If he were ill-disposed toward me, he would not have taken on my flesh and blood."[5] We, too, should contemplate these words, "And was made human," with reverent awe and sing them with long notes as is done in church.[6] This is proper and right, since all our comfort and joy against sin, death, devil, hell, and despair revolve about them and nothing else.

5. PL 183:792. Bernard, furthermore, identified Christ's incarnate mortality as the gift presented to us as the human heirs who otherwise had no claim on heaven, an exchange motif Luther developed in *The Freedom of a Christian*, as mentioned in the introduction. In general, Bernard's poetic preaching on the sufferings of Christ in the flesh inspired poetry and hymnody well known in Lutheran tradition, such as "Wide Open Are Thy Hands" and especially the chorale beloved by J. S. Bach, "O Sacred Head, Now Wounded." In sum, Luther quoted and praised Bernard often in his writings, although not for his devotion to the Virgin Mary, as several studies have fully documented, for example, Franz Posset, *Pater Bernhardus: Martin Luther and Bernard of Clairvaux* (Kalamazoo, MI: Cistercian Publications, 1999).

6. Namely, the Nicene Creed (see pp. 438–39 and n. 3 above).

[Examples of Irreverence and Reverence]

The following tale is told about a coarse and brutal lout. While the words "And was made human" were being sung in church, he remained standing, neither genuflecting nor removing his hat. He showed no reverence, but just stood there like a clod. All the others dropped to their knees when the Nicene Creed was prayed and chanted devoutly. Then the devil stepped up to him and hit him so hard it made his head spin. He cursed him gruesomely and said: "May hell consume you, you boorish ass! If God had become an angel like me and the congregation sang: 'God was made an angel,' I would bend not only my knees but my whole body to the ground! Yes, I would crawl ten yards down into the ground. And you vile human creature, you stand there like a stick or a stone. You hear that God did not become an angel but a human like you, and you just stand there like a stick of wood!" Whether this story is true or not, it is nevertheless in accordance with the faith (Rom. 12:6). With this illustrative story, the holy fathers wished to admonish the youth to revere the indescribably great miracle of the incarnation; they wanted us to open our eyes wide and ponder these words well.

I have also read of a number of people who, when persistently assailed by the devil, crossed themselves and spoke these words: "The Word became flesh," or the equivalent: "I am a Christian!" with the result that the devil was beaten and put to flight and their peace of mind was restored.[7] And I believe this to be true, so long as the words are spoken from a believing heart. Little is gained against the devil with a lengthy disputation; but a brief word and reply such as this is effective: "I am a Christian, of the same flesh and blood as my Lord Christ, the Son of God. You settle with him, devil!" Such a retort would soon make him depart.

7. The interesting example of a nun comes up on page 445.

It is certain that if anyone could speak these words, "And the Word became flesh," in true faith and with strong confidence in hours of the greatest temptation, he would be delivered from his trouble and distress; for the devil fears these words when they are uttered by a believer. I have often read and also witnessed it myself that many, when alarmed and distraught, spoke these words, "And the Word became flesh," and at the same time made the sign of the cross, and thereby routed the devil. Belief in these words was so powerful that it overcame the world and the devil. There is another story or legend which is told about the devil. He was listening unmoved as the initial words of the Gospel of St. John were being read: "In the beginning was the Word." But when the words "And the Word became flesh" were pronounced, he vanished. And again, whether this story is truth or fiction, the fact remains that the devil will surely take to his heels before anyone who speaks or meditates on these words in true faith. That the Son of God is the Light and Life of humankind is a thought he cannot bear. He chuckles contentedly inside himself when he observes that humanity does not accept Christ, as St. John declared in verse eleven of our chapter. But the words "God's Son became human"[l] knock all his thoughts to pieces.

l See WA 46:628,70.

It is, however, a frightful misuse and a piece of witchery to write the words "In the beginning was the Word" on a slip of paper, encase this in a quill or some other container, and hang it around one's neck or somewhere else; or to read these words as a protective charm against thunder and storm, as was customary in the papacy.[8] Sorcerers also have the habit of misusing the names of Jesus, Mary; of the four evangelists, Matthew, Mark, Luke, and John; of the holy three kings; also the words: "Jesus of Nazareth, the King of the Jews" in connection with their knavery and whoremongering.

The godless do this in imitation of the apostles, their disciples, and many pious bishops and saints of a later day, who performed signs and wonders if they spoke only a few words from the gospel. The godless also uttered these words with the intention of performing such miracles. The Jews declare that Jesus had wrought miracles with the help of the Tetragrammaton.[9] And they supposed that by repeating this, though without faith, they could do the same thing. Luke cites an example in Acts 19:13.

But, brother, not that way. You are making it a work without faith. There is a world of difference between the words of a believer and those of an unbeliever. If faith is wanting, there is no power in the words. Unless the devil wants to strengthen an error thereby, he does not care at all if a godless papist or a sorcerer uses the same words that a Christian quotes in faith. A Christian's words, however, the devil cannot ignore. And if you speak the words in faith, it will be done to you in accord with those words; they cannot but be effective. Therefore, there is a great difference between him who speaks these words in faith and him who employs them for sorcery. Every sorcerer feigns holiness, saying: "You must recite the Lord's Prayer three or five times and pronounce the names Jesus, Mary, Luke, and John; also the words: 'The Word became flesh.'" Without these words, they say, their magic is impotent. They declare: "After all, those are good words, found in Holy Scripture." May the devil take such wisdom! These words were not given for you to misuse; you are to believe them, in order that you may get your wish and desire in and through faith. But your disregard of faith and your practice of sorcery and monkey business is a shameful abuse of these words.

Such a fellow was Simon Magus. When he observed that the Holy Spirit was imparted visibly through the laying on of the

8. The *Malleus Maleficarum* II.2.7 prescribed saying exactly these words as a defense against hailstorms, and claimed that this was a catholic practice. The passage from the *Malleus* was also quoted by Luther's adversary, Silvestro Mazzolini Prierias, *De Strigimagarum demonumque mirandis libri iii* (Rome: Antonius Bladis de Asula, 24 Sept 1521), sigs. ff ii^v and following.

9. The four-letter Hebrew name for God sometimes rendered Yahweh or Jehovah. See Exod. 3:14.

apostles' hands (Acts 8:18-19), he offered them money, saying: "Give this power to me, too, that anyone on whom I lay my hands may receive the Holy Spirit." He did not care about faith; his sole concern was the acquisition of the power to transmit the Holy Spirit to others. This gift he wanted to purchase from the apostles; then he wanted to work miracles without faith. He wanted to degrade it to an object of barter, convert it into a fair, where he would fleece others with this gift. St. Peter answered him severely, saying (Acts 8:20): "Your silver perish with you, because you thought you could obtain the gift of God with money." The words of our text are meant for those who believe them, not for those who mumble them without faith. But since these knaves discovered that the holy fathers used these words for their protection, they began to practice magic with them.

One reads of a holy nun who said no more than "I am a Christian" when assailed by the devil.[10] And with these words she protected herself against the devil, who was forced to leave her. I am inclined to believe this story; for many a pious soul was

Satan tempts Jesus in the wilderness, illustrating the petition in the Lord's Prayer, "Lead us not into temptation." Woodcut from Luther's *Large Catechism* (1531).

10. Earlier, Luther commented that the key phrase "the Word became flesh" has an equivalent, "I am a Christian." In itself, this is a striking equivalency, and it shows in another way that Luther considers the incarnation at the heart of Christian identity. Also striking is this glimpse of "a holy nun" who used the latter phrase to repel the devil. Although Luther here says he is "inclined to believe this story," we might miss its importance to him if we only see this one brief mention. But this was one of Luther's favorite stories, shared almost twenty times early and late in his career, in sermons, treatises, lectures and "table talks." Sometimes she is a holy virgin, sometimes a nun; sometimes she is named Mechthild or Metildis, sometime Megdilla or Machilde; sometimes she adds "I have been baptized." But always she says "I am a Christian," and this alone thwarts the devil and the temptation to despair or give up the faith. Here, her comment is taken as the functional equivalent of the central Christian conviction that "the Word became flesh," a small phrase but powerful when spoken in faith. See Carolyn M. Schneider, *I Am a Christian: The Nun, the Devil, and Martin Luther* (Minneapolis: Fortress Press, 2010).

kept wonderfully in the true faith through God's grace while in the papacy, as Abraham was in Ur of the Chaldees and Lot in Sodom. It is true that whoever could sing such words against the terrors of the devil and against the evil world would never be duped by the devil. It is a small word, but it is pregnant with meaning and power. Wherever it is spoken in faith, the devil cannot abide. But in the mouth of an adulterer, a whoremonger, or a miser the word profits nothing.

Therefore, we should constantly have such and similar words in our heart and on our lips. We should learn not to argue with the devil when he tempts us; for he surpasses us by far in might, cunning, and understanding—even of Holy Scripture. We should beat him off curtly with the words "The Word became flesh" or "I am a Christian" or "I believe in Jesus Christ, our Lord, who was conceived by the Holy Spirit, born of the Virgin Mary, and became human." Then see what he will accomplish!

It is not surprising if an unbeliever parrots these scriptural words of a believer without effect, for there is no power without faith. Therefore, the dear fathers accomplished much by writing so much and so often about these words: "The Word became flesh"; "And was made human." This was done to inculcate reverence for them. Formerly, during the papacy, one uncovered the head, genuflected, or, in some places, even knelt during the chanting or reading of these words. Now we can sing and hear them with far greater and holier joy, because today, thank God, we know and understand what an indescribable treasure is offered, yes, is given us through these words. For those who accept and retain them in faith are the children of God.

[Summary]

To summarize, no angel, much less a prophet or apostle, can fully express the truth that the eternal Son of God, who, according to Isa. 53:9 and 1 Pet. 2:22, "committed no sin, and no guile was found on his lips," and, for that reason, was not guilty of death, yet became incarnate for our comfort and salvation. Yes, he became a curse and sin for us, in order to deliver us from the eternal curse and to justify us (Gal. 3:13; Rom. 8:3; 2 Cor. 5:21).

Thus, the evangelist John preached of the Word, which was in the beginning, which was with God the Father, which was eternal God with the Father, through which all things were created, which was the Life and Light of humankind shining into the darkness, which came into the world, which dwelt among humans, and, in spite of this, was not recognized by humanity. However, that he might be made manifest, God sent John the Baptist to go before him to bear witness to him. But the great multitude paid John's testimony no heed. And when Christ came into his own, preached, and worked miracles, his own did not accept him. But to those who did receive him he gave power to become the children of God. All this we have now covered in detail.

John fails to mention Mary, the Lord's mother, with as much as a word.[11] Luke, however, does write at some length in his second chapter about Christ's birth from her in Bethlehem. John gave the mother scant attention. Paul also disposes of her with the brief words "born of a woman" (Gal. 4:4). For the greater the men of God and the larger the measure of the Spirit in them, the greater the diligence and attention they devote to the Son rather than to the mother. The outstanding men have always

A finely detailed engraving of the madonna with the Christ Child by Martin Schongauer (1450–1491)

11. Here Luther does not mind that John's Gospel pays little attention to Mary, indeed none at all in the prologue or about the incarnation itself and only later when Jesus seems to chide her at Cana. Of course, he says that Luke pays her more tribute, and he himself commented on her "Magnificat" quite eloquently. But even greater than Luke's perspective is the perspective of John and also Paul (who barely alludes to Mary), since the proper focus should be on Christ, the fruit of her womb, and not on her for herself, although she was a "holy, pure, and chaste virgin." His Christmas homilies and the tract *That Jesus Christ Was Born a Jew* (TAL 5:391–439) give Mary a central human place, with detail and conviction, but John's silence on Mary serves Luther well in the context of Roman Catholic devotion to her in her own right as mediator. Overall, her role is essential as anchoring the full humanity of Christ, but in this literary and historical context she receives little mention at all.

insisted that we fasten our gaze on the fruit, that is, the Son of God, who made and created all, who is the Light of the world, and who became truly human. To be sure, Mary was a holy, pure, and chaste virgin, favored among women, as the angel assured her in Luke 1:42 and as she herself sang in her song: "Henceforth all generations will call me blessed" (Luke 1:48). But her one concern was the incarnation of the true Son of God. John refers to Mary in chapter two of his Gospel. Here he reports that Christ almost chided her at the marriage at Cana, saying to her: "O woman, what have you to do with me?" His one purpose was the proper portrayal of the person of Christ.

"And the Word became flesh"

The evangelist states: "The same Word of which I declared that it was in the beginning, through which all things were made, which was the Life and Light of humanity, became flesh." In scriptural parlance, "flesh" denotes a complete human being, as in John 3:6, where we read: "That which is born of the flesh is flesh." It goes without saying that of a woman both body and soul are born, not an inanimate mass of flesh, a physical being of flesh and blood, designated by Scripture with that one word "flesh." Similarly, fleshly wisdom, glory, power, and strength are the equivalent of what we in the German tongue call human wisdom, glory, power, and whatever may be great and glorious in the world.

Thus, the most precious treasure and the strongest consolation we Christians have is this: that the Word, the true and natural Son of God, became human, with flesh and blood like that of any other human; that he became incarnate for our sakes in order that we might enter into great glory, that our flesh and blood, skin and hair, hands and feet, stomach, and back might reside in heaven as God does, and in order that we might boldly defy the devil and whatever else assails us. We are convinced that all our members belong in heaven as heirs of heaven's realm.

We have already heard how Arius, Cerinthus, and other Heretics impugned the article concerning the deity of Christ.[12] Heretics also arose to call his humanity into question. They asserted that Christ, the true Son of God, was without a soul, inferring this from the fact that the evangelist failed to make mention of a

12. As he says, Luther had already discussed and dismissed Arius (c. 250–336) and others who did not confess Christ as fully divine, the presenting issue at the Council of Nicaea in 325. A very recent sermon had presented Arius and "Arians" quite thoroughly: they grant that Christ was divine, but not equal to the Father, thus not fully divine, more a creature than the creator. Yet John has said, "All things were made through him," a "strong testimony and incontrovertible proof against the Arians" (LW 22:75). "Cerinthus" (c. 100) was named by Irenaeus (*Against Heresies* I, 26) as a chief proponent in apostolic times of the extreme view that Christ was not God, but merely human, and not born of a virgin, as Luther covered in his first sermon (LW 22:7).

Emperor Constantine and the Council of Nicaea. The burning of Arian books is illustrated below. Illustration on vellum dating to c. 825 from a book of canon law.

soul but merely said: "And the Word became flesh." Thus, the Apollinarists alleged that Christ adopted only a human body, but not both body and soul; they declared that his divinity replaced the soul.[13] They were stupid asses. It would be just as logical to say that Christ had no body either; for "flesh" and "body" are not identical. But we cannot be mistaken, because we follow Scripture, which says in the story of the creation of Adam and Eve: "They will become one flesh" (Gen. 2:24). In our language we translate this: "Adam and Eve will become one body." In scriptural usage, the word "flesh" embraces both body and soul, for without the soul the body is dead.

In spite of the fact that throughout Scripture body and soul, together with all their capacities, are called flesh, those stupid

13. Since the preacher had already addressed those who qualified or denied the full divinity of Christ, he here gives more attention to the other side of the story, those who qualify or deny the full humanity of Christ. Apollinaris (d. c. 390), eager to ensure the full divinity of Christ, had argued that the divine Word had adopted a human body but not the (rational) soul, since the Word in effect replaced the human mind or soul. The second ecumenical Council at Constantinople (381) reaffirmed that Christ was fully divine, equal to the Father, *and* asserted against Apollinaris that Christ was also fully human, of body and human soul, as confirmed in the later Council of Chalcedon (451). Luther here makes the same argument not by citing the councils, as he does elsewhere, but by way of biblical language and common usage. "The Word became flesh" signals humiliation and mortality, not a body separated from the soul.

asses take the word to mean the kind of flesh dogs and wolves have. Those people have no understanding of Scripture. The text "The Word became flesh" supports our position. "The Word," that is, the eternal Son of God, "became flesh," that is, became human, born of the Virgin Mary. In the German language the word "body" does not denote a corpse; it denotes a living person in possession of body and soul. Therefore, the view referred to is rank heresy and is easily detected. And we should gladly hear sermons on this article of faith, accept it in true faith and with a happy heart, and praise and thank God for inviting us to this blessed proclamation.

It is true, the evangelist might have said: "The Word became human." However, he adapts himself to scriptural parlance and says: "He became flesh." He does so to point out its weakness and its mortality. For Christ took on the human nature, which was mortal and subject to the terrible wrath and judgment of God because of the sins of the human race. And this anger was felt by the weak and mortal flesh of Christ.

With that word "flesh" the evangelist wanted to indicate this inexpressible humiliation. Isaiah says (53:10): "When you make his soul," that is, his life, "an offering for sin, he shall see his seed; he shall prolong his days." And St. Paul writes to the Galatians (3:13): "Christ redeemed us from the curse of the law, having become a curse for us."

But we are not to assume that the evangelist used the word "flesh" lightly. Human reason cannot comprehend the magnitude of God's anger over sin. Therefore, it does not fathom Paul's full meaning when he says that God had made Christ a sin and curse for our sakes (2 Cor. 5:21; Gal. 3:13). But the dear Lord was fully aware of this; he felt and endured the great and terrible wrath of God so that "His sweat became like great drops of blood" and an angel from heaven appeared to strengthen him (Luke 22:43-44).

"And dwelt among us"

The same Word, which became human, Mary suckled and carried in her arms as any other mother does her child. He came to humans, lived and dwelt among them. Thus, it was no ghost but a true human, "taking the form of a servant," as St. Paul says (Phil. 2:7), "being born in human likeness" with regard to seeing, hearing, speaking, eating, drinking, sleeping, and waking, so that all who saw and heard him were constrained to confess and say that he was a true and natural human. He did not withdraw from people, retire into some shelter, escape into the desert, where no one could hear, see, or touch him. But he appeared publicly, preaching and performing miracles, thereby enabling all the people who were about him, among whom he moved and lived, to hear and touch him. Thus, John says in the beginning of his epistle: "That which was from the beginning, which we have heard, which we have seen with our eyes, which we have looked upon and touched with our hands" (1 John 1:1). And at the same time he was the Word of life and the Creator of all creatures. All this is what the evangelist wants to convey with the words: "And dwelt among us." He was no ghost; he was a true human. St. Paul bears this out in Phil. 2:6, where he says: "Though he was in the form of God, he did not think it robbery to be equal with God but took upon himself the form of a servant and was like any other human."

The heretical Manichaeans, knaves that they were, took offense at the assertion that the Son of God had become human.[14] To embellish their error, they feigned great saintliness and profound wisdom, saying that it was an insult to the divine majesty to claim that he had been born from poor and sin-corrupted, impure, and mortal flesh, and from the flesh of a woman at that. They protested that it was impossible that the divine purity, which exceeds the brightness of the sun, should submerge itself into this vile slime. Therefore, they averred that Mary was not the true, natural, and physical mother of Christ. They used the analogy of a piece of red glass, which casts a red shadow on the wall, where it can be clearly seen although the wall is, in fact, not red in color; or of a sunbeam, which shines through a piece of blue glass and casts a blue reflection. Thus, they claimed, a shadow or phantom passed through Mary, like a ghost that has no real body or soul. They claimed that Christ had only resembled a human, but in reality was no true human. Thus, they reduced him to a ghost; this implies, of course, that the Jews crucified an incorporeal phantom.

In this way they tried to make their heresy palatable. And, in fact, they did succeed in seducing many good people; for this is a glittering and glistening heresy. St. Augustine lay ensnared in it for nine whole years, and he would have remained there

14. As with the Apollinarists, the Manichaeans objected to the incarnation but even more so, since the divine in their view can have no commerce with the material of humanity. To these extreme, even cosmic, dualists, the spiritual and the material are completely alien to each other, even stemming from two separate sources or gods. In such a view, obviously the divine cannot become flesh. Luther sees clearly the immense implications of such an extreme dualism, for if there is no incarnation there is no real crucifixion or resurrection. Further, they disparage Mary as a real embodied woman who really gave birth and nursed the baby Jesus.

15. That St. Augustine was freed from the seductive Manichaean lies about embodiment including Mary is nicely credited to another woman, his mother, Monica (322–387) (*Confessions*, Book 4). With Augustine and the Creed, Luther affirms often that Christ became "a natural human like any other human of flesh and blood," yet without sin. Otherwise, the faith falls apart, for there can be no resurrection without a real death, and no real death without a fully embodied human life.

The Saint Augustine Taken to School by Saint Monica. Painting by Nicolo di Pietro (c. 1415).

had not the assiduous praying of his mother, Monica, liberated him.[15] It sounds shocking when these people claim that Christ neither ate nor drank and that the Jews crucified a phantom, not the real Christ. By their denial of Christ's humanity, at which they took offense, they wished to pay homage to God.

But we believe the Scriptures and confess with holy Christendom, which existed at all times and will endure till the end of the world, that this article of our holy Christian creed, together with all others, is firmly and solidly established by the testimony of the holy prophets and apostles, the spokesmen of the Holy Spirit: that Christ, our Lord and God, assumed true human nature, not the nature of an immaterial phantom, and that he became a natural human like any other human of flesh and blood. He did not flutter about like a spirit, but he dwelt among people. He had eyes, ears, mouth, nose, chest, stomach, hands, and feet, just as you and I do. He took the breast. His mother nursed him as any other child is nursed. He acted as any other human does. He was born as a true human from the Virgin Mary; the one difference, however, was that he was not born in sin as we are, that "He committed no sin, and no guile was found on his lips" (Isa. 53:9; 1 Pet. 2:22).

When the evangelist declared that Christ dwelt among us, he meant to say: "He did not appear like the angel Gabriel, who came to Mary with God's command and then soon departed from her; for angels do not tarry long in visible form among humankind. Christ, however, remained with us according to his human nature, which was inseparably united with the divine since his incarnation. Into his thirty-fourth year he ate and drank with us, he was angry and sad, he prayed and he wept. He executed his Father's mission, suffered persecution and death in the end at the hands of his own people. And thus the Jews crucified the true Son of God, the Lord of Glory (1 Cor. 2:8); and we saw his blood oozing forth and flowing to the ground."

This is the article of faith which we Christians believe, which is our greatest consolation, and by means of which we become children of God. We should not engage in lengthy debates about whether the fact that God became human redounds to God's glory or to his disgrace; but we should accept it gladly and with all our hearts as something for our welfare and comfort, and we should thank God for it sincerely.

Now there follows: *"We have beheld his glory."*

What does this mean? The evangelist wants to say that Christ not only demonstrated his humanity with his actions, by dwelling among the people so that they could see him, hear him, speak with him, and live near him until his thirty-fourth year, by suffering cold, hunger, and thirst in this feeble and wretched human form and nature, but that he also displayed his glory and power in proof of his divinity. Of this he gave proof with his teaching, his preaching, his signs and wonders, convincing anyone of his Godhead who was not blinded and hardened by the devil, as the high priests and scribes were. By word and deed he proved that he was God by nature: he healed the sick and raised the dead; in short, he wrought more and greater miracles than any prophet before him, in fact, than any other human being ever was able to do.

By way of illustration, as God brought forth heaven and earth through the Word, that is, through him, even so he, too, performed all that he wished by uttering a word. For instance: "Little girl, I say to you, arise" (Mark 5:41); and: "Young man, I say to you, arise" (Luke 7:14); and: "Lazarus, come out!" (John 11:43); and to the paralytic: "Rise, take up your bed and go home, be delivered of your sickness" (Matt. 9:6); and to the lepers: "Be clean!" (Matt. 8:3; Luke 17:14). In a similar way he fed five thousand men with five loaves of bread and two fish, prompting those who witnessed this miracle to say: "This is indeed the prophet who is to come into the world" (John 6:14). When a great storm arose on the sea and the Lord rebuked the winds and the sea, all those in his ship marveled, saying: "What sort of man is this, that even winds and sea obey him?" (Matt. 8:27). With his words he also exorcised the evil spirits. All this he could accomplish with a single word.

"As of the only-begotten of the Father"

This is the first time John calls the Word the only-begotten Son of the Father. In these words: "As of the only-begotten of the Father" you have the evangelist's own explanation and the answer to your question regarding the meaning of his words: "In the beginning was the Word"; "All things were made through the Word"; "He was the Life and Light of all people." Here you hear his own interpretation of them: "The Word, which was with the Father from eternity and is the Light of humanity, is called the Son, yes, the only-begotten Son of God. He alone is that, and no one else." Here we find the idea clearly stated which the evangelist wanted to convey earlier with the term "Word." Henceforth, he intends to preach plainly of the kingdom of Christ. Until now he has done so with odd and obscure expressions which lack clarity in any language. But now he says: "This is God's only-begotten Son."

God has many sons and daughters besides; but he has only one only-begotten Son, of whom it is said that all was created through him. The other sons are not the Word, through which all things were made; but they themselves were created through this only-begotten Son, who is coequal Creator of heaven and earth with the Father. All others became sons through the only-begotten Son, who is our God and Lord. There are many begotten sons; he alone is the only-begotten Son, begotten in the Godhead from eternity.[16] Thus, the Word, through which all things are made and preserved, was made flesh, that is, human, was born according to the flesh from the seed of Abraham and David, dwelt among us, and redeemed us from the curse and the power of the devil. By virtue of his incarnation and his eternal and glorious divinity we poor mortals who believe in his name become children of God, and God becomes our Father. We emphasize that Christ alone is, as St. Paul declares (Rom. 1:4), the only-begotten Son of God, through whom God creates, rules, and makes all things.

We must treasure this text and take comfort from it in hours of sadness and temptation. Whoever lays hold of it in faith is lifted out of his distress, for he is a child of eternal bliss. And to this honor he falls heir through the only-begotten Son, who is God from eternity. Now this Gospel begins to be lucid and clear. Until now the evangelist employed peculiar expressions, uncommon in any language, saying: "In the beginning was the Word"; "through the Word the world was made"; and "the Word became flesh." Whoever heard such speech before? But now all becomes plain and evident. Now the evangelist says: "The Word, of which

16. Here Luther pauses to clarify the phrase "only-begotten Son." Although God has many sons and daughters, he says, meaning us as children of God through Christ, only one is *uniquely* begotten in the sense of God's own self expression as the Son or Word from all eternity. Alternating the language of Son and Word reinforces the message that the text refers to God's self-expression. When we, too, "give our word" we give ourselves in a way, and some sons even today are named for their fathers (with "junior" added) as a form of paternal self-expression. Luther appreciates the Johannine language of the Word, with God from the beginning and by whom all creation came into being, as indicating the uniqueness of this begetting, unlike the rest of us sons and daughters begotten and children of God in a different and derivative way.

I have spoken to you, is the only-begotten Son of God, true God and Creator with the Father, differing only in this, that he was born of the Father, and the Father not from him." Thus, we confess and pray: "And in Jesus Christ, His only-begotten Son." In Gen. 1:3 we find a similar expression: "God said." And, as already stated, John here adds the explanation.

That Jesus Christ is very God and very human, the only-begotten Son of the Father, begotten of him in eternity, and born of the Virgin Mary in time, and that believers in him are redeemed from sin and all evil—this is our Christian faith.[17] This alone makes us Christians. It makes us adopted sons of God, but not his natural children; for Christ, our Head, alone is the natural, true, and only-begotten Son of God the Father. This gospel should be highly prized and regarded by us, as the holy fathers also regarded it. For whoever has the Son is free from trouble, for

Christ the Savior (Pantokrator), a sixth-century encaustic icon from Saint Catherine's Monastery, Mount Sinai. The halo is a representation of the divine *logos* of Christ, and the two different facial expressions on either side emphasize Christ's dual nature as both divine and human.

17. Here at the end, Luther again identifies the incarnation as our Christian faith, as what makes us Christians as adopted children of God. Yet the incarnation for Luther is more than a single event, however pivotal for world history. It is also a way to understand other occasions of the divine meeting the human. "Fully divine and fully human" can also characterize Luther's understanding, for example, of the biblical word as God's Word and yet also as human words. The Bible is both. This relationship of divine and human is like a red thread running through many doctrinal topics in Luther, or, as Johann Anselm Steiger calls it, the "axle and motor" of his theology. "The *communicatio idiomatum* as the Axle and Motor of Luther's Theology," *Lutheran Quarterly* 14 (2000): 125–58.

As in the paramount case of the incarnation itself, the claim of "fully divine" needs to be held together with the claim of "fully human." Holy Scripture, to continue that example, is not only the Word of God; to be expressed and heard, it needs to be fully human as well, articulated out of concrete human contexts and expressed in concrete human conditions. The same goes for preaching, since Luther had a strong conviction that the proclamation of the gospel, in obviously human words such as his own, was God's very word both of law and of gospel. Hearing the preacher's word, the hearers of the gospel were hearing God's own Word, and should trust that their forgiveness thus came from God's own voice. See H. S. Wilson, "Luther on Preaching as God Speaking," in *The Pastoral Luther*, ed. Timothy J. Wengert (Grand Rapids: Eerdmans, 2009), 100–114, with further bibliography. This high view of the Word

then he is a child of God. Although he is not the only-begotten Son of God, he nonetheless becomes a son of God through him, and as such he is his co-heir and brother.

The evangelist also stated that "the Word became flesh and dwelt among us," as any human being dwells among humans. We have learned that Christ was a natural human, and then we also beheld his glory as that of the only-begotten Son of the Father. This glory was demonstrated when he raised the dead and when he himself arose from the dead by divine power. Thus, he said in John 10:18: "I have power to lay my life down, and I have power to take it again." After his resurrection he showed himself alive for forty days, imparting the Holy Spirit. Thus, the same Word that became incarnate is "full of grace and truth." Accordingly, the evangelist differentiates between Christ and the patriarchs, Moses, and all the prophets; he exalts him above all the others. It is as if he were saying: "In all ages there have been great men, though in some more than in others. For example, there were Adam, Noah, Abraham, Isaac, Jacob, Moses, Joshua, Samuel, David, Elijah, Elisha, all of whom proved by word and deed that they were friends and children of God. God worked many great miracles through them; they preached and taught, and their sermons and teachings were passed on to us as our inheritance through the records of Holy Writ. For this reason they were excellent and great men even in the eyes of the world. They believed in Christ as their Savior who was to come; and thus they were children of God, born of and from God, the same as we. They proved themselves by word and deed; and the glory we perceive in them is divine, not physical and earthly. The Old Testament Scriptures also bear witness to this. Nevertheless, they are in no respect comparable to the Word that became flesh."

becoming human words extended, for Luther, to the words of explicit absolution and also to the personal words a pastor (or a parent) can give someone in need of forgiveness.

Not only Scripture, preaching, and other pastoral acts, but the church itself was in one way divinely founded and assured of divine favor and in another way an assembly of the sinful arrayed in human weakness. Of course, the two sacraments also shared this parallel with the dynamics of "fully divine and fully human." Baptism is God's adoptive embrace *and* the human community's initiation at the same time. So, too, but more complicated, with the Lord's Supper. The body of Christ is received along with real bread; to deny the former was the error of the (Zwinglian) sacramentarians, in Luther's view, and to deny the latter, thinking that what *looks* like bread no longer has the *substance* of bread, was the unhelpful philosophical explanation of transubstantiation according to Scholastic theology. Even Luther's ethics and humor, says Steiger, presuppose this same incarnational paradigm of fully divine *and* fully human. Thus, the incarnation for Luther has immense implications for the Christian message and the Christian life, although not all of them can come out in any one sermon.

Preface to the Epistle to the Romans

1522, and as revised 1546

EUAN K. CAMERON

INTRODUCTION

The Epistle to the Romans is probably the most important single book of Scripture for the history of the Reformation in Europe. It was commented upon, preached over, expounded, and argued over endlessly, especially for those passages that seemed to contain the decisive proof texts for the Reformation doctrines of justification and salvation. Yet the letter to the Romans is far from a clear or simple pastoral epistle. Although placed first in the traditional listing of Paul's epistles, some scholars believe that it may have been the last, or nearly the last, of the authentic letters of Paul to have been written. It was written to a church that Paul had not founded. It does not concentrate on specific issues in church government or conduct. Rather, it embodies a highly sophisticated theology of the relationship between Paul's Jewish heritage and the emerging movement of Jewish and non-Jewish followers of Jesus. Its primary purpose or object has been and continues to be debated.

Perhaps because of its considerable rhetorical and theological complexity, the epistle had been studied in many different ways by Christian exegetes down the centuries. The early fathers, Augustine (354–430) especially, reflected extensively on the epistle. For the antecedents of Luther, the most important thread of exposition was probably that which led from Hugh of Saint-Cher (c. 1200–1263) through Thomas Aquinas (1224–1274) to Nicholas of Lyra (1270–1349). Lyra's *Literal Postill* was complete by 1331, and embodied his characteristic approach of favoring the "literal" reading, with the assumption that the literal sense of Scripture comprehended its spiritual and prophetic senses. However, Lyra's theological analysis of the believer's growth in faith, where faith was formed by charity, would serve as a provocation to Luther's quite different interpretation.[a]

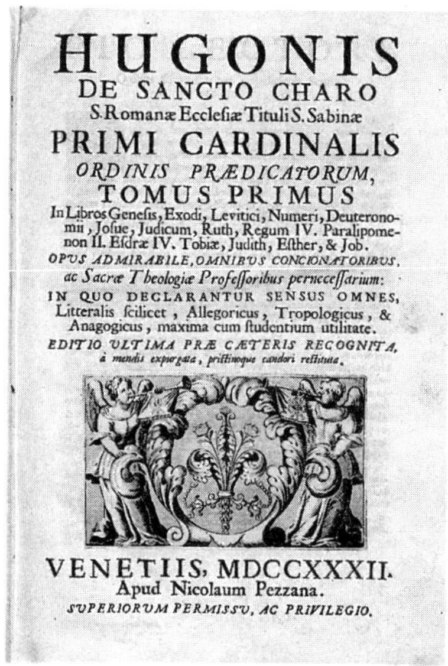

HUGONIS
DE SANCTO CHARO
S. Romanæ Ecclesiæ Tituli S. Sabinæ
PRIMI CARDINALIS
ORDINIS PRÆDICATORUM,
TOMUS PRIMUS
In Libros Genesis, Exodi, Levitici, Numeri, Deuteronomii, Josue, Judicum, Ruth, Regum IV. Paralipomenon II. Esdræ IV. Tobiæ, Judith, Esther, & Job.
OPUS ADMIRABILE, OMNIBUS CONCIONATORIBUS, ac Sacræ Theologiæ Professoribus pernecessarium:
IN QUO DECLARANTUR SENSUS OMNES, Litteralis scilicet, Allegoricus, Tropologicus, & Anagogicus, maxima cum studentium utilitate.
EDITIO ULTIMA PRÆ CÆTERIS RECOGNITA, à mendis expurgata, pristinoque candori restituta.

VENETIIS, MDCCXXXII.
Apud Nicolaum Pezzana.
SUPERIORUM PERMISSU, AC PRIVILEGIO.

Hugh of Saint-Cher was a French Dominican friar and later a cardinal. He wrote extensively on the Bible. This is his *Opera Omnia in universum Vetus et Novum Testamentum,* published in Venice in 1732.

An even greater provocation to Luther was presented by Erasmus of Rotterdam (1466–1536), in his introduction and paraphrase on Romans, which appeared as the first of Erasmus's New Testament paraphrases late in 1517 or early in 1518.[b] When Erasmus's paraphrase appeared, Luther had already been lecturing on Romans in his theological faculty at Wittenberg since 1515,

a Mark W. Elliott, "Romans Commentaries in the Later Middle Ages," in William S. Campbell, Peter S. Hawkins, and Brenda Schildgen, eds., *Medieval Readings of Romans* (New York: T&T Clark, 2007), 182–201, at 182–87.

b [Erasmus], *In Epistolam Pauli Apostoli ad Romanos Paraphrasis, per Erasmum Roterodamum . . .* (Basel: Froben, January 1518).

though these lectures would remain unpublished for centuries after Luther's death.[c] By this time Luther had already developed the hermeneutic key that one sees in this preface. Luther read the letter to the Romans chiefly, if not exclusively, for the insights that it gave into Paul's teaching about the justification of sinners through faith. Erasmus, in contrast, took a quite different approach. The preface ("*argumentum*") to his paraphrase, following Lyra, first dwelt at some length on Paul's change of name from Saul to Paul. Erasmus then embarked on a discussion of what he saw as the defining context for the letter: the tension between Jewish and non-Jewish followers of Jesus in the first decades of the Christian movement. Paul was aware of the number of Jewish people in Rome, and that the presence of this large community had implications for differing responses to the message of Jesus. So he wrote the letter to both communities:

> One whyle therfore chydeth he one sorte, another whyle, another, and anone after againe comfortably encourageth them bothe. The Gentiles pride he abated, declaryng, that neither the lawe of nature, nor their Philosophie, wherof they were so proude, auayled them so, but that they fell nethelesse into all kyndes of mischief. Checkyng againe and reprouyng the Iewes arrogant myndes, whiche through theyr affiaunce in the law had lost the chiefe grounde therof, that is to wete, fayth in Iesus Christ, he teacheth them, that the ceremonies of Moses lawe are abolished through the bright beames of the gospell of Christ, whom the shadowes of the lawe rudely represented, with diuers other thynges, as the reste of the sabboth day, the displeasure and paine of circumcision, the comyng about of the calendes, the holy dayes, whiche thrise yerely came againe.[d]

EXIMII DOCTORIS HIERONYMI STRIDONENSIS VITA EX IPSIVS POTISSIMVM LITTERIS CONTEXTA PER DESYDERIVM ERASMVM ROTERODAMVM.

Acknowledgment page
of Erasmus's Greek New Testament,
engraved and published by
Johannes Froben, 1516

Erasmus continued to develop the theme of relations between Jewish and non-Jewish followers of Jesus in the *Annotations* that

c A translation of the 1515 Romans lectures is found in LW 25.

d [Desiderius Erasmus], *The seconde tome or volume of the Paraphrase of Erasmus vpon the Newe Testament conteynyng the epistles of S. Paul, and other Apostles: wherunto is added a paraphrase vpon the reuelacion of S. John* (London: Edwarde Whitchurche, 1549), sig. Cii^{v}.

he adapted and edited from the work of Lorenzo Valla (1407–1457).[e] He also emphasized—no doubt to Luther's exasperation—the rhetorical complexity and obscurity of Paul's language in parts of the epistle. At some points Erasmus's paraphrase turned out considerably longer than the text that it expounded.

By the time of Luther's translation of the New Testament (the September Testament), in which the preface to Romans first appeared, the great public rupture with Erasmus of 1524–1526 had not yet taken place. Nevertheless, some scholars suspect that Luther's preface to Romans was intended at least in part as a rebuttal of Erasmus's (and others') emphasis on what, for Luther, were peripheral issues. Unlike any of his other prefaces to books of the New Testament, Luther's preface to Romans consists, in effect, of a miniature theological treatise on justification, embedded within a chapter-by-chapter summary of the epistle. It drew chiefly on Luther's own cumulative body of work on grace and justification, which had been his driving preoccupations for nearly a decade. The preface may have owed quite a lot to the first edition of Philip Melanchthon's *Loci Communes* (*Common Places*), which had appeared in 1521 and earned Luther's enthusiastic approval.[f] When Luther stressed that one must understand "what St. Paul means by the words: 'law,' 'sin,' 'grace,' 'faith,' 'righteousness,' 'flesh,' 'spirit,'" he echoed Melanchthon's semantic approach. Some would see Luther's dialectical analysis of "law" versus "gospel" as a further outcome of his conversations with Melanchthon (1497–1560).[g]

Luther argued that "the law" in Romans could not be understood merely, as Lyra and Erasmus had argued, as a reference to the ceremonial demands of the Mosaic code. "Law" meant above all God's just demand that human beings live up to a standard of moral perfection, which our fallen natures made it quite impossible for us to attain. The function of "law," therefore, was to drive us to despair of our own "works," of our own moral capacities

e Multiple editions of this work appeared. See, e.g., *Des. Erasmi Roterodami in Novum Testamentum Annotationes*, 4th ed. (Basel: Froben, 1527).

f The edition cited here is that in MSA, vol. II, part i. For a more recent edition, see also Philipp Melanchthon, *Loci Communes 1521: Lateinisch–Deutsch*, ed. Horst Georg Pöhlmann (Gütersloh: G. Mohn, 1993).

g See L. C. Green, *How Melanchthon Helped Luther Discover the Gospel* (Fallbrook, CA: Verdict Publications, 1980).

and achievements. Only when a human being utterly despairs of human righteousness is such a person ready to receive in its fullness the message of forgiveness contained in the gospel.

Luther went on to articulate with exceptional precision, but in accessible terms in the vernacular, the distinction between "grace," which is God's gift of perfect forgiveness given for Christ's sake, and the "gifts," which are the imperfect and incomplete signs of spiritual growth and renewal seen in the lives of the faithful as the products and consequences of grace. As Luther insisted, "the gifts and the Spirit increase in us every day, but they are not yet perfect since there remain in us the evil desires and sins that war against the Spirit." In technical theological language "grace" means justification; the "gifts" mean sanctification. Here Luther set out the conceptual distinction between these two divine gifts to the believer with lucid clarity.

Luther reprinted this preface with only modest changes throughout the editions of the German Bible that appeared in his lifetime. The preface enjoyed a significant afterlife in its own right. When the Church of England under Edward VI (r. 1547–1553) decided to issue the paraphrases of Erasmus on the New Testament in English translation in 1548–1549, an edited and slightly amplified but fully recognizable version of Luther's preface to Romans was added, without attribution, before Erasmus's *argumentum* to Romans at the beginning of the second volume.[h] Thus, Luther's theology of justification entered anonymously into the early teachings of the reformed English church. Famously, on 24 May 1738, John Wesley (1703–1791), who had been falling under the influence of the Moravian Church since a visit to the American colonies, went "very unwillingly" to a religious society in Aldersgate Street, where "one was reading Luther's Preface to the Epistle to the Romans." It was during this reading that he reported that "I felt my heart strangely warmed. I felt I did trust in Christ, Christ alone for salvation, and an assurance was given me that he had taken away my sins, even mine, and saved me from the law of sin and death."[i]

h [Erasmus], *The second tome . . . of the Paraphrase*, Sigs. ✠ iiii r– ✠✠ vi r: "A Prologe . . . to the Romaynes."

i [John Wesley], *The Works of John Wesley*, vol. 18: *Journals and Diaries I, 1735–1738*), ed. Albert C. Outler, et al. (Nashville: Abingdon, 1984–), 248–50.

The "Aldersgate Flame" commemorates Wesley's spiritual experience at Aldersgate Street and features text from Wesley's journal describing it.

In the latter half of the twentieth century, theological and biblical scholarship, even in many Lutheran circles, has rather turned away from Luther's reading of Paul in Romans. What has become known as the "New Perspective on Paul" focuses the reader's attention, once again, back to Jewish-Gentile relations in the early Jesus movement. In so doing, this approach actually returns to the emphases of Lyra and even more to that of Erasmus, although with a much more constructive and ecumenical regard for Judaism than any premodern exegete could attain to. The new perspective draws attention to Paul's evident desire in Romans to hold up and to affirm both the Jewishness of Jewish followers of Jesus, and the accessibility of the gospel to Gentile followers. Over all, the grace of God—a concept that derived from Judaism—took precedence as the source of salvation.[j]

j For a brief discussion of this interpretative movement see Campbell, Hawkins, and Schildgen, eds., *Medieval Readings of Romans*, 207–12.

For Luther, of course, the primary antithesis to justification by grace was not, in this particular instance, any alleged Jewish dependence on works (despite whatever deplorable things Luther wrote about Judaism elsewhere in his writings). The primary target for Luther's critique was medieval Christian theology, with its doctrine of salvation where growth in merit, grace, faith, and godly living mysteriously collaborated to raise up the saved soul. That doctrine, Luther argued, was based in turn on concepts of virtue derived from Aristotle's *Ethics*. Luther stressed that *nothing* of what actually determined human justification depended on any increase in personal virtue. As such, the entire edifice of medieval piety, above all so-called works of supererogation, such as monasticism, fell to the ground.

Did Luther critically misrepresent Paul? Certainly so, if one focuses on the fact that Paul, to state the obvious, did not live in the sixteenth century. Paul could never have anticipated, let alone addressed, the extravagant forms that late medieval Catholic piety had assumed by 1500. On the other hand, let us suppose that Luther misconstrued (or just regarded as irrelevant) the ecclesial and community context that called forth the letter to the Romans. The fact remains that Paul in Romans solved his dilemma of Jewish-Gentile relations not merely by pastoral exhortation, but by framing a highly sophisticated theology of grace to address the paradox, to subsume Jewish and Gentile believers in the same scheme of salvation. Luther—and the countless other preachers and theologians of the Reformation who followed him—saw the theology more clearly than the context, and adapted it to their own passionately felt spiritual needs in their own times.

PREFACE TO THE EPISTLE TO THE ROMANS[k]

THIS EPISTLE is really the chief part of the New Testament, and is truly the purest gospel. It is worthy not only that every Christian should know it word for word, by heart, but also that he should occupy himself with it every day, as the daily bread of the soul. We can never read it or ponder over it too much; for the more we deal with it, the more precious it becomes and the better it tastes.

Therefore I, too, will do my best, so far as God has given me power, to open the way into it through this preface, so that it may be the better understood by everyone. Heretofore it has been badly obscured by glosses[l] and all kinds of idle talk, though in itself it is a bright light, almost sufficient to illuminate the entire Holy Scriptures.

To begin with, we must have knowledge of its language and know what St. Paul means by the words "law," "sin," "grace," "faith," "righteousness," "flesh," "spirit," and the like. Otherwise no reading of the book has any value.[1]

The little word "law" you must here not take in human fashion as a teaching about what works are to be done or not done. That is the way with human laws; a law is fulfilled by works, even though there is no heart in the doing of them. But God judges //[m] according to what is in the depths of the heart.[2] For this reason, his law, too, makes its demands on the inmost heart; it cannot be satisfied with works, but rather punishes as hypocrisy and lies the works not done from the bottom of the heart. Hence, all men

1. As observed in the introduction, this approach, which begins with accurate definition of terms as the basis for theology, appears to follow the approach used by Philip Melanchthon in the *Loci communes* (*Common Places*), of which the first edition appeared in 1521, shortly before this preface was written.

2. This distinction between the demands of human and divine law, in terms of the disposition of the one keeping the law, was very important to the reformers. Interestingly, John Calvin, in the fourth book of the *Institutes*, would draw a similar distinction between obedience to civil laws (where mere performance was sufficient) and spiritual or church discipline, where a grumbling acquiescence in the demands of church discipline was insufficient and unacceptable. See Calvin, *Inst.*, IV.xi.3–4; IV.xii.1–4.

k This edition is based on that in LW 35:365–80, and compared with the edition of the original text in WA DB 7:3–27.

l For an alphabetical listing of commentaries on Romans, including a considerable number from periods prior to the Reformation, see H. A. W. Meyer, *Critical and Exegetical Handbook to the Epistle to the Romans*, trans. William P. Dickinson (New York: Funk and Wagnalls, 1884), xv–xxiii. For the medieval exegesis of Romans—especially some of those exegetes whom Luther turned against—see Campbell, Hawkins, and Schildgen, eds., *Medieval Readings of Romans*.

m WA DB 7:4–5.

are called liars in Ps. 116[:11],[n] because no one keeps or can keep God's law from the bottom of the heart. For everyone finds in himself displeasure in what is good and pleasure in what is bad. If, now, there is no willing pleasure in the good, then the inmost heart is not set on the law of God. Then, too, there is surely sin, and God's wrath is deserved, even though outwardly there seem to be many good deeds and an honorable life.

Hence, St. Paul concludes, in chapter 2[:13], that the Jews are all sinners, saying that only the doers of the law are righteous before God. He means by this that no one, in terms of his works, is a doer of the law. Rather, he speaks to them thus, "You teach one must not commit adultery, but you yourself commit adultery" [2:22]; and again, "In passing judgment upon another you condemn yourself, because you, the judge, are doing the very same things" [2:1]. This is as if to say, "You live a fine outward life in the works of the law, and you pass judgment on those who do not so live. You know how to teach everyone; you see the speck that is in the eye of another, but do not notice the log that is in your own eye" [Matt. 7:3].

For even though you keep the law outwardly, with works, from fear of punishment or love of reward, nevertheless you do all this unwillingly, without pleasure in and love for the law, but with reluctance and under compulsion. For if the law were not there, you would prefer to act otherwise. The conclusion is that from the bottom of your heart you hate the law. What point is there then in your teaching others not to steal, if you yourself are a thief at heart, and would gladly be one outwardly if you dared? Though, to be sure, the outward work does not lag far behind among such hypocrites! So you teach others, but not yourself; nor do you yourself know what you are teaching—you have never yet understood the law correctly. Moreover, the law increases sin, as St. Paul says in chapter 5[:20], because the more the law demands of people what they cannot do, the more they hate the law.

For this reason he says, in chapter 7[:14], "The law is spiritual." What does that mean? If the law were for the body, it could be satisfied with works; but since it is spiritual, no one can satisfy it—unless all that you do is done from the bottom of your heart. But such a heart is given only by God's Spirit, who

n Vulgate version, Ps. 115:11; cf. KJV.

fashions a person after the law, so that he or she acquires a desire for the law in his or her heart, doing nothing henceforth out of fear and compulsion but out of a willing heart.[3] The law is thus spiritual in that it will be loved and fulfilled with such a spiritual heart, and requires such a spirit. Where that spirit is not in the heart, there sin remains, also displeasure with the law and hostility toward it even though the law itself is good and just and holy. //[o]

Accustom yourself, then, to this language, that doing the works of the law and fulfilling the law are two very different things. The work of the law is everything that one does, or can do, toward keeping the law of his own free will or by his own powers. But since in the midst of all these works and along with them there remains in the heart a dislike of the law and compulsion with respect to it, these works are all wasted and have no value. That is what St. Paul means in chapter 3[:20], when he says, "By works of the law will no one be justified in God's sight." Hence, you see that the wranglers and sophists practice deception when they teach people to prepare themselves for grace by means of works. How can we[p] prepare ourselves for good by means of works, if we do good works only with aversion and unwillingness in our hearts? How shall a work please God if it proceeds from a reluctant and resisting heart?[4]

To fulfill the law, however, is to do its works with pleasure and love, to live a godly and good life of one's own accord, without the compulsion of the law. This pleasure and love for the law are put into the heart by the Holy Spirit, as St. Paul says in chapter 5[:5].[5] But the Holy Spirit is not given except in, with, and by faith in Jesus Christ, as St. Paul says in the introduction. Faith,

o WA DB 7:6–7.

p The singular masculine in the original text is here rendered as inclusive plural.

3. Compare, for example, Luther's exposition of the great psalm in praise of the law, Psalm 119. Luther makes a similar point in his 1513–1515 lectures on verse 10 of this psalm, though with a very different technique (see LW 11, on Psalm 119, the second part).

4. The theology of the Ockhamist school, in which Luther was educated in his student days at Erfurt, argued that it was possible, if only momentarily, for a person in his or her natural state (*in puris naturalibus*) to achieve spontaneous love of God and abhorrence of sin. Such a momentary state of pure love could of itself earn a "congruent" merit, merit "of-the-right-kind," even though it was not in itself sufficient or "condign" merit for salvation. God, it was believed, would graciously respond to such quite insufficient "merit" by a gift of grace and the spirit, which would grow within the believer and enhance his or her worthiness before God to a point that God could accept as meeting the demands of divine righteousness. Luther, however, could never believe that a fallen person could seek to do God's will with anything other than "a reluctant and resisting heart." As early as his first lectures on the Psalms in 1513–1515, Luther concluded that the only true preparation for grace was that the sinner must acknowledge one's utter insufficiency, inadequacy, and worthlessness before the demands of the law.

5. God's grace poured into the soul through the Holy Spirit formed a key theme of Luther's lectures on Romans from 1515 onward. Although Luther later (as here) stressed the imputation of "alien" righteousness as the cause of justification, he never minimized the importance of the indwelling spirit for sanctification.

moreover, comes only through God's word or gospel,[6] which preaches Christ, saying that he is God's Son and a man, and has died and risen again for our sakes, as he says in chapters 3[:25], 4[:25], and 10[:9].

So it happens that faith alone makes a person righteous and fulfills the law. For out of the merit of Christ it brings forth the Spirit. And the Spirit makes the heart glad and free, as the law requires that it shall be. Thus, good works emerge from faith itself. That is what St. Paul means in chapter 3[:31]; after he has rejected the works of the law, it sounds as if he would overthrow the law by this faith. "No," he says, "we uphold the law by faith"; that is, we fulfill it by faith.

Sin, in the Scripture, means not only the outward works of the body but also all the activities that move people to do these works, namely, the inmost heart, with all its powers. Thus, the little word "do"[q] ought to mean that a person falls all the way and lives in sin. Even outward works of sin do not take place, unless one plunges into it completely with body and soul. And the Scriptures look especially into the heart and single out the root and source of all sin, which is unbelief in the inmost heart. As, therefore, faith alone makes a person righteous, and brings the Spirit and pleasure in good outward works, so //[r] unbelief alone commits sin, and brings forth the flesh and pleasure in bad outward works, as happened to Adam and Eve in paradise, Genesis 3.

Hence, Christ calls unbelief the only sin, when he says in John 16[:8-9], "The Spirit will convince the world of sin . . . because they do not believe in me." For this reason, too, before good or bad works take place, as the good or bad fruits, there must first be in the heart faith or unbelief. Unbelief is the root, the sap, and the chief power of all sin.[7] For this reason, in the Scriptures it is called the serpent's head and the head of the old dragon, which the seed of the woman, Christ, must tread under foot, as was promised to Adam, Gen. 3[:15].

q *Thun*, i.e., "commit sin."

r WA DB 7:8-9.

6. This phrase also alludes to Rom. 10:17: "So faith comes from what is heard, and what is heard comes through the word of Christ" [NRSV]. A classic exposition of this theme is Ernst Bizer, *Fides ex auditu. Eine Untersuchung über die Entdeckung der Gerechtigkeit Gottes durch Martin Luther*, 3d ed. (Neukirchen-Vluyn: Neukirchener Verlag, 1966).

7. Luther had been emphasizing that unbelief was the root cause and the chief of all sin for several years before this point. See, for instance, "it is not the so-called actual sins that are censured in this epistle but the greatest sin, namely, the sin of unbelief," in his *Lectures on Hebrews* (LW 29:182), on Heb. 6:8.

Between grace and gift there is this difference.[8] Grace actually means God's favor, or the good will[s] which in himself he bears toward us, by which he is disposed to give us Christ and to pour into us the Holy Spirit with his gifts.[9] This is clear from chapter 5[:15], where St. Paul speaks of "the grace and gift in Christ," etc. The gifts and the Spirit increase in us every day, but they are not yet perfect since there remain in us the evil desires and sins that war against the Spirit, as he says in Rom. 7[:5ff.] and Gal. 5[:17], and the conflict between the seed of the woman and the seed of the serpent, as foretold in Gen. 3[:15]. Nevertheless, grace does so much that we are accounted completely righteous before God.[10] For his grace is not divided or parceled out, as are the gifts, but takes us completely into favor for the sake of Christ our Intercessor and Mediator. And because of this, the gifts are begun in us.

In this sense, then, you can understand chapter 7. There St. Paul still calls himself a sinner; and yet he can say, in chapter 8[:1], that there is no condemnation for those who are in Christ

Woodcut titled "Law and Grace" ("Fall and Redemption") by Lucas Cranach the Elder (1529/30)

s *Gottes Hulde oder Gunst.* Luther deliberately uses nontheological language here.

8. This paragraph contains the core of Luther's mature theology of justification, which developed in the 1518–1521 period and was expressed technically in the reply to Jacobus Latomus (c. 1475–1544), written at the Wartburg in 1521 (see *Against Latomus* [1521], LW 32:133–259). The conceptual distinction between "grace" and "gifts," in effect between justification and sanctification, is crucial for Luther's developed thought.

9. The redefinition of "grace" as God's "favor" toward human beings marked a major theological shift. "Grace" had previously been considered a transmissible quality that could be conferred and infused into the believer by the Spirit of God, and increased by acts of piety. By defining it simply as God's attitude of favor toward human beings, the whole theological principle of "acquiring" and "increasing" grace was stripped away. This point was made especially clearly in the first edition of Melanchthon's *Loci Communes* (see MSA, II.i.85–88). Melanchthon so interpreted the Greek χάρις and the Hebrew *chen* (חֵן).

10. Compare Luther's later teaching in the Genesis lectures from c. 1535: "There are two kinds of saintliness. One is the Word, which is saintliness itself. But this saintliness is *imputed* to those who have the Word. A person is simply *accounted* saintly, not because of us or because of our works but because of the Word. Thus the whole person becomes righteous. . . . If we do not glory in this saintliness, we do wrong to the true God, who sanctifies us with His Word. . . . 'But I am a sinner,' you will say. 'I know that you are a sinner, and if you were not, I would not want to sanctify you; you would have no need of the Word. But because you are a sinner,

simply because of the incompleteness of the gifts and of the Spirit. Because the flesh is not yet slain, we are still sinners. But because we believe in Christ and have a beginning of the Spirit, God is so favorable and gracious to us that he will not count the sin against us or judge us because of it. Rather, he deals with us according to our faith in Christ, until sin is slain.[11]

Faith is not the human notion and dream that some people call faith. When they see that no improvement of life and no good works follow—although they can hear and say much about faith—they fall into the error of saying, "Faith is not enough; one must do works in order to be righteous and be saved." This is due to the fact that when //[t] they hear the gospel, they get busy and by their own powers create an idea in their heart which says, "I believe"; they take this then to be a true faith. But, as it is a human figment and idea that never reaches the depths of the heart, nothing comes of it either, and no improvement follows.

Faith, however, is a divine work in us which changes us and makes us to be born anew of God, John 1[:12-13]. It kills the old Adam and makes us altogether different, in heart and spirit and mind and powers; and it brings with it the Holy Spirit. O, it is a living, busy, active, mighty thing, this faith. It is impossible for it not to be doing good works incessantly. It does not ask whether good works are to be done, but before the question is asked, it has already done them, and is constantly doing them. Whoever does not do such works, however, is an unbeliever. A person gropes and looks around for faith and good works, but knows neither what faith is nor what good works are. Yet that one talks and talks, with many words, about faith and good works.

Faith is a living, daring confidence in God's grace, so sure and certain that the believer would stake one's life on it a thousand times.[12] This knowledge of and confidence in God's grace makes people glad and bold and happy in dealing with God and with all creatures. And this is the work which the Holy Spirit performs in faith. Because of it, without compulsion, a person is ready and glad to do good to everyone, to serve everyone, to suffer everything, out of love and praise to God who has shown this grace. Thus, it is impossible to separate works from faith, quite as impossible as to separate heat and light from fire. Beware, therefore, of your own false notions and of the idle talkers who

t WA DB 7:10-11.

I sanctify you,' says God. . . . The other saintliness is a saintliness of works. It is love, which does what is pleasing. But because weakness clings to us, this righteousness is not pure" (see Luther on Gen. 28:12-15, in LW 5).

11. Numerous phrases in this preface echo the language of Luther's reply to Latomus, written in the previous year in much more technical language and in Latin (see n. 8, p. 468). Compare LW 32:28: "Here we see plainly that sin remains, but it is not imputed. The two reasons were mentioned above. First, because we believe in Christ, who, through faith, takes our place and covers our sin with his innocence; second, because we battle unceasingly against sin, to destroy it." Again, LW 32:249: "So sin is truly sin, but because grace and the gift are within me, it is not imputed; not on account of its innocence—as if it were not harmful—but because grace and the gift reign within me."

12. This definition of faith as, ultimately, trust in the grace of God would come to be known by the Latin term *fiducia* in Lutheran orthodoxy. Compare Melanchthon's *Loci Communes* in MSA II.i.92, 115-16.

imagine themselves wise enough to make decisions about faith and good works, and yet are the greatest fools. Pray God that he may work faith in you. Otherwise you will surely remain forever without faith, regardless of what you may think or do.

Righteousness, then, is such a faith. It is called "the righteousness of God" because God gives it, and counts it as righteousness for the sake of Christ our Mediator,[13] and makes us[u] to fulfill our obligations to everybody. For through faith we become free from sin[v] and come to take pleasure in God's commandments, thereby we give God the honor due him, and pay him what we owe him. Likewise, we serve others willingly, by whatever means we can, and thus pay our debts to everyone. Nature, free will, and our own powers cannot bring this righteousness into being. //[w] For as no one can give himself faith, neither can he take away his own unbelief. How, then, will he take away a single sin, even the very smallest? Therefore all that is done apart from faith, or in unbelief, is false; it is hypocrisy and sin, Rom. 14[:23], no matter how good a showing it makes.

13. The "righteousness of God," understood as the righteousness with which God makes us and accounts us righteous, was a crucial interpretative point for Luther, to which he would return again and again. Compare Luther's 1515 *Lectures on Romans* (LW 25) on 15:33: "[God] does this, when we believe His words; for through such believing He justifies us, that is, He accounts us as righteous. Hence it is called the righteousness of faith and the righteousness of God which works effectively in us."

Flesh and spirit you must not understand as though flesh is only that which has to do with unchastity and spirit is only that which has to do with what is inwardly in the heart. Rather, like Christ in John 3[:6], Paul calls everything "flesh" that is born of the flesh—the whole person, with body and soul, mind and senses—because everything about us longs for the flesh. Thus, you should learn to call one "fleshly," too, who thinks, teaches, and talks a great deal about lofty spiritual matters, yet does so without grace. From the "works of the flesh" in Gal. 5[:19-21], you can learn that Paul calls heresy and hatred "works of the flesh." And in Rom. 8[:3] he says that "the law is weakened by the flesh"; yet this is said not of unchastity, but of all sins, and above all of unbelief, which is the most spiritual of all vices.

On the contrary, you should call a person "spiritual" who is occupied with the most external kind of works, as Christ was when he washed the disciples' feet [John 13:1-14], and Peter when he steered his boat and fished. Thus, "the flesh" is a person who lives and works, inwardly and outwardly, in the service of the

u The singular masculine in the original text has been rendered as an inclusive plural in this sentence and the next.

v *Wird on sünde.*

w WA DB 7:12–13.

flesh's gain and of this temporal life. "The spirit" is the one who lives and works, inwardly and outwardly, in the service of the Spirit and of the future life.

Without such a grasp of these words, you will never understand this letter of St. Paul, nor any other book of Holy Scripture. Therefore beware of all teachers who use these words in a different sense, no matter who they are, even Origen, Ambrose, Augustine, Jerome, and others like them or even above them.[14] And now we will take up the epistle.[15]

It is right for a preacher of the gospel in the first place by revelation of the law and of sin to rebuke and to constitute as sin everything that is not the living fruit of the Spirit and of faith in Christ, in order that people should be led to know themselves and their own wretchedness, and to become humble and ask for help. This is therefore what St. Paul does. He begins in chapter 1 to rebuke the gross sins and unbelief that are plainly evident.[16] These were, and still are, the sins of the heathen who live without God's grace. He says: Through the gospel there shall be revealed the wrath of God from heaven against all because of their godless lives and their unrighteousness. For even though //[x] they know and daily recognize that there is a God, nevertheless nature itself, without grace, is so bad that it neither thanks nor honors God. Instead it blinds itself, and goes steadily from bad to worse until, after idolatry, it blatantly commits the most shameful sins, along with all the vices, and also allows others to commit them unreprimanded.

In chapter 2 he extends his rebuke to include those who seem outwardly to be righteous and who commit their sins in secret. Such were the Jews and such are all the hypocrites who without desire or love for the law of God lead decent lives, but at heart hate God's law, and yet are quick to judge other people. This is the nature of all hypocrites, to think of themselves as pure, and yet to be full of covetousness, hatred, pride, and all uncleanness, Matt. 23[:25-28]. These are they who despise God's goodness, and in their hardheartedness heap wrath upon themselves. Thus, St. Paul, as a true interpreter of the law, leaves no one without sin, but proclaims the wrath of God upon all who would live well simply by nature or of their own volition.[y] He makes them

x WA DB 7:14–15.

y *Aus natur oder freiem willen.*

14. Church fathers: Origen (c. 185–c. 254), Ambrose (c. 340–397), Augustine (see p. 457 above), Jerome (c. 347–419). While Luther and the reformers had a high opinion of the fathers, especially Augustine, the authority of previous expositors was never allowed to determine their exegesis. There existed a copious patristic body of interpretation of Romans, which Luther was quite ready to set aside for the sake of what he perceived as the core message of the gospel.

15. Luther regards everything up to this point as a spiritual prologue or preliminary exposition. From this point he explores and expounds the epistle chapter by chapter. Luther would almost certainly have known that the chapter divisions were not original to the text, but uses them for convenience.

16. Note here that Luther interprets even the opening passages in Romans, which could be considered as circumstantial pastoral commentary on the life of the community, in terms of his theological principles. That was probably not what Paul had in mind in writing as he did.

to be no better than the obvious sinners; indeed, he says they are stubborn and unrepentant.

In chapter 3 he throws them all together in a heap, and says that one is like the other: they are all sinners before God. Except, the Jews have had the word of God. Though not many have believed that word, this does not mean that the faith and truth of God are exhausted. He quotes incidentally a verse from Ps. 51[:4], that God remains justified in his words. Afterward he comes back to this again and proves also by Scripture that all people are sinners, and that by the works of the law nobody is justified, but that the law was given only that sin might be known.[17]

Then he begins to teach the right way by which all must be justified and saved. He says: They are all sinners making no boast of God; but they must be justified without merit [of their own][18] through faith in Christ, who has merited this for us by his blood, and has become for us a mercy seat by God. God forgives all former sins to demonstrate that we are helped only by his righteousness, which he grants in faith, and which was revealed at that time through the gospel and was witnessed to beforehand by the law and the prophets. Thus, the law is upheld by faith, though the works of the law are thereby put down, together with the boasting of them.

After the first three chapters, in which sin is revealed and faith's way to righteousness is taught, St. Paul begins in chapter 4 to meet certain remonstrances and objections. First, he takes up the one //[z] that all commonly make when they hear that faith justifies without works. They say, "Are we, then, to do no good works?" Therefore Paul himself takes up the case of Abraham, and asks, "What did Abraham accomplish, then, with his good works? Were they all in vain? Were his works of no use?" He concludes that Abraham was justified by faith alone, without any works, so much so that the Scriptures in Gen. 15[:6] declare that he was justified by faith alone even before the work of circumcision. But if the work of circumcision contributed nothing to his righteousness, though God had commanded it and it was a good work of obedience, then surely no other good work will contribute anything to righteousness. Rather, as Abraham's circumcision was an external sign by which he showed the righteousness

z WA DB 7:16–17.

17. Luther appears here to be addressing Rom. 3:19-20 in particular.

18. The German reads "*mussen aber on verdienst rechtfertig werden.*" The passage in square brackets serves to make Luther's intentions clearer but is not in the original.

that was already his in faith, so all good works are only external signs which follow out of faith; like good fruit, they demonstrate that a person is already inwardly righteous before God.

With this powerful illustration from the Scriptures, St. Paul confirms the doctrine of faith which he had set forth in chapter 3. He cites also another witness, David, who says in Ps. 32[:1-2] that a person is justified without works—although that one does not remain without works when he or she has been justified. Then he gives the illustration a broader application, setting it over against all other works of the law. He concludes that the Jews cannot be Abraham's heirs merely because of their blood, still less because of the works of the law; they must inherit Abraham's faith, if they would be true heirs. For before the law—before the law of Moses and the law of circumcision—Abraham was justified by faith and called the father of all believers. Moreover, the law brings about wrath rather than grace, because no one keeps the law out of love for it and pleasure in it. What comes by the works of the law is thus disfavor rather than grace. Therefore faith alone must obtain the grace promised to Abraham, for these examples, too, were written for our sakes [Rom. 15:4], that we, too, should believe.

Abraham's covenant with God (Genesis 15). Woodcut from a seventeenth-century publication by Christoph Weigel (1654–1725).

In chapter 5 he comes to the fruits and works of faith, such as peace, joy, love to God and to every person, as well as confidence, assurance, boldness, courage, and hope amid tribulation and suffering. For all this follows, if faith be true, because of the superabundant goodness that God shows us in Christ, causing Christ to die for us before we could ask it of him, indeed, while we were still enemies. Thus, we have it that faith justifies without any works; and yet it does not follow that we are therefore to do no good works, but rather that the genuine works will not be lacking.[19] Of these the work-righteous saints know nothing. //[a] They dream up works of their own in which there is no peace, joy, confidence, love, hope, boldness, or any of the qualities of true Christian work and faith.

19. Here and elsewhere Luther gives no room for what would later be called the "antinomian" argument, that one who is justified by faith needs no good works, or the claim that would later be made—attributed to Nikolaus von Amsdorf (1483–1565)—that good works might be harmful to salvation. Faith cannot fail to be active.

a WA DB 7:18–19.

After this he digresses and makes a pleasant excursion,[b] telling whence come sin and righteousness, death and life, and comparing Adam and Christ. He means to say that Christ had to come as a second Adam bequeathing his righteousness to us through a new spiritual birth in faith, just as the first Adam bequeathed sin to us through the old fleshly birth. Thus, he declares and proves that no one by his own works can raise himself out of sin into righteousness, any more than he can prevent the birth of his own body. This is proved also by the fact that the divine law—which ought to assist toward righteousness, if anything can—has not only not helped, but has even increased sin. For the more the law forbids, the more our evil nature hates the law, and the more it wants to give reign to its own lust. Thus, the law makes Christ all the more necessary, and more grace is needed to help our nature.

In chapter 6 he takes up the special work of faith, the conflict of the spirit with the flesh for the complete slaying of the sin and lust that remain after we are justified. He teaches us that we are not by faith so freed from sin that we can be idle, slack, and careless, as though there were no longer any sin in us. Sin is present; but it is no longer reckoned for our condemnation, because of the faith that is struggling against it. Therefore we have enough to do all our life long in taming the body, slaying its lusts, and compelling its members to obey the spirit and not the lusts. Thus, we become like the death and resurrection of Christ, and complete our baptism[20]—which signifies the death of sin and the new life of grace—until we are entirely purified of sin, and even our bodies rise again with Christ and live forever.

All this we can do, he says, because we are under[c] grace and not under law.[21] He himself explains what this means. To be without the law is not the same thing as to have no laws and to be able to do what one pleases. Rather, we are under the law when, without grace, we occupy ourselves with the works of the law. Then sin certainly rules [us] through the law, for no one loves the law by nature; and that is great sin. Grace, however, makes the law dear to us; then sin is no longer present, and the law is no longer against us but one with us.

20. This, perhaps of all Luther's interpretations, feels authentically Pauline.

21. This passage appears to refer to 6:15.

b Ger.: "*lustigen Ausbruch und Spaciergang*"; this refers to 5:12-21.

c Editions prior to 1546 read "in" rather than "under." WA DB 7:9 nn.29–30.

This is the true freedom from sin and from the law. //[d] He writes about this down to the end of the chapter, saying that it is a freedom only to do good with pleasure and to live well without the compulsion of the law. Therefore this freedom is a spiritual freedom, which does not overthrow the law but presents what the law demands, namely, pleasure [in the law] and love [for it], whereby the law is quieted and no longer drives people or makes demands of them. It is just as if you owed a debt to your overlord and could not pay it. There are two ways in which you could rid yourself of the debt: either that overlord would take nothing from you and would tear up the account, or some good person would pay it for you and give you the means to satisfy the account. It is in this latter way that Christ has made us free from the law. Our freedom is, therefore, no carefree fleshly freedom which is not obligated to do anything, but a freedom that does many works of all kinds, and is free of the demands and obligations of the law.[22]

In chapter 7 he supports this with an analogy from married life. When a man dies, his wife is also alone, and thus the one is released entirely from the other. Not that the wife cannot or ought not take another husband, but rather that she is now for the first time really free to take another—something which she could not do previously, before she was free from her husband. So our conscience is bound to the law, under the old man of sin; when he is slain by the Spirit, then the conscience is free, and the one is released from the other. Not that the conscience is to do nothing, but rather that it is now for the first time really free to hold fast to Christ, the second husband, and bring forth the fruit of life.

Then he depicts more fully the nature of sin and of the law,[e] how by means of the law sin now stirs and becomes mighty. The old man comes to hate the law all the more because he cannot pay what the law demands. Sin is his nature and of himself he can do nothing but sin; therefore the law to him is death and torment. Not that the law is bad, but the old man's evil nature cannot endure the good, and the law demands good of him; just as a sick man cannot stand it when he is required to run and jump and do the works of a well man.

d WA DB 7:20–21.

e Rom. 7:7 and following.

22. In this sense the response of the faithful believer to the grace of justification arises out of gratitude. This interpretation has affinities (perhaps surprisingly) with Peter Abelard's (c. 1079–1142) subjective theory of the atonement, though Luther would stress that the faithful response is itself a gift of the Spirit.

Therefore St. Paul here concludes that the law, correctly understood and thoroughly grasped, does nothing more than remind us of our sin, and slay us by it, making us liable to eternal wrath. All this is fully learned[f] and experienced by our conscience, when it is really struck by the law. Therefore a person must have something other than the law, something more than the law, to make him righteous and save him. But they who do not correctly understand the law are blind. They go ahead in their presumption, thinking to satisfy the law by means of their deeds, not knowing how much the law demands, //[g] namely, a willing and happy heart. Therefore they do not see Moses clearly; the veil is put between them and him, and covers him [Exod. 34:29-35; 2 Cor. 3:12-16].

Then he shows how spirit and flesh struggle with one another in a person.[23] He uses himself as an example, in order that we may learn how properly to understand the work of slaying sin within us. He calls both the spirit and the flesh "laws"; for just as it is in the nature of the divine law to drive people and make demands of them, so the flesh drives us and makes demands. It rages against the spirit, and will have its own way. The spirit, in turn, drives us and makes demands contrary to the flesh, and will have its own way. This tension lasts in us as long as we live; though in one person it is greater, in another less, according as the spirit or the flesh is stronger. Nevertheless, the whole person is both spirit and flesh, and we[h] fight with ourselves until we become wholly spiritual.

In chapter 8 he comforts these fighters, telling them that this flesh does not condemn them. He shows further what the nature of flesh and spirit is, and how the Spirit comes from Christ. Christ has given us his Holy Spirit; he makes us spiritual and subdues the flesh, and assures us that we are still God's children, however hard sin may be raging within us, so long as we follow the spirit and resist sin to slay it. Since, however, nothing else is so good for the mortifying of the flesh as the cross and suffering,[24] he comforts us in suffering with the support of the Spirit

23. Verses 14 and following.

24. Verses 18-25. Note that Luther does not take up the cosmic dimension of Paul's thought here, though he might consistently have done so.

f *Leret* may have been introduced for the sake of rhyming with the following word *erferet;* in editions prior to 1530 the word had been *lernt*. WA DB 7:21 n.34.

g WA DB 7:22-23.

h Singular masculine pronouns in the original rendered as inclusive plural in this sentence.

of love, and of the whole creation, namely, that the Spirit sighs within us and the creation longs with us that we may be rid of the flesh and of sin. So we see that these three chapters (6–8) drive home the one task of faith, which is to slay the old Adam and subdue the flesh.

In chapters 9, 10, and 11 he teaches of God's eternal predestination—out of which originally proceeds who shall believe or not, who can or cannot get rid of sin—in order that our salvation may be taken entirely out of our hands and put in the hand of God alone.[25] And this, too, is utterly necessary. For we are so weak and uncertain that if it depended on us, not even a single person would be saved; the devil would surely overpower us all. But since God is dependable—his predestination cannot fail, and no one can withstand him—we still have hope in the face of sin.

Here, now, for once we must put a stop to those wicked and high-flying spirits who first apply their own reason to this matter. They begin at the top to search the abyss of divine predestination, and worry in vain about whether they are predestinated.[26] They are bound to plunge to their own destruction, either through despair, or through throwing caution to the winds.[i] //[j]

But you had better follow the order of this epistle. Worry first about Christ and the gospel, that you may recognize your sin and his grace. Then fight your sin, as the first eight chapters here have taught. Then, when you have reached the eighth chapter, and are under the cross and suffering, this will teach you correctly of predestination in chapters 9, 10, and 11, and how comforting it is. For in the absence of suffering and the cross and the perils of death, one cannot deal with predestination without harm and without secret anger against God. The old Adam must first die before he can tolerate this thing and drink the strong wine. Therefore beware that you do not drink wine while you are still a suckling. There is a limit, a time, and an age for every doctrine.[27]

In chapter 12 he teaches what true worship is, and makes all Christians priests.[28] They are to offer not money or cattle, as under the law, but their own bodies, with slaying of the lusts. Then he describes the outward conduct of Christians, under the spiritual government, telling how they are to teach, preach,

i *Sich in die freie schantz schlahen.*

j WA DB 7:24–25.

25. Here Luther, presumably intentionally, overlooks Paul's preoccupation with the status of the people of Israel. It seems safe to assume that he avoided it because he was addressing the pastoral needs of a lay readership who were not Jewish, and did not need to read the text historically. The "clay and the potter" phrase was often used in medieval discussions of predestination.

26. Luther here warns against introspection and the so-called practical syllogism: "do I show within myself sufficient evidence to be confident that I am predestinated?" Calvin makes a very similar warning (*Inst.* III.24.4). He notes also that election may not be visible until very late in someone's life: *Inst.* III.24.10.

27. Again, Luther shows little interest in the question of the salvation of Israel versus the salvation of the Gentiles. See n. 25 above.

28. Luther made the point that there was no spiritual distinction among the baptized between priests and laity in his *To the Christian Nobility of the German Nation*, inaugurating the so-called "priesthood of all believers" (see TAL 1:369–465; LW 44:115–217). It is a little hard to see how it fits with Paul's text here, but its presence shows the importance of the doctrine for Luther.

rule, serve, give, suffer, love, live, and act toward friend, foe, and all people. These are the works that a Christian does; for, as has been said, faith takes no holidays.[29]

In chapter 13 he teaches honor and obedience to worldly government. Although worldly government does not make people righteous before God, nevertheless it is instituted in order to accomplish at least this much, that the good may have outward peace and protection and the bad may not be free to do evil in peace and quietness, and without fear. Therefore the good, too, are to honor it even though they themselves do not need it.[30] Finally, he comprehends it all in love, and sums it up in the example of Christ: as he has done for us, we are also to do, following in his footsteps.

In chapter 14 he teaches that consciences weak in faith are to be led gently, spared, so that we do not use our Christian freedom for doing harm, but for the assistance of the weak. For where that is not done, the result is discord and contempt for the gospel; and the gospel is the all-important thing. Thus, it is better to yield a little to the weak in faith, until they grow stronger, than to have the teaching of the gospel come to nothing. And this work is a peculiar work of love, for which there is great need even now, when with the eating of meat and other liberties, people are rudely and roughly—and needlessly—shaking weak consciences, before they know the truth.

In chapter 15 he sets up Christ as an example: we are to tolerate also those other weak ones who fail in other ways, in open sins or in unpleasing habits. We are not to cast them off, but to bear with them until they, too, grow better. For so Christ has done with us, //[k] and still does every day; he bears with our many faults and bad habits, and with all our imperfections, and helps us constantly.

Then, at the end, he prays for them, praises them, and commends them to God. He speaks of his own office and of his preaching, and asks them kindly for a contribution to the poor at Jerusalem. All that he speaks of or deals with is pure love.[l]

29. "*Glawb feyret nicht.*" Luther writes as though this expression were a common proverb. However, most of the recorded instances of the expression derive from Luther's own writings: it is found, for example, in Luther's postil for Quasimodo Sunday 1533, as in WA 52:275. Quasimodo Sunday, the first Sunday after Easter, is so named because the introit text for that day, "quasi modo geniti infantes" from 1 Pet. 2:2.

30. Luther would develop this theme in his treatise *On Secular Authority: To What Extent It Should Be Obeyed*, published in the following year, 1523 (see TAL 5:79–129; LW 45:75–129, esp. 93–95).

k WA DB 7:26–27.

l *Ist eyttel lieb davon er redet und da mit er umbgeht.*

The last chapter is a chapter of greetings. But he mingles with them a noble warning against human doctrines,[31] which break in alongside the teaching of the gospel and cause offense. It is as if he had certainly foreseen that out of Rome and through the Romans would come the seductive and offensive canons and decretals and the whole squirming mass of human laws and commandments which have now drowned the whole world and wiped out this epistle and all the Holy Scriptures, along with the Spirit and faith itself; so that nothing remains anymore except the idol, Belly,[m] whose servants St. Paul here rebukes. God save us from them. Amen.

In this epistle we thus find most abundantly the things that a Christian ought to know, namely, what is law, gospel, sin, punishment, grace, faith, righteousness, Christ, God, good works, love, hope, and the cross; and also how we are to conduct ourselves toward everyone, be he righteous or sinner, strong or weak, friend or foe—and even toward our own selves. Moreover, this is all ably supported with Scripture and proved by St. Paul's own example and that of the prophets, so that one could not wish for anything more. Therefore it appears that he wanted in this one epistle to sum up briefly the whole Christian and evangelical doctrine, and to prepare an introduction to the entire Old Testament. For, without doubt, whoever has this epistle well in his heart has with him the light and power of the Old Testament. Therefore let all Christians be familiar with it and exercise themselves in it continually. To this end may God give his grace. Amen.[32]

31. Cf. Luther's treatise *Avoiding the Doctrines of Men* (1522) in LW 35:125–53. One presumes that Luther had verses 17-20 in mind at this point. Even so, it may seem a little fanciful to read into Paul a prediction of medieval Catholicism.

32. In editions prior to 1539 the order of these last two paragraphs is exactly reversed, so that the one here given last comes before rather than after the one which here immediately precedes it.

m Phil. 3:19; cf. Rom. 16:18.

In this woodcut from 1477, the apostle Paul sits at a desk with an open book before him. He was commonly depicted as holding a sword, representing the weapon believed to have been used when he was martyred in Rome under Nero.

Lectures on Romans 3:20-27

1515–1516

PIOTR J. MAŁYSZ

INTRODUCTION

Having received his doctoral degree in 1512, Luther was appointed lecturer on the Bible at the University of Wittenberg, which was founded a mere decade earlier. Luther's lectures on St. Paul's letter to the Romans were only the second lecture cycle, following the Psalms, that the new professor offered. Luther lectured on St. Paul's epistle from spring 1515 until fall 1516.

Unlike a number of later cycles, published and readily available already in Luther's lifetime, the lectures on Romans did not come out in print until 1908, while a critical edition appeared as late as 1938. Luther himself, it seems, never intended the material for publication in its original form. He preserved his notes, however, with the possible goal of eventually revising them for a print edition.

As was the medieval custom, Luther's lecture notes consist of handwritten glosses on St. Paul's text, as well as longer, interpretive scholia on select passages.[a] The lecturer would ordinarily dictate the glosses to be inserted by the students, as annotations,

a For a view of such glosses on Luther's Psalms commentary, see pp. 213–14 in this volume.

between the lines or in the margins of a specially printed section of Paul's letter. The scholia, by contrast, were the lecturer's own preparatory notes for the lectures to be followed or departed from at the lecturer's discretion. The selection presented here is from Luther's scholia.

Also in keeping with the custom of the day, Luther supported his interpretation of St. Paul's letter by appealing to a variety of authorities. Those include, first and foremost, the Bible, the church fathers, as well as more recent interpreters. In the selection offered here, for example, Luther quotes Augustine[1] (approvingly) and cites Peter Lombard[2] (polemically). The biblical text, beyond the scriptural passage under consideration, remains the single most quoted authority.

What makes Luther's approach different already in those early years of his academic career is that, in his engagement with Scripture, Luther does not utilize the longstanding model of fourfold interpretation (historical, allegorical, tropological, anagogical), an approach whose roots go back to Christian antiquity. Neither does he follow the more recent school of literal historical exegesis, associated with Nicholas of Lyra (1270–1349). What defines and distinguishes Luther's interpretation is, instead, a christological lens focused on Christ's redemptive work.

Besides Luther's critical approach to received commentatorial practices, a similarly critical attitude can be observed in his use of vocabulary. He continues to draw on the conceptual repertoire of medieval theology, but the terms acquire new dimensions of meaning and are often employed to criticize the very theology of which they are a part.

The most significant such shift occurs in Luther's understanding of faith, works of the law, and their relation to justification. On the face of it, Luther seems to embrace the received view of faith as a disposition that requires its exercise by the believer. Only as so exercised, it was widely held, does faith justify.[b] Luther's apparent acceptance of the notion is actually driven by a complex critique. This critique is oriented both to what Luther believes ought to be excluded, given precisely this understanding of faith, as well as to the understanding itself.

1. The writings of St. Augustine, bishop of Hippo (354–430), had a great influence on Luther's biblical and theological perspectives. See Piotr J. Małysz, "Luther's Trinitarian Hermeneutic of Freedom," in D. R. Nelson and P. Hinlicky, eds., *Oxford Research Encyclopedia of Martin Luther* (Oxford: Oxford University Press, 2017), available at http://religion.oxfordre.com/page/martin-luther.

2. Peter Lombard (c. 1096–1160) was the initiator of the custom of gathering and compiling sayings from the church fathers and then commenting on them. This is how the foundational theological perspectives were identified and collected, ones that students had to master. Lombard's own collection, his four-part commentary *Sententiae in IV libros distinctae*, remained highly popular and influential well into the 16th century. Luther himself lectured on Lombard's *Sentences* early in his career.

b E.g., Thomas Aquinas, STh, II-ii, q.4.

Specifically, Luther's insistence that faith has works of its own leads him, first of all, to reject the more recent, nominalist theology, known as the modern way (*via moderna*). This, it should be noted, was the theology that formed the backbone of Luther's own university training. Nevertheless, Luther takes St. Paul's exclusion of the works of the law from God's justification of the sinner and uses it against the nominalist view that a person can, by one's natural power, turn to God, and by doing one's utmost, merit, however incongruously, the gift of divine grace. As the nominalist slogan put it, God does not withhold grace from those who do their best.[c] To this Luther responds by asserting the worthlessness of works of the law: works done outside of and without reference to faith. Luther, to be sure, does not question the possible inherent worth of such works themselves. They may in fact be of genuine moral worth and command admiration. What he does focus on is the spiritual toll—in the form of ungodly pride—that works outside of faith take on those who through them seek to rectify their relationship with God.

The same concern about pride remains evident when Luther proceeds to analyze faith's character and faith's own works, seeking to clarify the nature of both, their mutual relation, and ultimately the believer's role in divine justification. This latter, internal critique leads Luther to begin articulating a stronger notion of faith than that furnished even by the old way (*via antiqua*) and its chief exponent, St. Thomas Aquinas (1224–1274). Keeping in mind the subtle opposition to God's self-giving that pride entails, Luther now downplays the dispositional understanding of faith as a habit in need of practice. He begins, instead, to move increasingly closer to a christological view of faith as fundamentally trust in God's own work. If faith has a dispositional aspect, Luther argues, it is humility. But humility is a disposition that paradoxically hides from view, and even undermines, its own dispositional nature. On the one hand, it leads one, before God, to consider even works done in faith as works of the law, and so of no value. Faith is certainly living and active, but it comes before God empty-handed, aware of the complexity of even the believer's own motivations. On the other hand, and even more

This page from *Summa Theologiae* by Thomas Aquinas is from an early printed edition published in Mainz by Peter Schöffer in 1471.

c For a standard account of the late medieval notion of doing one's best (*facere quod in se est*), see Heiko A. Oberman, *The Harvest of Medieval Theology* (Cambridge: Harvard University Press, 1963), 131–45.

important, faith is disposed to apply to oneself all there is to believe about Christ and his work. Humility thus does justice to God, to God's being and work. Pride, by contrast, rather than being a mere character flaw, finds its inevitable corollary in heresy, for it is unable to accept the entirety of Christ's work on one's behalf.[3]

Luther's theology of humility, articulated in his lectures on Romans and soon to be echoed in the *Heidelberg Disputation* (1518), is an important step toward his later notion of faith as receptive trust rather than a virtue. Faith, Luther will come to claim in his mature lectures on Galatians of 1531 (published in 1535), is given concreteness—given form, or its very identity—not through works of love but through trust in God's work alone. Christ with his work on the sinner's behalf is the form of faith.[d]

The selection offered here marks an important transition from a medieval theology of faith as the lowest of the theological virtues, a habit in need of exercise, to Luther's mature understanding of faith's central place. Faith, as Luther will come to understand it, is that which becomes what it is only in grasping Christ as a gift to the believer and as such, without remainder, makes the Christian into a Christian.[e]

3. Luther used the language of justifying, or doing justice to, God (*Deum iustificare*) through one's faith as early as his first lectures on the Psalms (see, e.g., the scholion to Psalm 51 in LW 10:235–43; also pp. 216–28 in this volume). He continues to employ this language in the Romans commentary, and will do so occasionally throughout his career (e.g., commenting on Gal. 3:6, in LW 26:227–33). In a gloss on Rom. 3:7, Luther explains: "God is justified and shown to be truthful . . . in an effective way, that is, when we cannot be justified of ourselves and come to him, so that he himself makes us righteous when we confess that we cannot overcome our sin. He does this, when we believe his words; for through such believing he justifies us, that is, he accounts us as righteous. Hence it is called the righteousness of faith and the righteousness of God which works effectively in us" (LW 25:205–6).

d LW 26:122–38.

e For further reading, see Berndt Hamm, "Why Did Luther Turn Faith into the Central Concept of the Christian Life?," *The Early Luther*, trans. M. J. Lohrmann (Grand Rapids: Eerdmans, 2014), 59–84.

LECTURES ON ROMANS 3:20-27[f]

20. THE QUESTION[4] IS ASKED, "How can justification take place without the works of the law, and how *by the works of the law* can there be no justification, since Jas. 2:26 clearly states: 'Faith apart from works is dead' and 'a person is justified by works,' using the example of Abraham and Rahab (Jas. 2:23-25)?" And Paul himself in Gal. 5:6 speaks of "faith working through love," and above in chapter 2:13 he says that "the doers of the law will be justified before God." The answer to this question is that the apostle is distinguishing between the law and faith, or between the letter and grace, and thus also between their respective works. The *works of the law* are those, he says, which take place outside of faith and grace and are done at the urging of the law, which either forces obedience through fear or allures us through the promise of temporal blessings. But the *works of faith*, he says, are those which are done out of the spirit of liberty and solely for the love of God. And the latter cannot be accomplished except by those who have been justified by faith, to which justification the works of the law add nothing, indeed, they strongly hinder it, since they do not permit a person to see oneself as unrighteous and in need of justification.[5]

Here is an example. If a layman should perform all the outward functions of a priest, celebrating Mass, confirming, absolving, administering the sacraments, dedicating altars, churches, vestments, vessels, etc., it is certain that these actions in all respects would be similar to those of a true priest, in fact, they might be performed more reverently and properly than the real ones. But because he has not been consecrated and ordained and sanctified, he performs nothing at all, but is only playing church and deceiving himself and his followers. It is the same way with

f The following translation is based on LW 25:234-54 with some modifications.

4. Luther introduces his exposition in dialectical fashion to identify the central issue posed by the passage. Dialectic was a common medieval form of theological discourse, typified most famously by Thomas Aquinas's *Summa Theologiae*. The expositor proceeds from a question, through apparent negative answers, to an affirmation of the opposite view, reaffirming what the question already suggests to be the case, all backed up with relevant authorities. The centerpiece is an extended response that supports the assertion to the contrary, followed by specific replies to the initial objections.

5. Though Luther alludes here to the Augustinian distinction between the letter and grace (or spirit), he departs from the standard medieval view that "works of the law" are the ceremonies of the Old Covenant, whereas the "works of faith"—as works of love—bring out the true, spiritual dimension of the old law and the prophets. Rather, in Luther's definition of the law's works, one can see the kernel of what Luther will later call the civil, or political, use of the law. Here all law—not only ceremonial but also moral—serves as a restraint on transgression, but neither leads one to faith nor aids faith. It may actually hinder faith, insofar as those who do the works of the law "regard [them] as the reason for their justification, and by [their] performance . . . consider themselves righteous," as Luther cautions below. This already suggests that works of faith, in opposition to those of the law, are not works that are simply moral or more spiritual, but have an altogether different character. See P. J. Małysz, "Apostolic Council of Jerusalem: Middle Ages and Reformation," in Christine Helmer, et al., eds., *Encyclopedia of the*

the righteous, good, and holy works which are performed either without or before justification. [. . .][g]

Therefore,[h] when St. James and the apostle [Paul] say that a person is justified by works, they are contending against the erroneous notion of those who thought that faith suffices without works, although the apostle does not say that faith justifies without its own works (because then there would be no faith, since, according to the philosophers, "action is the evidence that form exists"), but that it justifies without the works of the law. Therefore justification does not demand the works of the law but a living faith which produces its own works.[6]

But if faith justifies with its own works, but without the works of the law, then why are heretics regarded as beyond justification, since they also believe and from this same faith produce great and sometimes even greater works than the other believers? And all the people in the church who are spiritually proud, who have many and great works which also surely proceed from faith, are such people also unrighteous? Does something other than faith in Christ with its good works seem to be required for justification?

James answers the question briefly: "Whosoever . . . fails in one point has become guilty of all of it" (2:10). For faith is indivisible.[7] Therefore it is either a whole faith and believes all that is to be believed, or it is no faith, if it does not believe one part. The Lord thus compares it to one pearl, to one grain of mustard, etc. Because "Christ is not divided" (cf. 1 Cor. 1:13), therefore he is either completely denied in one unit, or else he is completely affirmed. He cannot be at the same time denied in one word and confessed in another. But heretics are always picking out one thing or many from those which are to be believed, against which they set their minds in their arrogance, as if they were wiser than all the rest. And thus they believe nothing which is to be believed and perish without faith, without obedience toward God, while still in their great works, which are so similar to the real ones. [. . .] So also every proud person in his or her own mind always opposes either the precept or the counsel of one who is correctly

g This bracketed ellipsis indicates that a portion of the LW text has been deleted.

h LW 25:235, para. 3.

Bible and Its Reception (Berlin: de Gruyter, 2016), vol. 13, cols. 1102–5.

6. Luther's terminology, to be sure, reflects the medieval view of faith as a theological virtue, a disposition that, once present, required intentional exercise. But Luther's critique of works of the law, as devoid of faith and so also the love of God, does not suggest a preference for the *via antiqua* over the more recent, nominalist thought. Luther does not go on to argue simply for the necessity and primacy of grace, outside of which a person's works remain strictly nonmeritorious. He instead reformulates the dispositional character of faith to suggest an altogether different kind of faith work from what falls within the realm of command, whether ceremonial or moral. To wit, already here, and explicitly below, Luther challenges the Aristotelian notion that doing makes a doer by asserting that doing is, rather, evidence of the doer's already established identity. Luther emphasizes this point in the course of his exposition by moving away from *charity* as that which gives faith its concreteness to *humility*, which makes no claim on any of its own works, as the proper work of faith. The doer—the believer, as Luther will say later—is established in his or her identity purely by deferring to and claiming God's mercy and gift of Christ. See LW 26:256.

7. James is actually addressing the law's comprehensive demand that requires the law's keeping in its entirety. Luther extends this to faith (with the help of 1 Cor. 1:13) to argue that humility alone, as faith's proper work, receives God's work without reservation, even if it should mean setting aside the person's own works.

guiding the person to salvation. Since they[i] do not believe this counsel, they likewise believe nothing, and their entire faith perishes because of the tenacity of one thought. We must always humbly, therefore, give way in our thinking, lest we stumble over this rock of offense, that is, the truth which in humility stands against us and opposes our own thinking. For since we are liars, the truth can never come to us except as an apparent adversary to what we are thinking, for we presume that we think the truth, and we wish to hear and see as truth only that which agrees with us and applauds us. But this cannot be.

The works of all of these persons, therefore, are the works of the law, not of faith or of grace; indeed they are opposed to and in conflict with faith. Thus, justification not only can but must take place without them, and with the apostle must "be counted as refuse for the sake of Christ" (Phil. 3:8).

Corollary[8]

It is always safer to listen to things which are contrary to our own thinking, than to listen to those things which approve and applaud our ideas and are in agreement with us.

Indeed, unless we[j] learn to listen gladly to things that are against us, and unless we enjoy argument against our own opinions and are happy in being contradicted, and on the other hand, unless we are fearful and sorry, or at least suspicious when our word, our opinion, and our work are approved, praised, and upheld, we certainly cannot be saved. For there is no more faithful testimony to the fact that our thinking, our word, and our work are from God than if they are blamed and condemned. For everything which comes from God (as is obvious in the case of Christ) is condemned by us, as stones by the builders. But if it is not from God, then it is much safer, indeed it is necessary, that it be rejected, lest he who continues in it should perish. [. . .]

22. *The righteousness of God through faith.* This teaches: Since the faith in Christ by which we are justified is not a matter of believing only in Christ or in the Person of Christ, but in all things

i The singular masculine pronoun is here rendered as plural.

j The original masculine nouns and pronouns are rendered as first-person plural through this paragraph.

8. This entire section, correlating pride with rejection of the truth, anticipates Luther's famous distinction, in the *Heidelberg Disputation* (1518), between the theologian of glory, who cannot see things for what they are, and the theologian of the cross, who recognizes the actual truth of things beneath their commonsensical appearance. See TAL 1:98–101; LW 31:52–54 (theses 19-22).

which pertain to Christ, the proud and the heretics are deceived and yet pleased in their deception that they believe in Christ but are unwilling to believe the things which pertain to him.

Thus, they plainly divide Christ when they say that it is one thing to believe in Christ and another to believe in the things which pertain to Christ; but actually "Christ is not divided" (1 Cor. 1:13), as the apostle says; and as we have said above, faith in Christ is similarly indivisible, just as Christ and the things which pertain to him are one and the same thing.

Thus, the heretics confess and brag that they believe in Christ according to what the gospels say of him, that he was born, suffered, died, etc. But they do not believe in those things which pertain to him. And what are these things? The church, of course, and every word which proceeds from the mouth of a leader of the church or from the mouth of a good and holy man are the word of Christ, for he has said, "He who hears you hears me" (Luke 10:16). They who withdraw themselves, therefore, from church leaders and are unwilling to listen to their words, but follow their own ideas, how do such people believe in Christ, I ask? Or do they believe that he was born and suffered, but not believe the person who teaches it to them? Therefore, "Is Christ divided" (1 Cor. 1:13) because they believe in him in one place and deny him in the other? God forbid. But actually in this way they deny Christ entirely, for he cannot be denied and confessed at the same time. [. . .]

If[k] these things are so, we must humble ourselves greatly. For since we are unable to know whether we really do live in every word of God and deny none (since many words are spoken by the spiritual leader, many by the brethren, many in the gospel and in the writings of the apostles, and many to us inwardly by God) we can never know whether we are justified or whether we believe. We should, therefore, consider our works as works of the law and humbly admit that we are sinners, seeking to be justified solely by his mercy. For although we are sure that we believe in Christ, yet we are not certain that we believe in all the words which pertain to him. And thus it is uncertain that we "believe in him."[9]

For even in the prophets there is no complaint except that the voice of the Lord is not heard by his people. But one who

k LW 25:238, para. 3.

9. Luther emphasizes here the precarious nature of faith when approached subjectively. The object of faith—Christ's work for the believer's sake—alone makes faith into what it is. When approached from the believer's perspective, faith will always seem lacking, whether in love or in commitment. Luther will continue to underscore this point, not only with medieval theology in view, but also that of the radical reformers and their inevitable turning of faith itself into a work possessed of certain subjective manifestations. See, e.g., *Concerning Rebaptism* (1528), LW 40:229–62.

fears and humbly confesses will be given grace, that she may be justified and her sins forgiven, even if occasionally she has done something through hidden or uninformed unbelief. Thus, for example, Job was afraid of all his actions. And the apostle was not conscious of any wrong he had done, but yet he did not think that he was thereby justified. And thus righteousness must be left to Christ alone, and to him alone the works of grace and of the Spirit. But we ourselves are always under the works of the law, always unrighteous, always sinners, as it says in Ps. 32:6, "Therefore let everyone who is godly offer prayer to you." [. . .]

20.[l] *Through the law comes the knowledge of sin.* This knowledge through the law comes in two ways, first, through contemplation, as we read below in chapter 7:7, "I should not have known what it is to covet if the law had not said, 'You shall not covet.'"

Second, through experience, that is, through the work of the law, or through the law that has been adopted together with the work. For in this way the law becomes an occasion for sinning, since human will, which is prone to evil, is driven toward the good through the law and thus becomes disinclined toward the good and tired of trying to do good, because it hates to give up what it loves, and it loves evil, as Scripture says. But yet, if it works and does what it is unwilling to do, compelled by the law, then we understand how deeply sin and evil are rooted in us, which we would not have understood if we did not have the law and had not attempted to work in accordance with it. The apostle passes over this idea briefly at this point, because he will go into detail on the matter below in chapters 5 and 7. Here he is satisfied with briefly answering the objection that the law is not of any use because the works of the law do not justify. Whenever a precept or a prohibition meets us, therefore, and we feel ourselves hostile toward it, let us recognize the fact that we do not love the good, but rather the evil. By this very fact, therefore, we recognize that we are wicked sinners, since one is not a sinner unless that one is unwilling to fulfill the law, which prescribes good works and forbids evil. For if we were righteous and good, we would consent to the law with ready will and delight in it, just as we now delight in our sins and evil desires. Hence: "Oh, how I love your law!" (Ps. 119:97), and again: "But his delight is in the law of the LORD" (Ps. 1:2). Behold, thus it has come to pass that

l LW 25:240, para. 2.

through the law there is knowledge of the sin which is in us, that is, of our evil will which inclines toward the evil and abhors the good. How useful this knowledge is![10] For all[m] who recognize it cry to God and in humility beg that this will may be lifted up and healed. But those who do not recognize it do not ask, and those who do not ask do not receive, and thus they are not justified because they are ignorant of their own sin. Hence, to say "Through the law is the knowledge of sin" is the same as saying "Through the law is the knowledge of sinners." For through this, that we are evil and that evil is in us, we recognize that we are sinners and that sin is in us.

Corollary

We do not apply the term "works of the law" to those works which are preparatory to acquiring righteousness, but to those which are regarded in themselves as being sufficient for righteousness and salvation.[11]

Because he who so conducts himself that through these works he has prepared himself for the grace of justification is already righteous in a certain sense. For a large part of righteousness is the will to be righteous. Otherwise the words and cries of all the prophets by which they called for Christ would have been in vain, and the laments of all the penitents would be fruitless. In vain would Christ and John have taught: "Repent, for the kingdom of heaven is at hand" (Matt. 3:2). Indeed, if all the righteous performed such works for no other purpose than that they might be more and more justified, no one would be righteous. Their works, therefore, are good because they do not trust in them but rather through them prepare themselves for justification, in which they trust alone for their future righteousness. But those who conduct themselves in this way are not under the law, because they desire grace and hate the fact that they are sinners.[12]

For the "works of the law" are one thing and the "fulfilling of the law" another. For grace is the fulfilling of the law, but not works. Well does he say "works of the law" and not "will of the

m Here and in the following sentence the original masculine pronoun is rendered as plural.

10. Luther will later refer to this sin-disclosing function of the law as the law's chief, theological use. In *The Bondage of the Will*, he will call the law-wrought despair over one's capacity to earn or retain God's favor "salutary despair" (LW 33:190). Importantly, as Luther goes on to suggest, the law is fulfilled not through graced works of charity, as if one could at any point be in control of one's deep-seated attitudes and so achieve righteousness, but through humility, which, in that it is prepared to receive from God, brings about one's righteousness as a gift.

11. Luther's discussion pivots on the distinction between good works in their external, objective character and what they subjectively accomplish. This latter aspect is what is at stake here. Luther distinguishes between, on the one hand, the work of the law, which the law itself performs and whose goal is to make one despair of one's ability to keep the law, and, on the other hand, works of the law, which, strictly speaking, engender just the opposite attitude. A person's good works turn into works of the law when, instead of the law speaking and working through them, they are allowed to deceive one into believing that they have the capacity to establish one's righteousness.

12. Insofar as the work of the law makes one despair of one's works and recognize their complex underlying motivations, and insofar as it thus leads one to humble oneself and yearn for righteousness, the law, as preparatory for the gospel, establishes a preliminary righteousness that is a matter of hope. The schema of righteousness as yearned for under the law and righteousness as conclusively bestowed by the gospel constitutes Luther's critical response to the theology of the *via antiqua*. To

This woodcut, printed in a work by Martin Luther on the Decalogue (1518), shows a horned Moses holding the two stone tablets of the law. Moses is depicted as horned in medieval Christian iconography because the Hebrew word קרן (*qaran*) was mistranslated as *cornuta* ("horned") in the Vulgate Bible in Exodus 34:29-35.

the duality of justification in medieval theology, see Heiko A. Oberman, "'*Iustitia Christi*' and '*Iustitia Dei*': Luther and the Scholastic Doctrines of Justification," in *The Dawn of the Reformation* (Edinburgh: T&T Clark, 1992), 104–25. Even as he retains a duality of justification (of sorts), Luther rejects the notion that initial righteousness is established by the infusion of grace which enables the believer to merit justification through works of charity. Rather, if the law has truly performed its office, one must regard all of one's good works as works of the law, that is, as deceitful and flawed, and, recognizing one's unrighteousness, seek for righteousness beyond the self. Insofar as faith then grasps the entirety of Christ's person and work and in this way bestows on the believer Christ's own complete righteousness, the law with its demand of righteousness can be said to be fulfilled by grace.

law," for they do not will what the law wills, although they do perform what the law commands. But the law wills and demands our will.

Other people work in such a way that they think they are fulfilling the law and thus are righteous, even though they neither desire grace nor realize and hate the fact that they are sinners; because they have worked according to the outward form of the law, they do not dispose themselves to seek righteousness but rather boast as if through these works it were already in their possession, being totally unaware in their thinking that they are observing the law either with no will or with a will which is unwilling and hostile, or at least out of love and desire for earthly things, but not out of a love for God. And thus they stand still, content and without plans for works worth seeking in behalf of grace, by which they might have also willingness in the law. The fact is that neither the works that precede nor those which follow justify. How much less the works of the law! The works which precede do not justify because they prepare for righteousness; those which follow do not justify because they demand a justification which has already been accomplished. For we are not made righteous by doing righteous works, but rather we do righteous works by being righteous. Therefore grace alone justifies.

22. *Through faith in Jesus Christ.* This statement is a useful addition against the rebellion of the proud, if they should say: "We agree that we are unrighteous of ourselves, and we believe that we are prone to evil and hostile to the law in our hearts. Therefore we believe that we must be justified by God, but we ourselves will obtain this as we pray to him and lament and confess. But we do not want Christ, for God can give us righteousness without Christ."

The answer to this is that he neither wills nor can do this. For Christ also is God. Righteousness will not be given except through faith in Jesus Christ. So it has been established, so it pleases God, and it will not be changed. For who can resist his will? This is only supreme arrogance to wish to be justified without Christ.

But at this point let those who open their eyes of whom I spoke above, who believe in Christ but not in the word of Christ, who will not heed their spiritual leader but have their pleasure in themselves and in their own ideas. They trust in themselves and not in the word of their pastor or of some good man, that is, the Christ who speaks in such men, for they presume that they can be justified without this obedience, without this faith in God and by performing their own good works. But this cannot be, for the statement still stands: "the righteousness of God by faith in Jesus Christ." [. . .]

Just[n] as the expression "without the law" means without the cooperation of the law and the works of the law, so also belief in Christ means faith in him wherever he is and through whomsoever he speaks. [. . .]

21.[o] *The law bears witness.* As Hab. 2:4 says: "The righteous shall live by his faith"; Hos. 2:20: "I will betroth you to me in faithfulness"; and Jer. 31:31-33: "I will make a new covenant with the house of Judah . . . I will write my law upon their hearts, etc." We also have in Genesis the example of Abraham and the others who were justified by faith.

Jesus faces Satan in an area outside of what is presumably Jerusalem (in the background), and protects his flock of sheep from the lion at Satan's side, a scene that illustrated the petition in the Lord's Prayer, "And do not bring us to the time of trial." Woodcut from a 1530 printing of Luther's *Large Catechism*.

n LW 25:242, para. 6.

o LW 25:243, para. 2.

Blessed Augustine in the 13th chapter of his *On the Spirit and the Letter* says: "What the law of works commands by its threats, this the law of faith accomplishes by believing. The one says: 'You shall not covet' (Exod. 20:17); the other says: 'When I knew that I could not otherwise be restrained except God gave it . . . I went to the Lord and begged him, etc.' (Wisd. of Sol. 8:21). And through this law of works God says: 'Do what I command.' But by the law of faith we can say to God in humble prayer: 'Give me what you command.' For the law commands in such a way that it tells faith what to do (that is, what it ought to do), in other words, so that if the one who is commanded cannot as yet fulfill the command, he may know what he should ask." [. . .]

But[p] now who will reveal to us all the tricks of the messenger of Satan by which he is trying to deceive us? We all pray: Give what you command, and yet we do not receive this power. We all believe and speak,[13] we confess and act, and yet we are not all justified. Others who are still rather inexperienced Satan deceives in this way, that they do not see their own weaknesses and the inclination of their wicked will, nor have they analyzed themselves to see how unwillingly they obey the law and how little they love it, but actually they believe and act out of a servile fear; yet they think that they are doing enough and that they must therefore be regarded as righteous before God, because they believe and act; yet they are in no way anxious to do this work so as to do it gladly in joy and love and with full will, or even to see their need of God's grace to accomplish it. But trusting only in their own powers they go about doing their works, although always with tedium and difficulty, when actually they ought to be seeking God with earnest prayers that he might take this tedium from them and fill their will with happiness and through grace take from them their inclination toward evil. For this, I say, there must be earnest prayer, earnest study, earnest work and reproof, until this old habit is eradicated and a newness of will comes into being. For grace is not given without this self-cultivation. But they are snoring so loudly, they have become so lukewarm, so stultified, so arid, and so obdurate, that finally they have lost their faith and have become full of impatience and evil desires, "unfit for any good deed" (Titus 1:16).

13. "Give what you command" is a famous quotation from Augustine, Confessions, X.29: "*Da quod iubes, et iube quod vis.*" Luther's Augustinian hearers would surely have recognized the quote.

In what follows, Luther analyzes the way in which believers' works may turn into works of the law because the work of the law, condemning human self-satisfaction and pride, goes unrecognized in them. The need for faith—which alone brings about the law's fulfillment by granting the believer Christ's own righteousness—is thus also set aside. Here Luther is again implicitly critical of the *via antiqua* understanding of faith which must be rendered concrete though the believer's works of charity.

p LW 25:244, para. 2.

But other people who are more discerning Satan deceives by a subtler delusion. He makes these people do their good works with joy and happiness, so that under this pretense he may hide their weakness from them, so that they thus come to believe that they have grace, and in this subtle manner they come to be more pleased with themselves than with others and are proud, until they have become completely taken up with their own uniqueness and superstition, as is often the case with heretics and stubborn people under the appearance of truth and righteousness in a "zeal which is not enlightened" (Rom. 10:2). Then they become rebels and under the appearance of obedience and fear of God they become disobedient and disdainful of the men of God, that is, Christ's vicars and ambassadors. If we examine ourselves carefully, therefore, we shall always find in ourselves at least vestiges of the flesh by which we are afflicted with self-interest, obstinate over against the good, and prone to do evil. For if there were not this kind of remnant of sin in us and if we were seeking only God, surely this mortal being would quickly be dissolved, and our soul would fly to God. But the fact that the soul does not take to flight is a sure sign that it still clings to the filth of the flesh until it may be freed by the grace of God, and this is to be awaited in death. [. . .] For God has not yet justified us, that is, he has not made us perfectly righteous or declared our righteousness perfect, but he has made a beginning in order that he might make us perfect. Hence, we read in Jas. 1:18: "That we should be a kind of first fruits of his creatures." This is pointed out in the story of the man half-dead who was brought to the inn. After his wounds had been bandaged he was not yet cured, but he was on the way to being made whole.

But it is easy, if we use any diligence at all, to see the depravity of our will in our love of sensual evils and our flight from things that are good, if, for instance, we are drawn toward lust, greed, gluttony, arrogance, love of honor, and we abhor chastity, generosity, sobriety, humility, shame; but it is easy, I say, to understand how in these things we seek our fulfillment and love ourselves, how we are turned in upon ourselves and become ingrown at least in our heart, even when we cannot sense it in our actions.

In spiritual matters, however (that is, in our understanding, our righteousness, our chastity, our piety), it is most difficult to see whether we are seeking only ourselves in them. For the love of these things, since it is honorable and good, often becomes an end in itself for us and does not permit us to regulate them in accord with God and refer them to him, so that as a result we do them not because they are pleasing to God but because they delight us and quiet the fears of our heart, because we are praised by others, and thus we do them not for the sake of God but for ourselves. And this proves to be a temptation. For if we are condemned because of this or if God takes away our enjoyment of these things and the pleasure which they give to our heart, then we neglect to do them or return the condemnations in kind and defend ourselves.

Corollary

Through such presumptuousness and pride it comes about that even the works of grace are turned into works of the law and the righteousness of God is turned into human righteousness, because, when people in grace have done good works, they become pleased with themselves thereby and stop right there and are unwilling to go forward, as if they had thus laid complete hold on righteousness, when actually they should have been progressing and should have been looking upon these good works as only preparatory. Indeed, all righteous works and works which are done in grace are only preparatory for the growth of righteousness which follows, according to the statements "Let the righteous still do right" (Rev. 22:11) and "They go from strength to strength" (Ps. 84:7) and "from one degree of glory to another" (2 Cor. 3:18), with the apostle "straining forward to what lies ahead, forgetting what lies behind" (Phil. 3:13) or has preceded. Thus, not one of the saints thinks or says that he is righteous but rather always prays and waits to be justified, and for this reason he is regarded by God as righteous, because God has regard for the humble.[14] [. . .]

How[q] then can we exalt ourselves against others as if we were more righteous than them? When we not only can do the same as others do, but also in our hearts actually do the same before God as the others do before people. Therefore no one should ever despise one who sins, but one should kindly help the person as

14. For Luther, the believer thus subjectively remains a sinner, while objectively already being righteous, even when the believer may abound and keep increasing in good works.

q LW 25:248, para. 2.

one who shares a common misery, and we should help each other just as two people who are caught in the same mire help each other. Thus, "we bear one another's burdens and so fulfill the law of Christ" (Gal. 6:2). But if we despise the other person, we shall both perish in the mire.

23. *And fall short of the glory of God.* The term "glory" must be understood here in the sense of glorying. And the expression "they fall short" is taken in the sense of being deprived of something, that is, they are empty or have no share. So the meaning is: They do not have a righteousness of which they can glory before God, as we read in 1 Cor. 1:29: "So that no human being might boast in the presence of God." [. . .]

25. The Master of the Sentences[15] and certain other writers construe and interpret the passage *in his divine forbearance he had passed over former sins* as meaning that God shows his righteousness, that is, his truth, for the sake of the remission of the sins of those who went before (that is, the fathers under the old law), whose sins he remitted "in forbearance," that is, for the sake of the coming satisfaction of Christ. [. . .]

15. Peter Lombard. See n. 2, p. 482 above.

But[r] it makes better sense if the term "He passed over former sins" be taken as an adjective and a substantive, so that the meaning is: God through the remission of the sins which we have committed in the past shows that he is the justifier of all. And thus the remission of sins proves that he is righteous and that he is able to justify. As has been said above: "That you may be justified in your words" (v. 4), which he repeats here by saying:

26. *That he himself is righteous and that he justifies.* He speaks of "former sins," however, because he does not forgive all sins, lest someone should say: "If sins are taken away through Christ, let us then do whatever we wish, for no one can now sin," as those people do who surrender the Spirit for "an opportunity for the flesh" (Gal. 5:13) and make their liberty a cloak for evil (cf. 1 Pet. 2:16). For grace and forbearance are not given in order that we may sin or act as we want to, as he later points out when he says that we are not under the law: "What then? Are we to sin because we are not under law?" (Rom. 6:15). And he answers: He does not remit sins in such a way that he no longer regards the work of anyone as sin and simply takes the law away, but he does not punish the sins of the past which he has patiently endured, in

r LW 25:249, para. 2.

order that he may justify. He therefore is not indulgent toward us in order that we may do as we please.

Similarly, it is obvious from this text that God is called righteous by the apostle because God justifies or makes us righteous, as has been said above. And thus it is also evident from the apostle, who interprets himself, that "righteousness of God" (v. 21) is a term which describes that by which he makes us righteous, just as the wisdom of God is that by which he makes us wise.

Through this term "former sins," therefore, the apostle is opposing the foolish and carnal understanding which would interpret the apostle's words thus: "God has fulfilled the law, he no longer imputes sin, he no longer wishes to regard as sin that which he formerly held to be sin. Therefore, let us perform in safety the same deeds as we did formerly, but now they are not sin."

The expression "to uphold the law" (v. 31) is understood in two ways, namely, intrinsically and extrinsically. Intrinsically, the law was formally established when the tenor and the words of the law were put into use, so that it points out and indicates what must be done and what omitted. On the other hand, the law is "overthrown" when it is done away with and abrogated, so that it no longer binds and people are permitted to act contrary to it. And in this way carnal people could get the idea that the apostle is overthrowing the law because he says that we are not justified by the law, but that "apart from the law the righteousness of God has been manifested and given" (v. 21). In another way, extrinsically and by way of example, the law is established and confirmed when we carry out and perform what the law has prescribed or else omit what the law has forbidden. [. . .] The law, therefore, is overthrown extrinsically, when what it commands or forbids is either not done or is done. The apostle is speaking of this matter when he says: *On the contrary, we uphold the law* (v. 31), that is, we assert that it is fulfilled and confirmed by faith. But you people destroy it when you do not fulfill it. You even teach that it should not be fulfilled when you teach that the works of the law are sufficient even without faith. Below, in chapter 8:3, we read: "For what the law, weakened by the flesh, could not do. . . ." [. . .]

Thus[s] the law is upheld both in itself and in us. In itself, when it is promulgated; in us, when we fulfill it with our will and our

Unfinished drawing
of Christ's crucifixion
(c. 1502) by Lucas Cranach the Elder

s LW 25:251, para. 2.

works. But apart from faith no one does this. We always make the covenant of God null and void, therefore, if we live without the grace of God through Christ.

27. *On what principle? On the principle of works? No, but on the principle of faith.* The principle of works of necessity puffs us up and makes for glorying, because he who is righteous and fulfills the law doubtless has something of which to glory and exalt himself. Now those people of whom we have been speaking believe that they are of this class, because they have fulfilled outwardly what the law demands and forbids. For this reason they do not humble themselves, they do not despise themselves as sinners. They do not seek to be justified, they do not cry out for righteousness, because they are confident that they already possess it.

Hence, we must note, as we have said above in quoting blessed Augustine,[16] that "the principle of works says: 'Do what I command,' but the principle of faith says: 'Give what you command.'" And thus the people of the law say to the law and to God, who speaks in the law: "I have done what you have commanded; it is done as you have ordered." But the people of faith say: "I cannot do, I have not done, but give me what you command; I have not done it, but I desire to do it. And because I cannot, I beg and plead you for the power whereby I may do it." And thus the former is made proud and boastful, and the latter humble and vile in his own eyes. And thus there is a very real difference between these classes of people, because the one says: "I have done it," and the other says, "I beg that I might be empowered to do it"; the one says: "Command what you do wish, and I will do it," the other says: "Give what you have commanded in order that I may do it"; the one is confident in the righteousness which he already possesses, the other prays for the righteousness which he hopes to acquire.

For this reason the whole life of the new people, the faithful people, the spiritual people, is nothing else but prayer, seeking, and begging by the sighing of the heart, the voice of their works, and the labor of their bodies, always seeking and striving to be made righteous, even to the hour of death, never standing still, never possessing, never in any work putting an end to the achievement of righteousness, but always awaiting it as something which still dwells beyond them, and always as people who still live and exist in their sins.[17] Thus, when the apostle says that a person is justified *apart from works of the law* (v. 28), he is not

16. Compare to n. 14, p. 495 above. Here Luther acknowledges that he is quoting Augustine and provides a fuller use of the famous phrase from Confessions X.29.

17. Luther retains the dynamic aspect of justification, characteristic of all medieval theology. But he does so to emphasize not its progressive achievement but rather justification's external, gift character. Justification is never earned, or possessed, or pursued in order to become one's possession. Rather, it is always divinely given, coming from beyond the person. Embraced in faith, as something constantly sought, it thus reorients and gives shape to "the whole life of the new people." See in this connection, Luther's understanding of repentance in the first of the *95 Theses*; LW 31:25; also TAL 1:34.

speaking about the works which are performed in order that we may seek justification. Because these are no longer the works of the law but of grace and faith, since we who perform them do not trust in them for our justification, but we want to be justified and we do not think that through these works we have fulfilled the law, but we seek its fulfillment. But Paul calls those works the works of the law which those who do them regard as the reason for their justification, and by the performance of which they consider themselves righteous. They do not do these works, therefore, in order to seek justification, but that they may glory in the righteousness which they already possess. Therefore, after they have performed these works, they come to a stop, as if, now that the law has been entirely fulfilled, no other justification were necessary. And surely this is a proud and arrogant attitude. Indeed, it is also utterly wrong to think that the works of the law could fulfill the law, for the law is spiritual, demanding a heart and a will which we do not possess by ourselves, as we have often said previously. Thus, these people do the outward works of the law but not the inner desires of the law. And thus the people of faith spend their whole life seeking justification. This is their prayer: "Draw me after thee" (Song 1:3). [. . .]

For[t] those[u] who thus seek in heart and work, by the very fact that they seek to be justified and do not think that they are righteous, are doubtless already righteous before God. For they do not confess themselves to be sinners in such a way that they want to keep their sins and depart from God, but rather that they may be freed from them and be justified, always saying: "Forgive us our debts" and "Hallowed be your name" (Matt. 6:12, 9). [. . .]

There[v] is a difference, therefore, between sinners and sinners. Some are sinners and confess that they have sinned, but they do not desire to be made righteous; instead, they despair and keep on sinning, so that in death they despair and in life they are slaves to the world. Others, however, are sinners and confess that they sin and have sinned, but they grieve about it and hate themselves for it and desire to be made righteous and constantly pray and

t LW 25:253, para. 5.

u In this paragraph masculine singular nouns in the original are rendered as plural.

v LW 25:253, para. 8.

cry to God for righteousness. These are the people of God, who bear the judgment of the cross like a yoke upon their shoulders.

In the same way there is also a difference between some righteous and others who are righteous. For some affirm that they are righteous and do not care to be justified, but rather they expect to be rewarded and crowned as kings. Others deny that they are righteous and fear condemnation and desire to be justified.

Therefore the fact that we are sinners does not harm us as long as we strive with all our strength to be made righteous.[18]

18. Note the passive voice. The striving does not produce or merit righteousness, but, rather, brings with itself the recognition that righteousness is thoroughly a gift.

The devil, therefore, that master of a thousand tricks, lays traps for us with marvelous cleverness. He leads some astray by getting them involved in open sins. Others, who think themselves righteous, he brings to a stop, makes them lukewarm, and prompts them to give up the desire for righteousness, as Rev. 3:14ff. speaks of the angel of Laodicea. A third group he seduces into superstitions and ascetic sects, so that, for example, in their greater degree of holiness and in their imagined possession of righteousness, they do not at all grow cold but feverishly engage in works, setting themselves apart from the others, whom they despise in their pride and disdain. A fourth class of people he urges on with ridiculous labor to the point where they try to be completely pure and holy, without any taint of sin. And as long as they realize that they are sinning and that evil may overwhelm them, he so frightens them with the judgment and wears out their consciences that they all but despair.[19] He senses the weakness of each individual and attacks him in this area. And because these four classes of people are so fervent for righteousness, it is not easy to persuade them to the contrary. Thus, he begins by helping them to achieve their goal, so that they become overanxious to rid themselves of every evil desire. And when they cannot accomplish this, he causes them to become sad, dejected, wavering, hopeless, and unsettled in their consciences.

19. Luther will much later, in 1545, echo this concern in reflecting on his time as an Augustinian friar: "Though I lived as a monk without reproach, I felt that I was a sinner before God with an extremely disturbed conscience. I could not believe that he was placated by my satisfaction." See *Preface to the Latin Writings*, LW 34:336; also TAL 4:501.

Then it only remains for us to stay in our sins and to cry in hope of the mercy of God that he would deliver us from them. Just as the patient who is too anxious to recover can surely have a serious relapse, we must also be healed gradually and for a while put up with certain weaknesses. For it is sufficient that our sin displeases us, even though we do not get entirely rid of it. For Christ carries all sins, if only they are displeasing to us, and thus they are no longer ours but his, and his righteousness in turn is ours.

Commentary on 1 Corinthians 15:16-23, 51-57

1534

PIOTR J. MAŁYSZ

INTRODUCTION

Luther's commentary on the fifteenth chapter of Paul's First Letter to the Corinthians was originally a series of seventeen sermons that Luther preached, as a running exposition of the chapter, between August 1532 and April 1533. Luther began the series, as an extended meditation on the meaning of Christian death and hope, only days before the death of the Saxon elector John the Steadfast (1468–1532) and the succession of his son, John Frederick (1503–1554). Luther himself was struggling with poor health at the time, exacerbated further by unrelenting overwork. The sermons were preserved by Luther's secretary, Georg Rörer (1492–1557) and soon edited for publication by Luther's colleague Caspar Cruciger (1504–1548).

Avoiding explicit polemics, Luther's sermons reflect a profound pastoral spirit. On the one hand, their backdrop was increasing confidence in the success of the Reformation's cause, following the presentation of the Augsburg Confession in 1530 before Emperor Charles V (1500–1558), the formation of the Schmalkaldic League for the defense of the Lutheran territories (1531), and, more generally, the continuing spread of Reformation ideas. On the other hand, the larger context of Luther's sermons was the now intractable theological refraction of the

Engraving (1699) of Caspar Cruciger the Elder. It is one of a large number of engravings published by Jean-Jacques Boissard, Theodor de Bry, and others under the title *Bibliotheca chalcographica* in the mid-seventeenth century.

Reformation; the realization that the Reformation lent itself to a variety of agendas, not all of them theological; and the frustration of the Wittenberg reformers with continued theological illiteracy and frequent indifference to the Reformation among the populace. "The peasant in the village, the citizen in the towns, the nobility in the country," as the preface notes, "lead such an infamous life, with no regard for God and God's word . . . [and] die as they lived, that is like sows and cows." Luther's emphasis, in this light, is on the faithfulness of pastors: "if only the pastors remain faithful and preserve the doctrine, God will bestow his grace that there will always be a number to accept it."[a]

In the sermons, Luther expresses his unflinching conviction that doctrine and life are intimately connected. He indicates, specifically, that to believe in the bodily resurrection of Jesus Christ is to assume a critical posture to life, to the world, and to one's own self—and in consequence to suffer. The Christian finds himself or herself assaulted by the world, which resents and despises the Christian's belief in the life to come. Further, the Christian personally cannot but feel the enormity of divine wrath and displeasure over sin, the accusation leveled by God's law, which leaves the conscience agitated and without respite. Finally, the Christian knows how all these are skillfully used by the devil to tempt the Christian into fixation on his or her own unenviable plight and to make the Christian yearn for immersion in unreflective worldliness.

In the midst of the Christian's *tentatio*, doctrine—specifically, belief in Christ's resurrection—becomes the best and, indeed, only response, a way for the Christian to leave one's self behind or, rather, to find the truth of one's self in the risen and living Christ. Luther takes the Christian's ability to respond to the varied assaults quite literally. His sermons are replete with dialogue: Christ responding to the devil, Christ addressing the Christian, the Christian, in turn, addressing the sources of his or her suffering and, in the face of adversity, boldly claiming the benefits of Christ. Luther thus gives his hearers/readers the very words to use and, in doing so, demonstrates the deep practical relevance of the Christian confession.

a LW 28:62. For a similar sentiment, see also Luther's preface to the *Small Catechism* (1529).

Given this emphasis on the relevance of doctrine for the Christian life, it is hardly surprising that major elements of Luther's mature theology all make their appearance. First, Luther repeatedly cautions against trusting in one's own reason and points rather to the actuality of Christ's work. In more concrete terms, he directs the Christian from the inscrutability of God's work in the world to the clarity of his work in Christ. The Christian need not seek forgetfulness through pleasure when faced with the world. When it comes to Christ, Luther stresses, above all, his victory over sin, death, and the devil and his lordship over the law—only to apply this victory to the believer. He points to the happy exchange between Christ and the believer.[1] Finally, to

Woodcut depicting the crucifixion of Christ, from a volume by Johann Eck published in 1532

make things even more concrete, Luther repeatedly draws attention to the preaching of the gospel, the administration of Baptism, and the celebration of the Lord's Supper as those actions by means of which God actually grounds the believer within the reality of Christ's resurrection. Through word and sacrament, God incorporates the believer into Christ's resurrection as a member of a body whose head is already born to a new life. The conscience and the heart that embrace Christ find themselves with him on the other side of death, while that which remains on this side is now saturated with God's continuing healing work.

1. Luther's teaching on *fröhlicher Wechsel*, *admirabile commercium*, or *feliciter commutans*, describes Christ's work of salvation as his assumption of all that human beings have, including, in particular, their sins, and in turn bestowing on humans all that Christ is and has (see *Sermon on Two Kinds of Righteousness*, TAL 2:8–24; *The Freedom of a Christian*, TAL 1:499–507).

The Christian can thus say with confidence, "I am no longer a child of man, but a child of God, for I am baptized in his blood and on his victory, and I am vested with all his possessions."

The only note of pessimism that can be heard in Luther's commentary—a note which is, however, good news for the afflicted Christians—is Luther's conviction that the greatest believers may all already be gone, that Christ "already owns the greatest part of his body," and that it is "only a short leap to the end." To be sure, Luther expects more people to be born and further believers to be incorporated into Christ's resurrection. But the apparent victory of the Reformation's cause and his own role in it are, as such, not a sign of hope for Luther. Luther finds in his movement no special source of optimism, and he shows no confidence in a Christian society. As the hour of death draws near, Christ alone, Luther insists, is the Christian's hope.

COMMENTARY ON 1 CORINTHIANS 15:16-23[b]

16-19. For if the dead are not raised, then Christ has not been raised. If Christ has not been raised, your faith is futile and you are still in your sins. Then those also who have fallen asleep in Christ have perished. If for this life only we have hoped in Christ, we are of all people most to be pitied.

[. . .][c]

WE CAN GATHER FROM THIS that [the Corinthians] did not take this article seriously and that St. Paul was vexed to see them treat it so coldly and indifferently, moreover, put it in

b The following is based on LW 28:100–123 with some modifications.

c The bracketed ellipsis here and elsewhere indicates breaks in the text, where some amount of text has been eliminated.

doubt, indeed, that some spoke of it so carelessly and even heathenishly, as though it were nothing at all. There are still many who do not believe this in their hearts and secretly regard this as a big laugh, especially those who claim to be smart and very intelligent and who measure and judge God's word with their reason. They are like the Sadducees and their disciples in the days of Christ, who spread that poison among God's people. This had already been disseminated widely. It necessarily follows, especially where factious spirits arise, who agitate this and spew it out among the people, that the majority remain steeped in such shameful unbelief, live riotously, and care neither about God nor about the life beyond, just as though there were neither hell nor heaven; and yet they are called Christians and are baptized. And no matter how much they are preached to, all is preached to deaf ears. [. . .]

St. Paul[d] here names the parts one after the other and arrays them *per impossible* [. . .]. In the first place, if the dead do not arise, it follows that Christ, too, did not arise. Reasoning: Christ is, as we know, also one of the dead; indeed, he is the Head of us all and, as he says later, "the first fruits," who was to rise. And if this article is not true in him, it is true in no one.

In the second place, it would also follow that our preaching is in vain. For why should we bestow such pains, why hazard to preach, to encumber ourselves with so much toil, and all of this at the risk of life and limb and all sorts of danger, if this were naught but an empty, worthless, and useless bauble? Indeed, then we should hold our tongue and forsake pulpit with Baptism, Sacrament [Lord's Supper], and Scripture. [. . .]

Therefore,[e] if we knew of no other life, we should also hold our peace and let the people live like cows and pigs, which probably also know very well what is good for them. We should let it rest at that and neglect pulpit and all. We should not devote so much attention to it as to create such a stir over it in the world, if it were but effort lost and if it would serve and help neither this nor that life. Therefore, if you desire no other life nor believe in it, just disregard preaching. If you do not care to have a God, you also do not need to hear us, nor need we preach to you. For, God

d LW 28:100, para. 3.

e LW 28:101, para. 2.

be praised, we are not so stupid that we should wish to propagate this doctrine in vain, or only to regulate this body and this life with it. No, we find that ordered very well already by the heathen and by reason. Our only concern is to teach how—after our Baptism—we may get from this to yonder life. To that end we have to preach and to admonish daily. But if there were nothing to the resurrection, all of that would be entirely in vain and futile.

In the third place, Paul said, your faith would be futile and nothing but an empty and worthless idea. For if the resurrection is nothing and yet I believe in it, what is that but a mere dream with sequel? Then all of Christendom from the beginning of the world would have followed a false belief, and all would be poor, bewitched people who permitted themselves to be fooled and misled by an empty dream and phantom, one for which people had to endure every persecution, distress, and torture. And after hoping for and relying on this for a long time, they would have had to depart this life and die in that confidence and then find themselves deceived shamefully. If it were true, as some people declare, that this article is false and that there is nothing to a life beyond, this would constitute the greatest deception ever perpetrated on earth. [. . .]

In[f] the fourth place, St. Paul says, we, too, would be false witnesses, we who say and teach that Christ has arisen, if the dead do not arise. And as that belief would be false, we, too, would be nothing but the devil's buffoons and liars, who speak of themselves and babble of things of which they know nothing. As base liars and rascals they invent things, cheating people out of their lives and out of all they have. We are, however, Christ's apostles and faithful witnesses. We can prove that we were called and commissioned by God and that we proclaim the truth, so that many people, mightily persuaded, join us of themselves and because of this suffer all that befalls us. This demonstrates that we are in earnest about this and do not joke or engage in trickery, as though we were vagrants or charlatans.

The fifth part follows. If there is nothing to the resurrection, St. Paul says, "you are still in your sins," both you and all those "who have fallen asleep in Christ." Then Christ would be of no avail at all to you. For what good would you derive from the fact

f LW 28:102, para. 3.

that you proclaim and believe you were redeemed from sin and were justified by his resurrection, if there is nothing to that resurrection and if you were not also redeemed from death and would not rise and live again? That you and all other Christians from the beginning were baptized on this, heard the gospel, and lived as Christians who had remission of sin from their Lord would all be in vain. Believing that all ends with death, you would die like the cattle and have no more than the heathen and unbelievers. It would be disgraceful indeed to declare that Christ is nothing and that he does not help either the living or the dead.

The sixth and final point with which St. Paul concludes is: "If in this life only we have hoped in Christ, we are of all people most to be pitied." That is tantamount to saying: "If it were true that there is no life after the present one, I should gladly forgo Baptism, pulpit, and all of Christianity." For observe a Christian and compare him with people who do not believe. The latter live in a whirl of pleasure; they have and they do what they please, and when they have lived their life, "they perish forever without any regarding it," as Job 4:20 says. They never experience what real suffering or sadness, misery and grief are. In contrast to them, we who want to be Christians endure all kinds of troubles and misfortunes, so that people despise and vilify, revile and slander us. The world is so hostile to us; it begrudges us our very life on earth. Daily we must be prepared for the worst that devil and world can inflict on us. In the face of this, who would be stupid enough to be a Christian if there were nothing to a future life? Who would not say: I, too, want to have good times and revel as those people do? With what wrongdoing do I charge myself that I let myself be tormented so and endure such sorrow, spite, hatred, and envy from the world? In addition to this, a Christian must suffer so much inward grief and heartache, such fear and terror of death, of sin, and of God's wrath. These are real blows indeed.

For that external suffering is only child's play, it is only the ABC of a Christian's misery and trouble with which the world persecutes him, exiles him, and displays all sorts of malice. But this fear and woe caused by God's wrath really pierce his heart: the fear of eternal death, of becoming partners of the devil in the abyss of hell. This haunts him day and night. Against this the Christian has to contend, well-nigh sweating blood. I should much rather lie in jail for a year, suffer hunger and thirst, than endure such mortal fright with which the devil afflicts Christians, who, after all, believe and are certain of the future resurrection and of eternal life awaiting them and, on the other hand, of judgment and eternal fire awaiting the evildoers. And just because they know that, they have no rest until they are rescued from this vale of tears. For here the two paths lie before them; in addition, the devil and their own conscience attack them, telling them that they are not pious and calling Scripture to witness that we are all sinners and guilty of damnation. The devil knows how to turn that to account and to torment a person so that he breaks out in cold sweat. Therefore it is necessary for a person to struggle and contend, lest he be engulfed in sadness and fear, but that he may instead remain confident that God is gracious to him and wants to take him unto himself in heaven. The others, the great multitude, know nothing of this. They fear neither God's wrath and judgment nor devil or death. They think that their own death is not unlike the death of a cow. In the meantime, they are secure and happy and experience nothing at all of such a heartache. Therefore a Christian is an especially wretched person, suffering more of whatever may be termed misery than others. His heart is daily roasted on the fire. He must[2] always be terrified, fearful, and trembling when the thought of death and God's severe judgment occurs to him. He must always worry that he has angered God and merited hell, although he may be pious and well practiced in faith. For such thoughts will not cease; rather, they are felt more and more and always become stronger than the good thoughts. Therefore we behold some people who are so depressed and so beaten and so assailed and wretched in their hearts that they can impart this to no one. They are bereft of all joy and happiness and do not care to live.

Therefore, St. Paul says, we would be mad and foolish to subject ourselves to such misery, fear, sadness, and distress and never be safe from death and devil for a moment, if we had nothing but this life. What could we possess on this earth, even though we might acquire all the goods of the world, to compensate for being Christians and cumbering ourselves with such suffering? Who would want to bear that and spend his life thus in nothing but misery and distress and not get anything but this life in return?

The heathen said very wisely: "he who fears death is a fool, for thereby he loses his own life." It would indeed be well spoken, if

2. Here Luther's stress is less on obligation and more on what inevitably will be the case, whether one wishes for it or not.

A peddler is stalked by death in this 1549 engraving by Hans Holbein

anyone could do it. [. . .] They[g] advise that there is nothing better than simply to cast all such fears aside, to force them from your mind, and think: "Why should we worry about this? After we are dead, we are dead." Just as the Corinthians said, as St. Paul indicates later (v. 32): "Let us eat and drink, for tomorrow we die, etc." That is making short shrift of it and extinguishing God's wrath, hell, and damnation completely.

However, Christians cannot do that. They cannot dismiss this so from hearts which would gladly believe. On the contrary, the more faith struggles and would strengthen itself, the more this is felt. Thus, it is not sure of life for a moment, and God's judgment and the pit of hell always stare it in the face. Such people must be comforted with this message: "My dear man, you may feel this very much, and it may pain you uninterruptedly to live thus, and, admittedly, you are a poor, miserable person; but be patient and be assured that this must be because you are a Christian. Otherwise you would not be so tormented. However, you must fend this off and cling with a firm faith to the fact that your Christ has risen from the dead. He, too, suffered such anguish and fear of hell, but through his resurrection he has overcome all." Therefore, even though I am a sinner and deserving of death and hell, this shall nonetheless be my consolation and my victory that my Lord Jesus lives and has risen so that he, in the end, might rescue me from sin, death, and hell.

The resurrected Christ, with an Easter lily on one side of his head and a sword on the other, sits above a scene depicting the resurrection of the dead. Woodcut from Luther's *Ain trostlichs büchlein* (1520). The image appears to be based on a famous image by Michael Wolgemut, found in Hartmann Schedel's *Nuremberg Chronicle* (1493).

With such faith Christians must soothe and assuage their suffering and check their unhappiness. Otherwise it would be impossible to comfort a saddened and frightened heart or to divert the thoughts with any earthly joy. This, however, is effected when the Man Christ declares that he is the God and Savior of the wretched. Not those who live in security, in a whirl of pleasures, and free of all fear, but those who fear the devil

g LW 28:105, para. 1.

and hell must occupy themselves with Baptism, the pulpit, and the gospel and conclude thus: "The fact that I feel this fear of hell and of God's judgment is a reliable sign that I am also a Christian and have some faith; for whoever is terrified by this must surely believe that there is a heaven and a hell. On the other hand, whoever does not fear these does not believe anything. For that reason I must comfort myself in such terror and fear, pull myself together by faith, and say to the devil and to my heart: 'You frighten me with sin and hell, but Christ tells me of heaven, righteousness, life, and eternal bliss. He must have greater weight with me than all my feelings and ideas.'" And thus we must ever struggle and resist, firmly holding and clinging to this article. This will be necessary both in life and in death.

So you see that St. Paul spoke the truth when he said: "If for this life only we have hoped in Christ, we are of all people most to be pitied," and we are also the greatest fools, for we alone renounce all goods and comforts, all joy and happiness of this life and of all creatures, we expose ourselves to every peril of life and limb in vain and for nothing and to the terrible and unspeakable terror of hell, so that we have to live in contempt and in misery before the world and in eternal fear before God. After all, there is no trouble or misfortune, no fire, no rope, no sword on earth comparable to this plague. And should we go into this or remain in it voluntarily? We should rather imitate the world or our rabble today and say: "Why do you make such a great ado about the gospel and faith? If I but had enough money to count out, etc." "But be off, dear brother, with your crowd. Be of good cheer as long as it lasts. Because you are no Christian and believe nothing regarding God or devil, it is easy for you to revel. Nobody is there to assail you. But if you, too, want to be a Christian and strive earnestly for the life to come, you will surely feel the devil pressing you and all Christians hard with every creature which he can use for that purpose. He will terrify you, aggrieve you; he will choke you that you will find rest neither by day nor by night. And your own experience will constrain you to profess that there is no life or existence on earth more wretched than that of a Christian." For all of this misery and grief arises because of Christ. It is due to the fact that the devil is hostile to him and to his word and to his rule, to Baptism, and to all of Christendom. We have to suffer for that now; and we must not imagine that we will have happiness and peace here on earth. [. . .]

20-21. But in fact Christ has been raised from the dead, the first fruits of those who have fallen asleep. For as by a man came death, by a Man has come also the resurrection of the dead.

[. . .] Here [St. Paul] presents the only true consolation against such external appearances and feelings. For, as I said, Christians have to have a stronger consolation than gold and silver, singing and dancing, and all that the world possesses. A miser can be consoled with money, a sick person with medicine, a beggar or a hungry person with a piece of bread; but none of these can help a Christian. For because we[h] believe and know that God has both a heaven and a hell, we are immediately terrified by God's wrath; we become timid and dejected people. Therefore we find joy and solace only in the promise of the life to come as we hear this article which informs us that Christ has risen from the dead, that he will also awaken us and transport us from death and every misfortune to joy eternal.

[. . .] [Christ][i] came forth alive from the grave in which he lay and destroyed and consumed both devil and death, who had devoured him. He tore the devil's belly and hell's jaws asunder and ascended into heaven, where he is now seated in eternal life and glory. This is to be comfort and defiance. For on his name we are baptized, and we hear and profess his word. After him we are called Christians, and for his sake we suffer every misfortune and grief from the hand of the devil. For this is not aimed at us but at him and his kingdom, whose enemy the devil is. He tries to destroy it, and he treats us so roughly and wearies us with pursuit, harassment, and death so that we might forsake Christ.

But we will confront him confidently and say: "No, you despicable, vile devil, you will not bring matters to such a pass that I surrender Baptism and the name of my Lord for your sake. If you can defiantly rely on and make an uproar with your death, fire, water, pestilence, and hell, we can defiantly rely on this Lord Jesus Christ, who has vanquished you. He can again destroy you and cast you into hell eternally—as he in fact will do—and wrest us alive from your jaws. Therefore devour us if you can, or hurl us into the jaws of death, you will soon see and feel what you have

h In this paragraph the original singular masculine pronoun is rendered as inclusive plural.

i LW 28:108, para. 2.

done. We, in turn, will cause such a great disturbance in your belly and make an egress through your ribs that you wish you had rather devoured a tower, yes, an entire forest. For you previously consumed a Person and put him under the ground, but he was too strong for you. To your great disgrace you had to return him although you blasphemed defiantly: 'He saved others; he cannot save himself, etc.' (Matt. 27:42). But now he defies you in return; he has become your death and hell. And soon he will overthrow you completely through us on the day of judgment."

You, of course, will say: "It is easy for Christ to defy the devil and death, for he is enthroned on high where no one can harm him. But what do I gain thereby? Or, how will I obtain that? As you can see, I remain behind." St. Paul replies with one short statement, saying: "Christ has been raised from the dead, the first fruits of those who have fallen asleep." For with the words "first fruits" he implies that Christ is not the only one to arise but that others will follow later. You must not regard this Man as one who arose for himself alone. We would be but poorly comforted if his resurrection had no sequel. Then we would derive no more benefit from this than if he had never become man.

It was not necessary for him to die for himself, because he was born without sin and the devil had no claim on him. Moreover, he was Lord over devil and death, so that the devil did not dare to attack him. Christ might well have defied the devil and challenged him to touch one little hair of his head. This is the way he repelled the Jews in the Garden when he said: "I am he" (John 18:5). No, we must view him in this light, that this dying and rising again were for your benefit and mine. As he died and lay under the sod as you and I must die and be buried, thus he also rose again for our sakes and made an exchange with us; as he was brought into death through us, we shall be restored from death to life through him.[3] For by his death he has devoured our death, so that we all will also arise and live as he arose and lives. Therefore Christ is rightly called *Primitiae*, "the first fruits of those who have fallen asleep," since he takes the lead and draws the whole throng after him. For whenever a first one is mentioned, it is implied that more than one are involved. [. . .]

What was a true and eternal death prior to this and without Christ is now, since Christ has passed from death to life and has arisen, no longer death; now it has become merely sleep. And so the Christians who lie in the ground are no longer called dead,

3. In his lectures on Galatians, delivered the preceding year, Luther articulated the nature of this exchange even more pointedly: "By this fortunate exchange with us he took upon himself our sinful person and granted us his innocent and victorious Person" (LW 26:284). See also n. 1, p. 503 above.

but sleepers, people who will surely also arise again. For when we say that people are asleep, we refer to those who are lying down but will wake up and rise again, not those who are lying down bereft of all hope of rising again. Of the latter we do not say that they are sleeping but that they are inanimate corpses. Therefore by that very word "asleep" Scripture indicates the future resurrection.

And what is more than that, by calling Christ "the first fruits of those who have fallen asleep," Paul wishes to signify that the resurrection is to be viewed and understood as having already begun in Christ, indeed, as being more than half-finished, and that this remnant of death is to be regarded as no more than a deep sleep, and that the future resurrection of our body will not differ from suddenly awaking from such a sleep. For the main and best part of this has already come to pass, namely, that Christ, our Head, has arisen. But now that the Head is seated on high and lives, there is no longer any reason for concern. We who cling to him must also follow after him as his body and his members. For where the head goes and abides, there the body with all the members must necessarily follow and abide. As in the birth of human beings and of all animals, the head naturally appears first, and after this is born, the whole body follows easily. Now since Christ has passed over and reigns above in heaven over sin, death, devil, and everything, and since he did this for our sake to draw us after him, we need no longer worry about our resurrection and life, though we depart and rot in the ground. For now this is no more than a sleep. And for Christ it is but a night before he rouses us from the sleep.

Now if I know this and believe it, my heart or conscience and soul have already passed through death and grave and are in heaven with Christ, dwell there and rejoice over it. And in that way we have the two best parts, much more than half, of the resurrection behind us. And because Christ animates and renews the heart by faith, he will also surely drag the decomposed rascal after him and clothe him again, so that we can behold him and live with him. For that is his word and work on which we are baptized and live and die. Therefore this will surely not fail us, as little as it failed him. No matter when or how God ordains that we die, whether in bed or in the fire, in the water, by rope or by sword, the devil, death's master and butcher, will surely see to killing us and carrying out his trade, so that we will not be able to choose or select a mode of death. But no matter how he executes us, it shall not harm us. He may give us a bitter potion, such as is administered to put people to sleep and make them insensitive, but we will wake up again and come forth on that day, when the trumpet will sound. That the devil shall not prevent, because even now we are more than halfway out of death in Christ, and he will not be able to hold back this poor belly and bag of maggots either.

Behold, thus we must view our treasure and turn away from temporal reality which lies before our eyes and senses. We must not let death and other misfortune, distress, and misery terrify us so. Nor must we regard what the world has and can do, but balance this against what we are and have in Christ. For our confidence is built entirely on the fact that he has arisen and that we have life with him already and are no longer in the power of death. [. . .]

In[j] the face of this, why should we let the devil terrify us and make us so despondent, even though he comes face to face with us and reaches out to us, as though he would rob us of everything; even though he kills wife and child, torments our heart with all sorts of misery and sorrow, and in the end also destroys our body, assuming that he has thereby taken everything away?[4] [. . .]

4. Luther's argument here evokes the language of the fourth stanza of his hymn "Eyn feste Burg."

But[k] with all that done, he has still stripped us of nothing. For the goods and the treasure which we Christians have are not those which the world seeks and possesses in this life on earth. No, we have already secured our possession against the devil, so that he cannot take it from us. It is in safe custody in this first fruits of the dead, who is seated on high, who has ascended from the den of murderers and has taken our life and all with him. We defiantly boast of that and, in addition, scoff at the devil, saying: "Because you hanker so to devour us Christians and assume that you are acquiring a dainty morsel, go ahead and kill and butcher us, fry us and devour us hide and hair. [. . .] It will be far from satisfying your insatiable appetite. For you will not find what you are seeking and desiring, and that is the best and greatest part of us, indeed, our whole life and treasure, namely, this article of the resurrection in Christ. Through this we have already been

j LW 28:111, para. 3.

k LW 28:112, para. 1.

wrested from your teeth and have been moved too far on high. For this treasure does not reside with us or in us—if it did, you would soon tear it away from us—but on high in Christ. There you will have to let it rest unassailed and without any thanks. What does it harm us that you now kill our body? For the only thing you effect thereby is to help this poor sack of maggots out of its misery and arrive at its destination, where the head, the heart, and everything is except all misfortune. That we look forward to daily and that we desire. Then you shall perceive and feel what you have eaten. It will be most distressing to no one but only you. The very pestilence and poison that you gave us you yourself will have to eat and devour and guzzle down, and it will tear both your jaws and your belly, putting an end to your raging." Behold, thus we must fend off and defy all terror of the vile enemy, because he can after all but afflict us with all distress and grief. This he does to distract our eyes and our heart from this article and the first fruits, Christ, making us forget whose we are or what we have and what we are called.

In this way St. Paul demonstrated that Christ's resurrection is the reason for ours. He now expounds and illustrates that further with an example, saying: "For as by a man came death, by a Man has come also the resurrection of the dead." That is to say: "Just as Adam was the beginning, the first man, through whom we must all die as he died, so Christ is the first Man through whom we are all to arise to a new life as he arose first." [. . .]

Here St. Paul places these two types over against each other. He wants to say: "Through one man, Adam, so much was effected that all people must now die, both he and all of us who, after all, did not commit or perpetrate the offense but came into sin and death solely because we are descended from him." Although this happens after the fall, yet it is no longer the sin of another, but it becomes our own when we are born. That is a miserable deal and an awful judgment of God; and it would be still more terrible if we were all to remain in death eternally. But now God placed a second Man, called Christ, over against the first one, so that, just as we die without any fault of our own by reason of the first man, we shall live again by reason of Christ and without our merit. And as we in Adam have to pay solely for the fact that we are his members or his flesh and blood, so we enjoy our advantage here in Christ also solely by virtue of his being our Head. It is pure grace and gift, so that we have no works or merits to boast of

This frontispiece depicts Adam and Eve after the Fall, as indicated by the skeleton (representing death), the serpent, and the piece of forbidden fruit at their feet. They look into the heavens at the resurrected Christ enthroned among the clouds. The inscription from 1 Corinthians 15 invokes Christ as the "new" Adam. From a prayer book published in 1784 by Paul Wright (d. 1785).

here, as our monks and false saints teach. For how should we who are born in sin and belong to death, being of Adam's flesh and blood, manage to liberate ourselves by our cowls or other works both from sin and death, emerging alive from dust and ashes, brighter and more beautiful than the sun and the rest of creation? That can, of course, not be achieved by human power and strength or by that of all creatures, not even by the angels in heaven, but exclusively by God himself. There must be another Man who can achieve that and bring it about, a Man who is called Christ, God's Son and Lord over sin, death, devil, and over all things,[5] as St. Paul will say of him later (v. 27). It is he who acquired this article and initiated it in himself and presented it to us, so that we, too, might attain it through him, solely because we are incorporated in him through baptism and were called to this article and engrafted in it, so that we will arise and live by the same power and merit by which he arose and lives.

And now since this is not at all our doing, both that we came into death and that we came into life, our consolation is all the stronger, as is also our hope that we shall have life through Christ as surely as we now have and feel sin and death through Adam. For if it would rest with us and depend on us to work our way out of sin and death and to obtain life by our own doing, we could not be at ease our whole life. We should have to torment and terrify ourselves with works incessantly. And after we had thus tortured ourselves to death, and even if one person were to produce the holiness of the whole world, we could still not be certain and sure that we had done enough and sufficient to satisfy God. Therefore God granted us the mercy to impose all of this on one Man, who acquired all of this without us and ahead of us, so that it is assured us and cannot fail us. Therefore we come into this entirely without our doing. Nothing that we do or are able to do contributes toward our obtaining grace and resurrection; although we do and must do good works. This is the same as when we become sinners without our doing and must die. For

5. This passage echoes the second stanza of Luther's "Ein feste Berg."

we had no hand in Adam's eating the apple and falling into sin, although we do admittedly commit sin after the fall. In that way everything that pertains to sin and to righteousness, to death and to life, resides solely in those two men, as St. Paul now elaborates further.

22. For as in Adam all die, so also in Christ shall all be made alive.

Here St. Paul is still speaking only about those who are Christians. These he wants to instruct and console with this article. For although also the non-Christians must all arise, this will not be to their comfort and joy, since they will arise for judgment and not for life. Therefore to hear this article does not bring comfort and joy to the world and the ungodly people of today either. This I experienced in my own case when I tried to be a holy monk and when I was most pious. I would much rather have heard about all the devils in hell than about the last day. My hair stood on end when I thought of it.[6] For aside from the fact that the whole world is loath to relinquish this life and to die and is frightened when one speaks of death and of yonder life, we are all submerged in the mire of our own holiness, and we are of the opinion that we might silence God's judgment and merit heaven with our life and works. And yet all that we accomplish thereby is that we become ever more averse and hostile to this day. I will say nothing of that great vulgar throng which seeks its pleasure and consolation only here, which condemns God's word and cares not a mite for God and his kingdom. It is not surprising that such people are annoyed to hear of the blessed resurrection; for us, however, it is pure joy, because we hear that our greatest Treasure, over which we rejoice, is already in heaven above, and that only the most insignificant part remains behind; and that he will awaken this, too, and draw it after him as easily as a person awakens from sleep. There will no longer be any grief or suffering, and neither world nor devil will plague and sadden us anymore. Now they are persecuting and tormenting us, but then tables will be turned on them. Their lot will be everlasting lamentation, but we will rejoice eternally. For since Christ is to be the judge both of the good and of the evil, they, too, will have to come forth on that day to receive their judgment and their punishment for whatever they perpetrated in their impenitent and devilish malice against Christ and us.

6. In 1545, toward the end of his life, Luther reflected famously on the anguish which he, as an Augustinian friar, experienced while contemplating divine justice: "Though I lived as a monk without reproach, I felt that I was a sinner before God with an extremely disturbed conscience. I could not believe that he was placated by my satisfaction" (*Preface to the Latin Writings*, LW 34:336; also TAL 4:501). Whereas Luther eventually came to see divine justice as primarily passive, offering itself as a gift, here he does not deny that it will also have an active, judicial aspect.

It is a ridiculous message that St. Paul conveys here, telling us where both death and eternal life originate. To clever reason and worldly wisdom it seems to be a great and strong lie that the entire human race must die for the guilt of another, of one single man. It seems too unfair and too absurd that God should treat this matter so strangely and take this silly position in his judgment. Because Adam bit into an apple, he is supposed to have effected that all human beings are doomed to die to the end of the world. But what is to be our position in this matter? That death befalls us we can all see clearly. But that this is due to one minor sin sounds too odd. When we explain this with words and compare the two, this does appear disproportionate.

For at the time Adam had, after all, not committed murder or adultery, he had not stolen or robbed anyone, he had not blasphemed God or committed any similar sins, wicked and horrible sins such as abound in the world today. All he did was to bite into an apple,[7] persuaded to do this and deceived by the devil through his wife. Reason asks whether so much importance had to be attached to that one apple that the whole world had to pay for it and that so many fine, excellent, and wise people, indeed, God's Son himself, together with all the prophets, fathers, and saints, had to die. Yes, if nothing more than death were involved here, as the world and wise people say, who console themselves over against death with the assumption that it ends all misfortune! If some better fate should await them after death, as they hope, they are willing to accept it, too. Still they cannot conclude that with any degree of certainty; and of the resurrection they know nothing whatsoever. But the thought that we all deserve eternal punishment and damnation and suffering in hell because of the sin of someone else, and all of that by reason of just one sin—that is still harder for the human heart to accept. For this judgment on the part of such an exalted Majesty, which is the highest Wisdom and Goodness, seems too unfair, and the action too merciless.

As we have said, we must all profess that it seems so ridiculous that we all must die; however, that this derives from Adam we must learn to believe here. For no human heart or wisdom ever devised or thought this out, that death is a penalty for sin. No, everybody thought and regarded death as man's natural lot, comparable to the death of a dog or a pig or any other animal, or comparable to the rising and the setting of the sun, or the grow-

7. On the belief that the forbidden fruit was an apple, see above n. *a*, p. 157.

ing or the withering of grass. All things are considered perishable by nature, vanishing again as they came. However, Scripture teaches us that our death and dying does not come in a natural way but that this is a fruit of and the penalty for our father Adam's sin. He offended the Sublime Majesty so outrageously that he and all who are descended from him and are born on earth must die eternally. No one on earth can escape or ward off this calamity.

And again it sounds so absurd and so false to the world, yes, much more incredible, when Paul declares here that in one Man all men shall rise again; that both death and life rest with and depend on one man; that the whole world is unable to do anything in this matter; that no man's power or might, no saint's life, virtue, and work, are adequate reason for rising from the dead; that this is absolutely beyond the ability and the merit of every other human being and is centered solely in one single Man, who was unknown to the world and despised by it, who, moreover, died a most shameful and miserable death. To him all the world is to accord honor, and he is to be regarded as the One by whom we all rise again. No holy monk, Carthusian,[8] yes, no prophet, apostle, or martyr, can contribute anything toward this or merit it with all his doings. This appears preposterous as we ponder it. It often appeared strange and odd to me myself. It is surely hard to convince the heart of this article. When I behold a corpse carried out and buried, it is hard to go my way and believe and think that we will some day rise together. How so, or by what power? Not by myself or by virtue of any merit on earth, but by this one Christ. And that is indeed certain, far more certain than the fact that I will be buried and see someone else buried, which I know with certainty and behold with my eyes. Therefore this is a sermon for Christians and an article of faith. All who are of the world regard this as sheer fraud. They argue that it is impossible for God to be so foolish and to condemn the whole world without distinction for the sake of one man, or, on the other hand, to save all people without any merit of theirs for the sake of one Man.

[. . .] What[l] sort of a God would he be who let us instruct him, or who would be directed by us and work according to our wisdom? But as it is, he works in a manner in which his wisdom remains profounder than ours; we have to surrender to it and

8. An order founded by Bruno of Cologne (1030–1101) in 1084 in the mountainous region near Grenoble, France. The Carthusians were known for their almost total seclusion from the world.

l LW 28:117, para. 3.

desist from criticizing. We must say: "According to my wisdom this does not seem good; however, since You say it, it is just and good." Those who will not do that but instead place their own wisdom before and above God's and judge him accordingly, let them beware what they are doing.[m] We, however, will confine our wisdom to things here below and apply it to cows and horses, trees, houses, fields, etc. In this area you may be smart and judge and rule as you will, and you may stick to your opinion. But we must not interfere with his wisdom and rule.[9] That is too high and far removed for us, since we are under him and he is over us as our Creator and Lord. Therefore we must give ear to him and believe what he says, so that his honor remains unsullied and his grace and mercy alone prevail, without any glory or merit of ours. [. . .]

9. Luther alludes here to the medieval adage, "the things above us are of no concern to us [*quae supra nos nihil ad nos*]," which he invoked and discussed in *The Bondage of the Will* (1525), warning against the rationalization of God's actions (see LW 33:139).

Meanwhile,[n] [the non-Christians and unbelieving saints] run to and fro in their fright, first to this saint, then to another. They look for one work here, for another there. But a Christian leaves all of that out of consideration, for we have learned and experienced that there is no help on earth against death, which is innate in us. In fact, a Christian must also bear and suffer death the same as others. And of course it frightens and pains us.[n] But we cry solely to God, believing that he will deliver us from death through Christ. In that way we Christians strengthen ourselves daily until we pass from this life.

Furthermore, we enjoy the advantage of which I spoke earlier, namely, that in Christ death has lost its meaning even today and that a part of the resurrection has already taken place—really the best and foremost part—and that we have received a taste of this in our hearts through Christ, and that we, praise be to God, have arrived at the point where the enemy has practically no more teeth and where he has lost his sword. For if we figure it out, we find that he has already almost devoured the world and has emptied the keg down to the very dregs, that he has killed the larger part of the human race, the head, the chest, the belly, and the legs, almost the feet, too. For today we are no more than the last toes of the great image of which Daniel speaks in chapter 7.[10] For the four monarchies, or empires, are already past history,

10. Luther presumably means the "great image" in Daniel chapter 2. In chapter 7 the four monarchies are represented by four monstrous beasts. See above, pp. 383–86, 389–91.

m The original singular masculine pronouns in this section and the next have been rendered as plural.

n LW 28:119, para. 1.

and all the prophets and fathers and Christ himself with his apostles and saints are all gone. In brief, the largest part of the entire body of Christendom and, in addition, the greatest and wisest princes and lords and kings are gone, so that only the last little drink remains to be taken, and it is only a short leap to the end. [. . .]

Daniel's vision of the four beasts (kingdoms) in Daniel 7. Sixteenth-century woodcut by Hans Holbein the Younger.

[Christ][o] already owns the greatest part of his body, that is, Christendom, through its belief in his resurrection, so that not more than a leap, yes, a moment, remains until his own, whose bodies still repose in the grave, arise completely. For all of these, excepting a small number, have been taken from their misery, and more than half of them are alive in Christ, because they lived and persevered in the faith. [. . .] Therefore we who have now reached the end of the world have the defiant comfort that it will be but a little while, that we are on our last lap, and before we are aware of it, we shall all stand at Christ's side and live with him eternally. [. . .]

We[p] received all of this free and gratis. We contribute nothing except that we are baptized, hear the gospel, and adhere to Christ—all of which is no work of ours but only God's grace. So we contribute nothing to the fact that we fall into sin in Adam except that we are born of him through a father and a mother and cling and stick to him as his flesh and blood. For he has led us all after himself. He is like a person who goes up a high mountain and in the ascent tumbles down and pulls all who followed him down to the bottom with him. And now, as I have acquired death through Adam, I acquire life through Christ. I on my part contribute nothing to the latter; I merely accept this or receive it by faith. [. . .]

23. But each in his own order: Christ the first fruits, then at his coming those who belong to Christ.

Here St. Paul does not discuss the question whether several others arose from the dead and are in heaven with Christ. He speaks solely of Christ as of one Man. For he wants to present

o LW 28:120, para. 1.

p LW 28:121, para. 1.

this article exclusively and purely according to its substance, making the one Man, Christ, the Origin and the Beginner of life, or of the resurrection. Therefore, whether several saints, for instance, Enoch and Elijah, ascended into heaven before Christ or whether several people were resurrected by him or arose with him is not the question under discussion here. [. . .]

St. Paul[q] says that the resurrection will not take place in this manner, that Christ will immediately take all who died before him with himself; nor will he awaken the Christians who die after him individually and one after the other. No, he was to be the Precursor and the Head, acquiring for all Christians, both those who preceded and those who succeed him, the ability to live in him spiritually during their appointed time here on earth. And when the time comes, he will on one day bid all who belong to him come forth, and then he will lead them with him. He arose when his hour was at hand. And thus we, too, shall arise when our hour comes and follow him. For he will not awaken us before all who are his own have been gathered together. And since many are yet to be born, both we and those who preceded us in death must wait until these are also added and death, which slays us daily, ceases entirely and is abolished, as St. Paul will tell us a little later.

That is what is meant here when we read: "each in his own order." These words differentiate between his resurrection and ours. For the order demands that he be the first; he must blaze the trail and produce life. After that he will gather all those who are his members and belong to the resurrection, one after another, so that they all come forth together on one day appointed by him and live with him eternally. [. . .] This will not happen in secret or in some nook or corner, one arising here and another person there; no, this will be a public spectacle viewed by the whole world, when death, sin, and every evil will end and all will be sheer life and joy. Furthermore, our bodies, together with those of all creatures, will possess a new clarity in keeping with his promise. Therefore the question whether several people rose separately is not to be dragged in here, as I said; for in these this is not yet manifest, nor is the final existence which will prevail at that time.

q LW 28:122, para. 3.

COMMENTARY ON 1 CORINTHIANS 15:51-57[r]

51-53. Lo! I tell you a mystery. We shall not all sleep, but we shall all be changed, in a moment, in the twinkling of an eye, at the last trumpet. For the trumpet will sound, and the dead will be raised imperishable, and we shall be changed. For this perishable nature must put on the imperishable, and this mortal nature must put on immortality.

[. . .]

SINCE [ST. PAUL] SAID that no one can enter heaven with this perishable animal body and that a new spiritual body will have to come from this natural body, someone might fret and ask what will happen to those still living on the last day. Will they remain thus, or will they also rise, though they are not buried and do not decay as the others who died previously?

Paul reveals this secret by way of reply. He says that this is the way things will happen: "We shall not all sleep, but we shall all be changed, etc." That sounds as though not all of us will die. In fact, some people did juggle the words to mean this. However, St. Paul's meaning is this, that the last day will come as suddenly as a snare—as he said elsewhere (Luke 21:35)—before anyone is aware of it and when the whole world feels secure. Then all will be changed in a moment. That does not negate that we must all die. No, Paul says that we shall not all sleep. That is to say that those who are struck in the final hour will not depart this life as a person does otherwise on his or her deathbed, nor will they be placed in a grave or buried under the soil. For Scripture applies the term "sleep" to those who are placed into coffin and grave. These people, however, will pass from this life into yonder life without being buried in a grave. They will simply be transformed, or changed.

The Greek word found here means chiefly to change so as to be moved from one place to another, for instance, from the water to dry land, from the earth into the air. Similarly, then we, too,

r The following is based on LW 28:199–213 with some modifications.

will be found elsewhere and in a different condition in the twinkling of an eye. The very hour before we were here on earth in a house or in a field. Suddenly we are removed from table or bed or from our work, as we happen to be walking, standing, sitting, or lying, so that we are dead and alive again in a moment, changed in every way, and soaring up in the clouds. Those are the changes Paul has in mind here. To be sure, he encompasses also the other changes *qualitatis*, of the form. Of these he already remarked earlier that the body will put on a different dress, that is, that it will be glorified and bright, much more resplendent and beautiful than the sun. But that will not happen while the body is still sojourning in this inn and garbed in this dress. No, it will first be divested of everything and become naked in the same moment and be burned to powder and be carried away.

Detail from Michelangelo's Last Judgment scene in the Sistine Chapel (1537–1541) depicting the resurrection of the dead

Paul explains this himself in greater detail in 1 Thess. 4:15-17, where he says: "We who are alive, who are left until the coming of the Lord, shall not precede those who have fallen asleep. For the Lord himself will descend from heaven with a cry of command, with the archangel's call, and with the sound of the trumpet of God. And the dead in Christ will rise first; then we who are alive, who are left, shall be caught up together with them in the clouds to meet the Lord in the air, etc." There he points out that everything will happen together and in the twinkling of an eye. The dead will be removed from their graves, and we will be carried away with them, however or wherever we may be found. We will be torn from this mortal life and existence, and all will be glorified together. [. . .]

To[s] be sure, God will not carry this out on the last day in a manner that might be intelligible to you now. In fact, there is no other article of faith either which can be understood or comprehended by reason. We cannot even understand our own

s LW 28:201, para. 2.

nature in body and soul, which we see before our eyes and feel. We cannot understand how it happens that we see, hear, talk, think, grow, etc. What, then, might we understand of such lofty things which we cannot see or feel, things that we must apprehend solely by faith?[11] [. . .]

54-55. When the perishable puts on the imperishable, and the mortal puts on immortality, then shall come to pass the saying that is written: Death is swallowed up in victory. O death, where is thy victory? O death, where is thy sting?

[. . .] Note[t] how St. Paul speaks about this life and existence. He views it not as [the essence of] humanity itself but as a dress that he must wear now but discards later and replaces with another. He makes no more of death and grave than he does of taking off an old torn garment and casting it away. To him the resurrection is like putting on a beautiful new garment called *immortalitas*, incorruptibility or immortality. It is spun and woven by Christ's victory. For the victory of Christ, who overcame all in himself, was wrought for the purpose of clothing you with it and of cleansing you from your sin and death, so that nothing of your corruptible body remains or of anything that the devil infused in you or that derives from him, all sorts of misfortunes and frailties, error and folly, everything except your natural and true body as created by God. For God did not create humans that they should sin and die, but that they should live.[u] But the devil inflicted so much shameful filth and so many blemishes on nature that humans must bear so much sickness, stench, and misfortune about their neck because they sinned. But now that sin is removed through Christ, we shall be rid of all of that, too. All will be pure, and nothing that is evil or loathsome will be felt any longer on earth. However, this is not brought about in any other way than that we first shed this old, evil garment through death. We must be divested of it entirely, and it must turn into dust.

t LW 28:202, para. 3.

u The singular masculine references are here rendered as plural.

11. The point that Luther makes here belongs to the theological repertoire of Christian apologetic. As Gregory of Nazianzus (c. 325–390) put it already in the fourth century, "If you have traversed the air and reckoned up all it involves, come now with me, touch heaven and things celestial. Faith rather than reason shall lead us, if that is, you have learned the feebleness of reason to deal with matters quite close at hand and have acquired enough knowledge of reason to recognize things which surpass reason. If so, it follows that you will not be a wholly earthbound thinker ignorant of your very ignorance." "Oration 28: On the Doctrine of God," in *On God and Christ*, ed. L. Wickham (Crestwood, NY: St. Vladimir's Seminary Press, 2002), 60, cf. 52–62.

When that comes to pass, Paul says, this will be fulfilled; now we say: *Scriptum est*, but then we shall say: *Factum est*. The time will come when that which is now always preached and spoken about will actually happen and be carried out. And what is that? It is the fact recorded in the words "Death is swallowed up in victory." St. Paul states that these words are found in Scripture; I really do not know where in Scripture. They seem to be taken from the prophet Hosea, chapter 13:14, where we read: "Shall I ransom them from the power of Sheol? Shall I redeem them from Death? O Death, I will be your poison. O Sheol, I will be your plague (or pestilence)." That is to say: "I will kill you and do away with you." [. . .]

However,[v] I believe that St. Paul's eyes ranged further and that he wished to include, in addition to Hosea's statement, all similar ones contained in Scripture; for instance, above all the chief verse from which many others are derived, Gen. 3:15, where God says to the serpent: "I will put enmity between you and the woman, and between your seed and her Seed; he shall bruise your head, and you shall bruise his heel."[12] In the Hebrew we find the same word for both *zertreten* and *stechen*. That word really means to bite as a serpent bites as it shoots the venom in. It means to say that the serpent will bite Christ's heel, but he, in turn, will bite its head, that he will be a mortal venom and a pestilence for it, as Hosea interprets from this text. And this verse now prompts this proclamation of St. Paul: "Death is swallowed up in victory." [. . .] In this way we can relate all similar verses found throughout the prophets to this one. They all flow from this one and into this one, so that all of them comprise but one text. For according to his rich Spirit he melts many verses into one and molds a text from these which is supplied by all of Scripture and expresses the meaning of all of Scripture. [. . .]

Note[w] how forcefully [Paul] speaks of death on the basis of Scripture. He pictures him [that is, death] as entirely swallowed up and devoured, with nothing remaining of him who himself devoured and swallowed up all people on earth. We hear furthermore that Christ himself will be a poison to death and a pesti-

12. As early as the 1523 edition of the Pentateuch, Luther identified Gen. 3:15, in a marginal note, as the first gift of the gospel (*protoevangelium*) and promise of Christ who was to overcome sin, death, and hell. This note was retained in subsequent editions of the Luther Bible (see pp. 149–50, 195–201 in this volume; WA DB 8:44–45).

v LW 28:203, para. 3.

w LW 28:204, para. 3.

lence to hell, which will consume all the poison with which the devil killed and destroyed people. For this poison is nothing else than the curse which has passed on to the whole world. It was blown and beaten into us by the devil, and we must all die from it. That is the drink he offered Adam and we all partook of with Adam when we were born. It has coursed through our body and all its members, and it also manifests itself externally by means of all sorts of distress and sorrow. However, Scripture discloses a salutary medicine and a precious antidote, given us by God in the word, in which he assures us that he will kill death in return and that he also gives the devil a drink with which he will have to drink himself to death forever. He himself will have to devour his poison, curse, sin, hell, and death which he attached to nature, while we will be saved from these eternally by believing and adhering to the Seed.

Eve shares a piece of forbidden fruit with Adam as the nearby serpent tempts them. Woodcut from a Bible published in Mainz (1534) by Johann Dietenberger, who translated and published a Catholic competitor for Luther's Bible.

"I myself will do that," he says; "I will be your death and your pestilence." He applies these ugly words, death and pestilence, to himself; and yet they are so immeasurably comforting. For note what and whom he refers to with these words. He is not a foe of nature. No, he shows that he wishes to help nature and subdue its enemy, death and devil. He has compassion with our misery, for he sees that we are now drowned by the devil's poison and by death and are so submerged in it that we cannot extricate ourselves. He wants to wreak vengeance on him as on his own foe, who poisoned and spoiled his work. Therefore this is a real divine antidote, not taken from a physician's pharmacy but prepared by heaven and given to us through Christ's resurrection. It will be harmless for us, but it will kill and ruin only him who gave and served us this poison. And now, when we begin to believe the article of Christ, the potion is already mixed and drunk which eliminates the poison that he injected into my heart and conscience and also into my body. Now we are saved from the curse, and the same poison which we have in us is now poured out for the devil, so that he has to eat death by us. Thus, we have drunk a salutary medicine in Baptism and the Sacrament,[13] which expels and removes our poison. This does not kill me but the very enemy who intended to kill me with it. You see, that is why God employs such figurative language and calls himself a poison, not a poison for us poor people who once

13. The Lord's Supper.

were cumbered with death and pestilence, but a poison against the poison of death and hell.[14] Now we who feel such poison and plague can take comfort from that, assured that God befriends us so greatly that he completely removes these from our body and soul and feeds these to devil and death, that his belly is rent by them.

Poison and pestilence are a death which does not kill suddenly and abruptly; but it kills nevertheless. It gradually makes its way through the whole body until it reaches the heart. That is the way God also treats us. He does not want to carry out the victory over death and devil all of a sudden, but he has this proclaimed for a while for the sake of the elect who are yet to be born. So he begins to mix and prepare the potion to be a *purgatio* or a medication for us, to refresh and to invigorate us but to be poison and death for the devil. This is comparable to a potion prescribed by a physician. This is conducive to a patient's health, but it is poison to a fever. Thus, he could well call his medicine or antidote a poison or a pestilence. Here, too, it is true that one poison expels another, that one pestilence kills the other.

This also applies to Christendom now, when word, Baptism, and the Sacrament are administered and nothing is proclaimed but that Christ died and rose again. That is the only prescription or *purgatio* for our sin and death. That we must take daily and let it work, in order to drive the poison from our heart and take us from death and hell to eternal life. He promised us that; and he commanded us to proclaim it and to believe it. Thereby he brings it about in us daily that it penetrates like a leaven (as Christ says in Matt. 13:33). Then the heart grows and grows in faith and learns to despise and overcome this life and its hardships.

That is the victory by which death is to be swallowed up, so that we need fear death no longer or remain in it. For the heart is already saturated by the gospel, which shall be poison and pestilence to death. It weakens death from day to day and deprives him of his strength, until he is submerged entirely and disappears. For although he is not yet entirely swallowed up in us, the victory gained by Christ is already present, and through gospel, baptism, and faith it has become our victory. On the last day, when we have taken off the old, terrestrial, perishable garment and put on a new celestial one, we can destroy him completely with this victory. Then we will remain in life forever; then we will behold and perceive life as we now behold and feel the reverse,

14. See also *Lectures on Galatians*, which Luther delivered the preceding year: "[Christ] became law to the law, sin to sin, and death to death, in order that he might redeem me from the curse of the law, justify me, and make me alive. And so Christ is both: While he is the law, he is liberty; while he is sin, he is righteousness; and while he is death, he is life. For by the very fact that he permitted the law to accuse him, sin to damn him, and death to devour him, he abrogated the law, damned sin, destroyed death, and justified and saved me. Thus Christ is a poison against the law, sin, and death, and simultaneously a remedy to regain liberty, righteousness, and eternal life" (LW 26:163).

namely, that death is in us and that we are stuck in death. The victory appears to be his alone, as he as the lord of the world devours and consumes one person after another up to the last day. But nevertheless we know from Scripture that victory was wrested from him by Christ, who began to swallow him up in himself. And through him we, too, are spiritually victorious over him. Later we will bury death also physically and do away with him entirely, so that nothing will be seen or known of him any longer. Instead, we will have nothing but life and bliss. [. . .]

56-57. The sting of death is sin, and the power of sin is the law.
But thanks be to God, who gives us the victory
through our Lord Jesus Christ.

[x][. . .] Sin is nothing but spear and cannonball, indeed death's thunder and lightning, through which he carries out his work. But where does sin come from? Or how does it happen that it is so very strong and able to kill and slay? St. Paul says: "I shall tell you: 'The power of sin is the law.'" Who has ever heard that said about God's commandment and law, which, after all, was given and instituted as holy and good by God? And still St. Paul can say that sin would be feeble and dead and could effect nothing if it were not for the law. The law renders sin alert and strong and prompts it to cut and to pierce. If it depended on us, sin would very likely remain dormant forever. But God is able to awaken it effectively through the law. When the hour comes for sin to sting and to strike, it grows unendurable in a moment. For the law dins this into your ears and holds the register of your sins before your nose: "Do you hear? You committed this and you committed that in violation of God's commandments, and you spent your whole life in sin. Your own conscience must attest and affirm that." In that way sin already shows its power. It frightens you so that the whole world becomes too confining for you. It agitates and strikes until you must needs despair. And there is neither escape nor defense here. For the law is too strong, and your own heart supports it, which itself denounces you and condemns you to hell. Therefore sin requires nothing else than God's law. Where that enters the heart, sin is already alive and

x LW 28:208, para. 3.

able to kill us if it wants to, unless we lay hold of this victory, which is Christ, our Lord.

If the law has such bad results, why, then, did God issue it? Would it not be far better if there were no law? To be sure, it would be better for us. And yet it cannot be dispensed with. For it is incompatible with God that he should be pleased to let us have our way and do as we wish. It is true that God is longsuffering with us all before he manifests his wrath. God permits many people to follow their own course, who never feel the law and sin or ever think of God's wrath, but, instead, disdain the law and sin and, moreover, deride them, no matter how one threatens them with death and hell. But finally God is constrained to show them what both the law and sin are able to do, to deter them from making sport of it. To be sure, God may wink at this for a while, but when the hour comes in which the law really raps at your door to find you at home and demands an accounting, it will not be so easy to ignore it. Then one begins to lament and wail: "Alas! What did I do? What will become of me now?" Then we observe the meaning of the words: "The law is the power of sin." That is why St. Paul elsewhere also calls it a law of death and an office of death, which proclaims death and is the cause of death. Even if there were no other sermon or rule, the entire world could be preached to death solely with this.

For the one follows the other: When the law shines into one's heart and reveals sin, the latter immediately becomes alive and strong; and sin brings death with it. Therefore it is pertinent to say that sin is the sting of death, that sin alone, and no one else, kills. But sin comes from nothing else than the law. This does not mean that the law first creates and makes sin. No, sin is existent already before the law appears, and it remains with us, because it is born with us and we are conceived in sin. It means that sin is not properly recognized and felt unless this light is kindled in the heart; nor can sin attain its power unless it is awakened by the law. But when the law appears, it shows us that we are completely steeped in sin and lying in God's wrath, so that we must say, as St. Bernard[15] says of himself: "I thought I was sitting in a rose garden, and am not aware that I am sitting among murderers." [. . .]

[St. Paul's] sermon is different from that of Moses, for it reveals the Christians' consolation against death's sting and sin's power. It is true and necessary and right that the law reveals

15. St. Bernard of Clairvaux (1090–1153) was an important reformer of the Cistercian Order. Among later medieval theologians, Bernard is the one whom Luther most frequently cites approvingly.

your sin and accuses you; and sin, in turn, has the right to kill you and death to devour you. That is beyond dispute and argument. For both your own testimony and God's word are against you there. However, there is help in the fact that the man Jesus Christ has come and has assumed and borne our sin and death, which we had justly deserved, and that he now steps forth on our behalf, confronts the law, sin, and death, and says: "I am of the same flesh and blood; these are my brothers and sisters. What they did I did; and I paid for it. Law, if you want to condemn them, condemn me. Sin, if you want to bite and kill them, bite me. Death, if you want to consume and devour, devour me." That is what happened when he stood before the judge, Pilate. There he was accused and sentenced to death as a sinner. Therefore he also calls himself a sinner in Scripture. In Ps. 41:4: "O Lord, be gracious to me; heal me, for I have sinned against you." Also in Ps. 69:9: "The insults of those who insult you have fallen on me," that is, "Whatever they did against you to deserve death, that I did." Therefore also the law attached itself to him and condemned him, sin crucified him and pierced him to death, and death carried him under the sod. They did everything to him, everything they were capable of. For God "did not spare his own Son," St. Paul declares in Rom. 8:32, "but gave him up for us all." They all tested their might on him.

Left: St. Bruno of Cologne with his attributes, a book and a cross. Right: St. Bernard of Clairvaux with his attributes, the instruments of the passion. From *Le Tableau de la Croix* (1625) by François Mazot.

But thereby they failed by far to accomplish what they had intended to do. For through the very event by which they expected to exterminate him and to win the victory he emerged again and said to the law, sin, and death: "Do you not know that I am your Lord and God? What right do you have to accuse and to slay your Lord? Therefore you shall do this no more; but, rather, I will accuse and condemn you and dispatch you so thoroughly that you will henceforth have no claim on anyone who believes in me. For what I did, I did for their sake." For his own person this would not have been necessary, and they would have been obliged to let him go unharmed. But now he has stepped into our place, and in our behalf he has let the law, sin, and death pounce on him. He has not only removed these from us, but he has also vanquished them completely and cast them at his feet. Now they are overcome for us and no longer have any right to or power over us. In that way we have a complete victory in Christ, now spiritually by faith but later also physically and visibly.

Now we Christians must learn to apprehend this and to avail ourselves[y] of it when the battle is joined and the law attacks us and tries to accuse us, when sin wants to slay us and thrust us into the jaws of hell, and when our own consciences tell us: "You have done this, and you have done that; you are sinners and are deserving of death, etc." Then the Christian should answer confidently: "It is unfortunately true that I am a sinner and that I have surely deserved death. So far you are right. But still you shall not condemn and slay me. Another, who is named my Lord Christ, shall stay your hand. You accused and you murdered him innocently. But do you remember how you vainly dashed full tilt against him and burned yourself and thereby forfeited all your rights to me and to all Christians? For he both bore and overcame sin and death not for himself but for me. Therefore I concede you no rightful accusation against me. I can, rather, justly assert my rights against you for trying to attack me without cause and despite the fact that you were already condemned and overcome by him, which deprived you of any right to assail and accuse me. And although you may now attack and devour me according to the flesh, you shall not accomplish or gain anything by this. You must eat your own sting and choke to death on it. For I am no longer the one you are looking for; I am no longer a child of man, but a child of God, for I am baptized in his blood and on his victory, and I am vested with all his possessions." [. . .]

This is the beautiful sermon for Christians which shows us how we, through Christ's victory, rid ourselves of sin's sting, which kills us, and of the power of the law, which drives this sting into us. And it shows us that in the end this sting will be completely destroyed in us. And now St. Paul appropriately concludes with a song which he sings: "Thanks and praise be to God, who gave us such a victory!" We can join in that song and in that way always celebrate Easter, praising and extolling God for a victory that was not won or achieved in battle by us—it is far too sublime and great for that—but was presented and given to us

y In this sentence the original singular masculine is rendered as plural.

by the mercy of God. He had compassion with our misery, from which no one could rescue us, and he sent his Son and let him enter the battle. He laid these enemies, sin, death, and hell, low and retained the victory. He transferred this victory to us, so that we may say it is our victory. It is just as if it had been gained by us. The only condition is that we must accept this sincerely and not give God the lie, as they do who presume to overcome their sin and death by themselves. Nor dare we be found ungrateful for this, as vulgar, false Christians do, but we must keep this in our heart in firm faith and confirm ourselves in this and always be engrossed in such a message of thanks and sing of this victory in Christ. And in faith in this we must cheerfully depart this life, until we experience this victory also in our own body. May God help us to that end through the same dear Son. To him be glory and honor forever. Amen.

The Sacrament of Baptism
(woodcut, 1534)

Title page of the first Low German edition of the Luther Bible. The woodcut border illustrates scenes from the Bible, including the creation, the resurrection of Lazarus, the Garden of Eden, the crucifixion, and Moses receiving the Ten Commandments. The woodcuts in this 1533 Bible are the work of the German artist Erhard Altdorfer (d. 1561).

Lectures on Galatians 2:15-16

1519

SIMO PEURA WITH KIRSI I. STJERNA

INTRODUCTION

Luther was a dedicated doctor of the Holy Scriptures. For him, being a doctor meant more than being learned. To be a doctor and a professor at the University of Wittenberg brought a binding responsibility. Luther's task was to interpret Scripture.[a] That meant accepting the common faith of the church, and it laid a foundation for the proclamation of the gospel. Later, in his introduction to the *Large Catechism* (1529), Luther refers to his doctorate and his mission as a preacher, and he exhorts priests to practice a continuous, lifelong meditative study of the Bible and the central principles of faith.

Luther lectured from the Psalms for the first time in 1513–1515, followed by lectures on Paul's letter to the Romans. After that he lectured on Galatians from 27 October 1516 until 13 March 1517. In the beginning, typical lectures lasted two hours. On summer days the lectures would begin at 6 AM, and one hour

a For a source on the background information of Luther's early commentary on the letter to the Galatians, see Brecht 1:286–97. For the letter to the Galatians and Luther, see Kenneth Hagen, *Luther's Approach to Scripture as Seen in His Commentaries on Galatians, 1519–1538* (Tübingen: J. C. B. Mohr [P. Siebeck], 1993).

later in winter months. From 1516 the lectures were offered at 1:00 in the afternoon.

Luther prepared for his lectures by printing selected texts with wide margins and spaces on which the notes could be written. Short and simple explanations of the words were inserted between the lines (Ger.: *Interlinearglossen*) and the more extensive notations could be written in the wider margin space (Ger.: *Randglossen*).[b] Luther used this method also when lecturing on Galatians. From the beginning of 1516, Luther had available to him the new edition of the New Testament by Erasmus of Rotterdam (1466–1536).[1] Other tools Luther drew from were the biblical interpretations of the church fathers and Scholastic theologians. All of these sources Luther engaged independently and critically (as will become evident with the text at hand).

1. The most important academic achievement of Erasmus is his critical edition of the New Testament in Greek, published in 1516 with the title *Novum Instrumentum*. The print was prepared by the Froben printhouse, and the text edition is based on three Koine Greek manuscripts from the twelfth century.

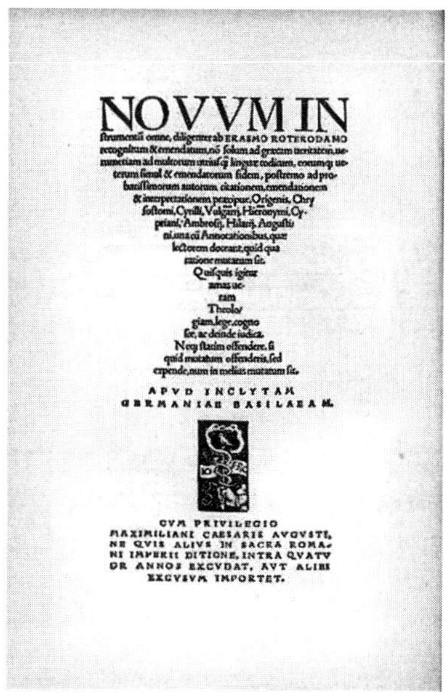
NOVVM IN
strumentũ omne, diligenter ab ERASMO ROTERODAMO
recognitum & emendatum, nõ solum ad græcam ueritatem, ue-
rumetiam ad multorum utriusq; linguæ codicum, eorumq; ue-
terum simul & emendatorum fidem, postremo ad pro-
batissimorum autorum citationem, emendationem
& interpretationem, præcipue, Origenis, Chry
sostomi, Cyrilli, Vulgarij, Hieronymi, Cy-
priani, Ambrosij, Hilarij, Augusti
ni, una cũ Annotationibus, quæ
lectorem doceant, quid qua
ratione mutatum sit.
Quisquis igitur
amas ue-
ram
Theolo-
giam, lege, cogno
sce, ac deinde iudica.
Neq; statim offendere, si
quid mutatum offenderis, sed
expende, num in melius mutatum sit.
APVD INCLYTAM
GERMANIAE BASILAEAM.
CVM PRIVILEGIO
MAXIMILIANI CAESARIS AVGVSTI,
NE QVIS ALIVS IN SACRA ROMA-
NI IMPERII DITIONE, INTRA QVATV
OR ANNOS EXCVDAT, AVT ALIBI
EXCVSVM IMPORTET.

Title page of Erasmus's New Testament (1516)

Toward the end of 1518, Luther planned to develop his lectures on Paul's letter to the Galatians into a commentary. This letter offered Luther a ready opportunity to present his own particular theological viewpoints. Leading up to this, Luther had already been criticizing church practices, and he had published

b On the medieval use of *glossae* by Martin Luther, see Brecht 1:128–30.

his *95 Theses* on 31 October 1517.[c] The indulgence controversy[2] continued until the summer of 1518 and eventually led to a judicial investigation against Luther, initiated by Rome.

Galatians in Context

The Galatians commentary arose during a very stormy period for Luther. He was accused of heresy and of showing a demeaning and disrespectful attitude toward the papal power of the keys. The accusation was founded in the statement by the papal court theologian Sylvester Prierias (c. 1456–1527).[3] Luther was ordered to arrive in Rome within sixty days of the invitation. The interaction between the two men led nowhere.

After many developments, Luther's hearing was moved from Rome to Augsburg, Germany. Luther was examined from 12–14 October 1518 by the papal delegate, Thomas de Vio (Cardinal Cajetan, 1469–1534). Luther was accused of erring on two

This sixteenth-century woodcut depicts Luther (left) being questioned by Cardinal Cajetan (seated at right).

c See Luther's *95 Theses* and other explosive texts from 1517 in TAL 1:13–46.

2. Indulgences had been used in the Western church since the eleventh century, as a way to relieve temporal penalties (or works of satisfaction) for personal sins. Their dogmatic or ecclesial/legal definition, however, occurred only gradually. Luther deemed that, from the proper understanding of repentance, indulgences were harmful, especially when financial motivations were involved in the selling of them. In the fall of 1517 he wrote a treatise about the indulgences, followed by his *95 Theses*. He blamed Archbishop Albrecht of Mainz (1490–1545), in particular, for allowing the questionable selling of indulgences. Rather than responding to Luther directly, Albrecht sent the material he had received all the way to Rome. This led to the heresy accusations against Luther and, eventually, to the papal bull declaring Luther a heretic, if he did not recant his words.

3. The pope appointed Sylvester Prierias as the professor of Thomist theology in Rome in 1515. His statement *In presumptuosas Martini Lutheri conclusiones de potestate papae Dialogus* (1518) was the first written reaction from Rome to the issue of Luther. As the title of the statement reveals, the controversy over the indulgences was closely related to the issue of papal authority.

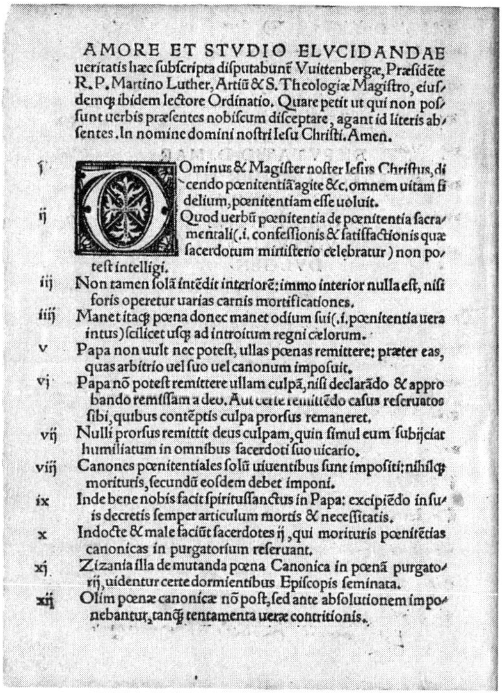

AMORE ET STVDIO ELVCIDANDAE ueritatis hæc ſubſcripta diſputabunt Vuittenbergæ, Præſidēte R. P. Martino Luther, Artiũ & S. Theologiæ Magiſtro, eiuſdemq; ibidem lectore Ordinatio. Quare petit ut qui non poſſunt uerbis præſentes nobiſcum diſceptare, agant id literis abſentes. In nomine domini noſtri Ieſu Chriſti. Amen.

j Dominus & Magiſter noſter Ieſus Chriſtus, dicendo pœnitentiā agite &c. omnem uitam fidelium, pœnitentiam eſſe uoluit.

ij Quod uerbũ pœnitentia de pœnitentia ſacramentali (.i. confeſſionis & ſatiſfactionis quæ ſacerdotum miniſterio celebratur) non poteſt intelligi.

iij Non tamen ſolā intēdit interiorē: immo interior nulla eſt, niſi foris operetur uarias carnis mortificationes.

iiij Manet itaq; pœna donec manet odium ſui (.i. pœnitentia uera intus) ſcilicet uſq; ad introitum regni cælorum.

v Papa non uult nec poteſt, ullas pœnas remittere; præter eas, quas arbitrio uel ſuo uel canonum impoſuit.

vj Papa nō poteſt remittere ullam culpā, niſi declarādo & approbando remiſſam a deo. Aut certe remittēdo caſus reſeruatos ſibi, quibus contēptis culpa prorſus remaneret.

vij Nulli prorſus remittit deus culpam, quin ſimul eum ſubijciat humiliatum in omnibus ſacerdoti ſuo uicario.

viij Canones pœnitentiales ſolũ uiuentibus ſunt impoſiti; nihilq; morituris, ſecundũ eoſdem debet imponi.

ix Inde bene nobis facit ſpiritusſanctus in Papa: excipiēdo in ſuis decretis ſemper articulum mortis & neceſſitatis.

x Indocte & male faciũt ſacerdotes ij, qui morituris pœnitētias canonicas in purgatorium reſeruant.

xj Zizania illa de mutanda pœna Canonica in pœnā purgatorij, uidentur certe dormientibus Epiſcopis ſeminata.

xij Olim pœnæ canonicæ nō poſt, ſed ante abſolutionem imponebantur, tanq; tentamenta ueræ contritionis.

The first page of the Basel pamphlet edition of *95 Theses* (1517)

points: first, he had denied papal authority in using the church's spiritual treasures toward satisfaction for temporal punishments for sin; second, he had insisted on the importance of firm faith for receiving the sacraments properly. The first and main issue pertained to church law; the second, a more theological position of Luther, was deemed by Cajetan to clash both with the Bible and the teaching of the church. On the next day, Professor Luther offered in writing his response to the cardinal's accusation.

Luther rejected his church's teaching that satisfaction for temporal punishments for sins would have a biblical basis in church law. On this point, however, there was no irreconcilable conflict between Luther and the church. The latter question, on sound or firm faith and justification, was non-negotiable for Luther.

Luther and Cajetan did not find common ground on either of the issues. Professor Luther left Augsburg on 20 October, and the cardinal demanded that Elector Frederick the Wise (1463–1525) surrender the rebellious monk to Rome, or at least expel him from his electoral duchy. It was clear, after the *95 Theses* and the questioning by Cajetan, that Luther's criticism attacked not only the predominant Scholastic theology but also addressed papal power and church leadership. Luther had seriously questioned papal hegemony, and he never recanted any of his statements. The papal-led church really had no other alternative but to launch a judicial investigation to issue a ban against Luther.

Editing the Commentary

The editing of the lectures toward a commentary began in earnest in the early part of 1519. The public questioning by Cajetan and the clash with Rome were the immediate context for the commentary. This work is the first broader exposition of Luther's theology. In the work, he assesses papal authority in light of the gospel and the commands of Christ, with a conclusion that the papal authority is a threat to Christian freedom. At the same time, he distinguishes between the powers claimed by the papal curia and the Roman Church itself. The latter, even if in distress, is still the true church, the bride of Christ.

Luther worked on editing this commentary from February until April 1519, without being able to devote all his time to the task. The printing was completed in May 1519, thanks to Melchior Lotter (1490–1542) in Leipzig. Short on time, Luther needed help in securing the necessary information and formal conditions for a commentary. His colleague Philip Melanchthon (1497–1560) obtained patristic material and also proofread the whole manuscript. Luther welcomed his linguistically gifted and skilled colleague's knowledge of the Greek language. When relating to the work of Erasmus, Melanchthon complemented Luther. The many differences between Erasmus's and Luther's views were more or less minimized. Regardless, Melanchthon did not water down Luther's polemics, and he did not alter Luther's theological arguments.

The Central Theme of Justification

The actual central theme of the commentary is justification that is based on Christ and his salvific work. On this foundational teaching rest all the numerous other themes present in the commentary. Luther consistently rejects *any ability* of human beings to collaborate or assist in their own salvation by meeting the expectations of God's law. Because of their sin, human beings cannot love God above all or their neighbors as themselves. Rather, they selfishly seek for their own benefit. True righteousness thus does not arise from human effort; rather, righteousness is granted from above, descending to humans from heaven. It is founded on grace and received by faith, and these are what make a Christian one with Christ. Faith means participation in Christ and in Christ's righteousness.

From this union with Christ flow the many aspects of justification. For Luther, justification means both being declared righteous and being made righteous. The former is holistic in character, whereas the latter is completed in this life only in part. Justification effects a change in a Christian, so that one, at least momentarily, does good deeds freely and without coercion. From these themes it is only a small step to Luther's main writings of 1520.

Striking in the treatise is Luther's criticism of Scholastic theology and, related to that, a view of justification that relies on Aristotelian philosophy. In this regard, the commentary does not bring forward anything new but, rather, reiterates Luther's criticism already familiar from earlier works. Drawing from Augustine,[4] Luther rejects synergism, according to which human salvation would result from a collaboration between God and human beings.[5]

4. Bishop Augustine of Hippo (354–430), a North African-born theologian and philosopher who, after his conversion to Christianity, became the most influential thinker and shaper of Christian theology, particularly on the topic of grace.

5. Luther represents the Augustinian tradition that strictly rejects any form of Pelagianism or semi-Pelagianism, orientations named after Augustine's British-born opponent, moral theologian Pelagius (c. 354–c. 420), in their famous, and decisive, debate on the freedom of the will in relation to grace. See also Luther's *Treatise on Good Works* (TAL 1:257–367) and *The Freedom of a Christian* (TAL 1:467–538).

A Salty Commentary

It was not until September 1519 that Luther was finally ready to send forth his "salty" commentary. After just a few weeks, however, he was no longer satisfied with the product but wished to express his thoughts more clearly and expansively. He felt that Paul's views were more understandable "now" than ever before. Later, Luther sharpened his critical arguments. He considered his commentary to be weak because it (still) included too many concessions regarding the pope. He was also not satisfied with his development of the doctrine of justification; he feared it was not clear enough.

Luther's contemporaries thought differently. Martin Bucer (1491–1551) esteemed the commentary as a rich treasure of true theological dogmas. With Bucer's input, a new printing was produced in Strassburg in 1520. Ulrich Zasius (1461–1535), a jurist in

Engraving of Martin Bucer at age 53 by René Boyvin (1525–1598)

Freiburg, for his part praised the commentary especially because of its imbedded doctrine of justification and teaching of the law. The work was reprinted again in 1523, in an edition without references to the contemporary context or the names of individuals.

Luther's earlier commentary on the letter to the Galatians has remained in the shadow of his later commentary on the same text. The work that was published in 1535 is typically called Luther's "large" commentary on the letter to the Galatians. However, there are reasons to consider Luther's 1519 commentary an exposition of his early theology. It expresses his love for Pauline theology. In 1531, after his personal life had changed significantly—upon marriage—Luther uttered in few words his affection toward the letter to the Galatians: "The epistle to the Galatians is my epistle, toward which I feel trust, my Käthe von Bora."[6]

Portrait of Katharina von Bora (1528) by Lucas Cranach the Elder

6. Katharina von Bora (1499–1552) and Martin Luther married on 13 June 1525. The wedding was officiated by a friend and a colleague, city pastor Johannes Bugenhagen (1485–1558), in the presence of just a few closest friends; Melanchthon and his wife were notably absent. The formal and more public ceremony took place on 27 June, with the participation of a large number of guests, including Martin's parents. This was a scandalous and attention-getting wedding of a runaway nun and an ex-monk who had publicly criticized the monastic lifestyle and celibacy.

LECTURES ON GALATIANS 2:15-16[d]

15. We ourselves are Jews by nature and not Gentile sinners.

PAUL COMPARES the Jews and the Gentiles. "It is true," he says, "that we, who are Jews by nature, excel the Gentiles, who are sinners if they are compared with us, in the righteousness[e] of the law, since they have neither the law nor the works of the law. But this does not make us righteous before God. This righteousness of ours is external."[f] In Rom. 1:18ff. and 2:17ff. Paul discusses this thought most fully. Here he declares first that the Gentiles were the greatest sinners;[g] but in the second chapter he turns to the Jews and asserts that even though they are not such sinners as he had described the Gentiles to be, they are sinners nevertheless;[7] in their glorifying of the law, they have kept the law outwardly but not inwardly, and they have thus dishonored God by transgressing the law.[8]

16. Yet we know that one is justified not because of the works of the law but through faith in Jesus Christ; we believe in Christ Jesus, in order to be justified because of faith in Christ, and not because of the works of the law.

"We are righteous,"[h] says Paul, "inasmuch as we are by nature Jews, not sinners, like the Gentiles"; but it is a righteousness of the works of law, and on the basis of this righteousness no one

7. Luther uses the Jewish interpretation of Scripture, as he understands it, as an example of the futile use of the law. See *How Christians Should Regard Moses* (TAL 2:127-51), and selections in TAL 5:391–666.

8. With Paul, Luther underscores human beings' inability to keep the law. Even if the Jews, unlike the Gentiles, know the law and seek to obey it, they can only keep it externally. Because of sin, no human being can ever meet the expectations of the law internally, against any illusions about this. As becomes evident later in the text, to keep the law internally requires holistic and pure love of God and one's neighbor.

d This translation and annotation by Simo Peura with Kirsi I. Stjerna are based on LW 27:218–25, with updates.

e Lat.: *iustitia*.

f Lat.: *Externa est ista iusticia nostra*.

g Lat.: *maximos peccatores*.

h Lat.: *Iusti, inquit, sumus*.

has ever been justified in relation to God. For this reason we, too, like the Gentiles, consider our own righteousness as dung and seek to be justified through faith in Christ—we who are as much sinners as the Gentiles are and similarly justified as the Gentiles are; namely, God "made no distinction between us and them," as Peter says in Acts 15:9, "but cleansed their hearts by faith."[9] But because this passage seems absurd to those who have not yet become accustomed to Paul's theology, and because even St. Jerome[10] expends much effort in trying to understand this, we shall expand the comments we began to make above about the traditions of the fathers. Among the extant authors I do not find anyone except Augustine[11] alone who treats this thought in a satisfactory manner; and even he is not satisfactory

Engraving of the apostle Paul (1514) by Albrecht Dürer

9. Justification requires purification from sin that has attached itself in and corrupted the human nature. With this argument Luther seeks support from the apostle Peter, who says that God has purified the hearts of both Jews and Gentiles with the faith of the heart (Acts 15:9). Luther's focus, then, is the renewal of the human being, that is, justification. In any other way, meeting the expectations of the law is impossible.

10. Erasmus (see n. 1, p. 236 above) published an edition of St. Jerome's (c. 347–420) works in 1516. Luther carefully studied his writings, which he furnished with annotations in 1516–1517. Jerome's theology, however, he rejects: Luther considers St. Jerome as an unacceptable example of synergism, that is, of the viewpoint that the salvation and justification of a human being results from one's collaboration with God. Medieval Scholastic authors drew from Jerome's teaching that God does not expect from human beings impossible things but that they fulfill the law. God could not deny grace from a person who does one's best when aspiring to keep the law (*facere quod in se est*). The roots of this opinion, however, are found in Pelagius (see below). See in detail: Leif Grane, *Contra Gabrielem. Luthers Auseinandersetzung mit Gabriel Biel in der Disputatio contra Scholasticam Theologiam 1517.* Acta Theologica Danica 4. Diss. (Copenhagen: Gyldendal, 1962), 183–84, 215, 244–46.

11. St. Augustine of Hippo is a rare late ancient author whom Luther considered trustworthy. He held the church father in great esteem, not the least because of his rebuttal of the Pelagian views. Luther himself was an Augustinian hermit monk (from 1505) and thus well versed in Augustine's theology.

everywhere. But where he opposes the Pelagians,[12] the enemies of God's grace, he will make Paul easy for you and opens him up for you.

Above all, therefore, it is necessary to know that there are two ways in which a human being[i] is justified,[j] and these two ways are totally contrary to each other.

In the first place, there is the external way, by works, on the basis of one's own strength.[13] Of such a nature are the kinds of human righteousness that are acquired by practice[k] (as it is said) and by habit.[l] This is the kind of righteousness Aristotle and other philosophers[14, m] describe: the kind produced by laws of the state and of the church in ceremonies, the kind produced

Luther had, however, reservations about certain viewpoints of Augustine, as is evident with this text.

12. Augustine was determined to refute Pelagius and his opponents. Several councils of the church condemned Pelagius as a heretic. Luther considers Pelagianism to be a central heresy. Pelagius's error was that he deemed human reason able to know and fulfill God's law. In essence, this would mean denial of grace. Even if he mentions Pelagius by name, Luther's actual targets are his more contemporary theologians, such as Gabriel Biel (c. 1414–1495) and Erasmus of Rotterdam. In his *Disputation against the Scholastic Theology* (1517), MLStA 1:165–72, Luther names Biel as his chief opponent because of Biel's synergism. See also n. 32, p. 551.

13. The first kind of righteousness, external righteousness, is based on what the human being is able to achieve on the basis of the natural abilities of one's soul (*ex puris naturalibus*). One becomes righteous by repeating the "right" deeds. Background for this thought is in Aristotle's *Nicomachean Ethics* 2, 1: "by performing just works, we become just, and acting reasonably, we become reasonable. . . ."

14. For Luther, philosophy has many dimensions and meanings. When he critiques earlier philosophers, such as Aristotle, his target is really the different medieval schools of interpretation on Aristotle's philosophy. Most famously, Thomas Aquinas (1224–1274) built his theology on the foundation of Aristotle's philosophy and metaphysics. Luther deemed that philosophy could well serve theology, but it should never become a universal metaphysical model for explaining reality. Luther, quite

i Lat.: *homo*.

j Lat.: *iustificatur*.

k Lat.: *usu*.

l LW 27 translates the Latin words *consuetudine comparatae* with "by habit." Whereas the word *habitus* does not appear in the original text, the meaning of "permanent, acquired quality" is evident. *Habitus* is an "accident" (*accidens*): it exists only when attached to another being (*ens in alio*).

m On Luther's relation to the philosophy of the Renaissance, see Kari Kopperi, "Luthers theologische Zielsetzung in den philosophischen Thesen der Heidelberger Disputation," in *Nordiskt forum för studiet av Luther och luthersk teologi* 1. Referate des ersten Forums für das Studium von Luther und lutherischer Theologie in Helsinki 21.–24.11.1991. Hrsg. von Tuomo Mannermaa mit Petri Järveläinen und Kari Kopperi. *Schriften der Luther-Agricola-Gesellschaft* 28 (Helsinki: Luther-Agricola-Gesellschaft 1993), 67–103; also "Luther and Renaissance Philosophy: Open Problems," in *Widerspruch–Luthers Auseinandersetzung mit Erasmus von Rotterdam*. Referate des dritten Nordischen Forums für das Studium von Luther und lutherischer Theologie in Magleäs, Dänemark 2.–5.3.1995. Hrsg. von Kari Kopperi. *Schriften der Luther-Agricola-Gesellschaft* 37 (Helsinki: Luther-Agricola-Gesellschaft, 1997), 92–116.

at the behest of reason and by prudence.[15] For they think that one becomes righteous by doing righteous things,[n] temperate by doing temperate things, and the like. This is the kind of righteousness the law of Moses, even the Decalogue itself, also brings about, namely, when one serves God out of fear of punishment or because of the promise of a reward,[16] does not swear by God's name, honors one's parents, does not kill, does not steal, does not commit adultery, etc. This is a servile righteousness;[o] it is mercenary, fake,[p] specious, external, temporal, worldly, human. It profits nothing for the glory to come but receives in this life its reward, glory, riches, honor, power, friendship, well-being, or at least peace and tranquility,[q] and fewer evils than do those who act otherwise. This is how Christ describes the Pharisees and how St. Augustine describes the Romans in the eighth chapter of the first book of *The City of God*.[r] Strangely enough, this

n Lat.: *operando iusta iustum fieri.*

o Lat.: *Haec est iusticia servilis.*

p Lat.: *ficta.*

q Lat.: *pacem et tranquillitatem*, translated in LW 27 as "peace and quiet."

r Augustine, *City of God* (*De civitate Dei*), 1, 8.

freely, uses different philosophers' views on theological reasoning: either to refute a doctrine of grace he considered erroneous or to give grounding for a "right" view of justification. For example, in his *Heidelberg Disputation* (1518), TAL 1:67–119; MLStA 1:190–218), Luther refers to Aristotle, Anaxagoras, and Plato. He was familiar with the Neoplatonic thinker Pseudo-Dionysius, as well as Occamism.

15. Human righteousness is a result of good deeds. According to the Scholastic theologians, human beings' natural reason can discern what they should do (*dictamen rationis*), and human beings' natural will (*voluntas*) can adapt to the work in question (*actus voluntatis*). In this, the Scholastics drew support from Aristotle's philosophy and doctrine of virtues. When repeating a good deed often enough, a respective *habitus* is born in human being. In the model of an Aristotelian metaphysics, righteousness appears as a quality, which human beings acquire by the way of their own natural abilities (*operando iusta iustum fieri*). The infusion of grace, then, perfects the acquired *habitus* in a human being and enables repeating of the good deed in the future. On this in Gabriel Biel's theology, see Grane, *Contra Gabrielem*, 251–52, 257–58.

16. The problem with human righteousness is that it is not born from a good heart and freely. Human beings try to fulfill the law only because of the fear of punishment or hope of a reward. This kind of righteousness is useless in the sight of the glory of the future life. However, it does generate temporary benefits. According to Luther, human righteousness expresses itself in this kind of self-love and in aiming for one's own benefit, which is at the core of sin.

righteousness deceives even those who are wise and great, unless they have been well instructed in the sacred texts.[17]

Jeremiah (2:13) calls this kind of righteousness "a broken cistern that holds no water"; yet, as he says in the same chapter (v. 23), it causes people to presume that they are without sin.[18] It is completely like the actions which we see done by a monkey when it imitates human beings, or like those displayed by actors on stages and in plays. It is entirely characteristic of hypocrites and idols. Consequently, in the Scriptures it is called a lie and an iniquity; thus, the name *Bethaven*, "house of iniquity."[s] To their kind belong also those who deceive minds today, who in reliance on their free will make a good resolution (as they say) and, after eliciting from their natural powers the act of loving God above all else,[t] at once take for granted in the most shameful manner that they have obtained the grace of God. These are the people who strive to cure the woman with an issue of blood (that is, a guilty conscience) by means of works and, after[19,u] exhausting her resources, make her worse (Mark 5:25-26).

In the second place, there is the inward way, on the basis of faith and of grace, when a human being utterly despairs of his former righteousness,[20] as though it were the uncleanness of a woman in menstruation, and casts oneself down before God, sobs humbly, and, confessing that one is a sinner, says with the publican: "God, be merciful to me a sinner!" (Luke 18:13). "This

17. Lat.: *sacris literis*. This could mean the Holy Scriptures, or sacred texts of the early teachers in general.

18. Aspirations to fulfill the law and earn righteousness lead human beings to imagine (*praesumptio*) that they are without sin. That is, however, only imitation of good works, akin to a monkey mimicking human actions or an actress acting on stage.

19. This is a summary of how human righteousness, which Luther criticizes, comes about. Human beings imagine that they can meet the demands of the law and form, with their free will, a good intent (*bona intentio*). This means that human love aims toward what is good and right and, eventually, the highest good (*summum bonum*)—God. Some Scholastic theologians taught that human beings can, with their natural capabilities, choose and produce an act with which to love God above all else (*actus diligendi deum super omnia*). Even an attempt to love God would suffice. God will not refuse grace from human beings, who do what is possible for them (*facere quod in se est*). For Luther, this is not "real" fulfillment of the law and does not lead to righteousness. It only produces a misconception of oneself and one's abilities regarding the law's expectations (*praesumptio*).

20. Human beings' attempts to fulfill the law may lead to despair (*desperatio*). Despair results when sinners notice that they actually do not love God above all but, rather, love themselves. In Lutheran language, this revealing of sin is called the second, or spiritual, use of the law. Law alone kills. God's alien work (*opus Dei alienum*) has, however, a positive meaning from the perspective of justification, as long as the sinners hear

s LW 27:220 n.27: "Luther is thinking of passages like Josh. 7:2; Hos. 4:15, etc."

t Lat.: *diligendi deum super omnia*.

u For more on Luther's criticism of Scholastic theology, see Grane, *Contra Gabrielem*, 320–22, 335–37; and Simo Peura, *Mehr als ein Mensch? Die Vergöttlichung als Thema der Theologie Martin Luthers von 1513 bis 1519*. Veröffentlichungen des Instituts für Europäische Geschichte Mainz, Band 152: Abteilung Religionsgeschichte (Mainz: von Zabern, 1994), 179–88.

man [the publican]," says Christ, "went down to his house justified" (v. 14).[21] For this righteousness is nothing else than a calling upon the name of God.[22] Now the name of God is mercy, truth, righteousness, strength, wisdom, and the accusation of one's own name. On the other hand, our name is sin, falsehood, vanity, and folly, as is written: "All people[v] are liars" (Ps. 116:11) and "Everyone walks in a vain show" (Ps. 39:6).

"God, be merciful to me, a sinner" (Luke 18:13). Woodcut of the parable of the Pharisee and the tax collector from a 1544 printing of Luther's *Interpretation of the Epistles and Gospel Texts, from Easter to Advent.*

v Lat.: *homo.*

the gospel in time. Through God's alien work, human beings are made sinners "for real": they become nothing also in their own self-perception (*redactio ad nihilum*). On *nihil* in Luther's theology, see Sammeli Juntunen, *Der Begriff des Nichts bei Luther in den Jahren von 1510 bis 1523*. Schriften der Luther-Agricola-Gesellschaft 36. Diss. (Helsinki: Luther-Agricola-Gesellschaft, 1996), 353–58.

21. True righteousness is based on God's grace and on faith. It is preceded by despair over one's righteousness, confessing one's sinful nature, and holding only God's name true and righteous. In other words, a human being's understanding of both God and self has to change radically. This is expressed in the petition that God would be merciful "for me"; in that petition, a human being's assessments of oneself and of God's righteousness are in harmony and reflects the actual reality.

22. In Luther's theology, God's name entails the idioms of God's nature and being, such as grace, truth, righteousness, power, and wisdom. In several of his writings, Luther describes the characteristics of God with these terms, e.g., the *Heidelberg Disputation* (1518), TAL 1:67–119; StA 1:207,29—208,8; *Sermon on Two Kinds of Righteousness* (1519), TAL 2:9–23; WA 2:147,36—148,5; and *Operationes in Psalmos* (1519–1521), AWA 2:345,16–31; 447,1-5. See also Peura, *Mehr als ein Mensch?*, 196–98; Juntunen, *Der Begriff des Nichts bei Luther*, 358–63. Luther is not that interested in what God is in God's own majestic being apart from human beings. His attention is directed on how this righteous God acts in relation to a sinner, that is, how God makes a sinner righteous with God's own righteousness. This he sees

But calling upon the name of God, if it is in the heart and truly from the heart, shows that the heart and the name of the Lord are one and cling to each other.[23,w] For this reason it is impossible for the heart not to share in the virtues in which the name of the Lord abounds. But it is through faith that the heart and the name of the Lord cling together (cf. Rom. 10:17).[24] Faith, however, comes through the word of Christ, by which the name of the Lord is preached, as is written: "I will tell of your name to my [sisters and] brothers" (Ps. 22:23), and again: "That people may declare in Zion the name of the LORD" (Ps. 102:21). Therefore, just as the name of the Lord is pure, holy, righteous, true, good, etc., so, if it touches, or is touched by, the heart (which happens through faith), it makes the heart entirely like itself. Thus, it comes about that for those who trust in the name of the Lord all sins are forgiven, and righteousness is imputed to them "for your name's sake, LORD" (Ps. 25:11), because this name is good. This does not come about because of their own merit, since they have not deserved even to hear of it. But when the heart has thus been justified through the faith that is in God's name, God gives them the power to become children of God[x] (John 1:12) by immediately pouring into their hearts God's Holy Spirit (Rom. 5:5),[25] who fills them with God's love and makes them peaceful, glad, active in all good works, victorious over all evils, contemptuous even of death and hell. Here all laws and all works of laws soon cease; all things are now free and permissible, and the law is fulfilled through faith and love.[26]

Behold, this is what Christ has merited for us, namely, that the name of the Lord (that is, the mercy and truth of God) is preached to us and that whoever believes in this name will be

w For more on the idea of Christ-oneness, see Simo Peura, "The Church as Spiritual Communion in Luther," in *The Church as Communion: Luther's Contribution to Ecclesiology*, ed. Heinrich Holze, LWF Documentation 42/1997 (Geneva: LWF 42, 1997), 104–20. On union and on participation in divine nature in Luther's theology, see Tuomo Mannermaa, "Justification and Theosis in Lutheran-Orthodox Perspective," in *Union with Christ: The New Finnish Interpretation of Luther*, ed. Carl E. Braaten and Robert W. Jenson (Grand Rapids: Eerdmans 1998), 32–36; Tuomo Mannermaa, *Christ Present in Faith: Luther's View of Justification*, ed. Kirsi Stjerna (Minneapolis: Fortress Press, 2005), 16–22; Peura, *Mehr als ein Mensch?*, 213–31.

x Lat.: *filios dei fieri*.

possible when a Christian, through faith, participates in Christ. Kenosis is central in Luther's theology: Christ's human nature assumes the form of a slave (Phil. 2:5-8) and hides his divine nature. As such, Christ is the object of faith.

23. From the inner logic of justification, it is decisive that Christ and human being become united through faith. The *unio cum Christo* idea originates from Paul and is quite prevalent in medieval theology. When one with Christ, the Christian participates (*participet*) in God's "being" and names, that is, in God's righteousness and grace. The idea of participation in divine nature has biblical roots (2 Pet. 1:4). The concept of participation appears frequently in Luther's theology. In his *Large Catechism*, when explaining the Third Article of the Creed, Luther emphasizes the meaning of the church in generating this Christ-oneness: when the church proclaims the gospel and distributes the sacraments, a faith is born in us and we become participants in the Christ-treasure.

24. It follows from participation that a Christian is transformed into a likeness of God's names. See Peura, *Mehr als ein Mensch?*, 232–43; Juntunen, *Der Begriff des Nichts bei Luther*, 357–61.

25. To Luther, justification is both about (1) a person's sins being forgiven and Christ's righteousness being imputed (*imputatio*), and (2) the person being made righteous (*iustum facere*). The Christian thus becomes a child of God and receives the infusion of Christ's Holy Spirit.

26. The changes that occur in justification and as effected by the Holy Spirit then manifest in the human being's ability to do good deeds and meet the expectations of the law.

saved. Therefore, if your conscience troubles you and you are a sinner and are seeking to become righteous, what will you do? Will you look around to see what works you may do or where you may go? No. On the contrary, see to it that you hear or recall the name of the Lord, that is, that God is righteous, good, and holy; and then cling to this, firmly believing that God is such a One for you. Now you are at once such a one, like God.[y] But you will never see the name of the Lord more clearly than you do in Christ. There you will see how good, pleasant, faithful, righteous, and true God is, since God did not spare God's own Son (Rom. 8:32). Through Christ God will draw you to God's self. Without this righteousness it is impossible for the heart to be pure.[27] That is why it is impossible for the righteousness of human beings to be true. For here the name of the Lord is used for the truth; there it is used for an empty show. For here a human being gives glory to God and confusion to oneself; there one gives glory to oneself and insult to God. This is the real cabala of the name of the Lord, not of the *Tetragrammaton*, about which the Jews speak in the most superstitious manner.[28] Faith in the name of the Lord, I say, is the understanding of the law, the end of the law, and absolutely all in all. But God has placed this name of God's own on Christ, as God foretold[z] through Moses.

This is a righteousness[a] that is bountiful,[b] freely given,[c] firm, inward,[d] eternal, true, heavenly, divine;[e] it does not earn, receive, or seek anything in this life. Indeed, since it is directed toward Christ and his name, which is righteousness, the result is that the righteousness of Christ and of the Christian are one and the same, united with each other in an inexpressible way.[29] For it flows and gushes forth from Christ, as he says in John 4(:14): "The water that I shall give will become in them a spring of living water welling up to eternal life." Thus, it comes about that just

y Lat.: *similis eius.*
z Lat.: *praedixit.*
a Lat.: *iusticia.*
b Lat.: *liberalis.*
c Lat.: *gratuita.*
d Lat.: *interna.*
e Lat.: *coelestis, divina.*

Freedom and free-from-coercion are characteristic to true good deeds. Luther describes this same theme in more detail in his treatise *The Freedom of a Christian* (1520), TAL 1:467–538.

27. *Unio cum Christo*—this idea is important also for pastoral reasons. When the conscience accuses the Christian, one is to pay attention only to the reality of God's righteousness and that God is righteous especially toward the sinner. Believing with this kind of faith, the Christian is one with Christ and the Christian's heart is pure, which is a prerequisite for the fulfillment of the law.

28. Tetragrammaton: God's name in Hebrew is transliterated with the letters YHWH, pronounced as Yahweh (or JHVH, Jehovah). For more about Luther's view of the Jewish use of the Tetragrammaton, see *On the* Schem Hamphoras *and On the Lineage of Christ* (1543), TAL 5:653–58.

29. With the *unio cum Christo* idea Luther is able to explain, diverting from the Scholastics, how exactly a human being can participate in God's righteousness. Luther's model is not based on Aristotelian metaphysics (with *habitus* and *accidens* terminology) but, rather, on the biblical language and Christology. Luther does not aim to give a detailed explanation of the nature of union in Christ; that is beyond words (*ineffabiliter*) anyway. In his lectures on the letter to the Hebrews (1517–1518), Luther writes on how the human heart and God become one through the effect of faith, and how the divine righteousness "in a certain way" (*quodammodo*) becomes the righteousness of the human heart. Similarly, as Christ is one in his humanity united with his divinity, also the Christian united in Christ is righteous with Christ's righteousness (WA 57H:187,5–188,3).

Woodcut depicting the union of the Trinity (1512) by Lucas Cranach the Elder

as all became sinners because of alien[f] sin, so by alien righteousness[30] all become righteous, as Rom. 5:19 says: "As by one person's disobedience many were made sinners, so by the righteousness of one human being,[g] Christ, many are made righteous."[h] This is the mercy predicted by all the prophets; this is the blessing promised to Abraham and to his seed, as we shall see later.

Coming back now to the text, we see how right the apostle is when he says: "Knowing that a human being[i] is not justified by works of the law but, as is obvious, only by faith in Jesus Christ,[j] we, too, believe in Christ Jesus that we may be justified by faith in Jesus Christ,[k] not because of the works of the law." In these words he describes both kinds of righteousness.[l] He rejects the former

30. Luther uses the term *iustitia aliena* already in his *Sermon on Two Kinds of Righteousness* (1519), TAL 2:9-24; StA 1:221,5-18. This term expresses the origins of righteousness but does not mean that Christ's righteousness would remain external to or outside the human being; quite the contrary. Union is a permanent condition for the Christian's participation in Christ's righteousness.

f Lat.: *alieno, aliena*, translated in LW 27 as "another."

g Lat.: *per unius hominis.*

h Lat.: *per unius hominis Christi iusticiam iusti constituuntur multi.*

i Lat.: *homo.*

j Lat.: *ex fide Iesu Christi.*

k Lat.: *et nos in Christo Iesu credimus, ut iustificemur ex fide Iesu Christi.*

l Lat.: *utranque hanc iusticiam designat.*

and embraces the latter. May you do likewise, beloved fellow-Christian.[m] First hear that "Jesus" means salvation[n] and that "Christ" means "the anointing of mercy";[o] then firmly believe this unheard-of salvation and mercy, and you will be justified.[p] That is, believe that Christ will be your salvation and mercy, and beyond all doubt Christ will be. Therefore it is altogether godless[q] and exceedingly heathenish to teach that remission of sins takes place through petty little works of satisfaction[r] and through compulsory acts of contrition,[31] and the doctrine of faith in Christ[s] is completely neglected, while the vulgar sententiarists[32] peddle their theology today.

Peter Lombard was a Scholastic theologian, the bishop of Paris, and author of *Four Books of Sentences*, which became the standard textbook of theology.

m With *charissime frater* (Lat.), Luther addresses the reader in general. In LW 27, the translation for the reader is "dearest brother," following the convention of using masculine pronouns and expressions for human beings.

n Lat.: *salutem.*

o Lat.: *unctionem misericordiae.*

p Lat.: *et iustificaberis.*

q Lat.: *impie.*

r Lat.: *satisfactiunculas.*

s Lat.: *hac fidei in Christum doctrine prorsus omissa.*

31. Here Luther refers to his time's Catholic teaching of repentance and confession. It included three parts: the heart's contrition (*contritio cordis*), confessing sins aloud (*confessio oris*), and works of satisfaction (*satisfactio operis*). Luther deemed this practice to lead to works righteousness. In his *95 Theses* (1517), Luther stressed that the entire Christian life is repentance (*poenitentia*). In his debate with the Catholic Johannes Eck (1486–1543) in Leipzig (1519), he underscored that neither fear nor love of righteousness would lead to genuine repentance. It is born only out of grace, which is in Christ.

32. "*Sententiastri*" is a nickname of scorn for commentators. They gathered and compiled sayings from the church fathers and then commented on them. This is how the foundational sources on dogmatics were formed, ones that students had to master. The initiator of this custom was Peter Lombard (c. 1096–1160), with his four-part commentary *Sententiae in IV libros distinctae*. Luther criticizes particularly Gabriel Biel, whose *Collectorium in quattuor libros Sententiarum* he had thoroughly studied. Biel had a significant impact on Luther's notion of the Scholastic theology.

Nevertheless, it should be noted here that the apostle does not reject the works of the law, as Jerome also points out in this connection; rather, he rejects reliance[t] on the works of the law. That is, he does not deny works per se, but he denies that anyone could be justified through them. Therefore one must read the apostle's statement with emphasis and close attention when he says: "A human being is not justified by the works of the law"; as if Paul were saying: "I admit that works of the law are to be done; but I say that a human being is not made righteous because of them[u] except in one's own sight and before other human beings and for[v] a reward in this life. Let there be works of the law, provided that one knows that in the sight of God they are sins and no longer true works of the law." In this way Paul totally demolishes our reliance on our own righteousness,[w] because a vastly different righteousness beyond all works of the law is required: truly, a righteousness of the works of God and God's grace.[x]

Furthermore, you must also observe that Paul speaks of "works of the law" in general, not merely of those that relate to the ceremonial law, but certainly also of all the works of the Decalogue.[33,y] For these, too, when done apart from faith and the true righteousness of God,[z] are not only insufficient; but in their outward appearance they even give hypocrites false assurance. Therefore who wants to be saved must lose one's hope[a] in all [human] strength, works, and laws.

Moreover, you will observe the manner of speaking peculiar to this apostle, that he speaks of works of the law not as others do, as those things by which the law itself is fulfilled. For this sense is the reason why many people do not understand the apostle, those who understand the works of the law as only righ-

33. Luther typically separates the Jewish ceremonial laws from the Decalogue. The heart of the Decalogue is the twofold commandment of love and the Golden Rule. The Golden Rule can be considered as the summation of the entire Christian life.

t Lat.: *fiducia*, meaning faith, reliance, assurance, trust.

u Lat.: *dico eis non iustificari hominem*.

v Lat.: *pro*.

w Lat.: *iusticiae nostrae*.

x Lat.: *iusticia . . . operibus dei et gratie*.

y For more on the Golden Rule, see Antti Raunio, *Summe des christlichen Lebens: Die "Goldene Regel" als Gesetz der Liebe in der Theologie Martin Luthers von 1510–1527*, Reports from the Department of Systematic Theology, University of Helsinki XIII. Diss. (Helsinki: Yliopistopaino, 1993), 252–86.

z Lat.: *extra fidem et iusticiam*.

a Lat.: *Desperandum*.

teous and good,[b] since the law itself is good and righteous: thus, they are compelled to understand [Paul as speaking of] the ceremonial laws, since those were then evil and dead. However, they are mistaken: the ceremonial law, just as it was, so is it now good and holy, since it was established by God.[c]

The apostle consistently declares that the law is fulfilled only through faith, not through works.[d] Because the fulfilling of the law is righteousness[e] and this is surely a matter of faith, not of works,[f] one cannot understand the works of the law to mean those works by which the law is satisfied. What then? The apostle's rule is this: It is not works that fulfill the law, but the fulfillment of the law produces works. One does not become righteous by doing righteous deeds; rather, one who has [first] been made righteous [then] performs righteous deeds. Righteousness and fulfillment of the law[g] come first, before the works are done, because the latter flow out of the former.[34] That is why Paul calls them "works of the law" in distinction from works of grace or works of God: for works of the law are really the law's works, not ours; they are not done by the operation of our will but because the law extorts them through threats or elicits them through promises. But whatever is not done freely of our own will but is done under the compulsion of another[h] is no longer our work. No, it is the work of those who require it. For works belong to those at whose command they are done. But they are done at the command of the law, not at the pleasure of one's own will.[i] It is clear enough that if a person were free to live without the law, one would never do the works of the law spontaneously. Hence, the law is called an enforcer when in Isa. 9:4 it is spoken of as "the staff for his shoulder, the yoke of his burden, the rod of his oppressor, as on the day of Midian." For on account of the child[j] who was given to us (Isa. 9:6) and in whom we believe,[k]

34. Luther does not deny the need to fulfill the law. It is decisive, however, how it takes place. He refutes the Scholastics' view that the law would be kept by repeating good works. In Luther's view, a Christian person first needs to be made righteous (justified). Only then can one do righteous deeds. From a changed way of "being" follows "doing" accordingly.

b Lat.: *opera legis non nisi iusta et bona intelligere possunt.*

c Lat.: *ab ipso deo statutat*; LW 27 translates this "by God Himself."

d Lat.: *per opera . . . per fidem.*

e Lat.: *Quia impletio legis est iusticia.*

f Lat.: *sed haec non est operum, immo fidei.*

g Lat.: *plentitudoque legis.*

h Lat.: *alio exigente.*

i Lat.: *non lubente voluntate.*

j Lat.: *per parvulum.*

k Lat.: *in quem credimus.*

we become free and take pleasure in the law,[l] and the law no longer owns us but we own the law.[m] And our works are not works of the law but works of grace, from which spring up freely and pleasantly the kinds of deeds that formerly the law squeezed out of us with harsh force.[35]

You will understand this if you arrange works in four categories: (1) works of sin, which are done under the domination of concupiscence,[36] with no resistance on the part of grace; (2) works of the law, which are done when concupiscence is externally coerced but glows all the more inwardly and hates the law, that is, works that are good in appearance but bad[n] in the core;[o] (3) works of grace, which are done when lust resists, but the spirit of grace is victorious; (4) works of [a soul at] peace and perfectly healed,[p] which are done with the fullest ease and pleasantness after lust has been extinguished; this is how it will be in the life to come,[q] here is only the beginning.[37]

therefore, by works of the law shall no one be justified.

Paul draws the same conclusion in Rom. 3:9ff. And there he proves it extensively on the basis of Ps. 14:3: "There is no one who is righteous, who does good." Therefore the works of the law must be sins; otherwise they would certainly justify. Thus, it is clear that Christian righteousness and human righteousness are not only altogether different but are even opposed to each other, because the latter comes from works, while works come from the former. No wonder, therefore, that Paul's theology vanished entirely and could not be understood after Christians began to be instructed by those who failed completely to understand either Aristotle or Christ and declared falsely that Aristotle's ethics are entirely in accord with the doctrine of Christ and of Paul. For our righteousness looks down from heaven and

35. True fulfillment of the law entails that the human being wants to do so, freely and without coercion. This is possible for the Christian only if one believes in Christ. When the Christian becomes one with Christ, one does good deeds willingly, freely, and with joy. For more, see Raunio, *Summe des christlichen Lebens*, 227–28. Luther focuses on this with detail in his treatise *The Freedom of a Christian* (1520), TAL 1:467–538; StA 2:263–309.

36. Desire (Lat.: *concupiscentia*) is a sinful lust; when it controls the human being, it distorts the person's deeds into sin. In his *Lectures on Romans* (1515–1516), Luther uses concupiscence as the synonym for the essence of sin. It makes the human being turn into oneself (*incurvatio in seipsum*) and forget God and neighbors. See WA 56:304,25–29; 356,4–10; 361,11–18.

37. A Christian's works belong mostly in the third category, the reason being the incompleteness of one's righteousness and the remaining sin (*peccatum manens*). A Christian is simultaneously partially righteous (*partim iustus*) and partially sinner (*partim peccator*). The spirit of grace, however, is stronger than the remaining evil lust, and this is why Christians can perform the deeds of grace. Occasionally, Christians perform also the works of the fourth category. he quality of the works is bound to the nature of the one who works.

l Lat.: *efficimur liberi ac lubentes in legem.*

m Lat.: *nos non legis sumus, sed lex nostra est.*

n Lat.: *mala*; in LW 27 translated as "evil."

o Lat.: *in corde*, literally, "in the heart."

p Lat.: *sanitas.*

q Lat.: *Opera peccati, Opera legis, Opera gratiae, Opera pacis et perfectae sanitatis.*

descends to us.[r] But those godless[s] ones have presumed to ascend into heaven by means of their righteousness and from there to bring the truth which has arisen among us from the earth.[38,t]

Therefore Paul stands resolute: "No flesh is justified on the basis of works of the law," as Ps. 143(:2) also says: "No living being will be justified before you." The only thing left is that the works of the law are not works of righteousness—except of the righteousness that is of our own making.

38. Theologians who rely on Aristotle imagine they can ascend to heaven on the basis of their own righteousness, whereas the true righteousness looks down from heaven and descends to people. Luther addresses this polarity between the theology of glory and the theology of the cross already in his *Heidelberg Disputation* (1518), TAL 1:67–120. Whereas the theologian of glory seeks to know God through God's invisible (to human) characteristics, the theologian of the cross looks to God who is hiding in Christ's humanity and weakness. Human love is born from its object—an object that the theology of glory holds worthy of love and attaining. According to the theology of the cross, then, God's love creates its objects. It aims down toward sinners and evil persons in order to make them righteous, good, and wise.

r Lat.: *Nostra enim iusticia de coelo prospicit et ad nos descendit.*

s Lat.: *impii.*

t For more on the theology of glory and the theology of the cross, see StA 1:207,25–208,13; 212,1–19 (1518); also Tuomo Mannermaa, *Der im Glauben gegenwärtige Christus—Rechtfertigung und Vergottung: Zum ökumenischen Dialog*, Arbeiten zur Geschichte und Theologie des Luthertums N.F. Band 8 (Hannover: Lutherisches Verlagshaus, 1989), 130–45.

Image Credits

xii, xiii (maps): © 2006 Lucidity Information Design, LLC. Used by permission.

3: Wikimedia Commons / {PD-1923}.

7, 20, 23, 28, 42, 59, 71, 81, 117, 130, 133, 134, 138, 141, 161, 197, 227 (Hus), 248, 256, 273, 281, 297, 303, 320 (Haetzer), 321, 325, 341, 347, 357, 372, 377, 379, 385, 390, 393, 400, 404 (Ptolemy VI), 406, 410, 412, 417, 420, 434, 435, 439, 447, 449, 452, 455, 458, 459, 462, 468, 483, 496, 501, 508, 521, 524, 536, 537, 538, 540, 541, 543, 550: Wikimedia Commons / public domain.

13, 39, 57, 92, 95, 111, 121, 127, 154, 188, 202, 206, 215, 217, 223, 227, 229, 231, (Bernard), 263, 269, 278, 312, 320 (Prophet's title page), 329, 334, 371, 380, 383, 387, 424, 427, 430, 445, 491, 493, 503, 509, 527, 533, 534, 547: Courtesy of the Richard C. Kessler Reformation Collection, Pitts Theological Library, Candler School of Theology, Emory University.

15, 74, 440: Wikimedia Commons / Web Gallery of Art.

34: Wikimedia Commons / private collection of S. Whitehead.

43: Historical Image College by Bildagentur-online / Alamy Stock Photos.

44: FALKENSTEINFOTO / Alamy Stock Photos.

49: Art Resource, NY.

68: Wikimedia Commons / Till Niermann.

69: Wikimedia Commons/ Museo Poldi Pezzoli.

77: Everett Collection Historical / Alamy Stock Photos.

79: Courtesy National Gallery of Art, Washington, DC.

84: Wikimedia Commons / sgFbOi8a8sxcjg at Google Cultural Institute.

89: Wikimedia Commons / www.geheugenvannederland.nl.

93: 115, 146, 359: Wikimedia Commons / The Yorck Project: 10,000 Meisterwerke der Malerei.

99: Wikimedia Commons / LQG_SIsDPpL2aQ at Google Cultural Institute.

104, 123, 211, 226, 397, 473, 480, 516, 531: Courtesy of Pitts Theological Library, Candler School of Theology, Emory University.

109: Wikimedia Commons / www.culture.pl.

113: Bridwell Library Special Collections, Perkins School of Theology, Southern Methodist University.

120: age fotostock / Alamy Stock Photo.

122, 166, 260, 291, 299: INTERFOTO /Alamy Stock Photos.

142: Wikimedia Commons / Cranach Digital Archives.

173: Wikimedia Commons / themorgan.org at Google Cultural Institute.

183: Wikimedia Commons / courtesy Bizzell Bible Collection, University of Oklahoma Libraries.

207: Wikimedia Commons / GNU Free Documentation License.

214: Herzog August Bibliothek Wolfenbüttel (www.hab.de), reprinted by permission.

242: Wikimedia Commons / Museum purchase provided by the W. Alton Jones Foundation Acquisition Fund, 1998.

244: Wikimedia Commons / Honolulu Museum of Art.

249: Wikimedia Commons / Wenceslas Hollar Digital Collection.

315: Wikimedia Commons / National Library of Israel Succoth Collection.

340: Wikimedia Commons / Hermitage Torrent.

344: Wikimedia Commons / ULB Darmstadt.

361: Wikimedia Commons / Marie-Lan Nguyen, 1910: bequeathed by George Salting.

404: (Antiochus coin), Wikimedia Commons / Classical Numismatic Group, Inc. www.cngcoins.com.

551: bilwissedition Ltd. & Co. KG / Alamy Stock Photo.

Index of Scriptural References

OLD TESTAMENT
HEBREW BIBLE

GENESIS

APOCRYPHA
DEUTERO-CANONICAL BOOKS

NEW TESTAMENT

Index of Names

Index of Works by Martin Luther and Others

Index of Subjects